Lecture Notes in Computer Science 5622

Commenced Publication in 1973
Founding and Former Series Editors:
Gerhard Goos, Juris Hartmanis, and Jan van Leeuwen

Randall Shumaker (Ed.)

Virtual and Mixed Reality

Third International Conference, VMR 2009
Held as Part of HCI International 2009
San Diego, CA, USA, July 19-24, 2009
Proceedings

 Springer

Volume Editor

Randall Shumaker
University of Central Florida
Institute for Simulation and Training
3100 Technology Parkway and 3280 Progress Drive, Orlando, FL 32826, USA
E-mail: shumaker@ist.ucf.edu

Library of Congress Control Number: Applied for

CR Subject Classification (1998): H.5, H.4, I.3, I.2, C.3, I.4, I.6

LNCS Sublibrary: SL 3 – Information Systems and Application, incl. Internet/Web
and HCI

ISSN   0302-9743
ISBN-10   3-642-02770-9 Springer Berlin Heidelberg New York
ISBN-13   978-3-642-02770-3 Springer Berlin Heidelberg New York

springer.com

© Springer-Verlag Berlin Heidelberg 2009
Printed in Germany

Typesetting: Camera-ready by author, data conversion by Scientific Publishing Services, Chennai, India
Printed on acid-free paper   SPIN: 12708710   06/3180   5 4 3 2 1 0

Foreword

The 13th International Conference on Human–Computer Interaction, HCI International 2009, was held in San Diego, California, USA, July 19–24, 2009, jointly with the Symposium on Human Interface (Japan) 2009, the 8th International Conference on Engineering Psychology and Cognitive Ergonomics, the 5th International Conference on Universal Access in Human–Computer Interaction, the Third International Conference on Virtual and Mixed Reality, the Third International Conference on Internationalization, Design and Global Development, the Third International Conference on Online Communities and Social Computing, the 5th International Conference on Augmented Cognition, the Second International Conference on Digital Human Modeling, and the First International Conference on Human Centered Design.

A total of 4,348 individuals from academia, research institutes, industry and governmental agencies from 73 countries submitted contributions, and 1,397 papers that were judged to be of high scientific quality were included in the program. These papers address the latest research and development efforts and highlight the human aspects of the design and use of computing systems. The papers accepted for presentation thoroughly cover the entire field of human–computer interaction, addressing major advances in knowledge and effective use of computers in a variety of application areas.

This volume, edited by Randall Shumaker, contains papers in the thematic area of Virtual and Mixed Reality, addressing the following major topics:

- Interaction and Navigation in Virtual and Mixed Environments
- Design, Development and Evaluation of VR Environments
- Haptics and Tactile Interaction in VR
- Vision in Virtual and Mixed Reality
- VR Applications

The remaining volumes of the HCI International 2009 proceedings are:

- Volume 1, LNCS 5610, Human–Computer Interaction—New Trends (Part I), edited by Julie A. Jacko
- Volume 2, LNCS 5611, Human–Computer Interaction—Novel Interaction Methods and Techniques (Part II), edited by Julie A. Jacko
- Volume 3, LNCS 5612, Human–Computer Interaction—Ambient, Ubiquitous and Intelligent Interaction (Part III), edited by Julie A. Jacko
- Volume 4, LNCS 5613, Human–Computer Interaction—Interacting in Various Application Domains (Part IV), edited by Julie A. Jacko
- Volume 5, LNCS 5614, Universal Access in Human–Computer Interaction—Addressing Diversity (Part I), edited by Constantine Stephanidis
- Volume 6, LNCS 5615, Universal Access in Human–Computer Interaction—Intelligent and Ubiquitous Interaction Environments (Part II), edited by Constantine Stephanidis

- Volume 7, LNCS 5616, Universal Access in Human–Computer Interaction—Applications and Services (Part III), edited by Constantine Stephanidis
- Volume 8, LNCS 5617, Human Interface and the Management of Information—Designing Information Environments (Part I), edited by Michael J. Smith and Gavriel Salvendy
- Volume 9, LNCS 5618, Human Interface and the Management of Information—Information and Interaction (Part II), edited by Gavriel Salvendy and Michael J. Smith
- Volume 10, LNCS 5619, Human Centered Design, edited by Masaaki Kurosu
- Volume 11, LNCS 5620, Digital Human Modeling, edited by Vincent G. Duffy
- Volume 12, LNCS 5621, Online Communities and Social Computing, edited by A. Ant Ozok and Panayiotis Zaphiris
- Volume 14, LNCS 5623, Internationalization, Design and Global Development, edited by Nuray Aykin
- Volume 15, LNCS 5624, Ergonomics and Health Aspects of Work with Computers, edited by Ben-Tzion Karsh
- Volume 16, LNAI 5638, The Foundations of Augmented Cognition: Neuroergonomics and Operational Neuroscience, edited by Dylan Schmorrow, Ivy Estabrooke and Marc Grootjen
- Volume 17, LNAI 5639, Engineering Psychology and Cognitive Ergonomics, edited by Don Harris

I would like to thank the Program Chairs and the members of the Program Boards of all thematic areas, listed below, for their contribution to the highest scientific quality and the overall success of HCI International 2009.

Ergonomics and Health Aspects of Work with Computers

Program Chair: Ben-Tzion Karsh

Arne Aarås, Norway
Pascale Carayon, USA
Barbara G.F. Cohen, USA
Wolfgang Friesdorf, Germany
John Gosbee, USA
Martin Helander, Singapore
Ed Israelski, USA
Waldemar Karwowski, USA
Peter Kern, Germany
Danuta Koradecka, Poland
Kari Lindström, Finland

Holger Luczak, Germany
Aura C. Matias, Philippines
Kyung (Ken) Park, Korea
Michelle M. Robertson, USA
Michelle L. Rogers, USA
Steven L. Sauter, USA
Dominique L. Scapin, France
Naomi Swanson, USA
Peter Vink, The Netherlands
John Wilson, UK
Teresa Zayas-Cabán, USA

Human Interface and the Management of Information

Program Chair: Michael J. Smith

Gunilla Bradley, Sweden
Hans-Jörg Bullinger, Germany
Alan Chan, Hong Kong
Klaus-Peter Fähnrich, Germany
Michitaka Hirose, Japan
Jhilmil Jain, USA
Yasufumi Kume, Japan
Mark Lehto, USA
Fiona Fui-Hoon Nah, USA
Shogo Nishida, Japan
Robert Proctor, USA
Yongho Rhee, Korea

Anxo Cereijo Roibás, UK
Katsunori Shimohara, Japan
Dieter Spath, Germany
Tsutomu Tabe, Japan
Alvaro D. Taveira, USA
Kim-Phuong L. Vu, USA
Tomio Watanabe, Japan
Sakae Yamamoto, Japan
Hidekazu Yoshikawa, Japan
Li Zheng, P.R. China
Bernhard Zimolong, Germany

Human–Computer Interaction

Program Chair: Julie A. Jacko

Sebastiano Bagnara, Italy
Sherry Y. Chen, UK
Marvin J. Dainoff, USA
Jianming Dong, USA
John Eklund, Australia
Xiaowen Fang, USA
Ayse Gurses, USA
Vicki L. Hanson, UK
Sheue-Ling Hwang, Taiwan
Wonil Hwang, Korea
Yong Gu Ji, Korea
Steven Landry, USA

Gitte Lindgaard, Canada
Chen Ling, USA
Yan Liu, USA
Chang S. Nam, USA
Celestine A. Ntuen, USA
Philippe Palanque, France
P.L. Patrick Rau, P.R. China
Ling Rothrock, USA
Guangfeng Song, USA
Steffen Staab, Germany
Wan Chul Yoon, Korea
Wenli Zhu, P.R. China

Engineering Psychology and Cognitive Ergonomics

Program Chair: Don Harris

Guy A. Boy, USA
John Huddlestone, UK
Kenji Itoh, Japan
Hung-Sying Jing, Taiwan
Ron Laughery, USA
Wen-Chin Li, Taiwan
James T. Luxhøj, USA

Nicolas Marmaras, Greece
Sundaram Narayanan, USA
Mark A. Neerincx, The Netherlands
Jan M. Noyes, UK
Kjell Ohlsson, Sweden
Axel Schulte, Germany
Sarah C. Sharples, UK

Neville A. Stanton, UK
Xianghong Sun, P.R. China
Andrew Thatcher, South Africa

Matthew J.W. Thomas, Australia
Mark Young, UK

Universal Access in Human–Computer Interaction

Program Chair: Constantine Stephanidis

Julio Abascal, Spain
Ray Adams, UK
Elisabeth André, Germany
Margherita Antona, Greece
Chieko Asakawa, Japan
Christian Bühler, Germany
Noelle Carbonell, France
Jerzy Charytonowicz, Poland
Pier Luigi Emiliani, Italy
Michael Fairhurst, UK
Dimitris Grammenos, Greece
Andreas Holzinger, Austria
Arthur I. Karshmer, USA
Simeon Keates, Denmark
Georgios Kouroupetroglou, Greece
Sri Kurniawan, USA

Patrick M. Langdon, UK
Seongil Lee, Korea
Zhengjie Liu, P.R. China
Klaus Miesenberger, Austria
Helen Petrie, UK
Michael Pieper, Germany
Anthony Savidis, Greece
Andrew Sears, USA
Christian Stary, Austria
Hirotada Ueda, Japan
Jean Vanderdonckt, Belgium
Gregg C. Vanderheiden, USA
Gerhard Weber, Germany
Harald Weber, Germany
Toshiki Yamaoka, Japan
Panayiotis Zaphiris, UK

Virtual and Mixed Reality

Program Chair: Randall Shumaker

Pat Banerjee, USA
Mark Billinghurst, New Zealand
Charles E. Hughes, USA
David Kaber, USA
Hirokazu Kato, Japan
Robert S. Kennedy, USA
Young J. Kim, Korea
Ben Lawson, USA

Gordon M. Mair, UK
Miguel A. Otaduy, Switzerland
David Pratt, UK
Albert "Skip" Rizzo, USA
Lawrence Rosenblum, USA
Dieter Schmalstieg, Austria
Dylan Schmorrow, USA
Mark Wiederhold, USA

Internationalization, Design and Global Development

Program Chair: Nuray Aykin

Michael L. Best, USA
Ram Bishu, USA
Alan Chan, Hong Kong
Andy M. Dearden, UK

Susan M. Dray, USA
Vanessa Evers, The Netherlands
Paul Fu, USA
Emilie Gould, USA

Sung H. Han, Korea
Veikko Ikonen, Finland
Esin Kiris, USA
Masaaki Kurosu, Japan
Apala Lahiri Chavan, USA
James R. Lewis, USA
Ann Light, UK
James J.W. Lin, USA
Rungtai Lin, Taiwan
Zhengjie Liu, P.R. China
Aaron Marcus, USA
Allen E. Milewski, USA

Elizabeth D. Mynatt, USA
Oguzhan Ozcan, Turkey
Girish Prabhu, India
Kerstin Röse, Germany
Eunice Ratna Sari, Indonesia
Supriya Singh, Australia
Christian Sturm, Spain
Adi Tedjasaputra, Singapore
Kentaro Toyama, India
Alvin W. Yeo, Malaysia
Chen Zhao, P.R. China
Wei Zhou, P.R. China

Online Communities and Social Computing

Program Chairs: A. Ant Ozok, Panayiotis Zaphiris

Chadia N. Abras, USA
Chee Siang Ang, UK
Amy Bruckman, USA
Peter Day, UK
Fiorella De Cindio, Italy
Michael Gurstein, Canada
Tom Horan, USA
Anita Komlodi, USA
Piet A.M. Kommers, The Netherlands
Jonathan Lazar, USA
Stefanie Lindstaedt, Austria

Gabriele Meiselwitz, USA
Hideyuki Nakanishi, Japan
Anthony F. Norcio, USA
Jennifer Preece, USA
Elaine M. Raybourn, USA
Douglas Schuler, USA
Gilson Schwartz, Brazil
Sergei Stafeev, Russia
Charalambos Vrasidas, Cyprus
Cheng-Yen Wang, Taiwan

Augmented Cognition

Program Chair: Dylan D. Schmorrow

Andy Bellenkes, USA
Andrew Belyavin, UK
Joseph Cohn, USA
Martha E. Crosby, USA
Tjerk de Greef, The Netherlands
Blair Dickson, UK
Traci Downs, USA
Julie Drexler, USA
Ivy Estabrooke, USA
Cali Fidopiastis, USA
Chris Forsythe, USA
Wai Tat Fu, USA
Henry Girolamo, USA

Marc Grootjen, The Netherlands
Taro Kanno, Japan
Wilhelm E. Kincses, Germany
David Kobus, USA
Santosh Mathan, USA
Rob Matthews, Australia
Dennis McBride, USA
Robert McCann, USA
Jeff Morrison, USA
Eric Muth, USA
Mark A. Neerincx, The Netherlands
Denise Nicholson, USA
Glenn Osga, USA

Dennis Proffitt, USA
Leah Reeves, USA
Mike Russo, USA
Kay Stanney, USA
Roy Stripling, USA
Mike Swetnam, USA
Rob Taylor, UK

Maria L.Thomas, USA
Peter-Paul van Maanen, The Netherlands
Karl van Orden, USA
Roman Vilimek, Germany
Glenn Wilson, USA
Thorsten Zander, Germany

Digital Human Modeling

Program Chair: Vincent G. Duffy

Karim Abdel-Malek, USA
Thomas J. Armstrong, USA
Norm Badler, USA
Kathryn Cormican, Ireland
Afzal Godil, USA
Ravindra Goonetilleke, Hong Kong
Anand Gramopadhye, USA
Sung H. Han, Korea
Lars Hanson, Sweden
Pheng Ann Heng, Hong Kong
Tianzi Jiang, P.R. China

Kang Li, USA
Zhizhong Li, P.R. China
Timo J. Määttä, Finland
Woojin Park, USA
Matthew Parkinson, USA
Jim Potvin, Canada
Rajesh Subramanian, USA
Xuguang Wang, France
John F. Wiechel, USA
Jingzhou (James) Yang, USA
Xiu-gan Yuan, P.R. China

Human Centered Design

Program Chair: Masaaki Kurosu

Gerhard Fischer, USA
Tom Gross, Germany
Naotake Hirasawa, Japan
Yasuhiro Horibe, Japan
Minna Isomursu, Finland
Mitsuhiko Karashima, Japan
Tadashi Kobayashi, Japan

Kun-Pyo Lee, Korea
Loïc Martínez-Normand, Spain
Dominique L. Scapin, France
Haruhiko Urokohara, Japan
Gerrit C. van der Veer, The Netherlands
Kazuhiko Yamazaki, Japan

In addition to the members of the Program Boards above, I also wish to thank the following volunteer external reviewers: Gavin Lew from the USA, Daniel Su from the UK, and Ilia Adami, Ioannis Basdekis, Yannis Georgalis, Panagiotis Karampelas, Iosif Klironomos, Alexandros Mourouzis, and Stavroula Ntoa from Greece.

This conference could not have been possible without the continuous support and advice of the Conference Scientific Advisor, Prof. Gavriel Salvendy, as well as the dedicated work and outstanding efforts of the Communications Chair and Editor of HCI International News, Abbas Moallem.

I would also like to thank for their contribution toward the organization of the HCI International 2009 conference the members of the Human–Computer Interaction Laboratory of ICS-FORTH, and in particular Margherita Antona, George Paparoulis, Maria Pitsoulaki, Stavroula Ntoa, and Maria Bouhli.

Constantine Stephanidis

HCI International 2011

The 14th International Conference on Human–Computer Interaction, HCI International 2011, will be held jointly with the affiliated conferences in the summer of 2011. It will cover a broad spectrum of themes related to human–computer interaction, including theoretical issues, methods, tools, processes and case studies in HCI design, as well as novel interaction techniques, interfaces and applications. The proceedings will be published by Springer. More information about the topics, as well as the venue and dates of the conference, will be announced through the HCI International Conference series website: http://www.hci-international.org/

General Chair
Professor Constantine Stephanidis
University of Crete and ICS-FORTH
Heraklion, Crete, Greece
Email: cs@ics.forth.gr

Table of Contents

Part II: Design, Development and Evaluation of VR Environments

Part III: Haptics and Tactile Interaction in VR

Part IV: Vision in Virtual and Mixed Reality

Part V: VR Applications

Part I
Interaction and Navigation in Virtual and Mixed Environments

Part I

The 'H' in HCI: Enhancing Perception of Interaction through the Performative

Simon Biggs, Mariza Dima, Henrik Ekeus, Sue Hawksley,
Wendy Timmons, and Mark Wright

University of Edinburgh and Edinburgh College of Art, UK
Mark.Wright@ed.ac.uk

Abstract. Motion sensing technologies are well developed at the bio-mechanical (motion capture) and geo-locative (GPS) scales. However, there are many degrees of scale between these extremes and there have been few attempts to seek the integration of systems that were designed for distinct contexts and tasks. The proposition that motivated the Scale project team was that through such systems integration it would be possible to create an enhanced perception of interaction between human participants who might be co-located or remotely engaged, separated in either (or both) time or space. A further aim was to examine how the use of these technologies might inform current s discourse on the performative.

Keywords: multi-modal, scaleable, interactive environments, interdisciplinary research, perception.

1 Introduction

CIRCLE is a group engaged in Creative Interdisciplinary Research into Collaborative Environments. CIRCLE's members work at Edinburgh College of Art and the University of Edinburgh in the visual and media arts, dance and performance, architecture and sound, informatics and social sciences. They seek to undertake collaborative research at the juncture of the creative arts and sciences and across disciplines. The CIRCLE website is at http://www.eca.ac.uk/circle/. The Scale research laboratory was designed as a prototype research laboratory. In this paper we describe the undertaking and outcomes of some of the laboratory sessions. The intention is that having successfully completed the laboratory and arrived at some initial outcomes this work will serve as the basis for a more ambitious and rigorously framed research project.

2 Context

The Scale research laboratory was undertaken at a juncture of a number of research areas. These include research into choreography and cognition, interactive environments, dance education and motion capture in performance and animation. However, what bound these research foci together was a shared interest in how the perception of interaction, across interactive systems and medial modes, might be enhanced. The mix of disciplines might have been seen as a challenge but, as we found, was

R. Shumaker (Ed.): Virtual and Mixed Reality, LNCS 5622, pp. 3–12, 2009.

advantageous in addressing this overall aim. Since the 1990's there have been attempts to employ digital multimedia and imaging technologies in the recording, analysis and enhancement of physical performance. William Forsythe's Improvisation Technologies interactive CD-ROM [1] allowed users to navigate a non-linear database of the choreographer's work, learning choreographic and dance material, illustrated by the choreographer and his dancers. Scenes could be selected employing various angles of view. The dynamic use of graphical elements allowed the choreographer to visually illustrate the dynamics and character of particular movement sequences. Fundamental work informing research in visual motion analysis was undertaken by Gunnar Johansson [2] at Uppsala University. This work employed video recording of light points attached to moving bodies that is strikingly similar in effect to contemporary motion capture systems.

Scott deLahunta is a key researcher inquiring into physical performance, choreography and cognition. His most recent work in this area has evolved out of a working relationship he has developed with choreographer Wayne McGregor and researchers at the University of Cambridge [3]. Recently he has been furthering this work with Forsythe and choreographers Emio Greco and Siobhan Davies on the development of 'interactive choreographic sketchbooks' and other digital tools for the analysis and creation of dance [4]. Kate Stevens' [5] work seeks to elucidate dance, from a psychological perspective, as a domain of knowledge and signification. Her research focuses on how communication operates in dance and information is apprehended in a non-verbal environment. Similar to deLahunta, Stevens' work employs both conventional and digital notational and analytical systems in the analysis of physical performance, the objective being to comprehend how movement is perceived as meaningful. Significant artistic work has been undertaken with systems involving full-body interaction. David Rokeby [6] has worked with real-time video based motion analysis since the 1980's and his Very Nervous System software has been employed by numerous creative practitioners. Mark Coniglio, of dance company Troika Ranch, similarly works with self-authored tools to create interactive stage environments for the performers to inhabit and interact with. Coniglio's system Isadora [7] is used by numerous creative practitioners. Biggs has worked with unencumbered sensing systems in artist designed interactive environments for some years, developing his first 3D motion analysis system whilst artist fellow at the Commonwealth Scientific and Industrial Research Organisation's National Measurement Laboratories, Sydney in 1984 [8]. Currently he works with and contributes to the development of Myron [9], an open source video tracking system, primarily authored by Josh Nimoy and used by other artists and developers.

3 Aims and Objectives

The Scale research project sought to inquire into the following:

- How do multiple sensing and tracking systems permit the mapping of the human body at multiple simultaneous scales and what effect do such systems have on those being monitored and tracked within artistic installations and performative environments?

- What are the artistic possibilities, arising during the laboratory, involving scaleable representation of the human body in systems ranging from the subjective proprioceptive through to location specific human interaction and larger topographic environments?

The subsequent questions specifically addressed in this paper include:

- How do different actual, augmented and telematic environments affect inter-actors self-perception and interaction with other inter-actors, interactive systems and the environment?
- How do changes in telematic mediation affect inter-actor perception and behaviour (including agency) of themselves and others?
- Does co-locating pre-recorded motion capture data with real-time video tracking of an inter-actor enhance the inter-actor's capacity to understand and internalise the recorded movement?

4 Methods

The evaluation of the Scale research laboratory was carried out employing several interpretative practices aimed at gathering data for qualitative analysis. Since the interest was in how the constructed environments affected the inter-actors' behaviour we applied methods, drawing on ethnography, within an action research approach.

Ethnographic research practices permitted direct observation of the inter-actors by the researchers, who were also situated within the research environment as subjects. We sought to apprehend the various physical and emotional states the inter-actors experienced in response to various stimuli (visual, aural, verbal and tactile) and their empathy with one another and reflect upon our actions and responses as engaged artists, researchers and system developers. We sought to identify how the stresses and tensions of multi-tasking, problem-solving and categorising within a complex interactive environment might result in inter-actors and researchers experiencing a heightened awareness and sensitivity of self and others. This approach was helpful in identifying patterns of meaning creation by the inter-actors that informed our research objectives. In parallel to this data collection we employed hand-written notes and video recordings to record participants' observations derived from their "exhibited moment-by-moment improvised character" [10]. We also engaged with the inter-actors in short informal discussions and more formal interviews (Timmons, Hawksley, Wright, Ekeus), during and after the laboratory sessions, all of which were video recorded. It is proposed that these recordings will be subsequently digitised and annotated employing experimental video annotation tools in development at the University of Edinburgh. The inter-actors activities in the interactive environments and other systems were documented on video tape (including real-time frame sequence screen grabs of the projections) while photographs were taken throughout all sessions and during the final presentation to an invited audience (Dima, Biggs, Timmons). Video recordings of the researchers engaged in the research process were also made. The gathered material was analysed and coded by a team of informants during and after the research laboratory (Timmons, Hawksley). The team discussed, at each stage, their findings with the rest of the research team in an attempt to identify elements that could serve in designing the next stage. This iterative process allowed outcomes of early experiments to inform the design of the later experiments.

Selected sequences of digitised video material are included with the electronic version of this paper. Documentation of the laboratory sessions is also accessible at http://www.eca.ac.uk/circle/scale1.htm.

5 The Laboratory

The laboratory was carried out in the British Association of Sport and Exercise Sciences accredited Biomechanics Laboratory within the Physical Education, Sport and Leisure Studies department of the University of Edinburgh and was organised as a week long intensive, following on from several days prior setup and testing of the technologies employed. The laboratory involved a number of members of the CIRCLE group, each bringing their own expertise and disciplinary concerns to the project, as well as four inter-actors who were professional contemporary dancers from the Scottish dance company, Curve Foundation. The dancers were Ross Cooper (Director, Curve), Morgann Runacre-Temple, Ira Siobhan and Lucy Boyes. As professionals, all the dancers were highly skilled in movement and self-reflection, our reason for working with such professionals. Nevertheless, they each brought to the laboratory different prior experiences of working with set/choreographed and/or improvised material. Choreographic direction was by Hawksley. For some of the dancers adopting the role of inter-actor within a technologically mediated interactive environment was novel, demanding an approach and modality of self-reflection with which they were unfamiliar. This shift in their working patterns and self-awareness is reflected in the interviews conducted with them. The hardware and software systems developed for and employed during the research intensive laboratory were composed of three primary elements, as follows:

The Motion Capture System. The 3D motion of the inter-actors was captured using a Motion Analysis Corporation system, operated by Wright. Spherical reflective markers where attached, using Velcro, to worn motion capture suits. Eight infra-red cameras, with ring-array red LED lights, were used to illuminate and record the motion of the markers. The 3D position of the markers was calculated and recorded as an x, y, z coordinate set in each frame at 60 frames per second. The system was not real time and had a maximum capture time of approximately one minute. Individual dancers were initially recorded with a full 32 marker set. Further recordings were taken of multiple dancers employing reduced marker sets. The motion capture data was used in two ways. Firstly, it was viewed as point data within the motion capture system so as to permit evaluation of the inter-actors ability to recognise individuals from the data set. Secondly, the 3D data was transferred and parsed for use in the real-time interactive video environment.

Interactive Video Environment. Software and hardware systems were employed that allowed for the real-time playback of 3D motion capture data acquired from the motion capture system, combined with real-time video acquisition and image analysis. The software was composed of custom C++ code (Nimoy and Biggs) along with higher level Lingo (Adobe Director) code (Biggs). The system permitted full resolution acquisition of digital video which could be analysed in real-time to determine moving points of interest. Live acquired video bitmaps were encapsulated with corresponding 3D motion capture data-sets, allowing the isomorphic mapping of live acquired video to recorded 3D motion capture data and their object-oriented manipulation. Given real-time motion capture technology and appropriate interfacing this could be achieved with real-time motion capture data with little more development work.

The resulting composite digital video image was video projected life-size and co-located with the inter-actors who were the live subjects of the video acquisition system. The resulting effect was not unlike a digital mirror. The inter-actor would see elements of themselves, in real-time, mapped onto the recorded motion capture data. So long as the inter-actor closely mimicked the movements of the motion capture data then they could ensure that the corresponding anatomical elements would be synchronised with the corresponding motion capture points and thus each part could be graphically mapped to create a full image of themselves. In practice, the inter-actors rarely achieved perfect correspondence between their real-time and motion captured actions. The resulting asynchronous activity led to the emergence of a far richer visual effect than if the correspondence had been perfect. Indeed, to exploit this the software was modified such that a perfect spatial correspondence would not be possible. The image acquisition and motion capture tracking capability were designed to have a degree of spatial overlap. The visual effect caused by this was like a fragmenting tessellated mirror. The greater the asynchronicity of the inter-actor with the motion capture data the greater the fragmentation. When no synchronous activity was occurring the video would not be mapped to the motion capture data, causing elements of the inter-actor (at times, all elements) not to be mapped and thus for the live graphic image to be partial or blank. The greater the synchronicity the more data that would be visible and the more complete the mirroring effect achieved.

Visual Temporal Differencing System. This system was developed by Ekeus using Cycling 74's Max/MSP/Jitter development environment. A digital video feed of the inter-actors was acquired in real-time and a running average of the most recent frames calculated. The 'absolute difference' between this running average and the current image was calculated and output as a life-size projection. The effect was that stationary objects, including the floor and walls, 'disappeared', the projection showing only what had changed. If an inter-actor stood still, the running average of the frames would gradually match the current image seen by the camera and they would seem to 'disappear'. Similarly, when individuals who were rendered 'invisible' moved they seemed to re-appear and also leave a 'shadow' at their former position. This shadow would also fade away over the time-span of the running average.

The effect was that the system would show a 'memory' of movement in the space and the inter-actors could effectively interact with their earlier movements. Different temporal scales were used, ranging from 10 seconds down to 1 second. This related to similar temporal effects achieved with the interactive video environment system. It was found that shorter time spans tended towards the inter-actors making faster, more sudden gestures, and the longer spans towards slower, smoother movements.

6   The Experimental Sessions

An intention of the laboratory was to explore and exploit the diverse disciplines and skill sets of the team members. One method was for the researchers to shift roles within the team, and to rapidly test out of a range of ideas, with a view to maximizing opportunities for unforeseen convergences and outcomes. Most interview sessions with the inter-actors were held informally, within the studio space, as they cooled down, emphasizing an ethnographic rather than analytical approach.

In the initial laboratory session three of the four inter-actors learned two set/choreographed dance phrases, comprising easily assimilated, codified material; one static, one travelling. The inter-actors also created short personal 'signature' phrases of movements that they felt in some way represented themselves. These phrases were recorded as full 32 point marker sets of 3D motion capture data, the phrases being executed by the inter-actors individually, in duets and in trios. The inter-actors had not previously seen the motion capture suits or the floor space. The only constraint they were given was that their phrases were to be of no more than one minute in length, this relating to the 1 minute capacity of the motion capture system. The physical size of the capture space was a cubic volume of approximately 4 x 3 x 3 metres in a laboratory space of roughly 10 x 10 x 6 metres. The researchers observed how the inter-actors adapted the phrases to accommodate the constraints of the system, with consequent effects on the use of space and timing as the suits restricted the inter-actors' movements. They needed to move more slowly to avoid the Velcro marker attachments sticking, relocating or detaching and also limiting points of body contact with the floor in floor-work to avoid pain from rolling on the markers.

Some of the motion capture data was rendered as point-figures and projected life-size and deployed so as to manipulate live acquired digital video employing the Myron software. An unexpected outcome of this particular configuration was that in order to maintain a mirror-like video image, the inter-actor is obliged to track the motion captured figure in real-scale time and space. The three initial inter-actors reported that they felt their task was complicated by the demands of synchronising their actions with the live manipulated video imagery. However, the fourth inter-actor had not been present during the first day of the laboratory and thus we were able to observe her working within the immersive environment with no prior knowledge of how the interactivity worked, nor of the phrases. She was able to decipher some 85% of the movement material and spacing. She reported "finding it easy to follow lines in terms of structure, that was quite clear, but when it got confusing for me was when the movement became circular and things became curved, and the changing in directions, I was just totally lost" [11]. However, she indicated that the life-size scale of the projections were helpful, allowing us to speculate as to how such an experimental prototype could inform the design of a system for movement phrase learning. The inter-actors also performed more subtle dance improvisations emanating from focusing attention to self and surroundings, more like a 'movement meditation'. Wearing reduced marker sets (as few as 7), to facilitate ease and greater range of movement, the inter-actors freely improvised in the laboratory space. Sometimes they did this as solo activities, sometimes as duos and sometimes as trios. However, they were not informed when recording would start or stop.

Following these motion capture recordings, the inter-actors were shown data from a range of phrases and improvisations, displayed as point-light figures. They were asked to identify who they thought was performing each phrase and to explain how and why they drew their conclusions. They correctly and confidently identified most of the codified material and their personal 32 marker set phrases. The inter-actors' comments from the interviews indicate the phenomena by which they were able to make these identifications. When two of the inter-actors recognised another in the data sets and were asked why, one stated "the head's like this" [12] (physically demonstrating the movement) whilst another said "because I saw him perform the step and the third count of the second triplet was like how Ira did it" [13]. Ira then said "I think that it is (me) because of the space..." [14]. Further feedback, such as "Mannerisms, character, body shapes...the choice of the movements...there are certain things you can see, like the shape or height of someone's leg, or the line..." [12] and "...feet, demi-pointe not high...wider body shape...look at the arms, those arms are big" [14], represented typical reflections contained in the recordings with the inter-actors. The latter quote is particularly curious as the point-light figures did not contain explicit data from which a viewer, expert or otherwise, might be able to deduce the volume of an anatomical element, such as the size of an arm. It is possible the inter-actor was referring to the length of the arm but within the context of the recording session and given the physical attributes of the inter-actors we are reasonably confident he was referring to the physical volume of the arm. \Whilst the inter-actors succeeded reasonably well in identifying codified material they struggled to identify any of the 'movement meditations', which used reduced marker sets. They had little recollection of what movement they had done during these improvisations. This suggests that part of their recognition depended on 'somatic memory' of known material as well as a prior knowledge of the material they were observing. Typical feedback collected from the inter-actors evidence this, such as "that is just a mess" [13] and "I can't tell what dot is what part of the body" [12]. Asking the inter-actors to identify more abstract movement phrases, with which they had less familiarity, echoes Johansson's research, although contrasting with the simple canonical movements, such as walking, of his studies. However, as the different phrases were not presented to the inter-actors as comparable data-sets this aspect of the laboratory will hopefully be explored more thoroughly in the next iteration of the research process. A further set of experiments sought to explore how the inter-actors interacted with more remote non-visual forms of real-time information. The objective here was to observe how the inter-actors managed to work with interactive data originating at a greater distance and where the spatial envelope was at a scale far greater than the interactive space afforded in the studio environment. This involved some of the inter-actors working in the laboratory, within an immersive interactive audio-visual environment, which was connected by mobile phone to a remote inter-actor. Using a mobile phone's hands-free set connected to an audio amplification system in the interaction space, an audio link was established between the laboratory and a remote inter-actor. The local inter-actors could talk back to the remote inter-actor. The audio from the phone was fed into the Max/MSP/Jitter patch for the temporal visual differencing system and the amplitude of the incoming audio was mapped to a brightness parameter on the input camera feed. The projection's brightness would thus vary in conjunction with the voice of the remote inter-actor and the sound of their environment. In trials the remote inter-actor tended to create a demonstrative sound-scape, seeking to translate the auditory characteristics of phenomena and objects back to the laboratory. The inter-actor approached this task almost like a 'gaming' situation. On one occasion the remote inter-actor was not expecting to be called from the laboratory and the resulting spontaneity of the inter-actor's response lent a more vital element to the interaction between them and the other inter-actors. In particular the inter-actors reported a greater feeling of empathy and awareness to the remote inter-actor, each other and their environment. The temporal graphic effects of the system meant that the dancers could purposefully render themselves invisible in the projections, which "gave us a use and a purpose to 'no movement'" [13] and allowed us to develop "a sense of becoming quieter … less aware of the situation that we were in and very much involved" [11]. Throughout the laboratory the inter-actors were asked to engage in situations which required highly complex problem-solving and multi-tasking capabilities. The remote audio experiment required a particular interaction with an audio-visual environment in which they were asked to move, watch, listen and talk. Their solutions were creative and they coped by rapidly choosing to respond to only certain information sets. The inter-actors also quickly became adept at juggling multiple tasks and shifting between media, evidencing a visceral sense of medial transliteracy. As one inter-actor observed "I became aware of how listening and how answering Ira on the phone was affecting the group and how we were moving" [11]. One inter-actor commented "I didn't think of the movement in the sense of 'dancer making steps'. More relating to the sound…I didn't have a vocabulary" [13] and yet another observed "it felt more emotion oriented" [12].

7 Outcomes

The Scale research laboratory allowed the CIRCLE researchers to study how multiple sensing and tracking systems can permit the mapping of the human body at multiple simultaneous scales and to observe the effects such systems have on those being monitored and tracked. A number of different systems, artistic strategies and environments were tested during the laboratory and were subsequently evaluated for their future potential application in artistic projects. Our primary research question, whether an integrated multi-modal approach to designing interactive environments might enhance an inter-actor's perception of interaction, was not definitively resolved. However, the observations and data collected indicate that this is likely the case. The involvement of professional dancers as inter-actors offered an opportunity to collect the qualitative data required to arrive at these outcomes. The experiments allowed us to observe and evaluate how augmented environments can affect inter-actors self-perception and interaction with other inter-actors. Thus we were able to engage a number of questions, amongst them inquiring into how an inter-actor recognises their own or others movement characteristics. The responses from the inter-actors show that where they were aware of being recorded, and movement material was pre-learned and/or canonical, they were able to identify themselves, whilst when confronted with improvised movement phrases and where they had not been aware they were being recorded, they struggled to do so. We were also able to observe and analyse how co-locating pre-recorded motion capture data with real-time video tracking of an inter-actor can enhance an inter-actor's capacity to understand and internalise a recorded movement. That one of the inter-actors, who was not present during the first day when many of the movement phrases were developed and recorded, was able to learn sequences with relative ease through physically following and explicitly 'mirroring' the life-size projections of the motion capture data, through the device of having their own video image mapped in real-time and life-size to the 3D data points, is evidence of this. Tantalisingly, there appears to be significant potential value in further exploring this aspect of the research, focusing on variations of how the system might be designed and studying different modes of interaction with the system. However, whilst the inter-actor's perception and recognition of motion capture data, represented as simple motions of individuals, is coherent with Johansson's classic work complex motions with orientation changes were less successfully recognised, as was the case with the reduced marker sets. Further research will need to more rigorously address these issues. Experiments with multi-modal systems employing sound and image that is both co-located with and remote to inter-actors allowed us to evaluate how changes in telematic mediation can affect inter-actor perception and behaviour and, in this instance, choreographic decision making. The evidence acquired during these experiments suggests the quality of the inter-actors experience was not only a function of the level of veracity of a representational system (e.g.: how realistic the presentation of a virtual presence might be) but also of other phenomena that are of a more abstract nature. This experiment also suggested that it is not necessary for an inter-actor to experience phenomena as cohesive or unitary for them to gain an effective apprehension of an event and thus successfully interact with the various elements involved. However, it was also clear from the interviews with the inter-actors that such a situation was more demanding of their concentration and multi-tasking capability as the inter-actors reported experiences of breaks in their sense of presence and agency.

During the research laboratory some initial experiments were attempted that employed geo-locative positioning systems and remote site specific actions, the objective being to engage the inter-actors with information not spatially co-located with them. Due to time constraints these experiments did not lead to any outcomes of value to the questions addressed in this paper. However, the experiment involving the use of the telephone call indicates that this is another area of inquiry that is likely to deliver further valuable insights. The integration of GPS technologies with local sensing and interactive systems was achieved during the laboratory. Successful, but tentative, experiments with synchronised video recording of inter-actors interacting within a large architectural space were also completed. It is the intention to employ telematic, GPS and live video streaming systems in the next iteration of the research, seeking to fully integrate these with the multi-modal interactive systems deployed as well as with real-time motion capture systems.

As the first research project undertaken by the CIRCLE group the Scale laboratory sessions also, perhaps most importantly, allowed us to test whether a group of researchers and practitioners from diverse disciplinary backgrounds could work together constructively, often with diverging aims and objectives, and yet realise outcomes of use in each of our disciplines and which might inform interdisciplinary discourse and research. It is the intention of the CIRCLE group members to further pursue this aspect of our work in order to both facilitate our own effectiveness as a research group and to further inform discourse on what interdisciplinary research might be. The Scale research laboratory was funded by the University of Edinburgh's Collaborative Research Dean's Fund and Edinburgh College of Art's Research Fund. Many thanks to Simon Coleman, Sports Science, University of Edinburgh.

Dancer Ross Cooper within the motion capture environment

Image sequence generated within interactive video environment

Image sequence generated by the visual temporal differencing system

Dancers within the interactive environment

References

1. Forsythe, W.: William Forsythe's Improvisation Technologies, ZKM Karlsruhe and Deutsches Tanzarchiv, Cologne/SK Stiftung Kultur CD-ROM (Mac/PC) (1994), ISBN 3-7757-0850-2
2. Johansson, G.: Visual perception of biological motion and a model for its analysis. Perception and psychophysics 14(2), 201–211 (1973)
3. McCarthy, R.: Blackwell, deLahunta, Wing, Hollands, Barnard, Nimmo-Smith, Marcel, Bodies meet minds: choreography and cognition. Leonardo 39(5), 475–478 (2006)
4. deLahunta, S.: Choreographic resources agents, archives, scores and installations. Performance Research, Routledge 13(1) (2008)
5. Stevens, C., McKechnie, S.: Thinking in action: thought made visible in contemporary dance. Cognitive Processing 6(4), 243–252 (2005)
6. Rokeby, D., Fondation Langlois, http://www.fondation-anglois.org/html/e/page.php?NumPage=80#n1 (accessed January 2, 2009)
7. Coniglio, M.: http://www.troikatronix.com/isadora.html (accessed January 2, 2009)
8. Biggs, S.: http://hosted.simonbiggs.easynet.co.uk/right/CSIRO/index.htm (accessed January 2, 2009)
9. Nimoy, J.: http://webcamxtra.sourceforge.net/ (accessed January 2, 2009)
10. Suchman, L.: Plans and Situated Actions: The Problem of Human-Machine Communication. Cambridge University Press, Cambridge (1987)
11. Boyes, L.: Quoted in interviews (recorded August and December 2008)
12. Runacre-Temple, M.: Quoted in interviews (recorded August 2008)
13. Cooper R.: Quoted in interviews (recorded August and December 2008)
14. Siobhan, I.: Quoted in interviews (recorded August 2008)

Advanced Interaction Techniques for Augmented Reality Applications

Mark Billinghurst[1], Hirokazu Kato[2], and Seiko Myojin[2]

[1] The Human Interface Technology New Zealand (HIT Lab NZ),
University of Canterbury, Private Bag 4800, Christchurch, New Zealand
mark.billinghurst@hitlabnz.org
[2] Nara Institute of Science and Technology,
8916-5, Takayama, Ikoma, Nara, 630-0192 Japan
{kato,seiko-m}@is.naist.jp

Abstract. Augmented Reality (AR) research has been conducted for several decades, although until recently most AR applications had simple interaction methods using traditional input devices. AR tracking, display technology and software has progressed to the point where commercial applications can be developed. However there are opportunities to provide new advanced interaction techniques for AR applications. In this paper we describe several interaction methods that can be used to provide a better user experience, including tangible user interaction, multimodal input and mobile interaction.

Keywords: Augmented Reality, Interaction Techniques, Tangible User Interfaces, Multimodal Input.

1 Introduction

Augmented Reality (AR) is a novel technology that allows virtual imagery to be seamlessly combined with the real world. Azuma identifies the three key characteristics of Augmented Reality: combining real and virtual images, the virtual imagery is registered with the real world, and it is interactive in real time [1]. These properties were a key part of the first AR application created over 40 years ago by Sutherland [2], and since then many interesting prototype AR applications have been developed in domains such as medicine, education, manufacturing, and others.

Although AR has a long history, much of the research in the field has been focused on the technology for providing the AR experience (such as tracking and display devices), rather than methods for allowing users to better interact with the virtual content being shown. As Ishii says, the AR field has been primarily concerned with "..considering purely visual augmentations" [3] and while great advances have been made in AR display technologies and tracking techniques, interaction with AR environments has usually been limited to either passive viewing or simple browsing of virtual information registered to the real world.

For example, in Rekimoto's NaviCam application a person uses a handheld LCD display to see virtual annotations overlaid on the real world [4] and but cannot interact with or edit the annotations. Similarly Feiner's Touring Machine outdoor AR

R. Shumaker (Ed.): Virtual and Mixed Reality, LNCS 5622, pp. 13–22, 2009.

application [5] allowed virtual labels to be placed over the buildings in the real world, but once again the user could not manipulate the virtual content.

Before AR technology can be widely used, there is a need to explore new interaction methods that can provide an enhanced user experience. In this paper we describe several advanced interaction techniques that could be applied to the next generation of AR experiences, including tangible object input, multimodal interaction and mobile phone manipulation. The common thread through these techniques is that it is tangible interaction with the real world itself than can provide one of the best ways to interact with virtual AR content.

In the remainder of this paper we first review related work and describe the need for new AR interface metaphors. We then describe the Tangible AR interaction metaphor and show how it can applied in the MagicCup AR application. Next we show how speech and gesture commands can be added to the Tangible AR method to create multimodal interfaces. Finally we discuss how these same methods can be applied in mobile AR settings, and discuss directions for future research.

2   Background Research

When a new interface technology is developed it often passes through the following stages:

1. Prototype Demonstration
2. Adoption of Interaction techniques from other interface metaphors
3. Development of new interface metaphors appropriate to the medium
4. Development of formal theoretical models for user interactions

For example, the earliest immersive Virtual Reality (VR) systems were just used to view virtual scenes. Then interfaces such 3DM [6] explored how elements of the traditional desktop WIMP metaphor could be used to enable users to model immersively and support more complex interactions. Next, interaction techniques such as the Go-Go [7] or World in Miniature [8] were developed which are unique to VR and cannot be used in other environments. Now researchers are attempting to arrive at a formal taxonomy for characterizing interaction in virtual worlds that will allow developers to build virtual interfaces in a systematic manner [9].

In many ways AR interfaces have barely moved beyond the first stage. The earliest AR systems were used to view virtual models in a variety of application domains such as medicine [10] and machine maintenance [11]. These interfaces provided a very intuitive method for viewing three dimensional information, but little support for creating or modifying the AR content.

More recently, researchers have begun to address this deficiency. The AR modeler of Kiyokawa [12] uses a magnetic tracker to allow people to create AR content, while the Studierstube [13] and EMMIE [14] projects use tracked pens and tablets for selecting and modifying AR objects. More traditional input devices, such as a hand-held mouse or tablet [15][16], as well as intelligent agents [17] have also been investigated. However these attempts have largely been based on existing 2D and 3D interface metaphors from desktop or immersive virtual environments.

In our research we have been seeking to move beyond this and explore new interaction methods. Unlike most other desktop interface and virtual reality systems, in an AR experience there is an intimate relationship between 3D virtual models and physical objects these models are associated with. This suggests that one promising research direction may arise from taking advantage of the immediacy and familiarity of everyday physical objects for effective manipulation of virtual objects.

Recently researchers have been investigating computer interfaces based on real objects. For example in ubiquitous computing [18] environments the computer vanishes into the real world, while Tangible User Interface (TUI) [3] research aims to allow people to use real objects to interact with digital content. For example in the Triangles TUI interface [19], physical triangles with characters drawn on them are assembled to tell stories while a visual representations of the stories are shown on a separate monitor distinct from the physical interface. Similarly, in the Urp application [20] the user can manipulate real model buildings while seeing projections of virtual wind and shadow patterns appearing on a table under the buildings. In both of these examples the use of physical objects to control the interaction with the virtual content makes it very easy to intuitively use the applications. Although the use of tangible user interface metaphors have been explored in projected environments, they have been less used in AR applications.

In addition to using physical objects to interact with AR content, there is also interesting research that can be performed in involving other input modalities, such as adding speech and gesture input. For example, users could issue combined speech and gesture commands to interact with the virtual content.

One of the first interfaces to combine speech and gesture recognition was Bolt's Media Room [21] which allowed the user to interact with projected graphics through voice, gesture and gaze. Since then, speech and gesture interaction has been used in desktop and immersive Virtual Reality (VR) environments. Weimer and Ganapathy [22] developed a prototype virtual environment that incorporated a data glove and simple speech recognizer. Laviola [23] investigated the use of whole-hand gestures and speech to create, place, modify, and manipulate furniture and interior decorations.

However, there are relatively few examples of AR applications that use multimodal input. Olwal et al. [24] introduced a set of statistical geometric tools, SenseShapes, which use volumetric regions of interest that can be attached to the user, providing valuable information about the user interaction with the AR system. Kaiser et al. [25] extended this by focusing on mutual disambiguation between speech and gesture input to improve interpretation robustness. This research is a good start but more work needs to be done on how best to use speech and gesture input in an AR setting.

A final area of interest for advanced interaction techniques is in mobile and handheld AR. In recent years AR applications have migrated to mobile platforms, including Tablet PCs [26], PDAs [27] and mobile phones [28]. The mobile phone is an ideal platform for augmented reality (AR). The current generation of phones have full colour displays, integrated cameras, fast processors and even dedicated 3D graphics chips. Henrysson [29] and Moehring [28] have shown how mobile phones can be used for simple single user AR applications.

Most handheld and mobile AR applications currently use very simple interaction techniques. For example, the Invisible train AR application [27] uses PDAs to view AR content and users can select virtual models directly by clicking on the model with a stylus. The Siemen's Mosquito mobile phone AR game [30] shows virtual mosquitos that can be killed with a simple "point and shoot" metaphor, while the AR-PAD interface [31] is similar, but it adds a handheld controller to an LCD panel, and selection is performed by positioning virtual cross hairs over the object and hitting a button on the controller.

As more mobile devices are used to deliver AR experiences then there is an opportunity to explore improved interaction techniques that move beyond simple point and click. In section 5 we will discuss this in more detail.

3 Tangible Augmented Reality Interfaces

By considering the intimate connection between the physical world and overlaid AR content, we believe that a promising new AR interface metaphor can arise from combining the enhanced display possibilities of Augmented Reality with the intuitive physical manipulation of Tangible User Interfaces. We call this combination Tangible Augmented Reality [32].

Tangible AR interfaces are extremely intuitive to use because physical object manipulations are mapped one-to-one to virtual object operations. There are a number of good tangible design principles can be used to create effective AR applications. Some of these principles include:

– The use of physical controllers for manipulating virtual content.
– Support for spatial 3D interaction techniques (such as using object proximity).
– Support for multi-handed interaction.
– Matching the physical constraints of the object to the task requirements.
– The ability to support parallel activity with multiple objects
– Collaboration between multiple participants

In the next section we give a case study showing how these design principles are combined in an example AR application.

3.1 Case Study: The Magic Cup

A good example of how tangible interaction methods can be applied in an AR experience is with the MagicCup interface. The MagicCup is a cup-shaped handheld compact AR input device with a tracker that detects six-dimensional position and pose information (see figure 1). MagicCup uses the interaction method of "covering," which employs it novel "shape that can hold an object." The "shape that can hold an object" and the interaction method of "covering" are useful for the virtual objects within arm's reach. A human's action when using the cup is as follows. In an interaction with a virtual object, there is one action — "Cover." In the actions with just the cup, except for the general relocation action, the variety of actions is limited to about five actions — "Put," "Slide,""Rotate,""Shake," and "Incline." According to Tangible AR, we need to make natural reactions of the virtual objects responsive to these actions. This allows users to build the right mental model easily.

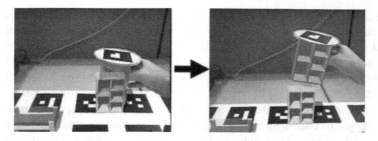

Fig. 1. MagicCup Input Device

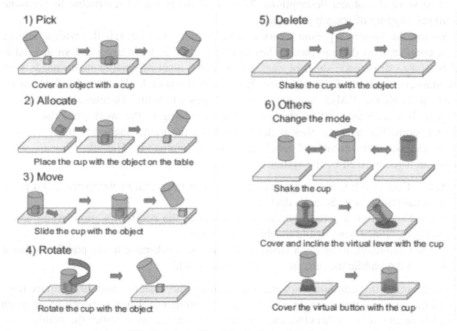

Fig. 2. Magic Cup Manipulation Methods

We assigned human actions to the reactions of the virtual object (Figure 2. A user holds the cup upside down and controls the virtual objects. (1) in Figure 2 shows selection. (2)(3)(4) show manipulation. (5)(6) show system control.

4 Multimodal Interfaces

Like the MagicCup example above, most of the current AR interfaces use a single input modality to interact with the virtual content. However Tangible AR interfaces have some limitations, such as only allowing the user to interact with the virtual content that they can see. To overcome these limitations we have been exploring speech and gesture interaction in AR environments.

Our example multimodal system is a modified version of the VOMAR application [33] for supporting tangible manipulation of virtual furniture in an AR setting using a handheld paddle. VOMAR is a Tangible AR interface that allows people to rapidly put together interior designs by arranging virtual furniture in empty rooms. Originally objects were manipulated using paddle gesture input alone and the AR Application is based on the ARToolkit [34] library and the VOMAR paddle gesture library.

To create a multimodal interface we added the Ariadne [35] spoken dialog system to allow people to issue spoken commands to the system using the Microsoft Speech 5.1 API as the speech recognition engine. Ariadne and the AR Application communicate with each other using the middleware ICE [36]. A Microsoft Access database is used to store the object descriptions. This database is used by Ariadne to facilitate rapid prototyping of speech grammar.

To use the system a person wears a head mounted display (HMD) with a camera on it connected to the computer. They hold a paddle in their hand and sit at a table with a large workspace sheet of markers on it and a set of smaller menu pages with six markers on each of them (Figure 3a). When the user looks at each of the menu pages through the HMD they see different types of virtual furniture on the pages (Figure 3b), such as a set of chairs or tables. Looking at the workspace they see a virtual room. The user can then pick objects from the menu pages and place them in the workspace using combined paddle and speech commands. The following are some commands recognized by the system:

– Select Command: to select a virtual object from the menu or workspace, and place it on the paddle, eg "Select a desk".
– Place Command: to place the attached object at the paddle location in the workspace, eg "Place here" while touching a location.
– Move Command: to attach a virtual object in the workspace to the paddle so that it follows the paddle movement, eg "Move the couch".

To understand the combined speech and gesture, the system must fuse inputs from both input streams into a single understandable command. When a speech recognition result is received from Ariadne, the AR Application checks whether the paddle is in view. Next, depending on the speech command type and the paddle pose, a specific

Fig. 3a. Using the system

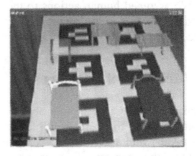

Fig. 3b. The user's view

action is taken by the system. For example, consider the case when the user says "grab this" while the paddle is placed over the menu page to grab a virtual object. The system will test the paddle proximity to the virtual objects. If the paddle is close enough to an object, the object will be selected and attached to the paddle. If the paddle is not close enough, the object will not be selected.

In a user study of the system [37], when using speech and static paddle interaction, participants completed the task nearly 30% faster than when using paddle input only. Users also reported that they found it harder to place objects in the target positions and rotate them using only paddle gestures, and they also said they liked the multimodal input condition much more than the gesture only input condition. These results show that by supporting multimodal input users are able to select the input modality that best matches the task at hand, and so makes the interface more intuitive.

5 Mobile AR Interfaces

As mentioned in the introduction there is a need for new interaction techniques for mobile AR experiences. There are a number of important differences between using a mobile phone AR interface and a traditional desktop interface, including:

- limited input options (no mouse/keyboard)
- limited screen resolution
- little graphics support
- reduced processing power

Similarly, compared to a traditional HMD based AR system, in an AR application on a phone the display is handheld rather than headworn, and the display and input device are connected. Finally, compared to a PDA the mobile phone is operated using a one-handed button interface in contrast to a two-hand stylus interaction.

These differences mean that interface metaphors developed for Desktop and HMD based systems may not be appropriate for handheld phone based systems. For example, applications developed with a Tangible AR metaphor [32] often assume that the user has both hands free to manipulate physical input devices which will not be the case with mobile phones.

We need to develop input techniques that can be used one handed and only rely on a joypad and keypad input. Since the phone is handheld we can use the motion of the phone itself to interact with the virtual object. Two handed interaction techniques [38] can also be explored; one hand holding the phone and the second a real object on which AR graphics are overlaid. This approach assumes that phone is like a handheld lens giving a small view into the AR scene. In this case the user may be more likely move the phone-display than change their viewpoint relative to the phone. The small form factor of the phone lets us explore more object-based interaction techniques based around motion of the phone itself (Figure 4).

We conducted a recent user study [39] exploring interaction techniques where a virtual block is attached to the mobile phone and the phone was moved to position the block. We found that people were able to accurately translate a block 50% faster when it was attached to the phone, than when using phone keypad input. However object-based interaction techniques were twice as slow for rotating objects compared

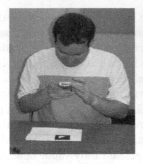 

Fig. 4. Interaction using a mobile phone

to keypad input. The results show that using a tangible interface metaphor provides a fast way to position AR objects in a mobile phone interface because the user just has to move the real phone where the block is to go. However, there seems to be little advantage in using our implementation of a tangible interface metaphor for virtual object rotation.

6   Conclusions

In order for Augmented Reality technology to become more mainstream there is a need for new interaction techniques to be developed that allow people to interact with AR content in a much more intuitive way. In this paper we review several advanced interaction techniques based on the tangible AR metaphor which combines tangible user interface input techniques with AR output.

The MagicCup application shows how using tangible AR design principles can produce a very intuitive user interface. Combining speech and gesture input can create multimodal interfaces that allow users to interact more efficiently than with either modality alone. Finally, we show how the tangible AR metaphor can also be applied in mobile AR interfaces to move beyond traditional input methods.

In the future more evaluation studies need to be performed to validate these techniques. User centered design approaches could also be applied to transfer these research ideas into commercial applications that meet the needs of a variety of application domains. Finally, formal theoretical models could be developed to predict user performance with a variety of tangible AR methods.

References

1. Azuma, R.: A Survey of Augmented Reality. Presence: Teleoperators and Virtual Environments 6(4), 355–385 (1997)
2. Sutherland, I.: The Ultimate Display. International Federation of Information Processing 2, 506–508 (1965)
3. Ishii, H., Ullmer, B.: Tangible Bits: Towards Seamless Interfaces between People, Bits and Atoms. In: Proceedings of CHI 1997, Atlanta, Georgia, USA, pp. 234–241. ACM Press, New York (1997)

4. Rekimoto, J.: The World Through the Computer: A New Human-Computer Interaction Style Based on Wearable Computers. Technical Report SCSL-TR-94-013, Sony Computer Science Laboratories Inc. (1994)
5. Feiner, S., MacIntyre, B., Hollerer, T., Webster, A.: A Touring Machine: Prototyping 3D Mobile Augmented Reality Systems for Exploring the Urban Environment. In: Proceedings of the 1st IEEE international Symposium on Wearable Computers, ISWC, October 13-14, 1997, IEEE Computer Society, Washington (1997)
6. Butterworth, J., Davidson, A., Hench, S., Olano, M.T.: 3DM: a three dimensional modeler using a head-mounted display. In: Proceedings of the 1992 Symposium on interactive 3D Graphics, SI3D 1992, Cambridge, Massachusetts, United States, pp. 135–138. ACM, New York (1992)
7. Poupyrev, I., Billinghurst, M., Weghorst, S., Ichikawa, T.: The Go-Go Interaction Technique. In: Proc. Of UIST 1996, pp. 79–80. ACM Press, New York (1996)
8. Stoakley, R., Conway, M., Pausch, R.: Virtual Reality on a WIM: Interactive Worlds in Miniature. In: Proceedings of CHI 1995, ACM Press, New York (1995)
9. Gabbard, J.L.: A taxonomy of usability characteristics in virtual environments. M.S. Thesis, Virginia Polytechnic Institute and State University (1997), http://www.vpst.org/jgabbard/ve/framework/
10. Bajura, M., Fuchs, H., et al.: Merging Virtual Objects with the Real World: Seeing Ultrasound Imagery Within the Patient. In: SIGGRAPH 1992, ACM, New York (1992)
11. Feiner, S., MacIntyre, B., et al.: Knowledge-Based Augmented Reality. Communications of the ACM 36(7), 53–62 (1993)
12. Kiyokawa, K., Takemura, H., Yokoya, N.: A Collaboration Supporting Technique by Integrating a Shared Virtual Reality and a Shared Augmented Reality. In: Proceedings of the IEEE International Conference on Systems, Man and Cybernetics (SMC 1999), Tokyo, vol. VI, pp. 48–53 (1999)
13. Schmalstieg, D., Fuhrmann, A., et al.: Bridging multiple user interface dimensions with augmented reality systems. In: ISAR 2000, IEEE, Los Alamitos (2000)
14. Butz, A., Hollerer, T., et al.: Enveloping Users and Computers in a Collaborative 3D Augmented Reality. In: Proceedings of IWAR 1999, San Francisco, October 20-21, pp. 35–44 (1999)
15. Rekimoto, J., Ayatsuka, Y., et al.: Augment-able reality: Situated communication through physical and digital spaces. In: ISWC 1998, IEEE, Los Alamitos (1998)
16. Hollerer, T., Feiner, S., et al.: Exploring MARS: developing indoor and outdoor user interfaces to a mobile augmented reality system. IEEE Computers & Graphics 23, 779–785 (1999)
17. Anabuki, M., Kakuta, H., et al.: Welbo: An Embodied Conversational Agent Living in Mixed Reality Spaces. In: CHI 2000, Extended Abstracts, ACM, New York (2000)
18. Weiser, M.: The Computer for the Twenty-First Century. Scientific American 265(3), 94–104 (1991)
19. Gorbet, M., Orth, M., Ishii, H.: Triangles: Tangible Interface for Manipulation and Exploration of Digital Information Topography. In: Proceedings of CHI 1998, Los Angeles (1998)
20. Underkoffler, J., Ishii, H.: Urp: a luminous-tangible workbench for urban planning and design. In: Proceedings of the SIGCHI Conference on Human Factors in Computing Systems: the CHI Is the Limit, CHI 1999, Pittsburgh, Pennsylvania, United States, May 15-20, 1999, pp. 386–393. ACM, New York (1999)
21. Bolt, R.A.: Put-That-There: Voice and Gesture at the Graphics Interface. In: Proceedings of ACM SIGGRAPH 1980, Computer Graphics, vol. 14, pp. 262–270 (1980)

22. Weimer, D., Ganapathy, S.K.: A Synthetic Visual Environment with Hand Gesturing and Voice Input. In: Proceedings of ACM Conference on Human Factors in Computing Systems, pp. 235–240 (1989)
23. Laviola Jr., J.J.: Whole-Hand and Speech Input in Virtual Environments. Master Thesis, Brown University (1996)
24. Olwal, A., Benko, H., Feiner, S.: SenseShapes: Using Statistical Geometry for Object Selection in a Multimodal Augmented Reality System. In: Proceedings of The Second IEEE and ACM International Symposium on Mixed and Augmented Reality (ISMAR 2003), October 2003, pp. 300–301 (2003)
25. Kaiser, E., Olwal, A., McGee, D., Benko, H., Corradini, A., Xiaoguang, L., Cohen, P., Feiner, S.: Mutual Dissambiguation of 3D Multimodal Interaction in Augmented and Virtual Reality. In: Proceedings of The Fifth International Conference on Multimodal Interfaces (ICMI 2003), pp. 12–19 (2003)
26. Träskbäck, M., Haller, M.: Mixed reality training application for an oil refinery: user requirements. In: ACM SIGGRAPH International Conference on Virtual Reality Continuum and its Applications in Industry, VRCAI 2004, Singapore, pp. 324–327 (2004)
27. Wagner, D., Schmalstieg, D.: First steps towards handheld augmented reality. In: Proc. of the 7th International Symposium on Wearable Computers (ISWC 2003), White Plains, pp. 127–137. IEEE Computer Society, Los Alamitos (2003)
28. Moehring, M., Lessig, C., Bimber, O.: AR Video See-Through on Consumer Cell Phones. In: Proc. of International Symposium on Augmented and Mixed Reality (ISMAR 2004), pp. 252–253 (2004)
29. Henrysson, A., Ollila, M.: UMAR - Ubiquitous Mobile Augmented Reality. In: Proc. Third International Conference on Mobile and Ubiquitous Multimedia (MUM 2004), College Park, Maryland, USA, October 27-29, 2004, pp. 41–45 (2004)
30. MosquitoHunt,
http://w4.siemens.de/en2/html/press/newsdesk_archive/2003/foe03111.html
31. Mogilev, D., Kiyokawa, K., Billinghurst, M., Pair, J.: AR Pad: An Interface for Face-to-face AR Collaboration. In: Proc. of the ACM Conference on Human Factors in Computing Systems 2002 (CHI 2002), Minneapolis, pp. 654–655 (2002)
32. Kato, H., Billinghurst, M., Poupyrev, I., Tetsutani, N., Tachibana, K.: Tangible Augmented Reality for Human Computer Interaction. In: Proc. of Nicograph 2001, Tokyo, Japan (2001)
33. Kato, H., Billinghurst, M., Poupyrev, I., Imamoto, K., Tachibana, K.: Virtual Object Manipulation on a Table-Top AR Environment. In: Proceedings of the International Symposium on Augmented Reality (ISAR 2000), October 2000, pp. 111–119 (2000)
34. ARToolKit, http://www.hitl.washington.edu/artoolkit
35. Denecke, M.: Rapid Prototyping for Spoken Dialogue Systems. In: Proceedings of the 19th international conference on Computational Linguistics, vol. 1, pp. 1–7 (2002)
36. ICE, http://www.zeroc.com/ice.html
37. Irawati, S., Green, S., Billinghurst, M., Duenser, A., Ko, H.: An evaluation of an augmented reality multimodal interface using speech and paddle gestures. In: Pan, Z., Cheok, D.A.D., Haller, M., Lau, R., Saito, H., Liang, R. (eds.) ICAT 2006. LNCS, vol. 4282, pp. 272–283. Springer, Heidelberg (2006)
38. Hinckley, K., Pausch, R., Proffitt, D., Patten, J., Kassell, N.: Cooperative Bimanual Action. In: ACM CHI 1997 Conference on Human Factors in Computing Systems, pp. 27–34 (1997)
39. Henrysson, A., Billinghurst, M., Ollila, M.: Virtual object manipulation using a mobile phone. In: Proceedings of the 2005 international conference on Augmented tele-existence, Christchurch, New Zealand, December 5-8 (2005)

Methods for Quantifying Emotion-Related Gait Kinematics

Elizabeth Crane[1], Melissa Gross[1], and Ed Rothman[2]

[1] Division of Kinesiology, University of Michigan,
Ann Arbor, MI USA
[2] Department of Statistics, University of Michigan,
Ann Arbor, MI USA
{bcrane,mgross,erothman}@umich.edu

Abstract. Quantitative models of whole body expressive movement can be developed by combining methods form biomechanics, psychology, and statistics. The purpose of this paper was to use motion capture data to assess emotion-related gait kinematics of hip and shoulder sagittal plane movement to evaluate the feasibility of using functional data analysis (FDA) for developing quantitative models. Overall, FDA was an effective method for comparing gait waveforms and emotion-related kinematics were associated with emotion arousal level.

Keywords: Whole Body Interaction, Motion Capture, Functional Data Analysis, Affective Computing.

1 Introduction

Integrating expressive whole body behavior into computer applications is an important feature for emerging applications ranging from the gaming industry to virtual environments. Many of these applications will need to recognize and produce emotionally expressive behavior for natural interaction between human and computer. Effective integration of these capabilities requires quantitative models of expressive behavior. To date, relatively few studies have used quantitative methods to investigate characteristics associated with expressive movement. Thus, the purpose of this paper is to demonstrate one possible approach to quantifying the effect of emotion on joint angular kinematics.

The approach presented in this paper for characterizing expressive behavior is multidisciplinary, combining methods from biomechanics, psychology, and statistics. From the field of biomechanics, the use of motion capture technology is an established method for gathering quantitative movement data. With this method, passive retro-reflective markers are placed on specific anatomical landmarks on the body and the position of each marker is tracked using high-speed video cameras. The centroid position of each marker is calculated for each instant in time. The three-dimensional coordinate data are used to demarcate body segments that are linked to form a representation of the body; each segment represents a bony segment of the musculoskeletal system. Therefore, motion capture can be used to describe body position and how it changes over time from three-dimensional coordinate data.

R. Shumaker (Ed.): Virtual and Mixed Reality, LNCS 5622, pp. 23–31, 2009.
© Springer-Verlag Berlin Heidelberg 2009

Motion capture is an effective method for describing body movement, but when the aim is to characterize expressive movement, methods from psychology can help ensure that the motion data contains the expressive signal. In brief, to identify emotion-related movement characteristics, the emotion signal must be in the motion data analyzed. Therefore, the emotion must be felt by the encoder and recognized by observers. Evaluating felt emotion is important for two reasons. Firstly, recent fMRI studies suggest a neurological basis for emotion affecting body movements in characteristic ways [1, 2]. Secondly, the quantitative difference, if any, of movements between felt and recognized emotions remains to be studied. Consequently, for studies that assume neurobiological changes due to emotion, it is especially important to ensure that the experience of emotion and associated bodily changes are captured [3]. Additionally, identifying trials that communicate the target emotion increases the probability that the data analyzed are representative of the actual emotion. Thus, validated methods from psychology can be borrowed for inducing and evaluating felt emotions as well as identifying motion stimuli that communicate target emotions.

The purpose of this paper is to provide a framework for characterizing emotion-related whole body movement and to demonstrate one potential statistical technique for quantifying emotion-related movement characteristics. First, the framework used for capturing emotion-related kinematic data is discussed. Second, functional data analysis methods are described. Finally, the results and conclusion of our analysis are presented.

2   Framework for Collecting Motion Data

Established methods from psychology can help ensure that motion data included in quantitative analyses contain the emotion-related signal. This section describes 1) the protocol used to capture motion data while participants experienced one of five target emotions, 2) the method used for evaluating felt emotion, and 3) the use of a social consensus paradigm to determine whether observers were able to accurately recognize the emotion portrayals.

Walking was studied because it is a well-documented whole body movement task in biomechanics and it is an emotionally neutral task. Further, studying a single movement task allows the expressive content to be separated from the task so that changes in the kinematics can be attributed to emotion difference. Previous studies have also demonstrated that emotions are recognizable in walking [4], suggesting that characteristics modifications in this task may be associated with specific emotions. Thus, walking is an ideal task to begin exploring the characteristic movement styles associated with specific emotions.

2.1   Motion Capture

The following methods were used to collect motion data, emotion elicitation data, as well as side-view video from walker participants. Further details about the methods used to collect these data are described in [3]. Walkers (n = 42, [5-7]52% female) were recruited from the University of Michigan undergraduate student population. Ages ranged from 18-32 years (20.1 $\pm$ 2.7 yrs.). All participants were able-bodied and no special skills were required. Prior to data collection, participants reviewed a description of the study and signed a consent form approved by the Institutional Review Board (IRB).

Upon arrival, the participants were informed that the study was about the expression of emotion and that video and motion capture data would be recorded during walking. They were informed that their faces would be blurred in the whole-body videos and these videos would be shown to peers in another study.

An autobiographical memories paradigm [5-7] was used to elicit emotions in participants. Participants were given as much time as needed to complete an autobiographical memories worksheet. They were informed that the worksheet was for their use only, to help feel emotions, and would remain confidential. On the worksheet, participants were asked to describe times in their own life when they felt two negative emotions (angry and sad), two positive emotions (content and joyful), and neutral emotion. Using only a few words, they were asked to indicate a) where they were, b) who they were with, and c) what caused the feeling/what was it about? For example, to elicit sadness, participants were asked to recall the following scenario.

> *Think of a time in your life when you felt in <u>despair</u>, for instance, when you felt <u>low</u> or <u>depressed</u>, or felt like you wanted to <u>withdraw from the world</u>.*

After completing the worksheet, participants changed into a special motion capture suit, and thirty-one passive retro-reflective markers (2 cm diameter) were placed on specific anatomical landmarks on the body in preparation for collection of motion capture data. The placement of the markers allowed the body to be demarcated into eight linked segments, each segment representing a bony segment of the musculoskeletal system.

Once the set-up was complete, participants were asked to walk at a self-selected pace approximately 5 meters after recalling a memory from their worksheet. Before each walking trial, the participants read their notes to help recall the specific memory. Memories were referred to as numbers rather than emotions to help ensure that a bias was not introduced. Participants began walking when they felt the recalled emotion as strongly as possible; they did not wait for a cue from the experimenter to begin and they did not have to provide a cue to indicate they were ready to walk. As each participant walked, side-view video and whole body 3-D motion capture data were recorded.

Participants performed three trials for each memory in a block to increase the probability that at least one trial would have usable video and motion capture data and that the target emotion would be felt.

2.2 Emotion Elicitation Evaluation

Subjective experience of emotion was assessed after each walking trial using a self-report questionnaire. The questionnaire included the four target emotions and four non-target, distracter emotions. The non-target emotions were selected for inclusion based on their similarity, in terms of valance and arousal, to the target emotions. After each walking trial, participants rated the intensity with which they felt each of the eight emotions using a 5-item likert scale (0 = not at all; 1 = a little bit; 2 = moderately; 3 = a great deal; 4 = extremely). After each emotion block, the walker was also asked to indicate the trial they felt was their best trial for that memory. The memory order was randomized for each participant.

One observation for each walker for each emotion was selected for inclusion in the final kinematic dataset (42 walkers x 5 emotions = 210 total observations). To be selected for inclusion in the dataset, a trial needed to have usable kinematic data and usable side-view video. If more than one emotion trial met these criteria for an individual emotion portrayal, the trial with the highest score for the target emotion item on the self-report questionnaire was selected. If two or more trials had the same score for the target self-report item, the self-selected best trial was used. If the self-selected best trial was not available, the trial with the lowest scores for all other questionnaire items was selected.

For each of the included walking trials, one gait cycle was selected (Heel strike or Toe off). Motion data was filtered to reduce noise in the signal with a 6Hz low pass Butterworth filter. For each trial the neck, trunk, shoulder, elbow, wrist, hip, knee, and ankle joint 3D kinematics were calculated, in addition to four 2D postural angles. All calculations were completed using C-Motion Visual 3D software package.

2.3 Social Consensus

Side-view video clips from the 210 trials (42 walkers x 5 emotions) selected in the walker protocol were shown to observers in a social consensus study to determine whether the emotion was recognizable. The walkers' faces were blurred to ensure that observers were not using information from facial expression to assess emotion, and the movement clips were looped three times. Two sets of observers (n=60 in each set) from the University of Michigan student population were recruited for participation in each study. Participants (n=60, 48% female) in the Recognition study ranged in age from 18-30 years (20.9 $\pm$ 2.7 yrs). No special skills were required. However, participants could not participate in the social consensus study if they participated as a walker. Displays were considered recognized if the observer recognition rate was greater than the chance recognition rate. Further details about the social consensus study are reported in [8].

3 Functional Data Analysis Methods

Joint angular data from hip and shoulder sagittal plane motion were included in a pilot study to assess the feasibility of quantitatively comparing gait waveforms using a functional data analysis (fda) approach. The object was to characterize the mean behavior in functional form for each emotion.

3.1 Inclusion Criteria

Motion in the sagittal plane for both joints was used in the analysis (flexion / extension). To be included in the analysis, emotion portrayals had to be considered felt by the walker and recognized by observers. For technical reasons, some emotion portrayals were missing motion data. This typically resulted from marker occlusion in the motion capture system. A cubic spline was used to interpolate missing data when

Table 1. Number of trials used in the fda analysis for each emotion for each joint

	Emotion				
	Angry	Joyful	Content	Neutral	Sad
Hip	15	20	22	25	22
Shoulder	16	22	20	17	23

appropriate according to standards in biomechanics. However, trials missing data after applying standard interpolation rules were additionally excluded from this analysis. Because of the strict criterion for inclusion in this analysis, it was particularly important to begin with a large sample size (Table 1).

3.2 Registration

Data were time normalized to ensure that gait cycle events occurred at the same point in time. Fig. 1 illustrates a common problem when analyzing gait data, the amount of time it takes to complete a single gait cycle can vary between trials and between participants. Data registration ensures that this does not confound the analysis. For each emotion portrayal, the data were time normalized to 100 samples per trial.

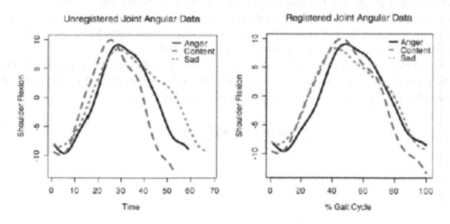

Fig. 1. Comparison of unregistered and registered joint angular data

3.3 Functional Form

A cubic B-spline was used to model the motion data in function form. Although other options such as polynomial functions could have been used to fit the data, these options lack the necessary stability and meaningful interpretations. In addition, using knots to demarcate the waveform into smaller sections can capture subtle features of the waveform. The *fda* library [9] in R version 2.5.0 was used for this analysis.

One primary goal of this analysis was to assess how joint angular kinematics change over time rather than assessing the angular position at the start and end of the gait cycle. Joint angles from human locomotion do not start and end at the exact same angular position. This is expected in human subject data due to naturally occurring variability in human motion resulting from both internal and external factors. However, the variability is expected to be within a small range. A test of the ranges between the start and end angles determined that this variability was not affected by emotion. Therefore, to simplify this pilot study the waveforms were adjusted to start at zero. This allowed us to apply a constraint to the function.

A cubic B-spline regression was used to fit a curve for each emotion group. Knots were visually selected for both the hip and shoulder joints. The object was to obtain a fit with extremely high r^2 (minimum acceptable value was .98), the squared correlation between the fitted values and actual values. In addition to the endpoint constraint, we also assumed that the first and second derivatives at each of the knots matched. A multivariate analysis was used to assess whether emotion affected each of the parameters.

4 Results

The overall results for the hip and shoulder analyses were the same. Three groups emerged based on arousal level: high arousal (anger and joy), moderate (neutral and content), and low arousal (sad).

Four knots were needed to fit the motion data. These knots were visually selected and occurred at 20, 40, 60, and 80 percent of the gait cycle. The shoulder analysis additionally included percent recognition in the regression analysis. Percent recognition was weighted so that portrayals with higher recognition rates had more influence on the fit of the model than those with lower recognition.

The fitted curve for the shoulder joint motion was defined as equation 1. The regression parameters are represented by β_i and the basis functions (Fig. 2) are represented by $\beta_i(x)$, where each is a truncated cubic polynomial.

$$f(x) = \sum_{i=1}^{8} \beta_i \bullet \beta_i(x) .$$

(1)

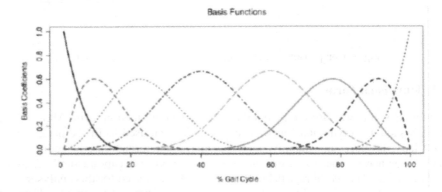

Fig. 2. Basis functions for shoulder joint angular data. Given the use of four knots and three constraints, there were a total of eight parameters.

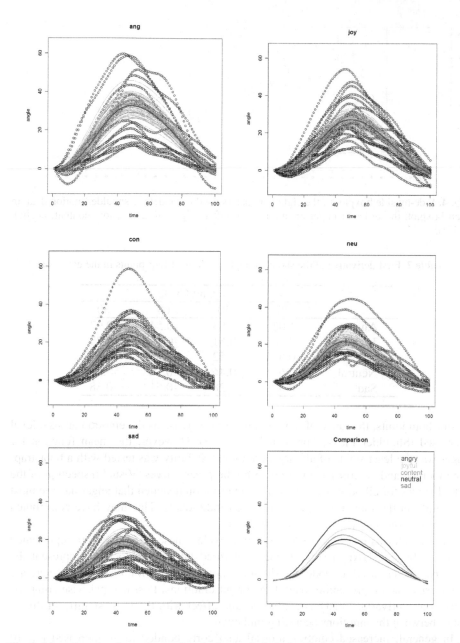

Fig. 3. Mean function for each emotion (red curve) plotted with the actual joint angular data for shoulder motion (black dots). The green curves represent the stability of the mean functional form; narrower bands indicate increased stability. The comparison plot represents the mean functional forms for each of the target emotions.

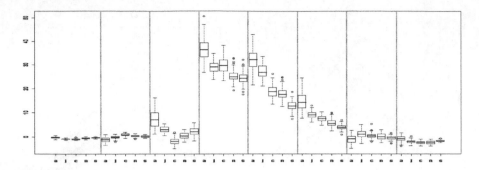

Fig. 4. Side-by-side boxplot of the eight parameters used to model the shoulder motion data. In each boxplot, the order of target emotions from left to right are anger, joy, content, neutral, and sad.

Table 2. First derivative of the shoulder angle position at four points in the gait cycle

	% Gait Cycle			
	20	40	60	80
Anger	1.02	0.63	-0.54	-0.97
Joy	0.76	0.61	-0.49	-0.75
Content	0.68	0.52	-0.55	-0.54
Neutral	0.62	0.46	-0.50	-0.51
Sad	0.63	0.28	-0.51	-0.38

For both joints, the range of motion tended to increase as the emotion arousal level increased (Shoulder Flexion presented in Fig. 3). However, the mean function for anger was the least stable of all target emotions. Stability was tested with a bootstrapping method and is represented in Fig. 3 by the green curves. Visual inspection of the actual angles for all portrayals of each target emotion revealed that anger had the most variability in the movement pattern between individuals. This may have contributed to the decreased stability of the mean function.

The waveforms tended to differ most mid cycle. These differences are represented in a side-by-side boxplot (Fig. 4) that is divided into eight blocks to represent the eight parameters used to model the shoulder motion data. Within each block there are five boxes, each representing one of the target emotions. Post-hoc pairwise comparisons of a multivariate analysis confirmed this effect with the most significant differences between the emotions occurring mid cycle.

In general, increased emotion arousal also corresponded to an increased rate of change in joint angular motion. The rate of change in joint angular motion for the shoulder joint was checked by calculating the first derivatives of the waveforms at the four knots which represent four unique points in the gait cycle (Table 2). With respect to biomechanics, this suggests that arousal is associated with joint angular velocity.

5 Conclusions

The results of this pilot study indicate that joint angular motion can be modeled in function form and gait waveforms can be quantitatively compared. Although the functional form was different for each joint, the differences between emotions were the same for both hip and shoulder kinematics. The high r^2 values (> .98) associated with the fitted models for the joint angular data combined with consistent results for the two joints suggest these findings are robust. The finding that differences were associated with arousal level may be related to changes in gait velocity. Indeed, in a previous study we determined that gait velocity was significantly greater for the high arousal emotions than the low arousal emotion sadness [10].

Based on the results of this pilot study, this method will be applied to assess joint angular data from additional limb and postural gait kinematics. It will also be important to assess the effect of gender, since one limitation of this analysis was that gender was not considered as a factor. Further evaluation is also necessary to determine whether cubic B-splines are the best choice for modeling the joint angular data.

References

1. de Gelder, B.: Towards the neurobiology of emotional body language. Nature Reveiws Neuroscience 7, 242–249 (2006)
2. Pichon, S., de Gelder, B., Grezes, J.: Emotional modulaton of visual and motor areas by dynamic body expressions of anger. Social Neuroscience (2007)
3. Crane, E.A., Gross, M., Fredrickson, B.L.: Feasibility of Concurrent Assessment of Dynamic Bodily and Facial Expressions (submitted)
4. Montepare, J.M., Goldstein, S.B., Clausen, A.: The identification of emotions from gait information. Journal of Nonverbal Behavior 11, 33–42 (1987)
5. Labouvie-Vief, G., Lumley, M.A., Jain, E., Heinze, H.: Age and gender differences in cardiac reactivity and subjective emotion responses to emotional autobiographical memories. Emotion 3, 115–126 (2003)
6. Levenson, R.W.: Emotion elicitation with neurological patients. In: Coan, J.A., Allen, J.J.B. (eds.) Handbook of emotion elicitation and assessment, pp. 158–168. Oxford University Press, Oxford (2007)
7. Levenson, R.W., Carstensen, L.L., Friesen, W.V., Ekman, P.: Emotion, physiology, and expression in old age. Psychology and Aging 6, 28–35 (1991)
8. Crane, E., Gross, M.: Expressive Movement Style Associated with Felt and Recognized Emotions (in preparation)
9. Ramsay, J.O., Silverman, B.W.: SpringerLink: Functional data analysis. Springer, New York (2005)
10. Crane, E., Gross, M.: Motion Capture and Emotion: Affect Detection in Whole Body Movement. In: Affective Computing and Intelligent Interaction, pp. 95–101 (2007)

Towards an Advanced Framework for Whole Body Interaction

David England, Martin Randles, Paul Fergus, and A. Taleb-Bendiab

School of Computing and Maths, Liverpool John Moores University,
Liverpool L3 3AF, UK
{d.england,m.j.randles,p.fergus,A.TalebBendiab}@ljmu.ac.uk

Abstract. Whole Body Interaction has emerged in recent years as a discipline that integrates the physical, physiological, cognitive and emotional aspects of a person's complete interaction with a digital environment. In this paper we present a framework to handle the integration of the complex of input signals and the feedback required to support such interaction. The framework is based on the principles of Autonomic Computing and aims to provide adaption and robustness in the management of whole body interaction. Finally we present some example case studies of how such a framework could be used.

Keywords: Whole Body Interaction, Motion Capture, Autonomic Computing.

1 Introduction

Bill Buxton [1] mused on what future archaeologist would make of today's humans extrapolating from our current computer technology and came up with a being with one eye, a dominant hand and two ears but lacking legs, and a sense of smell or touch. He argued for greater involvement in the whole person and their senses in human-computer interaction. Researchers and artists have responded to this challenge by exploiting the various technologies that fall under the general banner of virtual reality, and support whole body interaction. In our own work with artists [2] we have seen how they use camera vision and motion capture in novel interactions.

However, despite the technological and methodological advances we are still some way off from a completely integrated approach to Whole Body Interaction. Let us give a definition of Whole Body Interaction:

The integrated capture and processing of human signals from physical, physiological, cognitive and emotional sources to generate feedback to those sources for interaction in a digital environment.

From this definition we can see that some approaches to HCI do not give us an integrated view of interaction. For example, Ubiquitous Computing [3] is more concerned with the notion of 'Place' rather than capturing the full range of actions. Physical Computing [4] is more concerned with artifacts than the physical nature of humans. Of course it is the nature of research to focus on certain, measurable aspects of interaction within the scope of a research project. However, in doing so we can loose sight of the larger, richer picture and the possibilities of Whole Body

R. Shumaker (Ed.): Virtual and Mixed Reality, LNCS 5622, pp. 32–40, 2009.
© Springer-Verlag Berlin Heidelberg 2009

Interaction. For Whole Body Interaction to succeed requires an interdisciplinary approach and interactions between the following disciplines

- Physical – we need interaction with Sports, Movement Science and Artists on the physical capabilities and limitations human being
- Physiological – sharing with clinicians and psychologists on the reading and interpretation of physiological signals
- Cognitive – the long history interaction between cognitive psychologists and computer science has been the bedrock of HCI
- Emotional – Psychologists, Artists and Game Designers have sought to understand and introduce knowledge of human emotions into interaction design

From this collection of disciplines we can see there is quite a rich interplay of knowledge required before we can begin to support a truly integrated Whole Body Interaction system. It would also be the case that as further research is carried out in the contributing disciplines, our understanding of how can support Whole Body Interaction would evolve. Furthermore, there are a vast range of possible applications areas for Whole Body Interaction including, Games and Entertainment, Medical, Military, Education, Sports, Household, the Arts and so forth and each application area would have its own requirements as to accuracy of movement, the nature of any feedback and robustness of the system. And within each area individuals will learn and evolve their physical skills as they interact.

From this opening set of requirements we can see that we may need a complex system to manage Whole Body Interaction. However, if we are to allow domain experts to exploit Whole Body Interaction then we need an approach which allows them to express their domain knowledge; in movement, cognition, physiology, in their own terms.

The rest of the paper is structured as followed. In section 2 we explain Autonomic Computing as a basis for managing complex Interaction. In section 3 we present our framework based on Autonomic Computing. In section 4 we present some illustrative case studies, and final in section 5 we discuss our conclusions and the future implications of our work.

2 Autonomic Computing and Interaction

Autonomic Computing systems [5] were proposed by IBM as a way of managing the configuration and management of complex systems without continuing user human involvement. Such systems could include farms of servers, monitoring equipment in the field, Cloud-like distributed systems of services, wireless sensor networks and autonomous robots. Autonomic Computing systems borrow and adapt ideas from biological systems in order to support their on-going self-management. Thus such systems try to take care of:

- Reconfiguration in the event that one or more components fail or go off line
- Real-time service selection: as circumstances change new services may be selected to cope with them
- Self-Monitoring of the status of the whole system supporting self-repair

Though originally envisaged as supporting embedded or autonomous systems without much human involvement, the principles of Autonomic Computing have been used in complex interactive systems. Here the requirement is to support characteristics such as adaptability, robustness, self-repair and monitoring of the interaction. We require the system to be able to cope with emerging complex issues after it has been released to the end users without further monitoring or maintenance by the original development team. Ideally we would like the end users to provide their own on-going systems configuration based on their expert domain knowledge.

In our own work on post-operative Breast Cancer decision support [6] we used the mechanisms of Autonomic Computing to support the integration of components in a complex decision making process. The key challenges to such a system were:

- The modeling of clinical decision-making processes – these processes could evolve over time and vary from hospital to hospital
- The governance of adherence to guidelines and patient safety
- Integration of rule-based guidelines modeling with the data mining of historical treatments data to provide a cross-cutting approach to decision support
- Providing multiple views of decision data
- Generating user interface(s) to the above

The chief mechanism for our Autonomic User Interface Engine is the Situation Calculus. The Situation Calculus provides an extensible representation of system knowledge, ideal states and action sequences [7, 8] is used as a User Interface Description Language to provide the major specification formalism and reasoning mechanisms. Firstly the action-based semantics of the language provide an in-built description for every available user interactive action and system-generated event; unpredictable environmental events are also expressible in the formalism, at runtime, through action histories. Secondly the effects of user interactions are predictable through the use of successor state axioms; providing a context and prediction for the consequences of action choices: Uniquely, counterfactual reasoning with branching timelines is permitted, thus reasoning may proceed, completely automatically, based on "what-if" scenarios. Thirdly, there is no requirement for a complete state enumeration and transition model; rather what is true in the system can be logically stated reasoned upon and updated whilst behaviour follows by logical consequence: The Current circumstance (situation), for the production of a user interface, is conceived as a causal action (event) history. Fourthly, properties of the specification can be proved entirely within the logic, whereas other formalisms require a separate mechanism to prove correctness properties of the interface deployment. Fifthly, the user interface, described in Situation Calculus, is directly implementable through Neptune scripts, which are runtime generable and adaptable; allowing rapid uptake and updating of decision models with runtime reasoning to incorporate current application knowledge with historical data in an integrated, fully audited and provably correct manner.

We can learn general lessons about supporting the requirements for rich and complex interaction scenarios where we need to support evolving processes, quality criteria, the integration and cross-working of components and the engineering of the final user interface. These can be expressed in the Situation Calculus to support a wide range of complex interactions.

2.1 Autonomic Computing and Whole Body Interaction

From the opportunities and challenges posed by both Whole Body Interaction and Autonomic Computing we can see how the latter can support the former. For example, in using multiple sensors for motion capture (accelerometers, 3/5 axis gyroscopes, ultrasonic transducers etc) we face potential problems of the sensors malfunctioning, temporarily dropping signals or giving error-prone signals. So we need a sensor management layer to ensure the robustness of the input data. We can triangulate this data with data from, say, markerless camera-based motion capture or stored kinematics models to smooth and correct the data.

Our stored kinematics model may give us a generic model of possible and allowed motions that can be used to ensure the safety of the human operator. However, we may also wish to model an individual's patterns of motion to either compare them with some norm or adapt the responses of the system to the individual. So there would be a machine-learning layer to capture and analyse the individual's performance.

Equally, if we are considering the emotional state of the person, we may wish to collect patterns of psycho-physiological data in an attempt to infer emotional states. Again we would need the appropriate machine-learning component in our framework and a means to integrate the data from that component with the other components. So we could combine signals from the physical and physiological states adjust the responses of the system to the user, e.g. to recognize they are under stress and change the nature of the feedback given.

3 An Advanced Framework for Whole Body Interaction

The full details of the implementation are outside the scope of this paper, and further details are available in the given references. To summarize, the implementation is executed through the Cloud architecture; the federation of services (component agents) and resources, with appropriately derived user interface descriptions. It is defined to enable the autonomic framework to function as a User Interface production module using the specially developed language, Neptune that allows management objects to be compiled and inspected at runtime. A system space provides persistent data storage for service registration and state information giving the means to coordinate the application service activities into an object model and associated User Interfaces based on the recorded interaction model and functional requirements. Reasoning can then proceed based on the Situation Calculus model, whereby the user interface descriptions are derived, inferred or adapted. Neptune exposes policies and decision models for system governance, derived from the Situation Calculus/Extensible Decision model, as compiled objects that can be inspected, modified and executed at runtime. Thus the system can evolve as modelled by the logical specification in a safe and predictable manner giving the adjustable self-management required. Neptune objects are executed on demand through an event model exposed by the Cloud architecture.

The system controller with an associated Observation System controls access to and from the individual services and resources within the Cloud. It brokers requests

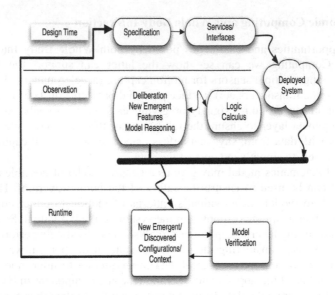

Fig. 1. The Observation system

to the system, through the contrived User Interface, based on system status and governance rules, in Neptune objects, derived from the deliberative process as stated above. An overview of the Observation system is shown in Figure 1.

Each service and resource when it first registers itself to the Cloud sends a meta-object serialized from an XML definition file. This meta-object contains the properties and state data of the service it is describing and is stored within the System Space at registration. Each service maintains its own meta-object and updates the System Space when changes in state occur. The XML definition file contains all information required for the Cloud to discover the service through registration contained in the service element and prepare the appropriate User Interface. In addition to the meta-objects exposing properties of a service within the Cloud, they also describe the interface events that can be fired, caught and handled, allowing multi-modal interfaces to be composed. The event model begins by the service informing the System Controller when an event is fired, which itself marshals this event to the System Space to provide the appropriate scope. It should be noted however, that the event model is abstracted from the components within the system, and is controlled by the Neptune scripting language that sends and receives the appropriate event calls to the controller. The Neptune scripting language is structured in terms of rules, conditional statements and variable assignments that are translated from the Situation Calculus specification to software system objects, encapsulating all the logical inference processes and variable instantiations for the production of the most relevant interaction model and associated interface. An overview of this process is shown in Figure 2.

In this way the base rules for deliberation to control the Cloud architecture, through enhanced user interaction, have been transcribed, from the Situation Calculus reasoned representation, into Neptune objects that can be modified as a result of Observation System deliberation on system events.

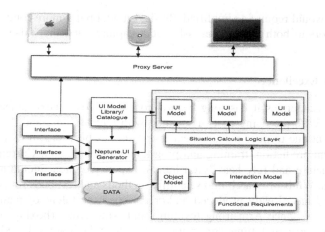

Fig. 2. User Interface Production at Runtime

4 Case Studies

To demonstrate the validity of the framework we present 3 case studies from current research work at Liverpool John Moores University.

4.1 Assessment of Risk of Falling in Older People

As the population in the more advanced countries ages there is an increasing burden on health services and budgets, not to mention personal risks and frustrations for older people. One of the major risks for older people is falling. Due to brittle bones, as a result of a fall, elderly people are more likely to break a major bone such as a hip or femur. They will then become bed-bound and loose their mobility and independence. The risk of premature death after a fall increases. These risks may be exacerbated by other factors such as diabetes, balance problems, Parkinson's disease and so on. At Liverpool John Moores the Caren platform [9] has been used to help measure issues or gait and balance. However, such platforms are large and expensive and thus not available to most clinicians who are diagnosing and caring for elderly people. It is also difficult to bring elderly people to such a facility. Ideally we would like a mobile system that would support:

- Research and Investigation of the general factors promoting the risks of falls
- A clinical diagnostic system that would help clinicians to identify at-risk individuals
- A personal mobile device that would warn elderly people that they were developing a fall risk

In the research system we are required to capture as much data as possible and compare it with existing models of potential fall situations and look for correlations with our clinical data, such as evidence of other diseases. We would need tools to visualize the data and help us refine our understanding of fall risks. For the diagnostic and alert models we would require a simplified physical model but a more robust management of the sensors to both ensure that risks were captured and that false positives were avoided.

4.2 Sports Excellence

In sporting academies it has long been a goal to discover next generation sporting champions. With the rising costs associated with their training and the potential loss of such talent due to poor management, attention has been drawn to scientific methods for talent prediction, training and programme development. Current methods are ad hoc in nature and rely heavily on human expert judgment including metrics and benchmarks. Whilst, research into scientific methods and test beds for sport science is not new and has already produced and/or enriched the talent of many world class names such as Lance Armstrong (cycling) and Amir Khan (boxing) to name but a few. Due to cost and time constraints often such laboratory based facilities are only available to the very few, and the techniques used are either intrusive or laboratory based, hence limiting their applicability to those sports that require mobile performance measurement (telemetry).

Using our framework we adopt a multidisciplinary approach where results from world-class research expertise in gait analysis for sportsmen, and advanced wireless body-area sensor networks and high-stream data analysis and visualisation are combined [10]. The framework aims to develop a fundamental understanding into full-motion modelling and analysis methods including associated test beds to support the prediction and follow up of potential sporting champions. Rather than utilising both marker and markerless motion capturing techniques we utilise advances in Micro-electromechanical systems that when connected to the body and switched on form an ad hoc peer-to-peer body area network. Ultrasonic transducer pairs, 3/5-axis gyroscopes, and accelerometers allow fully body motion to be captured. The challenge is to collect information from these data sources in real-time and perform predictive analysis of movements for the intended purpose of detecting movements, reactions and techniques typically associated with current and past world champions.

Using our novice and world champion martial arts collaborators we aim to evaluate the framework. Martial artists are equipped with body area sensor networks that dynamically connect to sub-networks in the gymnasium, such as gloves, footwear and the floor, including the sensors attached to the opponent. The sensors in one body area network form a coupling with another indicating that they are in combat mode. This allows attacks given by one subject to be compared against the defence techniques of the other. Building on techniques from artificial intelligence (neural networks) and autonomic computing a predictive module will collect information in real-time and rank the potential of new students using data from existing world champions.

4.3 Operator Performance in Simulators

Operators of complex systems, from automobiles, to aircraft to nuclear plants face they possibility of errors and mistakes when they become over-loaded or stressed. We can put operators in stressful but risk-free situations in simulators to assess people's reactions to stress and propose avoiding or alerting actions. Work on

Bio-cybernetic Control [11] has looked at the collection of physiological data such as heart rate, breathing rate and galvanic skin response to look for patterns in the data in moments of stress. However, such data does not always correlate with actual stress and potentially dangerous changes in operator behaviour in stressful scenarios. We would need to look for other factors such as body posture, head tilt and eye gazed to assess the alertness of the operator; have their physical responses to the controls changed, has their head titled forward due to fatigue or have their patterns of eye gazed changed from normal?

Once again we are looking at the integration of two types of input data with a view to discovering rich patterns of interaction, and our knowledge of both areas improves we would wish to update any stress monitoring and alerting system without re-writing the whole system.

5   Conclusions and Future Work

We have presented the beginnings of an advanced framework for whole body interaction. Having learned lessons from other domains we have applied the principles of Autonomic Computing to provide a framework that supports the requirements for system evolution, robustness and self-monitoring which are necessary in the complex field of Whole Body Interaction. Our illustrative case studies show such a framework could be used in a number of areas. These demonstrate the requirements for robustness in the use of sensor, pattern discovery and adaptability.

There are of course many challenges to the wider development and use of Whole Body Interaction systems. We need further investigation of the physical capabilities and limitations of humans in full body interaction. As Buxton [13] more recently observed we still only have a good knowledge of interaction involving the hands and arms but little beyond that. We are still at the early stages of understanding emotion in interaction let alone whole body interaction [12]. However, without a rich and evolvable framework, developments in these supporting areas will fail to provide the expected potential benefits.

Acknowledgements. The authors have benefit from discussions and presentations at the series of Whole Body Interaction workshops. The position papers for these workshops can be found here: http://lister.cms.livjm.ac.uk/homepage/staff/cmsdengl/WBI2009/.

References

1. Buxton, W.: There's More to Interaction than Meets the Eye: Some Issues in Manual Input. In: Norman, D.A., Draper, S.W. (eds.) User Centered System Design: New Perspectives on Human-Computer Interaction, pp. 319–337. Lawrence Erlbaum Associates, Hillsdale, New Jersey (1986)
2. England, D., Ruperez, M., Botto, C., Nimoy, J., Poulter, S.: Creative Technology and HCI. In: Proceedings of HCI 2007, Aveiro, Portugal (2007)
3. Weisner, M.: Some Computer Science Issues in Ubiquitous Computing. Communications of the ACM 36(7), 75–84 (1993)

4. Igoe, T.: Physical Computing: Sensing and Controlling the Physical World with Computers (Paperback), Course Technology PTR (2004)
5. Kephart, J., Chess, D.M.: A Vision of Autonomic Computing. IEEE Computing (January 2003)
6. Miseldine, P., Taleb-Bendiab, A., England, D., Randles, M.: Addressing the Need for Adaptable Decision Processes in Healthcare. In: Medical Informatics and the Internet in Medicine, March 2007, vol. 37, pp. 1–7. Taylor and Francis, Abington (2007)
7. Randles, M., Taleb-Bendiab, A., Miseldine, P., Laws, A.: Adjustable Deliberation of Self-Managing Systems. In: Proceedings of the 12th IEEE International Conference and Workshops on the Engineering of Computer-Based Systems (ECBS 2005), pp. 449–456 (2005)
8. Reiter, R.: Knowledge in Action. MIT Press, Cambridge (2001)
9. Lees, A., Vanrenterghem, J., Barton, G., Lake, M.: Kinematic response characteristics of the CAREN moving platform system for use in posture and balance research. Medical Engineering and Physics 29(5), 629–635 (2007)
10. Fergus, P., Merabti, M., El Rhalibi, A., Taleb-Bendiab, A., England, D.: Body Area Sensor Networks for Predicting Potential Champions. In: HCI 2008 Workshop on Whole Body Interaction, Liverpool John Moores University (September 2008)
11. Fairclough, S., Taleb-Bendiab, A., Tattersall, A.: Biocybernetic Control of Adaptive Automation, EPSRC Project (2002)
12. Crane, E., Gross, M.: Motion Capture and Emotion: Affect Detection in Whole Body Movement. Affective Computing and Intelligent Interaction, pp. 95–101 (2007)
13. Buxton, B.: Closing Keynote Talk. In: SIGCHI 2008, Florence, Italy (2008)

Evaluation of Body Sway and the Relevant Dynamics While Viewing a Three-Dimensional Movie on a Head-Mounted Display by Using Stabilograms

Kazuhiro Fujikake[1], Masaru Miyao[2], Tomoki Watanabe[3],
Satoshi Hasegawa[4], Masako Omori[5], and Hiroki Takada[6]

[1] Institute for Science of Labour, 2-8-14 Sugao, Miyamae-ku, Kawasaki 216-8501, Japan
k.fujikake@isl.or.jp
[2] Nagoya University, Furo-cho, Chikusa-Ku, Nagoya 464-8601, Japan
[3] Aichi Gakuin University, 12 Araike, Iwasaki-cho, Nisshin 470-0195, Japan
[4] Nagoya Bunri University, 365 Maeda Inazawa-cho, Inazawa, Aichi 492-8520, Japan
[5] Kobe Women's University, 2-1 Aoyama Higashisuma, Suma-ku, Kobe 654-8585, Japan
[6] Gifu University of Medical Science, 795-1 Ichihiraga Nagamine, Seki, Gifu 501-3892, Japan
takada@u-gifu-ms.ac.jp

Abstract. The viewers of three-dimensional (3D) movies often complain of blurring and bleeding. They sometimes experience visually induced motion sickness (VIMS). In this study, the effect of VIMS on body sway was examined using stabilograms. We measured the sway in the center of gravity before and during the exposure to images projected on a head-mounted display (HMD). While viewing, the subjects were instructed to remain in the Romberg posture for the first 60 seconds and maintain a wide stance (midline of the heels, 20 cm apart) for the next 60 seconds. Employing Double-Wayland algorithm, we measured the degree of determinism in the dynamics of the sway in the center of gravity with respect to viewing 3D movies on HMD. As a result, the dynamics of the sway during and before the exposure was considered to be stochastic. Thus, exposure to 3D movies would not change the dynamics to a deterministic one.

Keywords: Three-dimensional (3D) movie, Visually induced motion sickness, Stabilogram, Degree of determinism, Double-Wayland algorithm.

1 Introduction

The human standing posture is maintained by the body's balance function, which is an involuntary physiological adjustment mechanism called the righting reflex [1]. In order to maintain the standing posture when locomotion is absent, the righting reflex, centered in the nucleus ruber, is essential. Sensory signals such as visual inputs, auditory and vestibular inputs, and proprioceptive inputs from the skin, muscles, and joints are the inputs that are involved in the body's balance function [2]. The evaluation of this function is indispensable for diagnosing equilibrium disturbances such as cerebellar degenerations, basal ganglia disorders, or Parkinson's disease in patients [3].

R. Shumaker (Ed.): Virtual and Mixed Reality, LNCS 5622, pp. 41–50, 2009.
© Springer-Verlag Berlin Heidelberg 2009

Stabilometry has been employed to evaluate this equilibrium function both qualitatively and quantitatively. A projection of a subject's center of gravity onto a detection stand is measured as an average of the center of pressure (COP) of both feet. The COP is traced for each time step, and the time series of the projections is traced on an x-y plane. By connecting the temporally vicinal points, a stabilogram is created, as shown in Fig 1. Several parameters such as the area of sway (A), total locus length (L), and locus length per unit area (L/A) have been proposed to quantitize the instability involved in the standing posture, and such parameters are widely used in clinical studies. It has been revealed that the last parameter particularly depends on the fine variations involved in posture control [1]. This index is then regarded as a gauge for evaluating the function of proprioceptive control of standing in human beings. However, it is difficult to clinically diagnose disorders of the balance function and to identify the decline in equilibrium function by utilizing the abovementioned indices and measuring patterns in the stabilogram. Large interindividual differences might make it difficult to understand the results of such a comparison.

Mathematically, the sway in the COP is described by a stochastic process [4]–[6]. We examined the adequacy of using a stochastic differential equation and investigated the most adequate equation for our research. G(x), the distribution of the observed point x, is related in the following manner to V(x), the (temporal averaged) potential function, in the stochastic differential equation (SDE), which has been considered as a mathematical model of the sway:

$$V(\vec{x}) = -\frac{1}{2}\ln G(\vec{x}) + const. \tag{1}$$

The nonlinear property of SDEs is important [7]. There were several minimal points of the potential. In the vicinity of these points, local stable movement with a high-frequency component can be generated as a numerical solution to the SDE. We can therefore expect a high density of observed COP in this area on the stabilogram.

The analysis of stabilograms is useful not only for medical diagnosis but also for achieving the control of upright standing for two-legged robots and for preventing falls in elderly people [8]. Recent studies suggest that maintaining postural stability is one of the major goals of animals, [9] and that they experience sickness symptoms in circumstances where they have not acquired strategies to maintain their balance [10]. Riccio and Stoffregen argued that motion sickness is not caused by sensory conflict, but by postural instability, although the most widely known theory of motion sickness is based on the concept of sensory conflict [10]–[12]. Stoffregen and Smart (1999) report that the onset of motion sickness may be preceded by significant increases in postural sway [13].

The equilibrium function in humans deteriorates when viewing 3-dimensional (3D) movies [14]. It has been considered that this visually induced motion sickness (VIMS) is caused by the disagreement between vergence and visual accommodation while viewing 3D images [15]. Thus, stereoscopic images have been devised to reduce this disagreement [16]–[17].

VIMS can be measured by psychological and physiological methods, and the simulator sickness questionnaire (SSQ) is a well-known psychological method for measuring the extent of motion sickness [18]. The SSQ is used herein for verifying the occurrence of VIMS. The following parameters of autonomic nervous activity is appropriate for the physiological method: heart rate variability, blood pressure, electrogastrography, and galvanic skin reaction [19]–[21]. It has been reported that a wide stance (with midlines of the heels 17 or 30 cm apart) significantly increases the total locus length in the stabilograms of individuals with high SSQ scores, while the length in those of individuals with low scores is less affected by such a stance [22]. We wondered if noise terms vanished from the mathematical model (SDEs) of the body sway. Using our Double-Wayland algorithm [23], we evaluate the degree of visible determinism for the dynamics of the sway.

We propose a methodology to measure the effect of 3D images on the equilibrium function. We assume that the high density of observed COP decreases during exposure to stereoscopic images [14]. Sparse density (SPD) would be a useful index in stabilometry to measure VIMS. In this study, we verify that reduction in body sway can be evaluated using the SPD during exposure to a new 3D movie on an HMD.

2 Material and Methods

Ten healthy subjects (age, 23.6 ± 2.2 years) voluntarily participated in the study. All of them were Japanese and lived in Nagoya and its surroundings. They provided informed consent prior to participation. The following subjects were excluded from the study: subjects working the night shift, those dependent on alcohol, those who consumed alcohol and caffeine-containing beverages after waking up and less than 2 h after meals, those who had been using prescribed drugs, and those who may have had any otorhinolaryngologic or neurological disease in the past (except for conductive hearing impairment, which is commonly found in the elderly). In addition, the subjects must have experienced motion sickness at some time during their lives.

We ensured that the body sway was not affected by environmental conditions. Using an air conditioner, we adjusted the temperature to 25 °C in the exercise room, which was kept dark. All subjects were tested from 10 a.m. to 5 p.m. in the room. The subjects wore an HMD (iWear AV920; Vuzix Co. Ltd.) on which 3 kinds of images were presented in random order: (I) a visual target (circle) whose diameter was 3 cm; (II) a conventional 3D movie that shows a sphere approaching and moving away from subjects irregularly; and (III) a new 3D movie that shows the same sphere motion as that shown in (II). The last movie was created using the Olympus power 3D method [24].

2.1 Experimental Procedure

The subjects stood without moving on the detection stand of a stabilometer (G5500; Anima Co. Ltd.) in the Romberg posture with their feet together for 1 min before the sway was recorded. Each sway of the COP was then recorded at a sampling frequency of 20 Hz during the measurement; subjects were instructed to maintain the Romberg posture for the first 60 s and a wide stance (with the midlines of heels 20 cm apart) for the next 60 s. The subjects viewed one of the images, i.e., (I), (II), or (III), on the HMD from the beginning till the end. The SSQ was filled before and after stabilometry.

2.2 Calculation Procedure

We calculated several indices that are commonly used in the clinical field [25] for stabilograms, such as "area of sway," "total locus length," and "total locus length per unit area." In addition, new quantification indices that were termed "SPD", "total locus length of chain" [26] and the translation error [27] were also estimated.

3 Results

The results of the SSQ are shown in Table 1 and include the scores on nausea (N), oculomotor discomfort (OD), disorientation (D) subscale and total score (TS) of the SSQ. No statistical differences were seen in these scores among images presented to subjects. However, increases were seen in the scores for N and D after exposure to the conventional 3D images (II). In addition, the scores after exposure to the new 3D images were not very different from those after exposure to the static ones (I). Although there were large individual differences, sickness symptoms seemed to appear more often with the conventional 3D movie.

Typical stabilograms are shown in Fig. 1. In these figures, the vertical axis shows the anterior and posterior movements of the COP, and the horizontal axis shows the right and left movements of the COP. The amplitudes of the sway that were observed during exposure to the movies (Fig. 1c–1f) tended to be larger than those of the control sway (Fig. 1a–1b). Although a high density of COP was observed in the stabilograms (Fig. 1a–1b, 1e–1f), the density decreased in stabilograms during exposure to the conventional stereoscopic movie (Fig. 1c–1d). Furthermore, stabilograms measured in an open leg posture with the midlines of heels 20 cm apart (Fig. 1b, 1d, 1f) were compared with stabilograms measured in the Romberg posture (Fig. 1a, 1c, 1e). COP was not isotropically dispersed but characterized by much movement in the anterior-posterior (y) direction (Fig. 1b, 1e). Although this trend is seen in Fig. 1d, the diffusion of COP was large in the lateral (x) direction and had spread to the extent that it was equivalent to the control stabilograms (Fig. 1a).

Representative results of the Double-Wayland algorithm are shown in Fig. 2. Whether subjects was exposed to the 3D movies or not, E_{trans} derived from the temporal differences of those time series x, y was approximately 1. These translation errors in each embedding space were not significantly different from the translation errors derived from the time series x, y.

According to the two-way analysis of variance (ANOVA) with repeated measures, there was no interaction between factors of posture (Romberg posture or standing posture with their feet wide apart) and images ((I), (II), or (III)). Except to the total locus length of chain, a main effect was seen in the both factors (Fig. 3).

Table 1. Subscales of the SSQ after exposure to 3D movies [28]

Movies	(II)	(III)
N	11.4±3.7	10.5±4.4
OD	18.2±4.1	17.4±4.9
D	23.7±8.8	19.5±6.6
TS	19.8±5.3	18.0±4.9

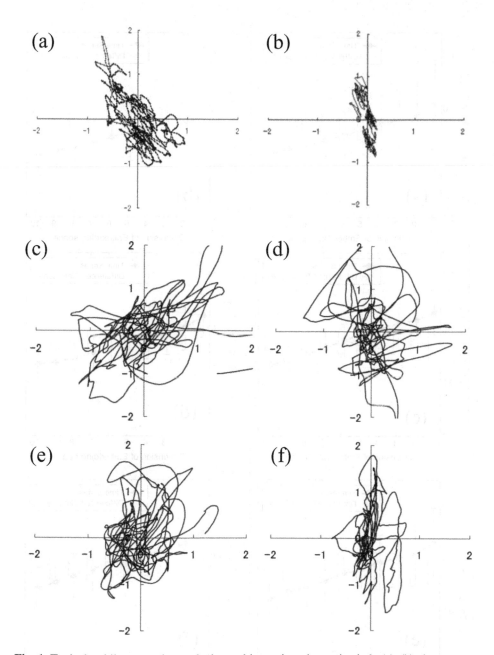

Fig. 1. Typical stabilograms observed when subjects viewed a static circle (a)–(b), the conventional 3D movie (c)–(d), and the new stereoscopic movie (e)–(f) [28]

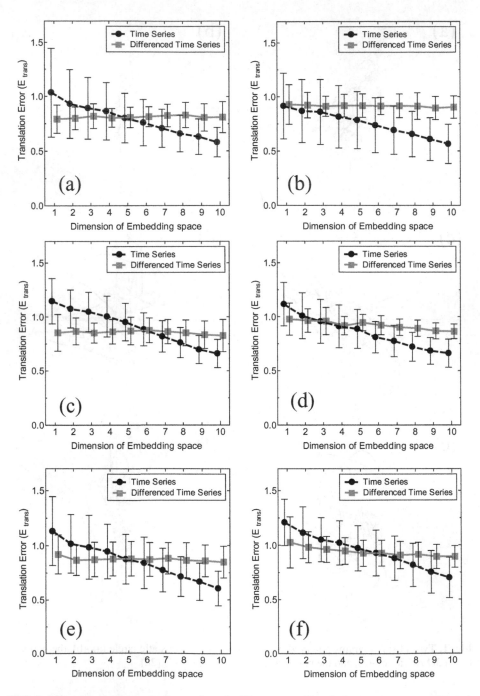

Fig. 2. Mean translation error for each embedding space. Translation errors were estimated from stabilograms that were observed when subjects viewed a static circle (a)–(b), the conventional 3D movie (c)–(d), and the new stereoscopic movie (e)–(f).

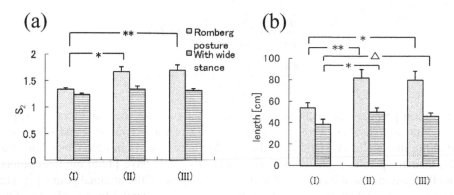

Fig. 3. Typical results of the two-way ANOVA with repeated measures for indicators [28]; the total locus length (a), the SPD (b)

4 Discussion

A theory has been proposed to obtain SDEs as a mathematical model of the body sway on the basis of the stabilogram.

In this study, we mathematically measured the degree of determinism in the dynamics of the sway of COP. The Double-Wayland algorithm was used as a novel method. $E_{trans} > 0.5$ was obtained by the Wayland algorithm (Fig. 2), which implies that the time series could be generated by a stochastic process in accordance with a previous standard [29]. The threshold 0.5 is half of the translation error resulting from a random walk. The body sway has been described previously by stochastic processes [4]-[7], which was shown with the Double-Wayland algorithm [30]. Moreover, $0.8 < E_{trans} < 1$ obtained from the temporal differences of these time series exceeded the translation errors estimated by the Wayland algorithm, as shown in Fig. 2b. However, the translation errors estimated by the Wayland algorithm were similar to those obtained from the temporal differences, except for Fig. 2b, which agrees with the abovementioned explanation of the dynamics to control a standing posture. The exposure to 3D movies would not change it into a deterministic one. Mechanical variations were not observed in the locomotion of the COP. We assumed that the COP was controlled by a stationary process, and the sway during exposure to the static control image (I) could be compared with that when the subject viewed 3D movies. Indices for stabilograms might reflect the coefficients in stochastic processes although the translation error did not exhibit a significant difference between the stabilograms measured during exposure to the conventional 3D movie (II) and the new 3D movie (III).

The anterior-posterior direction y was considered to be independent of the medial-lateral direction x [31]. Stochastic differential equations (SDEs) on the Euclid space $\mathbf{E}^2 \ni (x, y)$

$$\frac{\partial x}{\partial t} = -\frac{\partial}{\partial x} U_x(x) + w_x(t)$$

$$\frac{\partial y}{\partial t} = -\frac{\partial}{\partial y} U_y(y) + w_y(t)$$

have been proposed as mathematical models that generate the stabilograms [4]-[7]. Pseudorandom numbers were generated by the white noise terms $w_x(t)$ and $w_y(t)$. Constructing the nonlinear SDEs from the stabilograms (Fig. 1) in accordance with Eq. (1), their temporally averaged potential functions U_x, U_y have plural minimal points, and fluctuations could be observed in the neighborhood of the minimal points [7]. The variance in the stabilogram depends on the form of the potential function in the SDE; therefore, the SPD is regarded as an index for its measurement. Although, stereoscopic movies decrease the gradient of the potential function, the new 3D movie (III) should reduce the body sway because there is no disagreement between vergence and visual accommodation. The reduction can be evaluated by the SPD during exposure to the movies on an HMD screen. We have succeeded in estimating the decrease in the gradient of the potential function by using the SPD by performing a one-way analysis of variance.

Multiple comparisons indicated that the SPD S_2 during exposure to any of the stereoscopic movies was significantly larger than that during exposure to the static control image (I) when subjects stood in the Romberg posture. The same calculation results were also obtained for S_3. The standing posture would become unstable because of the effects of the stereoscopic movies. As mentioned above, structural changes occur in the time-averaged potential function (1) with exposure to stereoscopic images, which are assumed to reflect the sway in center of gravity.

Scibora et al. concluded that the total locus length of subjects with prior experience of motion sickness increases with exposure to a virtual environment when they stood with their feet wide apart [22], whereas, in our study, the degree of sway was found to be reduced significantly when the subjects stood with their feet wide apart than when they stood with their feet close together (Romberg posture). However, the total locus length during exposure to the conventional stereoscopic movie was significantly larger than that during exposure to the control image when they stood with their feet wide apart. As shown in Fig. 1d, a clear change in the form of the potential function (1) occurs when the feet are wide apart. The decrease in the gradient of the potential might increase the total locus length.

Regardless of posture, the total locus length during exposure to the conventional 3D movie (II) was significantly greater than that during exposure to the control image (Fig. 3b). Moreover, the total locus length of chain tended to increase when subjects were exposed to the conventional 3D images (II) compared that when they were exposed to (I). Hence, we noted postural instability with the exposure to the conventional stereoscopic images (II) by using these indicators involved in the stabilogram (total locus length and that of chain). This instability might be reduced by the Olympus power 3D method.

References

1. Okawa, T., Tokita, T., Shibata, Y., Ogawa, T., Miyata, H.: Stabilometry - Significance of Locus Length Per Unit Area (L/A) in Patients with Equilibrium Disturbances. Equilibrium Res. 55(3), 283–293 (1995)
2. Kaga, K.: Memaino Kouzo: Structure of vertigo. Kanehara, Tokyo pp. 23–26, 95–100 (1992)
3. Okawa, T., Tokita, T., Shibata, Y., Ogawa, T., Miyata, H.: Stabilometry-Significance of locus length per unit area (L/A). Equilibrium Res. 54(3), 296–306 (1996)
4. Collins, J.J., De Luca, C.J.: Open-loop and closed-loop control of posture: A random-walk analysis of center of pressure trajectories. Exp. Brain Res. 95, 308–318 (1993)
5. Emmerrik, R.E.A., Van Sprague, R.L., Newell, K.M.: Assessment of sway dynamics in tardive dyskinesia and developmental disability: sway profile orientation and stereotypy. Moving Disorders 8, 305–314 (1993)
6. Newell, K.M., Slobounov, S.M., Slobounova, E.S., Molenaar, P.C.: Stochastic processes in postural center-of-pressure profiles. Exp. Brain Res. 113, 158–164 (1997)
7. Takada, H., Kitaoka, Y., Shimizu, Y.: Mathematical Index and Model in Stabilometry. Forma 16(1), 17–46 (2001)
8. Fujiwara, K., Toyama, H.: Analysis of dynamic balance and its training effect-Focusing on fall problem of elder persons. Bulletin of the Physical Fitness Research Institute 83, 123–134 (1993)
9. Stoffregen, T.A., Hettinger, L.J., Haas, M.W., Roe, M.M., Smart, L.J.: Postural instability and motion sickness in a fixed-base flight simulator. Human Factors 42, 458–469 (2000)
10. Riccio, G.E., Stoffregen, T.A.: An Ecological theory of motion sickness and postural instability. Ecological Physiology 3(3), 195–240 (1991)
11. Oman, C.: A heuristic mathematical model for the dynamics of sensory conflict and motion sickness. Acta Otolaryngologica Supplement 392, 1–44 (1982)
12. Reason, J.: Motion sickness add –aptation: a neural mismatch model. J. Royal Soc. Med. 71, 819–829 (1978)
13. Stoffregen, T.A., Smart, L.J., Bardy, B.J., Pagulayan, R.J.: Postural stabilization of looking. Journal of Experimental Psychology. Human Perception and Performance 25, 1641–1658 (1999)
14. Takada, H., Fujikake, K., Miyao, M., Matsuura, Y.: Indices to Detect Visually Induced Motion Sickness using Stabilometry. In: Proc. VIMS 2007, pp. 178–183 (2007)
15. Hatada, T.: Nikkei electronics 444, 205–223 (1988)
16. Yasui, R., Matsuda, I., Kakeya, H.: Combining volumetric edge display and multiview display for expression of natural 3D images. In: Proc. SPIE, vol. 6055, pp. 0Y1–0Y9 (2006)
17. Kakeya, H.: MOEVision:simple multiview display with clear floating image. In: Proc. SPIE, vol. 6490, 64900J (2007)
18. Kennedy, R.S., Lane, N.E., Berbaum, K.S., Lilienthal, M.G.: A simulator sickness questionnaire (SSQ): A new method for quantifying simulator sickness. International J. Aviation Psychology 3, 203–220 (1993)
19. Holomes, S.R., Griffin, M.J.: Correlation between heart rate and the severity of motion sickness caused by optokinetic stimulation. J. Psychophysiology 15, 35–42 (2001)
20. Himi, N., Koga, T., Nakamura, E., Kobashi, M., Yamane, M., Tsujioka, K.: Differences in autonomic responses between subjects with and without nausea while watching an irregularly oscillating video. Autonomic Neuroscience. Basic and Clinical 116, 46–53 (2004)

21. Yokota, Y., Aoki, M., Mizuta, K.: Motion sickness susceptibility associated with visually induced postural instability and cardiac autonomic responses in healthy subjects. Acta Otolaryngologia 125, 280–285 (2005)
22. Scibora, L.M., Villard, S., Bardy, B., Stoffregen, T.A.: Wider stance reduces body sway and motion sickness. In: Proc. VIMS 2007, pp. 18–23 (2007)
23. Takada, H., Morimoto, T., Tsunashima, H., Yamazaki, T., Hoshina, H., Miyao, M.: Applications of Double-Wayland algorithm to detect anomalous signals. FORMA 21(2), 159–167 (2006)
24. Nishihara, T., Tahara, H.: Apparatus for recovering eyesight utilizing stereoscopic video and method for displaying stereoscopic video. US Patent 7404639 (2008)
25. Suzuki, J., Matsunaga, T., Tokumatsu, K., Taguchi, K., Watanabe, Y.: Q&A and a manual in Stabilometry. Equilibrium Res. 55(1), 64–77 (1996)
26. Takada, H., Kitaoka, Y., Ichikawa, S., Miyao, M.: Physical Meaning on Geometrical Index for Stabilometly. Equilibrium Res. 62(3), 168–180 (2003)
27. Wayland, R., Bromley, D., PickeTT, D., Passamante, A.: Recognizing determinism in a time series. Phys. Rev. Lett. 70, 530–582 (1993)
28. Takada, H., Fujikake, K., Watanabe, T., Hasegawa, S., Omori, M., Miyao, M.: On a method to evaluate motion sickness induced by stereoscopic images on HMD. In: Proceedings of the IS&T/SPIE 21st Annual Symposium on Electronic Imaging Science and Technology (to appear, 2009)
29. Matsumoto, T., Tokunaga, R., Miyano, T., Tokuda, I.: Chaos and Time Series. Baihukan, Tokyo, pp. 49–64 (2002) (in Japanese)
30. Takada, H., Shimizu, Y., Hoshina, H., Shiozawa, Y.: Wayland tests for differenced time series could evaluate degrees of visible determinism. Bulletin of Society for Science on Form 17(3), 301–310 (2005)
31. Goldie, P.A., Bach, T.M., Evans, O.M.: Force platform measures for evaluating postural control: reliability and validity. Arch. Phys. Med. Rehabil. 70, 510–517 (1989)

Estimation of User Interest from Face Approaches Captured by Webcam

Kumiko Fujisawa[1] and Kenro Aihara[1,2]

[1] The Graduate University for Advanced Studies, Sokendai
[2] National Institute of Informatics
2-1-2 Hitotsubashi, Chiyoda-ku,
Tokyo, Japan
{k_fuji,kenro.aihara}@nii.ac.jp

Abstract. We propose a methodology for estimating a user's interest in documents displayed on a computer screen from his or her physical actions. Some studies show that physical actions captured by a device can be indicators of a user's interest. We introduce the ongoing pilot study's results, which show the possible relationship between a user's face approaching the screen, as captured by a webcam, and their interest in the document on the screen. Our system uses a common user-friendly device. We evaluate our prototype system from the viewpoint of presuming an interest from such a face approach and the practicality of the system, and discuss the future possibilities of our research.

Keywords: Interface design, knowledge acquisition, user interest, motion capture.

1 Introduction

Although keyboards and mice are standard input devices for personal computers, many new devices are coming into regular use. Nintendo Wii's motion-sensitive controller is a popular example of such futuristic input devices. Video capturing devices can also be used as a means of input whereby people can control PC software, games, or other machines by moving their hands or bodies.

Techniques to detect and analyze body (including the face) movements are becoming more accessible. In particular, face tracking technologies are now used in household electronic goods [e.g., 1, 2, 3].

There has been a lot of research on new input devices and on using devices to detect user reactions in the field of human-computer interaction (HCI). These devices and systems tend to be heavy or distracting in some way, and user experiments involving them have had to be conducted under extraordinary conditions. To capture natural and emotional behaviors, more common situations are needed.

Our research focuses on how to capture the users' natural behaviors in response to information displayed on the screen via user-friendly (low impact) devices such as webcam. We are planning to identify user actions reflecting their interests using these devices and put them to practical use in the real learning situations. Therefore, we need light-weight and effective data for estimating the user's interest.

R. Shumaker (Ed.): Virtual and Mixed Reality, LNCS 5622, pp. 51–59, 2009.

We are proposing a methodology to estimate the users' interests by using face tracking data captured by a webcam. We describe our preliminary test results showing the potential effectiveness of such a methodology. This is part of our ongoing research on new interactive systems for supporting users in acquiring knowledge.

2 Previous Work

The topic of using sensors to recognize user actions has attracted the attention of researchers in the field of computer science for a long time, and quite a lot of devices have been developed. We will introduce some of these in the following paragraphs.

2.1 How to Capture User Actions

For a system to be able to capture whole-body movements, users sometimes have to wear sensor devices. For example, Sementile et al. [4] proposed a motion capture system based on marker detection using ARToolkit. The system consists of markers with patterns that act as reference points to collect a user's articulation coordinates. This system was used to generate humanoid avatars with similar movements to those of the user. Another example is the emotion recognition sensor system (EREC) that detects a user's emotional state [5]. It is composed of a sensor globe, a chest belt, and a data collection unit. Eye tracking cameras are often used, and the EMR eye tracker is one example [6]. This system uses a dedicated computer to make a head-mounted camera track the eye movements of the user.

Jacob categorized input devices in terms of the aspect of HCI [7, 8]. He studied the use of the hands, foot position, head position, eye gaze, and voice to manipulate a computer and described the devices that could be manipulated. Picard and Daily [9] summarized the body-based measures of an affect and described the typical sensor devices that can detect the action modalities, such as the facial or posture activities. They introduced video, force sensitive resistors, electromyogram electrodes, microphones, and other electrodes.

2.2 Body Action, Interest, and Capture Devices

Mota and Picard [10] described a system for recognizing the naturally occurring postures and associated affective states related to a child's interest level while he or she performed a learning task on a computer. Their main purpose was to identify the naturally occurring postures in natural learning situations. The device used in this research was composed of pressure sensors set in a chair. They used a hidden Markov model to remove the noise from the data and estimated the relationship between a posture and interest. They found evidence to support a dynamic relationship between postural behavior patterns and the affective states associated with interest.

Wakai et al. [11] proposed a technique for quantitatively measuring the change in interest from a portrait measured with a camera. They focused on the pose of eye gaze and the distance to the object. Their system detected eye gazes and the posture from the video image, and they succeeded in detecting changes in the direction of interest when the experiment's participants were asked to choose one favorite advertisement from a total of three. They used three cameras set behind each of the advertisements to detect the approach posture from the silhouette.

3 Proposed System

We propose a system that uses a familiar webcam to detect a user's face approaching the screen. We intend to use this system to select the natural movements which relate to the interest from a large amount of real-life samples. Figure 1 shows the basic structure of our prototype system.

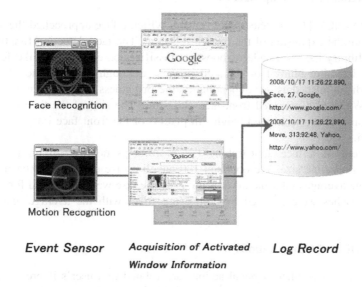

Fig. 1. Basic structure of prototype system

Fig. 2. Participants of the web experiment (left: with desktop PC; right: with notebook PC)

The webcam (Qcam E3500) mounted on the top of the screen (Fig. 2) captures the images of the user and the event sensor of the system detects the size of the face (face recognition part) and the body movements (motion recognition part). When the event sensor is activated, the log part records the timestamp in milliseconds, the active window's name, the URL (only when a browser is active), and the recognized face or motion size. The sensor detects the target event from each frame, and the maximum frame rate is 30 fps.

The image acquired from the camera is reduced to 1/2 size for the purpose of faster processing. The original image is 240 pixels in height by 320 pixels in width, and the converted image is 120 x 160 pixels.

3.1 Detection of Face Approaches

We used OpenCV [12] to detect the events in which a face approached the screen, as judged from the expansion of the recognized face. The face-detection function in the OpenCV library has a cascade of boosted classifiers based on Haar-like features. It excels at detecting blurred or dimmed images, although objects other than a face might be distinguished as one depending on the brightness difference in the rectangular area. We used a prepared front-face classifier. The size of the face is calculated from the sum of the width and height (in pixels) of the front face image detected by the system.

The event of a face approaching the monitor is determined on the basis of each user's baseline size. We obtained 100 baseline size data before starting the detection. The average and standard deviations of the size were calculated for each user. Face approaches were counted by comparing them with the average and standard deviations.

3.2 Detection of Other Actions

To investigate how other physical actions are related to a user's interest, the size of the user's body motions were also recorded. Body motions were calculated by summing up the widths and the heights of the motion segment detected by OpenCV.

4 Pilot Study Results

The implemented motion detector was tested in a pilot study. We evaluated its function and the relationship of the body movements to the user's interest.

4.1 Participants

Nineteen university undergraduate and graduate students from 19 to 31 years old (average age: 21.74 yrs.) participated in our preliminary test. All of them were right-handed. Seven of them did not use any visual correction devices, but the rest wore either contacts or glasses.

4.2 Procedure

Participants were asked to adjust their monitor and keyboard positions to suit their preferences. Then, they were asked to gaze at the monitor. This was the baseline session, and it lasted more than three minutes.

During the experimental session, the participants were asked to watch and evaluate the web pages according to the links on the screen. To distribute the degree of interest on a web page, we prepared 10 links to topics on the arts, academics, current news, fiction, and commercial goods. The participants were asked to visit all the links shown on the screen and other links if they wanted, and after visiting a link or viewing a new page, they were asked to rate on a scale of one to ten each page by using the following points: degree of reading (from 'did not read' to 'read carefully'), interest (from 'not interesting at all' to 'very interesting'), amusement (from 'not amusing at all' to 'very amusing'), novelty (from 'not novel at all' to 'very novel'), benefit (from 'not beneficial at all' to 'very beneficial') and easiness (from 'not easy at all' to 'very easy'). The duration of the experiment was around one hour. The face recognition and motion recognition parts of our system recorded data in both the experimental session and in the baseline session.

After this experimental session, all participants were asked whether they cared about the camera on the screen. We used these answers to evaluate the system's impact on the user.

4.3 Collected Data

The user's evaluation of each page and their actions (face approach and motion) while each page was being shown were totaled for reflecting whole tendency. The face size data in the experimental session was compared with a threshold value. We used the following function (1) and a size that was bigger than the threshold (T) value was counted as a face approach. T value was determined by adding on averaged x values in baseline period ($avg(X_{baseline})$) to standard deviation of x values ($stdev(X_{baseline})$) multiplied by coefficient α (from 1 to 3) value.

$$x = face.height + face.width$$
$$T = avg(X_{baseline}) + \alpha \times stdev(X_{baseline})\;.$$
$$f(x) = \begin{cases} 1 & if\ x_{experiment} > T \\ 0 & otherwise \end{cases}$$

(1)

We used only one threshold for the motion detection, because all of the users' avg. + 2 stdev. values and avg.+3stdev. values exceeded the maximum size of the recognition area (280 pixels), and most of the values recognized by the prototype system were near the maximum. We also measured the duration of each page's access.

4.4 Preliminary Results

We eliminated two of the 19 participants' log data because of a system failure in recording and an answering mistake. The face approaches were counted on each web page, and the Pearson's product-moment correlation coefficients between the counted

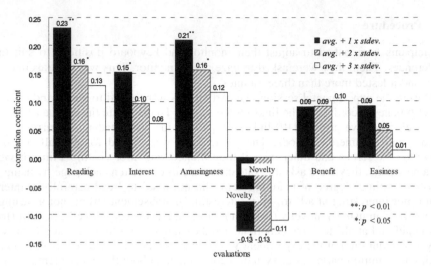

Fig. 3. Comparison of correlation coefficients between counted number of face approaches and each evaluation value from three different thresholds

Table 1. Matrix of correlation coefficients between variables

	Reading	Interest	Amusing	Novelty	Benefits	Easiness	Face	Motion	Duration
Reading	1.00	0.80(**)	0.75(**)	0.17(*)	0.50(**)	0.57(**)	0.23(**)	0.06	0.04
Interest	0.80(**)	1.00	0.87(**)	0.12	0.53(**)	0.58(**)	0.15(*)	0.04	0.07
Amusing	0.75(**)	0.87(**)	1.00	0.12	0.51(**)	0.55(**)	0.21(**)	0.10	0.08
Novelty	0.17(*)	0.12	0.12	1.00	0.32(**)	-0.07	-0.13(*)	-0.17(*)	-0.03
Benefits	0.50(**)	0.53(**)	0.51(**)	0.32(**)	1.00	0.09	0.09	0.07	0.07
Easiness	0.57(**)	0.58(**)	0.55(**)	-0.07	0.09	1.00	0.09	0.03	-0.02
Face	0.23(**)	0.15(*)	0.21(**)	-0.13(*)	0.09	0.09	1.00	0.47(**)	0.12
Motion	0.06	0.04	0.10	-0.17(*)	0.07	0.03	0.47(**)	1.00	0.07
Duration	0.04	0.07	0.08	-0.03	0.07	-0.02	0.12	0.07	1.00

** p < 0.01

* p < 0.05

number of face approaches and each evaluation value were calculated for three thresholds (Fig. 3).

For all the thresholds, all the coefficients showed the same tendency in positive and negative values. Face approach counts using avg.+1stdev. threshold showed these tendency more clearly. Significant ($p<0.01$) correlations were found between the face approach frequency and the degree of reading (0.23**) and amusement (0.21**) at the avg.+1stdev. threshold. The results at the avg.+2stdev. threshold showed similar tendencies. Although the level of significance was low ($p<0.05$), interest was positively correlated (0.15*) and the novelty was negatively correlated (-0.13*).

The face count, motion count, page access duration time, and all the page evaluation points are summarized in the correlation matrix (Table 1). The motion count and duration did not show any significant correlation to the reading, interest, or amusement factors, but the face approach and motion counts were significantly correlated. The N size of a motion was much smaller than the others', because four of the participants did not leave motion logs in the baseline period and their data was treated as a missing value. The reading, interest, and amusement factors highly correlated with each other.

Results from questions and answers about webcam were shown below (Table 2). Most participants said that the existence of the camera didn't matter to them. Even if they had no experience in using personal computers with a webcam, they could browse without being concerned. This result showed that the camera on the computer was not considered to be out of the ordinary.

Table 2. Questions and answers about webcam

	Did you care about the camera on the screen?	Have you ever seen a camera like this?	Have you ever used a PC with a camera like this?
Yes	3	13	6
No	16	6	13

N=19

5   System Evaluation

We evaluated our prototype system from the viewpoint of presuming an interest from the face approach frequency and the practicality of the system.

5.1   Effect of Interest Estimation by Using Face Approach

There was a positive correlation between the face approach frequencies acquired by the system and the degree to which the user had actually read the page and the degree of amusement they felt while viewing it. In addition, the reading factor was highly correlated to the interest and amusement factors. These results showed that our system could be used to estimate whether a user had actually read the contents with positive emotions such as interest or amusement. However, these relationships became vague as the threshold value increased.

Motion count and page access duration were not useful data for estimating the user's interest in this experiment. The size of the acquired motion or the range of the value might be the reason for this problem. It is necessary to reexamine the sensitivity of the system or the acquisition method for characterizing an individual's behavioral pattern for the precision enhancement in addition to the face approach.

5.2 System Practicality

In our experiment, most of the participants reported that the existence of the camera did not bother their activities when exploring the web. Although the data size of a captured image was very small, the results showed the possibility to estimate a user's emotional status. This prototype system seems to be applicable to the current PC environment.

Moreover, our system did not directly record facial images, but recorded only numeric size data. In addition to the familiarity of a device, such data might be comparatively less intrusive to the user. That is, it might be useful data for the information provider, and it can be collected while maintaining the user's privacy.

6 Conclusion

We described our prototype system to identify a user's interest in the target on a PC screen using a common webcam. Although our methodology is very easy to use, the preliminary results showed the possibility of using it to identify actions reflecting the user's interest in a target. For the detailed analysis, we will evaluate this tendency of each individual.

Analyzing the whole-body movement with dedicated equipment continues to have a very important role, because our experiment is based on the relations revealed by past experiments. On the other hand, experimental analyses using real-world equipment in real-life situations are becoming more and more important now that there is an ever-increasing variety of input devices. Developing an application for an actual environment will soon be an important issue.

This technique might could be applied to various fields, although it would be necessary to set the appropriate thresholds for judging face approaches under varying circumstances. The degree of reading showed a positive correlation, and this seemed to indicate the possibility of utilizing our technique for user profiling in systems that make recommendations. To estimate the user's interest in a website, researchers have used the viewing duration, mouse movement, or eye gaze [13]. If our system proves to be valid in future experiments, it may be useful for estimating users' actions on the web.

The results of our experiments are presently being validated in real-world learning situations. We plan to analyze additional movements and revise the prototype system while applying it in an actual environment.

References

1. NIKON COOLPIX 5900,
   http://www.nikon-image.com/jpn/products/camera/compact/
   coolpix/5900/features01.htm
2. Polaroid t831,
   http://www.polaroid.com/global/detail.jsp?PRODUCT%3C%3Eprd_i
   d=845524441767954&FOLDER%3C%3Efolder_id=282574488338793&bmUI
   D=1224770795670&bmLocale=en_US

3. OLYMPUS FE-360,
   http://olympus-imaging.jp/product/compact/fe360/
4. Sementille, A.C., Lourenço, L.E., Brega, J.R., Rodello, I.: A motion captures system using passive markers. In: Proceedings of the 2004 ACM SIGGRAPH International Conference on Virtual Reality Continuum and Its Applications in Industry, Singapore, June 16-18 (2004)
5. Kaiser, R., Oertel, K.: Emotions in HCI: an affective e-learning system. In: Goecke, R., Robles-Kelly, A., Caelli, T. (eds.) Proceedings of the Hcsnet Workshop on Use of Vision in Human-Computer interaction, Canberra, Australia, November 1, 2006. ACM International Conference Proceeding Series, vol. 56, 237, pp. 105–106. Australian Computer Society, Darlinghurst, Australia (2006)
6. Prendinger, H., Ma, C., Yingzi, J., Nakasone, A., Ishizuka, M.: Understanding the effect of life-like interface agents through users' eye movements. In: Proceedings of the 7th international Conference on Multimodal interfaces, ICMI 2005, Toronto, Italy, October 4-6, 2005, pp. 108–115. ACM, New York (2005)
7. Jacob, R.J.: Human-computer interaction: input devices. ACM Comput. Surv. 28(1), 177–179 (1996)
8. Jacob, R.J.: The future of input devices. ACM Comput. Surv. 28(4es), 138 (1996)
9. Picard, R., Daily, S.B.: Evaluating affective interactions: Alternatives to asking what users feel. In: The 2005 CHI Workshop Evaluating Affective Interfaces (2005)
10. Mota, S., Picard, R.W.: Automated posture analysis for detecting learner's interest level. In: 1st IEEE Workshop on Computer Vision and Pattern Recognition, CVPR HCI 2003 (2003)
11. Wakai, Y., Sumi, K., Matsuyama, T.: Estimation of Human Interest Level in Choosing from Video Sequence. In: The actual use of vision technology Workshop (2005)
12. OpenCV, http://opencv.jp/
13. Hijikata, Y.: User Profiling Technique for Information Recommendation and Information Filtering. Jinkouchinougakkaishi 19(3), 365–372 (2004)

Spatial Navigation in a Virtual Multilevel Building: The Role of Exocentric View in Acquiring Survey Knowledge

Zhiqiang Luo[1], Henry Been-Lirn Duh[2],
I-Ming Chen[1], and Wenshu Luo[3]

[1] Sch. of Mech. & Aerospace Enginerring, Nanyang Technological University, Singapore
zqluo@ntu.edu.sg, michen@ntu.edu.sg
[2] Dept. of Electrical & Computer Engineering, National University of Singapore, Singapore
eledbl@nus.edu.sg
[3] Centre for Research of Pedagogy and Practice, National Institute of Education, Singapore
wenshu.luo@nie.edu.sg

Abstract. The present study aimed to test the function of the exocentric view on the acquisition of survey knowledge during spatial navigation in a virtual multilevel building. Subjects navigated a virtual three-level building in three conditions. In the first condition, subjects navigated the building without any aid. In the second condition, subjects navigated the building with the aid of a three-dimensional (3D) floor map which illustrated the spatial layout on each level from one exocentric perspective. In the third condition, subjects could watch the spatial layout on each level from the exocentric perspective when traveling to another level by an elevator. After navigation, all subjects made the judgment of spatial relative direction. The analyses of the accuracy of spatial judgments showed that the accuracy of judgment of spatial horizontal direction was significantly improved when subjects observed the exocentric views of levels in the last two conditions; the judgment of spatial vertical direction was significantly worse in the 3D floor map condition than in other two conditions. Furthermore, the accuracy of judgment of both spatial horizontal and vertical directions was best in the direction faced by subjects when they first enter each level. The results suggested that the content of exocentric view should be carefully designed to improve the acquisition of survey knowledge. The application of the findings included the design of 3D map for the navigation in the virtual multilevel building.

1 Introduction

Spatial navigation in a multilevel building is one common task in people's daily life, such as the navigation in the subway station, shopping mall and the museums. A multilevel building is a constrained three-dimensional (3D) space with the constraints of walls, ceilings and floors. Navigation in a multilevel building is also limited within specific areas, such as on floors and staircases. Because of the constraints of building and navigation, it is very difficult for people to acquire the accurate survey knowledge of a multilevel building. When navigating the multilevel building in the virtual

R. Shumaker (Ed.): Virtual and Mixed Reality, LNCS 5622, pp. 60–69, 2009.

environment (VE) rather than in the real world, people encounter more problems in acquiring the survey knowledge. Previous studies [4, 13] have demonstrated that the exocentric views provided during the navigation on the level in one virtual building can facilitate the acquisition of survey knowledge of spatial layout in this level. Two questions are addressed in the present study: (1) Do the exocentric views facilitate the acquisition of survey knowledge in a virtual multilevel building; (2) what difference exists in survey knowledge if the way to provide the exocentric views is different during spatial navigation in the same virtual multilevel building.

Generally, there are two common ways to provide the exocentric views during spatial navigation in VE. The first way is to elevate the viewpoint in air. For example, subjects in study [13] study learned a virtual floor layout of building with one of three navigation training aids: local and global orientation cues, exocentric views, and a theme environment enhanced with sights and sounds, where subjects with the exocentric-view aid watched the layout from a viewpoint outside the building. The survey knowledge was tested after the navigation. The results indicated that the exocentric views were effective in improving performance on the survey knowledge tests. One extreme exocentric view of environment is a 3D model of environment, such as "world in miniature" (WIM, [10]) which can be changed at will simply by rotating or zooming in study [4] employed a 3D model of one floor of a building to assist their subjects' spatial learning, and the results indicated that this modal was even as good as a real-world environment for acquiring survey knowledge. Furthermore, they suggested that a VE training system that combines an immersive walk-through VE and a miniature-model VE could provide better training to achieve the survey knowledge than real-world training.

The second way is to draw the exocentric view of space into a 3D map, or called the exocentric map, on a computer screen or a paper. Compared with the 2D map, the 3D map preserves features of objects and integrates all three dimensions into a single rendering, thereby enhancing the shape and layout understanding [11]. Evidence for the benefits of the 3D map comes from the research on aviation displays for navigation in the unconstrained 3D natural space [3, 12] and the research on learning the building structure in the constrained building space [2]. For example, Fontaine [2] found that subjects using a 3D map could better elaborate the vertical relations between levels of a subway station than their counterparts without the map.

Although spatial learning from the exocentric views can facilitate the acquisition of survey knowledge, the orientation-dependent mental representation is still observed. Subjects in study [9] study learned the spatial layout on one floor in a large-scale virtual building environment from either the egocentric or exocentric perspective, and then performed the judgment of relative direction (JRD ,"Imagine you are standing at object A and facing object B, point to object C"). The accuracy of spatial judgment indicated that subjects judged the relative directions between objects more accurately when imagining facing the direction aligned with the initial orientation faced in this building. The experience of exploring spatial layout plays a critical role in defining the orientation-dependent property of mental representation of this environment [6].

The present study aimed to test the function of the exocentric view on the acquisition of survey knowledge of a virtual multilevel building. The exocentric view was acquired through the above two ways, the elevation of viewpoint in air and the 3D map. Specifically, the first way was realized by permitting subjects to observe the floor layout from the exocentric perspectives when they took the elevator to travel between levels in this multilevel building. The second way was to provide the 3D floor map which draws the floor layout from one exocentric perspective. The content of the 3D floor map would be updated when subjects arrive at a new level in this multilevel building.

Three hypotheses would be tested in this study. First, the exocentric views provided by above two ways could facilitate the acquisition of survey knowledge in the virtual multilevel building. Second, there was no difference between the survey knowledge when the exocentric views were provided by these two ways. Third, orientation dependent mental representation of the virtual environment would be build even though the exocentric views were provided during the spatial navigation.

2 Participant

Thirty undergraduate and graduate students (15 males, 15 females, all between 18 and 29 years of age, M =22, SD = 2.586) from Nanyang Technological University in Singapore participated in this experiment for monetary compensation. All participants had normal or corrected-to-normal vision.

3 Materials

A HP xw4300 workstation with a 19-in LCD monitor was used to display virtual environments (VEs) which were created by using EON software (Eon Reality Company, 2004). Movement through the VE was effected by pressing the arrow keys on the keyboard: the up and down arrows effected forward and backward movements, whereas the left and right arrows effected left and right rotations. Subjects could hold down the keys to obtain the continuous translation with 1 meter per second and rotation with 60^0 per second.

The multilevel VE was comprised of three vertically aligned rooms that formed a three-level building (see Figure 1). The room on each level was rectangular in shape and measured approximately 8m×6m×3m. In the middle of one of the shorter walls on each level was an elevator with a 2×2m floor, which connected the adjacent levels. The elevator had one door which was open to the room and close when the elevator moved between levels. In all but one experimental condition, the doors were opaque and subjects could not observe the outside when taking the elevator. Inside the elevator room, subjects could choose the target level by clicking on a level button. There were nine common household objects (e.g. chair, cabinet, etc) in the experimental building, three positioned in different locations in each room.

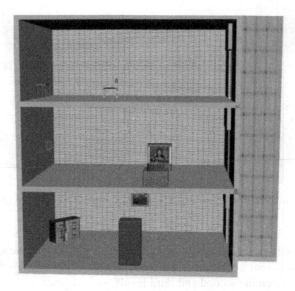

Fig. 1. The virtual three-level building

4 Design

The independent variables included one between-subjects variable and two within-subjects variables. The between-subjects variable defined three kinds of navigation treatment: no map, 3D floor map, and transparent conditions. Subjects were randomly assigned to each of three experimental conditions. The no map group was the control group, in which subjects explored the virtual building without any aid.

The 3D floor map presented the layout of each level from the viewpoint of 4 meters above that level, looking forward from the elevator. The geometric field of view (GFOV) of the exocentric map was set at 74^0 on the horizontal axis and 59^0 on the vertical axis to help with the depiction of spatial layout and to assist subjects with the position judgment.

In the 3D floor map condition, a small (10.2cm×8.1cm) map was embedded in the 3D immersive view and located in the top left of the computer screen. This method was based on the split-screen technique used in the design of aviation display (e.g., [7]). This design allowed subjects to go back and forth easily and quickly between exocentric views of maps of space and egocentric views derived from being in that space, which was effective for remaining oriented and learning the space. Specifically, the 3D floor map showed the layout of the level on which subjects were standing. When subjects arrived on a new level by taking the elevator, the content of map automatically changed to show the new level layout. The view of the second level in the 3D floor-map condition is shown in Figure 2(a).

In the transparent condition, the elevator door and its connected wall were transparent so that subjects could observe the room layout through the door when standing inside the elevator. The virtual building was not augmented with any map aid. But different from the no map condition, subjects in this condition could observe the room

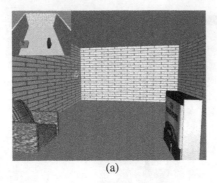
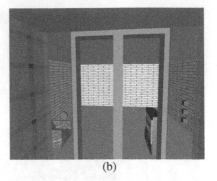

(a)   (b)

Fig. 2. The view of second level in (a) the 3D floor map condition and (b) the transparent condition

layout from exocentric perspectives as elevation changed. The view of the second level in the transparent condition is shown in Figure 2(b) when subjects took the vertical move between the second and third levels.

The two within-subjects variables defined the characteristics of probe questions to be asked in the judgment of relative direction task (JRD, "Imagine you are standing at object A and facing object B, point to object C",[1]): (1) the level difference between the target objects C and the reference objects A and B and (2) the imagined facing direction from object A to object B. The level difference along the vertical dimension could be two levels up, one level up, same level, one level down, two levels down, designed to reveal the vertical same level bias and downward bias in spatial memory. The imagined facing direction along the horizontal dimension could be forward (facing the room from the elevator), left/right, or backward (facing the elevator from the room), purported to reveal the preferred orientation in spatial memory.

To perform the JRD task, subjects were required to stand at one mark which was 1 meter in front of a vertically mounted board. A coordinate system was set up in this test environment. The original point of this coordinate system was the mark on the ground, the Z axis was defined to be vertical to the ground, the Y axis paralleled the front board, and the X axis was orthogonal to the front board. Therefore, each position in the test environment could be represented by a coordinate of this system (x, y, z). Moreover, the target object C in the JRD task were all in front of subjects as they imagined facing the reference object B, so subjects would not need to point to objects behind them. Subjects were required to use a laser pointer to project a point on the board, through which they could imagine seeing the top of the target assigned in the instruction. The experimenter recorded the coordinates of the eye and the point on the board. From this, the horizontal and vertical angles between the eye and the point in the coordinate system could be computed.

In this test, the dependent variables were the angular error and the response time. The angular error was measured as the absolute angular difference between the pointing direction and the actual direction where the target would have been. There were two angular errors: the error of horizontal angle and the error of vertical angle. The response time was measured as the time from the presentation of instruction to the end of the subject's response, which was recorded by a stop watch.

5 Procedure

Subjects were tested individually in a quiet room. In order to screen out subjects with the poor memory, all subjects first took a memory test. They were required to scan nine objects printed on a piece paper for 30 seconds and then generate these objects at the corresponding positions on a piece of blank paper with the same size. These nine objects were not used in the virtual building. All subjects could recall more than six objects in this test and were allowed to proceed to the next phase.

Subjects were then seated approximately 0.42 meters from the computer screen. They first observed the nine experimental objects printed as 3D objects on a piece of paper. After they were familiar with the objects and could associate each with a unique name, they started practicing the navigation in a practice building containing no objects. The practice building was the same as the experimental building except the spatial objects. Maps were not given to subjects in the 3D floor map condition at this moment and no time limit was imposed on this preliminary exploration. Subjects then navigated the experimental building with nine objects. They were told that each of nine objects would react if clicked by the mouse and they needed to go nearby to the objects to click on the objects. Subjects were instructed to explore all three levels freely in ten minutes and enter each room at least twice. They were told that the purpose of this exploration was to remember the locations of the nine objects and that they would later be asked to point out these locations.

After exploring the building, subjects were asked to perform the JRD task. The instruction of each trial was displayed on the computer. Subjects first took two trials in order to be familiar with the requirement and procedure of the JRD task. The performance in these two trials was not counted in the data analysis. The total time for the experiment was approximately 60 minutes.

6 Result

All dependent measures were subjected to analysis of variance (ANOVA) in terms of navigation treatment, level difference and imagined facing direction. Since the levels of the two within-subjects variables were not fully crossed, the interaction between them could not be tested. Therefore, in the customized analysis, only the main effects of the three independent variables and the interaction effects between navigation treatment and each of the two between-subjects variables were examined. A significance level $\alpha < .05$ was adopted for all these analyses.

6.1 The Judgment Accuracy of Horizontal Direction

The main effect of the navigation treatment was significant, $F(1, 27) = 3.82$, $p < .05$. Multiple comparisons showed that the performance was significantly worse in the no-map condition than in other two conditions; the remaining two did not differ

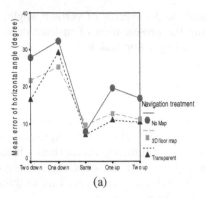
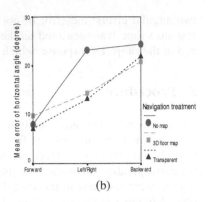

(a)   (b)

Fig. 3. Judgment of the horizontal direction. (a) Mean error of horizontal angle as a function of level difference and navigation treatment; (b) Mean error of horizontal angle as a function of imagined facing direction and navigation treatment.

significantly. As depicted in Figure 3(a), the main effect of level difference was significant, $F(4, 108) = 19.23$, $p < .01$. Multiple comparisons showed that (1) the best performance (least error) was observed when subjects pointed to objects on the same floor, and (2) the performance was better when pointing up than pointing down. The interaction between navigation treatment and level difference was not significant.

As depicted in Figure 3(b), the main effect of the imagined facing direction was significant, $F(2,54) = 41.80$, $p < .01$. Multiple comparisons suggested that the performance in the forward direction (i.e. the orientation from which subjects entered the room) was the best and in the backward (i.e. the orientation from which subjects exited the room) was the poorest. The interaction between navigation treatment and imagined facing direction was also significant $F(4,54) = 2.60$, $p < .05$. Further analyses in each navigation condition revealed that (1) in the no-map condition, the performance in the forward direction was better than those in the left/right and backward directions; (2) in the 3D floor map condition, the performance in the forward direction was better than those in the backward direction, while no significant difference was found between the left/right direction and other two directions.; (3) in the transparent direction, the performance was best in the forward direction, then in the left/right direction, and poorest in the backward direction.

6.2   The Judgment Accuracy of Vertical Direction

The main effect of the navigation treatment was significant, $F(1, 27) = 4.37, p < .05$. Multiple comparisons showed that the performance was significantly worse in the 3D floor map condition than in other two conditions; the remaining two did not differ significantly. As depicted in Figure 4(a), the main effect of level difference was significant, $F(4, 108) = 20.64$, $p < .01$. Multiple comparisons showed that (1) the best performance (least error) was observed when subjects pointed to objects on the same floor, and (2) the performance was better when pointing down than pointing up. The interaction between navigation treatment and level difference was not significant.

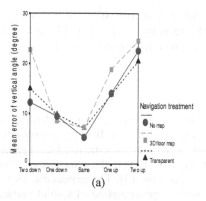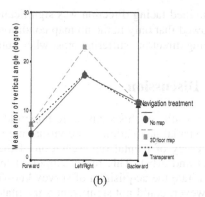

(a)   (b)

Fig. 4. Judgment of the horizontal direction. (a) Mean error of vertical angle as a function of level difference and navigation treatment; (b) Mean error of vertical angle as a function of imagined facing direction and navigation treatment.

As shown in Figure 4(b), the main effect of the imagined facing direction was significant, $F(2,54) = 52.78$, $p < .01$. Multiple comparisons suggested that the performance in the forward direction (i.e. the orientation from which subjects entered the room) was better than those in other two directions. The interaction between the imagined facing direction and the navigation treatment was not significant.

6.3 Response Time

Navigation treatment did not show significant main effect on response time. There was a significant effect of level difference, $F(4, 108) = 4.22$, $p < .01$, and pointing to objects on the same level was fastest, as shown in Figure 5(a). The interaction between navigation treatment and level difference was not significant.

As shown in Figure 5(b), the main effect of the imagined facing direction was significant, $F(2, 54) = 6.749$, $p < .01$. The interaction between navigation treatment and

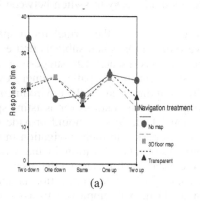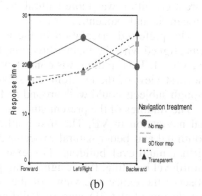

(a)   (b)

Fig. 5. Response time. (a) Response time as a function of level difference and navigation treatment; (b) Response time as a function of imagined facing direction and navigation treatment.

imagined facing direction was significant, $F(4, 54) = 3.98$, p < .05. Post hoc analysis showed that only in the no map condition was the response time affected by imagined facing direction, suffering most when subjects imagined facing left or right.

7 Discussion

The results of this study were threefold. First, the exocentric views provided during the spatial navigation in the virtual multilevel building can significantly improve the accuracy of mental representation of the spatial horizontal information (see Figures 3(a) and 3(b)). This result supported the first hypothesis that the exocentric views facilitate the acquisition of survey knowledge in space [8, 13]. The exocentric views, however, could not significantly facilitate the mental representation of spatial vertical information, which did not support the first hypothesis. The distinct effect of the exocentric view on the mental representations of spatial horizontal and vertical information demonstrated that spatial information on the horizontal and vertical dimensions is represented differently in memory.

Second, compared with the static exocentric views provided by the 3D floor map, the dynamical exocentric views provided during the vertical movement between levels in the transparent condition can better assist subjects to acquire spatial vertical information (see Figures 4(a) and 4(b)). This result did not support the second hypothesis.

Last, the orientation dependent mental representation was observed even though subjects could acquire the exocentric views of the virtual environment (Figure 3(b) and 4(b)). This result supports the third hypothesis. The extra exocentric views provided during the spatial navigation could not ensure the orientation-free mental representation of the virtual multilevel building.

In general, subjects in the transparent conditions perform best in the present experiment. The reason would lie in two aspects. First, compared with the 3D floor map condition, subjects in the transparent condition could acquire more exocentric views of each level. The increased number of exocentric views helped subject better observe the spatial layout. This result was consistent with our previous finding in the virtual room space [5]. Second, the way to provide the exocentric views in the transparent condition was more natural, and subjects would be easy to switch between the egocentric and exocentric views.

The preferred orientation in the mental representation of the virtual room space was aligned with the facing direction (the forward direction) when subjects first enter each level. This finding was consistent with the previous research [9], suggesting that the first view of the environment should be most salient in the spatial memory even though subjects could walk around and faced different directions in the environment.

The findings of the present study have two important implications for assisting spatial navigation in VE. The first implication is that VE designers should provide the continual and better natural exocentric views for users during their navigation in the virtual multilevel building. For example, when users take elevation in the virtual multilevel building, the designers can provide the escalator for users so that users can observe the exocentric views of the spatial layout. The second implication is about the design of the 3D map of building. When a 3D map is employed to assist the navigation in the virtual multilevel building, the 3D map should illustrate the vertical relationship between levels in a multilevel building (also see [2]). The present study has demonstrated that the 3D floor map which only illustrates the spatial layout on one level can impair the mental representation of spatial vertical information among three levels.

Our future work will further investigate the design of the 3D map for navigation in a virtual multilevel building. Some research questions are remained. Besides the requirement of illustration of spatial vertical relations between levels, what are other requirements? What is the effect of the 3D map of building on the wayfinding performance in the virtual multilevel building? Can users improve their wayfinding strategy in the virtual multilevel building if the 3D map is applied?

References

1. Easton, R.D., Sholl, M.J.: Object-array structure, frames of reference, and retrieval of spatial knowledge. Journal of Experimental Psychology: Learning, Memory, and Cognition 21(3), 483–500 (1995)
2. Fontaine, S.: Spatial cognition and the processing of verticality in underground environments. In: Montello, D.R. (ed.) COSIT 2001. LNCS, vol. 2205, pp. 387–399. Springer, Heidelberg (2001)
3. Hickox, J.C., Wickens, C.D.: Effects of elevation angle display, complexity, and feature type on relating out-of-cockpit field of view to an electronic cartographic map. Journal of Experimental Psychology: Applied 5(3), 284–301 (1999)
4. Koh, G., Wiegand, T.E.v., Garnett, R.L., Durlach, M.I., Shinn-Cunningham, B.: Use of virtual environments for acquiring configurational knowledge about specific real-world spaces: 1. Preliminary experiment. Presence: Teleoperators and Virtual Environments 8(6), 632–656 (1999)
5. Luo, Z.Q., Luo, W.S., Chen, I.M., Jiao, J.X.R., Duh, B.L.H.: Spatial representation of a virtual room space: perspective and vertical movement. International Journal of Human Computer Interaction (under review)
6. McNamara, T.P.: How are the locations of objects in the environment represented in memory? In: Freksa, C., Brauer, W., Habel, C., Wender, K.F. (eds.) Spatial Cognition III. LNCS, vol. 2685, pp. 174–191. Springer, Heidelberg (2003)
7. Olmos, O., Wickens, C.D., Chudy, A.: Tactical displays for combat awareness: An examination of dimensionality and frame of reference concepts and the application of cognitive engineering. The International Journal of Aviation Psychology 10(3), 247–271 (2000)
8. Rieser, J.J., Doxsey, P.A., McCarrell, N.S., Brooks, P.H.: Wayfinding and toddlers' use of information from an aerial view of a maze. Developmental Psychology 18(5), 714–720 (1982)
9. Shelton, A.L., McNamara, T.P.: Orientation and perspective dependence in route and survey learning. Journal of Experimental Psychology: Learning, Memory, and Cognition 30(1), 158–170 (2004)
10. Stoakley, R., Conway, M.J., Pausch, R.: Virtual reality on a WIM: Interactive worlds in miniature. In: The Computer Human Interaction, CHI 1995 (1995)
11. St. John, M., Cowen, M.B., Smallman, H.S., Oonk, H.M.: The use of 2D and 3D displays for shape-understanding versus relative-position tasks. Human Factors 43(1), 79–98 (2001)
12. Wickens, C.D., Prevett, T.: Exploring the dimensions of egocentricity in aircraft navigation displays. Journal of Experimental Psychology: Applied 1(2), 110–135 (1995)
13. Witmer, B.G., Sadowski, W.J., Finkelstein, N.M.: VE-based training strategies for acquiring survey knowledge. Presence: Teleoperators and Virtual Environments 11(1), 1–18 (2002)

A Real-World Pointing Device Based on an Optical Communication System

Yuichi Mitsudo

116-2 Kamedanakano-cho, Hakodate-shi, Hokkaido, Japan
Future University Hakodate
mitsudo@fun.ac.jp

Abstract. In the present paper, a new augmented reality environment that is based on an optical communication system is described. Optical communication devices have been used in several studies on ubiquitous computing. A novel physical structure of an optical communication system that enables the user to select the optical signal by simply pointing its transmitter with his/her finger is developed. In such an environment, the optical transmitter can be treated as a visual tag, referred to as a GhostTag, that includes continuous data, such as audio files. In addition, the PointSpeech application, which provides the user with audio assistant data via GhostTag, is presented herein.

1 Introduction

In the present paper, a new augmented reality environment, which enables the attachment of continuous data to real-world objects as an annotation, is presented. In some studies, RF tags or visual tags are used to attach small amounts of data to real-world objects[1,2,3]. The annotations are stored in the tags as a visual pattern on paper or as digital data in small circuits. The user must be close to the tag and readout the annotations. In the present system, the annotation is placed within the visual angle of the real-world object (Fig.1). The visual angle within which an annotation is placed is referred to as the **GhostTag**, and the user reads out the annotation by a pointing behavior, referred to as **TeleClick**.

This visual-angle-based annotation system is similar to a GUI system, in which the GhostTag corresponds to an icon, and the index finger corresponds to the cursor. TeleClick, in which the user overrup his/her index finger on the visual angle of object(Fig.1, Fig.3) is the method used to select an annotation.

2 GhostTag

GhostTag is essentially the visual angle around a tag. GhostTag can be generated by a simple combination of a transmitter, photo-detector and an image sensor. Figure 2 shows the system used to generate and read GhostTags.

An optical transmitter(tag), which transmits optical signal, is attached to a real-world object. When an image sensor observes the this transmitter, a photodetector, which is directed toward the surface of the image sensor, detects the

R. Shumaker (Ed.): Virtual and Mixed Reality, LNCS 5622, pp. 70–79, 2009.

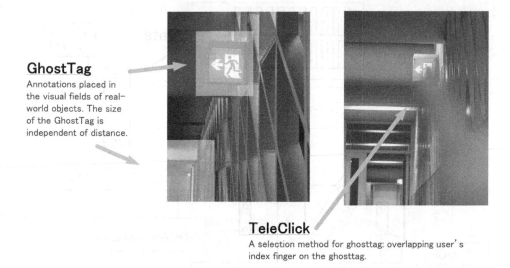

GhostTag

Annotations placed in the visual fields of real-world objects. The size of the GhostTag is independent of distance.

TeleClick

A selection method for ghosttag: overlapping user's index finger on the ghosttag.

Fig. 1. GhostTag: continuous data placed within in the visual angle, TeleClick: selection method of GhostTag

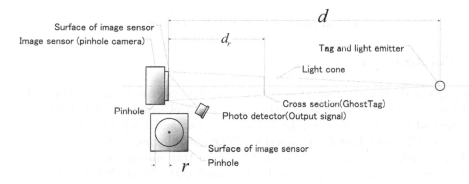

Fig. 2. Schematic diagram of the GhostTag setup

optical signal reflected by the surface of the image sensor. The optical signal is a cone-shaped and is symmetric about an axis formed by a line running from the center of the image sensor to the center of the light emitter. The cross section of this cone is GhostTag. The center of GhostTag is a light emitter on the tag, and the size of GhostTag is determined by the distance between the image sensor and cross section d_r. The visual angle of GhostTag, θ_r, is determined primarily by d_r.

Generally, optical communication systems that use transmitters and receivers have time-domain resolution, rather than spatial resolution. Owing to its simple structure, in which the photodetector is directed toward the image sensor and senses the signal reflected from the surface of the image sensor, the proposed system has both time-domain and spatial resolutions.

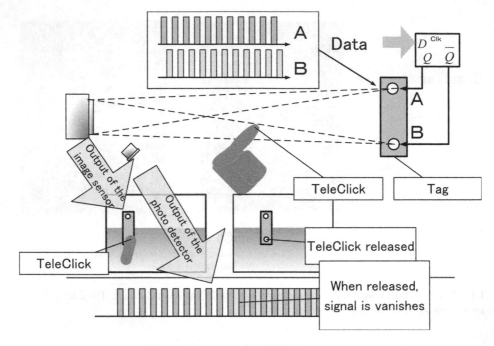

Fig. 3. Diagram of TeleClick operation

3   PointSpeech

PointSpeech is an application system that provides audio assistance to the user. The user obtains sound data from GhostTag by TeleClicking. In the following, the method used to detect a TeleClick by the user and read out the contents of the TeleClicked GhostTag is described. The optical transmitter, attached to real world object as a tag, has two LEDs: one for transmitting data signals (Q) and another for transmitting inverted data signals ($\bar{Q}$) (Fig. 3). When a receiver receives both these signals, it outputs a flat signal (data signal is eliminated). When a user blocks an inverted signal by TeleClicking as described above, the data signal can be observed by the receiver. In PointSpeech system, Pulse Width Modulation(PWM) is used to translate auditory data.

3.1   RealEyeCommunicator/VisionCommunicator

Receiver of PointSpeech system is implemented through RealEyeCommunicator(REC)/VisionCommunicator(VC), a receiver part(image sensor and photodetector) of GhostTag generator. VC includes a cell phone CCD as the image sensor , and the other receiver uses the eye of the user as the image sensor. By implementing through REC/VC system, PointSpeech does not require image processing to select and readout the data from GhostTag, althogh it is a

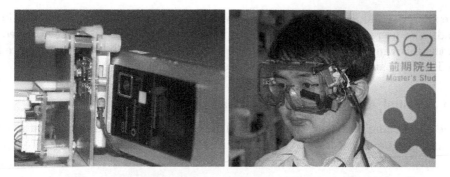

Fig. 4. A view of VisionCommunicator/RealEyeCommunicator

Fig. 5. A transmitter of VC/REC

vision-based pointing system. This enables the use of high-speed signals as an annotation, and helps to employ numerous optical systems, including the eye of the user as an image sensor.

4   System Implementation

PointSpeech was implemented in the proposed optical system. Audio data is broadcast from transmitters, and the user selects the transmitted signals by pointing at the transmitter. Two types of receivers, REC and VC are used.

5   Experiments

In this section, the visual angle of GhostTag and its pointing time are described through experiments. In the following subsections, an optical translator, for which the LED distance is 6.0 cm, is used as a tag. The tag emits a digital optical signal, the content of which is a sound generated by pulse width modulation (PWM).

Pulse width modulation is a popular digital modulation for conveying analog information over communication channels. Pulse width modulation uses a rectangle wave that is pulse width modulated such that the average value is equal to the source signal. By the principle of PWM, the following characteristics can be lead. The user can retrieve same sound weather which LED to be TeleClicked. In the following section, the visual angle of the GhostTag and the time required to TeleClick are obtained for several cases.

5.1   Visual Angle Required for Read out

The visual angle of GhostTag required in order for VisionCommunicator or RealEyeCommunicator to be used as a receiver is shown.

VisionCommunicator. The following experiment shows the visual angle of GhostTag when VisionCommunicator is used. The experiment is performed when $d_r = 0.4$m and a cursor of 16×10^{-3} m in diameter is used, and both the distance d and the position of the cursor are manipulated (Fig.6).

In this experiment, the integrated cell-phone camera (Fig. 4) with a resolution of 160×120 is integrated into the system. The experimental value is shown in Figure 11, and its view is shown in Fig. 7.

Before the cursor touches the optical signal, the voltage output by the receiver is flat. When the signal appears, that cursor position is left (right) edge of the GhostTag. The horizontal length of GhostTag is measured by this method.

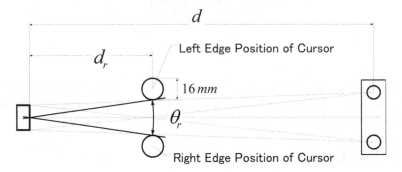

Fig. 6. Experimental setup

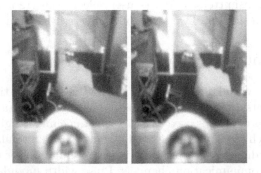

Fig. 7. Left and right edges of GhostTag

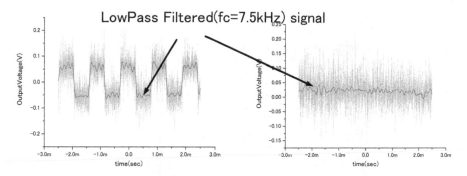

Fig. 8. Examples of output signals: clicked signal (left) and normal signal (right)

Figure 8 shows the normal and "clicked" signals.

Based on these experimental results, VisionCommunicator has sufficient spatial resolution to detect a TeleClick performed by the index finger of the user.

RealEyeCommunicator. Next, an experiment using the RealEyeCommunicator (REC) as a receiver. The REC uses the human eye as its image sensor. A glass-like interface is constructed and a photo-diode is attached near the eye of the user to receive a reflected optical signal from the eye (Fig. 4). Then, a ruler is placed behind the transmitter, and the position of the cursor is measured (Fig. 9). A graph of the position and the received signals when d =1.5m and d_r =0.4m is shown in Fig. 10. Both edges (W8 and E6) have a flat signal, and enough signal ($\geq$ 0.005V) to make sounds appeares from W7 to E4. The code

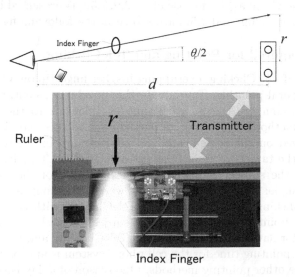

Fig. 9. A view of VisionCommunicator/RealEyeCommunicator

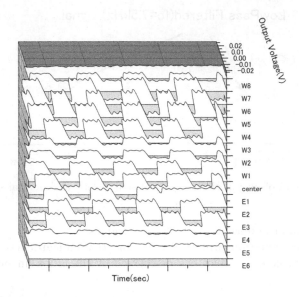

Fig. 10. A view of VisionCommunicator/RealEyeCommunicator

of W7 or E4, means 8.0×10^{-2}m left(or 6.0×10^{-2}m right) of the center. The visual angle of GhostTag(θ_r) can be calculated to

$$\theta_r = \arctan\frac{7}{150} + \arctan\frac{4}{150} - \arctan\frac{0.8}{40} = 3.1° \tag{1}$$

when $d = 150$cm. The last part of this equation, $\arctan\dfrac{0.8}{40}$ is the visual angle of index finger. The visual angles in case of d=2.0, 2.5m is presented in Fig.11. The visual angles for d =2.0m and 2.5m are shown in the following figure (Fig. 11)

5.2   Time Required for Pointing and TeleClicking

The movement of TeleClicking, overupping his/her fingertip on a target in view, is similar to natural pointing. To evaluate this novel movement, an experiment is conducted to compare the pointing time of TeleClick to the times for the other pointing methods. Five subjects participated in this experiment. A black circle is displayed on the screen, and the subjects are instructed to point to or TeleClicked the targets as quickly as possible(Fig. 12).The distance between the screen and the subject is 2.5m, and the diameter of the target is 0.6×10^{-2}m (visual angle: 2.5°). The experiments were carried out as follows: natural pointing, TeleClicking with natural view, TeleClicking with cell phone camera view, and laser pointing (Fig. 12) for five subjects. As shown in Fig. 12, the pointing times for natural pointing, natural TeleClicking, and laser pointing are similar, but the pointing time for the cell phone system is approximately double compared to the other pointing methods. One reason of delay is the low refresh rate of the cell-phone CCD.

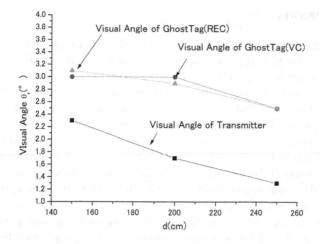

Fig. 11. Visual angles of GhostTag of VC and REC

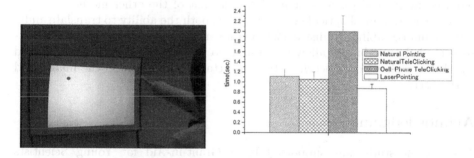

Fig. 12. Experimental view and results

6 Previous Work

Pierce present a interaction techniques called "Stickey Finger", overlapping user's index finger to the object in head-tracked immersive virtual world[4]. In this work, some other interaction techniques, Head Crasher, Framing, Lifting Palm, using 1st person view, are presented. Interactive Sight and TeleClick, which using user's viewfield, is presented in the authors previous work[5,6]. These system includes a receiver of Real Eye Communicator, but transmitter is not developed. A interaction method to optical signal with TeleClick behavior, has been developed in this paper. Ayatsuka presents finger point interaction with visual code, overlapping index finger on the code, in their paper[3].

In some studies, laser pointer, or narrow angle LED were mounted to user's index finger, to detect the target of natural pointing[7,8,9], and evaluating its pointing(motion) time. The pointing time of hand-held laser pointer is reported in several papers[10,11].

7   Conclusions

In the present paper, a real-world streaming data translator, that allows continuous data to be placed in a small visual angle to a real-world object, called PointSpeech, were developed. PointSpeech is based on a cell phone camera (VisionCommunicator) or the human eye (RealEyeCommunicator) with an added optical communication system, which receives optical signals from real-world tags. These optical signals, modulated in both temporal and spatial domains, appear its data part by detecting user's contact. The combination of transmitters and a receiver has sufficient ability to resolute user's contact with his/her index finger, this system can be used as a real-world pointing device, even though it is a data translator. The experimental results indicate that these systems, vision communicator and real eye communicaotr, have very similar characteristics with respect to resolution, data translation ability, and pointing ability. However, the systems differ in their practical applications. The pointing times for these systems are measured and compared to other pointing methods such as natural pointing and laser pointing methods. The results for the eye system are similar to those for the natural pointing and laser pointing methods. However, the time required by the cell phone system is double that of the other methods. In the present paper, a novel optical system that has both the ability to translate audio signals and the ability to distinguish a transmitter which visual angle is $2.8°$ is presented. These abilities allow the system to be used as a pointing device, and enables to realize PointSpeech system, to attach sound data on the image field of the user.

Acknowledgement

The present study was supported by a Grant-in-Aid for Young Scientists B(20700113).

References

1. Want, R., Fishkin, K.P., Gujar, A., Harrison, B.L.: Bridging physical and virtual worlds with electronic tags. In: CHI 1999: Proceedings of the SIGCHI conference on Human factors in computing systems, pp. 370–377. ACM Press, New York (1999)
2. Rekimoto, J., Ayatsuka, Y.: Cybercode: designing augmented reality environments with visual tags. In: DARE 2000: Proceedings of DARE 2000 on Designing augmented reality environments, pp. 1–10. ACM Press, New York (2000)
3. Ayatsuka, Y., Rekimoto, J.: Active cybercode: a directly controllable 2d code. In: CHI 2006: extended abstracts on Human factors in computing systems, pp. 490–495. ACM Press, New York (2006)
4. Pierce, J.S.: Image plane interaction techniques in 3d immersive environments. In: Proceedings of the 1997 symposium on Interactive 3D graphics (1997)
5. Mitsudo, Y., Mogi, K.: Real eye communicator: An eye-mediated real world pointing device. In: Proceedings of the First International Conference on Pervasive Computing (Short paper), in an informal companion volume of short papers, Zurich, pp. 112–118 (2002)

6. Mitsudo, Y.: Interactive sight: A new interaction method for real world environment. In: HCII 2003, vol. 2, pp. 746–750 (2003)
7. Sibert, J., Gokturk, M.: Natural pointing techniques using a finger-mounted direct pointing device. In: SIGGRAPH 1998: ACM SIGGRAPH 98 Conference abstracts and applications, p. 121. ACM, New York (1998)
8. Gokturk, M., Sibert, J.L.: An analysis of the index finger as a pointing device. In: CHI 1999: extended abstracts on Human factors in computing systems, pp. 286–287. ACM, New York (1999)
9. Tsukada, K.: Ubi-finger: Gesture input device for mobile use. In: Proc. of 5th Asia Pacific Conference on Computer Human Interaction, November 2002, vol. 1, pp. 388–400 (2002)
10. Dan, R., Olsen, J., Nielsen, T.: Laser pointer interaction. In: CHI 2001: Proceedings of the SIGCHI conference on Human factors in computing systems, pp. 17–22. ACM, New York (2001)
11. Myers, B.A., Bhatnagar, R., Nichols, J., Peck, C.H., Kong, D., Miller, R., Long, A.C.: Interacting at a distance: measuring the performance of laser pointers and other devices. In: CHI 2002: Proceedings of the SIGCHI conference on Human factors in computing systems, pp. 33–40. ACM, New York (2002)

VR Based Movie Watching Method
by Reproduction of Spatial Sensation

Kunihiro Nishimura[1], Aoi Ito[2], Tomohiro Tanikawa[1],
and Michitaka Hirose[1]

[1] Graduate School of Information Science and Technology, The Univeristy of Tokyo
[2] Graduate School of Interdisciplinary Information Studies, The University of Tokyo
7-3-1, Hongo, Bunkyo-ku, 113-8656, Tokyo, Japan
{kuni,aoi,tani,hirose}cyber.t.u-tokyo.ac.jp

Abstract. A conventional movie watching method is to view movies in front of a large screen such as theaters. Conventional presenting images in fixed position have a problem that it is easy for audiences to lose their spatial sensation of existing movies. In this paper, we propose a novel movie watching method in order to improve presence in existing media contents using virtual reality technology. We assumed when frames are presented with shooting angle based on audiences' looking position, their presence will be much higher. To represent the camera-shooting angle, we used a optical flow method. We proposed a movie watching viewing method based on the reconstructed camera shooting angle which is presented with a moving projector or a wall screen. We thought that our method made it possible to reconstruct lost spatial in movies.

Keywords: Presence, Camera Work, Roaming Images, a Moving Projector, and Spatial Sensation.

1 Introduction

Recently, displays and projectors have been improved recently. It leads users to buy projectors for their personal use in their home, for example, making a home theater. In addition, the media of movies are increased such as DVD and Blue-ray. We can enjoy high resolution and high quality movies with both projectors or displays and digital medias.

Displays and projectors are generally used to present images, and they come to enable users to feel presence. There are several ways to improve presence. Researches improved presence are followings; expression of immersion [1], image moseying for generating a large and high resolution images by integrating multiple images [2][3][4], and construction of 3D space from multiple images or movies[5][6]. Researches that relate to reconstruct 3D geometry using an optical flow have been conducted for many years [7][8]. Study about 3D reconstruction calculated by optical flow from pre correction camera [9][10].

In movie theatre, wide view screen and high resolution displays are introduced. With using a still projector that are used in general, shooting loses spatial sensation because presenting images cannot be moved. It leads to lose the spatial sensation that was taken at the movie shooting.

R. Shumaker (Ed.): Virtual and Mixed Reality, LNCS 5622, pp. 80–89, 2009.

Fig. 1. Proposed Method using a Moving Projector

In this paper, we propose a novel VR based movie-watching method of improving presence of existing media contents. Our proposal method makes it possible to reconstruct lost spatial sensation in the movie. By presenting frames with shooting angle based on audiences' looking position, lost spatial sensation can be reconstructed and audiences can feel higher presence. We reconstruct camera work and present images by roaming images with a moving projector based on camera work calculated from movies (Fig.1). We also present movies not only current frames but also past frames using a wall type display. The frames are presented in a wide view display based on the spatial angle.

2 Spatial Sensation and Camera Work in a Movie

2.1 Spatial Sensation

In this paper, spatial sensation is defined as extensity. That is to say, recognizing spatial sensation means to grasp the position of objects or situation with high accuracy. We consider recognizing spatial sensation make us feel high presence. However, the existing methods of movie appreciate are difficult to express accurate space in movies because the position of presenting images are fixed. Thus, we reconstruct the space of movie for grasping the position of objects or situation in movie with accuracy.

Our method helps to construct space in movie and to grasp spatial sensation intuitively. In a movie theatre, we can see a large wide view screen, which enable us to fell presence. However, we know presence consists of not only a large wide view but also a spatial sensation in a real world. We can feel directions of objects, position of objects, and relationship among them. We often remember the spatial relationship among objects. For example, there is a kiosk shop next to a station and there is a police station in front of the kiosk shop. We remember the position and the direction of such objects. We focused on this kind of sensation in order to improve presence. When we watch movies in a conventional movie watching methods, we have to reconstruct object positions in our mind. We have to remember the previous frames that present one object and have to grasp the camera work in order to know the relationship between the object and a new object. That is, we reconstruct our spatial sensation by ourselves.

2.2 Camera Work

Many movies with complex camera work are existed. However, according to "Grammar of the film Language" written by D.Arijon, the movements of camera itself are only panning (to rotate the camera angle with camera's position fixed), traveling (to move camera position) and zooming (to change focal distance of a lens) [11]. We consider the effective method of presenting images for every movement of camera. In this paper, we focus on panning and constructed the system applicable only for panning.

3   System

In our system, we calculated shooting camera angle from a movie to reconstruct spatial sensation that was lost by shooting. To present images based on estimated camera work can comprehend intuitively space in a movie.

Fig.2 shows a concept sketch of our system. Our system is composed of two parts; the process of calculating camera angle and the process of presenting images (Fig.3). In the process of calculating camera angle, we computed the camera angles when the movie was shot from a camera. In the process of presenting images, we projected movie frames at the position synchronized with calculated camera angles.

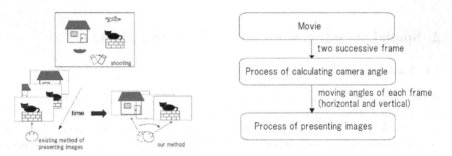

Fig. 2. Concept Image of Proposed Method   **Fig. 3.** System Overview

3.1   Process of Calculating Camera Angle

In this paper, spatial sensation is defined as extensity. That is to say, recognizing spatial sensation means to grasp the position of objects or situation with high accuracy. We consider recognizing spatial sensation make us feel high presence. However, the existing methods of movie appreciate In order to apply also to existing movies, we computed camera angles not by sensors such as gyroscope and accelerometer, but by optical flow (calculated velocity field between successive.) Because current movies did not taken with such sensors. Using optical flow enables to calculate differential angle between two successive frames.

We used OpenCV library that Intel Corporation have been developed and opened for image processing when we calculate optical flow between images. Optical flow has several methods--gradient method, Block-Matching method and so on. We use iterative Lucas-Kanade method in pyramids [12]. Lucas-Kanade method is one of the local gradient methods that is said to be one of the best algorithm for this usage because of high processing speed and high level of confidence [13]. This method

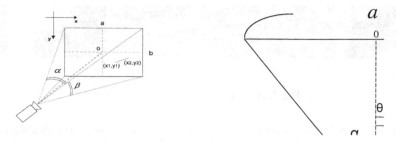

Fig. 4. The relationship between a camera and an image

can give us accurate movement of each feature point. We divide a movement into horizontal element and vertical element and respectively calculate differential angles by the angle of view of a camera and the size of a frame image. Fig 4 shows the relationship between a viewpoint and a frame.

Coordinate x_1, which represents the position of feature point of former frame and coordinate x_2, which represents that of latter frame can be calculated by using optical flow. Suppose that the angle of view of a camera (α) and the size of a frame image (a) are known. The differential angle (θ) is difference between θ_1, which is the angle between coordinate x_1 and the center of the image, and θ_2, which is the angle between coordinate x_2 and the center of the image.

$$\theta_1 = \arctan\left(\frac{x_1 - a/2}{l}\right) \qquad (1)$$

$$l = \frac{a/2}{\tan(\alpha/2)} \qquad (2)$$

l, which is the length from the center of the image to the camera is calculated by (2).

$$\theta_1 = \arctan\left(\frac{x_1 - a/2}{\dfrac{a/2}{\tan(\alpha/2)}}\right) \qquad (3)$$

θ_1 is calculated by (3). θ_2 can also be calculated by the same process. θ is difference of θ_1 and θ_2.

However, when we calculate camera angles only by a movie, we cannot know the angle of view of a movie. So, we calculate virtual camera angles using parameters of the projector. We use the angle of projection (α) and the size of projection (a) and calculate camera angles.

In our method, optical flow is calculated after extracting many feature points. There are several optical flows, so we average them as the difference angle between two frames. We calculate the difference angles between every two frames.

time

Fig. 5. Optical flows in the upper part of frames

However, when we don't account for moving objects, we can't calculate accurately the different angles because the optical flows of moving objects may be noises. Therefore, we focus only on stopped objects and calculate optical flows only from them.

For example, a movie scene sometimes does not have moving objects in the upper half of the frames. We should use the upper half of the frames for calculating the optical flow. We use equation (1)-(3) for calculating camera's relative moving angle. Fig 5 shows the picture of calculating the optical flow of the upper half of the frames.

3.2 Process of Presenting Images

In the process of presenting images, we used a moving projector "Active Vision" produced by TOSHIBA LIGHTING & TECHNOLOGY CORPORATION. The moving projector can change the direction of projection either horizontally or vertically. We reconstructed the shooting camera angles by directing the moving projector to the angle calculated by the process of calculating camera angle. The moving projector can move at most 80 degrees/sec. The size of presenting images depends on the size and the aspect ratio of the projector.

We need to revise the projecting images because the angle between the plane of projection and the line of projection is changed by moving the projector. We project the images revised by changing the shape of images, not by changing the parameter of the projector. Fig.1 shows the appearance of projecting images.

3.3 Process of Presenting Images with Frame Logs

In the process of presenting images, we also used a wall type screen. When we used a moving projector, we could know the spatiality because we could know the exactly presented angle. It was easy for us to grasp relationships among objects such as a buildings and road. However, a moving projector has a limitation. It can present images on a restricted area. We could not see the previous frames. We should remember the frames when presented images are moving. Thus we propose a new combine method in order to present both spatiality and frame histories. We used a wall type screen (9m wide x 2.7m height). The past frames are left on the wall screen. Thus audiences can easy to grasp the spatiality when a movie moves a lot.

3.4 Implementation Results

We applied our method to various movies. Fig. 6 shows the result of an applied movie. Our method helps to construct space in movie and to grasp spatial sensation intuitively.

Fig. 6. (left) The result of Roman Holiday[14] (right) Appearance of presenting images using moving projector

4 Evaluations

4.1 Evaluation of the Process of Calculation Camera Angle

We applied In order to meet our proposal purpose; we should calculate the camera-shooting angle precisely. In this section, we evaluated the process of calculating camera angle using the optical flow methods. The way of evaluation is by comparison between the result of calculation and the real movement angle. We calculated the camera angle when we took a movie with a panning. We compared the moving angle between observed and calculated angles.

We examined about seven movies that are different of movement angle at three different places. Table.1 shows the result of this examination. The ratio of the difference of the movement angle calculated by the theory and our system to theoretical movement angle is 7.5% on an average. This is sufficient accuracy to our study and this result implied that the process of calculating camera angle by optical flow revealed the effectiveness.

Table 1. Comparison between the translated angle calculated from theoretical and this system

The angle of theory (degree)	The angle of our system (degree)	error (degree)	The rate of error (percent)
38.7	35.1	3.6	9.3
29.7	27.3	2.4	8.1
16.0	14.3	1.7	10.6
21.3	21.8	-0.5	2.3
28.8	27.4	1.4	4.9
37.4	32.2	5.2	13.9
29.0	28.0	1.0	3.4

4.2 Experiment of Grasping the Objects' Position by Reconstruction Shooting Camera Angle

We as a pilot experiment, we examined on six subjects whether presenting images by a moving projector enables users to grasp accurately the position of objects in a movie by comparing two projection methods--projecting position is fixed and move to reconstruct the shooting camera angles.

Method of Experiment. First, we shoot three objects in a room by rotating camera horizontally. Second, subjects observe in two methods--projecting position is fixed and move to reconstruct the shooting camera angles calculated by optical flows. Third, the subjects draw the position of three objects in the movie and answer several questions. The subjects observe two movies--first, by the method of the fixed position of presenting images (non-moving) and second, by the method of the roaming images (moving). We categorized six subjects into two groups (group I, II) and change the order of presenting two movies (movie A, B), where the position of the three objects are different. Fig.7 shows the appearance of this experiment.

Result and examination. Fig.7 shows the difference of actual positions of the objects and written positions by a subject.

Table 2 shows the group I subjects experimental results, which is the angle between the position of objects in the real world and the written position of the objects by the subject. Table 3 shows the group II subjects experimental results for the sample. Fig 8 shows the graph of the same result of Table 2 and Table 3. Fig.8 shows

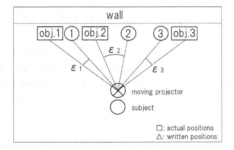

Fig. 7. The relationship between a camera and an image

Table 2. The angles of actual positions and written positions by group II

Group I subject	Non-moving (movie A)			Moving (movie B)		
	ε_1	ε_2	ε_3	ε_1	ε_2	ε_3
1	7.0	5.0	-30.0	-10.0	-10.0	-9.0
2	-14.0	-17.5	-20.0	16.0	5.0	20.0
3	7.0	6.0	-31.0	10.0	5.0	-3.0
Average (abs)	9.3	9.5	27.0	12.0	6.7	10.7
average	15.3			9.8		

Table 3. The angles of actual positions and written positions by group II

Group II subject	Non-moving (movie B)			Moving (movie A)		
	ε_1	ε_2	ε_3	ε_1	ε_2	ε_3
4	15.0	3.0	-8.0	10.0	10.0	-8.0
5	10.0	42.0	9.0	14.0	16.5	3.5
6	11.0	11.0	20.0	13.0	16.5	-12.0
Average (abs)	12.0	18.7	12.3	12.3	14.3	7.8
average	14.3			10.6		

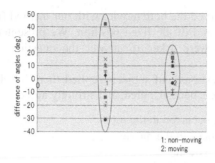

Fig. 8. The angles of actual positions and written positions by all subjects each case of non-moving and moving

Table 4. Answer of the question "Which task is easy for you to grasp the object position"

groupI	answer	groupII	answer
Subject 1	5	Subject 4	5
Subject 2	4	Subject 5	3
Subject 3	5	Subject 6	5

the angles of actual positions of objects and written positions by subjects (both group I and II) in each case of non-moving and moving. Many subjects can grasp more accurately the position of the objects in the case of moving than in the case of non-moving since the more the difference angle between actual and written objects close to 0 degree, the more the subjects grasp the positions of the objects.

We conducted questionnaires for subjects. Table 4 shows the result of the question; "Which task is easy for you to grasp the object position?" A result of questions suggests that the method of reconstructing the shooting camera angles got high valuation from most subjects. This means that subjects can grasp the positions of objects easily. We can suggest that roaming images is effective to improve presence and grasp the space precisely in the movie.

We shoot three objects in a room by rotating camera horizontally. Second, subjects observe in two methods--projecting position is fixed.

4.3 Experiment with Existing Movies

We compared two method applied for the existing movie. We employed six subjects and conducted the experiment that can compare subjects' feelings under two conditions; present images at a fixed position and presenting images based on the reconstructed camera work. Subjects were asked to answer several questions. The positions of the screen, the moving projector, and subjects were the same as the previous pilot experiment. We categorized six subjects into two groups (group I, II), used two different movies (movie A, B), and changed the order of presenting method as well as the pilot experiment. In group I, subjects observed the both movies with the method of the fixed position first and then observed the movies with our proposal method.

In group II subjects observed the both movies with our method first and then observed the movies with the method of the fixed position. We presented the movie a first in both methods. Subjects were asked to answer the questions after observing each movie four times.

We prepared five questions and subjects replied them by choosing five answers; strongly disagree, disagree, neutral, agree, and strongly agree.

- Could you grasp what occurred in the movie?
- Could you grasp the space in the movie?
- Did you feel the space is wide?
- Did you feel you observed in the space?
- Were you interested?

Moreover, subjects asked to answer the most impression point.

In each movies, five subjects thought it was possible to grasp the spaces in the movies using our method, thus it suggested that our method was effective to reconstruct the lost spatial sensation. In addition, five subjects in the case of movie A and four subjects in the case of movie B felt that they were there in our method. In each movie, one subject who answered "disagree" answered the same score or higher score in our method than the other method. Therefore, it was suggested that our method could improve presence.

In group I (with the method of the fixed position of presenting images first), the impressed objects in the movies were same in the case of our method and in the case of the method of the fixed position of presenting images, but in group II (with our method first), the impressed objects in the movies were different by two methods. Additionally, most subjects of group I were impressed by concrete objects in the movie, but most subjects of group II replied sensational answers. These results implied that subjects felt differently between the method of the fixed position of presenting images and the method of the moved position of presenting images.

5 Conclusion

In this paper, we proposed the novel presentation method of improving presence for existing media contents such as movies. The method includes a reconstruction of the lost spatial sensation in movies and presentation of images at the right direction which angles are calculated by optical flow. This method enables us to improve our sense of spatiality and presence. A pilot experiment indicated that present images based on the reconstructing camera work makes us more accurately grasp the space that are expressed in the movie than presenting images at a fixed position. In addition, an application for existing movies revealed that our method was effective in reconstructing the lost spatial sensation in movies and improving presence.

Acknowledgments. A part of this study is supported by JST CREST "Technology to Create Digital Public Art".

References

1. Hirose, M.: CABIN-A multiscreen display for computer experiments. In: 1997 Int. Conf. on Virtual Systems and MultiMedia, p. 78 (1997)
2. Chenm, S.E.: QickTime VR—an image-based approach to virtual environment navigation. In: Proc. SIGGRAPH 1995, pp. 29–38 (1995)
3. Sezliski, R., Shum, H.Y.: Creating full view panoramic image mosaics and environment maps. In: Proc. SIGGRAPH 1997, pp. 251–258 (1997)
4. DiVerdi, S., Wither, J., Hollerei, T.: Envisor: Online Environment Map Construction for Mixed Reality. In: IEEE Virtual Reality 2008, pp. 19–26 (2008)
5. Hoiem, D., Efros, A.A., Hebert, M.: Automatic photo pop-up. In: Proc. SIGGRAPH 2005, pp. 577–584 (2005)
6. Van de Hengel, A., Dick, A., Thormahlen, T., Ward, B., Torr, P.H.S.: VideoTrace: Rapid interactive scene modelling from video. In: Proc. SIGGRAPH 2007, p. 86 (2007)
7. Longuet-Higgis, H.C., Prazdny, K.: The interpretation of a moving retinal image. In: Proc. Roy. Soc. Lond., vol. B208, pp. 385–397 (1980)
8. Maybank, S.J.: The angular velocity associated with a optical flow field arising from motion through a rigid environment. Proc. Roy. Soc. Lond. A401, 317–326 (1985)
9. Brooks, M.J., Chojnacki, W., Baumera, L.: Determining the egomotion of an uncalibrated camera from instantaneous optical flow. J. Opt. Soc. Am., A 14-10, 2670–2677 (1997)
10. Viéville, T., Faugeras, O.D.: The first order expansion of motion equations in the uncalibrated case. Computer Vision Image Understanding 64(1), 128–146 (1996)
11. Arijon, D.: Grammar of the Film Language. Focal Press, London (1976)
12. Lucas, B., Kanade, T.: An Interative Image Registration Technique with an Application to Stereo Vision. In: Proc. The 7th International Joint Conf. on Artificial Intelligence, pp. 674–679 (1981)
13. Baron, J., Fleet, D., Beauchemin, S.: Performance of optical flow techniques. Int. J. Computer Vision 12(1), 43–77 (1994)
14. Wyler, W.: Roman Holiday (1953)

Comparison of Measurement of Accommodation between LCD and CRT at the Stereoscopic Vision Gaze

Masako Omori[1], Satoshi Hasegawa[2], Tomoyuki Watanabe[3],
Kazuhiro Fujikake[4], and Masaru Miyao[5]

[1] Faculty of Home Economics, Kobe University, 2-1 Aoyama Higashisuma,
Suma-ku, Kobe 654-8585, Japan
[2] Dept. of Information Culture, Nagoya Bunri University, 365 Maeda Inazawa-cho,
Inazawa, Aichi 492-8520, Japan
[3] Faculty of Psychological and Physical Science, Aich Gakuin University,
12 Araike, Iwasaki-cho, Nisshin 470-0195,Japan
[4] Institute for Science of Labour, 2-8-14 Sugao, Miyamae-ku,
Kawasaki 216-8501, Japan
[5] Information Technology Center, Nagoya University, Furo-cho, Chikusa-Ku,
Nagoya 464-8601, Japan
masako@med.nagoya-u.ac.jp, mmiyao@med.negoya-u.ac.jp

Abstract. In the present study, we examined the visual accommodation of subjects who were gazing fixedly at 3D images from two different displays: a cathode ray tube (CRT) while wearing special glasses and a liquid crystal display (LCD) while not wearing special glasses. The subjects in this experiment were two healthy people aged 22 and 39 years, all with normal vision. The instrument objectively measured visual accommodative changes of the right eye in both binocular and natural viewing conditions. The results suggested that it was easy and comfortable to focus on both the LCD and CRT. When the subjects viewed the progressively receding target, their accommodation was about 0.8 D at the presumed furthest points, a level at which the ciliary muscle is relaxed. The accommodative power differed by about 1.5 D from the near to far point. Thus, the ciliary muscle is repeatedly strained and relaxed while the subject views the moving target.

Keywords: Accommodation, binocular and natural viewing, stereoscopic image, display, LCD and CRT.

1 Introduction

Various studies have been performed on the influence of stereoscopic images on visual function [1] [2] [3]. Most prior studies discussed the effects of visual image quality and extent of physical stress. These studies have employed bioinstrumentation or surveys of subjective symptoms [4].

Under natural viewing conditions the depth of convergence and accommodation agreed. However, when viewing a stereoscopic image using binocular parallax, it has been thought that convergence moves with the position of the reproduced stereoscopic image, while accommodation remains fixed at the image display. As a result, there is

R. Shumaker (Ed.): Virtual and Mixed Reality, LNCS 5622, pp. 90–96, 2009.

contradictory depth information between convergence and accommodation, called discordance, in the visual system. With the aim of qualitatively improving stereographic image systems, bio measurements under stereoscopic viewing conditions are needed.

However, from objective measurements of the accommodation system it has been confirmed that there is a fluctuating link between accommodation and convergence [5]. To comfortably view a stereoscopic visual system, we are at the stage where we should view the qualitative improvements that need to be made from a different perspective. Therefore, to investigate the influence of stereoscopic images on visual function in humans, we measured accommodation in people gazing at a target under both binocular and natural viewing conditions.

The aim of this experiment was to verify whether there are differences in vision with stereoscopic images on different hardware: an LCD (EIZOS-1911SA-BK) and CRT (both with liquid-crystal shutter eyeglasses).

2 Method

2.1 Accommodative Measurement and Stimulus

Using an original accommodo-refractometer, we measured and recorded accommodation in the subjects while they were viewing stereoscopic images on the two different displays for 40-second periods: a cathode ray tube (CRT) while wearing special glasses and a liquid crystal display (LCD) while not wearing special glasses. Visual function was tested using a custom-made apparatus.

This combined an automated infrared accommodo-refractometer (Nidek AR-1100) and original binocular halfmirror system [6][7]. The display images were placed in front of the small mirror for the tests. Subjects gazed at each type of display through a

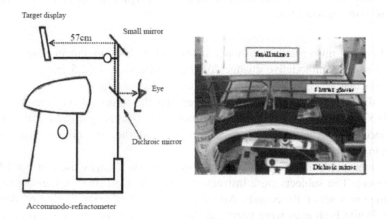

Fig. 1. A schematic view of the device developed for the present experiment. Apparatus to measure lens accommodation, modified for experiment.

Fig. 2. Experiment scenery of CRT and LCD

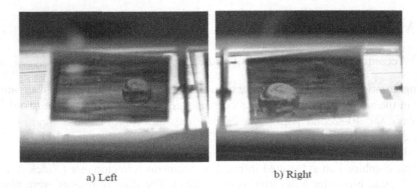

a) Left   b) Right

Fig. 3. The upper photograph is an image of the liquid-crystal shutter at which the testee gazes. a) is an image for the left eye and b) is an image for the right eye. The time of this figure is not the same as the right and left.

half (dichroic) mirror and an ordinary small mirror. The instrument objectively measured visual accommodative changes of the right eye at a 12.5 Hz sampling rate in both binocular and natural viewing conditions [8].

The distance between the subjects' eyes and the target on the screen was 57 cm (1.00/0.57 = 1.75 diopters (D)) (Note: diopter (D) = 1/distance (m); MA (meter angle) = 1/distance (m)). The scene for measurements and the measurement equipment are shown in Fig. 2.

The presented images were the same stereoscopic images used in the LCD/CRT experiment. The subjects were instructed to gaze at the center of the sphere, and the gaze time was set at 40 seconds. All subjects had a subjective feeling of stereoscopic vision. While both eyes were gazing at the stereoscopic image, the lens accommodation of the right eye was measured and recorded.

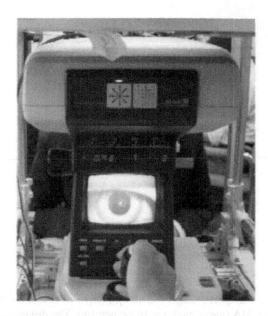

Fig. 4. The scene for measurements and the measurement equipment

2.2 Experiment Procedure

The subjects were 2 people aged 21 years and 39 years, with normal vision. The subjects' refraction was less than + 0.5 Diopter (D), so both were emmetropic. The stereoscopic sphere image used had a reciprocating movement with the image appearing to move on the LCD and CRT toward and away from the subjects in a ten-second period (Figure 5). Gaze time was 40 seconds, and the accommodation of the right eye was measured and recorded while the subjects gazed at the stereoscopic image with both eyes. The subjects were instructed to focus on the stereoscopic image on each display. They gazed at the open-field stereoscopic target under binocular and natural viewing conditions. We measured and recorded the change in accommodation of their right eye continuously over the 40 seconds.

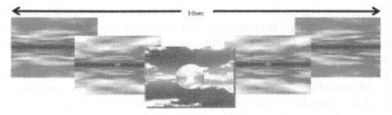

Note: It had a reciprocating movement with the image appearing to move on the LCD toward and away from the subjects in a ten-second period.

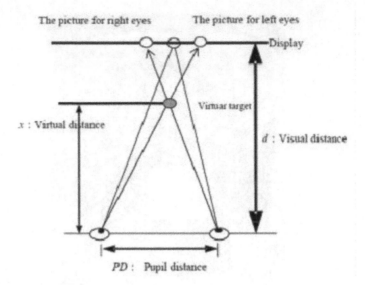

The picture for right eyes   The picture for left eyes

Display

x : Virtual distance

Virtual target

d : Visual distance

PD :   Pupil distance

Fig. 5. The stereoscopic sphere image and the principle of a parallax barrier. Note: diopter (D) = 1/distance (m); MA (meter angle) = 1/distance (m). The distance between the subjects' eyes and the target on the screen was 57 cm 1.00/0.57 = 1.75 diopters (D).

3 Results

When the subjects were viewing the stereoscopic image, the accommodation in the right eye corresponded to the time when the visual target was at the virtual nearest point with all of the displays, and accommodation occurred that led to focus in the distance. With the CRT, accommodation was from 3.2 D for far vision to 0.72 D for near vision. Thus, the focus accommodation was from 31 cm near the eyes to 1.4 m away from the eyes. With the LCD, accommodation was from about 2.5 D near the eyes to 0.5 D away from the eyes, so the focus changed from about 38 cm in front of the eyes to about 2.5 m at the far point (Figure 6).

In subject B, it was larger than the angle of convergence. With the CRT, accommodation was from 5.4 D for far vision to 1.0 D for near vision. Thus, the focus accommodation was from about 19 cm near the eyes to 1 m away from the eyes. With the LCD, accommodation was from about 4.5 D near the eyes to 0.9 D away from the eyes, so the focus changed from about 22 cm in front of the eyes to about 1.1 m at the far point (Figure 7). A tendency was thus seen to focus on a place more distant than the actual screen.

The above results indicate that focal accommodation in near vision did not differ greatly with the different types of display, but that in peak accommodation at the far point focal accommodation was more distant with the LCD than with the CRT. Thus, it was shown that accommodation is strongly influenced by angle of convergence when subjects gaze at a stereoscopic image. It was also shown, regardless of the whether or not liquid crystal shutter glasses were used, that accommodation was easy and comfortable when focusing on virtually distant movements on both the LCD and CRT.

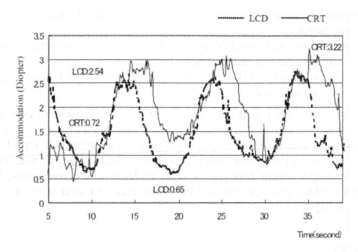

Fig. 6. Accommodative change of subject A – CRT and LCD - Note. X-axis shows time: 0-50 sec, Y-axis shows diopter: 0-4 diopter.

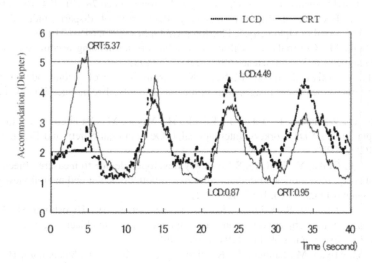

Fig. 7. Accommodative change of subject A – CRT and LCD -Note. X-axis shows time: 0-50 sec, Y-axis shows diopter: 0-4 diopter.

4 Conclusion

To investigate the effect of stereoscopic images on human visual function, we measured accommodation in both binocular and natural viewing conditions. Consequently, it was confirmed that when following a moving target accommodation changes to focus on far and near distances.

1. Thus, the ciliary muscle is repeatedly strained and relaxed while the subject views the moving target.
2. Irrespective of the use of liquid crystal shutter glasses, accommodation was shown to occur with both far and near virtual motion.
3. It was also confirmed that there was accommodation for still stereoscopic images with both distant and near images.

Therefore, it is assumed that the ciliary muscles of subjects who viewed the stereoscopic image moved repeatedly between stressed and relaxed stages. In other words, the ciliary muscle was stretched effectively. These results suggest that prolonged near work with computers may cause eyesight to shift toward a myopic state, and that the stereoscopic images might improve eyesight under working conditions. Moreover, repeatedly stretching between near and far vision may be useful in easing the fatigue of VDT work [5].

References

1. Heron, Charman, W.N., Schor, C.M.: Age changes in the interactions between the accommodation and vergence systems. Optometry & Vision Science 78(10), 754–762 (2001)
2. Schor, C.: Fixation of disparity: a steady state error of disparity-induced vergence. American Journal of Optometry & Physiological Optics 57(9), 618–631 (1980)
3. Rosenfield, M., Ciuffreda, K., Gilmartin, B.: Factors influencing accommodative adaptation. Optometry & Vision Science 69(4), 270–275 (1992)
4. Iwasaki, T., Akiya, S., Inoue, T., Noro, K.: Surmised state of accommodation to stereoscopic three-dimensional images with binocular disparity. Ergonomics 39(11), 1268–1272 (1996)
5. Omori, M., Watanabe, T., Takai, J., Takada, H., Miyao, M.: An attempt at preventing asthenopia among VDT workers. International J. Occupational Safety and Ergonomics 9(4), 453–462 (2003)
6. Miyao, M., Otake, Y., Ishihara, S.: A newly developed device to measure objective amplitude of accommodation and pupillary response in both binocular and natural viewing conditions. Sangyo-Igaku 34(2), 148–149 (1992)
7. Miyao, M., Ishihara, S., Saito, S., Kondo, T., Sakakibara, H., Toyoshima, H.: Visual accommodation and subject performance during a stereographic object task using liquid crystal shutters. Ergonomics 39(11), 1294–1309 (1996)
8. Otake, Y., Miyao, M., Ishihara, S., Kashiwamata, N., Kondo, T., Sakakibara, H., Yamada, S.: An experimental study on the objective measurement of accommodative amplitude under binocular and natural viewing conditions. Tohoku J. Experimental. Medicine 170(2), 93–102 (1993)

Is Embodied Interaction Beneficial When Learning Programming?

Pablo Romero[1], Benedict du Boulay[1], Judy Robertson[2],
Judith Good[1], and Katherine Howland[1]

[1] University of Sussex, Department of Informatics, Brighton BN1 9QH, UK
[2] Heriot-Watt University, Department of Mathematical and Computer Sciences Edinburgh
EH14 4AS, UK
pablor@sussex.ac.uk

Abstract. Embodied interaction has been claimed to offer important advantages for learning programming. However frequently claims have been based on intuitions and work in the area has focused largely around system-building rather than on evaluation and reflection around those claims. Taking into account research in the area as well as in areas such as tangibles, psychology of programming and the learning and teaching of programming, this paper identifies a set of important factors to take into account when analysing the potential of learning environments for programming employing embodied interaction. These factors are formulated as a set of questions that could be asked either when designing or analysing this type of learning environments.

1 Introduction

Often learning environments designed to introduce children to computer programming have used some form of interaction with the physical world. Efforts in this area have tended to concentrate on designing and building environments capable of this interaction but the motivation for the approach as well as the specifics of the instructional design have been driven largely by intuitions. Although there has been some research aimed at building theories and frameworks in areas such as tangibles in learning, computer programming poses specific challenges related to taking advantage of the concreteness of the physical world in order to understand and master an abstract task such as programming.

An embodied type of interaction aims to exploit the familiarity of physical world couplings between actions and their effects by employing analogies based on those couplings [1]. An example of exploiting familiar analogies are electronic organisers that can present documents in portrait or landscape mode depending on how they are physically orientated. Employing analogies of physical world couplings tends to work well for tasks that require a concrete, direct form of manipulation, however computer programming is not about direct manipulation.

Computer programming is related to specifying abstract behaviours to be performed by the computer. These behaviours are abstract because, for instance, they might take place in the future and / or might depend on certain conditions [2]. Programming activities are therefore radically different from direct manipulation tasks

R. Shumaker (Ed.): Virtual and Mixed Reality, LNCS 5622, pp. 97–105, 2009.

and it is not clear whether the benefits of familiar coupling analogies apply in this case. This paper analyses where the benefits of embodied interaction may lie by identifying a set of important factors to take into account when designing or analysing a programming learning environment with embodied interaction. The second section highlights some of the difficulties faced by novice programmers, the third section discusses some of the potential benefits that embodied interaction could offer to the learning of programming, the fourth section describes how embodied elements have been incorporated into learning environments for programming, the fifth presents a set of important factors to consider for this type of environments and the sixth discusses some important aspects of these factors.

2   The Difficulties of Learning Programming

Programming is hard precisely because, among other factors, its abstract nature prevents the use of direct manipulation [2]. Du Boulay [3] separates into five areas the difficulties facing those who are learning to program for the first time. First is a general orientation towards the nature of programming itself. It involves clarifying what programs are for, what can be done with them and what is the point and value of them. Second is the notional machine. This is the abstract machine which will execute the program. We do not mean the hardware or memory registers themselves. It is not about bits and bytes, but about the kind of activities that one can describe in the programming language being learnt. For example, printing a word, causing a Logo turtle to move forward, adding two numbers together, adding a value into a table and so on. The programming paradigm (declarative, functional, object-oriented) is determined by the particular instantiation of the notional machine. Third is the notation of the programming language, in other words the way that the programming language as a language is expressed the syntax, where the semantics is covered by the notional machine. Fourth is standard structures or programming plans [4, 5]. This is about how one puts standard phrases and sentences of the language together to make meaningful paragraphs or essays. For example, how one uses a looping construct to iterate through a list, or how one organises a program into separate methods or separate functions. Fifth is pragmatics: how one makes use of the overall environment (e.g. the editor and the compiler or the program development environment) to get from the idea for a program to a working program itself. Pragmatics also covers developing the skills of effective design and debugging to ensure that the program does what it is supposed to do. Frequently the importance of pragmatics or strategic programming knowledge is underestimated [6].

Typically when learning a second programming language, the general orientation and some aspects of the pragmatics can be generalised from what has already been learned, even if the new notation, the new notional machine and the new structures are quite different. And when learning a third language similarities of notation, notional machine and structures are likely to emerge to simplify and shorted the learning process.

Within a learning environment containing embodied or tangible elements, the question arises as to how far the inclusion of those embodied and/or tangible elements can assist in the mastering of a difficult task such as programming.

3 Potential Benefits of Embodied Interaction

Exploiting the familiarity of physical world couplings between actions and their effects by employing analogies and metaphors based on those couplings is important not only for embodied interaction in general but also for tangibles learning environments. These perceived couplings [7] are an important aspect of the meaningful interaction with the world to which embodied interaction aspires [1]. The couplings can be literal, when there is a close one-to-one mapping in the analogy, or more abstract, when the mapping is looser and the relationship between actions and effects has a certain degree of arbitrariness [8]. Abstract couplings are not necessarily negative, Hornecker and Buur [7] point out that many tangible environments aim for literal couplings missing out on opportunities to exploit people's imagination or to provide useful re-representations of information.

The relationship between actions and effects in abstract couplings is usually mediated by a representation. The more arbitrary the representation the more abstract the coupling. The correspondence could be based on symbols, which have an arbitrary structure, or on icons, which have a more direct perceptual correspondence, for example [9, 10]. Hurtienne and Israel [11] propose that physical manipulations can be employed not only for literal but also for abstract correspondence. They propose to employ the concept of Image Schemas [12], abstract representations of recurring dynamic patterns of bodily interactions, as a sound basis to provide abstract couplings in tangible environments. According to them, Image Schemas capture patterns of sensory-motor experiences, exist beneath conscious awareness and can be represented visual, haptic or kinesthetic way for example. The container schema, for example, is a pattern characterised by comprising an outside, an inside and a boundary between them and is derived from our daily experience with houses, rooms, boxes, cars, etc. Image Schemas can have a central importance in taking advantage of the concreteness of the physical world in order to support the learning of an abstract task such as programming.

Frequently embodied environments mix representations of different types in the perceived couplings, for example, the shape of a toy car could communicate how it could be used but it could also have an attached printed label with symbols to for example, indicate additional functions or characteristics. There are potential advantages and disadvantages in mixing representations of different types; one representation could, for example, constraint the interpretation of another and in this way support the learner [10].

Besides aspects associated with the notion of perceived couplings, embodied interaction can offer other benefits that could be particularly important for programming learning environments. Important aspects in this sense are those that have to do with social interaction and motivation. Embodied interaction has a strong potential for enabling collaboration, which is an important aspect when learning to program [13]. Being able to interact with the environment from multiple points, the inherent visibility of actions and events happening in the physical world and the sheer size of objects and physical environments [7] make embodied interfaces especially suitable for enhancing communication and collaborative learning.

Embodied interaction and its potential for collaboration may also support the understanding of abstraction in a more direct way. Deictic references to physical objects and gestures performed while communicating have been found to support the emergence of scientific languages and ontologies in school children [14]. Verifying whether this is also the case when using embodied interaction for the learning of programming would be of central importance for the area.

The potential of embodied interaction for motivation was highlighted in one of the first environments employing tangible elements [15]. Embodied interaction was claimed to increase the feelings identification with the characters of the environment and in this way the level of absorption in the task. Additionally, embodied interaction can enable performative action [7], which in turn has been suggested as capable of inducing motivating experiences [16].

4 Embodied Interaction in Programming

The discussion above suggests that there are three important dimensions to consider when employing embodied interaction in learning programming environments: where the embodied element is located (a) pragmatically and (b) conceptually, and (c) what its nature is. The embodied element could target any of the five sources of difficulty for novice programmers outlined in Section 2. For example the embodied element could aim to provide cues about the workings of the notional machine or about the nature of the notation. In practical terms, the embodied element could be associated with any of the elements of the environment: the input, the output, the editor, the debugger, etc. Finally the nature of the interaction could be predominantly haptic or kinesthetic but could combine these with symbolic or iconic elements.

For example, in Logo and its follow-up versions [15, 17–20], the embodied element is associated with their output, a tangible robotic system. Logo aimed to teach programming concepts to children by controlling a robotic turtle. The only tangible element in Logo was its output (the robotic system). The program had to be written by conventional means (typing code to a computer) and the notation was a simplified version of Lisp. Other versions such as the Button Box [18] and Quetzal [20] had additional embodied elements. The button box was a device employed to enable children to control the turtle without having to learn how to type commands on a keyboard. It had a series of buttons that had a one to one mapping with the main controlling functions. Additionally, there was a record button that enabled children to record a sequence of commands and a play button that allowed the command sequence to be played. Although still using a type of keyboard as input, the couplings between actions and effects where more direct than those of a conventional keyboard.

Quetzal is an interesting system that allows children to edit Lego Mind-storms [19] programs with tangible tokens representing keywords of a textual programming language. Children create program statements by physically connecting tokens to form chains that describe the flow of control of the program, similarly to the way textual programs are written as a sequence of statements on the screen with conventional textual languages. In this case there are two independent embodied elements, one is related to the editor of the environment and the other to its output. The editor uses a combination of symbolic and tangible elements.

Another example with a different combination of embodied elements are tangible programming environments. Usually in these systems the focus of the embodied element is the notation. One typical tangible programming environment is the Electronic Blocks system [21]. Electronic Blocks uses Lego blocks augmented with sensors, actuators and logic circuits to enable children to program logical behaviours by joining blocks that perform simple operations. In this case the notation uses a combination of symbolic, iconic and haptic elements. The notation has symbolic elements as blocks of different colours belong to different categories. It also has iconic aspects as the shapes of the blocks indicate their use (for example those shaped as cars can run on wheels). Finally it is haptic as statements of the language are constructed by physically joining the blocks.

The three dimensions discussed in this section plus some of the factors described in previous sections can be used to analyse the learning potential of embodied environments for programming. The following section offers an initial framework that can be used when designing or analysing a programming learning environment with an embodied style of interaction.

5 Important Factors for Embodied Environments for Learning Programming

A set of important factors for programming learning environments with an embodied style of interaction are illustrated on Table 1. These factors could be classified as technical and social. Technical factors could be further classified into those related with the nature of the interaction and those associated with the place where interaction occurs. Social factors could also be further classified into collaborative and those related to motivation. This section talks about them in terms of questions that can be asked when designing or analysing a programming learning environment using embodied interaction.

5.1 Nature of the Interaction

These factors have to do with the type of the perceived couplings, how abstract they are and the type of support they could offer.

- What is the nature of the bodily interaction? It could be symbolic, iconic, haptic, kinetic, gestural, or a combination of them.
- How literal or abstract are the action-effect couplings provided in the environment? If they are abstract are they based on a sound framework of correspondence such as Image Schemas for example?
- What is the support intended through the bodily interaction type? if the interaction type is mixed (iconic and haptic for example), there might be benefits associated with external representations, one representation constraining the interpretation of another for example. This could enable, for example, to allow a progression from understanding more concrete to more abstract notations.

Table 1. Some important factors for programming environments with embodied interaction

Technical	Nature	Interaction type
		Degree of abstraction
		Representational support
	Focus	Programming concepts
		Environment elements
Social	Collaboration	Affordances of embodiment
		Scaffolding abstraction
	Motivation	Possibility of performative action
		Body-syntonic

5.2 Focus of the Interaction

These factors refer to the place where the embodied element occurs. The place could be conceptual (one of the difficult aspects of learning programming) or related to the programming environment (input, output, editor, etc.).

- What programming concept understanding is the bodily interaction aiming to support?
- Do familiar coupling analogies:
- Help to visualise the scope and general orientation of the system?
- Provide cues about the workings of the notional machine and the nature of the notation?
- Constrain or direct users into producing valid structures?
- Offer guidance to perform practical tasks?
- Where in the programming environment is the bodily interaction taking place? It could take place in the input, editor, output, debugger, etc.
- What is the relationship between the targeted concept and the place of the environment where the bodily interaction takes place? For example, is a tangible output aimed to support the understanding of the notional machine?

5.3 Collaboration

One of the most important characteristics of embodied environments is their potential for collaboration. Here we consider, besides the generic collaborative affordances, those that could support the understanding of abstraction.

- What are the collaborative affordances of the bodily interaction style? For example, is the sheer size of the tangible elements conducive to collaboration?
- Are collaborative activities aimed at scaffolding the mastering of abstraction? For example deictic references to physical objects and gestures have been found to support the emergence of scientific language and ontologies in science learning. They might play a similar role in understanding how to specify abstract behaviours.

5.4 Motivation

Similarly to collaboration, motivation is an important factor for embodied environments. For programming, performative action [7] and body-syntonic relations [15] are particularly important.

- Does the system give opportunities for performative action when carrying out the programming task? Combining programming and performative action might induce motivating experiences and appeal to segments of the population who are not usually attracted to programming.
- Is the type of interaction aimed at producing body-syntonic relations with users?

6 Discussion

This paper offers an initial framework that can be useful for analysing the learning potential of programming environments employing an embodied type of interaction. Perhaps more importantly, the initial framework can be used before any system has been built to maximise the learning potential of such environments.

The factors taken into account by the initial framework can be classified into technical and social. Within the technical factors, an important consideration is the degree to which the action-effect couplings provided by the environment are literal or abstract. As mentioned above, embodied interaction aims to exploit the familiarity of physical world couplings but programming, on the other hand, could benefit from employing abstract couplings as a way of specifying abstract behaviours. A concept that can bridge this apparent mismatch is Image Schemas [12]. Image Schemas capture patterns of recurring bodily interactions and therefore encapsulate important aspects of our familiarity with the physical world. At the same time, they are generic enough to be employed for abstract couplings. Image Schemas have been employed to provide abstract couplings in tangible environments [11]. However, they have not, to the best of our knowledge, been employed in programming environments employing an embodied type of interaction. The potential of Image Schemas for this type of environments needs to be evaluated empirically.

Social factors can be particularly important as they can address sociological barriers to programming such as lack of social support and compelling contexts [22]. Social support can be enhanced by the potential of embodied environments for collaboration. The degree of collaboration can be increased if the embodied elements are associated with the actual environment rather than just with its output. Traditional tangible robotic systems, for example, limit the potential for collaboration by employing a conventional desktop setup for the actual programming environment.

Finally performative action can be an important factor for providing compelling contexts. Unfortunately most of the current embodied environments for programming do not provide many opportunities for performative action. These opportunities can be enhanced by environments which embed their embodied elements in large physical spaces (rooms for example) [23] or by those that enable whole body interaction [24].

7 Conclusion

This paper has motivated and presented a set of important factors to take into account when analysing the learning potential of programming environments employing an embodied type of interaction. These factors are classified into technical and social. Technical factors are further classified into those related with the nature of the interaction and those associated with its focus. Social factors have been classified into collaborative and those related with motivation.

The factors are presented as a set of questions that could be asked when designing or analysing programming learning environments employing an embodied type of interaction.

These factors and questions suggest that if the potential of embodied interaction is maximised, the learning of programming would be much more compatible with a studio approach and in many ways similar to learning in disciplines such as architecture or product design. It would be similar not only because the end product could be tangible, but also because of the emphasis on a hands-on approach, on collaboration and on performative action. However this is a conjecture, work that focuses not only on system-building but also on empirically evaluating the benefits and implications of embodied interaction in the learning of programming is needed.

References

1. Dourish, P.: Where the action is: the foundations of embodied interaction. MIT Press, London (2001)
2. Blackwell, A.: What is programming? In: Kuljis, J., Baldwin, L., Scoble, R. (eds.) Proceedings of the 14th annual workshop of the Psychology of Programming Interest Group, pp. 204–218 (2002)
3. du Boulay, B.: Some difficulties of learning to program. In: Soloway, E., Spohrer, J. (eds.) Studying the Novice Programmer, pp. 283–299. Lawrence Erlbaum, Hillsdale (1989)
4. Rist, R.S.: Plans in programming: definition, demonstration and development. In: Soloway, E., Iyengar, S. (eds.) Empirical Studies of Programmers, first workshop, pp. 28–47. Ablex Publishing, Norwood, New Jersey (1986)
5. Gilmore, D.J., Green, T.R.G.: Programming plans and programming expertise. Quarterly Journal of Experimental Psychology 40A, 423–442 (1988)
6. Gilmore, D.J.: Expert programming knowledge: a strategic approach. In: Hoc, J., Green, T.R.G., Samurcay, R., Gilmore, D.J. (eds.) Psychology of Programming, pp. 223–234. Academic Press, London (1990)
7. Hornecker, E., Buur, J.: Getting a grip on tangible interaction: a framework on physical space and social interaction. In: CHI 2006: Proceedings of the SIGCHI conference on Human Factors in computing systems, pp. 437–446. ACM Press, New York (2006)
8. Price, S.: A representation approach to conceptualizing tangible learning environments. In: TEI 2008: Proceedings of the 2nd international conference on Tangible and embedded interaction, pp. 151–158. ACM Press, New York (2008)
9. Purchase, H.: Defining multimedia. IEEE MultiMedia 5, 8–15 (1998)
10. Ainsworth, S.: Deft: A conceptual framework for considering learning with multiple representations. Learning and Instruction 16, 183–198 (2006)

11. Hurtienne, J., Israel, J.H.: Image schemas and their metaphorical extensions: intuitive patterns for tangible interaction. In: TEI 2007: Proceedings of the 1st international conference on Tangible and embedded interaction, pp. 127–134. ACM Press, New York (2007)
12. Johnson, M.: The Body in the Mind: The Bodily Basis of Meaning, Imagination, and Reason. The University of Chicago Press, Chicago (1987)
13. McDowell, C., Werner, L., Bullock, H., Fernald, J.: The impact of pair-programming on student performance, perception and persistence. In: Clarke, L., Dillon, L., Tichy, W. (eds.) Proceedings of the 25th International Conference on Software Engineering, pp. 602–607. IEEE Computer Society, Washington (2003)
14. Roth, W.M., Lawless, D.: Scientific investigations, metaphorical gestures, and the emergence of abstract scientific concepts. Learning and Instruction 12, 285–304 (2002)
15. Papert, S.: Mindstorms: Children, Computers, and Powerful Ideas. Basic Books, New York (1980)
16. Lindley, S.E., Couteur, J.L., Berthouze, N.L.: Stirring up experience through movement in game play: effects on engagement and social behaviour. In: CHI 2008: Proceeding of the twenty-sixth annual SIGCHI conference on Human factors in computing systems, pp. 511–514. ACM Press, New York (2008)
17. Resnick, M., Martin, F., Sargent, R., Silverman, B.: Programmable bricks: toys to think with. IBM Systems Journal 35, 443–452 (1996)
18. McNerney, T.S.: From turtles to tangible programming bricks: explorations in physical language design. Personal Ubiquitous Computing 8, 326–337 (2004)
19. Boogaarts, M., Daudelin, J.A., Davis, B.L., Kelly, J., Levy, D., Morris, L., Rhodes, F., Rhodes, R., Scholz, M.P., Smith, C.R., Torok, R.: The lego mindstorms nxt idea book: design, invent, and build. Ubiquity 8, 2 (2007)
20. Horn, M.S., Jacob, R.J.K.: Tangible programming in the classroom with tern. In: CHI 2007: extended abstracts on Human factors in computing systems, pp. 1965–1970. ACM Press, New York (2007)
21. Wyeth, P., Purchase, H.C.: Tangible programming elements for young children. In: CHI 2002: extended abstracts on Human factors in computing systems, pp. 774–775. ACM Press, New York (2002)
22. Kelleher, C., Pausch, R.: Lowering the barriers to programming: A taxonomy of programming environments and languages for novice programmers. ACM Computing Surveys 37, 83–137 (2005)
23. Montemayor, J., Druin, A., Chipman, G., Farber, A., Guha, M.L.: Tools for children to create physical interactive storyrooms. Comput. Entertain. 2, 12–12 (2004)
24. Romero, P., Good, J., Robertson, J., du Boulay, B., Reid, H., Howland, K.: Embodied interaction in authoring environments. In: Ramduny-Ellis, D., Hare, J., Gill, S., Dix, A. (eds.) Proceedings of the second Workshop on Physicality, pp. 43–46. UWIC Press, Lancaster (2007)

Mobile Interfaces Using Body Worn Projector
and Camera

Nobuchika Sakata, Teppei Konishi, and Shogo Nishida

Division of Systems Science and Applied Informatics Graduate
School of Engineering Science, Osaka University,
Machikaneyama-cho 1-3, Toyonaka city, Osaka 560-8531 Japan
{sakata,konishi,nishida}@nishilab.sys.es.osaka-u.ac.jp

Abstract. Unlike most desktop computer and laptop, mobile interface are designed to facilitate user operating the information easily with various situations that is standing, walking, and moving. However, almost mobile devices such like cell phones have a small key pad and small display because those devices should keep compact and light weight for bringing and pocketing. Therefore, they impose a lot of burdens to users in terms of watching a small display and typing with a small keyboard. Such devices do not focus to provide implicit and awareness information. In this paper, we describe features of body worn projector, which has capability for projecting information to user's peripheral vision, and body worn camera, which has capability for recognizing user's posture and estimating user's behavior, is suitable interface for providing awareness, implicit, and even explicit information. Finally, we propose two mobile interfaces which are "Palm top display for glance information" and "Floor projection from Lumbar mounted projector".

Keywords: Mobile AR, Wearable Computer, Mobile Interface, Mobile Projector, and Procams.

1 Introduction

Unlike most desktop computer and laptop, mobile interface are designed to facilitate user operating the information easily with various user's situations that is standing, walking, and moving. However, almost mobile devices such like cell phones have a small key pad and small display because those devices should keep compact and light weight for bringing and pocketing. Therefore, they impose a lot of burdens to users in terms of watching a small display and typing with a small keyboard. Also, they are designed for providing explicit information such like "search result of user's input" and "mail for you", needs user's deeply attention. For example, when user supposes to get restaurant information, user push a small button for inputting the restaurant name and gaze a small display for confirming the search results. Existent those devices do not focus to provide implicit and awareness information. For example, if the current cell phones provide "Good restaurant around you" via character information with the small display when user walks around the good cuisine and the user storages the cell phone in user's pocket, the cell phone should vibrate itself, ring or flash for awaking to the explicit information, and then, user should take the device

R. Shumaker (Ed.): Virtual and Mixed Reality, LNCS 5622, pp. 106–113, 2009.

from user's pocket to confirm the information. However, in case of user does not suppose to get restaurant information, it bothers the user. In this paper, we report that a combination of body worn projector, which has capability for projecting information to user's peripheral vision, and body worn camera, which has capability for recognizing user's posture and estimating user's behavior, is suitable interface for providing awareness, implicit, and even explicit information.

2 Related Works

Real world based interface, which aim to provide information based on user's behavior and circumtance around a user in real world, has been researched as good piece of supporting IT usability[1-8][10][13][15]. In the fields of wearable and mobile computer such like cell phones, providing information based on the place, pose and circumstances of mobile user, real world based interface has a possibility to boost usability dramatically. Also estimating user's purpose and circumstance by means of multimodal interface, several researches[3][4][5][6][8-12][16][17][19-21] provide information corresponding to the estimated purpose and circumstance. In those researches, some works adopted projector as display interface. Projecting information to various place and parts of human body, user can obtain the projected information with various postures such like standing, walking, running and crouching. Following paragraph introduce some details of above relate works.

Assaf Feldman presents "ReachMedia"[5], a system for seamlessly providing just in-time information for everyday objects, built around a wireless wristband with an RFID reader to detect objects that the user is interacting with. It enables hands and eyes- free interaction with relevant information using a unique combination of audio output and gestural input, allowing socially acceptable, on-the-move interaction. Toolstone[8], the system applies only the information of object poses. However, these researches do not apply 3D spatial relation between the held object and a user. One of ways of recognizing user's condition and situation is identifying a held object and using it as input to a system. Tsukubu[7] proposed that a system comprised from a visible and an infrared camera estimates user's status with a held object and offers a teaching video. Ueoka [6] presented "I'm here" to support a user's memory where he placed an object by displaying the last video scene of the object he handled. The system enables users to retrieve certain information from a video database that has recorded a set of the latest scenes of target objects which were held by the user and observed from the user's viewpoint. As mentioned above, those researches recognize just a held object. 'SIXth Sense'[22][23] bridges these digital devices and interaction with the physical world by augmenting the physical world around us with digital information and proposing natural hand gestures as the mechanism to interact with that information. 'SIXth Sense' projects information to any surface, walls, and the objects around us, and to interact with the information through natural hand gestures, arm movements, or with the object itself. However, 'SIXth Sense' treats explicit information by explicit gesture mainly.

Those works indicated providing a information based on user's posture and gesture is good way to boost IT usability. However, those works mainly focused to explicit information based on explicit user's gesture and posture.

3   Mobile Interface by Body Worn Projector and Camera

Commercial projector such like mobile LED projector become small enough to attach a human body, recently. One big feature of body worn projector is projecting to various places, such as floor and wall, and even human body parts which are arms, palms, fingers and back of the hands. It enables to provide information via any surface around a user. In section 3.1, we suggest "Palmtop display for glance information" for mobile interface of shoulder or breast worn projector and camera. In section 3.2, we suggest "Floor Projection from lumbar worn projector" for mobile interface of lumbar worn projector and stabilization method for lumbar mounted projector using internal inertial Sensor.

3.1   Palmtop Display for Glance Information

With attaching a projector on user body, it causes occlusion problem by user's own body. Mayol[18] conducts the simulation to measure a level of decoupling of camera movement from the wearer's posture and motions by a combination of inertial, visual sensor feedback and active control. In terms of field of view of the handling space and amount of camera motion during walking, around a breast and shoulder is suitable place for deploying wearable visual robot which has 2-axis actuator, some sensors and a camera. We assume that cell phone installed a projector module is attached to user's shoulder. In that situation, we suggest "Palmtop display for glance information". We define information which needs short time to view and understand as the glance information. For example, when getting a spam mail on cell phone, in case of using current cell phone, user should bring out a cell phone from own pocket or bag, and then user watch small display. Finally, user recognizes the information is no worth to browse. However, using a palm top display, user just holds up own palm to certain position, and then the cell phone projects header information to user's palm. Consequently, user can cut out motion of bringing out cell phone from own pocket and bag. This way of viewing information is suitable for time, short message, mail subject, and memo information (fig.1). Note that in case of that the projected information is worth for replying and operating, user just takes a cell phone from shoulder, and then, user operates by old fashion ways such like pushing buttons. Therefore, this mobile interface just boosts ease of viewing information and cuts out bothersome motions to bring out a cell phone from own pocket and bag, it does not deny current operating of cell phone.

We conduct a user study to assess performance of "Palmtop display for glance information" with qualitative and quantitative analysis. We set "on shoulder condition" and "in pocket condition" as comparative conditions. "Palmtop display condition" is that user just hold up own palm to certain position and view the projected information on user's own palm under wizard-oz-way. "On shoulder condition" is that user detach semi-fixed cell phone from own shoulder and view a display of the cell phone. "In pocket condition" is that user brings out cell phone from shoulder and view a display of the cell phone. Ten males served as subjects (age:21-24).

The sampling data are completion time of viewing and completion time of motion. Completion time of viewing is time through a signal of starting, viewing the information on cell phone display or user's palm and telling the information to observer.

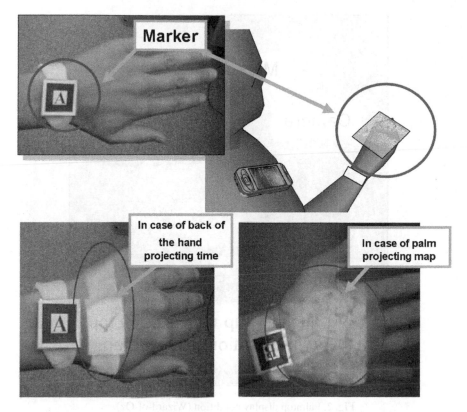

Fig. 1. Palm top display for glace

Completion time of motion is time through a signal of starting, viewing the information on cell phone display or user's palm, telling the information to observer, fixing cell phone to pocket or shoulder (in case of palmtop display, putting back own palm to original position). Also, to measure the performance of palm top display purely, we conduct Wizard-of-OZ test in "Palmtop display condition". Actually, in "Palmtop display condition", to compensate a problem of stability of projected information by user's motion, we fixed camera and projector with tripod instead of attaching to user's body. Note that we do not disrespect the stabilize problem. We believe that it is necessary to solve the problem for realizing palmtop display. We put ARToolkit[21] Marker to user's wrist (fig.3) for recognizing 3D posture and position of user's palm by the camera. After the user test, we conduct questioners to subjects.

Fig 3 shows a result of the user test. In case of "Palmtop Display condition", completion time of viewing and completion time of motion mark shortest time as shown in the upper side of fig. 3. Lower side of fig. 3 shows a result of questionnaire. "Palmtop display condition" marks less bothers. In this result, we can confirm possibility that palmtop display realize ease of viewing information and reduce bothers to bring out a cell phone from own pocket and bag.

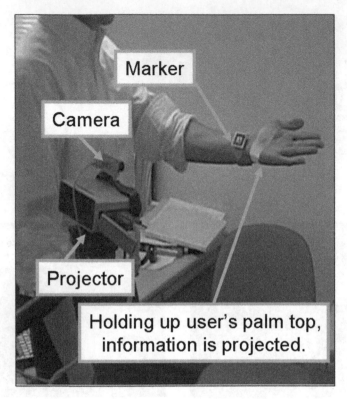

Fig. 2. Palmtop display condition (Wizard-of-Oz)

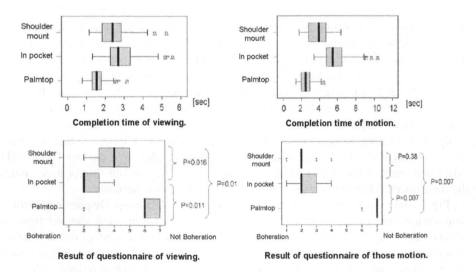

Fig. 3. Result of user test of palm top display for glance

3.2 Floor Projection Using Internal Inertia Sensor

Almost mobile device provide information to user via small own LCD. To use such mobile device, user must hold the device by one-handed and gaze installed small display even while user walking and running. However, risks of collision and falling are increased with gazing and holding the device by one-hand. Furthermore, it is difficult to provide the information based on real-world situation such like AR information. Also, the devices are designed for providing explicit information such like "search result of user's input" and "mail for you". Such style information needs user's deeply attention. Those devices have no focus to provide implicit and awareness information. Therefore, we propose "Floor projection" from lumbar mounted projector. This projecting way realizes hands, eye, and head free interface with current social acceptance. In section 3.1, we assume that cell phone installed a small projector and a camera are attached to user's shoulder. However, considering social acceptance, we assume that people storage the cell phone in a pocket or fix the cell phone to own belt such like current mobile style in early age of spreading cell phone with projection capability. The common feature of body worn projector enables to provide information via any surface around a user. With using body worn projector, implicit and awareness information are projected to on a part of floor where user watches by user's peripheral vision. Explicit information is projected to a part of floor where user watches by user's central vision (Fig. 4).

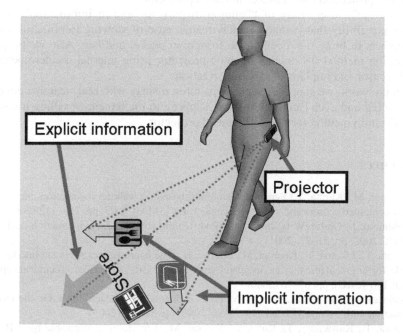

Fig. 4. Projecting explicit and implicit information from lumbar mounted projector

However, lumbar as mounting position loses a stability of projection comparing to shoulder, breast and head mounting. In particular, during walking and running, the projected information becomes unstable extremely. Therefore, we propose stabilization method for lumbar mounted projector using internal sensor. Actually, accelerometer and attitude sensor which be installed to a lumbar mounted projector measure translation and rotation of the lumbar mounted projector. Also we focus to periodicity of walking for applying compensations of time and spatial displacement by means of active noise cancel (ANC). Finally, according to measured translation and rotation, the projected information is moved on pixel of projector coordinate to cancel motion of lumbar mounted projector. Currently, we implement canceling a projector rotation. As a result, we can prevent that the projected information drop from user's peripheral while walking. However, it still involves stabilization problems. We should implement canceling translation by means of ANC.

4 Conclusion

In this paper, we describe features of body worn projector, which has capability for projecting information to user's peripheral vision, and body worn camera, which has capability for recognizing user's posture and estimating user's behavior, are suitable interface for providing awareness, implicit, and even explicit information. Finally, we propose two mobile interfaces which are "Palmtop display for glance information" and "Floor projection from Lumbar mounted projector".

Conducting a user study of "Palmtop display for glance information", we can confirm possibility that palmtop display realize ease of viewing information and reduce bothers to bring out a cell phone from own pocket and bag. Also we propose a stabilization method for lumbar mounted projector using internal accelerometer and attitude sensor and implement canceling rotation.

In future work, we suppose to realize palmtop display with real wearable condition while waling and even running. Also, we suppose to implement canceling translation of stabilization method for lumbar mounted projector.

References

1. Kourogi, M., Kurata, T.: Personal positioning based on walking locomotion analysis with self-contained sensors and a wearable camera. In: ISMAR 2003, pp. 103–112 (2003)
2. Rekimoto, J.: GestureWrist and GesturePad: Unobtrusive wearable interaction devices. In: ISWC 2001, pp. 21–27 (2001)
3. Kurata, T., Okuma, T., Kourogi, M., Sakaue, K.: The hand-mouse: A human interface suitable for augmentedreality environment enabled by visual wearables. TechnicalReport of IEICE (PRMU), pp. 69–76 (2000)
4. Feldman, A., Tapia, E.M., Sadi, S., Maes, P., Schmandt, C.: ReachMedia: On-the-move interaction with everyday objects. In: ISWC 2005, pp. 52–59, (2005)
5. Ueoka, T., Kawamura, T., Kono, Y., Kidode, M.: I'm Here!: a Wearable bject Remembrance Support System. In: MobileHCI 2003, Fifth International Symposium on Human Computer Interaction with obile Devices and Services, pp. 422–427 (2003)

6. Tsukubu, Y., Kosaka, T., Kameda, Y., Nakamura, Y., Ohta, Y.: Video-Based Media for Gently Giving Instructions: Object change detection and working process identification. In: PRMU 2004, pp. 13–18 (2004)
7. Rekimoto, J., Sciammarella, E.: ToolStone: Effective Use of the Physical Manipulation Vocabularies of Input Devices. In: Proc. of UIST 2000, pp. 109–117 (2000)
8. Kourogi, M., Sakata, N., Okuma, T., Kurata, T.: Indoor/Outdoor pedestrian navigation with an embedded gPS/RFID/Self-contained sensor system. In: Pan, Z., Cheok, D.A.D., Haller, M., Lau, R., Saito, H., Liang, R. (eds.) ICAT 2006. LNCS, vol. 4282, pp. 1310–1321. Springer, Heidelberg (2006)
9. Sakata, N., Kurata, T., Kato, T., Kourogi, M., Kuzuoka, H.: WACL: Supporting Telecommunications Using Wearable Active Camera with Laser Pointer. In: ISWC 2003, NY, USA, pp. 53–56 (2003)
10. Yamamoto, G., Xu, H., Sato, K.: PALMbit-Silhouette. In: Interaction 2008, pp. 109–116 (2008) (in Japanese)
11. Yamamoto, G., Nanbu, S., Xu, H., Sato, K.: PALMbit-Shadow: Accessing by Virtual Shadow. In: The 6th IEEE and ACM International Symposium on Mixed and Augmented Reality, Nara, Japan (2007)
12. Starner, T., Weaver, J., Pentland, A.: Real-time American SignLanguage recognition using desk and wearable computer-based video. IEEE Trans. Patt. Analy. and Mach. Intell. 20(12) (1998)
13. Mann, S.: Smart Clothing: TheWearable Computer and WearCam. Personal Technologies 1(1) (1997)
14. Starner, T., Auxier, J., Ashbrook, D., Gandy, M.: The gesture pendant: A self-illuminating, wearable, infrared computer vision system for home automation control and medical monitoring. In: The Fourth International Symposium on Wearable Computers, ISWC 2000 (2000)
15. Kolsch, M., Beall, A., Turk, M.: Postural comfort zone for reaching gestures. In: Human Factors and Ergonomics Society Annual Meeting (2003)
16. Kolsch, M., Beall, A., Turk, M.: An objective measure for postural comfort. In: Human Factors and Ergonomics Society Annual Meeting (2003)
17. Wither, J., DiVerdi, S., Hollerer, T.: Evaluating Display Types for AR Selection and Annotation. In: International Symposium on Mixed and Augmented Reality (2007)
18. Mayol, W.W., Tordoff, B., Murray, D.W.: Designing a miniature wearable visual robot. In: ICRA, pp. 3725–3730 (2002)
19. Chaffin, D.B.: Localized Muscle Fatigue Definition and Measurement. Journal of Occupational Medicine 15(4), 346–354 (1973)
20. Wither, J., Di Verdi, S., Hollerer, T.: Evaluating Display Types for AR Selection and Annotation. In: International Symposium on Mixed and Augmented Reality 2007, pp. 95–98 (2007)
21. ARToolkit Website, http://www.hitl.washington.edu/artoolkit/
22. Mistry, P., Maes, P., Chang, L.: WUW: Wear Ur World - A Wearable Gestural Interface. In: CHI 2009 extended abstracts on Human factors in computing systems, Boston, USA (to appear, 2009)
23. Maes, P., Mistry, P.: The Sixth Sense. TED talk in Reframe session. In: TED 2009, Long Beach, CA, USA (2009)

Relationship between Physiological Indices and a Subjective Score in Evaluating Visually Induced Motion Sickness

Norihiro Sugita[1], Makoto Yoshizawa[2], Akira Tanaka[3], Makoto Abe[1],
Shigeru Chiba[4], Tomoyuki Yambe[5], and Shin-ichi Nitta[5]

[1] Graduate School of Engineering, Tohoku University, Aoba 6-6-05,
Aoba-ku, Sendai 980-8579, Japan
[2] Cyberscience Center, Tohoku University, Aoba 6-6-05,
Aoba-ku, Sendai 980-8579, Japan
[3] Faculty of Symbiotic Systems Science, Fukushima University,
Kanayagawa 1, Fukushima 960-1296, Japan
[4] Sharp Corporation, Nakase 1-9-2, Mihama-ku, Chiba 261-8520, Japan
[5] Institute of Development, Aging and Cancer, Tohoku University,
Seiryo-machi 4-1, Aoba-ku, Sendai 980-8575, Japan
sugita@yoshizawa.ecei.tohoku.ac.jp

Abstract. Visual environments are evolving rapidly along with the popularization of high resolution and wide field-of-view displays. However, there is a concern that these environments may give negative effects on viewers' health such as visually-induced motion sickness (VIMS). Previous studies reported that some physiological indices were useful to assess the effect of visual stimulation. However, we have little knowledge about temporal relationship between the severity of sickness and the change in the physiological indices. In this study, the average mutual information has been employed to investigate this relationship. The analysis of experimental data has suggested that there is a possibility to detect a sign of VIMS prior to the development of symptoms of VIMS with the physiological indices.

Keywords: visually-induced motion sickness, physiological index, subjective score, averaged mutual information.

1 Introduction

In recent years, people are often exposed to a moving picture taken by an amature cameraman who does not have any special knowledge for filming. This is because a video camera has come down in price and posting private videos on the Internet has been expanded. In this situation, some cases were reported in which people suffered from visually-induced motion sickness (VIMS) during or after watching a video including unexpected whole image motion and vibration [1]-[4].

Some previous studies reported that not only questionnaires but also physiological indices were useful to detect the symptoms of VIMS. In particular, variations in the parasympathetic cardiac activity [5]-[6], skin conductance [7]-[8] and gastric

R. Shumaker (Ed.): Virtual and Mixed Reality, LNCS 5622, pp. 114–119, 2009.

tachyarrhythmia [7][9]-[10] are considered to be affected by VIMS. The authors also proposed a physiological index (ρ_{max}) and reported that this index decreased significantly when people suffered from VIMS [11]-[14]. However, the temporal relationship between the change in the physiological state and the development of VIMS based on a subjective score has not been clarified yet.

The aim of this study is to reveal the temporal relationship between the physiological indices and the subjective score obtained from subjects suffering from VIMS. In the experiment of this study, both the subjective score and the physiological parameters were measured simultaneously, and the average mutual information [15] was calculated to measure the statistical dependence between them.

2 Methods

2.1 Experiment

Fifty-one healthy adults (22 males and 29 females; 26.6 ± 9.3 years) participated in the experiment. A 37-inch liquid crystal display (resolution: 1920×1080 pixels, brightness: 100 cd/m^2) was used to show a video to each subject. The subject sat on a chair placed 70cm away from the display, which gave 60.5×40.3 degree field of view, and watched a self-produced video for 27min30s after adaptation to darkness. The video included unexpected whole image motion and vibration (20min) which would induce VIMS. Before and after the moving image, a wholly gray screen with no image was presented to the subjects for 5min30s and 2min, respectively.

During the experiment, biological signals were measured in the way hereinafter described. ECG and finger photo-plethysmogram were measured by physiological amplifiers (ECG100C, PPG100C; BIOPAC System Inc.), and they were stored by a data recording device (MP-100; BIOPAC System Inc.), whose voltage resolution and sampling rate were 16bit and 1kHz, respectively. The subject rated the symptom of VIMS on a scale of zero to four with a joystick every 1min. It is regarded that the higher this subjective score (SS) was, the more severe the symptom of VIMS was.

Informed consent was obtained from each subject before the experiment. And the experimental protocol was approved by the University's Internal Review Board.

2.2 Data Analysis

Only 23 subjects' data (10 males and 13 females; 27.6 ± 10.0 years) could be analyzed because artifacts, measurement noise or mistakes in measuring were found in the other subjects' data.

In this study, to investigate the relationship between the subjective score and the physiological index, the averaged mutual information (I) which shows the statistical dependence between changing patterns (increased, decreased or changed little) of variables was calculated. Heart rate variability (HRV), its low-frequency component (LF_{HR}) from 0.05 Hz to 0.15Hz and high-frequency component (HF_{HR}) from 0.15 Hz to 0.45Hz were chosen as the physiological index to calculate I. In addition to these indices, ρ_{max} was also chosen. The index ρ_{max} is defined as the maximum cross-correlation coefficient between heart rate and pulse transmission time whose frequency components are limited to Mayer wave-related frequencies.

By its nature, I between arbitry variables X and Y does not contain directional information, in other word, I does not show causality between X and Y. Whereas, it is possible to detect causality between X and Y by the calculation of I using X_L instead of X. X_L is the time series which lags behind X by L [16].

3 Results and Discussion

Figure 1 a) shows changes in ρ_{max} and SS of a subject. SS increased at 8min, 11min, 19min and 22min, and ρ_{max} decreased at around these points of time. Fig.1 b) shows the average mutual information I between SS and ρ_{max} of this subject. In this figure, I was the highest at time lag L=-1min. This result means that his physiological state had changed 1 minute before he felt the sensation of VIMS.

Figure 2 shows relationships between time lag L and the mean values of I calculateded from four physiological indices a) ρ_{max}, b) HRV, c) LF_{HR} and d) HF_{HR}. In these figures, the mean I at an arbitrary time lag L_0 was obtained as the value averaged only in subjects whose I were the highest at L_0.

In Fig.2, I obtained from ρ_{max} and HF_{HR} showed higher level than those from other physiological indices. This agrees with the results of previous studies which reported that the changes in ρ_{max} and HF_{HR} were associated with the development of motion sickness [5]-[6] [11]-[14].

Meanwhile, between ρ_{max} and HF_{HR}, there was a difference in the time lag when the relation of the physiological index with SS was strengthened. This means that the physiological reaction seen in HF_{HR} appeared at almost the same time as the subjective evaluation changed, while the reaction in ρ_{max} appeared before or after the subjective evaluation changed. The cause of this result has not been clear. However, the

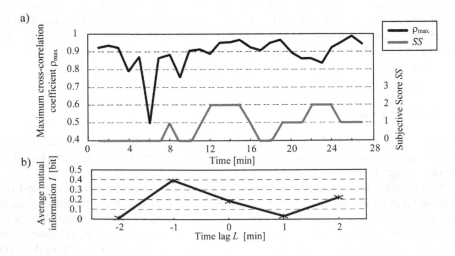

Fig. 1. a) Changes in ρ_{max} (black line) and subjective score SS (gray line) of a subject and b) the average mutual information I between them

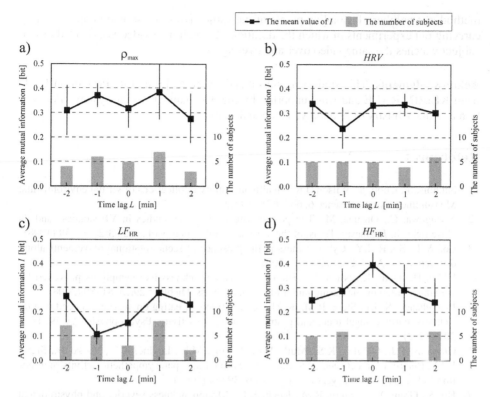

Fig. 2. The mean values of the average mutual information I between subjective score SS and four physiological indices a) ρ_{max}, b) HRV, c) LF_{HR} and d) HF_{HR}. Bar graph at each time lag represents the number of subjects whose I were the highest at that time lag.

difference in the autonomic nervous activity may be a candidate of the causes. It is well known that HF_{HR} reflects the parasympathetic nervous activity while ρ_{max} is obtained from Mayer wave component which is related to both the sympathetic and the parasympathetic nervous activities [17]-[19].

In general, the dependence between the physiological index and the subjective score is not necessarily linear. However, this problem can be avoided by analyzing I which shows the statistical dependence of the two variables.

4   Conclusion

In this study, the average mutual information was employed to investigate the temporal relationship between a subjective evaluation score and some physiological indices. The result showed that the physiological states of some subjects changed prior to the development of VIMS symptoms.

In future works, it is necessary to analyze other physiological indices in the above way, such as gastric tachyarrhythmia which has been frequently reported to have relationship with motion sickness. Moreover, to confirm the validity of the proposed method, the number of sampling points of the subjective score should be increased by carrying out experiments in which the duration of watching a video is extended or one subject watches the same video over and over again.

Acknowledgments. This study was subsidized by JKA through its Promotion funds from KEIRIN RACE and was supported by the Mechanical Social Systems Foundation and the Ministry of Economy, Trade and Industry.

References

1. Nichols, S., Cobb, S., Wilson, J.R.: Health and safety implications of virtual environments: Measurement issue. Presence 6, 667–675 (1997)
2. Nakagawa, C., Ohsuga, M.: The present situation of the studies in VE-sickness and its close field (in Japanese). Trans. of the Virtual Reality Society of Japan 3(2), 31–39 (1998)
3. Lo, W.T., So, R.H.Y.: Cybersickness in the presence of scene rotational movements along different axes. Appl. Erg. 32, 1–14 (2001)
4. Ujike, H., Ukai, K., Nihei, K.: Survey on motion sickness-like symptoms provoked by viewing a video movie during junior high school class. Displays 29(2), 81–89 (2008)
5. Uijtdehaage, S.H.J., Stern, R.M., Koch, K.L.: Effects of eating on vection-induced motion sickness, cardiac vagal tone, and gastric myoelectric activity. Psychophysiology 29, 193–201 (1992)
6. Gianaros, P.J., Quigley, K.S., Muth, E.R., Levine, M.E., Levine, R.C., Vasko Jr., Stern, R.M.: Relationship between temporal changes in cardiac parasympathetic activity and motion sickness severity. Psychophysiology 40, 39–44 (2003)
7. Hu, S., Grant, W.F., Stern, R.M., Koch, K.L.: Motion sickness severity and physiological correlates during repeated exposures to a rotating optokineic drum. Aviation, Space, and Environmental Medicine 62, 308–314 (1991)
8. Miller, J.C., Sharkey, T.J., Graham, G.A., McCauley, M.E.: Autonomic physiological data associated with simulator discomfort. Aviation, Space, and Environmental Medicine 64(9), 813–819 (1993)
9. Stern, R.M., Koch, K.L., Leibowitz, H.W., Lindblad, I.M., Shupert, C.L., Stewart, W.R.: Tachygastria and motion sickness. Aviation, Space, and Environmental Medicine 56, 1074–1077 (1985)
10. Himi, N., Koga, T., Nakamura, E., Kobashi, M., Yamane, M., Tsujioka, K.: Differences in autonomic responses between subjects with and without nausea while watching an irregularly oscillating video. Autonomic Neuroscience: Basic and Clinical 116, 46–53 (2004)
11. Sugita, N., Yoshizawa, M., Tanaka, A., Abe, K., Yambe, T., Nitta, S.: Evaluation of effect of visual stimulation on humans based on maximum cross-correlation coefficient between blood pressure and heart rate (in Japanese). J. Human Interface Society of Japan 4(4), 39–46 (2002)
12. Sugita, N., Yoshizawa, M., Abe, M., Tanaka, A., Yambe, T., Nitta, S., Chiba, S.: Biphasic Effect of Visually-induced Motion Sickness Revealed by Time-Varying Correlation of Autonomic Nervous System. In: 10th International Conference on Human - Computer Interaction, LasVegas (2005) (CD-ROM)
13. Sugita, N., Yoshizawa, M., Tanaka, A., Abe, K., Yambe, T., Nitta, S.: Evaluation of the Effect of Visual Stimulation on Humans by Simultaneous Experiment with Multiple Subjects. In: 27th Annual International Conference of the IEEE Engineering in Medicine and Biology Society, Shanghai (2005) (CD-ROM)

14. Sugita, N., Yoshizawa, M., Abe, M., Tanaka, A., Watanabe, T., Chiba, S., Yambe, T., Nitta, S.: Evaluation of adaptation to visually induced motion sickness based on the maximum cross-correlation between pulse transmission time and heart rate. J. NeuroEngineering Rehabilitation (Online) 4(37) (2007),
    http://www.jneuroengrehab.com/content/4/1/35
15. Shannon, C.E.: The mathematical theory of communication. Bell Syst. Tech. J. 27, 379–423 (1948)
16. Tanaka, N., Okamoto, H., Naito, M.: Detecting and Evaluating Intrinsic Nonlinearity Present in the Mutual Dependence between Two Variables. Physica D 147, 1–11 (2000)
17. Malliani, A., Pagani, M., Lombardi, F., Ccrutti, S.: Cardiovascular neural regulation explored in the frequency domain. Circulation 84(2), 482–492 (1991)
18. Berntson, G.G., Bigger, J.T., Eckberg, D.L., Grossman, P., Kaufmann, P.G., Malik, M., Nagaraja, H.N., Porges, S.W., Saul, J.P., Stone, P.H., DerMolen, M.W.: Heart rate variability: Origins, methods, and interpretive caveats. Psychophysiology 34, 623–648 (1997)
19. Malliani, A., Montaro, N.: Heart rate variability as a clinical tool. Ital. Heart J. 3, 439–445 (2002)

Effect of a Stereoscopic Movie on the Correlation between Head Acceleration and Body Sway

Hiroki Takada[1], Tetsuya Yamamoto[1], Masaru Miyao[2], Tatehiko Aoyama[1],
Masashi Furuta[3], and Tomoki Shiozawa[4]

[1] Gifu University of Medical Science, 795-1 Ichihiraga Nagamine,
Seki, Gifu 501-3892, Japan
[2] Nagoya University, Furo-cho, Chikusa-Ku, Nagoya 464-8601, Japan
[3] Aichi University of Education, 1 Hirosawa, Igaya-cho, Kariya, Aichi 448-8542, Japan
[4] Aoyama Gakuin University, 4-4-25 Shibuya, Shibuya-ku, Tokyo 150-8366, Japan
takada@u-gifu-ms.ac.jp

Abstract. Visually induced motion sickness (VIMS) is caused by sensory conflict, the disagreement between vergence and visual accommodation while observing stereoscopic images. VIMS can be measured by psychological and physiological methods. We quantitatively measured the head acceleration and body sway before and during exposure to a conventional 3D movie. The subjects wore a head mount display and maintained the Romberg posture for the first 60 s and a wide stance (midlines of the heels 20 cm apart) for the next 60 s. Head acceleration was measured using an Active Tracer with 50 Hz sampling. The Simulator Sickness Questioner (SSQ) was completed immediately afterward. For the SSQ sub-scores and each index for stabilograms, we employed two-way ANOVA with leg postures and presence/absence of stereoscopic images as factors. Moreover, we assumed that the input signal was the head acceleration in the transfer system to control the body sway and estimate the transfer function.

Keywords: visually induced motion sickness, stabilometry, sparse density, head acceleration, transfer function analysis.

1 Introduction

The human standing posture is maintained by the body's balance function, which is an involuntary physiological adjustment mechanism termed the righting reflex [1]. To maintain a standing posture when locomotion is absent, the righting reflex, centered in the nucleus ruber, is essential. Sensory signals such as visual inputs and auditory and vestibular inputs as well as proprioceptive inputs from the skin, muscles, and joints are involved in the body's balance function [2]. The evaluation of this function is indispensable for diagnosing equilibrium disturbances such as cerebellar degenerations, basal ganglia disorders, and Parkinson's disease in patients [3].

Stabilometry has been used to evaluate this equilibrium function qualitatively and quantitatively. A projection of a subject's center of gravity onto a detection stand is measured as an average of the center of pressure (COP) of both feet. The COP is

R. Shumaker (Ed.): Virtual and Mixed Reality, LNCS 5622, pp. 120–127, 2009.

traced for each time step, and the time series of the projections is traced on an x-y plane. By connecting the temporally vicinal points, a stabilogram is created. Several parameters such as the area of sway (A), total locus length (L), and locus length per unit area (L/A) have been proposed to quantify the instability involved in the standing posture, and such parameters are widely used in clinical studies. The last parameter, in particular, depends on the fine variations involved in posture control [1]. This index is then regarded as a gauge for evaluating the function of the proprioceptive control of standing in human beings. However, it is difficult to clinically diagnose disorders of the balance function and to identify the decline in equilibrium function by utilizing the abovementioned indices and measuring patterns in the stabilogram. Large interindividual differences might make it difficult to understand the results of such a comparison.

The analysis of stabilograms is useful not only for medical diagnosis but also for achieving control of upright standing by two-legged robots and for preventing elderly people from falling [4]. Recent studies suggest that maintaining postural stability is a major goal of animals [5] and that they experience sickness symptoms in circumstances where they have not acquired strategies for maintaining their balance [6]. Riccio and Stoffregen argued that motion sickness is not caused by sensory conflict but by postural instability, although the most widely known theory of motion sickness is based on the concept of sensory conflict [6]–[8]. Stoffregen and Smart (1999) reported that the onset of motion sickness may be preceded by significant increases in postural sway [9].

The equilibrium function in humans deteriorates when viewing three-dimensional (3D) movies [10]. This visually induced motion sickness (VIMS) has been considered to be caused by a disagreement between vergence and visual accommodation while viewing 3D images [11]. Thus, stereoscopic images have been devised to reduce this disagreement [12]–[13].

VIMS can be measured by psychological and physiological methods, and the simulator sickness questionnaire (SSQ) is a well-known psychological method for measuring the extent of motion sickness [14]. The SSQ is used herein for verifying the occurrence of VIMS. The following parameters of autonomic nervous activity are appropriate for the physiological method: heart rate variability, blood pressure, electrogastrography, and galvanic skin reaction [15]–[17]. A wide stance (with midlines of the heels 17–30 cm apart) reportedly results in a significant increase in the total locus length in the stabilograms for individuals with high SSQ scores, while the length in those of individuals with low scores is less affected by such a stance [18].

By using the SSQ and stabilometry, in this study, we examined whether the VIMS was induced by a stereoscopic movie. We also investigated the relationship between the body sway and head acceleration by using transfer function analysis.

The correlation between head movement and the movement of the center of gravity has been investigated in general, and a corporative effect was seen in their relationship [19]. By showing a stereoscopic movie to the subjects, Takeda et al. verified that there is a corporative correlation between the head movement and the sway [20]. We herein assume that the input signal, x(t), is the head acceleration in the transfer system to control the body sway as shown in Fig. 1. In this figure, we denote the Fourier transform by a capital letter corresponding to the letter of function being transformed (such as y(t) and Y(f)). The transfer function H(f) is defined as a Fourier transform of the impulse response h(f). In our experiments, we cannot observe the output signal of the transfer system but only the signal added to the noise n(t). Based on a theorem (Winner-Khinchine):

$$W_{xx} = |X(f)|^2 = \sigma_x^2 \mathscr{F}(R_{xx}),$$ (1)

we can easily estimate a power spectrum W_{xx}. On the right-hand side of Eq.(1), σ_x expresses the standard deviation and $\mathscr{F}(R_{xx})$ means the Fourier transform of the auto-correlation function with respect to the signal x(t) [21]. In this study, we estimate the transfer function that controls the sway as follows.

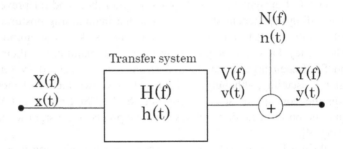

Fig. 1. A transfer system and its output, y(t)

2 Materials and Methods

Ten healthy subjects (age, 23.6 ± 2.2 years) voluntarily participated in this study. All of them were Japanese and lived in Nagoya and its surrounding areas. They provided informed consent prior to participation. The following subjects were excluded from the study: subjects working in the night shift, those dependent on alcohol, those who consumed alcohol and caffeine-containing beverages after waking up and less than 2 h after meals, those who had been using prescribed drugs, and those who may have had any otorhinolaryngologic or neurological diseases in the past (except for conductive hearing impairment, which is commonly found in the elderly). In addition, the subjects must have experienced motion sickness at some time during their lives.

We ensured that the body sway was not affected by environmental conditions. By using an air conditioner, we adjusted the room temperature to 25 °C and kept the room dark. All subjects were tested from 10 a.m. to 5 p.m. in the room. The subjects wore an HMD (iWear AV920; Vuzix Co. Ltd.) on which 2 kinds of images were presented in a random order (Fig. 2): (I) a visual target (circle) whose diameter was 3 cm; (II) a conventional 3D movie that shows a sphere approaching and moving away from subjects irregularly (Fig. 3).

Fig. 2. The setup of the experiment [22]   **Fig. 3.** A scene in the movie [22]

2.1 Experimental Procedure

The subjects stood without moving on the detection stand of a stabilometer (G5500; Anima Co. Ltd.) in the Romberg posture with their feet together for 1 min before the sway was recorded. Each sway of the COP was then recorded at a sampling frequency of 20 Hz during the measurement, while the head acceleration was simultaneously recorded by the active tracer (AC-301A; GMS Co. Ltd.) at 50 Hz; subjects were instructed to maintain the Romberg posture for the first 60 s and a wide stance (with the midlines of heels 20 cm apart) for the next 60 s. The subjects viewed one of the images, i.e., (I) or (II), on the HMD from the beginning until the end. The SSQ was filled before and after stabilometry.

2.2 Calculation Procedure

We calculated "total locus length," which is commonly used in the clinical field for stabilograms [23]. In addition, new quantification indices termed "SPD" were also estimated [24].

When subjects stood with their feet close together (Romberg posture), the coherence function between the head acceleration $x(i)$ and the movement of the centre of gravity $y(j)$ was estimated as

$$\mathrm{coh}_{x(i)y(j)}(f) = |W_{x(i)y(j)}|^2 / (W_{x(i)x(i)}\, W_{y(j)y(j)}), \qquad (2)$$

where i and j expressed the component (1: lateral, 2: anterior/posterior). By using the Fast Fourier transform algorithm, power spectrums $W_{x(i)x(i)}$, $W_{y(j)y(j)}$ were estimated. On the basis of Eq.(1), we calculated cross spectrums $W_{x(i)y(j)}$. The coherence means an index for the degree of the linear correlation between input and output signals

$(0 \leq coh \leq 1)$. There exists a completely linear correlation between these signals when coh $=1$. In this study, we assumed that a linear system intervenes between the head and the body sway only if coh ≥ 0.12 (significant correlation coefficient for N = 512, p < 0.01). Moreover, we estimated the transfer function as follows:

$$H(f) = W_{x(i)y(j)} / W_{x(i)x(i)},$$

and the transfer function gain (TFG) $|H(f)|$.

3 Results and Discussion

Scores for SSQ-N (nausea), SSQ-OD (eyestrain), SSQ-D (disorientation), and SSQ-TS (total score) were 11.4 ± 3.7, 18.2 ± 4.1, 23.7 ± 8.8, and 19.8 ± 5.3, respectively. Sickness symptoms seemed to appear with the exposure to the stereoscopic images although there were large individual differences.

Typical stabilograms are shown in Fig. 4. In these figures, the vertical axis shows the anterior and posterior movements of the COP, and the horizontal axis shows the right and left movements of the COP. The amplitudes of the sway that were observed during exposure to the movies (Fig. 4c–4d) tended to be larger than those of the control sway (Fig. 4a–4b). Although a high density of COP was observed in the stabilograms (Fig. 4a–4b), the density decreased in stabilograms during exposure to the conventional stereoscopic movie (Fig. 4c–4d).

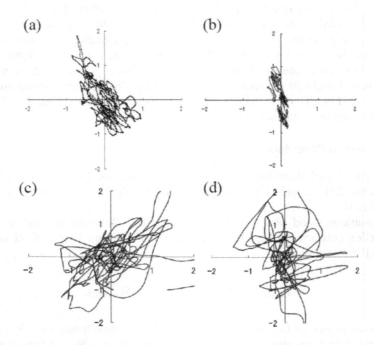

Fig. 4. Typical stabilograms observed when subjects viewed a static circle (a)–(b) and the conventional 3D movie (c)–(d) [22]

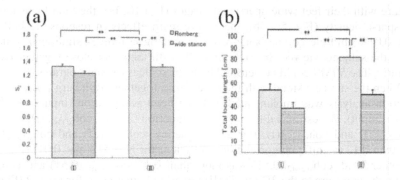

Fig. 5. Typical results of two-way ANOVA with repeated measures for indicators; the total locus length (a) and the SPD (b)

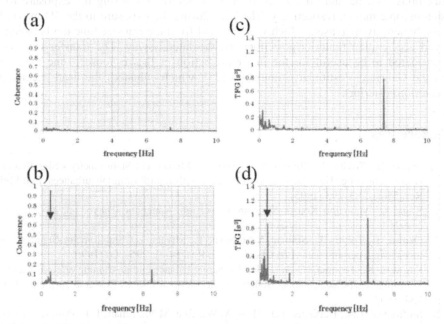

Fig. 6. Representative examples of the distributions of coherence function (a), (b) and transfer function gain (c), (d) between the head acceleration (anterior/ posterior) and the lateral sway

Furthermore, stabilograms measured in an open leg posture with the midlines of heels 20 cm apart (Fig. 4b, 4d) were compared with those measured in the Romberg posture (Fig. 4a, 4c). COP was not isotropically dispersed but was characterized by considerable movement in the anterior-posterior (y) direction (Fig. 4b, 4d). Although this trend is seen in Fig. 4d, the diffusion of COP was larger in the lateral (x) direction and had spread to the extent that it was equivalent to the control stabilograms (Fig. 4a)

According to the two-way analysis of variance (ANOVA) with repeated measures, there was no interaction between the factors of posture (Romberg posture or standing posture with their feet wide apart) and images (I or II). For the total locus length and the sparse density (Fig. 5a, 5b), there were main effects in response to both factors (p < 0.01). Multiple comparisons revealed that these indices significantly increased when the subjects viewed the 3D movie (II) with their feet close together (Romberg posture). The VIMS could be detected by these indices for stabilograms.

When the subjects stood with their feet close together (Romberg posture), transfer function analysis was implemented with the head acceleration (input) and the body sway (output). We estimated the coherence function (2), i.e., $coh_{x(1)y(1)}(f)$, $coh_{x(1)y(2)}(f)$, $coh_{x(2)y(1)}(f)$ and $coh_{x(2)y(2)}(f)$. For any frequency, $coh_{x(1)y(1)}(f)$ and $coh_{x(1)y(2)}(f)$ were less than 0.12 (significant correlation coefficient for N = 512, p < 0.01) (Fig. 6a). On the other hand, $coh_{x(2)y(2)}(0.51)$ was more than 0.12. $coh_{x(2)y(j)}(0.51)$ and $coh_{x(2)y(j)}(7)$ during the exposure to the 3D movie (II) remarkably increased for j = 1, 2 (Fig. 6b).

While watching the 3D movie, the lateral sway might become dependent on its transverse component of the head movement. Moreover, we estimated the transfer functions. Fig. 6c and 6d showed their TFG before and during the exposure to the stereoscopic movie, respectively. The TGF during the exposure to the 3D movie (II) simultaneously increased, which was obtained from the transfer function between the head acceleration (anterior/posterior) and the lateral sway. The transfer function is considered to be useful for the linear prediction of the response to the load, such as the Galvanic Vestibular Stimulation [25], which enhances the head acceleration (anterior/posterior).

References

1. Okawa, T., Tokita, T., Shibata, Y., Ogawa, T., Miyata, H.: Stabilometry - Significance of Locus Length Per Unit Area (L/A) in Patients with Equilibrium Disturbances. Equilibrium Res. 55(3), 283–293 (1995)
2. Kaga, K.: Memaino Kouzo: Structure of vertigo. Kanehara, Tokyo, pp. 23–26, 95–100 (1992)
3. Okawa, T., Tokita, T., Shibata, Y., Ogawa, T., Miyata, H.: Stabilometry-Significance of locus length per unit area (L/A). Equilibrium Res. 54(3), 296–306 (1996)
4. Fujiwara, K., Toyama, H.: Analysis of dynamic balance and its training effect-Focusing on fall problem of elder persons. Bulletin of the Physical Fitness Research Institute 83, 123–134 (1993)
5. Stoffregen, T.A., Hettinger, L.J., Haas, M.W., Roe, M.M., Smart, L.J.: Postural instability and motion sickness in a fixed-base flight simulator. Human Factors 42, 458–469 (2000)
6. Riccio, G.E., Stoffregen, T.A.: An Ecological theory of motion sickness and postural instability. Ecological Physiology 3(3), 195–240 (1991)
7. Oman, C.: A heuristic mathematical model for the dynamics of sensory conflict and motion sickness. Acta Otolaryngologica Supplement 392, 1–44 (1982)
8. Reason, J.: Motion sickness add–aptation: a neural mismatch model. J. Royal Soc. Med. 71, 819–829 (1978)
9. Stoffregen, T.A., Smart, L.J., Bardy, B.J., Pagulayan, R.J.: Postural stabilization of looking. Journal of Experimental Psychology. Human Perception and Performance 25, 1641–1658 (1999)
10. Takada, H., Fujikake, K., Miyao, M., Matsuura, Y.: Indices to Detect Visually Induced Motion Sickness using Stabilometry. In: Proc. VIMS 2007, pp. 178–183 (2007)

11. Hatada, T.: Nikkei electronics 444, 205–223 (1988)
12. Yasui, R., Matsuda, I., Kakeya, H.: Combining volumetric edge display and multiview display for expression of natural 3D images. In: Proc. SPI, vol. 6055, pp. 0Y1–0Y9 (2006)
13. Kakeya, H.: MOEVision: simple multiview display with clear floating image. In: Proc.SPI, vol. 6490, 64900J (2007).
14. Kennedy, R.S., Lane, N.E., Berbaum, K.S., Lilienthal, M.G.: A simulator sickness questionnaire (SSQ): A new method for quantifying simulator sickness. International J. Aviation Psychology 3, 203–220 (1993)
15. Holomes, S.R., Griffin, M.J.: Correlation between heart rate and the severity of motion sickness caused by optokinetic stimulation. J. Psychophysiology 15, 35–42 (2001)
16. Himi, N., Koga, T., Nakamura, E., Kobashi, M., Yamane, M., Tsujioka, K.: Differences in autonomic responses between subjects with and without nausea while watching an irregularly oscillating video. Autonomic Neuroscience. Basic and Clinical 116, 46–53 (2004)
17. Yokota, Y., Aoki, M., Mizuta, K.: Motion sickness susceptibility associated with visually induced postural instability and cardiac autonomic responses in healthy subjects. Acta Otolaryngologia 125, 280–285 (2005)
18. Scibora, L.M., Villard, S., Bardy, B., Stoffregen, T.A.: Wider stance reduces body sway and motion sickness. In: Proc. VIMS 2007, pp. 18–23 (2007)
19. Sakaguchi, M., Taguchi, K., Ixhiyama, T., Netsu, K., Sato, K.: Relationship between head sway and center of foot pressure sway. Auris Nasus Larynx 22(3), 151–157 (1995)
20. Takeda, T., Izumi, S., Sagawa, K.: On the correlation between the head movement and the movement of the center of gravity using HMD. In: Proceedings of the 1995 IEICE General Conference, p. 203 (1995)
21. Kido, K.: Digital Fourier Transform (II), pp. 68–102. Corona Publishing, Tokyo (2007)
22. Takada, H., Fujikake, K., Watanabe, T., Hasegawa, S., Omori, M., Miyao, M.: On a method to evaluate motion sickness induced by stereoscopic images on HMD. In: Proceedings of the IS&T/SPIE 21st Annual Symposium on Electronic Imaging Science and Technology (to appear, 2009)
23. Suzuki, J., Matsunaga, T., Tokumatsu, K., Taguchi, K., Watanabe, Y.: Q&A and a manual in Stabilometry. Equilibrium Res. 55(1), 64–77 (1996)
24. Takada, H., Kitaoka, Y., Ichikawa, S., Miyao, M.: Physical Meaning on Geometrical Index for Stabilometly. Equilibrium Res. 62(3), 168–180 (2003)
25. Day, B.L., Severac Cauquil, A., Bartolomei, L., Pastor, M.A., Lyon, I.N.: Human body-segment tilts induced by galvanic vestibular stimulation: a vestibularly driven balance protection mechanism. J. Physiol. 500, 661–672 (1997)

AR City Representation System Based on
Map Recognition Using Topological Information

Hideaki Uchiyama[1], Hideo Saito[2], Myriam Servières[3], and Guillaume Moreau[4]

[1,2] Keio University, 3-14-1 Hiyoshi, Kohoku-ku 223-8522, Japan
{uchiyama,saito}@hvrl.ics.keio.ac.jp
[3,4] Ecole Centrale de Nantes-CERMA, 1, Rue Noë 44300 Nantes, France
{myriam.servieres,guillaume.moreau}@ec-nantes.fr

Abstract. This paper presents a system for overlaying 3D GIS data information such as 3D buildings onto a 2D physical urban map. We propose a map recognition framework by analysis of distribution of local intersections in order to recognize the area of the physical map from a whole map. The retrieval of the geographical area described by the physical map is based on a hashing scheme, which is called LLAH. In the results, we will show some applications augmenting additional information on the map.

Keywords: GIS, Augmented Reality, LLAH.

1 Introduction

Geographical Information Systems (GIS) have become essential tools for studying, handling and planning urban development. GIS can superimpose layers (representing homogeneous information) that are fused together to generate maps. GIS data can be updated any time and are thus more up-to-date than traditional paper maps. They can moreover be adapted in real time to meet the user's need.

One of the research issues in GIS community is GeoVisualization, which is a way of designing an interface and displaying and handling the spatial and temporal GIS data on the interface [1, 2]. The advantages of using Augmented Reality (AR) techniques to display digital information on standard paper maps have been shown, because AR enables 3D data to be manipulated easier [3, 4, 5]. Moreover, GIS need a shift towards 3D to be compatible with sustainable development concerns. To manage increasing complexity of sustainable development requirements, spatial and temporal queries have to be handled to compute new indicators that are now being defined. For instance, a thermal comfort indicator could be 'walls that have more than 8 hours sunlight in winter and less than 2 hours in summer'. Visualizing the results of such a query requires 3D representation way because sunlight exposure is dependent on building height and neighboring buildings. 3D virtual environments are not easy to manipulate for local authorities. That is why we assume that the use of AR maps will facilitate the display of such results by letting the user manipulate both a paper map and the viewpoint in a natural way.

In this paper, we propose a framework of map recognition technique to establish a correspondence between the image of a real map captured with a camera and a GIS.

R. Shumaker (Ed.): Virtual and Mixed Reality, LNCS 5622, pp. 128–135, 2009.

Intersections are extracted from the input image, and then matched with the GIS data, as in the problem of "Document image retrieval" [6]. We are then able to compute the camera position and orientation with respect to the map assuming that a map is flat, and display more information from the GIS. In experimental results, we will show that our framework is compatible with AR system and some applications.

The rest of the paper is organized as follows: we will first briefly present related works that can be used to match images representing the same objects, i.e. compute the geometric transformation that links the two images. We will then provide an overview of our system in Section.4 and the algorithm in Section.5. Finally, experimental results will be presented and discussed.

2 Related Works

The problem of finding a match for a query object using feature points has been addressed in various ways. The feature points can be described using rich descriptors such as SIFT [7] or SURF [8], that typically use image patches. These descriptors are robust in terms of change of illumination, scale and rotation and describe them with high-dimensions vectors. The search methods have then to deal with the problems of nearest neighbor search in high dimensions with approximate nearest neighbor searching [9] or locality-sensitive-hashing [10].

Rich descriptors are well suited to the retrieval of images near-identical to the ones in the database, with few repetitive texture patterns. By contrast, 2D maps can be presented in different ways, according to the manufacturer, and the retrieval method needs then to focus on the geometry of the urban environment they describe. For this reason, the feature points need to be specific to urban environments and the location of intersections are used in this paper.

It is not possible to distinguish an intersection query using only the location of a single intersection. For this reason, the essential information in retrieval is the arrangement of the features points. Such an arrangement, in our case, must be invariant to the orientation of the camera relative to the map.

One of the recognition methods by geometrical information is Geometric hashing (GH) [11]. GH is such a general model-based object recognition method widely used in computer vision as well as in other domains. The introduction of a geometric invariant yields a computational cost quite important, that is unsuitable for an augmented reality application. A probabilistic reduction of the number of feature points results in accuracy degradation and has led to the introduction of "Locally Likely Arrangement Hashing" (LLAH), which outperforms GH in both processing time and required amount of memory [6]. In this scheme, neighboring points are considered for the calculation of an affine invariant used as a key in a hashing table. A voting technique is employed for retrieval, insuring efficiency and robustness against erasure of feature points. We use a combination of this method and a more traditional tracking technique to first recognize the area in the camera filed of view, then overlay 3D buildings in real-time.

3 System

The user has a hand-held device equipped with a camera coupled with a computer, for example a cellular phone or a see-through HMD. In our experimental setup, we use a digital camera and a laptop (Fig.1 (a)).

The physical map can be displayed on a desktop, on a wall or any flat surface. At the beginning of the use, the camera needs to be in a position more or less parallel to the map, so that perspective distortion is not too important (Fig.1 (b)). After that, the user can move more freely (Fig.1 (c)) to watch the 3D buildings and the GIS data in real-time on the screen of the device (Fig.1 (d)). All physical maps should be registered in the database beforehand. The user can select a map from the registered map for watching its visual aids.

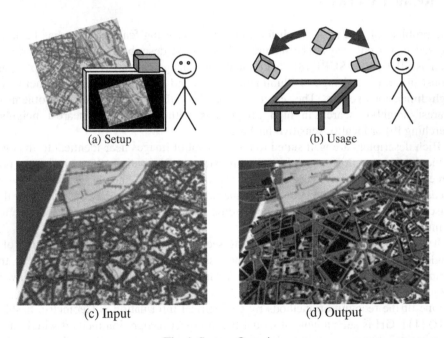

(a) Setup   (b) Usage

(c) Input   (d) Output

Fig. 1. System Overview

4 Algorithm

4.1 Overview

In the off-line process, the initial database of LLAH features of all intersections in GIS is generated beforehand. In the on-line process, the same process is executed at every frame (Fig.2). From a captured image, intersections are extracted by using simple color segmentation because their color was determined beforehand. Since another automatic intersection extraction method has been proposed [12], we focus on map image retrieval by distribution of intersections. For each intersection, the corresponding intersection is retrieved from the database by using the LLAH features. Based on the number of the retrieved intersections, the area of the map can be determined. In addition, the camera pose can be computed by using the retrieved intersections for displaying 3D GIS data of the area. At the same time, LLAH features of each intersection in the captured image are updated.

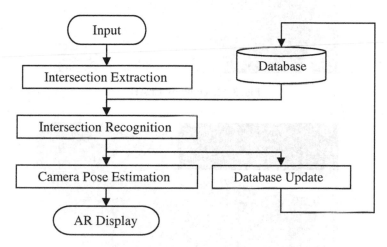

Fig. 2. Algorithm

4.2 GIS Data

Real GIS data of a large French city is used. GDMS [13] is used to process the data in two ways:

- with a simple query, all intersections are extracted from the road network to build the features points that are used in the method.
- following Neubauer and Zipf's idea [14], we have built an XML style file that describes how the GIS database will be rendered in the virtual environment, i.e. whether a polygon layer should be rendered with flat surfaces or extruded polygons, and additional information such as the color to use. We have thus built a VRML builder above GDMS that transforms GIS data according to the XML file and generates a VRML file.

The area described by the data can in theory be very large, and must be sub-divided in sub-areas that correspond to the size of the physical maps used as queries. These sub-areas are defined by a specific ID with intersection's IDs such as (Area ID, Intersection ID1, Intersection ID2 ...). Each Intersection is stored with its belonging area such as (Intersection ID, Area ID). Additional information of the map such as 3D models of buildings is also tagged with its belonging area ID to be able to retrieve the information from area ID.

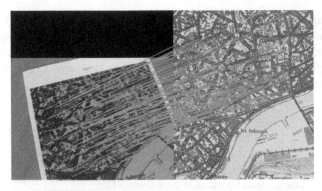

Fig. 3. Matching by LLAH

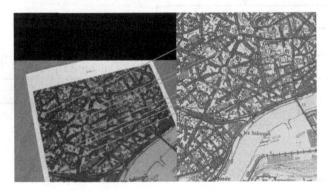

Fig. 4. Outlier Removal by RANSAC based Homography Computation

4.3   Intersection Recognition

From a captured image, red intersections are extracted by finding red region. For each intersection's region, the center is computed. Based on LLAH [6], the corresponding intersection of each extracted intersection is retrieved from the database. As a result, some intersections are correctly matched and other intersections are wrongly matched (Fig.3). Since there are similar arrangements of intersections, the result of LLAH sometimes includes wrongly matched intersections. For removing these wrongly matched intersections, we use RANSAC based homography computation [15].

Since the map is 2D, the correspondence between the map in the database and the map in a captured image can be described by homography. For computing a homography, several intersections are randomly selected and evaluated in the RANSAC process. After that, high confidential intersections are selected (Fig.4).

After the homography is computed, the homography can be converted into a camera position and orientation [16], which is equivalent to camera pose estimation.

4.4   Database Update

Since the initial database is generated by using intersections in GIS, we can say that the LLAH features in the initial database are generated by using a top view image. If we use only the initial database, the retrieval of intersections will succeed in case of near top view including many points. By adding new LLAH features according to the changes of the user's viewpoint, the retrieval will still work when the captured image is not close to the top view image.

When the homography is computed in Intersection Recognition, the intersections in the database can be reprojected onto the captured image by using the homography. If a distance between the reprojected intersection and an extracted intersection in the image is within a threshold, the extracted intersection is matched with the reprojected intersection. Thanks to the reprojection, many intersections which are not matched with corresponding intersections in GIS by LLAH can be matched.

5 Experimental Results

5.1 Computational Costs

For evaluating computational costs of AR display, 100 frames are captured in order to compute the average computational costs. Our device is composed of a laptop (Intel Core 2 Duo 2.2GHz and 3GB RAM) with a firewire camera.

The computational costs of Intersection Recognition and Database Update depend on the number of extracted intersections, which can be represented by $O(N)$ in the case that the number of extracted intersections is N. In our algorithm, total computational costs are 46 msec (more than 20fps). However, 3D Model Rendering took most computational costs because GIS data includes detailed polygons. The content should be appropriately selected depending on computational costs.

Table 1. Computational Costs

Process	Time (msec)
Intersection Extraction	11
Intersection Recognition	22
Camera Pose Estimation	3
Database Update	10
3D Model Rendering	102

5.2 Application

Since the camera pose against the map is estimated, any virtual object can be overlaid at an appropriate position. In this section, we will introduce one application for AR geovisualization.

Fig.5 shows a system for displaying a picture at the captured place on the map. If a user takes a picture with its information of the captured place and input it into the application, the application displays the picture at the captured place on the map (Fig.5 (b)). The user can recognize the places and their relationships where the user captured pictured.

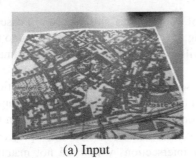 

(a) Input   (b) Tagged images

Fig. 5. Display of tagged images on a map

6 Conclusions

In this paper, we have presented an AR representation system for 3D GIS that are based on the augmentation of a physical map including intersections. It provides a natural device for 3D GIS information representation and manipulation. Intersection recognition is based on LLAH framework by using geometrical relationship with neighbor intersections. For free camera moving, update of LLAH features is adapted.

Our future work will be centered on two main topics. First, we will be using a real physical map, easier to manipulate, but requiring more image processing to recover the features needed in the initialization phase. Second, a map contains more information than just intersections, and this could be used to extract other features such as connectivity.

Acknowledgement

This work is supported in part by a Grant-in-Aid for the Global Center of Excellence for high-Level Global Cooperation for Leading-Edge Platform on Access Spaces from the Ministry of Education, Culture, Sport, Science, and Technology in Japan.

References

1. Wilson, D.C., Lipford, H.R., Carroll, E., Karr, P., Najjar, N.: Charting new ground: modeling user behavior in interactive geovisualization. In: Proc. the 16th ACM GIS (2008)
2. Wood, J., Dykes, J., Slingsby, A., Clarke, K.: Interactive visual exploration of a large spatio-temporal dataset: Reflections on a geovisualization mashup. IEEE Trans. VCG 13, 1176–1183 (2007)
3. Romao, T., Dias, E., Danado, J., Correia, N., Trabuco, A., Santos, C., Santos, R., Nobre, E., Camara, A., Romero, L.: Augmenting reality with geo-referenced information for environmental management. In: Proc. the 10th ACM GIS (2002)
4. Hedley, N.R., Billinghurst, M., Postner, L., May, R., Kato, H.: Explorations in the use of augmented reality for geographic visualization. Teleoperators and Virtual Environments 11, 119–133 (2002)

5. Reitmayr, G., Eade, E., Drummond, T.: Localisation and interaction for augmented maps. In: Proc. ISMAR, pp. 120–129 (2005)
6. Iwamura, M., Nakai, T., Kise, K.: Improvement of retrieval speed and required amount of memory for geometric hashing by combining local invariants. In: Proc. BMVC, pp. 1010–1019 (2007)
7. Lowe, D.G.: Distinctive image features from scale-invariant keypoints. IJCV 60, 91–110 (2004)
8. Bay, H., Tuytelaars, T., Van Gool, L.: SURF: Speeded up robust features. In: Leonardis, A., Bischof, H., Pinz, A. (eds.) ECCV 2006. LNCS, vol. 3951, pp. 404–417. Springer, Heidelberg (2006)
9. Arya, S., Mount, D.M., Netanyahu, N.S., Silverman, R., Wu, A.: An optimal algorithm for approximate nearest neighbor searching fixed dimensions. J. of the ACM 45, 891–923 (1998)
10. Datar, M., Indyk, P., Immorlica, N., Mirrokni, V.S.: Locality-sensitive hashing scheme based on p-stable distributions. In: Proc. SCG, pp. 253–262 (2004)
11. Lamdan, Y., Wolfson, H.: Geometric hashing: A general and efficient model-based recognition scheme. In: Proc. ICCV, pp. 238–249 (1988)
12. Chiang, Y.Y., Knoblock, C.A.: Automatic extraction of road intersection position, connectivity, and orientations from raster maps. In: Proc. ACM GIS (2008)
13. Bocher, E., Leduc, T., Moreau, G., Cortés, F.G.: Gdms: An abstraction layer to enhance spatial data infrastructures usability. In: Agile 2008 (2008)
14. Neubauer, S., Zipf, A.: Suggestions for extending the OGC styled layer descriptor (SLD) specification into 3D – towards visualization rules for 3D city models. In: Proc. UDMS, Stuttgart, Germany (2007)
15. Fischler, M.A., Bolles, R.C.: Random sample consensus: a paradigm for model fitting with applications to image analysis and automated cartography. C. of the ACM 24, 381–395 (1981)
16. Uematsu, Y., Saito, H.: Vision based registration for augmented reality using multi-planes in arbitrary position and pose by moving uncalibrated camera. In: Proc. MIRAGE, pp. 99–1019 (2005)

Estimation of Visually Induced Motion Sickness from Velocity Component of Moving Image

Hiroyasu Ujike

Institute for Human Science and Biomedical Engineering
National Institute of Advanced Industrial Science and Technology
Central 6, 1-1-1 Higashi, Tsukuba 305-8566 Japan
h.ujike@aist.go.jp

Abstract. The purpose of the study is to examine whether the effects of global motion, (GM), on visually induced motion sickness, (VIMS), found with visual stimulus consisting of simple global motion will be applied to the effects of moving images including combination of global motion on VIMS. We, previously, found that velocity, but not temporal frequency component, of GM dominates subjective scores related to VIMS in the experiments presenting simple GM. To achieve the purpose, I made a model to estimate discomfort level of a standard observer during watching a moving image. The model, at the beginning, analyses GM included in the movie; and then, the time-series of velocity data in each element of analyzed GM is compared with the characteristics of simple GM on VIMS for estimating discomfort level. The validity of the model was examined by comparing the estimated discomfort level and actually measured average discomfort level using identical video movie which rather easily inducing VIMS. As a result, the model well estimates the values of subjective score actually measured during observers watching video movies.

1 Introduction

Because of recent evolution of moving image technology, we can enjoy, communicate with, and learn from a variety of real and dynamic moving images. However, we may sometimes suffer from motion-sickness-like symptoms. The symptoms that are obtained when people are watching moving images are called visually induced motion sickness, or VIMS. Actual incident of VIMS was reported by news media in Japan in 2003, in which 36 students of 294 who watched a 20-minutes movie displayed on a large screen were treated at a hospital for a symptom of VIMS [2]. The cause is supposed to be frequent visual motion included in the footages, which was induced by jaggy and dynamic motion of handheld video camera.

There are many factors that possibly affect VIMS. As Lo and So [1] reported, the factors may be categorized in the following three: (i) how moving image is presented, (ii) who watches moving image, and (iii) what is presented as moving image. Among the factors, the trigger of VIMS can be visual motion, especially global motion or optic flow, which belongs to the item (iii) above. The literature actually reported effects of image rotation along each of the three axes, yaw, pitch and roll, on visually

R. Shumaker (Ed.): Virtual and Mixed Reality, LNCS 5622, pp. 136–142, 2009.

induced motion sickness [1, 3, 4, 5]. They reported that: (i) visual roll motion can be the most effective and visual yaw motion can be the least effective, and (ii) a certain range of rotational velocity is effective for VIMS. Moreover, our recent data indicated that the dynamic visual motion can affect temporal variations of subjective discomfort ratings (Ujike, 2007), which can be well associated with VIMS.

The present study investigates whether what we have found about VIMS with simple GM can be applied to discomfort induced by moving images, such as movies. In another word, I examined how global motion velocity affect VIMS from actual moving images. To do this, I developed and examined the validity of a model estimating time-varying discomfort level based on velocity components of GM.

2 Procedures

2.1 Model Development

As a tool to examine how global motion velocity affect VIMS in actual moving images, I tried to find out a mathematical function that connects camera motion velocity of a movie and discomfort subjective ratings that are experimentally obtained with the movie. For the camera motion, we use the term pan, tilt, roll, which correspond to yaw, pitch, roll in global motion, respectively.

To investigate the mathematical function of the model, I used a movic produced by computer graphics, which includes the identical camera motion of a movie provoking an incident of VIMS in Japan, 2003. Input of the model is the camera motion velocity, which can be obtained by analyses of local motion vector (LMV) and global motion vector (GMV) of the movie. Output of the model will be fitted to subjective discomfort rating, which is experimentally obtained every one minute during observer watching a video movie.

As a first step, in this study, instead of using camera motion velocity, we used video frame count that contains camera motion velocity included in the range of provocative to VIMS.

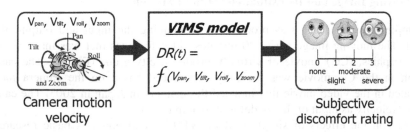

Camera motion velocity   Subjective discomfort rating

Fig. 1. A model connecting camera motion velocity as input and subjective discomfort rating as output

Fig. 2. City scene image presented to observer. The image was textured to inside wall of a sphere, at which center a virtual camera was set to make a movie image. The camera motion applied to the scene is shown in Fig. 3.

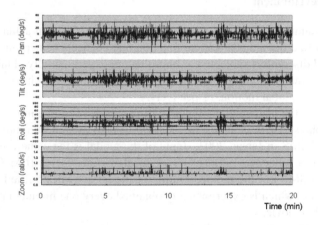

Fig. 3. Camera motion included in the moving image used in the study. The camera motion originated from the global motion analyzed from the movie of the incident in Japan in 2003.

2.2 Moving Image and Its Estimated Camera Motion

A sample moving image was produced for obtaining the input and output of the model. The moving image was a 20-minutes video footages that was made as computer graphics, (CG), movie of virtually produced city scene (Fig. 2). The camera motion in the CG movie was basically reproduced based on the camera motion estimated in the video movie that induced the incident in Japan in 2003. The camera motion velocity as input of the model is shown in Fig. 3.

Based on the effects of simple GM on VIMS found previous basic researches, number of frames that include camera motion velocity within the range provocative to VIMS was obtained and shown in Fig. 4. From this graph, large number of frames appeares at around 7 min and 16 min.

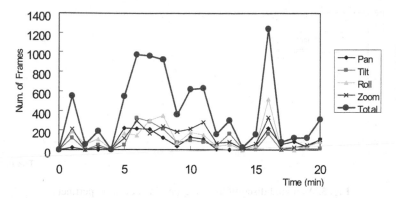

Fig. 4. Number of frames that include camera motion velocity within the range provocative to VIMS found by basic researches

2.3 Measurements of Subjective Discomfort Rating

The visual stimulus was video image that was comprised of five-minutes gray image, 20-minutes video footage described in the former section, and another two-minutes gray image, which were presented in this order. Four different small experimental booths were set up side by side; each of the booths was mostly enclosed by blackout curtain, was set up with a LC display, the chin-, head- and arm-rests, with a viewing distance of 1.0 m. There were two different size of the LC display, 20 inch (or 22.7 x 17.0 deg) and 37 inch (or 34.1 x 25.9 deg). The height of the LC display was adjusted so that the center of the display was the same as vantage point of observers. The experimental room was light-proofed, and the light other than the display was turn off during the experiment.

On one of the armrest, a response box was fixed. The response box has a button and a four-way joystick. The button was pressed when a small red dot was appeared for a short period on a movie image, in order to keep the observers eyes on the display screen. The joystick was used for observers to evaluate discomfort in a four point scale.

Thirty-three adults, aged 19-52 years (mean: 36.2, SD: 8.7; 24 females and 9 males), participated in the study as observers, after giving their informed written consent in accordance with the Helsinki Declaration, and were free to withdraw at any time during the experiment. The study was approved by the Ethics Committee of the National Institute of Advanced Industrial Science and Technology. The observers were naïve as to the purpose of the experiments, and had normal or collected-to-normal visual acuity.

Each experimental session started with asking observers to do Simulator Sickness Questionnaire, and then, observers fix their heads at chin- and head-rests, and their arms on armrests. They watched the video movie for 27 minutes; during this time, observers were asked, every one minute, to report about one of SSQ score, "General discomfort" in four alternatives: "None," "Slight," "Moderate," and "Severe"; they report the score using the four-way joystick. The observers also need to respond by pressing the button on the response box when a small red dot was appeared for a short

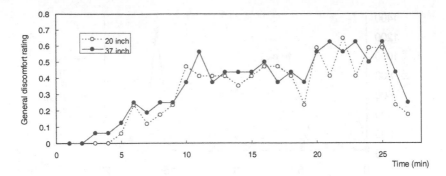

Fig. 5. Averaged discomfort rating obtained in the experiment

period on a movie image; the position and time (three times every minute) of the appearance of the was randomized. Just after finishing watching the video movie, they started, again, SSQ, and then they did it another three times every 15 minutes.

The measurement results are shown in Fig. 5, in which averaged value of general discomfort ratings are plotted against time.

3 Analyses for Modeling

When the frame count based on camera motion velocity data in Fig. 4 and the subjective discomfort rating in Fig. 5, the following two can be pointed out:

1. When the frame count increases, the discomfort rating increases.
2. The rating gradually increases with time, despite no-increment of the frame count.

These points may indicate that there are two different time components of development of VIMS. The first one is transient component, and the second one is accumulated component.

To develop a model estimating discomfort level, I examined whether subjective discomfort rating can be reproduced by weighted average of the frame count data. Considering the two possible components described above, I adopted the followingg mathematical expression. That is, the discomfort rating at time tn:

$$DR(t_n) = FC(t_n) *w_n + FC(t_{n-1}) *w_{n-1} + FC(t_{n-2}) *w_{n-2} + \cdots$$

while,

$$FC(t_n) : \text{Frame count at time } t_n$$

The function was obtained by multiple regression analysis. Because of the collinearity problem (condition index <5.0), we adopted one present and three previous values of frame count.

$$DR(t_n) = \sum_n (FC\ (t_n)\ {}^*w_n + FC(t_{n-1})\ {}^*w_{n-1} + \cdots + FC(t_{n-3})\ {}^*w_{n-3})$$

$$W_n = 0.319,\ W_{n-1} = 0.164,\ W_{n-2} = 0.068,\ W_{n-3} = 0.139$$

The difference between the discomfort ratings and the regression has linear trend:
(Difference) = 16.361xTime - 171.86.

This trend can not be simply explained by the sum of the weighted average of frame count values. This may represent the accumulation effect: after some exposure to visual motion, the rating becomes larger for the same range of camera motion velocity. Then, I combined the multiple-regression function obtained above and the residual liner trend.

Therefore, the discomfort rating can be formulated as follows:

$$DR(t_n) = \sum_n (FC\ (t_n)\ {}^*w_n + FC(t_{n-1})\ {}^*w_{n-1} + \cdots + FC(t_{n-3})\ {}^*w_{n-3} + A{}^*t_n) + B$$

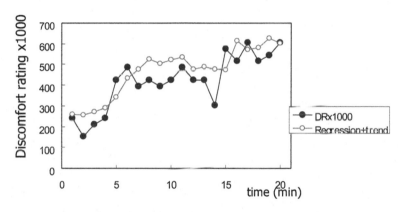

Fig. 6. Comparement of the Discomfort ratings and estimated scores obtained by the model

4 Summary

With multiple regression of camera motion velocity data to subjective discomfort rating, I have developed the model estimating valid values of discomfort level caused by moving images. Moreover, during the development of the model, I found two different temporal components of discomfort related to VIMS.

In the study, discomfort induced by moving images can be mostly determined by the velocity and time period of GM in a moving image.

Acknowledgement

This study was subsidized by JKA through its Promotion funds from KEIRIN RACE and was supported by the Mechanical Social Systems Foundation and the Ministry of Economy, Trade and Industry.

References

1. Lo, W.T., So, R.H.Y.: Cybersickness in the presence of scene rotational movements along different axes. Applied Ergonomics 32(1), 1–14 (2001)
2. Ujike, H., Ukai, K., Nihei, K.: Survey on motion sickness-like symptoms provoked by viewing a video movie during junior high school class. Displays 29, 81–89 (2008)
3. Ujike, H., Yokoi, T., Saida, S.: Effects of virtual body motion on visually-induced motion sickness. In: Proceedings of the 26th Annual International Conference of the IEEE EMBS, pp. 2399–2402 (2004)
4. Ujike, H., Ukai, K., Saida, S.: Effects of motion types and image contents on visually-induced motion sickness. Transactions of the Virtual Reality Society of Japan 9(4), 377–385 (2004)
5. Ujike, H., Kozawa, R., Yokoi, T., Saida, S.: Effects of rotational components of yaw, roll and pitch on visually-induced motion sickness. In: Proceedings of the 11th International Conference on Human-Computer Interaction (2004)

Part II
Design, Development and Evaluation of VR Environments

Part II

Supporting Reusability of VR and AR Interface Elements and Interaction Techniques

Wolfgang Broll and Jan Herling

Collaborative Virtual and Augmented Environments
Fraunhofer FIT
53754 Sankt Augustin, Germany
{Wolfgang.Broll,Jan Herling}@fit.fraunhofer.de

Abstract. In contrast to 2D environments which apply well established user interface elements and generally accepted interaction techniques, VR and AR applications typically provide rather individual and specific realizations. This often leads to inconsistent user interfaces and a long and cumbersome development process. In this paper we show how we extended our approach on modeling VR and AR interface elements and interaction techniques represented by interaction and behavior objects by some simple yet powerful mechanisms: modules, templates, and inheritance. We will also show how specific examples could benefit from that approach.

Keywords: Virtual Reality, Augmented Reality, Mixed Reality, 3D User Interfaces, Multi-modal User Interfaces, Interaction Techniques.

1 Introduction

The majority of the overall effort and time required to develop Virtual Reality (VR) and Augmented Reality (AR) applications is spent for the development of specific user interface elements and underlying interaction techniques [2]. The first issue is also true for many traditional 2D desktop applications, although it is generally easier there due to the availability of appropriate user interface design tools and well established design guidelines (both not available for VR and AR). However, when it comes to interaction techniques, the difference is even more obvious. While in 2D desktop environments applications usually rely on the well known and well established WIMP metaphor, no standard interaction techniques for VR and AR exist [4]. In contrary, they often depend on the specific (3D) input devices available, the user's preferences as well as the specific requirements of the application. Further, most users have no or little experience using VR and AR technology and related devices and interaction techniques. This additionally complicates the user interface design and often results in either rather poor user interfaces or several iterative user trial and update cycles requiring a high implementation effort.

Existing approaches to overcome this problem include user interface description languages such as UIML [1] and InTML [7], authoring tools such as DART [13] or iaTAR [11], scene graph related approaches such as Behavior3D [6] and YABLE [5], and component based approaches such as BodyElectric [10] or Unit [12].

R. Shumaker (Ed.): Virtual and Mixed Reality, LNCS 5622, pp. 145–153, 2009.

Our original approach [4] combines synchronous control and data flows with asynchronous event and network distribution. It is based on a predefined yet extendable set of components representing integral parts of VR/AR interaction techniques and related device handling. Several of these components are combined into a so called interaction or behavior object (aka interactive bit). These objects react to event input from input devices or other objects, or depend on the elapsed time or are synchronized with per frame scene updates.

While the overall approach has already proved to be quite powerful for fast and easy realization of application prototypes, reusability of already realized interaction techniques going beyond simple copy and paste has been a major request by the users.

In this paper we will present our recent extensions allowing for easy and powerful reusability of user interface elements and interaction techniques. In section 2 we will briefly explain the major concepts and components of our original approach. In section 3 we will then present our extensions allowing for an efficient reusability of interaction and behavior objects. In section 4 we will provide some example scenarios to demonstrate how specific user interfaces and interaction techniques can benefit from the approach, before concluding and looking at some future work in section 5.

2 Our Original Approach

In our original approach [4] we used a component based approach allowing for modeling rather than programming 3D user interfaces and interaction techniques by assembling interaction and behavior objects from a set of pre-defined components. These components represent integral parts of autonomous object behavior, user interface elements, and interaction techniques. Generally we distinguish between seven component categories:

- Base components, for receiving and sending events and to query information or register for updates or changes at other system components. This for instance allows for registering for an input device and to manipulate a scene graph object accordingly.
- Execution components are used to influence the control flow and to perform calculations or even more complex behavior by scripting.
- Time-dependent components are invoked independent of user input at specific timestamps or after certain periods, etc.
- Key-value mapping components are in particular used for realizing animations, but also for mapping between different data sets and for autonomous behavior based on state machines.
- Device input calculation components allow for easy calculation as necessary for using 2D devices in 3D interaction techniques and for modifying 3D input data. This includes components for transforming and filtering data.
- Data storage components, allow for temporal (memory) and permanent (file) storage and retrieval of data.
- Networked components, finally provide enhanced versions of other components for better supporting their usage in networked environments allowing for more advanced distributed interaction mechanisms than by replicated scene graphs only.

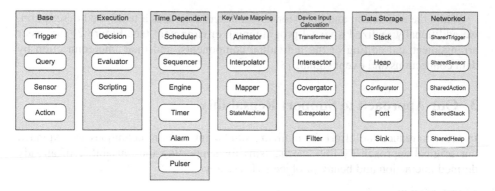

Fig. 1. Component hierarchy for assembling interaction and behavior objects

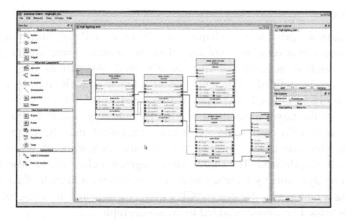

Fig. 2. Visual programming environment for defining interaction and behavior objects

Figure 1 provides an overview of the currently supported components.

Each interaction and behavior object may use an arbitrary number of components of each type, which are connected by a signal/slot mechanism. This mechanism allows us to transfer data values (such as integers, floats, strings, vectors, matrices, etc.) between the individual components. In order to specify the control flow for the execution of the individual components, event signals are used (also specified by the signal/slot mechanism). However, these mechanisms apply for the internal communication between the individual components of a single object only. For external communication, i.e. access to input and output devices, scene graph objects, or services such as object picking or collision detection, an asynchronous event based mechanism is used. Thus, it allows for easy application of the approach to networked/distributed environments, where events will need some time to be transmitted. This event based mechanism is also used for communication between different interaction and behavior objects.

While the interaction and behavior object description uses a text based description, we additionally realized a visual programming environment (see Figure 2) for easier arrangement and editing of the individual components, and their interconnection by data connections and event signals [3].

3   Our Approach to Support Reusability

In order to reduce the effort for realizing similar interaction techniques we extended our original approach by four mechanisms for supporting the reusability of already defined interaction and behavior objects. These are:

- Instantiation
- Templates
- Modules
- Inheritance

By instantiation we provide a mechanism which allows for easy attachment of interaction techniques to several user interface elements at once. Therefore a master object is defined, which is actually not immediately used. As part of the definition an attachment rule is defined. Whenever the attachment rule is fulfilled, a instance (copy) of the object defined is created and attached to the objects specified. As the specification of the target attachment is quite flexible (e.g. specifying specific scene graph objects by wild cards) and the actual attachment may be either explicit or implicit (e.g. whenever a new object is created), this mechanism allows for easy reuse of elements already defined. The short coding fragment below shows how an object is specified to be dynamically attached to objects in a certain branch of an X3D scene graph having a name with the prefix "CHAIR". The attachment is re-evaluated each time a file is loaded or a node is added to the scenegraph.

```
Behavior {
    targets XSG:X3D::MY_ROOM/FURNITURE/CHAIR*
    attachment [LOAD_FILE, ADD_NODE]
...
// definition of individual components follows here
Sensor GRAB {
    ...
}

Action MOVE {
    targets .   // i.e. the local entity the
                // behavior is attached to
    ...}
```

Further, we developed two template mechanisms: one for entire interaction and behavior objects and one for individual components. The first one allows for specifying a full object with additional parameters applied during initialization. Upon instantiation the parameters are then used to create the actual object. The individual components of such a template are invisible and cannot be accessed directly within the instantiated object. A simple example would be a behavior simulating the movement caused by a parabolic flight. As a parameter you may specify the velocity (direction and amount).

The second template mechanism applies to individual components. A component template is always based on one or several already existing components (or component templates). In addition to parameters a component template has to define the data and control flow interfaces of the new template component. Those are mapped to the corresponding data and signal slots of the underlying sub-components. This allows us to combine several components into a new component template, which then may be used similar to built-in components.

Further, our approach supports a mechanism for realizing interface and interaction technique modules. It may be used to include previously defined interaction and behavior objects or templates. It allows for the provision of frequently used interaction and interface modules (e.g. for rigid 3D manipulation such as positioning and rotating, support for tangible user interface elements, or individual navigation styles for specific types of input devices).

Finally we provide an inheritance mechanism. It allows us for the reuse of already defined behaviors object, enabling the rapid construction of new objects with rather small modifications (either replacing parts of their behavior or by applying additional features). For example, a standard object behavior which highlights a scene graph objects upon selection can be easily modified and extend to use a color frame and a sound feedback instead, while the underlying selection mechanism is kept). Inheritance applies during instantiation of an object and applies to any part of its definition.

A big advantage of the four approaches presented is their ability to be combined and even nested arbitrarily.

4 Example Scenarios

In this section we would like to present and discuss some example scenarios. In particular we will show how those examples benefited from the mechanisms introduced in this paper.

4.1 Autonomous Behavior

In this little demo example we realized an arena containing a configurable yet arbitrary number of autonomous robots. Each robots goal is to explore the given arena and to kill as many other robots as possible. The entire demonstration scenario is based on two 3D files (one containing the geometry of the arena and one for the geometry of a robot), three behavior objects (in a single file) and a couple of sound files representing the individual activities of the robots. The three behavior objects are:

- One defined as template, where the actual instance used allows for specifying the number of robots and the size and location of the area for their potential initial starting position. This one will include the robot file as many times as specified, giving each of them an individual name (ROBOT1 ... ROBOTn) and define an arbitrary starting position for each robot.

- One for registering the virtual 3D scene with the tracked marker on the table. This is a standard marker tracking behavior which is loaded from an appropriate module using the include mechanism.
- One for the actual behavior of the individual robot. Its main component is a *State-Machine* (scan, fire, cruise, explode, idle) activating and deactivating individual tests (i.e. picking and/or collision detection) and animations. The behavior object is defined as master allowing for an automatic instantiation and attachment of an individual copy to each robot's geometry upon creation.

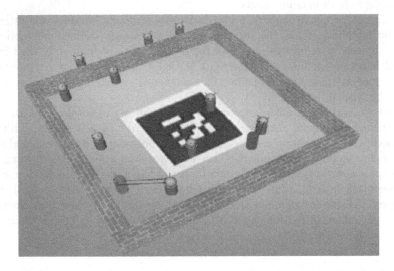

Fig. 3. Demo application showing autonomous robots trying to destroy each other

4.2 Application Specific Interaction Styles

TimeWarp [8] – an application showcase of the integrated project IPCity [9] - is a location-based Mixed Reality game where the players have to solve challenges in different locations distributed throughout the old part of Cologne. In addition to enhancing the real environment by the virtual challenges, the game takes the players to different epochs in the history of the city by augmenting the real environment visually and acoustically. Players use either head-mounted optical see-through displays or handheld ultra mobile PCs applying video see-through AR. While the individual challenges are quite different regarding their content, the interaction techniques for selecting and manipulating content are shared by all challenges. As each challenge typically is realized independently (even by different developers or game designers), it was important to ensure that the interaction techniques used are independent of the individual challenge. For that reason an interaction library module was created and included in each challenge implementation. This also ensured that changes to the interaction techniques apply to all challenges automatically. Specifically the reusability mechanisms also allowed us to support different flavors of the interaction techniques depending on the devices used. While for head-mounted displays we relied

Fig. 4. A virtual version of the famous Roman Dionysus mosaic in Cologne was modified and had to be re-arranged to represent the original figures by the players

on ray-based picking along the viewing direction in the center of the current view, ray-based picking on the handheld devices providing a touch screen was more flexible as objects could be directly selected by the players using their fingers. Thus, we just inherited and extended the original ray-based mechanism, adding the inherited interaction technique to the module.

Additional reusability mechanisms were applied to realize individual challenges. The challenge to reconstruct the original tiles of the famous Roman Dionysus mosaic (see Figure 4) consists of nine interactive tiles. Each of them may be turned by 180° based on user interaction. While each tile seems to consist of two faces, there are actually three different texture applied to each tile in a sequence. Thus, the behavior object for turning a tile and replacing the textures from a set uses the template mechanism to specify the individual texture as parameters.

4.3 Guided Tour

Another application we realized using the mechanisms presented was a guided tour for a stereoscopic 3D presentation of a reconstruction of the Bamiyan Buddha statues in Afghanistan for a museum (see figure 5). The camera was animated smoothly flying from one point of interest to the next one. This was the standard mode in the museum. For guided tours however, there was a SpaceTraveler as navigation device. By that, a guide could interrupt the animated camera at any point and continue individual navigation. The automatic animation of the camera would resume after a certain time of inactivity, flying smoothly to the next POI in line.

Here, the SpaceTraveler navigation is loaded from a navigation module containing navigation support for various input devices as template. The default 6-DOF

Fig. 5. Guided tour and interactive navigation for a presentation of the destroyed Bamiyan Buddha statues in the Gandhara region of Afghanistan

navigation provided by the device is reduced to 5-DOF by disabling the roll axis for easier use by occasional users, since user tests showed that they otherwise get easily lost in the scene. This was done by inheriting from the template a modified behavior template, thus combining the template and the inheritance mechanism.

5 Conclusion and Future Work

In this paper we introduced our approach on supporting the reusability of interaction techniques and user interface elements in VR and AR environments. We showed how the approach overcomes the limitations of existing approaches in respect to flexibility, scalability, and usability.

Beside the detailed introduction of the mechanisms applied, we presented several examples from ongoing projects, showing the actual feasibility of the individual mechanisms and the usability of the overall approach.

In our future work we will further extend the interface and interaction libraries of predefined behavior templates and base classes, reflecting all major 3D interaction techniques and interfaces. We further intend to combine this with a tutorial on best practice examples for easier use by new interface developers and in particular for using the approach for teaching VR and AR user interface classes.

Acknowledgments

The authors thank their colleagues at the Collaborative Virtual and Augmented Environments Department at Fraunhofer FIT for their comments and contributions. Special thanks to our colleagues Lisa Blum for her work on the visual programming environment, Richard Wetzel for realizing the TimeWarp Dionysus mosaic challenge and Robert Menzel who realized the Gandhara guided tour. They further wish to thank their project partners of the IPCity project for their ideas, cooperation, and their support. IPCity (FP6-2004-IST-4-27571) is partially funded by the European Commission as part of the 6th Framework.

References

1. Abrams, M., Phanouriou, C., Batongbacal, A.L., Williams, S.M., Shuster, J.E.: UIML: An Appliance-Independent XML User Interface Language. In: Proceedings of the Eighth International World Wide Web Conference, pp. 1695–1708. Elsevier, Toronto, Canada (1999)
2. Bowman, D.A., Kruijff, E., LaViola, J.J., Poupyrev, I.: 3D User Interfaces: Theory and Practice. Addison-Wesley, Boston (2004)
3. Broll, W., Herling, J., Blum, L.: Interactive Bits: Prototyping of Mixed Reality Applications and Interaction Techniques through Visual Programming. In: Proc. of the 3rd IEEE International Symposium on 3D User Interfaces 2008 (IEEE 3DUI 2008), pp. 109–115. IEEE Computer Society, Los Alamitos (2008)
4. Broll, W., Lindt, I., Ohlenburg, J., Herbst, I., Wittkämper, M., Novotny, T.: An Infrastructure for Realizing Custom-Tailored Augmented Reality User Interfaces. IEEE Transactions on Visualization and Computer Graphics 11(6), 722–733 (2006)
5. Burrows, T., England, E.: YABLE—yet another behaviour language. In: Proceedings of the Tenth international Conference on 3D Web Technology, Web3D 2005, Bangor, United Kingdom, March 29-April 01, 2005, pp. 65–73. ACM, New York (2005)
6. Dachselt, R., Rukzio, E.: Behavior3D: an XML-based framework for 3D graphics behavior. In: Proceeding of the Eighth international Conference on 3D Web Technology, Web3D 2003, Saint Malo, France, March 9-12, 2003, p. 101. ACM, New York (2003)
7. Figueroa, P., Green, M., Hoover, H.J.: InTml: a description language for VR applications. In: Proceeding of the Seventh international Conference on 3D Web Technology, Web3D 2002, Tempe, Arizona, USA, February 24-28, 2002, pp. 53–58. ACM, New York (2002)
8. Herbst, I., Braun, A., McCall, R., Broll, W.: TimeWarp: interactive time travel with a mobile mixed reality game. In: Proceedings of the 10th international Conference on Human Computer interaction with Mobile Devices and Services, MobileHCI 2008, Amsterdam, The Netherlands, September 2-5, 2008, pp. 235–244. ACM, New York (2008)
9. IPCity – Integrated Project on Interaction and Presence in Urban Environments, http://www.ipcity.eu
10. Lanier, J., Grimaud, J.-J., Harvill, Y., Lasko-Harvill, A., Blanchard, C., Oberman, M., Teitel, M.: Method and system for generating objects for a multi-person virtual world using data flow networks. United States Patent 5588139 (1993)
11. Lee, G.A., Nelles, C., Billinghurst, M., Kim, G.J.: Immersive Authoring of Tangible Augmented Reality Applications. In: Proceedings of the Third IEEE and ACM international Symposium on Mixed and Augmented Reality (ISMAR 2004), November 2-5, 2004, pp. 172–181. IEEE Computer Society, Los Alamitos (2004)
12. Olwal, A., Feiner, F.: Unit: modular development of distributed interaction techniques for highly interactive user interfaces. In: Spencer, S.N. (ed.) Proceedings of the 2nd international Conference on Computer Graphics and interactive Techniques in Australasia and South East Asia, GRAPHITE 2004, Singapore, June 15-18, 2004, pp. 131–138. ACM, New York (2004)
13. MacIntyre, B., Gandy, M., Dow, S., Bolter, J.D.: DART: a toolkit for rapid design exploration of augmented reality experiences. In: Proceedings of the 17th Annual ACM Symposium on User interface Software and Technology, UIST 2004, Santa Fe, NM, USA, October 24-27, 2004, pp. 197–206. ACM, New York (2004)

Development of 3D Avatars for Professional Education

Miglena Dontschewa, Andreas Künz, and Sabahat Kovanci

Vorarlberg University of Applied Sciences, UCT Research, Dornbirn, Austria
miglena.dontschewa@fhv.at, andreas.kuenz@fhv.at

Abstract. This article covers avatars as anthropomorphic tutors in learning processes within teaching and learning settings. Starting points and objectives are presented, as well as the requirements for the creation, the environment and the tools. The article focuses on the latter, the media-synergetic problems the different tools pose, and possible solutions to those problems.

1 Introduction: Avatars in Education

For the cognitive-emotional processing of information vital for learning, nonverbal impulses are of utmost importance. Such impulses are triggered by the form and modality of the communicating parties' gestural and mimic behavior. This is because nonverbal behavior has a greater impact on the regulation of relationships than verbal behavior. Thus some instructors are able to enhance the learning outcome by their demeanour alone. Others, while commanding the same expertise, achieve much lesser results - or even create counterproductive effects - just by the way they behave. In the design of human-machine-interaction this fact has played an important role from the beginning. Early on there have been attempts to design avatars capable of emulating the function of nonverbal behavior in the process of reception and storage of knowledge (MIT Media Lab, plus the universities Philadelphia, Northwestern and Stanford; in Germany the „Virtual Human Project").

However, multimedia specialists found in learning projects that the attempted implementations met with refusal by the users so that they did not meet expectations. The avatars used – e.g. the "assistants" used in commercial office systems – never rate better than "annoying gimmick".

Those hitherto disappointing results can be ascribed to the fact that the development work had almost exclusively been driven by engineers. Accordingly their focus was on the solution of (certainly non-trivial) technical problems like photorealistic renderings or optimizations of motion capture techniques. This led to the construction of avatars before it had been determined, which specific attributes of complex nonverbal behavior are responsible for cognitive and emotional reactions observed, which of those are supportive and which are disruptive factors for the learning process.

This approach had a particularly negative effect on the creation of the anthropomorphic avatars that are vital to learning processes. This is vividly demonstrated in the grave problem recently discussed under the label "Uncanny Valley".

If we are to successfully emulate the nonverbal behavioral patterns relevant to the information processing of the human brain, we must first develop profound knowledge of this centrally important component of communications behavior. In

R. Shumaker (Ed.): Virtual and Mixed Reality, LNCS 5622, pp. 154–158, 2009.

particular, we must learn which cognitive and emotional effects are triggered in the recipients by specific nonverbal behavioral patterns.

Only on the basis of this knowledge can we create avatars in Web 2.0 environments with two important properties: Firstly, to be able to keep a learner's attention and concentration on the learning matter, secondly, to kindle a learner's desire to learn, thus creating the precondition for their lasting and dedicated engagement with the learning matter.

2 Presentation of the Suitable Data Streams and Tools

2.1 Video

The sequences to be learned are recorded as a basis for the synthetic scenes that will be created. Naturally, the videos have to fulfil several requirements to serve appropriately. Primarily they have to show clearly and distinctly the motions of the nurse while executing certain operations. Close-ups of specific procedures performed on the patient are to be recorded in detail, using zooms and other video techniques. The video material serves both as general information and for the acquisition of 2D motion data of the nurse. That information is input in a special tool for rendering 3D motion data.

2.2 Tool to Generate 2D/3D Motion Data

The proprietary tool can show the videos in combination with a virtual stick-figure. Using that stick-figure, the operator can transfer the movement of the nurse seen on the video frame by frame to 3D space. To be as productive as possible the tool has to focus on the main task – the transformation of human motion from video sequences to three dimensional representations of the human skeleton. Thus a dataset of the 3D motion for use in a 3D animation system is created. The data has to be optimized and

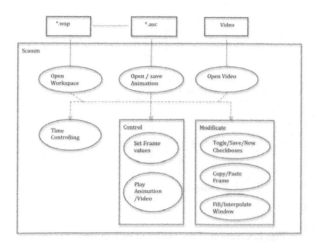

Fig. 1. Schematic view of the 2D/3D-transformation tool

structured to export it in a format that 3D applications can understand (see also point 2.3 and 3). In Figure 1 the combination of workspace data (*.wsp), rotational data of joints (*.asc) and the video-source is shown in a schematic view.

2.3 3D Computer Animation System

The project uses the well-known animation system Autodesk Maya to visualize the avatars. Maya works with *.ma files that contain all necessary information for the creation of a 3D computer animation. It is also possible to work with *.anim files, that predominantly contain the motion data of joints. It is necessary to develop adequate conversion tools and interfaces as a part of the discussed project. Their task is the transfer of the 3D motion data generated from the real life videos to the Maya system for creation of the desired learning sequences in Maya.

Computer animations are created by first modelling the characters and objects for the learning sequences as three dimensional geometric shapes, and then rigging and preparing them for animation.

Rigging is the construction of a skeleton with bones and joints and setting it up for animation. The properties of the rig define how the elements of a mesh (a polygon lattice) can be moved. Quite often the construction is oriented along the properties of a real skeleton, e.g. emulating a real thighbone or a real knee joint.

After the creation of the skeleton, the polygon mesh can be linked to it (skin binding). Often a further work step – called skinning – is required, eliminating the imperfections which can occur while linking mesh and bones.

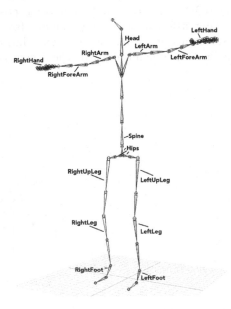

Fig. 2. Creation of the skeleton with correct naming

With the optimized motion data (see point 2.2) the motion of the characters can be controlled in detail. Additional visualization effects (e.g. illumination, camera moves) are added in the 3D computer animation system. In addition to Autodesk Maya the software Motion Builder will be used here. The character has to look in the direction of the positive z-axis and be in the T-stance: the avatar stretches its arms in a straight angle of 90°. Legs are close together (Figure 2). The FBX-plugin from Autodesk is used to interchange the data between Maya and Motion Builder.

3 Software Technologies

The following technologies are utilized:

- Programming language: C++
- Graphic user interface: QT V4.3.3
- 3D graphics engine: OpenGL
- Framework: Eclipse

The tool for generating 2D/3D motion data generates the data for the skeleton from a video sequence. The motions in the video are transferred to the avatar. Variations of these motions can be created within the tool.

The motion data must be importable to commercial animation software programs to visualise, shade and render the avatars appropriately. The imported data is applied to a skeleton. At this point the 3D-modeled surrounding can be added and the motion edited using commercial software. The tool for generating 2D/3D motion data is supposed to show the following features:

- Platform independence
- Efficiency
- Extensibility
- Maintainability
- User friendliness

Platform independence: Platform independence is exceptionally important, because there are plans to provide the software as a download on the internet so that several people around the world can transform the 2D video data to 3D rotational data. Therefore it is absolutely necessary to make the software available for users of all systems. The platform independence was achieved by the use of the GUI-library QT.

QT is a C++-library for platform independent programming of graphic user interfaces. There are interfaces to various programming languages.

Efficiency, Extensibility, Maintainability: The use of an object oriented programming language largely ensures efficiency, extensibility and maintainability of the software.

Two technologies were under consideration as the object oriented programming language: Java and C++.

Research showed that C++ is the best choice for the project because the use of OpenGL is not common in java programming and requires the special Java library JOGL. This turned out to be a particular disadvantage.

4 Objectives

The project includes and optimizes the following, among others:

- The collection and analysis of tools and appliances available for creating and appropriately animating 3D objects for use in teaching and learning scenarios in the area of nursery education.
- Development of a tool or a procedure for determining empirically which nonverbal interaction patterns help to foster an enduring interest in the use of web based teaching/learning scenarios.
- Use of the findings generated with the above mentioned tool for developing an avatar with a nonverbal behavior that is adjusted to the reception processes of users in a way that activates learning processes and supports them.

References

1. Dontschewa, M., Bolter, R., Kempter, G., Weidmann, K.-H., Künz, A.: Developments in the area of the virtual reality at the User Centered Technologies Research Institute, September 15-19, 2004, Ohrid, Macedonia (2004)
2. Dontschewa, M., Kempter, G., Künz, A., Marinov, M., Weidmann, K.-H.: Using Sensors from a Motion Capturing System for Morphological Movement Examination and Visualization Control. In: Proc. 13th International Scientific and Applied Science Conference - ELECTRONICS 2004, Sozopol, Bulgaria, September 22-24, 2004, pp. 88–93 (2004)
3. Dontschewa, M., Kempter, G., Weidmann, K.-H., Marinov, M.: Immersion research in the area of Virtual Reality at the User Centered Technologies Research Institute. In: HCI 2005, Las Vegas, USA, July 12-17 (2005)
4. Künz, A., Dontschewa, M., Weber, H.: Low Cost-Interactivity für 3D-Computeranimation mit Computerspiel-Engines, University of Applied Sciences Vorarlberg uDay V, Dornbirn, Austria (May 11, 2007)
5. Kempter, G.: Das Bild vom Anderen. Skriptanimation als Methode zur Untersuchung spontaner Attributionsprozesse, PABST, Germany (1999)
6. Trolltech (2009), http://doc.trolltech.com/4.3/aboutqt.html (February 20, 2009)

Rapidly Prototyping Marker Based Tangible User Interfaces

Maribeth Gandy[1], Brian Jones[1], Scott Robertson[1],
Tiffany O'Quinn[1], and Amos Johnson[2]

[1] Interactive Media Technology Center, Georgia Institute of Technology
{maribeth,brian,scott,tiffany}@imtc.gatech.edu
[2] Computer Science Department, Morehouse College
ajohnson@morehouse.edu

Abstract. Tangible user interfaces (TUIs) can create engaging and useful interactive systems. However, along with the power of these interfaces comes challenges; they are often so specialized and novel that building a TUI system involves working at a low level with custom hardware and software. As a result the community of people that are capable of creating TUIs is limited. With this project we aim to make a particular class of TUIs accessible to a broader range of designers and HCI researchers by exposing TUI specific tools in a mixed-reality rapid prototyping environment know as DART (The Designer's Augmented Reality Toolkit). In this paper we discuss the creation of a system for rapidly prototyping marker based tangible user interfaces. These prototyping tools were then used to create a set of TUI-based applications with the goal of raising students' interest in science via an exploration of fine art concepts.

Keywords: Tangible User Interfaces, rapid prototyping, mixed reality, toolkits.

1 Introduction

Tangible User Interfaces (TUIs) are a promising avenue for HCI research and a diverse array of TUI projects have been developed over the past fifteen years [6]. However, along with the unique power of these interfaces comes a drawback; they are often so specialized and novel that building a TUI system often involves working from scratch with custom hardware and software. As a result the community of people that are capable of creating TUIs is limited and the ability to iterate, test, and deploy them is also restricted. There has been considerable interest in the development of TUI toolkits that aid in the rapid prototyping and deployment of TUI systems [9], and there is still need for work in this domain. In particular there is a need for toolkits that enable TUI development by people without access to specialized hardware or low level programming expertise.

In this project we aim to make a particular class of TUIs accessible to a broader range of designers and HCI researchers by exposing TUI specific tools in a mixed-reality (MR) rapid prototyping environment know as DART (The Designer's Augmented Reality Toolkit). DART exposes a variety of tracking and MR prototyping services (e.g. "Wizard of Oz" support) that can be incorporated in standard Adobe Director applications; thus providing a mature rapid prototyping environment for

R. Shumaker (Ed.): Virtual and Mixed Reality, LNCS 5622, pp. 159–168, 2009.

augmented reality (AR). This tool provided a starting point for our work which was to identify the additional components that were needed to support the creation of TUIs with DART and to incorporate them into a toolkit we refer to as DART-TUI. In this paper we discuss the creation of this system for rapidly prototyping marker based tangible user interfaces. The resulting tool (DART-TUI) was then used as part of an initiative to create novel and engaging interactive experiences for students with the goal of increasing their interest in science via an exploration of fine art concepts.

In the following sections we will discuss further the need for this type of tool and the underlying architecture of DART. We will examine the similarities and differences between the needs for AR and TUI prototyping tools. Then we will discuss in detail the additional components we created for DART that supports TUI development. Lastly we will discuss the first application we have created with our toolkit; a suite of art-themed applications that let students use tangible interfaces to have a constructivist learning experience to explore scientific concepts such as optics and fractals.

2 Background

Many unique and inspired TUIs have been developed over the years; ranging from a marble based music composition tool [2], to Topobo, a robot construction kit [13], to Designer's Outpost which allows web designers to layout sites via post-it notes [8], to a physical system for developing multimedia narratives [11]. As TUIs these systems are defined by the fact that the user sends input and (possibly) receives output through physical objects. Therefore a key component of a TUI system is the ability to track various types of objects such as marbles [2], drinking glasses [16] and ping pong balls [7]. In the systems mentioned above the tracking is often achieved via RF tags placed on the objects [11] (or magnetic switches [13]) and surfaces that are capable of sensing them. Computer vision [8] and acoustics [7] based systems are also used. While these approaches provide a robust and unobtrusive solution, working with such technologies requires both expertise and resources that may not be available to everyone wanting to experiment with TUIs and the resulting systems are hard to duplicate and move.

However for over a decade AR researchers have been utilizing an open source toolkit that uses paper based markers for tracking, called the ARToolkit [5]. The ARToolkit can also be used as the method of tracking tangible objects in a TUI. Of course, there are drawbacks to the use of visual markers for this task. The markers must remain in view of the camera and the user may have a hard time detecting when they are not. A user's hand occluding part of the marker will stop the object from being tracked. Fast movement of the markers will affect the tracking as will light levels. There are limitations on the range of motion (particularly rotation) for an object since the entire marker must always be in view. Lastly having to place a relatively large marker on an object can detract from its aesthetic qualities and its affordances for manipulation. However, based on our experience with our science education application we feel that these drawbacks can be accounted for in the design of the TUI and that the advantages (inexpensive, easy to deploy and replicate) outweigh these disadvantages. Therefore in DART-TUI we leverage this simple tracking mechanism, which can be used for cheap and easy prototyping.

From the beginning, researchers have designed TUIs that utilize the tabletop paradigm. From Wellner's DigitalDesk [15] to table top tangible games such as fish pong [16], many TUI systems have been based on the user interacting with objects placed on a table-top surface. While TUIs can come in other forms (like Topobo) the tabletop interface is a common one and is amenable to the marker based tracking we were leveraging in DART-TUI .Therefore our components are specifically crafted for this table-top TUI approach.

This is not the first project to tackle the concept of TUI prototyping. For years researchers working in the TUI domain have recognized the need for prototyping tools. In fact DART was first discussed as a platform for TUI extensions at Pervasive Computing 2004 [3]. There is not room in this paper to catalog the variety of projects that have looked at the taxonomy of tangible interactions [14], user definable TUIs [12], and hardware prototyping [4] for example. However one toolkit is of particular interest in the context of DART-TUI. Klemmer's Papier-Mache is a tool with some similarities to DART but originally created with TUIs in mind [9]. Papier-Mache provides rapid prototyping services including Wizard of Oz functionality and supports an array of tracking and identification technologies. And the designer is able to swap out technologies throughout the design process (e.g. prototyping with bar codes and deployment with RFID).

3 DART

DART is a set of tools added onto Adobe (formerly Macromedia) Director that allows designers and non-technologists to rapidly prototype augmented reality (AR) applications [10]. DART (and DART-TUI) applications are created with "Actors" which are any sort of asset in the application (e.g. 3D object, audio clip, billboarded texture etc.) or physical object the user is interacting with. These Actors can be linked directly or indirectly to "Trackers" which are visual markers, a VRPN device, or a phidget sensor. "Cues" are used to generate events triggered by occurrences such as the appearance of a visual marker, two Actors within a specified proximity, the pressing of a button etc. "Actions" are what happen as a result of Cues (e.g. when a marker comes into view an audio clip is played or a virtual Actor becomes visible in the scene). In section 5 we will discuss how DART-TUI utilizes modified versions of these basic components for TUI specific functionality.

All the behaviors that are provided with Director (and are part of DART) are written in Lingo and editable by the user. Therefore a common approach is for developers to modify the standard behaviors while also writing their own from scratch. This is key to understanding the design of DART-TUI. We have created a suite of TUI specific scripts, but some of them were crafted for the specific needs of our initial application. This is not a shortcoming of the toolkit but rather is the standard way of working with Director. We provide a set of tools that may be useful "out of the box" to TUI designers however these scripts can be easily modified or built upon. In fact this process of building up a library of TUI components is an effective way of providing TUI tools. As discussed previously TUIs come in many different forms and it would be impossible to anticipate every component a TUI designer would need. The attempt to do so would either result in an overly complicated generalized system or one that is only of use in a particular type of application. Instead DART-TUI can evolve over time based on the needs of the user.

4 Requirements: AR vs. TUI

There are many similarities between the requirements of AR and TUI applications. Both require some sort of tracking technology. In AR applications the goal is to track the position of the user's eye so that virtual 3D graphics can be rendered such that they are properly registered with the physical world [1]. In AR applications that use marker tracking the goal is usually to register 3D content at the location of the markers. In TUIs the tracking needs are more focused on monitoring the position and orientation of the tangible objects the user is interacting with rather than the user's head/eye. While all the AR specific functionality of DART intended for head tracking and registering 3D graphics is still available to TUI developers our goal in with the DART-TUI additions was to provide components that fit with the "trackable objects" paradigm and make it easy for TUI developers to define the relationships between object location and application input. By using marker based tracking of objects this tool then allows designers to rapidly prototype a TUI by simply printing out a few markers and attaching them to the object they wish to track. The system then uses a webcam to track their positions. Of course this system restricts the types of TUIs that can be prototyped, but still supports a wide variety of interfaces. And marker tracking can be switched out for more sophisticated sensors in the DART-TUI application at any time.

In AR applications the output and rendering are typically focused on presenting 3D graphics overlaid on the live video stream. The display modalities and types of content presentation in TUIs are much more varied. Therefore DART-TUI decouples the tracking and presentation of content and allows the developer to more easily map tracker location to functions such as the movement of a 2D pointer.

Similarly since registration is often the goal in AR there are limits on the types of modifications you can make to tracker data that would impact the ability of the system to tightly link the graphics to physical objects. TUIs however do not have this constraint. Therefore the DART-TUI components let the designer apply transformations to the data such as smoothing so as to make the interactions more fluid for the user.

5 The DART-TUI Toolkit

Our prototyping system supports the creation of TUIs that have two main components: physical objects that will be manipulated by the user and a work area in which the user will interact with the objects. Contained within DART-TUI are behaviors that allow the designer to define the work area, the objects, and the application's response to object manipulation.

The first step in designing a TUI is defining the workspace in which a user will interact. One approach for defining a space is to use a book paradigm. The pages can have text, illustrations, and other guides printed on them but these pages also act as the trigger to expose a particular activity or interaction set to the user. Therefore we created the "BookTracker" behavior which is used to create a workspace that consists of one or more "pages"; each page has printed on it a unique marker. With the Book-Tracker it is up to the designer to define what the cue generated by the appearance of a page will trigger. In our applications we use the cue to advance the application to a new exercise. An advantage of using the book workspace is that since we wanted to create applications that could be replicated and moved (e.g. our science education app was to be deployed in various student computer labs) this approach lets us define a workspace without delicate calibration or setup. When using the BookTracker the designer can have all the other trackers in the application report their position and orientation relative to the page marker, therefore the correspondence between movements of the objects and input to the system will remain constant no matter the angle, position, or distance of the page relative to the webcam. The other advantage of the book workspace is that it supports natural navigation through an experience (e.g. flipping to another page to choose another exercise, moving back and forth between pages to review previous information) and allows for content physically printed on the page to enhance the tangible feel of the experience and supports the users' interactions with the objects.

The "TableTracker" is a behavior that is used to track any number of physical objects within the work space. The TableTracker has all the capabilities of the original "LiveTracker" from DART (see [10] for more detail), but with some TUI specific features. First, as mentioned previously, the coordinates of the physical objects are reported relative to the marker on the work area page so that the designer can rely on the objects reporting within a set range of values regardless of how the book/work area is placed under the camera. Unlike AR applications, TUI designers may often wish to ignore parts of the tracker information so as to limit the degrees of freedom of the physical objects. In our science education application it was common that for a particular activity we would simply need the position of an object; using rotation data only made the interaction more confusing to the user. Therefore the TableTracker lets the designer indicate which degrees of freedom she wishes to be reported by the system. The tracker data can also be passed through a filter component(s). Marker tracking often results in constant small pose estimate errors that manifest as jittering of the registered objects in AR. This jittering was less acceptable in a TUI where movements of the objects were transformed and then used to control various types of 2D and 3D interfaces. Therefore we created a "smooth" component that minimized these tracker errors. This type of filtering would be unacceptable in an AR system where the result would be a loss of registration between the marker and the 3D object, but it was very useful for TUI development. These filters are simply treated as trackers themselves that consume live tracker data and then pass it on to subscribers transparently. It is therefore possible to combine several filters together seamlessly. We created "smooth" and "delay" trackers to modify our TUI tracker data, but developers can easily create their own filters by using these basic scripts as templates.

For TUI control, the designer needs additional tools to transform the raw tracking information into meaningful control data for the application; the interface or application that is ultimately affected by the user's manipulation of the tangible objects does not have the natural correspondence between marker pose and virtual object rendering that an AR application has (in fact our science application uses both 2D and 3D environments as the output). In DART-TUI once the physical object information has been filtered it can be passed on to a variety of "controllers" that are fed into the interface of the designer's choice. It was important to build them with an architecture that makes it easy for designers to create controllers of their own since as previously discussed a characteristic of TUIs is the unique mappings between object interaction and application response. For example, in our application we created controllers that would transform the movement of objects into a change in camera field-of-view in a 3D scene, navigation of the virtual camera through a 3D scene, movement of a 2D pointer, rotation of a 3D object, and intensity of a light in a 3D scene among others.

Due to the structure of DART it is quite easy for a designer to add their own controllers to the existing set. A controller simply subscribes to a tracker (which may in fact be a filtered version of a live tracker) and, if needed, applies a "tracker specific transform" which maps the coordinates reported by the tracker into the coordinate system appropriate for this controller's function (e.g. a controller that controls the movement of a 2D point on the screen projects the reported points into 2D screen coordinates). The controller then has a set of properties related to its specific function. For example the Camera Controller that lets the user dolly a camera in a 3D scene asks the designer for the amount of time it should take the virtual camera to reach the next point. The controller will then interpolate between the current camera position and the new position so as to further smooth the movement in the world and to make the camera movements pleasing even if the user picks up a marker and moves it to another location. There is also a property that specifies whether the camera should always point at the origin or simply maintain its original orientation. The Rotation Controller which is used to rotate a 3D object lets the designer specify which actor to apply the rotation to and min/max angles of rotation for the 3 axes.

6 The STEM Application

Our first application created with DART-TUI presents students with a suite of activities which aim to teach them about science topics via art lessons (e.g. light, perspective, and fractal math). This work was sponsored via an NSF project led by Morehouse College that is studying the efficacy of using simulation environments that include artistic elements to enhance Science, Technology, Engineering and Mathematics (STEM) curricula at the high school level. An emphasis on creativity and passion was intended as an antidote to negative student attitudes about these fields.

To use the STEM application the student sits in front of a desktop computer; instead of a keyboard or mouse there is a physical book in front of her and a webcam is placed on the monitor such that is has a view of the book from above. The student accesses the activities by paging through the physical book (see Fig 1.). Each page contains printed illustrations and instructions to guide and enhance the activity. The student places various plastic paddles on the book page to interact in the activity. To

Fig. 1. A student interacts with an exercise in the Perspective module

get guidance with the system the student places a paddle with a "?" on the page it to access the help system. The TUI system allowed us to create an interface for the activities utilizing two handed interactions and direct manipulation. The student can experience a variety of activities such as subtractive color mixing, changing lighting effects in a still life, and using magic lenses to see paintings in new ways.

There are several advantages of this TUI approach for the exercises. In general we wanted to provide a novel and fun interface which would make these activities more engaging to the students than a typical desktop computer keyboard and mouse based application. Also, in the exercises the students are often manipulating multiple variables simultaneously (e.g. coordinated dollying and zooming of the virtual camera, generating seed values and iterations of a fractal) which is afforded by the two handed control of the TUI. The tangible interface also gives subtle and expressive control over the input parameters (e.g. color mixing). Since we are teaching via art it is fitting that the students have a sense of applying their own creativity (e.g. fractal creation, lighting a still life, camera effects etc.) to the experience. The TUI also allows us to convey spatial concepts through the interface (e.g. the student can understand the ratios of apparent size to distance from the viewer in the perspective module because she can see the relative distance the two paddles are from each other on the page). This tangible approach also allows us to leverage physical media such as the book pages (e.g. putting information, guides, and other content on the physical book pages). Lastly, the result is a natural interface that supports exploration (e.g. turn to another book page to go to another section, turn back and forth as you please, put the "?" paddle on the page to get help). The students can discover through experimentation how the tangible objects (paddles) affect the activity (e.g. multiple paddles defining fractal creation and magic lenses).

6.1 Application Interactions

In this section we will highlight a few of the thirteen exercises from three modules that make up the STEM application and discuss the tangible interfaces for each.

In the Perspective module the student does a variety of tasks that help illustrate the concept of perspective, how field of view of a camera affects our perception of it, and how depth is conveyed in 2D art via vanishing points. The first set of exercises take place in a 3D scene created from photographs of the Morehouse campus (not unlike a diorama) (See Fig. 1). In the fourth exercise in this module two paddles are used to change the camera location and the FOV in this scene. The student is challenged to recreate the "zoom in/ dolly out" style effect that is seen in movies such as "Vertigo" and "Jaws." Sliding paddle 1 vertically on the page will change the FOV while doing the same motion with paddle 2 will dolly the camera in and out. The mappings are defined such that moving the paddles in opposite directions will achieve the desired effect (e.g. "zooming in" by reducing FOV while simultaneously dollying the camera out).

The Light Module allows students to explore the concept of light, its importance to art and our perception of it. In one exercise the student is exposed to how the human eye works via a series of "magic lenses" that they can move over a painting via the paddles. First the student moves a lens over Seurat's "Sunday in the Park". The area under the lens is magnified. This allows the student to see how individual dots of different colors are perceived at a distance as a mixture of those colors. Then the student manipulates a series of lenses over a second painting (each paddle represents a different type of lens). Through the lenses she can see how a person with a vision impairment experiences a scene (color blindness, retinitis pigmentosa etc.)

In the Fractal module the student is able to create and modify fractals and learns how they appear in nature as well as art. In the first exercise the student creates an iterated function system (a method of generating fractals). Two paddles define a starting position and orientation of two block figures in 2D. The third paddle dynamically increases and decreases the number of recursive iterations of function generator. In another the students are exposed to fractals in art (architecture). Ba Ila villages in Zambia have a pseudo fractal pattern. The student builds her own Ba Ila village by placing huts in the scene (paddle 1 is used to move a hut around the world and when paddle 2 is placed on the page the hut is dropped) and a virtual village is generated around these starting conditions. The student can then browse their village via paddle 1 which is used to rotate the 3D scene.

7 Conclusion and Future Work

Through this process of design and implementation we have identified the components that are necessary to repurpose an AR design tool for use as a TUI prototyping system. In particular these components allow the designer to define a workspace, and map object position/orientation to arbitrary functions in the application. The DART-TUI toolkit is particularly useful for rapidly creating inexpensive and portable tabletop TUI prototypes. A designer can download the code, print out the markers, and then begin working with her own TUI environment. We have utilized our toolkit to create an educational system (the STEM application) that uses tangible interactions and fine-art concepts to expose students to science topics.

This STEM education application is in the process of being evaluated by Morehouse College researchers with high school students. In the future we plan to add additional exercises and to gather data on the usability and learning effects of our system. DART (with the DART-TUI components) is available for download and we are eager to see our toolkit applied to additional TUI applications.

Acknowledgements

The authors would like to acknowledge the students at Morehouse College who helped create the content for the STEM application. Also a special thanks to the all developers of DART over the years which include Prof. Blair MacIntyre who lead the original project and to Steven Dow who contributed significantly to its design and implementation. This work was funded by NSF Grant #0625731

References

1. Azuma, R.T.: A Survey of Augmented Reality. Presence: Teleoperators and Virtual Environments 6(4), 355–385 (1997)
2. Bean, A., Siddiqi, S., Chowdhury, A., Whited, B., Shaer, O., Jacob, R.J.: Marble track audio manipulator (MTAM): a tangible user interface for audio composition. In: Proceedings of the 2nd international Conference on Tangible and Embedded interaction, Bonn, Germany, February 18-20 (2008)
3. Gandy, M., Dow, S., MacIntyre, B.: Prototyping Applications with Tangible User Interfaces in DART,The Designer's Augmented Reality Toolkit. In: Toolkit Support for Interaction in the Physical World Workshop at IEEE Pervasive Computing 2004, April 20 (2004) (positional paper)
4. Greenberg, S., Fitchett, C.: Phidgets: easy development of physical interfaces through physical widgets. In: Proceedings of the 14th Annual ACM Symposium on User interface Software and Technology, Orlando, Florida, November 11-14 (2001)
5. Kato, H., Billinghurst, M.: Marker Tracking and HMD Calibration for a Video-Based Augmented Reality Conferencing System. In: Proceedings of the 2nd IEEE and ACM international Workshop on Augmented Reality, October 20-21 (1999)
6. Ishii, H., Ullmer, B.: Tangible bits: towards seamless interfaces between people, bits and atoms. In: Proceedings of the SIGCHI Conference on Human Factors in Computing Systems, Atlanta, Georgia, United States, March 22-27 (1997)
7. Ishii, H., Wisneski, C., Orbanes, J., Chun, B., Paradiso, J.: PingPongPlus: design of an athletic-tangible interface for computer-supported cooperative play. In: Proceedings of the SIGCHI Conference on Human Factors in Computing Systems: the CHI Is the Limit, Pittsburgh, Pennsylvania, United States, May 15-20 (1999)
8. Klemmer, S.R., Newman, M.W., Farrell, R., Bilezikjian, M., Landay, J.A.: The designers' outpost: a tangible interface for collaborative web site. In: Proceedings of the 14th Annual ACM Symposium on User interface Software and Technology, Orlando, Florida, November 11-14 (2001)

9. Klemmer, S.R., Li, J., Lin, J., Landay, J.A.: Papier-Mache: toolkit support for tangible input. In: Proceedings of the SIGCHI Conference on Human Factors in Computing Systems, Vienna, Austria, April 24-29 (2004)

10. MacIntyre, B., Gandy, M., Bolter, J., Dow, S., Hannigan, B.: DART: The Designer's Augmented Reality Toolkit. In: Proceedings of the 2nd IEEE/ACM international Symposium on Mixed and Augmented Reality, October 7-10 (2003)

11. Mazalek, A., Davenport, G., Ishii, H.: Tangible viewpoints: a physical approach to multimedia stories. In: Proceedings of the Tenth ACM international Conference on Multimedia, Juan-les-Pins, France, December 1-6 (2002)

12. Mugellini, E., Rubegni, E., Gerardi, S., Khaled, O.A.: Using personal objects as tangible interfaces for memory recollection and sharing. In: Proceedings of the 1st international Conference on Tangible and Embedded interaction, Baton Rouge, Louisiana, February 15-17 (2007)

13. Raffle, H.S., Parkes, A.J., Ishii, H.: Topobo: a constructive assembly system with kinetic memory. In: Proceedings of the SIGCHI Conference on Human Factors in Computing Systems, CHI 2004, Vienna, Austria, April 24-29 (2004)

14. Shaer, O., Leland, N., Calvillo-Gamez, E.H., Jacob, R.J.: The TAC paradigm: specifying tangible user interfaces. Personal Ubiquitous Comput. 8(5), 359–369 (2004)

15. Underkoffler, J., Ishii, H.: Urp: a luminous-tangible workbench for urban planning and design. In: Proceedings of the SIGCHI Conference on Human Factors in Computing Systems: the CHI Is the Limit, Pittsburgh, Pennsylvania, United States, May 15-20 (1999)

16. Wellner, P.: The DigitalDesk calculator: tangible manipulation on a desk top display. In: Proceedings of the 4th Annual ACM Symposium on User interface Software and Technology, Hilton Head, South Carolina, United States, November 11-13 (1991)

17. Yoon, J., Oishi, J., Nawyn, J., Kobayashi, K., Gupta, N.: FishPong: encouraging human-to-human interaction in informal social environments. In: Proceedings of the 2004 ACM Conference on Computer Supported Cooperative Work, Chicago, Illinois, USA, November 6-10 (2004)

Evaluation of Non-photorealistic 3D Urban Models for Mobile Device Navigation

Christos Gatzidis[1], Vesna Brujic-Okretic[2], and Maria Mastroyanni[2]

[1] Bournemouth University, School Of Design, Engineering And Computing,
Talbot Campus, Poole House, BH12 5BB, Poole, UK
cgatzidis@bournemouth.ac.uk
[2] City University, Department of Information Science, School Of Informatics,
EC1V 0HB, London, UK
vesna@soi.city.ac.uk, mastroyannim@blueyonder.co.uk

Abstract. This research presents a user evaluation study examining the effect different rendering styles of 3D virtual city models, as intended for navigational purposes, could potentially have on users with emphasis on non-photorealistically rendered (NPR) stylizations. The purpose of this experiment is to establish whether, particularly for the application area mentioned above, non-photorealistic, expressive rendering could provide alternative, more effective visual styles than the photorealistic representations of urban areas usually opted for by developers today. 50 participants were exposed to a predominably questionnaire-based study assessing various parameters by observation of the models on a UMPC (Ultra Mobile PC). The results of this research could potentially have significant implications on how future pedestrian navigational software should be visualized in the future.

Keywords: non-photorealistic rendering, mobile navigation, urban modeling, user studies.

1 Introduction

Despite of the fact that traditional computer graphics research to this day still focuses on the production and assessment of photorealism, a relatively new field, the one of non-photorealism (NPR), has produced results that focus on viewer engagement by the use of stylization, abstraction and expressiveness. This new field has been slowly gaining ground not only in research but also in commercial applications since the rich visual styles it can emulate are in many occasions more suitable for certain information visualization communication purposes. Examples include psychological applications ([1], [2], [3], [4], [5]), architectural applications [6], perception of space studies [7], texture-based depiction ([8], [9], [10]), medical applications [11], learning applications [12] and also weather / natural phenomenon visualization software [13].

In the field of mobile navigation and particularly in regards to 3D urban modeling, research has already been conducted offering conclusive evidence that, especially for remote visualization of large city models, NPR can have many potential benefits. A recent approach [14] used a feature-line NPR method for building facades, demonstrating that urban data content using this type of shading over a photorealistic one

R. Shumaker (Ed.): Virtual and Mixed Reality, LNCS 5622, pp. 169–178, 2009.

can be transmitted much faster over a limited-bandwidth network. Similar work [15] has also yielded positive results for NPR methods and mobile device rendering.

While the technical advantages of using NPR shading for 3D city models have been explored, there has not, to this day, been a cognitive study offering results and evidence to support the argument that indeed artistic rendering is not only less resource-heavy but also, because of its nature, more appropriate in conveying information to the average user of mobile 3D navigational software. Furthermore, the technical studies listed above only evaluated / visualized one NPR style on a mobile device rather than attempting to cover more of the many visual styles the area has to offer.

2 Methodology

Since the main objective of the project is to contrast photorealistic rendering and non-photorealistic rendering types in context with mobile urban navigation, it was evident that this research should consist of a mainly exploratory study regarding the users' preference. Then, it was decided that the main task of the study would be the viewing/observing of images depicting 3D urban environment (rendered in pre-selected rendering types) on a mobile device. The data would be collected through questionnaires after viewing the images but a face-to-face meeting with each of the participants was considered essential since the same means (a specific mobile device) should be used to view the rendered images. In other words, questionnaires would not be distributed by email or post since the images should be viewed on the same mobile device by all participants.

It is worth noting that 50 sample users participated in total. More specifically, 31 male and 19 female subjects took place in the experiment. The subjects involved were undergraduate students, postgraduate students and professionals and subject age was of a great range (18 to over 43). Moreover, it should be mentioned that all subjects had normal or corrected-to-normal vision. The sampling was randomly performed although the subjects were selected from various places in London and the greater area so that a further diversity of the population participated could be achieved.

The device used in the experiment was an Ultra Mobile PC (UMPC) and more specifically an ASUS R2Hv (with a 7-inch screen display). This device was chosen because the platform technology of such an ultra-mobile, ultra-portable PC with a small screen display is expected to be the norm over the next few years for pedestrian 3D navigation.

In order to contrast the normal shading rendering style with the non-photorealistic rendering styles, it was decided to use six rendering styles overall, representative of NPR styles in general. Thus, 3D rendered images have been created for each of these styles of an average central London urban area using the Virtual City Maker application [16]. The styles were the following; a) normal shading b) toon-shaded c) pen-and-ink with noise d) pen-and-ink e) line rendering and f) volume illustration. Figure 1 demonstrates a variety of the rendering styles used.

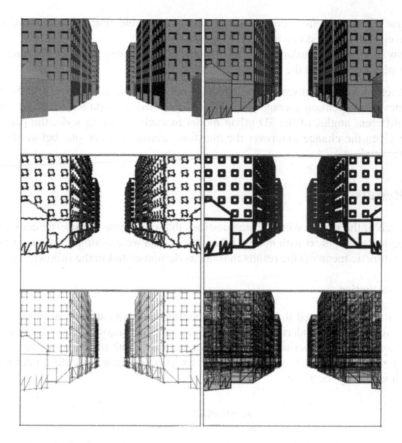

Fig. 1. The six rendering styles used in the experiment

A questionnaire was used for the collection of data. This included demographics such as general details of each participant (age, gender, occupation etc) and some questions regarding their previous experience regarding non-photorealistic rendering, navigation applications and mobile devices. The rest of the questionnaire was divided in six sections; one for each rendering type (normal shading, toon-shaded, pen-ink with noise, pen-ink, line rendering, volume illustration). Each section included seven (ordinal scale) questions, exactly the same ones for each rendering type as well as a special part at the end dedicated to any comments that could be left by the respondents (open question). All the questions were related to the efficiency of the rendering type in context with mobile 3D urban navigation. More specifically, the subjects were asked for each rendering type;

a. how they would rate the urban environment they see aesthetically
b. how easy they would be able to perceive distance in the urban environment given
c. how easy they would be able to perceive height in the urban environment given
d. how easy it would be to distinguish finer details in buildings such as doorways and windows in the urban environment given
e. how immersive they find the urban environment given

f. how effective in interaction with the user they would find the urban environment given if it was used in a navigation application

g. how appropriate and/or visible they think this rendering style is for small-screen display devices like the one used in the experiment

For each of the ordinal scale questions answers should be given from 1 to 5. 40 to 45 minutes were spent on average per subject. After observing on the UMPC device several different angles of the 3D urban model in each rendering style, the participants were given the chance to answer the questions above for each one before moving to the next style.

3   Results

For each of the seven ordinal scale questions that contribute to the efficiency of a rendering style in context with mobile urban navigation we can simply average (calculate the arithmetic mean of) the results in total, as demonstrated in the following sections.

3.1   Aesthetics

In Figure 2 it is noticed that the normal shading rendering style is aesthetically equal to the toon-shaded rendering style. That is to say, the majority of the population that participated in the experiment preferred aesthetically both of the aforementioned rendering styles. It is very interesting to see an average value on both rendering styles which is exactly the same.

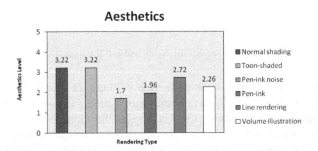

Fig. 2. User aesthetical preference

Furthermore, it is also noticeable that line rendering scores second as far as aesthetics is concerned. Volume illustration scores third aesthetically while from the two pen-and-ink styles the one without the noise scores higher leaving pen-and-ink with noise last. Interestingly, we notice that normal shading and toon-shaded rendering styles score equally aesthetically but much above the average of levels (ranging from 1 to 5 or "very poor" to "excellent") while line rendering comes second with some distinguishable difference from the first ones (but again above the average). The other styles score below the average, a fact that shows that they are not preferred aesthetically by the participants.

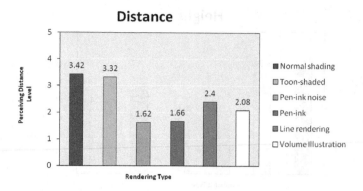

Fig. 3. Ability to perceive distance in rendering styles

3.2 Distance

In Figure 3, we notice that the toon-shaded rendering type is almost equal to the normal shading rendering type as far as distance perception is concerned. That is to say, the majority of the population that participated in the experiment suggested that they were able to perceive distance easier in both of the aforementioned rendering types than the other types with a slight preference of the normal shading over the toon-shaded. Again, it should be mentioned here that the average value in those types is almost the same. Line rendering scores third as far as distance is concerned. Volume illustration scores fourth while from the pen-and-ink styles the one without the noise scores higher leaving the style of pen-and-ink with noise last. Finally, the results indicate that the normal shading and toon-shaded rendering styles score almost equally and much above the average of levels (ranging from 1 to 5 or "very hard" to "very easy") while line rendering comes third with some distinguishable difference from the first ones (although slightly below the average). The other styles score below the average, a fact that shows that they are not preferred by the participants as satisfactory rendering styles as far as distance recognition is concerned.

3.3 Perceiving Height

In Figure 4, we notice that the toon-shaded rendering style is almost equal to the normal shading rendering style as far as height perception is concerned. That is to say, the majority of the population that participated in the experiment suggested that they were able to perceive height easier in both of the aforementioned rendering types than the other types with a slight advantage of the normal shading over the toon-shaded. Again, it should be mentioned here that the average value in those types is almost the same. Line rendering scores third as far as height is concerned. Volume illustration scores fourth while from pen-and-ink styles the one without the noise again scores higher leaving the style of pen-and-ink with noise last. The data indicate that the normal shading and toon-shaded rendering types score almost equally and much above the average of levels (ranging from 1 to 5 or "very hard" to "very easy") while line rendering comes third with some distinguishable difference from the first ones

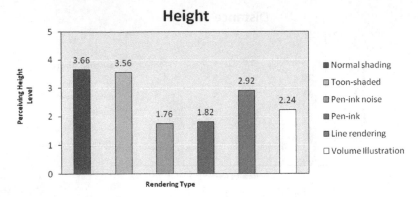

Fig. 4. Ability to perceive height in rendering styles

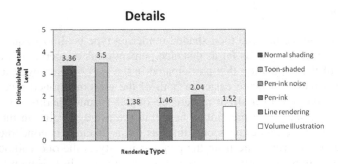

Fig. 5. Ability to distinguish finer details in rendering styles

(but above the average). All the other styles score below the average, a fact that shows that they are not preferred by the participants as satisfactory rendering styles as far as height is concerned.

3.4 Distinguishing Details

Interestingly in Figure 5, we notice that the toon-shaded rendering type scores higher than the normal shading rendering type as far as the details that can be distinguished is concerned. That is to say, the majority of the population that participated in the experiment suggested that details in buildings (windows, doorways etc.) were clearer to make out in the toon-shaded rendering style than the normal-shading. Line rendering scores third as far as the distinguishable details are concerned. Volume illustration scores fourth while from the two pen-and-ink styles the one without the noise scores slightly higher leaving the style of pen-and-ink with noise last. Finally, the data indicate that normal shading and toon-shaded rendering types score almost equally much above the average of levels (ranging from 1 to 5 or "very hard" to "very easy") while line rendering comes third with some distinguishable difference from the first ones (below the average). The other styles score below the average too, a fact that shows that they are not preferred by the participants as satisfactory rendering styles as far as making out details is concerned.

3.5 Immersiveness

In Figure 6, we notice that the toon-shaded rendering style scores slightly higher than the normal shading rendering style as far as immersiveness is concerned. That is to say, the majority of the population that participated in the experiment suggested that they have found the 3D urban environment given very immersive in both of the aforementioned rendering styles (since the difference between them is really small). Line rendering scores third as far as immersiveness is concerned. Volume illustration scores fourth while from the pen-and-ink styles the one without the noise scores higher leaving the style of pen-and-ink with noise last. Finally, the data indicate that normal shading and toon-shaded rendering types score almost equally much above the average of levels (ranging from 1 to 5 or "not at all" to "very much") while line rendering comes third with some distinguishable difference from the first ones (although slightly below the average). All the other styles also score below the average, a fact that shows that they are not preferred by the participants as satisfactory rendering styles as far as immersiveness is concerned.

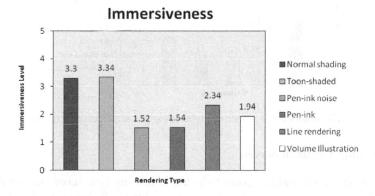

Fig. 6. Immersiveness of rendering styles

3.6 Interaction Effectiveness

In Figure 7, we notice that the normal shading rendering type scores slightly higher than the toon-shaded rendering type as far as the effectiveness in interaction with the user is concerned. That is to say, the majority of the population that participated in the experiment suggested that the user could be able to interact more effectively in the 3D urban environments relating to both of the aforementioned rendering styles (since the difference between them is really small). Line rendering scores third as far as the effectiveness in interaction with the user is concerned. Volume illustration scores fourth while from pen-and-ink styles the one without the noise scores higher leaving the style of pen-and-ink with noise last. Finally, the data indicate that normal shading and toon-shaded rendering types score almost equally and much above the average of levels (ranging from 1 to 5 or "not at all" to "very much") while line rendering comes third with some distinguishable difference from the first ones (although below the average). All the other styles score below the average.

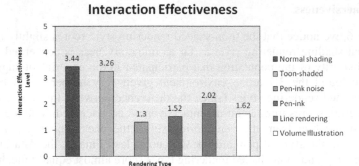

Fig. 7. Effectiveness of rendering styles in interaction with the user

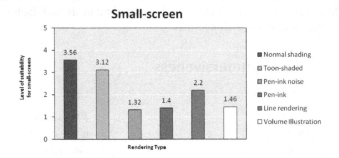

Fig. 8. Suitability of rendering styles for small-screen display device

3.7 Suitability for Small Screen

In Figure 8, we notice that the normal shading rendering type scores higher than the toon-shaded rendering type as far as its suitability for small-screen display devices is concerned. That is to say, the majority of the population that participated in the experiment suggested that both of the aforementioned rendering styles (since the difference between them is really small) are very appropriate and visible for usage on a small-screen display device. Line rendering scores third as far as the appropriateness/visibility for small-screen display is concerned. Volume illustration scores fourth while from the pen-and-ink styles the one without the noise scores higher leaving the style of pen-and-ink with noise last. Finally, the data indicate that normal shading and toon-shaded rendering types score almost equally and much above the average of levels (ranging from 1 to 5 or "not at all" to "very much") while line rendering comes third with some distinguishable difference from the first ones (but again below the average). All the other styles also score below the average.

4   Discussion of Results and Conclusion

The collected data was also analysed by a number of other ways (not shown in this publication) including averaging male-female population and using the one-way

ANOVA model. Overall, results agree on the following: the cartoon-shaded view (one of the NPR rendering styles) is efficiently equal or almost efficiently equal to the photorealistic shading in context with mobile urban navigation (i.e. in all categories examined). Notably, finer details of the 3D environment were more distinguishable to the subjects in the aforementioned NPR rendering style than in any of the others including the photorealistic view, meaning that building outlines, doorways, windows, street signs and other intricacies of the scene are more easily recognised with this visual representation. This style was also ranked as the most immersive according to user preference. These findings support the initial argument that a mobile navigation system with an expressively rendered view (a toon-shaded one in particular) has tangible advantages over the standard photorealistic shading on a cognitive level.

Currently a real-time navigation experiment is underway (as the second part of this study), where users are asked to walk a distance of approximately 100 metres in the same area, for each rendering style, with a mobile device (PDA) in hand, while observing the corresponding 3D model which is translated in real-time according to the subject's positioning and orientation. The mobile device comes equipped with a GPS and digital compass and is running a prototype of the LOCUS application [17]. The same seven areas with the study presented above will be researched again with similar questions post-tasks, after each one of the rendering styles. This way, a complimenting and contrasting study for real-time NPR results will emerge which can offer comparable results with the ones presented in this publication, leading to further discussion on the applicability of NPR to mobile navigation visualisation.

Acknowledgments

Fellow Bournemouth University, City University and ALCATEL Lucent Telecom UK Limited researchers are thanked for their support, guidance and assistance during the research work presented in this publication.

References

1. Duke, D.J., Barnard, P.J., Halper, N., Mellin, M.: Rendering and Affect. Computer Graphics Forum 22(3), 359–368 (2003)
2. Santella, A., Decarlo, D.: Visual Interest and NPR: an Evaluation and Manifesto. In: NPAR 2004, pp. 71–78. ACM Press, Annecy (2004)
3. Decarlo, D., Finkelstein, A., Rusinkiewicz, S., Santella, A.: Suggestive Contours for Conveying Shape. ACM Transactions on Graphics 22(3), 848–855 (2003)
4. Halper, N., Mellin, M., Herrmann, C.S., Linneweber, V., Strothotte, T.: Towards an Understanding of the Psychology of Non-Photorealistic Rendering. In: Workshop Computational Visualistics, Media Informatics and Virtual Communities, pp. 67–78. Deutscher Universitats-Verlag (2003)
5. Halper, N., Mellin, M., Herrmann, C.S., Linneweber, V., Strothotte, T.: Psychology and Non-Photorealistic Rendering: The Beginning of a Beautiful Relationship. Mensch & Computer, 277–286 (2003)
6. Schumann, J., Strothotte, T., Raab, A., Laser, S.: Assessing the Effect of Non-photorealistic Rendered Images in CAD. In: CHI 1996, pp. 35–42. ACM Press, New York (1996)

7. Gooch, A., Willemsen, P.: Evaluating Space Perception in NPR Immersive Environments. In: NPAR 2002, pp. 105–110. ACM Press, New York (2002)
8. Jackson, C.D., Acevedo, D., Laidlaw, D.H., Drury, F., Vote, E., Keefe, D.: Designer-Critiqued Comparison of 2D Vector Visualization Methods: A Pilot Study. In: ACM SIGGRAPH 2003 Conference Abstracts and Applications. ACM Press, New York (2003)
9. Kim, S., Hagh-Shenas, H., Interrante, V.: Conveying Shape with Texture: Experimental Investigation of Texture's Effects on Shape Categorization Judgments. IEEE Transactions on Visualization and Computer Graphics 10(4), 471–483 (2004)
10. Isenberg, T., Neumann, P., Carpendale, S., Sousa, M.C., Jorge, J.A.: Non-photorealistic Rendering in Context: An Observational Study. In: Fourth International Symposium on Non-Photorealistic Animation and Rendering (NPAR 2006), pp. 115–126. ACM Press, New York (2006)
11. Tietjen, C., Isenberg, T., Preim, B.: Combining Silhouettes, Shading, and Volume Rendering for Surgery Education and Planning. In: EuroVis 2005, pp. 303–310, 335. Eurographics Association (2005)
12. Gooch, B., Reinhard, E., Gooch, A.: Human Facial Illustrations: Creation and Psychophysical Evaluation. ACM Transactions on Graphics 23(1), 27–44 (2004)
13. Healey, C.G., Tateosian, L., Enns, J.T., Remple, M.: Perceptually-Based Brush Strokes for Nonphotorealistic Visualization. ACM Transactions on Graphics 23(1), 64–96 (2004)
14. Quillet, J.C., Thomas, G., Granier, X., Guitton, P., Marvie, J.E.: Using expressive rendering for remote visualization of large city models. In: 11th International Conference on 3D Web Technology, pp. 27–35. ACM Press, Columbia, Maryland (2006)
15. Diepstraten, J., Gorke, M., Ertl, T.: Remote line rendering for mobile devices. In: CGI 2004: IEEE Computer Graphics International, Crete, pp. 454–461 (2004)
16. Gatzidis, C., Brujic-Okretic, V., Liarokapis, F., Baker, S.: Developing a Framework for the Automatic Generation and Visualisation Of 3D Urban Areas on Mobile Devices. In: 10th Symposium For Virtual and Augmented Reality, Joao Pessoa, pp. 151–162 (2008)
17. Mountain, D., Liarokapis, F.: Interacting with Virtual Reality scenes on mobile devices. In: Mobile HCI 2005: 7th International Conference on Human Computer Interaction with Mobile Devices & Services, pp. 331–332. ACM Press, Salzburg (2005)

Integrating and Delivering Sound Using Motion Capture and Multi-tiered Speaker Placement

Darin E. Hughes

Institute for Simulation & Training
University of Central Florida
Orlando, Florida
dhughes@ist.ucf.edu

Abstract. Creating effective and compelling soundscapes for simulations is a challenging process that requires non-traditional tools and techniques outside the scope of standard production methods. In an immersive simulation, sound is at least as important as graphics; auditory cues can be heard from behind walls, around corners, and out of the line of sight. This paper describes a novel approach to interactive 3D sound design utilizing vision-based motion capture and multi-tiered, configurable loudspeaker delivery.

Keywords: Sound Design, Immersive Simulation, Motion Capture, 3D Sound, XACT.

1 Introduction

Sound is well understood in the film industry to be at least "50 percent of the experience" and as such a great deal of time and money are put into the scoring and sound designing of a major film production. Films are then released into sound treated rooms with powerful surround systems and bass transducers that can envelope the listener in an intense aural and tactile experience to complete the visual display on the screens in front of them.

It can be argued that sound is even more important in an interactive, multi-modal, and fully immersive simulation. Sound is an essential form of communication and can be used in both verbal and non-verbal forms, and in abstract and naturalistic presentations. Abstract sounds are used in many aspects of simulation and in general computer interaction. "Beeps and boops" let the user know when new messages or processes may require attention or some form of action. These sounds may also provide feedback when a user has made an erroneous command or has added a new device to a system. Naturalistic sounds are more common in gaming and simulation and may provide environmental details whereas linguistic sounds can give direct commands and communications to the user [1].

In fully immersive environments, sound provides a truly 360 degree, 3D sense. Humans can detect sounds all around them, in front or behind, as well as above and below head level. Eyes cannot see through walls or around corners but ears can hear sounds that are occluded by such obstructions thus providing a unique source of information that would otherwise be unavailable. Sound has been shown to greatly

R. Shumaker (Ed.): Virtual and Mixed Reality, LNCS 5622, pp. 179–185, 2009.

increase a sense of immersion and presence in simulation and is an essential component for situational awareness [2]. Additionally, temporal acuity is an order of magnitude greater with hearing than it is with sight in the human system and as such can be an essential first indicator of an important cue or event in a simulation or real-world situation [3].

Sound design is the art and science of capturing, synthesizing, mixing, integrating, and delivering sound into a particular form of media. Interactive, immersive simulation is one of the most challenging environments for a sound designer. Unlike a linear product such as film, a sound designer must craft the audio in such a way as to be responsive to unexpected and oftentimes unpredictable interactions. Where a sound designer for a film can hear the final product and tweak every last sound, a sound designer for interactive simulation will never hear a final product. Every time a simulation is run, a different set of outcomes and interactions will change the overall presentation of sound.

In order to provide a sound designer of interactive simulations with tools that can facilitate a successful outcome and effective final product, new capabilities must be developed that allow the designer to work in an environment similar to the listeners' environment. In other words, the sound designer must be able to design within the actual immersive and interactive world.

This paper provides an overview of the production pipeline for the sound design of interactive simulation and describes two new approaches for the integration and delivery of sound.

2 Audio Production Pipeline for Simulation

The sound design process for interactive simulation can be summed up in four main steps: capture and synthesis, mixing and mastering, integration, and delivery. The first two steps utilize standard production hardware and software and are consistent with most other media projects that have a sound design component. The final two steps require tools and processes that differ greatly from standard production and as such require a certain amount of research and innovation to produce a quality product.

2.1 Capture and Synthesis

Capture consists of recording (in the field or in the studio), gathering sound effects from available libraries, and synthesizing sounds utilizing hardware and software synthesizers. Field recording refers to on-location capturing of various kinds of sound effects or environmental sounds. This is typically done with mobile recording devices such as the Sony PCM-D1 or similar units. Field recording is essential for the capture of authentic soundscapes (some examples could include ambience in a remote forest, a dense urban cityscape, a shooting range, etc.). Studio recording is used for the isolated capture of discrete sound events such as voice or Foley (the recording of sounds to videos or animations, e.g. footsteps). The controlled environment of studio recording allows for a clean capture of very specific sound effects which can later be mixed into a larger soundscape.

Some sound effects cannot be captured because of budget or other practical limitations. These sounds can often be retrieved from sound effects libraries. For instance, if a simulation requires the sound of a 50 caliber machine gun, arranging to record this kind of sound will take a good deal of time, money, planning, and other logistical concerns. Adequate recordings of such sounds already exist in effects libraries that can be purchased for a greatly reduced cost. Finally, some sounds that may be necessary for a simulation don't exist in nature. For simulations that require abstract sounds (such as various kinds of "beeps and boops"), synthesis is a good approach. Synthesis can also be used to add an extra effect to real world sounds. For instance, most recordings of gun shots fail to capture the haptic component of a weapon being fired. A crafty sound designer can add a low-frequency "hit" into the sound of a gun firing to provide a richer and more true-to-life effect.

2.2 Mixing and Mastering

Mixing and mastering is the process during which all captured, gathered, or synthesized sounds are brought together and output to a set of finalized audio files that will be used in the simulation. Some sounds may be as simple as a single footstep while others may be 5 minute long, richly layered ambient tracks. This is the last step in the standard production process that a sound designer for simulation follows and in many instances this is the last step where a sound designer may be able to exert creative control.

2.3 Integration

Integration is the process where all sound effects are made accessible to the game engine or controlling code. Depending on the tools available to the sound designer, this could be as simple as handing over a folder with audio files to a programmer, or it could be a much more involved process using audio toolkits, scripting engines, or other methods of integration. The manner in which this is handled can be the difference between an elegant presentation of sound or a repetitive and annoying auditory experience. If the sound designer does not have the proper tools to test and tweak at this stage, the end product will suffer as a result.

2.4 Delivery

Delivery is the method through which sound goes from the computer to the user's ears. This can involve the use of headphones, loudspeakers, tactile transducers, hypersonic sound devices and other technologies. The main challenge for anyone designing sound for gaming and simulation is that it may not be known what hardware the end user will use. There are standards for movie theatres and even though the quality among them may vary, there is at least a minimum of expectation for what the delivery system will be. Sound designers for simulation cannot depend upon such expectations. As such, the delivery of sound must be made scalable to accommodate a wide variety of delivery formats. Even when simulation is not intended to be distributed and may only be experienced in set environments, the specific environments may vary greatly from the controlled space of a mixing room. For example, the final product may be in an elaborate MOUT facility or it may be a travelling simulation that is to be displayed at convention centers or exhibitions. These factors must be considered and addressed by the sound designer and resolved either programmatically or through creative hardware configurations.

3 Integration: XACT and Motion Capture

The integration process developed at the Media Convergence Laboratory (MCL) combines off the shelf technology and custom designed tools to place as much control as possible in the sound designer's hands. The XACT sound toolkit which is a part of Microsoft's XNA suite is utilized for the first step of the integration process. XACT allows the sound designer to create wave and sound banks from a collection of .wav files. The designer can create individual cues that reference one or multiple sounds within the banks. A number of built in features give the sound designer specific interactive controls that would typically be hard coded by a programmer and an auditioning feature that allows the designer to preview the results. Below is a brief list of a few key features currently being utilized by MCL's team:

- Looping
- Randomized playback
- Randomized pitch and volume shifting
- Distance attentuation
- Global dynamic variables

The XACT toolkit provides an excellent set of controls for the sound designer, especially for real-time and interactive audio cues. However, it still does not provide the designer with the ability to tweak and alter sounds from within the simulation environment.

3.1 Motion Capture

One of the biggest challenges for visual designers is the translation of motion capture to the simulation environment. Animations that may look good inside of Motion-Builder, Maya, or 3D Studio Max don't always translate properly to the actual simulation. This problem can be compared to the issues that sound designers face when the audio in a traditional production environment sounds much different than it does once integrated. Motion-captured animations are essentially pre-scripted sequences that can be triggered at certain times and looped if necessary. There is a similar need for these types of sequences in sound design. For instance, in a given simulation there may be a certain time when two helicopters are triggered to fly past each other. One way to handle this may be to place the sound of a helicopter on each model and when they are triggered, the sound moves with the models across the scene. This approach rarely yields satisfactory results. Ideally, the sound designer would be able to work directly in the environment and, by hand, move an evolving sound from its start to stop points.

Fig. 1. Sound Designing with Motion Tracking

The system designed by MCL allows the sound designer to do just this. Utilizing two inexpensive motion-capture cameras and retroreflective objects, the sound designer can attach a sound or sounds to a node or nodes and move them in real-time across the 3D space to achieve the precise effect desired for a given situation. In many instances, there are sounds that have no virtual model associated with them. For instance, in a given simulation it may be appropriate to have birds flying around through the soundscape. Hand crafted audio animations can be created while monitoring their effects in real-time to create a very compelling and realistic sounding spatial effects for this type and many other scenarios.

The system is designed to be size-scalable such that a sound designer can create a 200 foot long animation by merely moving a retroreflective object 20 centimeters. In other words, the animations can be created without having to get out of a chair and can be done on a desk table.

4 Delivery: Configurable Speaker Placement

Most audio APIs such as OpenAL or Creative's EAX don't provide support for alternate speaker arrangements. Speaker set-up is therefore determined by the sound card software. Typical sound cards will provide support for traditional set-ups including headphones all the way up to 7.1 configurations. However, it is assumed that the speakers will be set up on a single plane and according to conventional guidelines.

One huge limitation of these configurations is the inability to simulate sound in the y axis (i.e. above and below head level). For 3D simulation it is essential to have true 3D sound. This cannot be achieved with a single tier of speakers.

The system developed at MCL allows for the placement of speakers in non-standard configurations, including multiple tiers. Each individual output channel on a sound card can be assigned a specific location in 3D space. If a simulation is designed such that the user will remain still then the user location can be assumed to be stationary. However, if the simulation requires that the user move through out a physical environment, the user must be tracked and their location should affect the way in which the sounds are spatialized. In the system described here, this is handled by a ListenerObject which can either be placed at the point of origin (for desktop simulations with a stationary user) or can be placed on the user (for immersive simulations with a mobile user). The spatialization algorithm accounts for both the speaker locations and the user location in order to determine the output.

The most computationally and algorithmically complex part of the rendering pipeline is the spatialization computation for spatialized channels. The essence of the algorithm is the computation of a table of attenuation factors for each combination of source and speaker on that channel. This table is computed once per iteration of the channel thread, and then each sample in the block of samples read in that iteration is multiplied by the appropriate attenuation factor in the table. The computation of the attenuation factors is based on the techniques for spatialization described in [4]; the essence of it is that the dot product of the vector to the source and the vector to the speaker is used for attenuation, so that speakers in exactly the direction of the source play the sample at full volume, and the attenuation factor increases based on an increasing angle until at a difference of 90 degrees, the sample contributes nothing to that speaker. This also means that speakers at an angle of greater than 90 degrees— i.e., speakers in the opposite direction of the source, will not play those samples; this does lead to undesireable artifacts—for example, a sudden and jarring transition from the speakers on the left to those on the right when a source moves past the origin along the x-axis—but the simplicity of the technique makes it a desirable one to use despite the artifacts associated with it, and such effects can be avoided as long as the sound designer is careful to avoid having sources move very close to the origin. (OpenAL seems to exhibit the same artifacts, so it seems likely that the approach here is typical of spatialized audio applications.)

5 Conclusions and Future Work

Sound is crucial element in immersive simulation and should be given the same kind of consideration and effort as its visual counterparts. Providing sound designers with tools that facilitate the process and cater to the particularities of simulation will result in more effective and immersive simulations.

The current integration method described in this paper is a first step towards a better production process for sound design in simulation. Sound orientation has not yet been developed as part of this technique but should most definitely be implemented in the future. Additionally, a system that can self calibrate speaker locations without the need for measurement and placement within the scripting code would be a very useful development.

Acknowledgements

The research presented here is partially supported by the National Science Foundation (IIP0750551 and DRL0638977) and the Army Research and Development Command, Orlando.

References

1. McAdams, S.: Recognition of sound sources and events. In: McAdams, S., Bigand, E. (eds.) Thinking in sound: the cognitive psychology of human audition, pp. 146–198. Oxford University Press, Oxford (1993)
2. Soulodre, G.A., Lavoie, M.C., Norcross, S.G.: Objective measures of listener envelopment in multichannel surround systems. Journal of the Audio Engineering Society 51(9), 826–840 (2003)
3. Sanders, M.S., McCormick, E.J.: Human Factors in Engineering and Design, 7th edn. McGraw-Hill, Inc., New York (1993)
4. Naef, M., Staadt, O., Gross, M.: Spatialized Audio Rendering for Immersive Virtual Environments. In: Proceedings of the ACM Symposium on Virtual Reality Software and Technology, pp. 65–72 (2002)

The Design of a Virtual Trailblazing Tool

Daniel Iaboni and Carolyn MacGregor

Systems Design Engineering, University of Waterloo,
200 University Ave West, Waterloo, Canada, N2L 3G1
{diaboni,cgmacgre}@engmail.uwaterloo.ca

Abstract. Trails are a proven means of improving performance in virtual environments (VE) but there is very little understanding or support for the role of the trailblazer. The Use-IT Lab is currently designing a tool, the VTrail System, to support trailblazing in VE's. The objective of this document is to introduce the concept of trailblazing, present the initial prototype for a tool designed specifically to support trailblazing and discuss results from an initial usability study.

Keywords: trailblazing, virtual environments, wayfinding.

1 Introduction

A hurdle to the wide-scale adoption of 3D interfaces is the lack of tool specificity [1]. Current tools and techniques do not take into consideration the specific needs of the environment, the task or the user. Generality in 3D interaction design is evident within the development of tools for navigation tasks. Navigation is a complex task consisting of physical (travel) and cognitive components (wayfinding) [2]. One type of wayfinding that receives very little attention is trailblazing – allowing the user to mark routes traveled and places visited while traveling through an environment.

Trails remain a fundamental means of conveying directional information for the purpose of wayfinding. Whether the trail consists of footprints in the snow or breadcrumbs on a website, trails reduce the mental workload associated with wayfinding tasks. While there are efforts directed towards the design of improved methods of creating and presenting trails [3], [4], [5], there is a lack of research looking at the role of the trailblazer in virtual environments (VEs).

The Usability and Interactive Technology (Use-IT) Lab is currently developing a trailblazing tool called the VTrail Tool. The initial objective is to create the VTrail Tool to enhance wayfinding within current virtual training environments, like those being used by Department of Research Defense Canada (DRDC)-Toronto. Providing support for effective trailblazing and trail following tasks can lead to improved performance in virtual training applications [4].

2 Design of the VTrail Tool

The preliminary design for the VTrail interface was created based on scenario-based task analyses performed on a typical infantry training scenario provided by

R. Shumaker (Ed.): Virtual and Mixed Reality, LNCS 5622, pp. 186–195, 2009.

Fig. 1. Initial design for the default VTrail Tool; user related information located at the top center of the screen, trail information located on the bottom left, and the mini-map on the lower right corner

DRDC-Toronto. By applying an object-oriented task analysis to the military ground troop scenario, the key tools and behaviours to be included for the trailblazer were identified. For the initial interface design, the tools were categorized as providing information relevant to the user, the trail or the environment. These tools were combined and the resulting interface is show in Figure 1.

2.1 Trail Information

A key component to the VTrail tool is the information regarding the trail. The trail display, located in the lower left corner, provides information about the trail markers, information embedded in a marker, and a preview of environment at the markers' position.

A trail consists of at least two, and ideally more, markers. Each marker has an ID, position (x, y, z) and heading (in degrees) to find the next marker in the sequence. Two buttons with triangle icons (pointed up, pointed down) allowed the user to scroll through all the markers. Another button allows the trailblazer to remove the marker currently being viewed. For the initial implementation of the VTrail, the users are only provided with one type of trail marker. Limiting the user to one type of marker simplifies the controls needed to create the trail. The marker design is based on earlier studies [6].

To increase the utility of the markers, the users have the ability to embed additional information into the marker. The trailblazer may want to highlight a landmark, or provide a warning to the trail followers. Although the current implementation of the VTrail only supports text, future versions could include multimedia content to enhance the training potential of the VTrail tool.

A trailblazer may want to provide a trail follower the ability to preview the environment prior to arriving at the location. As such, the design of the VTrail marker includes a camera that provides a view of the environment in front of the marker. Furthermore, although the VTrail system is designed based on continuous movement through the environment, providing a preview of the environment with the marker camera reduces disorientation if the training program allows for teleportation as a means of travel.

2.2 User Information

To be able to localize within an environment a user must know his position and orientation.

In the real world, GPS data is presented in the conventional format of degrees: minutes: seconds, which can then be overlayed on to a map to indicated the user's position in the world. Without the aid of the map, the GPS data is difficult to interpret if the user has a desire to travel to a specific position in the world. Within VEs the positional information is presented using Cartesian co-ordinates (x, y, and z if necessary to represent vertical displacements). While positional data will indicate when a user reaches a desired destination, a compass is useful in indicating the direction necessary to reach the destination.

Using only a compass an expert wayfinder can successfully navigate to a desired location and back provided he keeps accurate track of the distance traveled and bearing. The simplest form of providing orientation information similar to a compass is to indicate heading information with text, i.e. 0° representing North, and 180° representing South. Displaying the heading in this manner allows the user to quickly and accurately align heading with the orientation of the trail marker provided by the trail display. Combining a compass with a map allows for position tracking and terrain prediction.

2.3 Environment Information

Providing a map to the users aids with planning, and reviewing of the trail as well as construction of a mental model of the environment. The VTrail includes two maps, a mini-map available while exploring the environment and a static world map. Both maps are created using an aerial photograph and are presented with a North up orientation. The mini-map, centered on the user represented by a dot, shows an exo-centric viewpoint of the environment up to 25m around the user.

3 Usability Study

The initial objective of this user study is to answer fundamental research design questions, such as; are there unnecessary features currently included in the standard design; are there features that should be added to the standard interface? Furthermore, user feedback will be used to evaluate the design of the independent interface components. For example, participants may provide insight with regards to the design of the map or the marker information provided. While a detailed and separate study can be performed on the design and validation of each individual component of the VTrail interface, the decision was made to test the interface in its entirety because of possible interactions between components. For example, use of a map is improved with the presence of a compass.

This study compared performance on creating trails to guide a user to multiple targets in the environment using either the interface with a minimum number of features or the current proposed default interface. The minimum interface is representative of performing the task with only a map and compass. The minimum interface is included for comparison to ensure that adding additional information into the user's visual field does not interfere with task performance.

Additional insight for modifications to the design may be gleaned from studying how individuals of different genders and spatial ability interact with the interface. There are known behavioural differences in navigation due to gender and spatial ability, but it is unknown if the differences will require changes to the standard interface to be more universal.

3.1 Participants

Twelve (6 male, 6 female) undergraduate students from the University of Waterloo agreed to participate. All participants were right hand dominant and had normal (20/20) or corrected to normal vision. When asked to rate their level of comfort on using the computer controls all participants rated themselves with a score of at least 3 on a 5-point Likert scale, indicating somewhat comfortable using computers.

3.2 Experimental Setup

The virtual world was generated using the Virtual Navigation and Collaboration Experimentation Platform (VNCEP) supplied by DRDC. VNCEP ran on Pentium™ 4 PC desktop computer with a 3.4 GHz processor and 3 GB of RAM. The computer uses Windows™ XP operating system with a Quadro™ FX 3450/4000 SDI (256 MB) from NVIDIA™. The large projection screen display was an 81" Fakespace® ImmersaDesk with 1280 by 1024 resolution at a 75Hz refresh rate. Non-stereoscopic vision was used to reduce possibility of simulator sickness [7]

Movement through the environment was similar to controls used in popular first person computer games. Participants used the "W", "A", S", and "D" keys on the keyboard to translate through the environment. The participant's walking speed was set to 1.5 m/s to simulate walking, but the participant could increase their speed to 3 m/s by pressing either "Shift" keys on the keyboard. Participants controlled their viewpoint through the mouse. Translating the mouse forward allowed participants to look up and translating the mouse backwards moved the viewpoint down. Left and right mouse movements controlled the viewpoint in their respective directions. The left mouse button was used to drop the trail markers and the right mouse button removed the marker nearest to the user. Travel was coupled with the gaze of the user. Participant movement was restricted to a single plane to simplify control and environment design.

The experimental environments consisted of three large-scale, approximately 300m x 300m, environments. Since there are no self-reported differences in wayfinding strategies between indoors and outdoors [8], the environments represented an outdoor rural setting. A rural environment was preferred over an urban environment because of the increased complexity of selecting a direction at a decision point. In an urban environment the decision may be constrained by the structure of the decision point (e.g. a 4-way intersection forces a choice between 3 directions). The environments were constructed in the form of a 3x3 matrix, consisting of nine square tiles each 100m x 100m. To reduce possible experimental bias due to the design of the world,

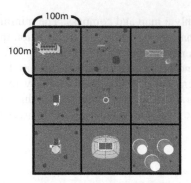

Fig. 2. Exocentric View of One of the Experimental Environments

the environments were created from a random arrangement of the nine tiles. Each tile contained a large feature (e.g. a building), a smaller feature (e.g. windmill), and assorted vegetation (e.g. trees and bushes). Participants were not able to enter the buildings. An exocentric view of an archetypal rural landscape is shown in Figure 2. Lighting simulated daytime levels.

3.3   Method

Upon arrival at the USE-IT Lab the participant was seated at a table approximately one meter in front of a large (81") projection screen. The participant was provided with an information letter describing the main objectives, the benefits of participating and the potential minimal risks of participating in a computer-based experiment. After reading the information letter the participant was asked to sign a consent form and complete a background questionnaire. The background questionnaire collected information on demographics (age, gender, computer experience, wayfinding experience), vision, and computing gaming experience. Participants completed the cube-comparison test [9]. Both tests are pencil and paper based and measure mental rotation, which has been linked to wayfinding ability [10]. Spatial ability will be studied as a covariate in these experiments as it may help explain individual differences in performance.

Two researchers were present during the study. One researcher was responsible for recording observations while the other researcher was responsible for running the study. Test scripts were used to reduce experimental variation. The participant was given an opportunity to learn how to use the VTrail interface during a familiarization in an environment similar to the experimental environment.

Upon completing the familiarization task, participants began the experimental trials. During the experimental trials participants were asked to use a "think aloud" protocol. The participant completed three (minimum/default/control interfaces) trials. For the minimum and default trials the trailblazing participant was asked to create a trail that would help someone deliver five packages to the appropriate locations. For example, the football would go to the stadium. At the beginning of each trial the trailblazer was provided a list of the delivery items and could either locate the five delivery targets and then create the trail or generate the trail while searching for the delivery locations. Once the participant was satisfied with the trail they could terminate the trial. The control condition was used to measure the participants' performance on the delivery task without the additional task of creating a trail. In the control condition the participant had to memorize the list of five items to be delivered. Upon locating all five locations, the participant was required to return to the starting location. Once the participant was back at the starting point the control trial was complete. Due to the differences in the task between the control trial and the minimum and default trials, the control trial was not included in the analysis. The control trial was included to determine if there are any baseline differences between the participants in this study and the participants selected for a planned study on trail following.

The order of minimum and default trials was random for the first two trials and the control was always the third trial. Performance on the control was not relevant in the comparison between the two VTrail interface designs but is used for another aspect of the study not discussed in this paper.

At the end of each trial the participant was asked to complete a subjective usability questionnaire on the interface they had just used. After completing the three trials the participant was thanked and provided with a general feedback letter outlining the benefits of the research.

3.4 Measures

There were two types of measures used in the assessment and comparison of the proposed interfaces; performance measures, and usability measures.

Performance Measures

The common method of quantitatively comparing interface designs is through task performance metrics. For this study the task metrics were time and distance travelled.

A more useful metric in assessing the effectiveness of the VTrail interface was the quality of the trail generated. A well-designed interface enables a trailblazer to create trails using an appropriate number markers that are placed in a manner that facilitates effective trail following. Poorly performed trailblazing will result in the placement of markers that are confusing or do not provide useful information. However, the literature does not provide any recommendations for assessing the quality of a trail from a user's perspective. Quantitatively it is possible to use graph theory to determine the number of markers dropped and positioned in the VE, as well as the distance between markers. However, such an approach does not view the trail within the context of the environment. The use of qualitative measures is likely to more suitable. The proposed approach to evaluating trail quality is based on modified criteria set by Parks Canada [11]. Modifications to the guidelines were required to due to physical requirements in the real world that are not applicable in virtual worlds, such as soil erosion. For this study, the virtual trails were evaluated on the following: marker placement (hard to spot, easy to spot), frequency of markers (too many, too few, appropriate number), length of trail (too long, not long enough), location of interest (e.g. start, finish, delivery location) indicated and overall impression of the trail quality. Graduate and Faculty members of the Use-IT lab were asked to independently review the created trails and evaluate the trails on a 5-point Likert scale based on a set of heuristics. One example of a heuristic is; "are the markers positioned in the environment so that the markers are easy to identify?" If all the markers are easy to identify, then the participant may receive a high score (around 5 on the scale) for the trail, whereas markers that are poorly positioned will result in a low score (around 1 on the scale). Averaging the ratings across the reviewers will contribute to an overall measure of the path quality.

Usability Measures
In addition to the task metrics an important source of data for evaluating interface design is user preference data captured through subjective questionnaires. The questionnaires were based on a 5-point Likert Scale, where 1 represents "strongly disagree" and 5 represents "strongly agree". For example, a question asks the participant to rate the usefulness of each tool provided. Participants were also asked to rate the overall interface. Space was provided for the student to add additional feedback.

Accumulated observational data, from the "think aloud" protocol and recorded observations during the trials provided additional insight into the effectiveness and usability of the components of the interface designs.

3.5 Results

The results of the pre-task mental rotation test were analyzed to determine if there were any differences in spatial ability between the genders. A T-Test comparing scores on the mental rotation task found no significant difference ($p > .05$) between the genders.

To determine trail quality four graduate members of the Use-IT lab (2 male, 2 female) received an hour-long training session involving a description of the trail quality metrics and practiced evaluating trails to ensure consistency. Trail evaluators then independently assessed all the trails in a random order. The final trail quality score was the average of individual evaluators scores.

A repeated measures analysis of variance (ANOVA) design was used to analysis the time spent trailblazing, distance traveled, and trail quality score, with factors being, Gender (2; male, female) X Interface (2;minmum, default) and spatial score as the covariate.

Analysis of the time and trail quality found no significant ($p > .05$) main effects or interactions. There was a significant interaction between gender and interface on the distance traveled while trailblazing, [$F(1,9) = 8.30$, $p < .05$]. On average, females traveled further (M = 37774m, SD = 14240) when using the minimum interface compared to the default interface (M = 23790m, SD = 10611).

Usability data was analysed using Friedman's test. Results indicate that the participants significantly, preferred using the default interface [mean rank = 1.75; c^2 (1, n=12) = 6.00, $p < .05$] compared to the minimum interface [mean rank = 1.25]. Participants also indicated that they did not like the embedded marker cameras, c^2 (2, n=12) = 6.50, $p < .05$.

4 Discussion

The objective of this initial study was to validate the current toolset provided in the default VTrail interface. In addition the study investigated the effect of providing additional information on trailblazing performance (minimum interface versus default interface). Due to known differences, gender and spatial ability were included as co-variates to gain insight on the impact of individual differences on interface design.

Some interface components were viewed as critical, such as the compass and mini-map. However, the features that participants responded to positively require further development. For example, the compass was provided in a strictly digital display, and a participant mentioned a preference of having a combined traditional dial compass for a relative sense of direction and digital information for improved accuracy. In addition, the marker camera feature was considered to provide of little or no support. While being able to view a location prior to teleporting reduces disorientation [12] the ability to teleport was not provide in this study and so this feature had limited use. However, other applications may allow users to jump between locations and so future VTrail interfaces may incorporate this feature that can then be customized to the needs of the specific application.

Participant feedback also led to some design considerations for the next version of the interface. The current interface provided users with a single type of trail markers to simplify the controls. However, participants expressed an interest in having another marker, one for conveying directional information, and another for marking important locations.

Previous studies [13], [14] reported that participants failed to create trails when asked to simply manually drop the markers. However in this study all the participants made use of the markers to create trails. The difference may be due to the fact that the primary task in this study was the creation of the trail whereas trailblazing was a secondary task in the previous studies. This suggests that users are capable of producing trails which may be more meaningful than a trail generated automatically based on an individual's travel history. However, based on trail quality results there is room for significant improvement to the quality of the trails generate, which can be achieved through improved awareness of the concept of trailblazing and further improvements to trailblazing support tools.

Despite the lack of difference in spatial ability, females tended to travel further when using the minimum interface compared to using the default interface. This suggests that providing additional information improves female performance on a trailblazing task, while males may achieve little performance gains from enhanced information on basic trailblazing tasks. Since the gender difference disappears when provided with additional support, this suggests that there is no need to consider the need for different interface designs for the different genders.

The small number of participants used in the study may be viewed as a limitation, particularly with a lack of significant results. However, this study is primarily a preliminary a design activity to determine interface design guidelines for the VTrail system. Similar to heuristic evaluation [15], individually participant feedback is incomplete, but the aggregated data of the 12 participants provided enough information to move forward with the next design cycle.

5 Conclusion

Initial results are encouraging and provide insight for the direction for future studies. Tools included in the original design have been identified as not useful and removed in the next design. Furthermore, feedback from the users has resulted in the inclusion of additional VTrail modifications such as the use of multiple trail marker types. Finally, this study demonstrated that providing additional information to the trail-blazer did not overload or hinder the performance on the trailblazing task. While the trails generated from trailblazing with the VTrail interface were not better than the trails with the minimum interface, this may be due to the participant's lack of trail-blazing experience.Further modifications to the trail quality heuristics may also be necessary in future studies. Feedback provided by participants will be reviewed and incorporated into the next version of the VTrail trailblazing interface.

The efforts of this research are directed towards the design of the VTrail Tool to aid in the generation of trails in virtual training environments. However, due to the lack of understanding on how to support trailblazing, this study and the others that follow will be setting the foundations for the understanding of trailblazing in the current known and future unknown environments.

Acknowledgements

We would like to thank the members of the Use-IT lab that assisted with data collection, industry partners DRDC and the Ontario Centre of Excellence for providing funding for this research.

References

1. Bowman, D.A., Chen, J., Wingrave, C.A.: New Directions in 3D. User Interfaces, The International Journal of Virtual Reality 5, 3–14 (2006)
2. Bowman, D.A., Koller, D., Hodges, L.: Travel in Immersive Virtual Environments: an Evaluation of Viewpoint Motion Control Techniques. In: Proceedings of the Virtual Reality Annual International Symposium, pp. 45–52 (1997)
3. Grammenos, D., Mourouzis, A., Stephanidis, C.: Virtual Prints: Augmenting Virtual Environments with Interactive Personal Marks. International Journal of Human-Computer Studies 64, 221–239 (2006)
4. Ruddle, R.A.: The Effect of Trails on First-time and Subsequent Navigation in Virtual Environments. In: Proceedings of IEEE Virtual Reality, pp. 115–122 (2005)
5. Ruddle, R.A.: Generating Trails Automatically, to Aid Navigation when you Revisit an Environment. Presence: Teleoperators & Virtual Environments 17 (2008)
6. Iaboni, D., MacGregor, C.: VTrail: The Design of Markers for Virtual Trailblazing. In: Proceedings of Association of Canadian Ergonomists (2007)
7. Häkkinen, J., Pölönen, M., Takatalo, J., Nyman, G.: Simulator Sickness in Virtual Display Gaming: A Comparison of Stereoscopic and Non-stereoscopic Situation. In: Proceedings of the 8th conference on Human-computer interaction with mobile devices and services, pp. 227–230 (2006)
8. Lawton, C.A.: Strategies for Indoor Wayfinding: The Role of Orientation. Journal of Environmental Psychology 16, 137–145 (1996)
9. Ekstrom, R., French, J., Harman, H.: Manual for Kit of Factor Referenced Cognitive Tests. Educational Testing Service, Princeton (1976)
10. Blajenkova, O., Motes, M.A., Kozhevnikov, M.: Individual Differences in the Representations of Novel Environments. Journal of Environmental Psychology 25, 97–109 (2005)

11. Faulkner, J.H.: Trail Manual, Parks Canada, QS 7053-000-BB-A1 (1985)
12. Elvins, T.T., Nadeau, D.R., Schul, R., Kirsh, D.: Worldlets: 3-D Thumbnails for Wayfinding in Large Virtual Worlds. Presence: Teloperators & Virtual Environments 10, 565–582 (2001)
13. Darken, R.P., Sibert, J.L.: A Toolset for Navigation in Virtual Environments. In: Proceedings of ACM User Interface Software & Technology, pp. 157–165 (1993)
14. De Roure, D., Hall, W., Reich, S., Hill, G., Pikrakis, A., Stairmand, M.: MEMOIR - an Open Framework for Enhanced Navigation of Distributed Information. Information Processing and Management 37, 53–74 (2001)
15. Nielsen, J., Molich, R.: Heuristic Evaluation of User Interfaces. In: Proceedings of the SIGCHI conference on Human factors in computing systems: Empowering people, pp. 249–256 (1990)

User-Centered Evaluation of a Virtual Environment Training System: Utility of User Perception Measures

Dawei Jia, Asim Bhatti, Chris Mawson, and Saeid Nahavandi

School of Engineering and Information Technology;
Centre for Intelligent System Research, Deakin University
dwj@deakin.edu.au

Abstract. This study assessed the utility of measures of Self-efficacy (SelfEfficacy) and Perceived VE efficacy (PVEefficacy) for quantifying how effective VEs are in procedural task training. SelfEfficacy and PVEefficacy have been identified as affective construct potentially underlying VE efficacy that is not evident from user task performance. The motivation for this study is to establish subjective measures of VE efficacy and investigate the relationship between PVEefficacy, SelfEfficacy and User task performance. Results demonstrated different levels of prior experience in manipulating 3D objects in gaming or computer environment (LOE3D) effects on task performance and user perception of VE efficacy. Regression analysis revealed LOE3D, SelfEfficacy, PVEefficacy explain significant portions of the variance in VE efficacy. Results of the study provide further evidence that task performance may share relationships with PVEefficacy and SelfEfficacy, and that affective constructs, such as PVEefficacy, and SelfEfficacy may serve as alternative, subjective measures of task performance that account for VE efficacy.

Keywords: User-based evaluation, Virtual Environment, Evaluation methodology.

1 Introduction

Immerging computing technologies, such as Virtual Reality (VR) is perceived to be effective in enhancing human abilities to complete complex tasks. A generic immersive VR system consists of a virtual environment (VE), advanced human-computer interface and models of interaction, these are useful for facilitating perception in such computer simulated 3D environments [18]. Enhanced perception is achieved through using displays that provide rich visual, auditory and haptics sensory information that allow human users to easily engage, immerse and interact with learning tasks [7]. A Virtual Environment (VE) is often used synonymously as VR to describe an environment based on real-world or abstract objects and data [17].

Effective design of a VE is often aimed at conveying to users the feeling of being "immersed", "present", "engaged", "satisfied", and or "enjoyed" in the simulated environment [9, 11, 12, 14, 16]. Moreover, to convey high level of self-efficacy- individual's beliefs of his or her capability to organize and execute the behaviors to performing tasks successfully [19] are thought to be useful. It has been speculated that facilitation this sense of self-belief not only leads to higher level of acceptance and adaption of computer technology [3, 5] but also enhance task performance and outcomes [2].

R. Shumaker (Ed.): Virtual and Mixed Reality, LNCS 5622, pp. 196–205, 2009.

In the field of VE understanding how to use immersive technology to support the learning of abstract concepts or tasks and evaluating the degrees of effectiveness of how well a system is in assisting a user to achieve the intended learning, this present a substantial challenge for designer and evaluators of this technology. The challenges include users understanding, transfer of training and retention of trained techniques. Further, it is unlikely that a single evaluation factor or criteria construct will be capable of adequately assessing VE efficacy [10, 15, 17]. Many orientational, affective, cognitive and pedagogical issues are considered fundamental to VE efficacy [10]. However, there is currently no standard on the "best" way to quantify VE efficacy [17].

1.1 Measures of VE Efficacy in User-Based Evaluation

Typically, VE is measured objectively on user task performance. Common task performance measures used to evaluate the effectiveness of VE include time on task, speeds of completion and numbers of errors [12]. Additionally, having computer event driven recordings of all the experiments details, allowing for the incorporation of more accurate performance evaluation of the VE is also used widely in usability evaluation. Other objective measures are derived from physiological factors involve recording, such as heart-beat, blood pressure or eye movement over the course of the experiment. These are useful for ergonomic assessment of VE as they allow us to link physical responses directly to VE. Quantitative data produced from these objective measures is useful in showing "what" the users did, but they cannot be used to explain "how" or "why" user performed in a certain manner [18].

On the other hand, subjective measures, such as self-report in behavioral interview and questionnaires involve collecting both quantitative and qualitative data during a usability evaluation or user modeling, in which user behaviors are collected and assessed. Self-report data through behavioral questionnaire, for example is useful in collecting data of subjective views on particular aspect of interaction and learning experience with computer systems. Various multiple response modes such as physiological, motoric, and cognitive behaviors can be gathered using questionnaire [18]. It has advantages, such as an efficient use of time for both evaluator and respondent, and standardization of questions. In the field of VE, questionnaires are used quite frequently to elicit information about subjective phenomena [17]. Well designed questionnaire, such as Presence Questionnaire (PQ) by Witmer and Singer (1998) [20] have wide reaching effects and have been adapted extensively in evaluation of VE. More importantly, insight of user perception and preference of an interactive computer system can not be explained fully if only objective measures are used. For these reasons, there has been a call for subjective measures of VE in the literature.

1.2 Quantifying VE Efficacy through User Perception

Empirical evidence illustrates that perceptions such as self-efficacy (beliefs) and perceived efficacy of computer systems (attitude) can be influenced by the system design features in performance of cognitive or procedural tasks [5]. Self-efficacy is defined as an individual's expectancy in his or her capability to organize and execute the behaviors needed to successfully complete a task [1]. Perceived self-efficacy has been used to predict performance in decision making, cognitive task performance, and mathematical test scores [19], as well as proven to be beneficial in increase in problem-solving efficiency [6]. Prior research has also shown that perceived self-efficacy and attitudes toward computer are predictive of performance in computer mediated learning [13]. Perceived VE efficacy refers to user perception of how effective a VE is in assisting their interaction and learning experience, as well as learning outcomes. As an affective construct, perceived VE efficacy assesses VE quality from the users' point of view.

Subjective perception of VE and rating techniques has shown benefits in evaluating VE system [15]. In the field of usability engineering, user perception of computer technology plays an important role in evaluation. For example, users' perception of immersion, presence, engagement, satisfaction and enjoyment are associated with system design features. Draw on Fishbein and Ajzen's (1975) attitude paradigm from psychology, Davis (1993) [3] developed a technology acceptance model that addresses the beliefs (e.g. self-efficacy) and attitudes (e.g. perception) of the software systems on users' actual system usage, this plays a significant role in users' adoption of computer systems. For example, a person's belief about behaviour refers to his or her subjective likelihood that performing the behaviour will lead to a specified outcome; and attitude toward a behaviour is an affective evaluation of that behaviour. Because of the hypothesized benefit to performance, beliefs of self-efficacy and attitude towards computer system have been generally accepted as an evaluation criterion for computer mediated learning. On this point, perceived self-efficacy (SelfEfficacy) and perceived VE efficacy (PVEefficacy) are important in measuring performance in VE training system. We also hypothesize that if a system is effective, users should have higher perception of usability and learnability; and higher attention, comprehension, but lower cognitive load. In the field of VE, it is surprising to see a lack of work on incorporate self-efficacy and user perception measures to quantify VE efficacy. In line with other researchers [10, 17], we believe a reliable, repeatable and robust measure is needed to quantify VE efficacy.

The primary goal of this research is two fold: first, to determine if construct of the user perception measures of self-efficacy scale and perceived VE efficacy scale, can be used to quantify VE efficacy of an object assembly task; second, to explore the hypothesized relationships between self-efficacy beliefs, user perception of VE efficacy and task performance.

2 Hypotheses

Task performance and user perception are significantly affected by subjects' prior experience of manipulating 3D objects (LOE3D) in gaming or computer environments. Higher performance and perception will be associated with higher LOE3D. In addition, VE efficacy score will be significantly positive related to performance and perception on the object assembly task. VE efficacy also was expected to be significantly positive related to LOE3D.

3 Experiment

The validation of the proposed hypothesis is performed by training users in object assembly simulation called Virtual Training Environment (VTE) developed at Centre for Intelligent System Research (CISR), Deakin University. In addition, an empirical assessment of the object assembly simulation, based on the proposed evaluation framework [8], has been carried out. Thirty volunteers with different levels of experience in manipulating 3D objects in gaming or computing environment (LOE3D) performed a series of object assembly tasks in a virtual training system. The task involved selecting, rotating, releasing, inserting and manipulating 3D objects these tasks required users to utilize a data glove, a haptics device, a 3D mouse and a head-mounted display (HMD). Subjective assessments of SelfEfficacy, PVEefficacy were recorded along with objective assessment of task performance.

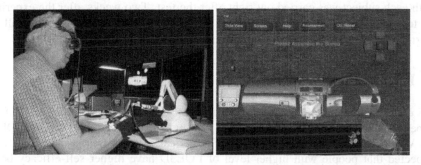

Fig. 1. Experiment setup (a) and training tasks (b)

Subjective measures on user perception of VE efficacy were captured through two questionnaires: Self-efficacy questionnaire (SEQ) or post-VE exposure questionnaire that measured self-efficacy (SelfEfficacy) and perceived VE efficacy questionnaire (PVEQ) or post-VE training test questionnaire that measured user perceived VE efficacy (PVEefficacy). Validation technique for questionnaire instrument [4] of factor analysis for data reduction of variables and Cronbach's Alpha for internal consistence were performed, which has shown the construct validity and reliability of these two measurement tools. Objective measure on task performance was captured through system logging file that automatically tracks user task performance and outcomes. A memory test was also conducted two weeks after the training test to assess users' long-term retention in the VE using a memory-test questionnaire (MTQ). Figure 2 represents the sequence of activities during the experiment. Upon entering the experimental environment, each subject was asked to complete a pre-test questionnaire (Pre-test Q). Each subject was then given a brief introduction of the system and performs a simple object assembly task, which serves as a pre-test of subject's ability to interact with, control and use various VE system control devices. SEQ was then filled out. Afterwards, a training test was presented to each subject, whom has 15 minutes to complete 7 object assembly tasks in the VE system. PVEQ was presented

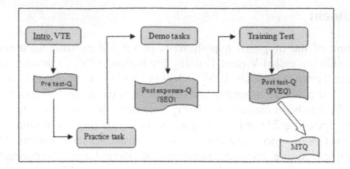

Fig. 2. Experiment Sequence

to the subject in the experimental environment. Lastly, an open-ended interview with each subject was carried out right after the test. Two weeks after the experimental test, subjects required to respond on the MTQ that requires them to recall their learning tasks or procedures in the VE training system.

4   Results and Discussion

VE efficacy was hypothesized to be significantly affected by different level of prior experience in manipulating 3D objects in gaming or computer environment (LOE3D). As VE efficacy was measured on TTS, SelfEfficacy, PVEefficacy and MMT, it was expected that people with higher level of LOE3D have higher self-efficacy beliefs, achieve better outome in training test, perceive the VE to be more effective and have higher achievement on the memory test.

4.1   Effect of Prior Experience

To assess the utility of prior experience for explaining task outcome, we used multiple predictors: computer use frequency (ComFreq), computer use history (CompHis), experience of manipulating 3D objects in gaming or computer environment (LOE3D), experience of manipulating 3D objects in VE environment (ExpVE). These were included in a multiple linear regression (MLR) model to predict training test score (TTS). Because of potential effects object assembly skills in real life may have influence on the subjects' performance in the VE, experience of using electronic tools for object assembly tasks (ExpTool), and perceived level of difficulty of assembly task (PdifTask) were included as predictors in this model. Finally, due to the potential effects of age and gender on training test score, and other response measures, these two variables were included in the model.

In general, the inclusion of these variables in the predictive model of training test score was aimed at avoiding biases in the parameter estimates; ComFreq, CompHis, LOE3D and ExpVE that might have occurred if variance due to prior object assembly skills (ExpTool, PdifTask) or individual differences were not taken into account However, it is anticipated that there were interrelationships among the variables. With this in mind, standard approach of multiple regression was performed, which allowed us to find out how the multiple predictors combine to influence the training test score. The regression model used to assess the utility of multiple predictors on training test score was structured as shown in equation 1.

$$TTS = \beta_0 + \beta_1 Age + \beta_2 Gender + \beta_3 CompFreq + \beta_4 CompHis \\ + \beta_5 LOE3D + \beta_6 ExpVE + \beta_7 ExpTool + \beta_8 PdifTask \tag{1}$$

Results of the standardized regression coefficients analysis indicated that this regression model predicts training test score well, F (2.404), $p<0.05$. Approximately 48% of the variability in training test score was explained by this model ($R^2=0.478$). The results also show that at the $\alpha=0.05$ level, LOE3D is the most important predictor of training test score ($Beta=0.567$, $p=0.032$). More important, LOE3D alone, account for 38% of the variance of training test score, $F=17.136$, $p=.000$. Surprisingly, of the eight predictors, only subjects' prior experience of manipulating 3D object in gaming or computer environment contributes significantly ($p=0.001$) to the model. Correlation analysis (1-tailed) also confirms that LOE3D was significantly and positively correlated with training test score, $r=.616$, $N=30$, $p=.000$. In other words, people who are more experienced in manipulating 3D objects in gaming or computer environment tend to achieve higher training test score. In addition, a moderate but significant linear relationship between gender and training test score ($r=0.321$, $N=30$, $p=0.042$), and between ExpVE and training test score ($r=.358$, $N=30$, $p=.026$) were found. These results show that male tend to outperform than female, and people with more experience in manipulating 3D objects in VE achieved higher training test score. In addition, younger people tend to have more experience of manipulating 3D objects in gaming or computer environment than elder ones, $r=0.508$, $N=30$, $p=0.004$.

4.2 Utility of User Perception Measures

To assess the utility of user perception measures, the response of self-efficacy questionnaire (SelfEfficacy) and perceived VE efficacy (PVEefficacy) were included in a multiple linear regression model to predict VE efficacy. Because of potential effects of the independent variable on VE efficacy and the other response measures, LOE3D also was included as a predictor in this model. Finally, memory test score (MTS) was added in the model to account for any susceptibility to cognitive learning outcomes that is essential in quantifying VE efficacy, as shown in equation 2.

$$VEefficacy= \\ \beta_0 + \beta_1 LOE3D + \beta_2 TTS + \beta_3 SelfEfficacy + \beta_4 PVEefficacy + \beta_{17} MMT + \varepsilon \tag{2}$$

Results of the standardized regression coefficients analysis indicated that the regression model adequately described self-efficacy believe, F (7.822), $p=0.000$. The results also shows that at the $\alpha=0.05$ level, training test score (TTS) (Beta=0.636, $p=0.000$) is the most important predictor of VE efficacy. Other predictors, memory test score (MMT) (Beta=0.266, $p=0.000$), perceived VE efficacy (PVEefficacy) (Beta=0.233, $p=0.000$), and self-efficacy beliefs (SelfEfficacy) contribute to the model slightly (Beta=0.193, $p=0.000$). However, LOE3D show no contribution to the model (Beta-.000, $p=.706$).

In addition, results of the Pearson correlation coefficients revealed strong, positive and significant relationships between VE efficacy and TTS (r=0.888, N=30, p=0.000), and between VE efficacy and MMT $(r$=0.766, N=25, p=0.000). Moreover, the result also shows a moderate, positive and significant linear relationship between VE efficacy and SelfEfficacy (r=0.637, N=30, p=0.000), and between VE efficacy and PVEefficacy (r=0.585, N=30, p=0.000). Interestingly, a moderate, positive and significant linear relationship also found between VE efficacy and LOE3D (r=0.506, N=28, p=0.000). These results shows people who achieve higher on training test (TTS) tend to have higher VE efficacy score. In addition, a moderately weak but positive linear relationship between PVEefficacy and TTS (r=0.384, N=30, p=0.036) suggests that people who perceive VE to be effective achieved higher TTS. A moderate and significant linear relationship also found between LOE3D and TTS (r=0.529, N=28, p=0.529), which suggest that people with high LOE3D tend to perform better than those with low and moderate LOE3D. Interestingly, no significant relationship found between self-efficacy (measured before the training test) and perceived VE efficacy (measured after the training test). Even thought a positive correlation exist between the two, but it is not significant, r=0.177, N=30, p=.175.

4.3 LOE3D on TTS, SelfEfficacy, PVE Efficacy and MMT

One-way analysis of variance (ANOVA) was performed and results show that there was significant effects of LOE3D on task performance, F=7.586, p<.05. Turkey Post Hoc test revealed that subjects performed task better (p<.05) under the moderate LOE3D (mean=82) than under the high (mean=85) and low LOE3D (mean=43). Counter to our expectations, results on SelfEfficacy and PVEefficacy revealed no significant effect (P>.05) of LOE3D. SelfEfficacy and PVEefficacy were observed as dependent measures in this study. People with low LOE3D have similar self-efficacy beliefs and perceive VE to be effective as these with moderate and high LOE3D. Mean score on TTS, SelfEfficacy and PVEefficacy indicate LOE3D have effects on these measures that account for VE efficacy as shown in Figure3. Additionally, one-way ANOVA analysis shows that there is no statistic significant difference on subjects' ability of recall in memory test (MMT) across LOE3D, F=1.852 p>.05. All subjects were able to recall learning task or procedures at high level, regards different ranges of LOE3D (mean>80).

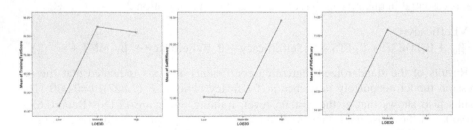

Fig. 3. Effects of LOE3D on TTS, SelfEfficacy and PVEefficacy

4.4 LOE3D on VE Efficacy

ANOVA analysis also shows that there is a statistic significant difference on VE efficacy score across LOE3D, F=4.42, p<.05. Tukey Post Hoc test further suggests that the differences lie between low and high experienced subjects, and no significant difference between moderate and high experienced subjects (p>.05). Mean results shows that moderate and high experienced subjects share similar VE efficacy sore (M>70), and low experienced subjects have lower VE efficacy score (M<60).

Table 1. Effects of LOE3D on VE efficacy

	Low Vs. Moderate	Moderate Vs. High	High Vs. Low
TTS	P<.05	P>.05	P<.05
SelfEfficacy	P>.05	P>.05	P>.05
PVEfficacy	P>.05	P>.05	P>.05
MMT	P>.05	P>.05	P>.05
VE efficacy	P<.05	P>.05	P>.05

4.5 Summary

We found that users with a different range of LOE3D had little to no effect on the self-efficacy and perceived VE efficacy in the VE. As mentioned above, different level of prior experience in manipulating 3D was gathered based on subjective self-report of their expertise. The manipulation of experimental group was affected by such information. With respect to LOE3D on TTS and VE efficacy, LOE3D of high, moderate and low ranges may not have been substantial enough to affect subject's ability to predict their performance and rate VE system efficacy. Besides, subjective perception may not be consistent with objective task performance measures. As in motivational/affect literature, self-efficacy and user attitude (perception) should be used as supplement of objective measures in evaluating VE system performance [10, 15]. Supported by the results of this study, we believe that user perception measures are equally important (if not superior) to assess system efficacy. Even though self-efficacy do not correlated with object measure of task performance significantly well, a positive relationship is detected between PVE and VE efficacy; and both user perception measures of self-efficacy and PVE efficacy are positively and strongly correlated with VE efficacy.

5 Conclusion

Various evaluation methodologies and techniques can be considered and applied for evaluating efficacy of VE systems designed for procedural task training. This paper has discussed issues related to the evaluation of this particular class of applications. Utility of user perception measures of self-efficacy and perceived efficacy based on our proposed evaluation methodology have shown significance in quantifying VE efficacy. The experiment confirms the general hypothesis that a positive correlation exists between subjective and objective measures designed specifically to quantify VE efficacy. Additionally, previous studies have not investigated a model of VE efficacy based on the combined objective measures of task performance and subjective measures of user perception. We also incorporated users previous experience in a computing environment, this past expertise possessed by the test subjects has not been done before when evaluating the effectiveness of a VE. As our research has found more study is required in this direction in order to clearly establish any relationships between self-efficacy, perceived VE efficacy and task performance.

References

1. Bandura, A.: Self-efficacy: the Exercise of Control. W.H. Freeman, New York (1997)
2. Bouffard-Bouchard, T.: Influence of Self-efficacy on Performance in a Cognitive Task. Journal of Social Psychology 130, 153–164 (1990)
3. Davis, F.D.: User Acceptance of Information Technology: System Characteristics, User perceptions and Behavioral impacts. International Journal of Man-Machine Studies 38, 475–487 (1993)
4. DeVellis, R.F.: Scale Development: Theory and Applications, 2nd edn. Sage Publications, Thousand Oaks (2003)
5. Hill, T., Smith, N.D., Mann, M.F.: Role of Efficacy Expectations in Predicting the Decision to Use Advanced Technologies: the Case of Computers. Journal of Applied Psychology 72, 307–313 (1987)
6. Hoffman, B., Schraw, G.: The influence of self-efficacy and working memory capacity on problem-solving efficiency. Journal of Learning and Individual differences 19(1), 91–100 (2009)
7. Isdale, J.: Introduction to VRTechnology. In: IEEE Virtual Reality Conference, p. 302. IEEE Computer Society Press, Los Alamitos (2003)
8. Jia, D., Bhatti, A., Nahanandi, S.: Computer-simulated Environment (VE) for training: Challenge of Efficacy Evaluation. In: The Simulation Technology and Training Conference (SimTecT 2008), p. 63. Simulation Industry Association of Australia (2008)
9. Lin, J.J.W.: Virtual Guiding Avatar: an Effective Procedure to Reduce Simulator Sickness in Virtual Environments. In: SIGCHI Conference on Human Factors in Computing Systems, pp. 719–726. ACM Press, New York (2004)
10. Mantovani, F.: VR Learning: Potential and Challenges for the Use of 3D Environments in Education and Training. In: Giuseppe, R., Carlo, G. (eds.) Towards CyberPsychology: Mind, Cognitions and Society in the Internet Age, pp. 207–226. IOS Press, Amsterdam (2001)
11. Moreno, R.: Does the Modality Principle Hold for Different Media? A Test of the Method-Affects-Learning Hypothesis. Journal of Computer Assisted Learning 22, 149–158 (2006)
12. Nash, E.B., Edwards, G.W., Thompson, J.A., Barfield, W.: A Review of Presence and Performance in Virtual Environments. International Journal of Human-Computer Interaction 12(1), 1–41 (2000)
13. North, M.M., Mathis, J.R., Madajewski, A., Brown, J.T., Cupp, S.M.: Virtual Reality and Transfer of Learning. In: Michael, J.S., Richard, J.K., Gavriel, S., Don, H. (eds.) Usability Evaluation and Interface Design: Cognitive Engineering, Intelligent Agents and Virtual Reality, vol. 1, pp. 634–638. Lawrence Erlbaum Associates, London (2001)

14. Papasratorn, B., Wangpipatwong, T.: The Effects of Self-Efficacy and Attitude on E-learning Outcomes. In: World Conference on E-Learning in Corporate, Government, Healthcare, & Higher Education, pp. 226–2270. Association for the Advancement of Computing in Education (AACE) (2006)
15. Riley, J.M., Kaber, D.B., Draper, J.V.: Situation Awareness and Attention Allocation Measures for Quantifying Telepresence Experiences in Teleoperation. Journal of Human Factors and Ergonomics in Manufacturing 14, 51–67 (2004)
16. Salzman, M.C., Dede, C., Loftin, R.B., Chen, J.: A Model for Understanding How Virtual Reality Aids Complex Conceptual Learning. Presence: Teleoperators and Virtual Environments, Special Issue on Education 8(3), 293–316 (1999)
17. Stanney, K.M.: Handbook of Virtual Environments Design, Implementation, and Applications. Lawrence Erlbaum Associates, London (2002)
18. Tesfazgi, S.H.: Survey on Behavioral Observation Methods in Virtual Environments. Research Assignment, Delft University of Technology (2003)
19. Wang, A.Y., Newlin, M.H.: Predictors of Web-student Performance: the Role of Self-efficacy and Reasons or Taking an On-line Class. Journal of Computers in Human Behavior 18, 151–163 (2002)
20. Witmer, B.G., Singer, M.J.: Measuring Presence in Virtual Environments: A Presence Questionnaire. Journal of Presence: Teleoperators and Virtual Environments 7(3), 225–240 (1998)

Emergent Design:
Serendipity in Digital Educational Games

Michael D. Kickmeier-Rust and Dietrich Albert

Department of Psychology, University of Graz
Universitaetsplatz 2, 8010 Graz, Austria
{michael.kickmeier,dietrich.albert}@uni-graz.at

Abstract. Using computer games for educational purposes is a fascinating idea that is getting increasingly popular amongst educators, researchers, and developers. From a technical as well as psycho-pedagogical viewpoint, today's educational games are at an early stage. Most products cannot compete with non-educational, commercial games and not with conventional educational software. Research must address fundamental challenges such as methods for convincing learning-game design or individualization of gaming experiences. An important key factor is development costs. To enter the market successfully requires reducing development costs significantly, however, without reducing gaming or learning quality. In this paper we introduce an approach of using existing methods for educational adaptation and personalization together with ideas of emergent game design.

Keywords: Digital educational games, game-based learning, adaptation, personalization, interactive storytelling, emergent game design.

1 Introduction

Computer games are a very successful element of the today's entertainment landscape and an integral part of everyday life. The young people, the so-called digital natives, spend a many hours on playing computer games. Thus, it is not surprising that educators developed an affinity to the idea of using computer games for educational purposes. The result is a significant hype over educational or serious games. Digital educational games (DEGs) are on their way to become a mainstream genre of educational technology. Of course, this idea is not new, educational games are as old as computer games. An early example is the game *Oregon Trail* released first in 1971 and re-released by the educational publisher *Brøderbund* for the *Apple II* in 1985. The game focused on teaching resource management. Today, the examples for educational games are manifold, ranging from so-called *moddings* (modifications of commercial, non-educational games) to games and simulations for primarily educational purposes. Also the scientific community addresses educational games for a while now, conducting research on the foundations of effective yet appealing DEGs. The reason for the hype, however, is not only the appeal of computer games to young people, computer games enable realizing elementary and essential pedagogical and didactical principles in a very natural way. Computer games, for instance, provide an emotionally and

R. Shumaker (Ed.): Virtual and Mixed Reality, LNCS 5622, pp. 206–215, 2009.

semantically appealing and meaningful context for learning, rich and immersive possibilities for visualizing contents, or the possibility for self-directed, active learning. In short, computer games do have the potential to make knowledge attractive, important, and meaningful.

Surveying the market as well as the body of scientific prototypes and projects, however, educational computer games are still at an early stage [8]. There exists a great many of small and simple games for the very young children and also "gameplay-enhanced" approaches with clear limitations in educational impact and gaming quality. However, there is a clear lack of DEGs that can compete with their "non-serious" counterparts in terms of gameplay, narrative, and visual quality as well as with conventional learning technology in their educational impact.

One fundamental problem of DEGs – and at the same time their most prominent advantage – is the intrinsic motivational potential of computer games. Children, adolescents, and adults play computer games voluntarily, for fun, and they spend a significant amount of time on playing. Today's gamers are used to an incredible visual quality and appeal of game play of entertainment computer games. However, if educational games cannot compete with this level of quality, the motivation to play them will be rather limited. Since the costs of current computer games are exploding – a good game might well cost 50 to 100 million dollars – educational publishers cannot keep up with game industry. Even worse, the "education" in educational computer games makes the development even more expensive. So it is clear that a prerequisite of commercial and educational success is cost-effectiveness. The consequence is that compelling DEGs are still rare. Quite in the contrary, more and more off-the-shelf entertainment games or modifications are used in class rooms.

An obvious idea to overcome the problem of cost-effectiveness is reducing the development costs. Unfortunately, this is most likely bound to reducing the quality of education, design, narrative, and game play. In conclusion, driving the establishment and quality of DEGs requires games that are effective from an educational point of view, effective from the development point of view, and competitive from the gaming point of view. And this is a non-trivial problem. In this paper we present an approach that, essentially, is based on a fusion of an intelligent in-game personalization and adaptation (in a psycho-pedagogical sense) with interactive storytelling and with ideas of emergence in game design.

2 Personalization in Digital Educational Games

Using "intelligent machines" for educational purposes has a long history; in fact, it can be traced back at least to 1926 when Sidney Pressey [12] tried to build a machine that presented multiple choice questions, their answers, and adequate feedback. The driving force behind intelligent educational systems is to provide individual learners with individual solutions, essentially because of the fact that meaningful and suitable one-on-one teaching is the most effective way of teaching. Unfortunately, a personal tutor is the most expensive way of teaching also. To address this problem with a technological solution, over the past decades several methods and frameworks for intelligent and adaptive tutorial systems were developed [2].

In contrast to conventional adaptive educational technology, for example learning management systems, DEGs are challenging the technological state-of-the-art by requiring a non-invasive assessment (e.g., of knowledge or learning progress) and adaptation. In simple words, typical assessment methods such as multiple choice questions or cloze texts cannot be utilized in immersive DEGs because, in all likelihood, popping-up assessments would immediately destroy game flow and immersion. The challenge is to find ways and methods to embed assessment subtly in the gameplay and narrative. In addition, the methods of personalization and adaptation must occur in a non-invasive way as well. Prominent methods are adaptive curriculum sequencing (selecting and re-ordering learning objects) and adaptive presentation (changing the look and feel of a learning environment). These methods (e.g., skipping a learning situation because the systems concludes that the learner already has the related knowledge) are hardly realizable in an immersive DEG because they would corrupt gaming experience and game flow, ending up with an implausible and confusing storyline without any motivational and educational potential.

Our solution is a non-invasive way of personalization and adaptation, that is, *micro adaptivity,* which was developed particularly for DEGs and which is related to techniques of adaptive problem solving support. The principle of micro adaptivity is to monitor the learner's behavior in the virtual world and to interpret the behavior in terms of available and lacking knowledge or in terms of specific inner states (e.g., motivation). To give an example, imagine a game-like exploratory learning situation within which the learner is required to narrow a light cone from a torch to a small light beam using a couple of blinds (see Figure 1). If the learner cannot narrow the light cone, we can conclude that this learner lacks the understanding of the blind principle. Of course, a single observation is not very significant but with an increasing number of actions, the (probabilistic) picture of the learner becomes continuously clearer and more valid. The micro adaptive assessment is complemented with subtle educational and motivational interventions, which are strictly embedded in the game.

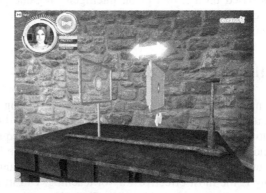

Fig. 1. Screenshot of a competitive educational game about the physics of optics. The game is a prototype developed in the context of the European ELEKTRA project (www.elektra-project.org).

An example is to provide the learner with feedback of the learning progress or hints. By aforementioned example, a non-player character (a NPC) might suggest the learner promising locations for the blinds. A more in-depth description of the micro adaptivity concept is provided by [6].

2.1 The Macro Level: Adaptive Storytelling

So far our concept of personalization and adaptation for DEGs just concerned assessment and interventions within specific limited and pre-defined learning situations. Educationally important techniques for personalization and adaptation such as adaptive sequencing of learning units (learning situations in a DEG) or adaptive presentation, however, are not addressed. To extend and enrich our approach to in-game personalization and adaptation, we aim for a fusion of the micro adaptivity concept with interactive and adaptive storytelling. In that way, we can realize a personalized sequencing of learning situations and units according to educational aspects as well as personalized adjustments of the game according to individual needs and preferences. In other words, we can shift in-game adaptation to the *macro level*.

In the literature several techniques for interactive or adaptive storytelling are described, varying in the openness of story generation and in their operational reliability. The approaches range from a recombining of self-contained story elements to an open-ended automated generation of "new" stories. For our goal of adaptation we rely on a robust approach based on the specification of atomic story-related entities (ranging from single spoken sentences to self-contained story units). In this context, a crucial aspect of interactive storytelling is to find an appropriate storyline on the basis of a pool of given atomic story or game elements. These entities can be compared to the rooms of a house and the furniture in those rooms, each entity has a specific goal (e.g., providing the learner with information, assessing internal states, or contributing to story and gameplay), specific characteristics and properties. During a gaming episode the single game entities must be adaptively re-combined and re-assembled into a meaningful storyline and a meaningful environment. The assembly is driven by specific sets of rules which refer to aspects of the game genre, the story model, educational aspects, and individual aspects.

The story model underlying our approach relies on a formalization of the classical *three-act structure* of *Aristotle* providing an arc model with 'exposition', 'rising action to climax', and 'denouement' (Figure 2, left panel). The related set of rules is supplemented with domain-related rules, defining the set of educationally meaningful sequences of learning, so-called *learning paths* through the learning situations of the game (or learning objectives of a conventional learning environment). This combination generates *game paths* (Figure 2, right panel), possible and meaningful paths through the game accounting for story model, learning objectives, and pedagogical interventions (see [7] for details).

The outlined approach, unfortunately, has an important drawback that is contracting our initial aim, the cost factor. A comprehensive adaptation throughout an entire game would require massive content (i.e., game elements) production. We address this problem by extending the approach of adaptive, educational storytelling with ideas of *emergent game design*.

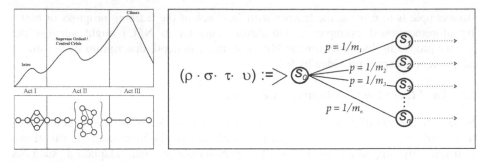

Fig. 2. The left panel shows the three act story model and its translation to a sequence of game entities. The right panel shows a formal representation of restrictions in the sequencing of story elements.

2.2 Emergence in (Educational) Game Design

A potential solution to the dilemma is making the game more "autonomous". In regular games, a sequence of scripted events occurs throughout the game. According to [15], however, this bears the downside that the game system has a limited awareness of what is happening and, more importantly, the game is lifelessly determined by what the designers think is exciting and fun. *Emergence*, on the other hand, occurs when more or less simple rules interact to give rise to behavior that was not specifically intended by the developer of a system. Emergence refers to the process of deriving new but coherent patterns or behaviors in complex systems. Emergent phenomena occur due to a non-trivial interaction of system components with each other and with the user. As [4] suggested, the collective of such kind of interactions forms novel, complex, and unexpected results. Emergent game design offers a ‚platform' and 'tools' for gaming, however, without any further blueprint; this is comparable to improvisational theatre or giving a kid a box of toy cars. The context is fixed but what happens occurs interactively and incidentally.

One method of realizing emergent game design is that gameplay is based on excellent and comprehensive simulations. Rich virtual worlds enable the player to interact with a large degree of freedom and, more importantly, to interact with game entities that respond in a realistic way. Examples might be *SimCity*, *The Sims*, or *Grand Theft Auto*. The key to emergent gameplay and emergent narrative is a meaningful and "intelligent" interaction with the game and within the game. The advantage is that players receive a very unique and personalized gaming experience as a direct result of their own behavior.

There exist several techniques from complex systems, machine learning, and artificial life that potentially enable emergent behavior in games. According to [16] some examples are flocking (simulating group behavior such as a flock of birds), cellular automata (discrete time models simulating complex systems), neural networks (machine learning techniques inspired by the human brain), or evolutionary algorithms (optimization techniques using concepts from natural selection and evolution to evolve solutions to problems). Some of those principles have already been transferred to real games; for example, *Half-Life* used flocking to give its monsters more lifelike responses. Another example is *Blade Runner*; here a pre-defined storyline is "enriched" or altered by accidental aspects, making the game different at each time. Important work in this area comes from [17] who developed and evaluated a technically sound framework for realizing emergent game design. Several authors claim that emergence is the direction game development is heading, which includes more flexible, realistic, and interactive worlds.

3 Educational Game Design

Realizing emergent game design requires a game context. Two fundamental dimensions of a game are gameplay and narrative. The gameplay determines the *what and how*, the narrative determines the *why*. Although both dimensions occur on a continuum, specific games are either gameplay-oriented (e.g., role playing games, action adventures, or campaign games) or narrative-oriented (e.g., simulation games, management games, or strategy games). To give very prominent examples, a game like *Tetris* is fundamentally driven by the gameplay without any story behind; adventure games such as the famous *Zak McKracken* are, almost like an interactive movie, driven by a story.

These dimensions also aroused some debate on which a game should focus more: The *ludologists* say that games should be played and not perceived like interactive movies. The *narratologists*, instead say, games should follow a red story thread. Both, the gameplay dimension as well as the narrative dimension can be described on a continuum between open/emergent and predefined/scripted.

When aiming for an effective and efficient design of DEGs, of course, more dimensions of computer games must be considered. A valuable contribution to formalizing viewpoints to computer games came from Smed and Hakonen [14]. These authors argue that the main dimensions of the computer game concept are linked together in a subtle way by the representation form (medium), by rules, by the goal definition, and by the absence or presence of opponents. Figure 3 illustrates these dimensions. A further important systematization of game genres we have to consider came from Lindley [10]. This approach begins with a classification of games on a 'plane' of ludology, narratology, and degree of reality (the author terms this 'simulation' or 'prosthetic reality'). In a next step, the model is extended by a 3rd dimension, that of chance (the author terms this 'gambling' or 'decisions about gain and loss'). The model manifests as a three-dimensional pyramid, which allows for classifying game types along its dimensions (Figure 3). Although Lindley's taxonomy offers a systematic approach that covers a wide range of aspects, the "purpose" aspect is not represented very well. Particularly educational aspects and intentions establish a micro universe of educational game types that must be considered in educational game design. With respect to the idea of emergence, finally, this dimension must be considered as well.

Emergent approaches involving intelligent gameplay and intelligent characters might play a crucial role in future mainstream game design, particularly in the context of serious games. The "intelligence" of game characters can be considered as essential factor. Those characters are supposed to behave flexible, challenging, unpredictable, or cunning [18]. An intelligent agent can be considered autonomous if it relies on its

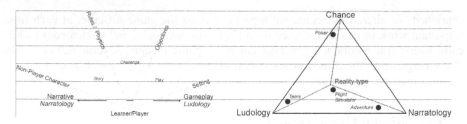

Fig. 3. The left panel shows the dimension of computer games according to [14], the right panel shows a different approach to describe game types according to [10]

own precepts and not on the predefined 'will' or 'knowledge' of the game designer [13]. Being autonomous, in turn, requires situational awareness. An example for such approach in an existing computer game is the agents in *Half Life*. Those characters "look" and "listen" to what is happening in their neighboring areas [9]. Still, the realization is rather simple; pre-defined check scripts are processed. In psychological terms, existing models perform a top-down approach driven by the designers/developers intelligence. The next generation of artificial in-game intelligence will rather purse a bottom-up approach by meaningful responses on changes in the agent's neighborhood.

3.1 Serendipity Instead of Emergence

If we consider emergence, as mentioned above, as a box of toy cars, certain rules and possibilities are fixed, what the play will be exactly is open – in other words, emerging. The problem is that this idea of openness is not compatible with (most) educational purposes. The existing ideas and approaches were developed in the context of entertainment games. Educational computer games cannot simply overtake such ideas since a distinct difference between the two kinds of games is that educational objectives require the learner to pass through certain learning situations following a certain curriculum. This means that pedagogical implications limit the degree of freedom and randomness in emergent approaches to game design. It is necessary that a learner is exposed to certain learning situations in a certain sequence.

Quite naturally, the question is arising whether both ideas can be merged into one game; the designers do not want to (and also must not) lose all control and system-only generated story plots are likely not very convincing. Thus, a subtle balance is required between a global idea of the story and emergent aspects; research proposed a dual layer model that separates a narrative layer and an agent/simulation layer [11]. The story generation is based on the interaction with the beholder, a story-ontology, and vectors of story elements and relationships.

To overcome the incompatibility of emergence and educational purpose while still taken advantage of an open approach, we generated a *narrative context model*. This model is based on the characteristics of the hero's journey [1] and the classical three-act story model. It determines a general red thread through the game and it defines the intro act and the closing act. As underlying data model we extended an ontological approach [5]. As shown in Figure 2, the atomic story elements provide the game with a certain degree of freedom of how the story proceeds and about what is happening in the game. To bring education into play, the story elements are mapped to educational objectives and pedagogical implications – utilizing a formal cognitive theoretical framework, that is, *Competence-based Knowledge Space Theory* [5], which establishes a structure of story/game elements that are meaningful in terms of education and in terms of story. The cognitive model reflects the psycho-pedagogical requirements and thus determines the admissible game parameters.

In a next step we introduce an *abstraction layer*. On an ontological basis we separate game play features, story features, and educational features from the game entities (story elements, in-game-objects, NPCs, etc.). As a result, we obtain a set of generic modules (cells), which can be "furnished" just-in-time in accordance with the ontological cognitive model and which can be sequenced in accordance with the narrative. The theoretical background of the generation of modules and their sequencing is similar to the principles of *cellular automata*. Many of today's approaches to modeling real-world phenomena, which aim to come up with accurate models, are based on this approach. Within games it is not necessary to be accurate in that sense; it is all about be consistent and credible. Forsyth [3], for example has described methods with which natural processes (e.g., fluid flow) can be simplified for games using cellular automata.

The game entities are seen as cells of a multi-dimensional grid. Each cell is in one of a finite set of admissible states (e.g., in terms of story or in terms of knowledge) and each cell has a set of update rules. The state of a cell is a function of the states of the neighboring cells and it is sensitive to the actions of the learner. This results in an *ebbing and flowing* of incidents and it allows an emergent development of game play as well as narrative – of course limited by the global red thread through the game and the educational objectives. The properties of cells can either be discrete or steady. For example, probability distributions over cells are used to estimate the learner's knowledge (in the sense of an associated memory). In such a way, actions of the user influence the properties of the cells (the present game state). In turn, altering the properties of a cell changes the properties of the neighboring cells, comparable to the propagation of waves when a stone hits the water surface. To give an example, if the learner fails to narrow a light cone properly, the next learning unit automatically adjusts itself to teach the learner about the blind concept.

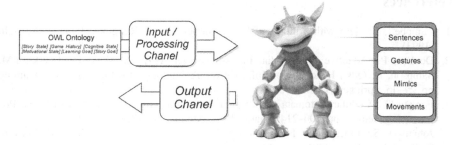

Fig. 4. Brief sketch of the architecture for an emergent behavior of the autonomous NPC – named Feon – that is currently developed in the 80Days project

What does this mean for our initial goal, reducing the costs of intelligent DEGs? The big advantage of this approach is that it is not necessary to develop all possible learning situations in a traditional sense. On this basis it suffices to develop a pool of assets (basic environments, objects, characters, sentences, etc.). The underlying intelligent technology autonomously builds the game upon the given assets.

4 Conclusion and Future Directions

To make effective and competitive DEGs mainstream educational technology, it is necessary to reduce the cost factor and to increase personalization and adaptation (which is likely even more important for DEGs than it is for conventional learning environments). The presented approach takes up existing intelligent technology for adaptation in the game-context and extends by a component of emergence – or rather *serendipity* (making fortunate discoveries by accident). We presented a hybrid model which tries to combine the best of both worlds, the author driven scripting of the global context (including the educator driven design of learning) as well as the degree of freedom and cost-effectiveness of emergent approaches to game design. Of course, the ideas and their technical realization are at an early level. Future work must extent the present theoretical approach, implement it, and evaluate its applicability. In the context of the European research project 80Days (www.eightydays.eu), we are currently focusing on an autonomous and intelligent NPC (Figure 4), which is supposed to serve as teacher in a competitive DEG. As outlined, the behavior of this character as a certain awareness of the game and learning progress and tailors its own behavior to those requirements. Thus, the script of what is happening when is not authored but emergent in the interaction with the learner. At the present stage, however, we have clear limitations in the variability of the overall story. Future developments will increase the freedom by extending the cellular network and by increasingly adding the so-called smart props.

Acknowledgements. The research and development introduced in this work is funded by the European Commission under the seventh framework programme in the ICT research priority, contract number 215918 (80Days, www.eightydays.eu).

References

1. Campbell, J.: Hero with a thousand faces. Harper Collins Religious, Pymble, Australia (1993)
2. De Bra, P.: Adaptive hypermedia. In: Adelsberger, H.H., Kinshuk, Pawlowski, J.M., Sampson, D. (eds.) Handbook on Information Technologies for Education and Training, pp. 29–46. Springer, Berlin (2008)
3. Forsyth, T.: Cellular Automata for Physical Modelling. In: Treglia, D. (ed.) Game Programming Gems 3, pp. 200–214. Charles River Media, Inc., Hingham (2002)
4. Johnnson, S.: Emergence: the Connected Lives of Ants, Brains, Cities and Software. Scribner, New York (2001)
5. Kickmeier-Rust, M.D., Albert, D.: The ELEKTRA ontology model: A learner-centered approach to resource description. In: Leung, H., Li, F., Lau, R., Li, Q. (eds.) ICWL 2007. LNCS, vol. 4823, pp. 78–89. Springer, Heidelberg (2008)

6. Kickmeier-Rust, M.D., Albert, D., Hockemeyer, C., Augustin, T.: Not breaking the narrative: Individualized Competence Assessment in Educational Games. In: Proceedings of the European Conference on Games based Learning (ECGBL), Paisley, Scotland, October 25-26 (2007)
7. Kickmeier-Rust, M.D., Göbel, S., Albert, D.: 80Days: Melding adaptive educational technology and adaptive and interactive storytelling in digital educational games. In: Klamma, R., Sharda, N., Fernández-Manjòn, B., Kosch, H., Spaniol, M. (eds.) Proceedings of the First International Workshop on Story-Telling and Educational Games (STEG 2008) - The power of narration and imagination in technology enhanced learning, Maastricht, The Netherlands, September 18-19 (2008)
8. Kickmeier-Rust, M.D., Hockemeyer, C., Albert, D., Augustin, T.: Micro adaptive, non-invasive assessment in educational games. In: Eisenberg, M., Kinshuk, Chang, M., McGreal, R. (eds.) Proceedings of the second IEEE International Conference on Digital Game and Intelligent Toy Enhanced Learning, Banff, Canada, November 17-19, 2008, pp. 135–137 (2008)
9. Leonard, T.: Building an AI Sensory System: Examining the Design of Thief: The Dark Project, Gamasutra, March 7 (2003)
10. Lindley, C.A.: Game Taxonomies: A High Level Framework for Game Analysis and Design. Gamasutra, October 3 (2003),
http://www.gamasutra.com/features/20031003/lindley_01.shtml
(retrieved October 23, 2008)
11. Peinado, F., Gómez-Martín, P.P., Gómez-Martín, M.M.: A game architecture for emergent story-puzzles in a persistent world. In: International DiGRA Conference, Vancouver, Canada, June 16-20 (2005)
12. Pressey, S.L.: A simple apparatus which gives tests and scores and teaches. School and Society 23(586), 373–376 (1926)
13. Russel, S., Norvig, P.: Artificial Intelligence: A Modern Approach. Prentice-Hall, Englewood Cliffs (2003)
14. Smed, J., Hakonen, H.: Towards a Definition of a Computer Game. Technical Report, Nr. 553, Turku Centre for Computer Science, Turku, Finland (2003)
15. Smith, H.: Systemic Level Design. In: The Game Developers Conference, San Jose, CA, March 21-23 (2002)
16. Sweetser, P.: Environmental Awareness in Game Agents. In: Rabin, S. (ed.) AI Game Programming Wisdom, vol. 3, Charles River Media, Inc., Hingham, MA (2006)
17. Sweetser, P.: An Emergent Approach to Game Design - Development and Play. Ph.D. Thesis. University of Queensland, Australia (2006)
18. Sweetser, P., Johnson, D., Sweetser, J., Wiles, J.: Creating Engaging Artificial Characters for Games. In: Proceedings of the Second International Conference on Entertainment Computing, pp. 1–8. Carnegie Mellon University, Pittsburgh (2003)

Intuitive Change of 3D Wand Function in Surface Design

Sang-Hun Nam[1], Hark-Su Kim[1], and Young-Ho Chai[2]

[1,2] The Graduate School of Advanced Imaging Science, Multimedia & Film
Chung-Ang University, 221 Heukseok-dong, Dongjak-gu,
Seoul 156-756, Korea
{sanghunnam,harksu}@gmail.com,
yhchai@cau.ac.kr

Abstract. According to the target model for a designer to sketch, an effective style or shape of input device can be defined differently. The spatial sketch system that supports various types of wand can help to sketch efficiently. We suggest the idea of changing wand style by altering the posture of a 3D wand. This method allows a designer to work in intuitive ways without being interrupted by complicated menus. We implement the surface drawing and merging technique with the grid based data structure which deals with multiple strokes from various types of wand.

Keywords: Virtual Reality, Virtual Conceptual Sketch, Surface Modeling, Interaction Technique.

1 Introduction

A number of tangible wands and software have been developed for sketching a model effectively in surface design. In hardware, a haptic device provides 3D interaction with force-feedback to users [1, 2] and enables them to reduce input errors in the depth position due to an incorrect cognition concerning depth cues [3, 4]. The similar shape of input device that user used to sketch on a 2D plane helps users to understand and adapt easily to a new device in spatial sketch system [5, 6]. In software, the wand shape in display can be changed for the purpose. BLUI [7] has a sphere-shaped wand and allow extruded surface to be created by moving a wand in space. Sketch-based 3D modeling systems, such as Teddy [8] and FiberMesh [9], enable the user to create a 3D model by inflating the region described by a silhouette. Thus, various styles of interaction with a 3D wand allow a designer to create spatial input suitable for different purpose. However, if it is necessary to navigate a complicated menu system to change the style of wand, the designer's train of thought will be interrupted. We propose a more intuitive method of changing wand brush style, based on the posture of the wand.

This research used a 3D input device that allowed designers to intuitively sketch within a spatial sketch system. Like the method through which a designer sketches on a 2D plane, the research used a method of drawing and deforming through the repetitive input of strokes [10, 11]. However, since curved lines and surfaces that are drawn overlapping, the drawing and merging algorithm is required to handle a large amount of data. Our system generates a model directly from the paths of different wand

R. Shumaker (Ed.): Virtual and Mixed Reality, LNCS 5622, pp. 216–224, 2009.
© Springer-Verlag Berlin Heidelberg 2009

brushes, each of which creates a different type of geometry. Our system uses a 3D input device to sketch and deform surfaces through a series of strokes. The drawing space contains pre-defined grids with movable internal vertices, which is similar to marching cubes [12].

This paper is comprised as follows. Chapter 2 explains the definition of wand brushes and the change of the brush style based on the posture of the wand. Chapter 3 explains surface modeling tool with multiple strokes. Chapter 4 explains the results of the paper.

2   Spatial Sketch Inputs with Various Brush Types

The way in which a designer uses a sketching system depends on the models they are trying to construct, and different types of brush would be appropriate for rectilinear and freeform models. Sketch systems therefore provide several brush types, for drawing different forms of geometry, such as curved lines and surfaces.

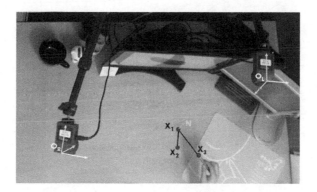

Fig. 1. Spatial sketch system

The position and posture of the wand is acquired by two infrared cameras which have three infrared reflection markers, as shown in Fig. 1. The velocity and acceleration of a moving wand can be calculated from a series of the position data. Also, the curvature (κ_w) and torsion (τ_w) of the wand can be calculated from (1). There are various kinds of brush types according to the relation between these properties and the changing rule of brush. We can associate three types of brush with a 3D wand, using rules which take account of the position and also the posture of the wand.

$$\kappa_w(t) = \frac{\|r'(t) \times r''(t)\|}{\|r'(t)\|^3}, \; \tau_w(t) = \frac{(r'(t) \times r''(t)) \cdot r'''(t)}{\|r'(t) \times r''(t)\|^2} \; . \tag{1}$$

First operation is used to define an initial swept cross-sectional curve as shown in Fig. 2(a). It is based on the Frenet formulas as shown in Fig. 2(b) and does not require menu interactions.

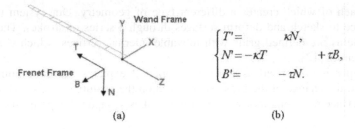

$$\begin{cases} T'= & \kappa N, \\ N'=-\kappa T & +\tau B, \\ B'= & -\tau N. \end{cases}$$

(a)   (b)

Fig. 2. Frenet frame and formulas

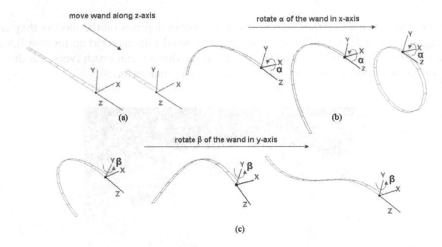

Fig. 3. Curve brush type

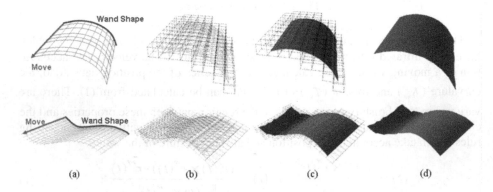

(a)   (b)   (c)   (d)

Fig. 4. Drawing surfaces with swept cross-sectional curves

As shown in Fig. 3(a), the length of the initial swept cross-sectional curve is adjusted by moving the wand in the z-direction. The curvature in the z-direction is created by the rotation α of the wand about the x-axis shown in Fig. 3(b), and the torsion in the z-direction is determined by the rotation β of the wand about the z-axis, as shown in Fig. 3(c). This arrangement can be changed at the beginning of the drawing process to be suitable for a designer.

A surface is defined by the swept cross-sectional curve shown in Fig. 4(a). This is then represented as polygons in the cells of the grid, as shown in Fig. 4(b). The rendered surface is shown in Fig. 4(c) and (d).

Second operation is a similar method to the first operation. However, this method has no need to make initial swept cross-sectional curves, because the cross-sectional curves are reshaped in proportion as the path of the wand automatically [8, 9]. As a designer moves the wand to draw a model in space, the operation gets the paths of the wand and calculates the curvature and torsion simultaneously in (1) as shown Fig. 5(a). The calculated curvature and torsion is applied to the Frenet formulas in Fig. 2(b). The designer can draw surfaces easily without the menu to change initial swept cross-sectional curves as shown in Fig. 5(b).

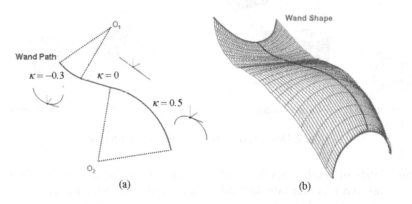

Fig. 5. Drawing a surface with automatic swept cross-sectional curves

Third operation is definition of the initial surface uses a similar method to that employed by the first brush, again using the Frenet formulas as shown in Fig. 2. Fig. 6(a) shows how the width of the initial surface is adjusted by moving the wand in the x and y-directions. The curvature in the y-direction is determined by the rotation α of the wand about the x-axis, and the curvature in the x-direction is determined by the rotation β of the wand about the y-axis, as shown in Fig. 6(b).

After the initial surface has been created, the designer moves the brush to the intended position and then stamps it. The surface is stored in the grid. Some rendered surfaces are shown in Fig. 7. This brush type is useful to draw shapes with simple geometries such as planes, cylinders, or spheres.

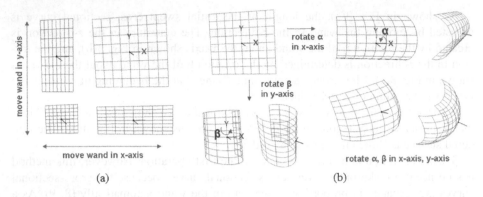

Fig. 6. Surface brush type

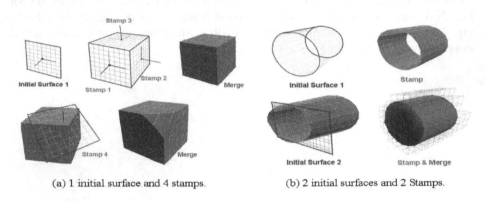

(a) 1 initial surface and 4 stamps.   (b) 2 initial surfaces and 2 Stamps.

Fig. 7. Drawing objects with a surface brush type

Three kinds of brush types have different advantage for use. So, it is useful to change brush types as occasion demands. Three kinds of brush types can be selected by the rotation of wand about the z-axis. A designer can change various brush types easily similar to changing initial curved lines and surfaces.

3 Surface Modeling with Grid-Based Data Structure

This paper suggests a modeling tool for conceptual surface design that draws a desired surface according to the distribution and the combination patterns of input data among grids, which is similar to marching cubes [12]. In the method using grids a surface is drawn based on the 3D input by applying to the spatial sketching a method for digitalizing a plane sketch into grid unit inputs. This has an effect on reducing the position errors caused by the repetitive input with additional stroke to modify a surface.

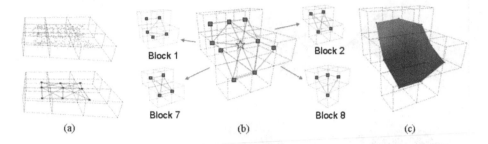

Fig. 8. The cubes with internal vertex and surface connected with internal vertices

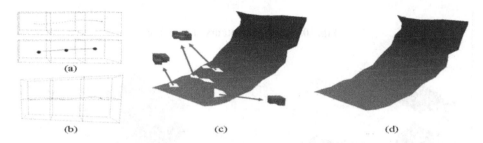

Fig. 9. A proper and improper input types in grids and a median surface regulation

As a designer moves the wand in drawing space, many points are inputted into grids from the input device and one internal vertex is calculated by a combination of input points in each grid and can be used as the real vertex of a real surface, as shown in Fig. 8(a). According to the relationship between the central grid and neighboring grids, a pre-defined pattern is selected as shown in Fig. 8(b). A surface is rendered by connecting the internal vertices with pre-defined patterns as shown in Fig. 8(c).

In a case in which an input stroke passes through grids that are simply connected as in Fig. 9(a), the intended curve can be easily drawn. However, as shown in Fig. 9(b), the input data can pass through the boundaries between the grids, or through the surrounding grids. In this case, the grids have unusual relationship with neighborhood grids, and so parts of surface with improper pattern are not drawn, as shown in Fig. 9(c). In order to minimize ambiguity by determining the valid grids, we regulate invalid parts of surface with the thinning algorithm [13]. However, the thinning algorithm erodes surface boundary well, which we want to preserve. We have extended thinning algorithm to preserve boundary and to avoid formation of a hole.

A designer sketches a model with multiple strokes with various wand brushes. Several surfaces with various shapes are inputted and merged to make a desired model. To connect and merge two surfaces, the modeling algorithm needs the relationships between both surfaces. So, we use the boundary contours for the regulation of grid based surface. When a surface is drawn by a stroke as shown in Fig. 10(a), the boundary cubes of outer boundary are searched as shown in Fig. 10(b). The boundary cubes are connected with near boundary cubes and made as a contour as shown in

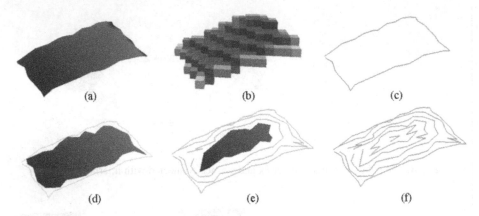

Fig. 10. Boundary contours of a surface

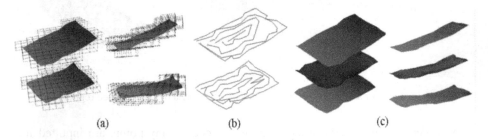

Fig. 11. Surface merging with parallel surfaces

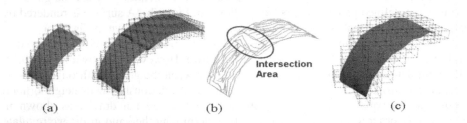

Fig. 12. Surface merging with intersected surfaces

Fig. 10(c). And the selected boundary cubes of the contour are removed as shown in Fig. 10(d). We make contours from the outer boundary one by one as shown Fig. 10(e) and (f).

There are two kinds of merging method in this paper. First method is merging two parallel surfaces. When a new surface is drawn, the new surface searches parallel surface with no intersection as shown in Fig. 11(a). If the parallel surface is found out, both surfaces make the boundary contours as shown in Fig. 11(b) and calculate the middle contours with both boundary contours. And a new surface is created with middle boundary contours as shown in Fig. 11(c). Second method is merging two surfaces that meet together. When a new surface meet existing surface as shown Fig. 12(a), both surface make the boundary contours and search intersection cubes as shown in Fig. 12(b). The intersection area is regulated with the thinning algorithm and the rule for removing protruding cubes as shown in Fig. 12(c).

4 Conclusions

This research adopted the idea that when a designer sketches a model, he/she uses various wand brush styles to draw it. Each brush style has advantages of drawing proper surfaces. It is useful for a designer to have several types of brush available as shown Fig. 13. We show how the style of brush can be selected by altering the posture of a 3D wand. This allows a designer to work in an intuitive way without being interrupted by complicated menus.

Our spatial sketch system simplifies the input data from different brush types by dividing the drawing space into a grid and makes an intended surface by regulating invalid cube patterns. We also use the boundary contours for surface merging.

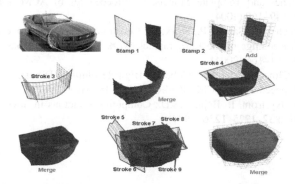

Fig. 13. Combination of surfaces with different brush types

Acknowledgments

This work is funded by KOSEF (Korea Science and Engineering Foundation). (No.R01-2007-000-20283-0)

References

1. McDonnell, K., Qin, H., Wlodarczyk, R.: Virtual clay: A real-time sculpting system with haptic interface. In: Proceedings of ACM Symposium on Interactive 3D Graphics, pp. 179–190 (2001)
2. Keefe, D., Zeleznik, R., Laidlaw, D.: Drawing on Air: Input Techniques for Controlled 3D Line Illustration. IEEE Transactions on Visualization and Computer Graphics 13, 1067–1081 (2007)

3. Fiorentino, M., Monno, G., Renzulli, P., Uva, A.: 3D Pointing in Virtual Reality: Experimental Study. In: XIII ADM–XV INGEFRAF International Conference on Tools and Methods Evolution in Engineering Design (2003)
4. Bowman, D., Johnson, D., Hodges, L.: Testbed Evaluation of Virtual Environment Interaction Techniques. Presence: Teleoperators and Virtual Environments 10, 75–95 (2001)
5. Schkolne, S., Michael Pruett, M., Schroder, P.: Surface Drawing: Creating Organic 3D Shapes with the Hand and Tangible Tools. In: Proceedings of the SIGCHI Conference on Human Factors in Computing Systems, pp. 261–268 (2001)
6. Keefe, D., Acevedo, D., Moscovich, T., Laidlaw, D.H., LaViola, J.: CavePainting: A Fully Immersive 3D Artistic Medium and Interactive Experience. In: Proceedings of ACM Symposium on Interactive 3D Graphics, pp. 85–93 (2001)
7. Brody, B., Harman, C.: Painting Space with BLUI. In: Proceedings of ACM SIGGRAPH Abstracts and Applications, p. 242 (2000)
8. Igarashi, T., Matsuoka, S., Tanaka, H.: Teddy: A Sketching Interface for 3D Freeform Design. In: Proceedings of ACM SIGGRAPH, pp. 409–416 (1999)
9. Nealen, A., Igarashi, T., Sorkine, O., Alexa, M.: FiberMesh: Designing Freeform Surfaces with 3D Curves. ACM Transactions on Graphics 26 (2007)
10. Kara, L., D'Eramo, C., Shimada, K.: Pen-Based Styling Design of 3D Geometry Using Concept Sketches and Template Models. In: Proceedings of ACM Solid and Physical Modeling, pp. 149–160 (2004)
11. Fleisch, T., Rechel, F., Santos, P., Stork, A.: Constraint stroke-based oversketching for 3D curves. In: Proceedings of the Eurographics Workshop on Sketch-Based Interfaces and Modeling, pp. 161–166 (2004)
12. Lorenson, E., Cline, E.: Marching Cubes: A High Resolution 3D Surface Construction Algorithm. In: Proceedings of ACM SIGGRAPH, pp. 163–169 (1987)
13. Borgefors, G., Nystrom, I., Baja, G.S.D.: Computing skeletons in three dimensions. Pattern Recognition 32, 1225–1236 (1999)

Software-Agents for On-Demand Authoring of Mobile Augmented Reality Applications

Rafael Radkowski

Heinz Nixdorf Institute, University of Paderborn
Fürstenallee 11
33102 Paderborn, Germany
Rafael.Radkowski@hni.uni-paderborn.de

Abstract. The paper presents an concept for the automatic authoring of augmented reality (AR) applications. The approach is based on software agents that provide different functions and content on demand for an AR application. Autonomous software agents encapsulate the specific functions of an AR application. It is distinguished between two kinds of software agents: So called provider-agents and user-agents. The user agent is configured by a human user, the provider-agent provides the functionality of an AR application. By communication and cooperation, provider and user agents form an AR application. The AR-based concept has been tested with the agent platform JADE.

1 Introduction

Augmented Reality (AR) is a human-computer-interface, which superimposes the perception of reality with computer-generated information [1]. The information is shown in the right context and with relation to a real world object. This information can be 3D models, text or annotations. To see them, special viewing devices are necessary. A classic viewing device is the head mounted display (HMD), a google-like thing that uses small displays instead of glasses. The user sees the reality as a video stream inside this displays, the computer-generated information superimpose the video stream.

Normally, most of the known AR applications are stand alone applications. These applications have a fixed set of functions as well as a fixed hardware setup at one certain location. These functions and the hardware setup form the configuration of the AR application. Figure 1 shows a schematic overview of a typical configuration of software components of an AR application. There are components for tracking, for interaction and for the content of the applications. To facilitate an AR application, the components exchange information. A tracking system tracks the position and orientation of the user and of real objects, surrounding the user. Content components for AR provide 2D visualizations, 3D models, annotations, and text information, etc. The content represents the information the AR application can present to the user. Interaction devices and the related software components provide the information from the hardware devices. All this information is processed in an application logic component, which manage the application and controls the renderer.

R. Shumaker (Ed.): Virtual and Mixed Reality, LNCS 5622, pp. 225–234, 2009.

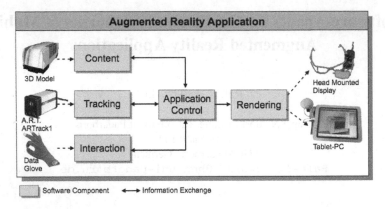

Fig. 1. Common component configuration of an AR application

Because AR applications present information about a localized real world object, a stand-alone application is suitable in many cases. But today, the mobile hardware devices become more and more smaller. In consequence, mobile, location based applications become important. If an AR application should facilitate information about more than on object, or should provide functions for more than one purpose, the configuration has to be changed.

There are two ways to change the configuration of an AR application: a programmer can reprogram the application or an AR-author uses an authoring tool. For a user of an AR application, e.g. a mechanics, an engineer or a medicine, these two ways are not adequate.

To get a dynamic change of the content, the tracking system, etc., different programming techniques exist. Software agents are one solution to achieve this. Software agents are autonomous computer programs that work according to the requirements of a user [2]. One feature of software agents is ability to communicate and cooperate with other software agents. In this paper, an agent-based AR software is described. First, the related work is discussed, and then the concept of the agent-based AR application is presented. Afterwards a software prototype of this concept is described and the first results are presented. At last, the results are summarized and an outlook is given.

2 Related Work

There are two research fields, which are related to the work, presented in this paper. These are software frameworks for AR applications and authoring tools. Both, software frameworks and authoring tools are used change the configuration of an AR application.

Software frameworks and APIs are the common way, because software developers create most of the developed and presented AR applications. They are the most flexible way to integrate new functions into an application, because new functionality is integrated by programming. This is flexible but very complex. At this place, only a few of them can be presented. One famous framework is Studierstube [3]. It is a framework for the development of mobile, collaborative and ubiquitous AR applications. The standard API is realized as a set of C++ classes built on top of the Open Inventor (OIV) graphics toolkit. It supports camera calibration and uses vision based pattern tracking. Because it is a programming interface it can be extended easily by adding new components. Another software for programming mobile AR applications is Tinmith [4]. Tinmith is a software architecture written in C++. It supports 2D and 3D rendering, tracker abstractions, object extensions etc.. The architecture has been designed and implemented for mobile outdoor augmented reality application. Interaction devices like data gloves can be easily integrated. To extend these two frameworks, it is necessary to program new functions or to integrate other software components by programming, too.

A framework, which can easily be extended by third-party components is DWARF [5]. DWARF is a CORBA based framework that allows the rapid prototyping of distributed AR applications. The framework is based on the concept of collaborating distributed services. The services are interdependent and expose their requirements with the help of service managers. It can be easily extended by integrated new services to the framework. With CORBA the development language can be chosen free from case to case. This framework simplifies the integration of new functions into an AR application and to design or setup a new application. But it doesn't work automatically.

Beside software frameworks and APIs, authoring tools are the second way to program a new application. But authoring tools have a fixed and limited set of functions, which can be configured by the user. If new functions are needed, they have to be programmed by the provider of the authoring tool or a computer scientist. For instance, authoring tools are DART (http://www.cc.gatech.edu/projects/dart/), AMIRE (http://www.amire.net/), and ARBlender (http://www.ai.fh-erfurt.de/arblender).

A work, which has the same aim is presented in [6], where a concept for ubiquitous tracking has been tested. Aim is to get data from widespread and diverse heterogeneous tracking sensors and automatically and dynamically fuse them, and then transparently provide them to applications. For tracking systems, the approach is close to the agent-based approach. But the agent-based approach extends it to content, interaction devices and the entire set of components necessary for an AR application.

3 Agent-Based AR Applications

Software agents have two features that facilitate a dynamic configuration of AR applications. It is their ability to communicate and to cooperate. If software agents encapsulate the functionality for an AR application, they are able to form an application only by communication. For that purpose, a proposal for an agent-based configuration is made and how the on-demand functionality can be achieved. Furthermore, a communication architecture is presented, that facilitates the dynamic connection of different components over TCP/IP or UDP/IP.

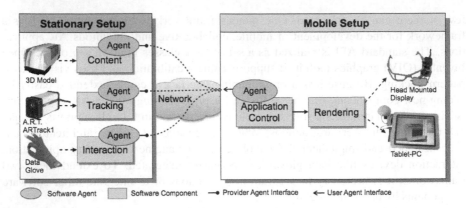

Fig. 2. Schematic overview of the agent-based approach for AR applications

3.1 Agent-Based Configuration

Figure 2 shows a schematic overview of the proposed agent-based configuration. Basic idea is, that software agents encapsulate the software components, necessary for an AR application. There need to be one agent for each component, which have to exchange data to the application control. Each agent knows the functionality of its related software component. Furthermore it knows the application context, in which the functions can be used.

The components of the AR application are separated into two classes: In components for a stationary setup and into components for a mobile setup.

Components of the stationary setup are localized. It is only reasonable to use them with relation to an appropriate place and an appropriate real world object. For instance a tracking system is localized. A hardware tracking system is installed and calibrated for one room. 3D models or text information should that an AR application shows should provide information about a real object. They are only reasonable at an appropriate location, too.

Components of the mobile setup are mobile. These are the application control and the rendering engine. The application control manages the information flow inside the application. For instance it shows or hide 3D models, annotate different real world objects, if they should be visible for the user. This managing component is only once needed. It must provide some basic functions (show/hide models, move models, change color, etc.), which can be selected by the content, tracking and interaction components. A rendering component is reasonable only in relation to a certain hardware device. Furthermore it don't need an agent, because their can be a point-to-point communication to the application control.

An AR application is realized by communication only. The task of the software agents is to found each other, to start an application and to initialize a communication process between the components. Initiate a communication process means, they agree about the values, the semantic of those values as well as about the communication protocol.

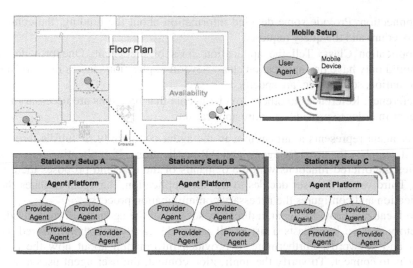

Fig. 3. Different stationary setups provide location-based functions for AR applications. If a mobile device comes close to a stationary setup, the user agent initiates the application.

3.2 On-Demand Authoring

On-demand in the context of AR applications means that a user can use a local referred application, if he is a) at the appropriate place and b) if he liked it. Authoring means that the content and functionality of an application and the necessary devices are changed in order to fulfill new requirements. This requires an infrastructure, that broadcast information about attainable applications and which informs the user, when a suitable application is attainable. To achieve this, two kinds of agents are proposed: the so called *provider agents* and *user agents*.

Provider agents provide information about the functionality of the location-based components (Fig. 3). There are two types of information: General information and communication information. General information provides data about the functionality of the agent and the application context. Communication information provides information about the data itself and about the binding procedure. In order to decide, which application or component is suitable for a user the general information is important.

The developer of the provider agent has to specify this information. Following information is proposed:

- ID: Each agent gets a unique id.
- Name: The name of the agent. The name can be chosen by the programmer of the agent
- Description: This is an annotation that should provide some further information about the agent.
- Keyword: Keywords, those provide a summary of the functions.
- Service Type: Specify the provider agent as provider of tracking functionality, interaction functionality or content.
- Server: Specify the url of the server, where the agent platform is located.

- Connection: Provide some detailed information about the binding, the connection procedure and the query requests.
- Application Class: Tell the application class of the agent. One provider agent should only have one application class. Several application classes like, art, fun, information, service, etc. are specified.
- Reference: References to other provider agents that functions are necessary for that agent in order to provide an entire application.

A user agent represents a human user in the agent community. It fulfills three tasks. First it searches for provider agents and AR applications. If applications are found, it verifies the offered functions with the demands of the user and proposes them to the user. Third, when the user decides to use the application, the agent initiates the AR application and configures the necessary communication process.

To localize a provider agent, a directory service of the agent platform is used. This directory service broadcasts a list of all available agents and their referred service types and keywords. Furthermore, it provides information about how the provider agent is to connect. To verify the application context, the user agent uses a keyword matching. Altogether, the user has to specify four type of information:

- Application Class: These keywords are similar to the applications classes of the provider agent. A user can specify as much keywords, as he wish to use.
- Keywords: These keywords should provide some detailed information about the applications, e.g. workshop, drilling machine, museum, etc. The keywords itself and their number can be chosen by the user.
- Human Factors: The most important human factors are, time, costs and location. By setting a time limit, the user tells the agent, how much time he want to spend for an application. Costs describe the prices that an user have to pay for an application. Location information help to find the application, It gives some detailed information about the location, e.g. a building or a room number.
- Hardware: Describes the hardware of the user. Most important values are the processing power, the available graphic capability, the memory and integrated interaction devices.

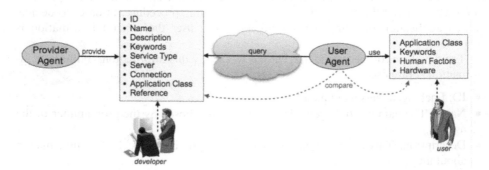

Fig. 4. Provider agent and user agent keep a set of data, the user agent compares this data to identify adequate applications

This keyword matching compares the application class of the provider agent and the keywords with keywords, entered by the user (Fig. 4).

3.3 Communication and Integration Architecture

If the user agent founds provider agents its user want to use, it has to setup an AR application. For that purpose, a communication server is used (Fig. 5). Main task of the communication server is to coordinate the data exchange between different software components. Software components can be tracking systems, software for interaction devices and the content. Because the AR applications should be realized by communication, the communication server is used as integration platform.

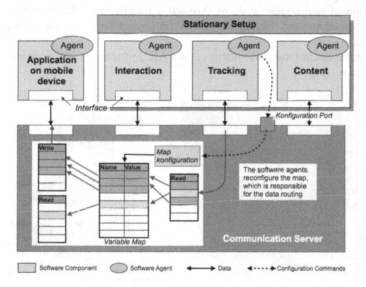

Fig. 5. A communication server is use to exchange the data between the components. The software agents send command to the server in order to configure the data routing.

To use the software agents itself for communication is not necessary. Main reason for that is the static communication between the components. Once, the communication is initialized, the attributes are fixed and will not be changed. An agents should be used only, if the values that are exchanged are not fixed. Furthermore, the time synchronize communication is better controllable over a central server.

Main part of the communication server is a variable map. Every variable that is exchange by the server is stored inside this map. The variables are stored by a unique name. This name is formed by the name of the component and a unique name for each variable

$$name\_of\_component.name\_of\_variable$$

Each component, which provides a variable, it is stored in the variable map. If a component needs variables, the communication server will send them to the component. Task of the software agents is to configure the read and write maps inside the communication server. If an user agent initialize an AR application, every provider agent declare the variables of the referred component to the server and start the application. After all variables are declared, the component starts to submit the data to the server. The user agent start to declare the date, its component needs to read.

4 Prototypical Realization

Aim of this work was to verify the agent-based architecture for AR applications and the keyword search for the on-demand configuration. For that purpose, a software prototype has been implemented. For that software prototype, an agent platform JADE (Java Agent DEvelopment Framework) has been used [7]. It simplifies the implementation of multi-agent systems through a middle-ware that complies with the FIPA specifications and through a set of tools that supports the debugging and deployment phases.

The test the agent-based architecture, two AR applications has been connected to software agents (Fig. 6).

a) AR to visualize the internal environment model of a soccer robot

b) An AR application, that visualize different cars. The user can change the color of the car.

Fig. 6. To test the agent-based architecture, two AR applications have been setup by software agents

The first AR application visualizes the internal environment model of autonomous soccer robots [8]. The second application shows different car models inside the real environment. To simulate different locations, each application has been installed in a different room. The 3D models, which present the environment to the user, and the car model have been encapsulated to software components. Moreover, two different tracking devices have been separated into two software components, which have been connected to a software agent. The soccer robots are tracked by an A.R.T. infrared tracking system [9], the car models are shown on ARToolkit pattern [10]. For the test, these four software components have been executed as stand alone applications, they communicate with the software agent via a TCP/IP socket. This was necessary to keep the existing applications and to allow software agents, written in JAVA to communicate with software, written in C++.

The AR rendering component has been programmed with OpenSceneGraph [11], an open source scenegraph programming library, written in C++. It runs as stand alone application and, for the tests, it communicates to a referred user-agent by a TCP/IP socket to. As hardware device a tablet PC (Compaq) has been used.

4.1 Results and Discussion

The application has been tested by a set of user. This test should show, if the user-agents are able to find the provider agents and if an AR application can be initialized by communication. The test show, that the software agents are able to configure the communication server and to initiate an AR application. Furthermore, they show that it is possible to separate a AR application in different independent running parts, which are integrated to an application, by communication and cooperation only. Existing agent frameworks like JADE allow a flexible cooperation between software agents. Further, they provide a service description and necessary functions to discover software agents on an agent platform.

One advantage of an agent-based concept is, that is separates the provider of the AR applications from the hardware of the user. Today, a provider of an AR application has to provide everything: the hardware, the rendering software, the tracking system, interaction devices and the content. There are no possibilities to separate these parts to different providers. For instance, one person/company could provide a tracking system on different places, and a provider of content, e.g. a museum, provide information to its paintings, based on the available tracking system. A visitor of this museum can use its on smart phone or tablet PC to use this AR application. Because people can user their own hardware theoretically, the provider of an AR application doesn't have to hold the hardware ready.

The big advantage is, that the agent-based approach facilitates a flexible framework for AR applications. Different agents form an AR application by communication only. If one component of the application should be exchanged, it is only necessary to change the software agent, encapsulate the needed functions. Of course, the software agents have to be prepared.

To achieve this flexibility, the communication protocol and agent service description must be standardizing. The general information the provider agent and user agent have been used is self-made. For the small controlled test, the keyword matching and the application classes work in order to found an application. But for a real world scenario, the information has to be standardized.

The agent-based AR applications aim to AR application in a workshop environment. Where a mechanics or an engineer use AR to analyze the behavior of a test bench or a mechanic maintenance a machine. This people use one hardware device only, but the need to use different content and different tracking systems. In such a not closed but limited environment, it is possible to have influence to the hardware, the communication protocol, and the service description. If these parts are under control, the agent-based AR application should facilitate flexible AR applications and an easy reconfiguration of the application without any assistance by an engineer of mechanics user.

5 Outlook

It is planed to use the agent-based architecture in an augmented reality-based experimental try-out environment for mechatronic systems. This environment is part of the collaborative research center 614 "Self-optimizing concepts and structure in mechanical engineering". Engineers use AR to analyze and test intelligent mechatronic systems. For that purpose, different extensions are planed.

First, the prototypical implementation must be extended. To test the architecture, a prototypical, not user-friendly software has been developed. This software serves for testing purposes only. For instance, the TCP based communication between software components of the AR application and the JADE agents is not sufficient. Therefore a wrapper API is planed.

Next, the information, which is exchange between the software agents and the keyword matching, should be extended. It is planed to use more than one model to describe the functionality of a software component. One model should provide information about the function, one model should describe the possible task, where the component can be reasonable used, and one model should describe the data.

In order to localize provider agent, a JADE agent platform needs to now the addresses of other reachable agent platforms. This way, a practical working service discovery cannot be realized. To improve this, the communication protocol, which the agents are used will be changed, of the agent platform will be changed.

References

1. Azuma, R.: A Survey of Augmented Reality. In: Presence: Teleoperators and Virtual Environments 6 (1997)
2. Jennings, N.R.: An agent-based approach for building complex software systems. Communications of the ACM 44(4), 7 (2001)
3. Schall, G., Newman, J., Schmalstieg, D.: Rapid and Accurate Deployment of Fiducial Markers for Augmented Reality. In: Proceed. of the 10th Comp. Vistion Winter Workshop, Zell an der Pram, Upper Austria (2005)
4. Piekarski, W., Smith, R., Thomas, B.H.: Designing Backpacks for High Fidelity Mobile Outdoor Augmented Reality. In: 3rd Int Symposium on Mixed and Augmented Reality, Arlington, Va (2004)
5. Bauer, M., Bruegge, B., Klinker, G., MacWilliams, A., Reicher, T., Riß, S., Sandor, C., Wagner, M.: Design of a Component-Based Augmented Reality Framework. In: Proceedings of The Second IEEE and ACM International Symposium on Augmented Reality (2001)
6. Newman, J., Wagner, M., Bauer, M., MacWilliams, A., Pintaric, T., Beyer, D., Pustka, D., Strasser, F., Schmalstieg, D., Klinker, G.: Ubiquitous Tracking for Augmented Reality. In: International symposium on mixed and augmented reality, Arlington, USA (2004)
7. Webpage of JADE, A open source plattform for peer to peer agent based applications (2009), http://jade.tilab.com/
8. Richert, W., Kleinjohann, B., Koch, M., Bruder, A., Rose, S., Adelt, P.: The paderkicker team: Autonomy in realtime environments. In: Proceedings of the Working Conference on Distributed and Parallel Embedded Systems, DIPES 2006 (2006)
9. Homepage of Advanced Realtime Tracing, http://www.ar-tracking.de/
10. Kato, H., Billinghurst, M.: Marker Tracking and HMD Calibration for a Video-based Augmented Reality Conferencing System. In: Proceedings of the 2nd International Workshop on Augmented Reality, IWAR 1999 (1999)
11. Webpage of OpenSceneGraph, http://www.openscenegraph.org

Multiuser Collaborative Exploration of Immersive Photorealistic Virtual Environments in Public Spaces

Scott Robertson, Brian Jones, Tiffany O'Quinn, Peter Presti,
Jeff Wilson, and Maribeth Gandy

Interactive Media Technology Center, Georgia Institute of Technology
85 5ᵗʰ Street NW, Atlanta GA 30308
{scott,brian,tiffany,peter,jeff,maribeth}@imtc.gatech.edu

Abstract. We have developed and deployed a multimedia museum installation that enables one or several users to interact with and collaboratively explore a 3D virtual environment while simultaneously providing an engaging and educational, theater-like experience for a larger crowd of passive viewers. This interactive theater experience consists of a large, immersive projection display, a touch screen display for gross navigation and three wireless, motion-sensing, hand-held controllers which allow multiple users to collaboratively explore a photorealistic virtual environment of Atlanta, Georgia and learn about Atlanta's history and the philanthropic legacy of many of Atlanta's prominent citizens.

1 Introduction

Multiuser Virtual Environments (MUVEs) enable multiple, simultaneous users to explore virtual worlds, interact with virtual objects and actors and participate in collaborative learning activities. Designing multiuser, collaborative virtual environments for public spaces such as museums is a challenging endeavor. Multimedia museum exhibits often only accommodate either single-user interaction (i.e. touch screen kiosk) or large groups of relatively passive viewers (i.e. theater video presentation). Our goal with this project was to create a multimedia museum experience that would enable one or several users to interact with and collaboratively explore a 3D virtual environment while simultaneously providing an engaging, theater-like experience for a larger crowd of passive viewers.

We were tasked with designing and implementing a shared virtual environment exhibit for the Millennium Gate and Museum of Atlanta, Georgia which would allow up to three users at a time to collaboratively visit and explore various important locations around Atlanta and to learn about the history, architecture, cultural and philanthropic heritage of Atlanta and its social, political and economic leaders over the past 150 years. Our primary target demographic was grade school through high school students, typically visiting the museum on field trips. The Millennium Gate Philanthropy Gallery (MGPG) system was developed to achieve these goals.

The MGPG system has been deployed in a theater-like space at the Millennium Gate museum and presents users with a large, high definition panoramic projection display showing interactive, photorealistic scenes around Atlanta, Georgia, a pedestal-mounted touch screen map used for gross navigation among various locations around

R. Shumaker (Ed.): Virtual and Mixed Reality, LNCS 5622, pp. 235–243, 2009.

Fig. 1. MGPG system panoramic display, pedestal touch-screen and motion-controllers

the metro Atlanta area and three motion-sensing, hand-held controllers derived from Nintendo Wii Remote game controllers (see Figure 1). Up to three active users utilize the touch screen map interface to travel from location to location around a virtual Atlanta with each location displayed on the projection screen as a full spherical panoramic image. Users use the three Wii Remote-based controllers to rotate the main projection screen camera view around and to find and select hidden "hot spots" and icons embedded each location scene, triggering the display of various media: photos, videos, text descriptions, quizzes, animations and audio clips. We found that the combination of gross navigation via touch screen and in-scene navigation and exploration with multiple hand-held controllers allowed several users to collaboratively explore the environments presented by the system.

We faced several major research challenges during the design and development of our project. This paper discusses the major technical and usability challenges we encountered and how we addressed each. In the following sections we present a description of the hardware and software architecture of the MGPG system, a description of how the MGPG system operates, including the educational content it showcases and a discussion of the user interaction challenges we faced and the solutions we developed. The last section discusses the conclusions we have reached thus far and possible future work for this project.

2   Related Work

Many museums have utilized technology to enhance the visitor experience, including the use of various virtual and augmented reality techniques [1][2]. Some museums and other public venues have also experimented with virtual reality environments and large public displays designed to encourage social interaction between on-site visitors or between on-site and on-line visitors [3]. Many studies of such systems have revealed difficulties in encouraging people to interact with them, especially in a public, social context. Brignull and Rogers' Opinionizer system [4], for example, investigated the causes of resistance by the public to participate in large display shared and social experiences and identified feelings of social embarrassment as a significant barrier. In designing our system we also considered ways of mitigating social embarrassment and encouraging collaborative participation. Our design strategies are presented in this paper.

Recent interactive installations have made effective use of hand-held tracking or pointing controllers, such as Wii Remote controllers to allow multiple users to collaborate and interact with large display walls. Infrared-filtered flashlights and camera tracking was used in the Beware Home demonstration [5] and Blitz Agency's "Adobe Creativity Conducted" interactive art wall [6] utilized multiple Wii Remote controllers to allow users to collaborative paint on a large display wall. The MGPG system is one the first permanent museum installations to use such technology. We purposely chose to use multiple Wii Remote controllers, a common paradigm from video game console systems, to appeal to young, game-savvy museum visitors and encourage them to interact with one another while exploring the system.

In designing the Millennium Gate Philanthropy Gallery System, we have attempted to address our client's desire to produce an entertaining and educational interactive experience for small groups of museum visitors, particularly grade school aged children. Given the design goal of multiuser collaborative exploration, we devoted considerable effort to developing and testing modes of system operation which would foster constructive social interaction among active and passive users.

3 System Hardware Architecture

Our system consists of several hardware components, including a high-definition, panoramic front projection display, a pedestal mounted touch screen, three Wii Remote-based motion-sensing input controllers and several CPUs to drive the displays and Wii Remote controllers.

3.1 Input Devices

We investigated a number of user input devices from touch screens to camera-based motion trackers before choosing the wireless, motion-sensing Wii Remote controllers used by Nintendo's Wii game system. Our main requirements for the input devices were to allow one to three simultaneous users to control the view of a virtual camera and to select and interact with graphical objects on a large projection screen. Wii Remote controllers naturally allow a "point and shoot" style interaction with large display screens which has proven to be good for object selection tasks [7]. We also found that the motion tracking Wii Remote controllers could allow several users to cooperate in controlling a virtual camera showing scenes around Atlanta and to explore and select graphical objects in each city scene. We briefly considered building custom motion tracking devices similar to Wii Remotes, but decided instead to modify the relatively inexpensive Wii Remote controllers, removing most buttons, replacing the battery power source with a hard-wired power cable that doubles as a security tether and fabricating new cases and buttons for the modified electronics. We also surmised that Wii Remote controllers would present a familiar and fun interaction mode to many, if not most of our target audience and that users not intimately familiar with using Wii Remotes would likely still find them intuitive to use as their size, shape and function is similar to television remote controls, a device that most of our users would be familiar with.

The Nintendo Wii Remote game controller contains traditional control buttons, a three-axis accelerometer, and an infrared fiducial tracking camera. These sensors allow the Wii Remote to be used as a "magic wand" pointing device. Wii Remotes report position, orientation and button data to the game console via a wireless Bluetooth connection. In our system, users simply aim the controller at a location on the large projection screen to control a cursor or reticle, which is used for discovering "hot-spot" objects, and use an eight-way direction pad button to rotate the virtual camera view to see different areas of the scene. Users activate the multimedia content attached to hot-spots either by dwelling their cursor over the hot-spot for a short time or by pressing a second button on the controller.

3.2 System Displays

The main projection screen in our system is quite large and high-resolution, utilizing two 1080P HD projectors. The two projectors' images are tiled side-by-side with image overlap and edge blending to create a seamless and extreme panoramic view (see Figure 1). The approximately twenty-feet wide and seven-feet tall screen is cylindrically curved and provides an immersive and theater-like experience to both active and passive viewers. Due to the rather shallow depth of the room in which our system is installed, most viewers stand close to the projection screen, between six to ten feet from the screen. This close proximity to such a large, high-definition cylindrical display produces an immersive experience similar to a CAVE [8].

We considered utilizing the large projection screen as the sole display, but ultimately decided to use a secondary pedestal-mounted touch screen for gross system navigation. The touch screen pedestal also houses cradles for the wired Wii Remote controllers. We fabricated retracting security and power cables for the Wiimote controllers to facilitate return of the control to its cradle, while constraining the use of the Wiimotes to be within optimal viewing range of the screen-mounted infrared tracking beacons and preventing their theft.

4 System Software Architecture

The MGPG system's hardware components are driven by a set of applications and servers running on three separate CPUs, including a high-power graphics workstation dedicated to driving the large projection display. The software architecture consists of a 3D graphics application, developed using the Unity 3D game engine, which drives the projection display, a separate Adobe Flash application displaying a map

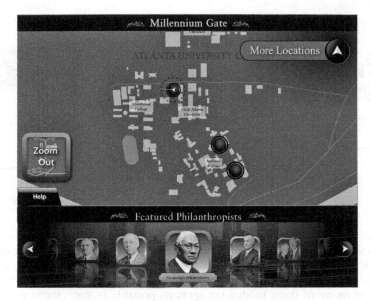

Fig. 2. Touch screen map showing panorama nodes

user interface on the pedestal touch screen, and a Wii Remote server application which is responsible for establishing and maintaining Bluetooth connections to the Wii Remote controllers and streaming tracking, orientation and button press data to the Unity application. The touch screen Flash map application, the projection display Unity application and the Wii Remote server communicate via socket messages.

The touch screen map application sends messages to the projection display application in response to touch screen input selections, sending commands to change city location, play and skip introduction videos, display help instructions, timeout the display systems when idle, etc. Figure 2 shows a sample map screen from the center console touch screen.

4.1 System Operation

The pedestal touch screen is used to navigate between the major city areas, or nodes, of Midtown Atlanta, Downtown Atlanta and the Atlanta University Center. Users zoom into individual city scenes by touch-selecting a major node icon (i.e. Downtown Atlanta), then a sub-node icon (i.e. Centennial Olympic Park) and finally touch icons for individual panoramic environments which display on the projection screen.

The projection display is used to show help instructions (see figure 3), node introduction videos, panoramic city scenes and all of their associated media and educational content. Users use the Wii Remote controllers' eight-way direction button to rotate the camera view. By aiming a controller at the projection screen each user controls a color and number coded cursor to select floating icons and hidden "hot spots" in the scene to activate various educational media content such as pop-up text and image "billboards", animations, videos, interactive quizzes and audio effects related to the location node the users are currently exploring. Some content naturally relates

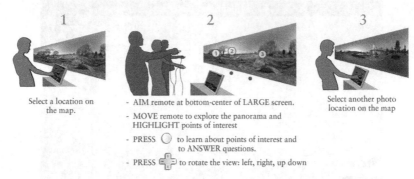

Fig. 3. Touch screen help screen showing system interaction instructions

to visible objects in each scene, a building or monument for example, and in these instances we create hidden "hot-spot" area triggers which, when "rolled" over with a user's Wii Remote cursor first highlight and after a dwell time threshold or controller button press activate or pop up the associated content object. We purposefully designed as many of these hidden hot-spots as possible in each scene to encourage exploration. Whenever there was not a large enough visible scene object or element to associate a media asset to, we instead designed a representative icon to insert into the scene and act as a hot-spot trigger.

4.2 System Media Content

The MGPG system allows users to explore a number of locations around the metro Atlanta, Georgia area. Each location was photographed using a high resolution digital

Fig. 4. Panoramic scenes with pop-up media activated

still camera and a spherical panorama tripod head to produce a 360° by 180° equirectangular image. These images are mapped to textured, environment maps to produce a photorealistic background for 2D and 3D overlay graphics. These photographic scenes are similar to Apple's Quicktime VR movies. Figure 4 shows example panoramic camera scenes with Wii Remote cursors and various activated media overlays.

A large database of photos, videos, audio clips and text scripts are embedded in the many city panoramic scenes. We worked with a team of museum exhibit designers, curators and subject matter experts who were responsible for the assembling the educational content of the project, including writing all scripts, researching and acquiring media assets and insuring that the presented content meets Georgia public school educational requirements.

5 System Design and Usability

We faced several major research challenges during the design and development of our project: How can we allow up to three people to simultaneously interact with and explore this shared virtual environment? What types of interactions will be pleasing to users, both those experienced in using the system and new visitors who walk up to the exhibit while it is currently in use by others? Can we provide an engaging experience for the one to three users actively interacting with the system as well as with a potentially large group of passive observers? How can we ensure usable navigation of the virtual environment for a single user as well as two or three users? Can normal social rules help mediate the interactions or will specific technology limitations need to be put in place? We developed a number of hardware and software solutions to address these challenges.

We chose to use Nintendo Wii Remotes for the major projection screen interaction and navigation because they have been proven to work well other multiple user applications, namely Wii video games. We were confident that most of our primary audience, grade school and high school children, would understand the Wii Remote interaction paradigm since many would certainly already be familiar with the operation of such controllers. We were pleased to discover after deployment of the system that most users, regardless of age or familiarity with video game systems, seemed to quickly learn how to use our controllers.

5.1 Usability Testing

Due to the limited budget and timeline and the manner in which components came together during the development and installation of the MGPG, we had little time or resources to conduct formal user studies. However, informal evaluation of the interactions was conducted during development to ensure the system would be usable and function as planned. We also were able to observe visitors to the museum interacting with the system during the opening weekend.

User Testing During Project Development. During project development we constructed a slightly scaled-down version of the museum's Philanthropy Gallery in our lab space using two 1080P home theater projectors. We used this development system to conduct informal usability testing with other IMTC personnel, Georgia Tech grad students and a group of visiting high-school students. Feedback from these users helped us define and refine the user interface components of the MGPG system.

Initial observation and feedback during testing of our simplified Wii Remote controllers by IMTC personnel and grad students revealed that while the controllers were quite good for navigating around a single city node, they did not afford intuitive navigation between different areas of the city or between multiple camera views, or sub-nodes, of an area. We ultimately decided to add a separate touch screen, map-based display for gross navigation. In further observation, interview and group review sessions with grad students and a group of high-school students we discovered that this configuration allowed two or three users to easily share control of the touch-screen while simultaneously exploring the main projection screen with their hand-held Wii Remote controllers.

User Testing After Deployment. In casual observations of user interactions during the opening weekend of the museum, we found that larger groups of passive viewers enjoyed the theater-like experience of watching the active users explore the extensive content. We also observed the Wii Remote controller users verbally negotiating and sharing control of the virtual camera view and touch-screen map navigation. Rather than devolving into conflict, the social interaction required of users allowed them to collaborate in exploring the virtual environments and, we suspect, created a better learning experience for them.

Brignull and Rogers [4] describe the "honey pot effect", a type of social affordance in which a number of people congregating near or using their Opinionizer system enticed a progressively increasing number of users to participate. We observed the same effect with the MGPG system. During the museum's opening weekend event, we repeatedly observed how one or two users actively controlling the system seemed to attract the interest of other visitors, friends and family and strangers alike. In some cases, children would operate the system while parents and grand-parents would give verbal directions for navigating the system. The active users would often take on a kind of tour guide role in their social interactions with passive users.

When visitors encountered the system without anyone actively using it, we often observed some hesitancy to begin interacting with the touch screen or Wii Remote controllers. This behavior may have been the result of visitors' fear of social embar-rassment [4] to be the first or only person in a group to attempt to operate the system. This reluctance was mainly observed in older adults and not younger adults and children, perhaps owing to younger users' comfort level with technology and video game controllers.

6 Conclusion and Future Work

We have developed and deployed a multimedia museum installation that enables one or several users to interact with and collaboratively explore a 3D virtual environment while simultaneously providing an engaging and educational, theater-like experience for a larger crowd of passive viewers. We have taken pains to insure that the em-ployed user interface technologies afford quick understanding of interaction paradigm by our target audience. Further, we made design choices to encourage people to feel comfortable using the system.

We hope to secure future funding to expand the scope of the MGPG system to include many more areas around Atlanta and to add more content features such as educational games, videos and quizzes. In future studies we also wish to investigate our hypothesis that the social interaction and cooperation required of users in controlling and navigating around in the MGPG system facilitates a better collaborative learning experience.

References

1. Woods, E., Billinghurst, M., Looser, J., Aldridge, G., Brown, D., Garrie, B., Nelles, C.: Augmenting the Science Centre and Museum Experience. In: Proceedings of the 2nd International Conference on Computer Graphics and Interactive Techniques in Australasia and South East Asia, Singapore (2004)
2. DiPaola, S., Akai, C.: Designing an Adaptive Multimedia Interactive to Support Shared Learning Experiences. In: ACM SIGGRAPH 2006 Educators Program, Boston, MA (2006)
3. Galani, A., Chalmers, M.: Far Away is Close at Hand: Shared Mixed Reality Museum Experiences for Local and Remote Museum Companions. In: Proceedings of ICHIM 2003. Archives & Museum Informatics, Europe (2003)
4. Brignull, H., Rogers, Y.: Enticing People to Interact with Large Public Displays in Public Spaces. In: Proceedings of Interact, pp. 17–24 (2003)
5. Kidd, C.D., Starner, T., Gandy, M., Quay, A.: The Beware Home: A Contextually Aware Haunted House. GVU Technical Report, Georgia Institute of Technology (2000)
6. Blitz Agency: Adobe Creativity Conducted. In: Adobe Max 2007 Conference, Chicago (2007)
7. Ballagas, R., Rohs, M., Sheridan, J.: Sweep and Point & Shoot: Phonecam-Based Interactions for Large Public Displays. In: CHI 2005 Posters, Portland, OR (2005)
8. Cruz-Neira, C., Sandin, D., DeFanti, T., Kenyon, R., Hart, J.: The CAVE®: Audio Visual Experience Automatic Virtual Environment. Communications of the ACM 35(6), 65–72 (1992)

A Design Method for Next Generation User Interfaces Inspired by the Mixed Reality Continuum

Jörg Stöcklein[1], Christian Geiger[2], Volker Paelke[3], and Patrick Pogscheba[2]

[1] University of Paderborn, Germany
`ozone@uni-paderborn.de`
[2] Duesseldorf University of Applied Sciences, Germany
`{geiger,Patrick.Pogscheba}@fh-duesseldorf.de`
[3] Leibniz University of Hannover, Germany
`Volker.Paelke@ikg.uni-hannover.de`

Abstract. In this paper we present a new approach to the systematic user centric development of next generation user interfaces (NGUI). Central elements of the approach are a conceptual model that extends the well established model view controller paradigm with an environment component, an iterative development methodology that guides development along the mixed reality continuum and tools to support the implementation. The approach is demonstrate with a concrete example of NGUI development.

Keywords: Mixed Reality, Next Generation User Interface Development.

1 Introduction

Next generation user interfaces (NGUI) diverge from the well known WIMP paradigm (window, icon, menu, pointer) and employ novel techniques like virtual, augmented and mixed reality interaction or tangible, embodied and multi-modal interfaces [1]. Achievements in recent years allow researchers to shift their focus from technical questions like IO devices, tracking and rendering to the design of such interfaces. However, they are faced with the challenge that NGUIs are less representational (no icons representing objects) and focus on reality-based interaction styles which leverage the user's built-in abilities by exploiting pre-existing skills and expectations from real-world experiences rather than computer trained skills. The proposed intuitiveness for end users has fundamental consequences for the designer. While design in other disciplines can draw on existing expertise to enable a streamlined, effective design processes without much experimentation, the lack of such expertise and the interdisciplinary nature of NGUI design requires a process based on iterative refinement and evaluation. The lack of a formal specification rules out the use of formal verification techniques and the limited design expertise limits the applicability of techniques like expert reviews for NGUI applications, leaving experimental evaluation through tests with potential end-users as the most promising option. However, a simple implement and test approach is not viable because the implementation of working prototypes is expensive and time consuming, limiting the number of concepts and designs that can be possibly explored. In order to evaluate the concepts

R. Shumaker (Ed.): Virtual and Mixed Reality, LNCS 5622, pp. 244–253, 2009.

under controlled conditions it is therefore necessary to remove technology problems from conceptual tests. To address these problems we developed a design process and corresponding support for NGUI design. The process is aimed at the fast development and evaluation of iteratively refined prototypes along a mixed reality continuum. This paper describes the principal idea of our design approach in section 3, and presents a project which was realized using our approach in section 4. We start with a short review of related work.

2 Related Work

A design approach for NGUI should be defined along three essential components. A conceptual model that allows to describe design entities for all stakeholders. A design process that provides a structured course of action and a technical framework that supports the efficient development of NGUI applications. The most prominent model for graphical user interfaces is the MVC paradigm originally defined for the Small-Talk80 programming language [2]. A model separates the data from its representation (view) and control elements (controller) provide for user interaction. Ishii extended this model to describe tangible user interfaces [3]. He adds a tangible / real representation to the digital view that is basically used as direct control mechanism. Real objects act as physical representations of interface elements and allow to use real and virtual elements in tangible user interfaces. Milgram's mixed reality continuum defines arbitrary combinations of real and virtual elements in more detail and ranges from virtual reality, augmented virtually, augmented reality to real reality [4]. Ourapproach uses this continuum as an additional dimension for the MVC model.

One of the earliest approaches towards a NGUI authoring framework was DART, an extension of Adobe Director by a number of AR features [5]. DART has been used in large projects and allows content experts to build AR worlds using Director's theatre metaphor as its conceptual model. Broll presented a visual authoring framework for 3D interaction techniques at 3DUI 2008 [6]. Their concept of "interactive bits" is a component-based approach to visually specify interactions techniques, object behavior or whole prototypes. The framework combines synchronous control and data flow with asynchronous event and network distribution and provides a XML-based description of the objects, components and the data/control flow. NIMMIT is a graphical notation for multimodal VR interaction techniques that is based on a state-chart model. Task chains between states define a linear control flow and high level variables (labels) allow data flow between tasks. Hierarchical task structures are supported and a tool allows to store the description in an XML file that can be loaded into a VE framework. A model-based design approach is nowadays mainly used for multi-device WIMP user interfaces but the declarative and visual description offers also benefits for NGUIs. Cuppens et al. presented a model-based framework for VR environments. They suggested to start with a task-related model that incrementally evolves towards the final user interface in an iterative design process [7]. Envir3D is a modeling tool, which enables users to visually specify 3D content, while preserving an underlying user interface model that can be used for evaluation and re-engineering. The model is used to generate VRML code that represents the 3D user interface. A number of relevant approaches, including model-based design, visual authoring and

HCI principles and guidelines for mixed reality user interface design was presented at the MRUI07 workshop at VR 2007 [8]. Due to space limitations we only give a reference to the proceedings that is one of the most relevant sources for our project. The main contribution of this paper is the combination of a extended 3D authoring framework with an iterative design approach that is based on a suitable conceptual model.

3   Design of Next Generation User Interfaces

While next generation user interfaces are often characterized by the employed technologies the ultimate aim is to create better interfaces for the user. It is therefore essential that a user centered design process is employed. At the same time the experimental nature of some base technologies must be adequately handled while the integration into larger systems requires the use of a systematic, controllable and manageable software engineering process. To address the need for experimentation within a structured development approach we structure our systems into loosely coupled components, using a model that extends the model-view-controller pattern with an additional component that captures the influence of the real world.

3.1   The MVCE Model

The model-view-controller pattern (MVC) structures user interfaces into three components and is popular in the development of user interfaces. The key benefit of this decomposition is that the visual and interaction aspects of a user interfaces can beisolated from the underlying application. The model (M) represents the application data and encapsulates the functionality of the application. The view (V) encapsulates the visual elements of the user interface, e.g. button widgets, text or visualizations. The controller (C) handles the interaction details, e.g. mouse events or text input and communicates necessary actions to the model. The MVC pattern enables modulardesigns in which changes in one component aren't coupled to other aspects. It alsoallows to provide multiple views and controllers for the same application/model. This is a desirable property, especially for multimodal interfaces that rely on specialized hardware that may not be available in all situations.

Figure 1a illustrates the communication between the three elements: When information in the model (e.g. application data) changes, the model notifies the view with a change_notification event. If an update of the presentation in the interface is required (e.g. this data is displayed) the view queries the model to retrieve the required

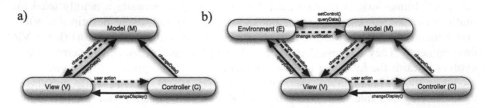

Fig. 1. a) The MVC model, b) The MVCE model

information and updates the information presentation accordingly. If the user interacts with the view (e.g. by clicking elements with the mouse) the controller is notified by user_action events. Depending on the semantics associated with the interaction event (the interaction technique encapsulated in the controller) the controller can change both data in the model (e.g. if the user inputs new values) or the presentation in the view (e.g. if the user changes the presentation).

One central feature of mixed-reality user interfaces is the integration with a real environment. The application requires information about objects and spaces, whose geometry and behavior is not under the control of the designer but must be acquired from the real environment. Real objects can be subject to real-world manipulation (e.g. in a maintenance task) or external forces. Therefore, it must be possible to track state changes in the environment. In practice the "real world" model of a mixed reality application often consists of a combination of static information (e.g. geometry of the environment that is assumed to be fixed) and dynamic information (e.g. position and orientation information for the user and central objects) that is acquired by sensors at runtime. While sensor information could be handled as controller events in the MVC model this can lead to complex and obscure models. We have therefore introduced an additional environment (E) component that captures the "real world" model of the application (see Figure 1b). A perfect real world model would contain all information about the real environment at the time of query. In practice both the amount of information required by the application and the amount actually accessible through sensors is limited.

The environment (E) is used similar to the model (M), with the main difference that the software has only a limited influence on the environment through dedicated controls, while the model is in theory completely controllable by software. Both the model (M) and the view (V) can query the environment (E). This allows to capture spatial association (e.g. the common augmented reality scenario in which a view object is fixed to a physical location or object) as well as control relations (e.g. objects in the real environment influenced by the application). Sensors in the environment can issue change_notification events to inform other components about detected changes, which can be used to implement tangible interaction techniques in which physical interaction with physical objects is interpreted as an action on software objects.

Using the MVCE structure, components can be refined independently. The current development state of a prototype can be characterized by the amount of complexity/ realism for each component, as visualized in the component refinement diagram in figure 2, where the center indicates the most abstract representation and movement along the MVCE axes represents in creasing refinement/ realism of the corresponding components. Each axis indicates the independent refinement state of the corresponding component. One key

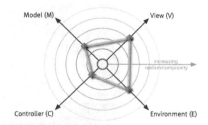

Fig. 2. Component refinement state diagram

benefit is the possibility to develop a user interface "along the mixed-reality" continuum, starting with a virtual environment in which the environment (E) is represented by a model. Testing mixed reality interfaces in a virtual environment allows to focus on interaction mechanisms and can provide controlled conditions for tests, while avoiding limitations of mixed reality technologies (e.g. tracking systems) that are often present in early development stages. Refinement of the E component ranges from more refined models to real-time data acquisition in the real environment. Arbitrary combinations of components are possible, e.g. it is sometimes useful to combine refined MVC components with a simple E model, for tests or demonstrations in later development stages.

The design approach needs adequate tool support that reflects the iterative nature of the process. Tools that support the efficient exchange of modules during iterative prototyping should fulfill a number of requirements: (1) a component-or building block-oriented system architecture, (2) a large component repository providing a variety of functions for NGUI design and (3) a visual authoring framework supporting quick prototyping. We provide such tool support with our HYUI system. More details about the underlying framework were presented in [9].

4   Example

We applied the iterative design approach as described in section 3 in an ongoing project where next generation user interfaces were developed along the mixed reality continuum. We used an indoor airship and are currently developing a training system that uses the complete MR continuum for different design variants. The idea is to train users of a radio-controlled indoor airship and develop new interaction techniques and training scenarios.

Technically the indoor airship is controlled by three propeller, as shown in figure 3a. The left and right propeller (figure 3b) can be rotated around the pitch axis (z). Both are connected to each other, thus the rotation speed and the pitch angle are the same. With these two propeller the zeppelin can navigate back and forth as well as up and down and diagonal. The third propeller is mounted at the back of the zeppelin (figure 3c) and is used for rotation around the yaw axis (y). Therefore the zeppelin has 3 degrees of freedom, translation on the x-and y-axis and rotation around the y-axis. The zeppelin can't directly move along the z-axis or roll and pitch.

Fig. 3. The real Zeppelin

For controlling the airship's propeller a radio-powered remote control is used. Steering the zeppelin with it is tricky and for simple movement users have to practice many hours. Difficult maneuvers like flying to a specific point with a certain orientation need even more practice. The development of such a training application was used to demonstrate our design process.

4.1 Prototype 1: Simple Virtual Reality

We started the first prototype with a small 3D scenario using a simple script that modifies the transformation matrix of the model. With the keyboard the user can move the airship around in a virtual environment. We specify the four different parts of our MCVE paradigm as followed: The model is the transformation matrix (position and orientation) which moves and rotates our virtual zeppelin. The environment consists of a virtual floor only and constrains the flight level. The view is the simplified 3D model of the airship, and the controller is the direct manipulation of the transformation matrix of our model. This is done using the computer keyboard.

Users can easily practice maneuvers and learn how to handle the zeppelin. A disadvantage is the use of a keyboard as input device, because it is very different to the remote control used for the real zeppelin. Figure 4 shows our simple application and the assignment in our component refinement state diagram. The model, the environment, the view and the controller are very basic, therefore all the points in the component refinement state diagram are near the center.

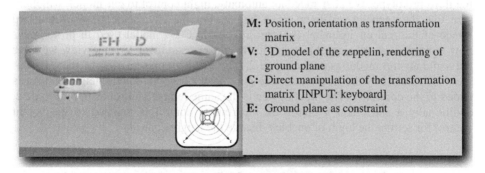

M: Position, orientation as transformation matrix
V: 3D model of the zeppelin, rendering of ground plane
C: Direct manipulation of the transformation matrix [INPUT: keyboard]
E: Ground plane as constraint

Fig. 4. Simple virtual reality application

4.2 Prototype 2: Game Physics

In the second prototype we tweaked the application towards more realism and complexity. As model we uses the Havoc game physic engine [10], which calculates the position and orientation of the airship (figure 5). We changes the environment to a static 3D CAD model of the real environment. The 3D model of the zeppelin is improved and the 3D model of building (the environment) is rendered. Forces of the propeller are visualized as vectors. For the controller we manipulate the 3 DOF of the zeppelin directly (rotor orientation, rotor speed, tail-rotor speed) and uses a remote control connected to the PC via USB for steering. In our component refinement state

M: Position, orientation as transform. matrix, controlled by game physics dynamics model
V: Refined 3D zeppelin model; rendering 3D model of env.; vector visualization
C: Direct control of 3 DOF (rotor orient. a. speed, tail rotor speed) [INPUT: remote control]
E: Static 3D CAD model of the environment

Fig. 5. Prototype using game physics

diagram all points placed one cycle away from the middle towards more realism and complexity. Now the user application can steer the zeppelin by using a standard remote control, which is more realistic than using the keyboard and thus better suited for training. Also the game physic engine create more realism in the motion-behavior.

4.3   Prototype 3: MATLAB/Simulink Simulation

Because the game physic engine is not as realistic as it should be, we build a MATLAB/Simulink [11] model for calculating the transformation and orientation in the third prototype. We also added an automatic hight control to our model, whichensure that the zeppelin retains a preset height. For the environment we uses a live image of the real environment (figure 6). The 3D CAD model used in prototype 2 now is needed as collision object and for height measurement. For the view we have the same airship-model as in prototype 2. The virtual representation of the environment is replaced by the live video. The parameter of the automatic height control is added to the controller. The input device is the same remote control as in prototype 2, additionally a slider and a button on the remote control is mapped to the height control for setting the hight or enable / disable the height control.

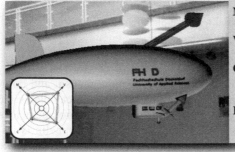

M: Transform. matrix controlled by physics model (Simulink); autom. height control
V: Zeppelin 3D model; vector visualization; live image as background
C: Direct control of 3 DOF (rotor orient. a. speed, tail rotor speed) [INPUT: remote control]
E: Static 3D model for collisions; live image of environment; height measurement

Fig. 6. Application using the MATLAB/Simulink model and a video background

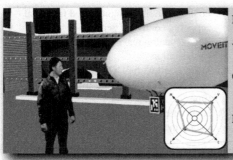

M: Position, orientation measured from real zeppelin; collision detection

V: Real zeppelin, rendering of virtual environment

C: Direct control of 3 DOF (rotor orient. a. speed, tail rotor speed) [INPUT: remote control]

E: Real-time tracking (6DOF), height measurement, static 3D model of environment

Fig. 7. AV scenario

4.4 Prototype 4: AV Scenario

In our next prototype we exchange the virtual model with the real zeppelin (figure 7). To minimize possible damage the airship fly in a large blue room with no obstacles. We added virtual obstacles to the scenario to build a parkour to fly through.

The MATLAB/Simulink model is replaced by the real zeppelin. It is tracked to get the actual position and orientation as transformation matrix. This transformation matrix is used by the collision detection, which controls the zeppelin when it collide with a virtual obstacle. This is done by calculating the collision vector and mapping it on the propeller of the zeppelin. At this point the user input is ignored and the collision detection takes over the control of the airship until the collision is resolved. For the environment we uses the real-time tracked zeppelin, the height measurement and the static 3D CAD model of the real environment. The real zeppelin itself is now handled as a part of the environment and only it's transformation matrix has to be acquired by appropriate tracking sensors. For the view we have the real zeppelin flying around in a virtual environment. The controller and input device is the same as in prototype 3.

4.5 Prototype 4: AR Scenario

In our last prototype (figure 8) the user control the real zeppelin in the real environment. We visualize the force vectors of all three propeller and the resulting force for the zeppelin as we did in prototype 3.

Our model consists of the position and orientation, which is tracked from the real zeppelin. The model itself is very simple compared to the model in MATLAB/Simulink, but as we control the real zeppelin, it is the most realistic one. The environment contains the real-time tracked zeppelin and the real environment. On the view-axis of our component refinement state diagram the environment and the zeppelin are real and in addition we have virtual visualization for the forces.

The controller is the same as in the AV prototype, which outputs the 3 DOF for controlling the zeppelin directly. As input device we first used the standard remote control, but then exchanged it by more complex input devices, including a gesture recognition using the Wiimote and a tracked TUI zeppelin model which is used to specify complete maneuvers (green dotted line in the diagram of figure 8).

M: Position, orientation measured from real
   zeppelin; control of zeppelin
V: Real zeppelin, real environment, vector
   visualization
C: Various, all with 3DOF output for direct
   control, either directly or over extended
   times
E: Real-time tracking of zeppelin (6DOF),
   height measurement

Fig. 8. Image of the AR application

5   Conclusion and Outlook

A key challenge in the development of mixed-reality (MR) applications is the use of ad-hoc development approaches and the lack of standardization and reuse. Most existing MR projects are research projects that focus on a single technology specific aspect and do not consider issues of tool development, content reuse and integration with other development processes. One area where this shortcoming is of central relevance is the reuse of software components in a flexible fashion. To exploit the full potential of MR interfaces a systematic development approach is required. In this paper we have presented an iterative development approach that is based on structuring MR applications into model, view, controller and environment components that can refined individually. We have shown how this model was used successfully to iteratively develop a variety of refinements of a NGUI to control a zeppelin and illustrated the benefits of component-wise refinement. The MVCE model helps to provide concrete support for software development and reuse in MR applications. In the future we aim to refine our process and experiment with extended tool support for MVCE applications. An area of development support that is still left largely unaddressed is thereuse of MR augmentation content between applications. A way to describe such models in a standardized and interchangeable format is still lacking and clearly requires more research in the future.

References

1. Shaer, O., et al.: User Interface Description Languages for Next Generation User Interfaces. In: CHI 2008 extended abstracts on Human factors in computing systems, ACM Press, Florence, Italy (2008)
2. Burbeck, S.: Applications Programming in Smalltalk-80: How to use Model-View-Controller, MVC (1992)
3. Ishii, H.: Tangible User Interfaces. In: Sears, A., Jacko, J. (eds.) Handbook of HCI, 2nd edn., Lawrence Erlbaum Association, Mahwah (2008)
4. Milgram, P., Kishino, F.: A taxonomy of mixed reality visual displays. In: IEICE Transactions on Information and Systems (1994)

5. MacIntyre, B., et al.: DART: A Toolkit for Rapid Design Exploration of Augmented Reality Experiences. In: User Interface Software and Technology, UIST 2004 (2004)
6. Broll, W., Herling, J., Blum, L.: Interactive Bits: Prototyping of Mixed Reality Applications and Interaction Techniques through Visual Programming. In: International Symposium On 3D User Interfaces, Reno, USA (2008)
7. Cuppens, E., Raymaekers, C., Coninx, K.: A model-based design process for interactive virtual environments. In: 12th International Workshop on DSVIS (2005)
8. Mixed Reality User Interfaces: Specification, Authoring, Adaptation. MRUI 2007. Charlotte, North Carolina, USA (2007)
9. Geiger, C., et al.: HYUI: a visual framework for prototyping hybrid user interfaces. In: TEI 2008: Proceedings of the 2nd international conference on Tangible and embedded interaction (2008)
10. Havok: Havok Physics (2009), http://www.havok.com
11. MathWorks, T.: MATLAB/Simulink (2009), http://www.mathworks.com

On a Qualitative Method to Evaluate Motion Sickness Induced by Stereoscopic Images on Liquid Crystal Displays

Hiroki Takada[1], Kazuhiro Fujikake[2], and Masaru Miyao[3]

[1] Gifu University of Medical Science, 795-1 Ichihiraga Nagamine,
Seki, Gifu 501-3892, Japan
takada@u-gifu-ms.ac.jp
[2] Institute for Science of Labour, 2-8-14 Sugao, Miyamae-ku, Kawasaki 216-8501, Japan
[3] Nagoya University, Furo-cho, Chikusa-Ku, Nagoya 464-8601, Japan

Abstract. Visually induced motion sickness (VIMS) is known to be caused by sensory conflict, which is the disagreement between vergence and visual accommodation while observing stereoscopic images. The simulator sickness questionnaire (SSQ) is a well-known method that is used herein for verifying the occurrence of VIMS. We quantitatively measure the sway of the centre of gravity of the human body before and during exposure to several images. During the measurement, subjects are instructed to maintain the Romberg posture for the first 60 s and a wide stance (midlines of the heels 20 cm apart) for the next 60 s. The stereoscopic images decrease the gradient of the potential function involved in the stochastic differential equations as a mathematical model of the body sway. We have succeeded in estimating the decrease in the gradient by using an index called sparse density.

Keywords: stabilometry, Simulator Sickness Questionnair, sparse density, stochastic differential equation, potential.

1 Introduction

The human standing posture is maintained by the body's balance function, which is an involuntary physiological adjustment mechanism called the 'righting reflex' [1]. In order to maintain the standing posture when locomotion is absent, the righting reflex, centred in the nucleus ruber, is essential. Sensory receptors such as visual inputs, auditory and vestibular functions and proprioceptive inputs from the skin, muscles and joints are the inputs to the body's balance function [2]. The evaluation of this function is indispensable for diagnosing equilibrium disturbances such as cerebellar degenerations, basal ganglia disorders, or Parkinson's disease in patients [3].

Stabilometry has been employed to evaluate this equilibrial function both qualitatively and quantitatively. A projection of a subject's centre of gravity onto a detection stand is measured as an average of the centre of pressure of both feet (COP). The COP is traced for each time step, and the time series of the projections is traced on an xy-plane. By connecting the temporally vicinal points, a stabilogram is composed. Several parameters such as the area of sway (A), total locus length (L) and locus

R. Shumaker (Ed.): Virtual and Mixed Reality, LNCS 5622, pp. 254–262, 2009.

length per unit area (L/A) have been proposed to quantitize the instability involved in the standing posture, and such parameters are widely used in clinical studies. It has been revealed that the last parameter particularly depends on the fine variations involved in posture control [1]. This index is then regarded as a gauge to evaluate the function of proprioceptive control of standing in human beings. However, it is difficult to clinically diagnose disorders of the sense of balance function and to identify the declines in equilibrial function by utilizing the abovementioned indices and measuring patterns in the stabilogram. Large interindividual differences might make it difficult to understand the results in comparison.

Mathematically, the sway in the COP is described by a stochastic process [4]-[6]. We examined the adequacy of using a stochastic differential equation and investigated the most adequate one for our research. G(x), the distribution of the observed points x, has the following correspondence with V(x), the (temporal averaged) potential function, in the stochastic differential equation (SDE) as a mathematical model of the sway:

$$V(\vec{x}) = -\frac{1}{2}\ln G(\vec{x}) + const. \tag{1}$$

The nonlinear property of SDEs is important [7]. There were several minimal points of the potential. In the vicinity of these points, the SDE shows local stable movement with a high-frequency component. We can therefore expect a high density of observed COP in this area on the stabilogram.

The analysis of stabilograms is useful not only for medical diagnosis but also for explaining the control of upright standing for two-legged robots and for preventing falls in elderly people [8]. Recent studies suggest that maintaining postural stability is one of the major goals of animals, [9] and that they experience sickness symptoms in circumstances where they have not acquired strategies to maintain their balance [10]. Riccio and Stoffregen argued that motion sickness is not caused by sensory conflict, but by postural instability, although the most widely known theory of motion sickness is based on the concept of sensory conflict [10]-[12]. Stoffregen and Smart (1999) report that the onset of motion sickness may be preceded by significant increases in postural sway [13].

The equilibrium function in humans deteriorates when observing 3-dimensional (3D) movies [14]. It has been considered that this visually induced motion sickness (VIMS) is caused by the disagreement between vergence and visual accommodation while observing 3D images [15]. Thus, stereoscopic images have been devised to reduce this disagreement [16]-[17].

VIMS can be measured by psychological and physiological methods, and the simulator sickness questionnaire (SSQ) is a well-known physiological method for measuring the extent of motion sickness [18]. The SSQ is used herein for verifying the occurrence of VIMS. The physiological methods measures autonomic nervous activity: heart rate variability, blood pressure, electrogastrography, and galvanic skin reaction [19]-[21]. It has been reported that a wide stance (with midlines of the heels at 17 cm or 30 cm apart) significantly increases total locus length in stabilograms of the high SSQ score group, while the low score group is less affected by such a stance [22].

This study proposes a methodology to measure the effect of 3D images on the equilibrium function. We assume that the high density of observed COP decreases during exposure to stereoscopic images [14]. Sparse density (SPD) would be a useful index in stabilometry to measure VIMS (Appendix). In this study, we show that reduction of body sway can be evaluated by the SPD during exposure to 3D movies on a Liquid Crystal Display (LCD).

2 Material and Methods

Ten healthy subjects (23.6 ± 2.2 year) voluntarily participated in the study. All of them were Japanese and lived in Nagoya and its surroundings. The subjects gave their informed consent prior to participation. The following were the exclusion criteria for subjects: subjects working the night shift, subjects with dependence on alcohol, subjects who consumed alcohol and caffeine-containing beverages after waking up and less than two hours after meals, and subjects who may have had any otorhinolaryngologic or neurological disease in the past (except for conductive hearing impairment, which is commonly found in the elderly). In addition, the subjects must not have been using any prescribed drugs.

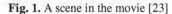

Fig. 1. A scene in the movie [23]   **Fig. 2.** The setup of the experiment [23]

We ensured that the body sway was not affected by environmental conditions. Using an air conditioner, we adjusted the temperature to 25 °C in the exercise room, which was kept dark. All subjects were tested from 10 am to 5 pm in the room. The subjects were positioned facing an LCD monitor (S1911- SABK, NANAO Co., Ltd.) on which three kinds of images were presented in no particular order (Fig. 1): (I) a visual target (circle) whose diameter was 3 cm; (II) a new 3D movie that shows a sphere approaching and going away from subjects irregularly; and (III) a conventional 3D movie that shows the same sphere motion as in (II). The new stereoscopic images (II) were constructed by Olympus Power 3D method. The distance between the wall and the subjects was 57 cm (Fig. 2).

2.1 Stabilometry

The subjects stood without moving on the detection stand of a stabilometer (G5500, Anima Co., Ltd.) in the Romberg posture with their feet together for 1 min before the sway was recorded. Each sway of the COP was then recorded with a sampling frequency of 20 Hz during exposure to one of the images. The subjects viewed a movie (image) on the LCD from beginning to end. SSQ was employed before and after this stabilometry.

2.2 Calculation Procedure

We calculated several indices that are commonly used in the clinical field [24] for stabilograms, such as "area of sway," "total locus length," and "total locus length per unit area." In addition, new quantification indices that were termed "SPD" and "total locus length of chain" [25] were also estimated (Appendix).

3 Results

The results of the SSQ are shown in Table 1 and include the scores on nausea (N), oculomotor discomfort (OD), disorientation (D) subscale and total score (TS) of the SSQ. No statistical differences were seen in these scores among images presented to subjects. However, increases were seen in the scores for N and D after exposure to the conventional 3D images (III). In addition, the scores after exposure to the new 3D images (II) were not very different from those after exposure to the static ones (I). Although there were large individual differences, sickness symptoms seemed to appear more often with the conventional 3D movie.

Typical stabilograms are shown in Fig. 3. In these figures, the vertical axis shows the anterior and posterior movements of the COP, and the horizontal axis shows the right and left movements of the COP. The amplitudes of the sway that were observed during exposure to the movies (Fig. 3c–3f) tended to be larger than those of the control sway (Fig. 3a–3b). Although a high density of COP was observed in the stabilograms (Fig. 3a–3d), the density decreased in stabilograms during exposure to the conventional stereoscopic movie (Fig. 3e–3f). Furthermore, stabilograms measured in an open leg posture with the midlines of heels 20 cm apart (Fig. 3b, 3e, 3f) were compared with stabilograms measured in the Romberg posture (Fig. 3a, 3c, 3e). COP was not isotropically dispersed but characterized by much movement in the anterior-posterior (y) direction (Fig. 3b, 3d). Although this trend is seen in Fig. 3f, the diffusion of COP was large in the lateral (x) direction and had spread to the extent that it was equivalent to the control stabilograms (Fig. 3a).

Table 1. Subscales of the SSQ after exposure to 3D movies

Movies	(II)	(III)
N	8.6±2.6	14.3±4.8
OD	17.4±3.4	16.7±4.0
D	16.7±6.2	22.3±9.3
TS	16.4±3.7	19.8±5.8

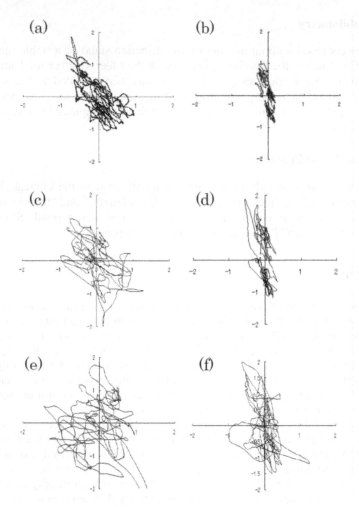

Fig. 3. Typical stabilograms observed when subjects viewed a static circle (a)–(b), the new stereoscopic movie (c)–(d), and the conventional 3D movie (e)–(f)

According to the two-way analysis of variance (ANOVA) with repeated measures, there was no interaction between factors of posture (Romberg posture or standing posture with their feet wide apart) and images ((I), (II), or (III)). Except to the total locus length per unit area and the total locus length of chain, main effects were seen in the both factors (Fig. 4). On the other hand, any indicators could find a main effect in the postural factor (p < 0.01).

4   Discussion

A theory has been proposed to obtain SDEs as a mathematical model of the body sway on the basis of the stabilogram. According to Eq. (1), there were several

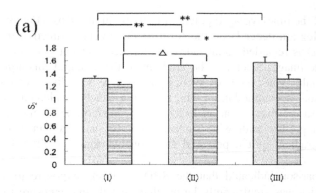

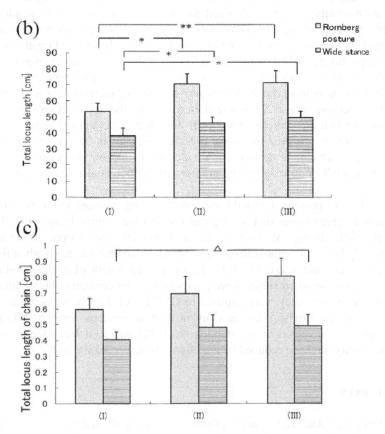

Fig. 4. Typical results of the two-way ANOVA with repeated measures for indicators [27]; the total locus length (a), the SPD (b), and the total locus length of chain (c) ($**p < 0.01, *p < 0.05$)

minimal points of the time-averaged potential function in the SDEs (Fig. 3). The variance in the stabilogram depends on the form of the potential function in the SDE; therefore, the SPD is regarded as an index for its measurement. The movies, especially stereoscopic images, decrease the gradient of the potential function. The new 3D movie (II) should reduce the body sway because there is no disagreement between vergence and visual accommodation. The reduction can be evaluated by the SPD during exposure to the movies on an LCD screen. Performing a one-way analysis of variance for a posture with wide stance, we have succeeded in estimating the decrease in the gradient of the potential function by using the SPD as shown in Fig. 4a ($p < 0.05$).

Multiple comparison indicated that the SPD S_2 during exposure to any of the stereoscopic movies was significantly larger than that during exposure to the static control image (I) when subjects stood in the Romberg posture (Fig.4a). The same calculation results were also obtained for S_3. The standing posture would become unstable because of the effects of the stereoscopic movies. As mentioned above, structural changes occur in the time-averaged potential function (1) with exposure to stereoscopic images, which are assumed to reflect the sway in center of gravity.

Scibora et al. concluded that the total locus length of subjects with prior experience of motion sickness increases with exposure to a virtual environment when they stood with their feet wide apart [22], whereas, in our study, the degree of sway was found to be reduced when the subjects stood with their feet wide apart (Fig.3b, 3d, 3f) than when they stood with their feet close together (Fig.3a, 3c, 3e). As shown in Fig. 3d and 3f, a clear change in the form of the potential function (1) occurs when the feet are wide apart. The decrease in the gradient of the potential might increase the total locus length.

Regardless of posture, the total locus length during exposure to the 3D movies was significantly greater than that during exposure to the control image (Fig.4b). However, the SPD during exposure to the conventional stereoscopic movie (III) was significantly larger than that during exposure to the control image (I) when they stood with their feet wide apart (Fig.4a). The total locus length of chain simultaneously tended to increase when subjects were exposed to the conventional 3D images (III) compared that when they were exposed to (I) (Fig.4c). Hence, we noted postural instability with the exposure to the conventional stereoscopic images (III) by using these indicators involved in the stabilogram (SPD and total locus length of chain). This instability might be reduced by the Olympus power 3D method.

References

1. Okawa, T., Tokita, T., Shibata, Y., Ogawa, T., Miyata, H.: Stabilometry - Significance of Locus Length Per Unit Area (L/A) in Patients with Equilibrium Disturbances. Equilibrium Res. 55(3), 283–293 (1995)
2. Kaga, K.: Memaino Kouzo: Structure of vertigo, Kanehara, Tokyo, pp. 23–26, 95–100 (1992)
3. Okawa, T., Tokita, T., Shibata, Y., Ogawa, T., Miyata, H.: Stabilometry-Significance of locus length per unit area (L/A). Equilibrium Res. 54(3), 296–306 (1996)

4. Collins, J.J., De Luca, C.J.: Open-loop and closed-loop control of posture: A random-walk analysis of center of pressure trajectories. Exp. Brain Res. 95, 308–318 (1993)
5. Emmerrik, R.E.A., Van Sprague, R.L., Newell, K.M.: Assessment of sway dynamics in tardive dyskinesia and developmental disability: sway profile orientation and stereotypy. Moving Disorders 8, 305–314 (1993)
6. Newell, K.M., Slobounov, S.M., Slobounova, E.S., Molenaar, P.C.: Stochastic processes in postural center-of-pressure profiles. Exp. Brain Res. 113, 158–164 (1997)
7. Takada, H., Kitaoka, Y., Shimizu, Y.: Mathematical Index and Model in Stabilometry. Forma 16(1), 17–46 (2001)
8. Fujiwara, K., Toyama, H.: Analysis of dynamic balance and its training effect-Focusing on fall problem of elder persons. Bulletin of the Physical Fitness Research Institute 83, 123–134 (1993)
9. Stoffregen, T.A., Hettinger, L.J., Haas, M.W., Roe, M.M., Smart, L.J.: Postural instability and motion sickness in a fixed-base flight simulator. Human Factors 42, 458–469 (2000)
10. Riccio, G.E., Stoffregen, T.A.: An Ecological theory of motion sickness and postural instability. Ecological Physiology 3(3), 195–240 (1991)
11. Oman, C.: A heuristic mathematical model for the dynamics of sensory conflict and motion sickness. Acta Otolaryngologica Supplement 392, 1–44 (1982)
12. Reason, J.: Motion sickness add –aptation: a neural mismatch model. J. Royal Soc. Med. 71, 819–829 (1978)
13. Stoffregen, T.A., Smart, L.J., Bardy, B.J., Pagulayan, R.J.: Postural stabilization of looking. Journal of Experimental Psychology: Human Perception and Performance 25, 1641–1658 (1999)
14. Takada, H., Fujikake, K., Miyao, M., Matsuura, Y.: Indices to Detect Visually Induced Motion Sickness using Stabilometry. In: Proc. VIMS 2007, pp. 178–183 (2007)
15. Hatada, T.: Nikkei electronics 444, 205–223 (1988)
16. Yasui, R., Matsuda, I., Kakeya, H.: Combining volumetric edge display and multiview display for expression of natural 3D images. In: Proc. SPIE, vol. 6055, pp. 0Y1–0Y9 (2006)
17. Kakeya, H.: MOEVision:simple multiview display with clear floating image. In: Proc. SPIE, vol. 6490, 64900J (2007)
18. Kennedy, R.S., Lane, N.E., Berbaum, K.S., Lilienthal, M.G.: A simulator sickness questionnaire (SSQ): A new method for quantifying simulator sickness. International J. Aviation Psychology 3, 203–220 (1993)
19. Holomes, S.R., Griffin, M.J.: Correlation between heart rate and the severity of motion sickness caused by optokinetic stimulation. J. Psychophysiology 15, 35–42 (2001)
20. Himi, N., Koga, T., Nakamura, E., Kobashi, M., Yamane, M., Tsujioka, K.: Differences in autonomic responses between subjects with and without nausea while watching an irregularly oscillating video. Autonomic Neuroscience: Basic and Clinical 116, 46–53 (2004)
21. Yokota, Y., Aoki, M., Mizuta, K.: Motion sickness susceptibility associated with visually induced postural instability and cardiac autonomic responses in healthy subjects. Acta Otolaryngologia 125, 280–285 (2005)
22. Scibora, L.M., Villard, S., Bardy, B., Stoffregen, T.A.: Wider stance reduces body sway and motion sickness. In: Proc. VIMS 2007, pp. 18–23 (2007)
23. Takada, H., Fujikake, K., Omori, M., Hasegawa, S., Watanabe, T., Miyao, M.: Reduction of body sway can be evaluated by sparse density during exposure to movies on Liquid Cristal Displays. In: International Federation for Medical and Biological Engineering (IFMBE) Proceedings, vol. 23, pp. 987–991 (2008)

24. Suzuki, J., Matsunaga, T., Tokumatsu, K., Taguchi, K., Watanabe, Y.: Q&A and a manual in Stabilometry. Equilibrium Res. 55(1), 64–77 (1996)
25. Takada, H., Kitaoka, Y., Ichikawa, S., Miyao, M.: Physical Meaning on Geometrical Index for Stabilometly. Equilibrium Res. 62(3), 168–180 (2003)

Appendix

Here, we describe the new quantification indices—SPD and total locus length of chain [25].

A Sparse density

SPD was defined by an average of the ratio $G_j(1)/G_j(k)$ for $j = 3, 4, ..., 20$, where $G_j(k)$ is the number of divisions having more than k measured points; a stabilogram was divided into quadrants whose latus was j times longer than the resolution. If the center of gravity is stationary, the SPD value becomes 1. If there are variations in the stabilograms, the SPD value becomes greater than 1. Thus, SPD depends on the characteristics of the stabilogram and the shift in the COP.

B Chain

The force acting on the center of gravity of the body was defined in terms of the difference in the displacement vectors. In particular, we focussed on singular points at which statistically large forces were exerted. On the basis of these forces, chains were eliminated from the stabilogram in the form of a consecutive time series. If the times measured at these points were in the temporal vicinity, these points were connected by segments (sequences). Figures formed by these sequences were called "chains" because of the shape of the connections. The figures of the sequences of points at which large forces were exerted show that the chain had a cusp pattern.

Balancing Design Freedom and Constraints in Wall Posters Masquerading as AR Tracking Markers

Ryuhei Tenmoku, Akito Nishigami, Fumihisa Shibata,
Asako Kimura, and Hideyuki Tamura

Ritsumeikan University 1-1-1 Nojihigashi, Kusatsu, Shiga, Japan
tenmoku@rm.is.ritsumei.ac.jp

Abstract. This paper describes how to construct a mixed reality (MR) environment by adopting a geometric registration method using visually unobtrusive flat posters on the wall. The proposed method is one of the several approaches of the semi-fiducial invisibly coded symbols (SFINCS) research project, the purpose of which is achieving a good balance between elegance with regard to the environment and robust registration. In this method, posters tentatively used for geometric registration are designed to blend with the environment. However, they are recognized as markers based on certain design rules. Posters in a real scene can be found in real time using these design rules. This paper introduces procedures for developing poster design rules using toolkits developed by us.

Keywords: mixed reality, geometric registration, poster, semi-fiducial, authoring tool.

1 Introduction

Mixed reality (MR), which can merge the real and virtual worlds in real time, have been suggested as a new technology for presenting the information [1, 2]. Geometric registration between the real and virtual worlds is one of the most important problems for realizing the MR environments. A variety of registration methods have been proposed worldwide.

In general, traditional methods can be classified into three types: sensor-based methods, image-based methods, and hybrid methods that integrate sensor-based and image-based technologies. Among them, image-based registration methods, which use markers placed in a real scene, have more potential because they do not require any sensors except a camera. In particular, ARToolKit [3] is globally known for its high quality and portability. However, there are many claims that such fiducial markers are not visually appealing.

Accordingly, we propounded semi-fiducial invisibly coded symbols (SFINCS) that are able to achieve a good balance between elegance with regard to the environment and robust registration. We attempted to realize SFINCS using the following two approaches: (1) using markers that are harmonious with the real scene, and (2) embedding information into objects that naturally exist in the real scene. Based on approach (1), we proposed a registration method using two-tone colored markers [4].

R. Shumaker (Ed.): Virtual and Mixed Reality, LNCS 5622, pp. 263–272, 2009.

This method is named SFINCS-TT. Our two-tone colored markers are similar in color to that of the background objects. These markers have the same hue value as the background color and differ slightly in brightness. T-shaped, L-shaped, I-shaped, and like markers are placed at the corners of flat colored plain surfaces of actual objects. On the other hand, as a concrete method based on approach (2), we developed a geometric registration system using visually unobtrusive flat posters arranged in the real world. This method is named as poster masquerading method (SFINCS-PM), which uses posters that have some common characteristics for geometric registration. These characteristics are used for finding the posters in real time.

This paper describes how to construct an MR environment using SFINCS-PM, i.e., how to decide the design rules, prepare the posters and calibrate them. This paper is structured as follows: Section 2 describes some related work. In section 3, an outline of the SFINCS-PM is described. Section 4 shows methods of constructing MR environments based on the SFINCS-PM. In Section 5 the present work is summarized and the future works are discussed.

2 Related Work

This section shows some traditional geometric registration methods for MR using computer vision techniques and the associated construction methods of an MR environment. A variety of vision-based methods have been proposed because of their affinity for video see-through displays.

As mentioned in the previous section, the most convenient vision-based method for MR is based on fiducial markers [5–7]. Such markers should have a common and obtrusive appearance so that they can be found from input images and should include unique IDs for identification. For example, ARToolKit markers [3] have black square frames of a certain width that can be identified based on the patterns placed inside the frames. These inside patterns are linked to the marker's position and angle in the world coordinate system. These fiducial markers are easy-to-use and robust, but are rigid for designing and affect the environment to a greater extent. In order to construct MR environments, where fiducial markers are arranged in the real world, the system requires a database of marker ID numbers and their 6DOF positions in the world coordinate system. In the case of ARToolKit markers, this database corresponds to the look-up table of the inside patterns and marker positions.

On the other hand, registration methods using natural feature points in a real scene [8–11] differ from the fiducial marker methods. These methods do not affect the environment, and on comparing with the fiducial marker methods, most of them do not show stability and robustness. These methods can be classified roughly into the following two technologies: 1) camera tracking without any environmental information [8, 9], and 2) measuring the absolute position and angle of the camera using a pre-constructed database of environmental information [10, 11]. Simply putting, the former technology estimates the camera position of the current frame, relative to that of the previous frame, by comparing the current image and previous camera images. In the latter method, it is somehow necessary to estimate the initial camera position.

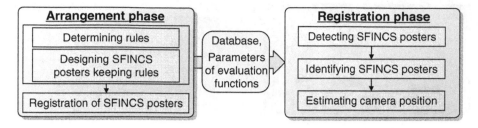

Fig. 1. Workflow of the arrangement phase and registration phase

Taketomi et al. [11] used a landmark database that included image templates around natural feature points and their 3D positions. However, constructing such a database requires much time and effort.

Consequently, some research projects try to maintain both eye appeal and robustness. Our SFINCS project is one of them. Nakazato et al. used retro-reflective markers on the ceiling and an infrared ray camera that focuses on the ceiling [12]. Saitoh et al. used pattern-coded wallpapers [13] to masquerade the coded patterns in the environments. In order to construct MR environments, the requirements for these intermediate methods are the same as that for the fiducial marker methods. However, in some methods [13], their IDs are not simple because of their unique complex encoding systems. The proposed method, described in this paper, SFINCS-PM, also adopts a complex encoding system.

3 SFINCS-PM

3.1 Outline of SFINCS-PM

SFINCS-PM is a geometric registration method that utilizes wall posters that can exist in the real environment naturally as augmented reality (AR) markers. This method holds the middle course between fiducial markers and natural feature points. The main idea of this method is that certain constraints for poster design are defined in advance to aid detection of posters. More specifically, design constraints are on the color or layout of components of the poster. We call these constraints as design rules.

The workflow of SFINCS-PM has two general phases, the arrangement phase and the registration phase (Fig. 1). In the arrangement phase the design rules are determined by the provider of the MR application by employing the proposed registration method. The provider also prepares wall posters that are used for geometric registration. We call such posters as "SFINCS posters." The order of these operations is determined depending on the rule scheme, as described in section 3.2. After these operations, the provider constructs a database that includes the ID numbers of SFINCS posters, their features, and their installation locations in the world coordinate system. The database and some parameters of the evaluation functions are handed over to the registration phase.

The following events take place in the registration phase sequentially. First, the SFINCS posters are detected from the input image. The detected SFINCS posters are

Fig. 2. Example images of SFINCS-PM

then identified according to the database and lastly, the absolute position and angle of the camera is estimated. Fig. 2 shows example MR images using SFINCS-PM.

As shown in Fig. 2, we assume that there are many notices and posters, including SFINCS posters, in the environment. In such a situation, it is important to determine how to detect only the SFINCS posters. In this research, the design of posters is restricted to enable detection of SFINCS posters. Accordingly, the degree of freedom for designing the posters decreases.

Here, we define some words that are used henceforth.

- **SFINCS poster** is the poster used for geometric registration in SFINCS-PM.
- **Design rules** are used for detecting SFINCS posters from the candidate regions displaying posters.
- **ID rules** are used to identify SFINCS posters. These rules change according to the design rules.
- **Common rules** are for all design rules. In the present system, we define the following two rules:

  - The shape of the SFINCS poster is rectangular whose aspect ratio is $1:\sqrt{2}$. (This is the popular paper aspect ratio in Japan.)
  - The background colors of SFINCS posters are not the same as that of the background object. This is based on the idea that all posters should be eye-catching.

- **Rule scheme** is the framework for establishing design rules and ID rules.
- **Rule set** is a set of design rules and ID rules established in the rule scheme.

3.2 Designing Rule Sets Using Rule Scheme

In the current system, we prepare a layout rule and a coloration rule scheme based on the idea that the design of each poster is determined by the layout of components and coloration. We think another rule scheme could be achievable.

Layout Rule Scheme. A Layout Rule Scheme uses a layout of poster components. We defined three types of components that are typical of posters, as follows:

- **Title component:** A title component is a single- or double-lined string drawn by a single color. The title color is highly visible against the background color.
- **Visual component:** A visual component is composed of a photograph. It uses multiple colors and has an outline box.

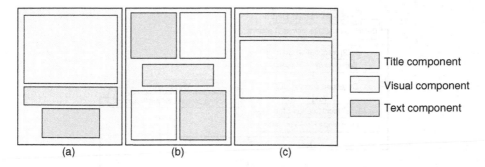

Fig. 3. Example design rules using layout of components

- **Text component:** A text component consists of multiple-lined strings drawn by a single color.

[Design rules]
Design rules are determined by a layout of these components. Some example of design rules using the layout of these components are shown in Fig. 3. If design rule (a) is adopted, the system recognizes posters that obey the following rules: the upper half is a visual component, the title component is below the visual component, and a text component is at the bottom.

[ID rules]
The provider can embed ID numbers into one or more of the following features: the hue value of the poster background, the title component, the text component, and the mode hue value of the visual component.

Coloration Rule Scheme. The coloration rule scheme uses coloration characteristics in a poster. For design rules, the system uses constraints on color histograms of the poster.

[Design rules]
Design rules are defined as conjunction of multiple constraints on the histograms of posters. Basic forms of these constraints are prepared in advance, and the provider has to decide the threshold of each constraint. Some examples of basic forms of constraints are listed below. Key colors A and B indicate the most-used and second-most-used chromatic color in the poster, respectively.

- The hue value of the key color A (B) is more (less) than x.
- The component ration of the key colors A (B) is more (less) than y.
- The sum (difference) of the component ration of key color A and B is more (less) than u.
- The component ration of chromatic (achromatic) colors is more (less) than v.

[ID rules]
The provider can embed ID numbers into one or more of the features noted in the design rules above.

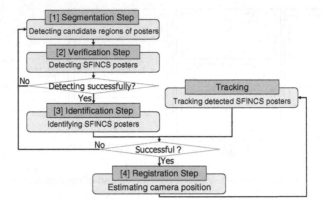

Fig. 4. Flowchart of the registration phase

3.3   Geometric Registration for Mixed Reality

Fig. 4 shows the flowchart of the registration phase in which four steps are processed sequentially. When the camera position in the previous frame is estimated, a tracking process runs to reduce the processing time and stabilize the detection of SFINCS posters. A camera tracking method using natural feature points [8, 9] is used for tracking the posters. The details of these steps are described below.

[1] Segmentation Step

As the first step, the system detects candidate regions of posters using the common rules. The system detects quadrangular regions whose areas are above a certain threshold as candidate regions. In order to detect quadrangular regions, the system operates the following processes:

- It applies an edge detector for the entire input image.
- It detects vertical line segments whose lengths are above a certain threshold.
- Every combination of two vertical line segments is investigated to see whether a line segment between each end point exists.
  The system detects a quadrangle if line segments between both upper and lower end points exist.

[2] Verification Step

Second, the system sifts detected candidate regions to SFINCS posters. This is realized by the following operations:

- The system applies inverse projective transformation for candidate regions of the posters. Here, the aspect ratio of SFINCS posters is used.
- The system verifies whether the candidate regions of the posters satisfy the design rules. Here, the common forms of evaluation functions are prepared beforehand. The parameters of these functions are passed from the arrangement phase. When a candidate region of a poster fulfills all design rules, the system recognizes it as a SFINCS poster.

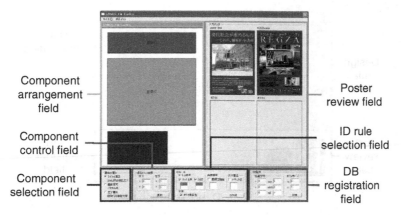

Component arrangement field

Poster review field

Component control field

ID rule selection field

Component selection field

DB registration field

Fig. 5. Support tool for layout rule scheme

[3] Identification Step

Third, the system estimates the ID numbers of detected SFINCS posters based on the database. Features of the detected posters are compared with those registered in the database to identify the detected posters. Here, the number of features used for identifying posters is n, the jth feature of the registered poster whose ID is i is defined as G_{ij}, and features of the detected posters are defined as G_j. The ID number of the detected poster is i which minimizes E_i in formula (1).

$$E_i = \sum_{j=1}^{n} |G_{i,j} - G_j| \tag{1}$$

[4] Registration Step

The position and angle of the camera in world coordinates is calculated based on the four corner positions of SFINCS posters registered in the database.

4   Constructing MR Environments

In order to construct an MR environment using SFINCS-PM, the three operations of the arrangement phase, described in Fig. 1, must be performed after the provider selects the layout or coloration rule scheme to be used. This section describes the procedures of the arrangement phase using the layout and coloration rule schemes.

4.1   Constructing MR Environments Using Layout Rule Scheme

When the layout rule scheme is selected, we assume that the provider creates MR environments as follows:

1. Determine design rules.
2. Design SFINCS posters that meet the design rules.
3. Define ID rules.
4. Register SFINCS posters.

We prepared an authoring tool that supports these procedures. Fig. 5 shows a sample image of this tool.

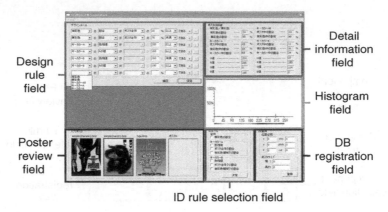

Design rule field

Poster review field

Detail information field

Histogram field

DB registration field

ID rule selection field

Fig. 6. Support tool for coloration rule scheme

First, the provider determines the design rules. Then he/she arranges the components in the component arrangement field. Radio buttons are used in the component selection field to choose the components. The provider can move and change the size of the arranged components using the component control field. After designing SFINCS posters, the provider can check whether the designed poster observes the design rules using this tool. In this case, the poster is presented in the poster review field. If the poster does not satisfy some rules, the unsuitable areas are shown by the authoring tool. For registration of the SFINCS posters, the provider has to input 6DOF parameters of the SFINCS posters and their sizes using the DB registration field.

Further, the tool generates the database including the ID numbers, some feature quantities, and position of each SFINCS poster. At the same time, the parameters of evaluation functions of SFINCS posters are decided. In the layout rule scheme, evaluation functions of the title, visual, and text components used in the verification step of the registration phase are prepared beforehand, and the system applies these functions based on these parameters. In the verification step, if all evaluation functions return "true," the system recognizes the poster as a SFINCS poster.

4.2 Constructing MR Environments Using Coloration Rule Scheme

In the case of the coloration rule scheme, the provider proceeds as follows:

1. Design posters.
2. Determine design rules by viewing posters.
3. Define ID rules.
4. Register SFINCS posters.

The tool supporting these procedures is shown in Fig. 6.

When the provider selects the coloration rule scheme, he/she has to prepare some posters at the beginning of the whole procedure. Next, the provider determines the design rules while viewing the prepared posters. Here, our tool enables an overview of these posters, shows detailed information, and the color histogram of the selected poster in the poster review field, the detail information field, and the histogram field, respectively. The design rules are represented as conjunctions of multiple constraints

<table>
<tr><td>(a) Example posters</td><td>(b) Example MR images</td></tr>
</table>

Fig. 7. Posters and MR images

on the histograms of posters. The provider can add or clear any constraint freely. Each constraint is designed by complementing the rule forms by choosing from options and filling in the blanks in a manner similar to that of a smart play list in iTunes. Defining ID rules and registration of SFINCS posters is the same as in the layout rule scheme.

In the coloration rule scheme, all possible evaluation functions, which check that the poster observes each constraint described in Section 3.2.2, are prepared in advance. The parameters of these functions (x, y, u, and v) are decided here.

4.3 Experiments of Constructing MR Environments

We made some rule sets and SFINCS posters using the support tools to validate our proposed procedures in constructing MR environments. The rule set of the coloration rule scheme is introduced here.

[Design rules]

- The component ration of chromatic colors is more than 50% of all colors.
- The sum of the component rations of key colors A and B is more than 80% of all colors.

[ID rules]
  The posters are identified using the hue value and the component ratio of the key colors A and B.

Example posters of this rule set are shown in Fig. 7 (a), and example images of the MR guide application using SFINCS posters based on this rule set are shown in Fig. 7 (b). Through these experiments, we validated that our proposed procedures can construct MR environments using SFINCS-PM.

5 Conclusions

This paper describes a method of constructing MR environments using SFINCS-PM. In SFINCS-PM, wall posters are used for geometric registration as AR tracking markers. These posters are designed in the framework of two rule schemes, the layout rule and coloration rule schemes. This paper introduces these two rule schemes and the associated procedures in constructing MR environments.

We assume a trade-off between the degree of freedom for poster design and the constraints used for detection. In other words, if the provider defines strict design rules, the degree of design freedom becomes low. Consequently, all SFINCS posters closely resemble each other. On the contrary, if the provider defines loose design rules, the degree of freedom increases. Accordingly, the provider should achieve a good balance of the two.

In the future, we will polish the proposed registration method. We will also construct other rule schemes.

Acknowledgment. The authors would like to thank Ms. Itsuki Morimoto for partly implementation.

References

1. Feiner, S., MacIntyre, B., Seligman, D.: I Knowledge-based augmented reality. Communications of the ACM 36(7), 52–62 (1993)
2. Azuma, R., Baillot, Y., Behringer, R., Feiner, S., Juiler, S., MacIntyre, B.: Recent advances in augmented reality. In: Proc. Int. Symp. on Augmented Reality, pp. 111–119 (2001)
3. Kato, H., Billinghurst, M., Imamate, K., Tachibana, K.: Recent advances in augmented reality. In: Proc. Int. Symp. on Augmented Reality, pp. 111–119 (2000)
4. Tenmoku, R., Yoshida, Y., Shibata, F., Kimura, A., Tamura, H.: Visually elegant and robust semi-fiducials for geometric registration in mixed reality. In: Proc. 6th Int. Symp. on Mixed and Augmented Reality, pp. 261–262 (2007)
5. Naimark, L., Foxlin, E.: Circular data matrix fiducial system and robust image processing for a wearable vision-inertial self-tracker. In: Proc. 1st Int. Symp. on Mixed and Augmented Reality, pp. 27–36 (2002)
6. Thomas, G.: Mixed reality techniques for TV and their application for on-set/pre-visualization in film production. In: DVD Proc. Int. Workshop on Mixed Reality Technology for Filmmaking, pp. 31–36 (2006)
7. Bianchi, G., Jung, C., Knörlein, B., Harders, M., Székely, G.: High-fidelity visuo-haptic interaction with virtual objects in multi-modal AR systems. In: Proc. 5th Int. Symp. on Mixed and Augmented Reality, pp. 187–196 (2006)
8. Gordon, I., Lowe, D.G.: Scene modeling, recognition and tracking with invariant image features. In: Proc. 3rd Int. Symp. on Mixed and Augmented Reality, pp. 110–119 (2004)
9. Reitmayr, G., Drummond, T.W.: Going out: Robust model-besed tracking for outdoor augmented reality. In: Proc. 5th Int. Symp. on Mixed and Augmented Reality, pp. 109–118 (2006)
10. Oe, M., Sato, T., Yokoya, N.: Estimating camera position and posture by using feature landmark database. In: Kalviainen, H., Parkkinen, J., Kaarna, A. (eds.) SCIA 2005. LNCS, vol. 3540, pp. 171–181. Springer, Heidelberg (2005)
11. Taketomi, T., Sato, T., Yokoya, N.: Real-time geometric registration using feature landmark database for augmented reality applications. In: Proc. SPIE Electronic Imaging, vol. 7238 (2009)
12. Nakazato, Y., Kanbara, M., Yokoya, N.: An initialization tool for installing visual markers in wearable augmented reality. In: Proc. 16th Int. Conf. on Artificial Reality and Telexistence, pp. 228–238 (2006)
13. Saito, S., Hiyama, A., Tanikawa, T., Hirose, M.: Indoor vision based localization using coded seamless pattern for interior decoration. In: Proc. IEEE Virtual Reality 2007, pp. 67–74 (2007)

Development of RFID Textile and Human Activity Detection Applications

Ryoko Ueoka[1], Atsuji Masuda[2], Tetsuhiko Murakami[2], Hideyuki Miyayama[3],
Hidenori Takeuchi[4], Kazuyuki Hashimoto[4], and Michitaka Hirose[5]

[1] Research Centre for the Advanced Science and Technology, the University of Tokyo,
4-6-1 Komaba Meguro-Ku Tokyo, 153-8904 Japan
[2] Industrial Technology Center of Fukui Prefecture 61 Kawaiwashizuka-cho,
Fukui-city Fukui, 910-0102 Japan
[3] Medical Japan Co., Ltd. 4-17-9 Asuwa Fukui –city Fukui, 918-8007 Japan
[4] UTIC Co., Ltd. 2-29-1 Tabata Harue-cho Sakai City Fukui, 919-0477 Japan
[5] Graduate School of Information Science and Technology, the University of Tokyo,
7-3-1 Hongo Bunkyo-Ku Tokyo, 113-8656 Japan
yogurt@cyber.t.u-tokyo.ac.jp,
{a_masuda,murakamitetsuhiko}@fklab.fukui.fukui.jp,
{takeuchi,h.kazu}@up-ut.com,miyayama@m-japan.co.jp
hirose@cyber.t.u-tokyo.ac.jp

Abstract. We developed RFID woven textile and a customized textile inspection machine with an automatic map making function. These developments
have potentials to extend location aware systems in real use. In this paper, we
present a process of the development of RFID, the developed map-making
system and an accuracy of the automatically made map and time saving effect.
And we outlined two prototypes of human activity detection using RFID textile.
One is a pilot application of a tracking system using 19-meter coated RFID
textile as a carpet. A person's tracking is detected by shoes that RFID readers
were embedded. Another one is a pilot application of a human-activity tracking
system using RFID textile wear. By wearing it, the predefined behaviour is detected by embedded RFID readers in the environment. In section 6 conclusions
and future works are discussed.

Keywords: RFID textile, Map making system, Human activity detection.

1 Introduction

Recent technological advancement makes the physical and digital worlds interlinked
and makes people, computers and environment seamlessly integrated in part of our
daily life. Thus human interface dealing with medium between people and computer
systems called context-aware technology is becoming important research area. Many
researches dealing with context-aware environments have concentrated on supporting
people at work as well as at home. [1][2] One example of a promising technology
for supporting interlinking physical and digital world is Radio Frequency Identification (RFID), which is an electronic tagging technology that allows the detection and
tracking of tags, and consequently the objects they are affixed to. Conventional
applications using RFID tags are frequently seen in the supply chain world for RFID

R. Shumaker (Ed.): Virtual and Mixed Reality, LNCS 5622, pp. 273–281, 2009.

attached object tracking.[3] The ability to do remote detection and tracking coupled with the low cost of passive tags has led to the widespread adoption of RFID in the field. On the other hand, massively distributed RFID tags are used to support the navigation of mobile devices, robot manipulation and tracking of a person.[4][5][6] .

These applications use RFID tags as position detection method by correlating physical coordinates with RF-IDs as a mapping table. By massively distributing RFID tags, each RFID tag acts as a position sensor in a way, which reacts depending on the position of a reader and responds to its unique ID. Though the method has high potential, the conventional method tends to need time and cost when to implement system into physical space. First of all, it is necessary to implement RFID tags. Secondly it is necessary to make a map integrating RFID tag ID and physical coordinates. Also conventional RFID based infrastructure is static so that once the RFID based environment is deployed, it is difficult to move. To solve these problems, authors developed RFID tag woven textile. Also authors developed a map-making system which automatically generates a map under the manufacturing process. RFID textile is flexible and light-weight position detection material which can be applied to RFID-carpet, curtain, cloth, chair or any other products using textile.

This paper is organized as follows. Related works are discussed in section 2. In section 3, we present the process of the development of RFID textile and in section 4 we present a developed map-making system and an accuracy of the automatically made map and time saving effect. In section 5, we outlined two prototypes of human activity detection using RFID textile. One is a pilot application of a tracking system using 19-meter coated RFID textile as a carpet. A person's tracking is detected by shoes that RFID readers were embedded. Another one is a pilot application of a human-activity tracking system using RFID textile wear. By wearing it, the predefined behaviour is detected by embedded RFID readers in the environment. In section 6 conclusions and future works are discussed.

2 Related Works

One of the authors developed RFID embedded outdoor space called PATIO.[4] 1,349 RFID active tags were embedded in the $1,700m^2$ floor space for position detection. These tags were arranged 2D lattice with 1.2 meter spacing. By having developed PATIO, compelling issues arose for achieving the practical use of position detection using RFID technology. These were those of dealing with replacing batteries of the Active RFID tags, the cost of the installation and maintenance of the larger tag area. Besides, once the RFID tag environment was deployed, it is difficult to reconstruct or move it to another space.

By implementing RFID textile system, authors reduce implementing time and cost as well as increase flexibility of the system. In addition, RFID textile is applied as material of many products. Willis et al. introduced an architecture and design using passive RFID information grid for location and proximity sensing for the blind user.[6] They were positive about using passive RFID tag for location detection from the perspective of maintenance and cost. Even though they presented the possibility of implementation of RFID tags as information grid both indoor and outdoor areas, their approach was not brought to realization. So the feasibility test of location detection was performed in comparatively small area. Bohn et al. also presented a potential of super-distributed RFID tag infrastructure over large areas or object surfaces.[7]

Their main contribution of the paper was the advocate of distribution schemas such as the density and structure of tag distributions and tag typing and clustering. They demonstrated the feasibility and versatility of their research by making prototype of a location –aware autonomous vacuum cleaner in small area. At this moment, we made 1.0m x 19.0m RFID textile which was performed as location detection carpet and were positive about making larger areas. Vorwerk, a German company, manufactured carpets sewn RFID tags for the intelligent navigation of service robots.[8] They demonstrated a navigation of a cleaning robot. They were the first commercial company advocating the possibility of RFID location detection method down to earth. However, sewing RFID tags on the carpet was expensive comparing to weaving if it becomes mass production.

Also the RFID textile could be adapted to many products other than carpets. But the Vorwerk system was targeted only to the carpet's infrastructure. Though no applications adapting RFID textile is not known, many researches dealing with detection of human activity by deploying RFID technology were advocated. iGlove and iBracelet were wearable RFID system for detecting human activity. [9] These wearable system deployed RFID reader system into wearable product such as a glove or a bracelet.

The system inferred people's actions from their effect on the environment such as objects with which they interact. Sixthsense was a human activity detection system under enterprise environment.[2] The interaction of a person and an object was detected by tagging office supplies and a person. These two researches challenged to detect human-activity by tagging a person and an object. The goal of our system is to make wearable RFID tag system as a normal cloth and embed RFID reader system in the environment. This may realize more unobtrusive human activity sensing system as well as have redundancy of the detection system since there are multiple RFID tags covered in a body.

Though there were many discussions about the effectiveness of massively distributed RFID tags for location detection, there were few discussions about map make efficiency. To correlate physical coordinates with RF-IDs as a mapping table is important as a basis of the system. Bohn et al. presented a prototype system for collaborative map making using mobile vehicles. [7] Multiple mobile vehicles move around the tag space starting from a known position, each vehicle chooses a random path through the area and thereby keeps track of the tags encountered and the relative inter-tag distances. The separate tag observations are subsequently merged by means of an efficient least-square coordinate transformation algorithm. Our map make system is a customized textile inspection machine. So the map make procedure is very different from it. Our proposing system automatically correlates RF-ID and physical coordinates under the ordinal manufacturing process. Thus it is possible to save time for running the location aware system immediately at the site.

3   RFID Textile Development

The goal of this development of RFID textile is to make automatic RFID textile manufacturing system with no RFID damage while weaving as well as doing after-treatment such as dying and coating. If the goal is accomplished, RFID textile could become commercial production for interior or apparel material.

Fig. 1. Prototype shirt (left) and vinyl covered textile carpet (right)

First of all, we used commercial RFID tags for making the textile by manually interlacing tags with polyester thread. We made two prototype rolls of RFID textile by inserting rows of 6 horizontal 5.3cm(width) x 0.35cm (height) tags every 10cm pitch with the size of 120cm(width) x 150cm(height). And two 1.0m x 30.0m RFID textile by inserting rows of 6 horizontal 5.3cm(width) x 0.35cm (height) tags every 10cm pitch were made.

Then authors made a sample RFID shirt to evaluate the probability of apparel use. No damaged tags are found while cutting, sewing and steam ironing and a carpet by sticking the textile on vinyl carpet. (figure 1)

However manual manufacturing is clearly unfit for mass-production. At least one person has to stick to the woven machine to insert tags every setting pitch.

For enabling automatic manufacturing, we developed a method for automatic weaving with RFID tag yarn. 1.0m x19.0m RFID textile woven RFID tag every 10.0cm both horizontally and vertically were prototypically manufactured at this moment.

4   RFID Map Making System Development

The goal of the system is to make automatic ID map making system during the process of manufacturing the textile. This allows users to apply RFID based positioning system more casually since it saves large amount of time for integrating global position data and RF-ID. We focused on the ordinal textile inspecting process which is done at the very end of shipping. Usual inspection purpose is to check if there are any damages or weaving irregularities on the surface of textiles and length and width is consistent by both automatically rolling textile and measuring length by digital length measuring machine as well as being inspected visually within the area of a flat board. If RFID readers are mounted horizontally in the board region, it is possible to read a unique ID of each RFID tag-arranged yarn woven into the textile while inspection. We invented an inspection system along with automatic map-making system by developing 20 multi-scan 4.0mm (width) x 6.0mm (height) size antennas mounted on a custom made inspecting machine. (figure 3)

As figure 2 shows, the 20 antennas read within small area of each region and the reader transmits tag IDs and antennas' numbers consecutively every 250 msec. Besides the digital length measuring machine transfers a present y position of the textile by counting the number of rotations of a roller. Then the computer system records the first and the last distance of each RFID tag and calculates centre y position. (figure 2 right) X position is automatically calculated from an antenna's number as it is a fixed mounted position. The 19 m automatically woven RFID textile is inspected. (10 antennas every 10 cm pitch) The speed of rolling textile is 0.5m/min which means that mapping data (RFID tag ID and two-dimensional position) is automatically calculated and saved within 40 minutes.

Whereas manual work for making a mapping data of the same RFID textile took 22 hours by one person. Reading RF-IDs took two hours, measuring position by hand took 16 hours and making one mapping data file by organizing tag IDs and position data took two hours. Definitely the map making system saves much time for making a mapping data.

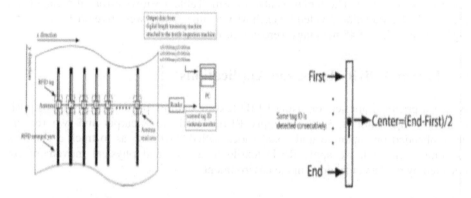

Fig. 2. Map-Making System Diagram (left) and vertical position calculation diagram (right)

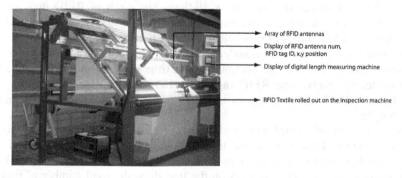

Fig. 3. Map-Making System

Table 1. Error ratio of measured by a map making system and measured by hand

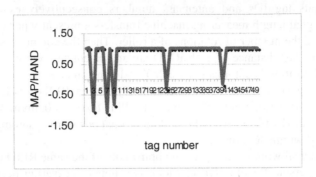

For evaluating the accuracy of the calculated position of map making system, we compared the positions manually recorded (HAND) and the positions automatically calculated by the map making system (MAP). Horizontal position of 50 RFID tags in one line is evaluated. The length is about 4.8m. Table 1 shows error ratio calculated from each HAND value divided by each MAP value. There were five errors out of 50 tags. The position of 45 read tags were correctly measured

5   Human Activity Detection Applications

As for a practical application using RFID textile, authors present two types of position-based applications. First we apply RFID textile to a carpet and two readers are embedded on Japanese traditional shoes called 'Geta' so as to track a person's movement. Second, we apply RFID textile to a shirt and physical movement are detected by readers embedded in the environment.

5.1   Tracking on a Carpet

System outline of the tracking on a carpet and prototype shoes are shown in figure 4. The RFID textile carpet size is 1.0m x 19.0 m. The pitch of RFID tags are every 100mm horizontally and every 100 mm vertically. RFID reader system is embedded on the bottom of left and right shoes. RFID reader is connected wirelessly to a server PC via Bluetooth ver 2.0 and transfers RFID tag ID by the request of the server PC consecutively. The average communication time between the server PC and the RFID reader to receive one RFID tag ID is 105msec (SD9.0msec) during 20000 trials. Coated RFID textile is shown in figure 5 left and tracking view is shown in figure 5 right.

The small scale of testbed were performed for evaluation of accuracy of position. The carpet size is 1.0m x 3.0m and tracking data of a left foot is recorded. Fig 6 shows a tracking of five straight steps. White line in the figure shows a tracking of 1.82m straight walking. The numbers on the line show the total number of times and locations RFID tags were detected. The reason that the tag detected numbers are more than the total number of walking steps is because the antenna consecutively calls

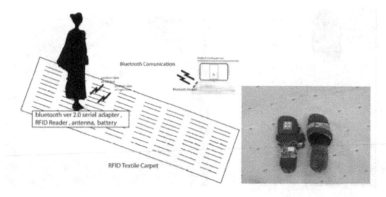

Fig. 4. System outline of a human-tracking system on a carpet and prototype shoes

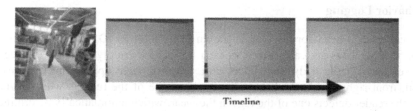

Fig. 5. A person walking on a RFID carpet (left) and tracking view (right)

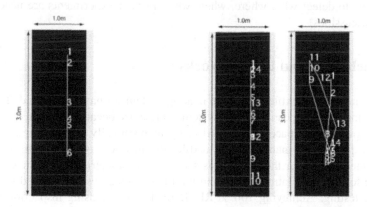

Fig. 6. 5 straight steps   **Fig. 7.** 10 straight and random steps

nearest tags so that any tags within accessible area is read even if the antenna is not touched on the carpet. However reading frequency is randomly occurred which means that it's necessary to fill the missing tracks by simulating the distance and direction. Fig 7 shows another tracking's trials of 10 straight and random steps.

Fig. 8. RFID textile shirt (left) and behavior logging environment (right)

5.2 Behavior Logging

System outline of a behavior tracking is shown in fig 8. A RFID textile shirt (Fig.8. left) has 55 tags. Tags are categorized as each body part. Prototypically, we categorized seven parts of the body. (left upper arm, left arm, right upper arm, right arm, front left, front right and back) If a wearer touches one of the readers while his/her activity, the reader detects one of the tags in the wear, which automatically determines which body part is touched. We tested one antenna embedded in a desk surface around a computer mouse area. We assume this system unobtrusively makes a behavior logging to detect who, where, when, what. Further experiments are necessary for further discussions.

6   Conclusions and Future Works

We presented RFID textile and a map making system we have developed. These were effective for making location aware systems in real use because RFID textile was possible to cover large space at once. Also, by automatically making a mapping table under the process of manufacturing textile, the location aware system was able to work immediately after the textile was set. These characteristics will save much cost and time for the installation. We found the map making system skipped reading RF-ID while testing. Achieving 100 % RF-ID read and increasing inspection speed are our next challenge. We also presented two prototypical location based applications. The basic function worked well for both applications. But there were some missing of RF-ID while walking when the shoe was in dead area of the beacon. We will perform further experiment to evaluate the error rate of it and challenge to decrease the error rate. As for RFID textile wear, the novel human activity tracking method is expected. We will continue to set up an experimental space in a laboratory room for logging an ordinary activity.

Acknowledgement

This research is funded by METI (Kansai Bureau of Economy, Trade and Industry), Japan under the title of "Newly Adopted Projects of Regional R&D Programs for FY2009 (Regional Innovation Creation R&D Programs) /Regional Resource Utilization R&D Programs".

References

1. Meyer, S., Rakotonirainy, A.: A Survey of Research on Context-Aware Homes. In: Workshop on Wearable, Invisible, Context-Aware, Ambient, Pervasive and Ubiquitous Computing, vol. 21, pp. 1–10 (2003)
2. Ravindranath, L., Padmanabhan, N.V., Agrawal, P.: SixthSense: RFID-based Enterprise Intelligence. In: Proceedings of MobiSys 2008, pp. 253–266. ACM Press, New York (2008)
3. Konomi, S., Roussos, G.: Ubiquitous computing in the real world: lessons learnt from large scale RFID deployments. In: Personal Ubiquitous Computing, pp. 507–521. Springer, Heidelberg (2007)
4. Amemiya, T., Yamashita, J., Hirota, K., Hirose, M.: Virtual Leading Blocks for the Deaf-Blind: A Real-Time Way-Finder by Verbal-Nonverbal Hybrid Interface and High-Density RFID Tag Space. In: Proceedings of the VR 2004, pp. 165–172. IEEE Publishing, New York (2004)
5. Gharpure, C., Kulyukin, V., Jiang, M.-h., Kutiyanawala, A.: Passive Radio Frequency Exteroception in Robot Assisted Shopping for the Blind. In: Ma, J., Jin, H., Yang, L.T., Tsai, J.J.-P. (eds.) UIC 2006. LNCS, vol. 4159, pp. 51–60. Springer, Heidelberg (2006)
6. Scooter, S., Helal, S.: A passive rfid information grid for location and proximity sensing for the blind user. In: University of Florida Technical Report number TR04-009 (2004)
7. Bohn, J., Mattern, F.: Super-distributed RFID Tag Infrastructures. In: Markopoulos, P., Eggen, B., Aarts, E., Crowley, J.L. (eds.) EUSAI 2004. LNCS, vol. 3295, pp. 1–12. Springer, Heidelberg (2004)
8. Smart carpet, vorwerk and co. (2006), http://www.vorwerk-teppich.de
9. Smith, R.J., Fishkin, P.K., Jiang, B., Mamishev, A., Philipose, M., Rea, D.A., Roy, S., Sundara-Raian, S.: Rfid-Based Techniques for Human-Activity Detection. Communications of the ACM 48(9), 39–44 (2005)

A Study on the Design of Augmented Reality User Interfaces for Mobile Learning Systems in Heritage Temples

Kuo-Hsiung Wang, Li-Chieh Chen, Po-Ying Chu, and Yun-Maw Cheng

Department of Industrial Design
Department of Media Design
Department of Computer Science and Engineering,
Tatung University, No.40, Sec. 3, Zhongshan N. Rd. Zhongshan District,
Taipei City, 104, Taiwan, R.O.C.
g9604020@ms.ttu.edu.tw,
{lcchen,juby,kevin} @ttu.edu.tw

Abstract. In order to reduce switching attention and increase the performance and pleasure of mobile learning in heritage temples, the objective of this research was to employ the technology of Augmented Reality (AR) on the user interfaces of mobile devices. Based on field study and literature review, three user interface prototypes were constructed. They both offered two service modes but differed in the location of navigation bars and text display approaches. The results of experiment showed that users preferred animated and interactive virtual objects or characters with sound effects. In addition, transparent background of images and text message boxes were better. The superimposed information should not cover more than thirty percents of the screen so that users could still see the background clearly.

Keywords: Mobile Learning, User Interface Design, Augmented Reality.

1 Introduction

With the advent of wireless network technologies, some heritage temples had begun to provide mobile devices for navigation and mobile learning. However, when visitors used the mobile device, their attention was divided into three parts, i.e., the environment, the user interface and digital contents on the devices, and other participants. Divided and distracted attentions reduced the usability and pleasure in using such systems. In order to reduce switching attention and increase the performance and pleasure of mobile learning, the objective of this research was to employ the technology of Augmented Reality (AR) on the user interfaces of mobile devices. With such user interfaces, the image and information can be superimposed on the background. Visitors could experience the rebuilt 3D images while some cultural heritage was damaged in the temples as well.

R. Shumaker (Ed.): Virtual and Mixed Reality, LNCS 5622, pp. 282–290, 2009.

2 Literature Review

Recently, AR technology had been applied in mobile devices successfully. Henrysson et al. (2005) constructed a system in which 3D content could be manipulated using both the movement of a camera tracked mobile phone and a traditional button inter-face as input for transformations. Liarokapis et al. (2006) developed the augmented reality interface that uses computer vision techniques to capture patterns from the real environment and overlay additional way-finding information, aligned with real imagery, in real-time. Liu et al. (2007) integrated the 2D barcodes, the Internet, aug-mented reality, mobile computing and database technologies to construct a mobile English learning system. Tarumi et al. (2008) developed a virtual time machine for edutainment on commercially available mobile phones. Their system displayed graphical images of a past scene within a given area, viewing from the location given by GPS and with arbitrary viewing angles. Users could virtually explore the past world with it. Schmalstieg and Wagner (2007) implemented a client-server architec-ture for multi-user applications and a game engine for location based museum games. After reviewing a great deal of existing AR systems for cultural heritage and museum guides, Damala et al. (2007) concluded that trying to make abstraction of the techno-logical constraints is of paramount importance for the development of Augmented Reality applications

3 Field Study

The authors first conducted a field study through observing the tourists' behaviors in a heritage temple, Lungshan Temple, located in Taipei. In addition, the authors inter-viewed some tourists and temple administrators to elicit the requirements of user interface design for mobile learning. This temple was founded in 1738 and dedicated

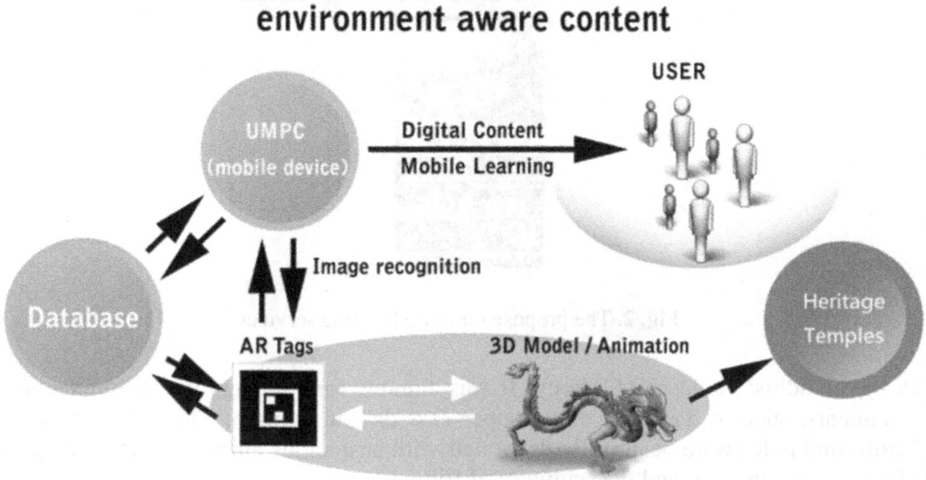

Fig. 1. System operating architecture

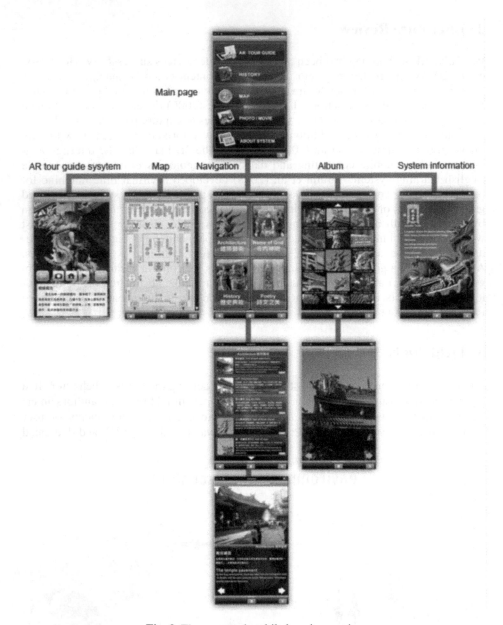

Main page

AR tour guide sysytem   Map   Navigation   Album   System information

Fig. 2. The proposed mobile learning services

to the Buddhist Goddess of Mercy. It was famous for its magnificent architectural ornaments, such as Taiwan's only copper-cast dragon column. The temple's doors, beams and poles were beautifully decorated with auspicious animals (such as dragon, phoenix, and unicorn) and the sculpture of folktales.

Fig. 3. A scenario with an augmented 3D dragon

Fig. 4. The screen shots of UI soncept 1

4 System Implementation

Based on the results of observation and interview, a user interface prototype was built on a Ultra Mobile PC (UMPC) with a 5.6 inch touch-screen and physical keyboards. Since the prototype weighed 600g, it should be held using both hands or carried by a dispatch bag. With this ergonomically designed bag, the tourists were able to enjoy the journey without worrying about how to carry it while walking in the crowded temple. Tourists could use the camera to capture the image of marks located near the spots with heritage features. The media introducing the heritage features would show up to provide augmented information superimposed on the corresponding background. In the media, animated characters or creatures in the folktales were re-built to deliver the story of the ancient. These contents help tourists understand the history and traditional culture of Taiwan. The user interface of Augmented Reality system was constructed based on ARToolKit and user interface widgets. The 3D digital skeleton models of characters and animals were created using Maya 8.5. Real-time rendering of these models were executed and displayed using graphic modules. In addition to the story contents, virtual direction arrows and landmarks were provided at each spot to help visitors navigate in the temple. Figure 1 demonstrated the system operating architecture. Figure 2 displayed the proposed services of a mobile learning system. The scenario with an augmented 3D dragon was presented in Figure 3.

Based on this architecture, three prototypes of user interfaces were constructed. They both offered two service modes but differed in the location of navigation bars and text display approaches. The first prototype superimposed digital images on the background and contained a navigation bar at the middle of the screen and a semi-transparent text message box at the bottom of the screen (Figure 4). Visitors could

Fig. 5. The screen shots of UI concept 2

Fig. 6. The screen shots of UI concept 3

switch between two services that had contents either relevant to the components of physical objects in the temple (left) or virtual characters that are cute versions of representative gods in the temple (right). Compared to the first prototype, the second prototype increased the percentage of transparency for the text box and displayed text in white color. In addition, the navigation bar was placed at the bottom of the page (Figure 5). In the third UI prototypes (Figure 6), the screen was divided into two windows. Furthermore, the background of the text message box was not transparent.

5   System Evaluation and Results

In order to test the advantages and disadvantages of proposed systems, ten students were invited to participate in the experiment of prototypes. During the experiments, video recording and audio recording were used to record the behaviors of participants. Interviews and post-test questionnaire surveys were used to obtain the opinions of participants after performing typical tasks. These tasks included locating some historical spots and reading the information through augmented contents. The results of experiments showed that, in general, the participants appreciated the new paradigm of interaction. Some participants indicated that locating marks and retrieving information through camera was intuitive. In addition, the connections between physical objects of the temple architecture and their detailed information were increased due to co-presence within a single screen at the same time. Furthermore, they could use the function of print screen to capture the image of superimposition. Some participants even creatively extended this function by asking their friends to stand aside the mark so that the background, the people, and the augmented contents appeared in the same picture, thus increasing the pleasure of visiting.

Table 1. Comments of two service contents

Comments	Virtual Objects	Virtual Characters
Advantages	Increase the immersion of visiting; Vivid and attractiveness; It's like a magic for kids	Cute and user friendly; The god characters had strong connectivity to the temple and the culture
Disadvantages	Large objects interfered the background; Difficult to distinguish physical and virtual objects; Serious and not user friendly	Proportion of virtual characters were too big; The form is too compli-cated; Lack of dynamic actions
Recommendation in Content Design	Cartoon version is more acces-sible; Decrease the proportion of ob-jects; Increase the dynamic actions of objects; Enhance the connection be-tween objects and text descrip-tions; Simple the form of objects	Add some dynamic actions to the characters; Two characters interact to each other; Make character interactive with users; Add sounds to enhance impression

Table 2. Comments of three UI concepts

Comments	Concept 1	Concept 2	Concept 3
Advantages	Icons are easy to be recognized; Color of text is legible	Text is clear and legible; Information is transparent; High quality	Color contrast of text is good; Option is clear
Disadvantages	Font is too small; Too many blocks; Big icons may cover background	Font is too small; The proportion of the text box is too big; Icons are too small to be overlooked	Font is too small; Too many menu icons; The proportion of the text box is too big;
Recommendation in UI Design	Place icons into the text box; Increase the font of text	Change the location of icons; Increase the size of icons	Make text box smaller and transparent; Reduce the num-ber of icons

The comments about two services provided by participants were presented in Tables 1. Their recommendations were summarized as follows:

1. The size of virtual objects should be limited to prevent coverage of background
2. Cute style and simple characters were more user-friendly
3. Animated objects were better
4. Sound effects and interactive virtual characters could increase the impression

The comments about two services provided by participants were presented in Tables 2. Their recommendations were summarized as follows:

1. Transparent background of virtual objects and text message boxes were better
2. Increase the size of font
3. Increase the size of menu
4. The proportion of text message boxes should be less than one-third of the screen

The ratings of performances among three UI concepts were showed in Table 3. Concepts 1 and 2 had higher ratings than concept 3. Separated screens and solid background color hampered the navigation and increase the perceived workload of participants.

Table 3. The mean and standard deviation of performance ratings for different UI concepts

Performance Measures	Concept 1	Concept 2	Concept 3
Navigation Aids	5.67(1.12)	5.78(0.83)	3.67(0.87)
Perceived Workload	2.22(0.67)	3.00(1.12)	4.44(0.73)

6 Discussion

Although the first attempt was successful, the participants still encounter some problems of carrying such a big device. For example, tourists always had their backpack or carried cameras. The dispatch bag of the device sometimes interfered with their personal equipment. In addition, even though the augmented contents were able to deliver virtual objects superimposed on the background, the shape and texture of these objects were still rough compared to the beauty of the temple architecture. The mark recognition process was too sensitive so that some users had difficulties in finding the right angle between the camera and the mark. Furthermore, the color contrast of the virtual foreground and the physical background were influenced significantly by the glare of light.

7 Conclusion and Future Work

The results of experiment showed that user prefer animated virtual objects or characters with sound effects. In addition, transparent background of images and text message boxes were better. The superimposed information should not cover more than fifty percents of the screen so that users could still see the background clearly.

Based on these findings, the research team had identified specific fields for further research to leverage between limited resources on current mobile devices and the design of user interfaces based on AR. First, the location and setup of marks deserve further experiments to avoid the influence of peripheral lighting. Second, the devices and algorithms for mark recognition need to be improved. Third, specific algorithms for real-time rendering of 3D models for AR should be developed. Fourth, the mapping of touch gestures and dynamics of content display should be addressed.

Acknowledgments

The authors would like to express our gratitude to the National Science Council of the Republic of China for financially supporting this research under Grant No. NSC97-2221-E-036-035.

References

1. Damala, A., Marchal, I., Houlier, M.: Merging Augmented Reality Based Features in Mobile Multimedia Museum Guides. In: Proceedings of the XXI International CIPA Symposium, Athens, Greece, October 1-6 (2007)
2. Henrysson, A., Ollila, M., Billinghurst, M.: Mobile phone based AR scene assembly. In: Proceedings of the 4th international conference on Mobile and ubiquitous multimedia, Christchurch, New Zealand, pp. 95–102 (2005)
3. Liarokapis, F., Brujic-Okretic, V., Papakonstantinou, S.: Exploring Urban Environments using Virtual and Augmented Reality. Journal of Virtual Reality and Broadcasting, GRAPP 2006 Special Issue 3(5), 1–13 (2006)
4. Liu, T.Y., Tan, T.H., Chu, Y.L.: 2D Barcode and Augmented Reality Supported English Learning System. In: Proceedings of the 6th IEEE/ACIS International Conference on Computer and Information Science, Melbourne, Australia, July 2007, pp. 5–10 (2007)
5. Schmalstieg, D., Wagner, D.: Experiences with Handheld Augmented Reality. In: Proceedings of the 6th IEEE and ACM International Symposium on Mixed and Augmented Reality, ISMAR 2007, November 13-16, 2007, pp. 3–18 (2007)
6. Tarumi, H., Yamada, K., Daikoku, T., Kusunoki, F., Inagaki, S., Takenaka, M., Hayashi, T., Yano, M.: Design and Evaluation of a Virtual Mobile Time Machine in Education. In: Proceedings of the International Conference on Advances in Computer Entertainment Technology, pp. 334–337. ACM, Japan (2008)

Part III
Haptics and Tactile Interaction in VR

Haptic Interaction and Interactive Simulation in an AR Environment for Aesthetic Product Design

Monica Bordegoni, Francesco Ferrise, and Marco Ambrogio

Politecnico di Milano, Dipartimento di Meccanica,
Via G. La Masa 34, 20156 Milano, Italy
{monica.bordegoni@,francesco.ferrise@,
marco.ambrogio@mail.}polimi.it

Abstract. Market rules show that most of the times the aesthetic impact of a product is an important aspect that makes the difference in terms of success among different products. The product shape is generally created and represented during the conceptual phase of the product and the last trends show that the use of haptic devices allows users to more naturally and effectively interact with 3D models. Nevertheless the shape needs to satisfy some engineering requirements, and its aesthetic and functional analysis requires the collaboration and synchronization of activities performed by various experts having different competences and roles. This paper presents the description of an environment named PUODARSI that allows designers to modify the shape of a product and engineers to evaluate in real-time the impact of these changes on the structural and fluid dynamic properties of the product, describing the choice of the software tools, the implementation and some usability tests.

Keywords: Mixed reality, haptic interaction, interactive simulation.

1 Introduction

The trends of the market suggest that a lot of importance in the whole Product Development Process (PDP) must be given to the definition of the aesthetical properties of the shape. The same product must be also efficient from the technological point of view and so requires some engineering tests to be done on it in order to be optimized. These requirements generate a process that can be imagined like a closed loop among designers that define the shape and engineers that analyze it. Despite the availability of new technologies like those of Virtual and Augmented Reality that can be considered as tools that enable a 'natural' interaction with computer generated worlds, the PDP in the world of industry is still based on old techniques and technologies that are considered robust and reliable. The designers use to work on physical prototypes and this is because some of them are manually skilled, or sometimes are used to define their shapes sketching on two dimensional papers. There are also CAD systems that help them to define computer geometrical models but they are still based on human computer interfaces like mouse and keyboards that often do not allow the designer to fully express his idea of shape and are not integrated with VR devices. The use of the CAD systems allows to get immediately, as a result of the modeling phase, a prototype that is more flexible than the physical ones because can be used some tests and evaluations.

R. Shumaker (Ed.): Virtual and Mixed Reality, LNCS 5622, pp. 293–302, 2009.

Regarding the engineering tests, the algorithms based on the Finite Element Method are helping to substitute the tests made in the past on physical prototypes. Some examples of this can be found in the Computational Fluid Dynamics analysis, known as CFD that is substituting the wind tunnel based analysis.

The integration of Virtual and Augmented Reality Technologies together with the use of virtual prototypes in the PDP and in particular in the phases when the shape is defined and analyzed would allow to reduce the time to market.

The paper describes a research carried out in the contest of the PDP with the aim of changing the way of defining a shape and of analyzing it, making it more easy and intuitive thanks to the use of VR/AR techniques and technologies together with some real-time analyses. In the first part a brief state of the art is presented, first on the VR/AR technologies and their usage in the contest of PDP and of the algorithms that enable the interactive simulations. The paper then describes how the classical process of shape modeling and engineering simulation can be virtualized, with issues and potentialities, and the solutions adopted in the contest of the PUODARSI project. So the paper describes the system that has been developed in order to prove the concept and run some usability tests. Then the conclusions are presented.

2   State of the Art of Haptic, AR Devices and Interactive Simulations in the Design Domain

There are some examples of the use of Virtual and Augmented Reality technologies supporting the PDP. Most of these applications are focused on the design review phase, i.e. when the product has been defined and just small changes can be taken. Our research aims at introducing the use of these technologies already in the preliminary phases of the PDP, i.e. in the conceptual and embodiment phases, where the product is still in its development phase. In the following a brief state of the art of the interested technologies is presented with regard to their application in the PDP.

2.1   Haptic Technologies

Haptic Interaction is meant as a way to add the sense of touch to Virtual Environments. There are many devices on the market, but basically point based and with three or more degrees of freedom [1]. The devices basically differ in terms of degrees of freedom in input and output, the work volume, and strength of the returned force. Among these devices the most used are the Phantom Sensable products [2], the Haptic Master-MOOG FCS [3], the devices of Force Dimension [4], and those distributed by Haption [5].

In the field of research some devices that return a linear contact-type [6] or surface contact-type with the virtual object have been developed, but at the time they're still prototypes. Haptic devices are generally provided with proprietary library for the development of applications, enabling in an easy way to create haptic environments, but with very low level visualization environments. However, there are some types of open source libraries, already integrated with high level visualization libraries and sound rendering and also algorithms for the creation of physics-based environments, which permit the development of applications regardless of device used. Examples of such libraries are CHAI3D [7], H3D [8], HaptikLibrary [9] and OpenSceneGraph Haptic Library [10].

In the specific area of design and product development there are a variety of applications ranging from the Virtual Sculpting commercial package FreeForm distributed by Sensable [2], which is the first application based on a physics-based interaction with a clay modeling tool, going up to the application that allows the Virtual Assembly in CATIA, a commercial CAD system, distributed by Dassault Systemes. Finally there are a number of research projects in which the haptic interaction is used in the creation of forms [11] by virtually replicating the behavior of some tools used by designers in the creation of forms from clay models, like the rake or the sanding tool. There's another example of a linear haptic device in a multimodal environment used as a means to return to the contact a characteristic line of a style surface in order to enable the qualitative assessment and modification of the same [12].

2.2 Augmented Reality Technologies

Augmented Reality (AR) allows to contextualize a Virtual Prototype in a real environment i.e. giving the opportunity to the user to see a digital model into a real scene. Nowadays computer graphics technology in fact is able to generate a photorealistic representation of the digital model but a good contextualization of the VP represents a challenge yet. The simplest architecture to realize an AR environment is composed by a camera and a monitor; the camera acquires the real scene then the image acquired is processed by the pc that merges digital model in the real environment.

In order to superimpose the virtual object in the real scene it is fundamental the use of a tracking system that provides the correct position and orientation of the virtual object respect to the user's point of view. The pioneer tracking system for AR is certainly represented by ARToolkit [13] library. This is a very simple tracking system that, by processing the camera video streaming, derives position and orientation of the virtual object by a 2D marker. Starting from this idea many other tracking libraries [14,15] have been developed to spending much effort to the marker-less tracking system and to improving precision and accuracy. Regarding the use of AR applications for PDP, in these years many research groups developed AR applications in order to improve, speed and simplify the different product development phases. Friedrich [16] describes a testing of AR application in development, production, and servicing of the product in use or the machines and systems required for service and production. Doil et al. [17] describes potential benefits and development of a prototypical AR-System for the support of manufacturing planning tasks. Santos et al [18] describes an application for collaborative mobile design review that allow to simplify the review procedures and to reduce the number of physical prototypes that are realized for review phase. Another interesting application is related to the exploitation of results of numerical simulation data. In [19] is presented a framework that allows to see the results of a CFD analysis directly on the physical prototype of the product in the developing phase by using a tablet pc. This framework is still used in the contest of the project described in this paper.

2.3   Interactive Simulation in CFD Analysis

In the PDP, numerical analyses are always used to verify and validate the virtual model of the product. The most used commercial software in industrial field for CFD analyses is Fluent, recently purchased by Ansys Inc. [20]. Moreover a number of open-source algorithms allow us to perform high accurate structural and CFD analyses and are widely used in the research field due to the fact that they are completely open and extensible. Regarding the CFD analysis we find, for example, OpenFOAM [21] and OpenFlower [22]. The analysis process is usually divided into three steps: pre-processing, analysis and post-processing. The first step consists of the discretization of the physic problem subject of the analysis, generally the geometric model and the control volumes around it for CFD analyses, and the definition of the initial conditions for the analysis. In the second step the software runs the numerical analysis and creates the results data. The third and last step represents the review of the output data obtained from analysis, which can be velocity and pressure distribution for CFD analyses. Generally, in the analysis phase of a product, a lot of time is spent by engineers, especially to correctly define the pre-processing parameters, but also to perform the analysis and find the solution of the problem, due to slow resolution algorithms developed in commercial software. Many studies have been done in order to speed-up the simulations, especially concerning the case of the simulation of the behavior of fluids, but all of these algorithms have been developed for Computer Graphics purposes. These algorithms, also if not suitable for pure engineering problems that sometimes need a high accuracy of results, are based on physical models and so are useful when, as in our research, the aim is to find a way to reduce the computational time of the analysis phase and the accuracy of the results is not the most important goal. Fournier and Reeves [23] describe a simple model to simulate the behavior of the surface of the Ocean that is based on Rankine model, where particles of water describe circular or elliptical orbits. Chen and Lobo define a new method [24] to perform in real-time three-dimensional CFD simulations in a dynamic virtual environment with moving obstacles. In the last years considerable improvements have been reached in the field of real-time fluid simulations, due to new programming technologies and different definitions of physical model of fluids. In particular Muller and Gross [25] describe a new method to simulate fluids with free surfaces, using Smoothed Particle Hydrodynamics. An example of fast engineering analyses based on classical CFD algorithms has been developed in the context of a research project where an engineering CFD tool has been optimized in order to perform fast analyses, connected to the change of the shape of style object [26], and the results show that fast analysis is possible if the phase of the creation of the mesh is optimized and the initial conditions are kept constant.

3   Issues in Virtualizing Some Real Tasks in the PUODARSI Solution

This section describes the implementation of the concepts highlighted above in particular presenting the PUODARSI solutions. The whole system is complicated and made of simpler and standalone modules, each for one purpose, and especially implemented in order to be reusable as additional tools for other existing applications. So all the modules share the same file format and communicate through server/client connections. Engineers and Designers make use of different representations and different language in order to express their concepts. In order to make them collaborate and work together, as will be described, an annotation tool has been added to the system.

3.1 Modification of the Shape

The Haptic module has been implemented in H3D. The module takes as input a STL file format and translates it in a X3D model. Then this object can be managed with a three-dimensional Gaussian modification tool where the user can choose some parameters like the width of the tool, and the softness of the material that he's managing. Every time that the model is modified, the system stores it in the RAM memory, in order to allow the undo/redo operations. When the desired shape is obtained then the designer freezes the model that is saved in a new file named VerN.stl where N is the number of times the file is saved, and sends it to the shared folder with the analysis tools. Figure 1 shows the user that is deforming a shape using a Sensable Phantom Omni device, in a Sensegraphics workbench.

Fig. 1. Example of the haptic modeling tool used for the modification phase

3.2 Simulation and Results

The simulation module has been defined taking into account problems regarding pre-processing step, simulation time, visualization and analysis of post-processing data. The implementation of the module for CFD analysis has been done using the open source OpenFOAM library, a set of different tools used to simulate specific problems in engineering mechanics, including computational fluid-dynamic problems. The choice of this library is attributable to the big amount of tools that can easily solve compatibility problems with the other modules, and also to the time performances of the solvers integrated in the library.

In order to share geometric models with the haptic module, it has been necessary to use tessellated surfaces, define a control volume around them and then create a three dimensional mesh on the volume obtained by the subtraction of the volume of the model from the control volume. This step has been done defining a C++ code to

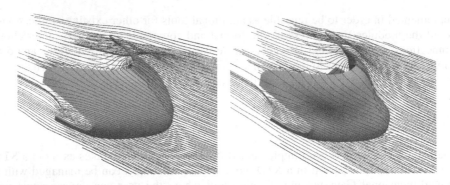

Fig. 2. CFD simulation on a windscreen before and after the modification

import tessellated geometries (STL files) and create the control volume in the software GMSH, used to generate the mesh of elements. To increase the velocity of the analysis, the initial conditions, like inlet velocity and outlet pressure, are automatically assigned to the corresponding surfaces of the control volume; in particular an inlet velocity of 30 m/s and atmospheric pressure are chosen for the analyses. Once chosen the geometry to analyze, the simulation module automatically runs all the steps described before and consequently launches the analysis.

When the analysis is complete, the results are sent to the Visualization System that renders these data. The results of the analysis are transformed into a format that is compatible with VTK. The Visualization Toolkit – VTK is an open source library for Scientific Visualization that allows developers to easily visualize data obtained from scientific simulations.

Figure 2 shows the results of the shape modification on the CFD analysis of the windscreen model.

3.3 Annotation Tool in AR and Exchange of Information

The annotation tool has been implemented in order to allow the exchange of information among the different users and has been connected to a Database that stores all the information of the PDP in order to allow a reuse of them. The annotation component has been developed in C++ using QT libraries. The idea was to create a VTK widget able to visualize only the visual links related to the annotations connected to the models, or the CFD/FEM analysis. Instead the annotation component has been implemented by means of a QT dialog box using which the user can create or manage annotations. In this way it is possible to exploit the QT library for defining the text-editing module and for integrating components to manage the threads of notes. Moreover QT supports easy integration of different multimedia files like audio, video or pictures related to the annotation. Both the VTK component and QT component access archives storing 3D models, analysis and annotations through a KM module developed to guarantee a transparent information retrieval with respect to technical details of the databases. The VTK objects are used then in the VTK4AR framework [19] that allows us to view and exploit the results in an intuitive way. Figure 3 shows an example of the annotation module in AR.

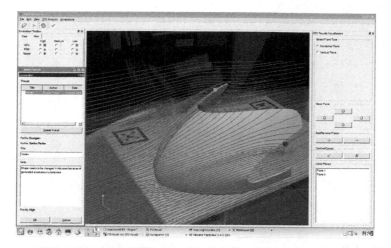

Fig. 3. Screenshot of the AR annotation tool, representing the results of the CFD analysis on the original model

4 Testing and Results

A prototype of the system has been developed in order to perform some usability tests and to get the impressions of the final user about the effectiveness of the approach. In the following a brief description of the testing phases and of the results is presented.

4.1 Description of the Usability Tests

The tests of the system have been articulated as following: ten users, five designers and five engineers had to perform the following tasks: 1) the designers were asked to change the shape of the windscreen as illustrated in the Figure 2; 2) the engineers were asked to verify the results on the CFD analyses in the AR environment; 3) engineers had to put some annotations on the geometry and on the streamlines in the AR environment and the designers had to read and add other notes. At the end of these tasks the users were asked to answer to some questions regarding the usability of the system for each task performed; the questions concerned their general impressions, knowledge acquisition, functionalities divided into systems components and GUI layout, goal achievements. The results are reported in the following section.

4.2 Results

After using the system, the testers were asked to answer to a questionnaire. Figure 3 reports the answers to the questions provided by the testers, scoring each question from 0 to 6. The general users' impressions about the system show that despite they like the concept and the innovation of the whole system, there is still some work to do on each module in order to reach a really usable system. From the data reported on the chart of Figure 3 it is possible to notice that the users perceive that the system can help to reduce the time needed to create and test the model, but they judge not so

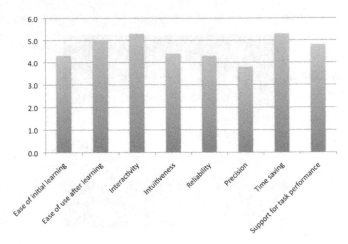

Fig. 4. Results of the general impressions of the users during the usability tests

efficient the precision and the reliability of the system. Then, the users state that the system is not so easy to use at the beginning of the tasks but after a period of learning it may become a good support for tasks performances thanks of the new kind of interaction implemented.

5 Conclusions

The paper described a contribution at the product development process innovation based on the use of VR and AR devices together with interactive simulation. The aim was to create a simulation aided design, and to bring closer the worlds of engineers and designers. A prototype has been build in order to test the effectiveness, to prove the concept and to get some initial feedbacks from the final users.

The tests show that far from being usable by the industrial world, the PUODARSI framework introduces some single innovations that if developed and exploited can become part of whole process. For example the users like the way of interacting with models thanks to the haptic or AR devices and this is because they consider the interaction more intuitive, but what they judge very important is the possibility to reduce the time needed to realize and test the product thanks to the collaboration of designers and engineers and this is mainly due to the reduction of the time for analyses and the exchange of information through the annotation system. So the next developments of the system will aim at introducing some adjustments at the interaction but also at the precision and reliability of the system.

Acknowledgments. Part of the research described in the paper has been developed in the context of the PUODARSI (Product User Oriented Development based on Augmented Reality and interactive SImulation) project (http://www.kaemart.it/puodarsi), partially funded by the Italian Ministry of University and Research.

References

1. Hayward, V., Ashley, O., Hernandez, M.C., Grant, D., RoblesDeLaTorre, G.: Haptic interfaces and devices. Sensor Review 24(1), 16–29 (2004)
2. PHANToM device, SenSable Technologies Inc.,
   http://www.sensable.com
3. FCS-HapticMaster, MOOG-FCS,
   http://www.moogfcs.com/robotics
4. Force Dimension Haptic devices,
   http://www.forcedimension.com/
5. Virtuose, Haption, http://www.haption.com/
6. Bordegoni, M., Cugini, U., Covarrubias, M.: Design of a visualization system integrated with haptic interfaces. In: Horvath, I., Rusak, Z. (eds.) Proocedings of the TMCE (2008)
7. CHAI3D Haptic Library, http://www.chai3d.org/
8. H3D Haptic Library, http://www.h3d.org/
9. Haptik Library, http://www.haptiklibrary.org/
10. OpenSceneGraph Haptic Library,
    http://sourceforge.net/projects/osghaptics
11. Bordegoni, M., Cugini, U.: Haptic modeling in the conceptual phases of product design. Virtual Reality Journal 9(1), 192–202 (2006)
12. Bordegoni, M., Ferrise, F., Shelley, S., Alonso, M., Hermes, D.: Sound and tangible interface for shape evaluation and modification. In: Proceeding of HAVE 2008 - IEEE International Workshop on Haptic Audio Visual Environments and their Applications (2008)
13. Kato, H., Billinghurst, M.: Marker tracking and hmd calibration for a video-based augmented reality conferencing system. In: International Workshop on Augmented Reality, p. 85 (1999)
14. Fiala, M.: Artag, a fiducial marker system using digital techniques. In: IEEE Computer Society Conference on Computer Vision and Pattern Recognition, CVPR 2005, June 2, 2005, vol. 2, pp. 590–596 (2005)
15. Schmalstieg, D., Fuhrmann, A., Hesina, G., Szalavari, Z., Encarnacao, L.M., Gervautz, M., Purgathofer, W.: The studierstube augmented reality project. Tech. Rep. TR-186-2-00-22, Institute of Computer Graphics and Algorithms, Vienna University of Technology (2000)
16. Wohlgemuth, W., Triebfürst, G.: Arvika: augmented reality for development, production and service. In: Proceedings of DARE 2000 on Designing augmented reality environments, pp. 151–152. ACM Press, New York (2000)
17. Doil, F., Schreiber, W., Alt, T., Patron, C.: Augmented reality for manufacturing planning. In: EGVE 2003: Proceedings of the workshop on Virtual environments 2003, pp. 71–76. ACM Press, New York (2003)
18. Santos, P., Stork, A., Gierlinger, T., Pagani, A., Paloc, C., Barandarian, I., Conti, G., de Amicis, R., Witzel, M., Machui, O., Jimanez, J., Araujo, B., Jorge, J., Bodammer, G.: Improve: An innovative application for collaborative mobile mixed reality design review. International Journal on Interactive Design and Manufacturing 1(2), 115–126 (2007)
19. Bruno, F., Caruso, F., Ferrise, F., Muzzupappa, M.: Vtk4ar: An object oriented framework for scientific visualization of cae data in augmented reality. In: Gallo, G., Battiato, S., Stanco, F. (eds.) Proceedings of Eurographics Italian Chapter Conference, Eurographics, pp. 76–81 (2006)
20. Fluent, by Ansys Inc., http://www.fluent.com/
21. OpenFOAM: The Open Source CFD Toolbox,
    http://www.opencfd.co.uk/

22. OpenFlower, http://openflower.sourceforge.net/
23. Fournier, A., Reeves, W.T.: A simple model of ocean waves. SIGGRAPH Comput. Graph. 20(4), 75–84 (1986)
24. Chen, J.X., da Vitoria Lobo, N., Hughes, C.E., Moshell, J.M.: Real-time fluid simulation in a dynamic virtual environment. IEEE Computer Graphics and Applications 17(3), 52–61 (1997)
25. Muller, M., Charypar, D., Gross, M.: Particle-based fluid simulation for interactive applications. In: Proceedings of the 2003 ACM SIGGRAPH/Eurographics symposium on Computer animation, Eurographics Association, pp. 154–159 (2003)
26. Bordegoni, M., Ferrise, F., Ambrogio, M., Bruno, F., Caruso, F.: A multi-layered modelling architecture for virtual design. In: Proceedings of IDMME Virtual Concept 2008 Conference (2008)

Evaluation of a Haptic-Based Interaction System for Virtual Manual Assembly

Monica Bordegoni, Umberto Cugini, Paolo Belluco, and Marcello Aliverti

Politecnico di Milano, Dipartimento di Meccanica,
Via G. La Masa 1, 20156 Milano, Italy
{monica.bordegoni,umberto.cugini}@polimi.it,
belluco@elet.polimi.it, marcello.aliverti@kaemart.it

Abstract. This paper describes a mixed reality application for the assessment of manual assembly of mechanical systems. The application aims at using low cost technologies and at the same time at offering an effective environment for the assessment of a typical task consisting of assembling two components of a mechanical system. The application is based on the use of a 6-DOF interaction device that is used for positioning an object in space, and a haptic interface that is closer to reality and is used for simulating the insertion of a second component into the first one while feeling a force feedback. The application has been validated by an expert user in order to identify the main usability and performance problems and improve its design.

Keywords: Virtual Manual Assembly, haptic-based interaction, VR system evaluation.

1 Introduction

Virtual reality tools and technologies are demonstrating to be useful and effective in various phases of product development. Several examples can be reported demonstrating the successful use of Virtual Reality (VR) for the early evaluation of various aspects of products, such as functional, ergonomics, usability, etc. [1]. Particularly complex are those situations where it is necessary to validate the interaction of humans with the designed products. Accessibility, reachability, usability are just few examples of issues where it is necessary to investigate the interaction of the user with the product. Most of VR systems based on pure visualization of objects do not allow us to fully validate these aspects. The recent introduction of haptic interfaces allows us to perform better and more comprehensive tests, including ergonomics and usability tests [2]. An additional situation where it is required the interaction of humans and products concerns the validation of the manual handling of products, such as assembling and disassembling and maintenance.

Several research works have addressed issues related to VR systems for the simulation of assembling and disassembling of components only based on digital simulation of the task, possibly including digital mannequins, but without any intervention from real users. Other works have integrated haptic technologies for the analysis of assembly tasks. The aim of the work presented in this paper is demonstrating the

R. Shumaker (Ed.): Virtual and Mixed Reality, LNCS 5622, pp. 303–312, 2009.

effectiveness of VR technologies for the validation of manual assembly processes in manufacturing industries. In particular, we address the problems related to the design review and validation of assembly of mechanical components. Currently mechanical systems tend to be compacted and occupy very limited space in order to allow more space to other components with which the users interact with. This fact generates assembling and disassembling problems, accessibility as well as maintenance problems. CAD tools allow engineers to perform static tests of parts assembling. They allow them to check collisions and interferences but do not allow the validation of assembling/disassembling procedures, i.e. mating trajectories, which are typically performed manually by skilled operators. Recently we are witnessing the development and evolution of sophisticated VR technologies in markets like games and infotainment. Actually, these technologies are performing although available at low and reasonable prices due to the dimension of their markets. Our intention is testing the use of these technologies in the technical and engineering domain related to product development, integrated with typical CAD-Computer Aided Design and PLM-Product Lifecycle Management tools. Our purpose is developing a mixed and heterogeneous experimental workbench where various technologies and interaction modalities can be easily developed and tested. This paper presents the workbench that has been implemented for the evaluation of assembly tasks performed by skilled operators. Typically assembly tasks are performed by operators by using both hands. The idea of our research is including the users (designers and individual assembly operators) in the validation loop so that functional, ergonomics and usability issues related to the assembly tasks can be tested in the virtual environment, before actually building the physical components constituting the system. This can be achieved providing users with two 6-DOF haptic devices for the manipulation of two components to assemble. Actually, this solution is quite expensive to implement. Therefore, we have been spurred to find an alternative solution but equally effective. Observing a real user during the assembly of two parts we have noticed that most of the times one hand is used to position and hold an object, and the other hand is used to insert a second object into the first one with sometime very complex trajectory guided by the force feedback generated by the contact between the two mounting parts. Therefore, we have thought of using a 6-DOF interaction device to position a part of a system, and a 6-DOF force feedback device for handling and assembling a second part or for simulating a machine tool, such as a drill, a welder, a wrench, etc. The VR environment has been tested by an expert user in order to identify main usability and performance issues. The final goal is accessing how effective would be a virtual manual assembly over a real physical assembly task, and compare human factors aspects.

2 Related Works

This section reports an overview of the virtual/mixed reality systems that make use of haptic interfaces for assembly simulation or manipulation tasks for testing or training purposes. Abhishek S. et al. [3] outline the problematic in virtual assembly applications that mainly regard the graphic visualization and rendering of the virtual scene, collision detection, physics-based modelling and haptic interaction. Stereo viewing, head tracking and instrumented glove interaction are all common components of many virtual reality applications.

Jayaram S. et al. [4] have developed VADE (Virtual Assembly Design Environment) a VR-based engineering application that allows engineers to plan, evaluate, and verify the assembly of mechanical systems. The Inventor Virtual Assembly system developed by Kuehne and Oliver [5] allows designers to interactively verify and evaluate the assembly characteristics of components directly from a CAD application.

The evolution of haptic technologies [6,7] has allowed researchers to study new interaction approaches between the users and the virtual tools concerning assembly tasks that may be performed through one-hand or two-hands. Applications based on two-hand interfaces have proved to be more effective and actually allow the implementation of additional tasks that cannot be performed by one hand alone.

The Sensable Phantom™ haptic device [8] has been used in several applications, like in virtual milling machines [9] and assembly training in the aeronautic environment where the device is used to simulate mounting and dismounting operations of different parts of an aircraft [10]. Recently it has been proposed a system that integrates mixed-reality and haptic feedback [11] based on the use of the Haptic Workstation™. The system consists of four devices manufactured by Immersion Corporation (www.immersion.com) and is able to acquire the position of the hand and to add force feedback for each finger in one direction, and it is also able to simulate the weight of the grasped objects. The major issue is related to the fact that the mixed-reality techniques based on optical see-through head mounted display are not precise enough to overlap correctly the real and virtual worlds. Another haptic device, which is used in the research presented in this paper, is the Virtuose manufactured by Haption (www.haption.com). The device has been used to develop an application described in [12] that consists of a complex virtual simulation dedicated to virtual assembly. The HapticMaster by Kyushu Institute of Technology, is used as a haptic interface in a tele-operation application. The user controls a manipulator on the basis of force and torque feedback provided by sensorized end-effectors; [13].

3   The Study Case

The Virtual Reality interactive workbench developed aims at simulating a typical environment where operators perform assembling tasks of mechanical components. The environment resembles the corresponding real environment and tasks without exactly replicating it. In fact, the purpose is allowing operators to test the efficiency and effectiveness of the workbench, its usability and intuitiveness.

We have developed a Study Case for performing manual tasks in a virtual environment. The scenarios are based on a combination of a virtual reality system and a haptic interface. The user can see the scene represented in real scale on a wall visualization system; his position is detected by a tracking system that allows him to change his point of view in respect to the scene. He can interact with the virtual objects using an input device, and can feel force feedback when grabbing and handling virtual components and virtual tools through the use of the haptic interface.

The Study Case consists of a two hands assembly task. Some components that are part of a mechanical system are positioned on a table. The system demonstrates the assembly procedure consisting of grabbing, holding and positioning a component (component A), grabbing a second component (component B) and assembling the two components. The user repeats the same task. He grabs and positions the component A using a 6-DOF interaction device, and then he grabs the component B using a 6-DOF haptic device, and assembles the component B into the component A.

4 The Virtual Reality System

We decided that the close correspondence between real and virtual is required for the hand that is performing the "primary" tasks. The primary task is the manipulation of the object (component B) to insert into the other component (component A). In this specific context the interaction with objects directly mimics the real world. Through the use of the haptic device, the user can feel the weight of the object and the collisions that occur when performing the insertion of the second object into the first one. Instead, the task performed with the other hand doesn't need to have a faithful resemblance with reality. An interaction device may be used for handling and orienting the first subject. Haptic feedback is not necessary, although appropriate feedback is required for informing the user about the system and the objects status.

Then, the application should have some features that help the user during the execution of the tasks. In particular the application should provide the following.

User's presence. The user should be represented in the virtual world by means of a visual representation. The interaction mainly consists of the manipulation of objects and occurs through the use of 6-DOF devices. The user's presence may be represented by visual rendering of the position and orientation of the device.

Haptic feedback. Haptic feedback is the sense of touch occurring when the user comes in contact with an object. Haptic feedback to user's interaction with scene objects may be provided either through the haptic device or through visual, sound, tactile (vibration) feedback.

Feedback of users' actions and on the effect of actions on objects. The user should be informed about the actions he is performing and about the effect that these actions have on the virtual objects.

Interactive techniques. Specific interaction techniques may be used for quickly reaching objects, zooming, and others.

Realistic graphical representation. The system should render photorealistic details of components that are important for the task that the user has to perform.

Information about the status of the environment and objects. The user should be always informed about the status of the environment and of the objects.

Affordances. The application should provide suggestions about usage, functions, actions to perform on objects.

4.1 Hardware and Software Components

The Virtual Reality system used for implementing the application consists of a real scale, stereoscopic visualization environment including an optical tracking system, and a haptic device. The hardware components of the system are shown in Figure 1.

The haptic interface consists of the Virtuose 6D35-45 ™ device from Haption. It is a 6-DOF haptic device with a large force-feedback field on all 6 DOF. For what concerns the input device simulating the use of the second hand we have used the relatively low cost WiiRemote™ device by Nintendo™. The Wii-mote has 3-axis accelerometer which transforms the user's physical motions to activities in the virtual environment. There are 12 buttons on the Wii remote. The Wii-mote is also equipped with a speaker. A very simple mechanism provides haptic feedback through vibration. It has an IR sensor and is connected to a computer via a Bluetooth wireless link. The tracking system is based on the use of ARTrack™. It is used for acquiring the user's head position and orientation. Three IR-cameras are oriented towards the user's working space. Some markers are positioned on the stereo glasses worn by the user. The user can move his head in order to see the objects in the virtual scene with different orientations and distance. The visualization of the virtual scene is provided by the Cyviz Viz3D™ display system (www.cyviz.com). A single PC with an nVidia Quadro FX5600™ graphics card provides the stereo image pairs and a CYVIZTM 3D stereo converter. Users wear simple polarized glasses to see the stereoscopic scene.

For what concerns the software platform, the application is based on Virtools from Dassault® Systèmes, which is a development system for creating interactive 3D applications. The Virtools allows developers to create immersive experiences based on stereo viewing scenes displayed on power walls integrated with a head-tracking

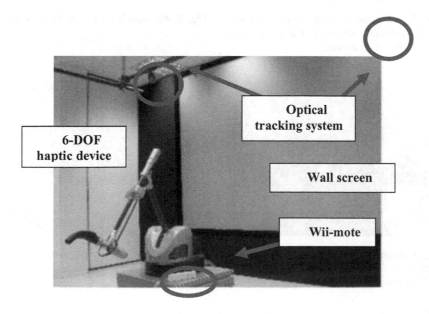

Fig. 1. Hardware components of the VR system

system and a real-time 3D application with haptic interaction (using IPP Interactive Physics Pack). It is possible to import several types of 3D files like: 3D XML (Dassault® CATIA®), 3ds Max®, Maya®, XSI®, Lightwave® and Collada®.

4.2 Study Case Implementation

This section reports the description of its implementation and the features of the study case described in § 3. The application displays some components of the mechanical system that are positioned on a table. The Wii-mote and the 6-DOF haptic devices are rendered on the screen through a visual reference frame (see Figure 2). The application demonstrates the assembly procedure consisting of grabbing, holding and positioning a component (component A), grabbing a second component (component B) and assembling the two components.

Fig. 2. Components of the mechanical system to assemble manually: the components are positioned on a table

Fig. 3. Wii-mote is used to grab component A

Fig. 4. Assembling task of two components: component A is hold using the Wii-mote and B is inserted into A using the haptic device

Fig. 5. Final assembly of the two components

The use's task consists of assembling the two components. First, the user grabs and positions the component A using the Wii-mote device (see Figure 3). The application provides feedback when the component A is grabbed: the component is highlighted in a different colour. Then, the user grabs the component B using the 6-DOF Haption haptic device. The application performs haptic feedback during the manipulation, so that the user can feel the weight and inertia of the grabbed objects. Then, the user starts assembling the component B into the component A (see Figure 4). When the two components collide the application provides proper feedback: the haptic device provides force feedback and the Wii-mote provides tactile feedback through vibration. The task is completed when the component A and B are properly assembled.The application records the tasks performed by the user. The data recorded are: trajectories of the two interaction devices, user's viewpoint, and trajectories of the manipulated objects.

5 Validation and Discussion

We are interested in testing the usability of the environment, according to the effectiveness, efficiency and satisfaction with which users reach the targeted objectives with the application context. According to Nielsen, heuristic evaluation can be performed by one usability expert although studies have shown that the effectiveness of the method is significantly improved by involving multiple evaluators [14]. In this first phase of the development and set-up of the system we have decided to run a preliminary evaluation asking an expert user to test the system, and using some of the heuristics proposed by Sutcliffe and Gault [15] for the evaluation of VR applications. The heuristics considered for assessing the quality of the application are the following (Table 1).

Table 1. Heuristics and description

Heuristic	Description
1. Natural engagement	Interaction should be as natural as the one in the real world.
2. Compatibility with the user's task and domain	The behaviour of objects should correspond to users' expectations of real world objects.
3. Natural expression of action	The virtual environment should be explored in a natural manner.
4. Close coordination of action and representation	The application should update the virtual environment without delay after user's movements and actions.
5. Realistic feedback	The effect of users' actions on virtual objects should be immediately visible.
6. Faithful viewpoints	User's head movements should coherently change the viewpoint without delay.
7. Navigation and orientation support	The application should support users in navigating and orienting themselves within the virtual space.
8. Support for learning	The application should provide explanations on how to interact with the virtual objects.
9. Sense of presence	The user should naturally feel as being in a real world.

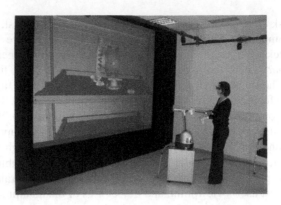

Fig. 6. Expert user assembling the components

The user is a mechanical engineer expert in using 3D application and with some expertise in using haptic devices and in assembly of parts (Figure 6).

The evaluation of the VR application started with the familiarization with the application and the interaction devices: the stereoscopic visualization wall, the change of viewpoint, the use of the two interaction devices. Then, the user was asked to perform the task: grab component A, then grab component B and assemble the two components. When the task was successfully performed, the user was asked to list the problems and to relate them to heuristics, also assigning a rate from 1 (very poor) to 4 (very good). The results are reported in Table 2.

Table 2. Heuristic rating and description of the problems

Heuristic	Rate	Problems
1. Natural engagement	2	No natural feedback is performed on the left hand.
2. Compatibility with the user's task and domain	3	Information when the task is completed.
3. Natural expression of action	3	Limited navigation within the virtual space due to fixed position of the haptic device.
4. Close coordination of action and representation	4	-
5. Realistic feedback	3	Force feedback is provided only on one hand.
6. Faithful viewpoints	4	-
7. Navigation and orientation support	2	Not intuitive. Rotation around y-axis is not activated directly but by means of pad.
8. Support for learning	2	Little assistance during the task execution.
9. Sense of presence	3	No realistic representation of the user

Then, we have mapped the less satisfactory aspects of the application into a list of features that may be improved. Table 3 lists the features and the related issues to address, including a reference to the heuristic that has originated it.

The following improvements have been taken into account in the implementation of the new version of the application.

Interaction. We may think of using sounds for mimicking the noise made by the various components when colliding also considering the kind of material they are made of, and also using sound for informing the user when the assembly is successfully completed. The navigation within the scene is going to be improved by adding functionalities for reaching objects, zooming the scene, etc. In addition, we are planning to implement a mechanism that moves the haptic device along a trajectory parallel to the virtual screen. The interaction limitations due to the use of the Wii-mote for moving and rotating the first component will be solved with the integration of devices equipped with a gyroscope capability.

Table 3. Classification of problems in respect to application features and importance rating

Application feature	Issue	Heuristic
1. Interaction	Provide feedback when the task is completed.	3
	Improve user's navigation within the virtual scene.	2
	Improve interaction performances of the Wii-mote.	7
	Better represent user's presence within the scene.	9
2. Action feedback	Improve feedback on virtual representation of Wii-mote and its interaction with object.	5
3. Haptic feedback	Better haptic feedback provided on the left hand.	1, 5
4. Affordances	Not enough assistance during task is provided.	8

Action feedback. The Wii-mote and the 6-DOF haptic devices are currently represented through a visual reference frame. A more intuitive and realistic visual representation may be implemented.

Haptic feedback. The aim of the application was to use a low cost device for providing feedback to the user about the actions performed on the secondary component during the execution of the assembly task. Tactile information, supported by the Wii-mote device, would be used more carefully to convey information about contacts and collisions with other components or with the environment.

Affordances. The object's affordance should also be improved, so that objects suggest how they can be used, also in perspective of more complex assembly tasks.

6 Conclusions and Future Works

This paper has described a low cost application developed for testing a mixed reality approach for the evaluation of manual assembly of mechanical systems. An application for evaluating manual assembly tasks typically require the simulation of haptic manipulation performed with both hands. In order to reduce the cost of the application, and limiting the application architecture to the use of one single 6-DOF haptic device, which is currently a rather expensive equipment, we have proposed a configuration where a Wii-mote device is used for positioning a first component and a 6-DOF haptic device used for performing the assembly of a second object into the first one. Major usability problems of the application have been identified through low cost tests by using a simple but effective evaluation methodology and involving one single expert user. From the results of this initial and preliminary evaluation we have modified the design of some features of the assembly application. Following activity plans to involve several evaluators for testing the system, with the aim of performing a more formal and comprehensive evaluation of the application. Once the platform has been set up and evaluated, we plan to implement additional industrial oriented applications also integrating other low cost interaction devices that in the meantime will become available. We are also planning to use the data recorded about assembly tasks performed by users for playing back the user's task using a virtual human with the aim of performing more accurate ergonomics analysis about user's postures and discomfort without engaging and bothering real users with exhausting testing sessions. The same data may be used for training purposes with novel users.

References

1. Sherman, W.R., Craig, A.B.: Understanding Virtual Reality – interface, application, and design. Morgan Kaufmann, San Francisco (2003)
2. Bordegoni, M., Cugini, U., Caruso, F., Polistina, S.: Mixed prototyping for rapid design review of information appliances. In: IDMME – Virtual Concept 2008, Beijing, China, October 8-10 (2008)
3. Abhishek, S., Hai-Jun, S., Judy, M.V.: Development of a Dual-Handed Haptic Assembly System: SHARP. J. Comput. Inf. Sci. Eng. 8(4) (December 2008)
4. Jayaram, S., Jayaram, U., Wang, Y., Tirumali, H., Lyons, K., Hart, P.: VADE: a Virtual Assembly Design Environment. In: Computer Graphics and Applications, November/December 1999, pp. 44–50. IEEE, Los Alamitos (1999)
5. Kuehne, R.P., Oliver, J.H.: Virtual environment for interactive assembly planning and evaluation. In: Proceeding of ASME Design Engineering Technical Conference, New York, USA, pp. 836–867 (1995)
6. Lin, M.C., Otaduy, M.: Haptic rendering: foundations, algorithms and applications (2008)
7. Burdea, G.: Force and Touch Feedback for Virtual Reality. John Wiley & Sons, New York (1996)
8. Massie, T., Salisbury, J.K.: The PHANTOM haptic interface: A device for probing virtual objects. In: Proceedings of the ASME Winter Annual Meeting: Symposium on Haptic Interfaces for Virtual Environment and Teleoperator Systems, pp. 295–300 (1994)
9. Michel, G., Burkhardt, J., Lécuyer, A., Dautin, J., Crison, F.: An Application to Training in the Field of Metal Machining as a Result of Research-Industry Collaboration. In: Proc. of the Virtual Reality International Conference, VRIC (2004)
10. Lécuyer, A., Kheddar, A., Coquillart, S., Graux, L., Coiffet, P.: A haptic prototype for the simulations of aeronautics mounting/unmounting operations. In: Proc. of the IEEE RO-MAN (2001)
11. Ott, R., Thalmann, D., Vexo, F.: Haptic Feedback in Mixed-Reality Environment. In: Proceedings of The 25th Computer Graphics International Conference, CGI 2007 (2007)
12. Sreng, J., Bergez, F., Le Garrec, J., Lécuyer, A., Andriot, C.: Using an event-based approach to improve the multimodal rendering of 6DOF virtual contact. In: Proc. of the 2007 ACM symposium on Virtual reality software and technology, pp. 165–173 (2007)
13. Horie, T., Abe, N., Tanaka, K., Taki, H.: Controlling Two Remote Robot Arms with Direct Instruction using HapticMaster and Vision System. In: 6th International Conference on Virtual Systems and MultiMedia, VSMM (2000)
14. Nielsen, J.: Usability Engineering. Academic Press, New York (1993)
15. Sutcliff, A., Gault, B.: Heuristic evaluation of virtual reality applications. Interacting with Computers 16, 831–849 (2004)

Transmission of Information through Haptic Interaction

Koichi Hirota and Yuichiro Sekiguchi

Department of Human and Engineered Environmental Studies
Graduate School of Frontier Sciences, University of Tokyo
5-1-5 Kashiwa-no-ha, Kashiwa, Chiba 277-8563, Japan
k-hirota@k.u-tokyo.ac.jp, sekiguchi@media.k.u-tokyo.ac.jp

Abstract. This paper describes a novel approach to haptic interface that transmits information through dynamic interaction. The approach is based on the idea of emulating an object that causes dynamic reaction, such as a box with content inside, using a mechanical device. Hence, the device should be designed as an object-oriented and self-contained form that can be handled similarly to the real object. Implementation of a prototype device that materializes this idea is introduced, and a possibility of expanding the idea into various scales of interaction and different modality is also discussed.

Keywords: Haptic device, haptic interaction, inertial force, virtual reality.

1 Introduction

It is interesting that we can estimate the content of a box or a bottle by shaking it. It is a common practice that we shake a bottle to know the remaining amount of drinks; also we often give a box a shake to know if the box is empty or not (Figure 1). If the bottle or the box is held just statically, it informs us of only gross weight of the container and the content; through dynamic interaction such as shaking, it provides more information which is helpful to know, for example, about the amount of liquid or approximate number of candies. This observation leads us to the idea of a novel haptic interface that transmits information through haptic interaction. This paper focuses mainly on the concept of such device.

Fig. 1. Box and bottle with content as passive haptic device

2 Background and Related Research

Although shaking a box or a bottle is frequently experienced, the mechanism of recognition about content is considered to be still not clear. According to knowledge

R. Shumaker (Ed.): Virtual and Mixed Reality, LNCS 5622, pp. 313–317, 2009.

from psychology, it is experimentally proven that human can tell the difference of the shape of solid objects by swinging them [9]. In the research of robotics, identifying inertial parameter of robot arm through experimental actuation of the mechanism is one of common technique. Estimating content of box or bottle is considered as an advanced task for human in that it involves dynamics of content and that the model of the content is not necessarily known.

From the viewpoint of haptic feedback, there are researches on presentation of dynamics model. Most of them are focusing on modeling and computation algorism of physics-based model, and carried out using general-purpose haptic device that is grounded to the environment. This implementation does not conform to our idea.

Box or bottle is considered as a kind of haptic device that respond to user's interaction and feedback force to the user. Hence, a device that emulates the box or the bottle must be implemented in a form that is compatible to the box or the bottle. In other words, the device must be an object that is handled and behaves similarly to the box or the bottle.

The idea of encounter type device has been proposed [3,5,8], however, it was mainly focused on presentation of surface. Also, there are many researches on portable and wearable haptic devices [1,2,6,10]; most of them are intended to transmit information such as intensity of force or direction of rotation through haptic sensation, and little of them were focusing on information that is transmitted by dynamic interaction. There are some researches that deals with dynamic interaction in shaking operation [7,11], however, the reaction of these devices were strictly limited to fit to the application of these researches.

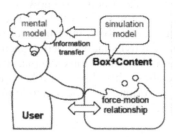

Fig. 2. Transmission of information through haptic interaction

3   Concept

The device that is based on our idea is considered to have two important aspects. One aspect is that, as stated above, it transmits information through haptic interaction, rather than through force or tactile sensation as independent sensory channel (Figure 2). There are various types of physical material and parameters that characterize each type of material. According to our experience, we can distinguish liquid, solid bodies, and powder as different type of content; also we will be able to approximately recognize parameters such as viscosity of liquid and size or weight of solid bodies. By mapping these types of material and parameters into information that is specific to application area, the device is expected to serve as a display that provides information through haptic interaction.

Another aspect of our idea is that it seeks for object-oriented device. Similarly to box or bottle, the device serves as a portable and self-contained object. Haptic interface of this approach is considered to be advantageous in case when it is integrated with a hand-held information device, such as cellular-phone and personal digital assistant.

4 Prototype

A prototype device that materializes the concept has been developed [4]. The device consists of a mechanism that moves mass, hence gravity center of the device, by one degree of freedom. Figure 3 shows the picture of the device, where 'frame' represents a part of box or bottle while the link that is parallel to the frame is the mass that is actuated to emulate the motion of content. Also, the device is equipped with an accelerometer that measures the acceleration of the frame.

Since the device virtually represents an object, the weight of the device is identical with gross weight of the object. Also, in the design of the prototype, a special attention was paid on the ratio of weigh of the frame and the moving mass; because, by allocating more weight as moving mass, the device becomes capable of providing interaction with larger content mass. In the prototype, the mechanism was implemented as a parallel-link mechanism where actuators were integrated into a part of the moving mass.

The control system consists of a servo system that actuates the device so that the motion of the gravity center of the device becomes identical with that of the object model. Also, external force, which is usually applied by the user, was estimated based on the acceleration of the frame of the device. The goal position of the gravity center is computed by using an object model based on the estimated external force.

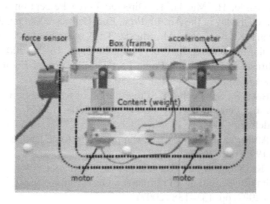

Fig. 3. Prototype device

5 Discussion and Conclusion

The prototype device has been designed following initial idea of emulating a box or a bottle, hence, design parameters such as movable mass and range of movement were determined assuming interaction using two hands. These design parameters must be determined based on modality of interaction that is required from its application. Device of various scales is conceivable, and also interaction style must differ from each other; a small device may be manipulated using fingers, on the other hand, larger device will require interaction using entire body (Figure 4). Implementation of these devices will be investigated in our future work.

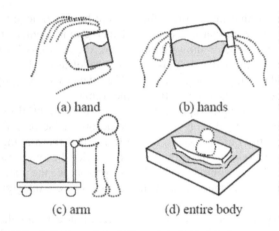

(a) hand   (b) hands

(c) arm   (d) entire body

Fig. 4. Scale and modality in interaction design

References

1. Amemiya, T., Ando, H., Maeda, T.: Directed Force Perception When Holding a Non-grounding Force Display in the Air. In: Proc. EuroHaptics 2006, pp. 317–324 (2006)
2. Ando, H., Obana, K., Sugimoto, M., Maeda, T.: A wearable force display based on brake change in angular momentum. In: Proc. ICAT 2002, pp. 16–21 (2002)
3. Hirota, K., Hirose, M.: Providing Force Feedback in Virtual Environments. IEEE Computer Graphics and Applications 15(5), 22–30 (1995)
4. Hirota, K., Sasaki, S., Sekiguchi, Y.: Presentation of force-motion relationship by inertial force display. In: Ferre, M. (ed.) EuroHaptics 2008. LNCS, vol. 5024, pp. 567–572. Springer, Heidelberg (2008)
5. McNeely, W.A.: Robotic graphics: a new approach to force feedback for virtual reality. In: Proc. VRAIS 1993, pp. 336–341 (1993)
6. Minamizawa, K., Kajimoto, H., Kawakami, N., Tachi, S.: A Wearable Haptic Display to Present the Gravity Sensation - Preliminary Observations and Device Design. In: Proc. World Haptics 2007, pp. 133–138 (2007)
7. Sekiguchi, Y., Hirota, K., Hirose, M.: The Design and Implementation of Ubiquitous Haptic Device. In: Proc. IEEE World Haptics 2005, pp. 257–258 (2005)

8. Tachi, S., Maeda, T., Hirata, R., Hoshino, H.: A Construction Method of Virtual Haptic Space. In: Proc. ICAT 1994, pp. 131–138 (1994)
9. Turvey, M.T.: Dynamic touch. American Psychologist 51, 1134–1152 (1996)
10. Yano, H., Yoshie, M., Iwata, H.: Development of a non-grounded haptic interface using the gyro effect. In: Proc. HAPTICS 2003, pp. 32–39 (2003)
11. Williamson, J., Murray-Smith, R., Hughes, S.: Shoogle: excitatory multimodal interaction on mobile devices. In: Proc. CHI 2007, pp. 121–124 (2007)

Development of Realistic Haptic Presentation Media

Yasushi Ikei

Tokyo Metropolitan University
6-6, Asahigaoka, Hino, Tokyo, Japan
ikei@computer.org

Abstract. This paper describes the development toward a realistic haptic presentation media---the haptic displays for surface textures. The display utilizes vibratory simulation that is efficient for cutaneous sensation. First, the characteristics of frequency mixture stimulation are demonstrated in terms of the amplitude modulation and the additive synthesis of 250 Hz and 50 Hz where the sensitivity of human skin takes peaks due to inherent mechanoreceptors. As a part of elucidation, the perception of 50 Hz under 250 Hz stimulation and its hardness sensation were measured. The amplitude modulation was more suitable for its small absolute limen while the additive synthesis was for softer sensation. In addition, the tactile/proprioceptive hybrid haptic display was investigated in terms of 3D texture perception. Spatial textures on surfaces of an icosahedron were matched and identified at about three levels of perception difficulty. Textures were discriminated moderately despite limited stimulators that suggested proper improvement.

Keywords: Haptic texture display, Frequency mixture, Sensation scaling, Texture discrimination/identification.

1 Introduction

A vibratory stimulus is effective to excite mechanoreceptors for imitating tactile images observed during the contact of a finger with real objects. Such a two-dimensional (2D) vibratory-pin stimulation display was developed in the late 1960s [1]. The stimulation was performed at a fixed optimal frequency around 250 Hz to deliver efficiently two dimensional character patterns. The drive data was obtained directly from a binarized visual image. The authors developed a 2D vibratory display [2] that produced multiple-intensity (amplitude) stimulation at a single 250 Hz frequency, to evoke a texture sensation based on the image data of a surface. Recently, a tactile array that produces stimuli in a range of frequency has been introduced [3] to investigate the dependency of tactile acuity on stimulus frequency, which suggested that better spatial acuity is observed in high frequency stimulation than in lower frequency. The result given in the paper was limited to the detection of simple motion at two frequencies. Haptic texture synthesis using the device remained for the future work.

In the present paper the current development of vibratory stimulation displays for tactile texture sensation in my laboratory is presented. The characteristics of a tactile display that operates at multiple vibratory frequencies have been investigated for

R. Shumaker (Ed.): Virtual and Mixed Reality, LNCS 5622, pp. 318–325, 2009.

imparting various sensations that we might receive in the real environment. Specifically, a synthesized stimulus based on two characteristic frequencies is discussed to provide the nature of tactile sensation from mixture of vibrations. In addition, the tactile texture exploration on a 3D object is investigated to show the accuracy of active touch on the spatial virtual textures.

2 Tactile Display for Realistic Haptic Sensation

2.1 Basic Frequency Characteristics of the Display

Tactile stimulation can effectively be performed by using vibratory pin array. A tactile display has been developed in this form by the author's laboratory. Figure 1 shows the display for tactile (cutaneous) sensation based on vibratory stimulus. The display has a window on the top board in which fifty vibratory pins are arranged in a 5×10 array with a 2 mm inter-pin distance. Each pin is driven by a piezoelectric actuator; the amplitude is controlled in 256 levels by changing the duty ratio of the PWM power output. The maximum amplitude as a function of drive frequency is depicted in Fig. 2. Around 280 Hz is there a resonant frequency above which the amplitude decreases monotonically. We set the upper limit of drive frequency at 410 Hz to maintain the maximum amplitude above at least 10 μm. As shown in the figure, the output frequency range is divided by a resonant frequency band into two portions: 40-260 Hz and 310-410 Hz. The lowest output frequency (40 Hz) is determined by the bit width of the controller register.

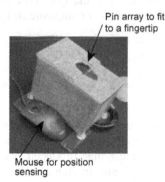

Fig. 1. Display for tactile stimulation (TextureDisplay2R

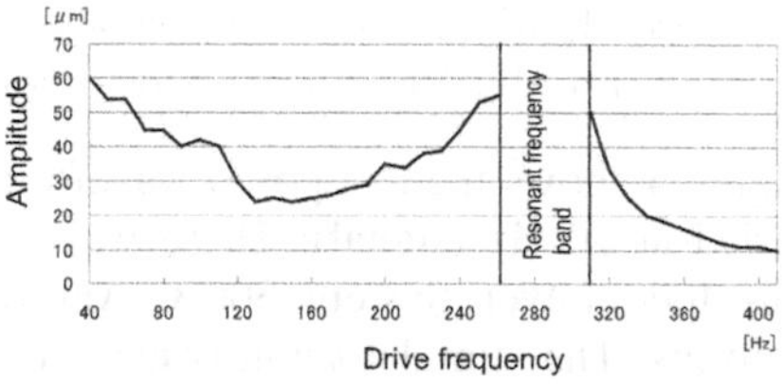

Fig. 2. Pin amplitude of the display as a function of drive frequency

Figure 3 shows sensation magnitude curves as a function of stimulus frequency, which indicates high frequency more than around 200 Hz is efficient. In the measurement, reference inputs were selected first at four amplitudes, 14.27, 11.01, 7.42, and 4.31 μm all with 250 Hz. This frequency is the original drive frequency of the Texture-Display as the highest cutaneous sensitivity was observed around it. We had collected the data of sensation scaling at the frequency. The data was obtained based on the method of adjustment. The curve with the lowest amplitude is the absolute threshold.

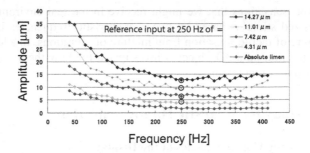

Frequency [Hz]

Fig. 3. Sensation magnitude curves. Four curves indicate amplitude at which the sensation magnitude is equivalent to the reference amplitude (four circles at 250 Hz) shown in the legend. The bottom curve represents the absolute limen.

The amplitude of equal sensation magnitude decreased almost monotonically to stimulus frequency. From this graph we can obtain the drive amplitude that generates an equivalent sensation magnitude at a different frequency. Of course in that case, the quality of sensation varies largely from the lower part to the higher part of the frequency range.

2.2 Frequency Mixture Stimulation

Two frequencies were mixed without other frequency in order to specify the mixture sensation of two components clearly. Two methods to mix the frequencies, an amplitude modulation and an additive synthesis shown in eqs. (1) and (2), respectively, were used to compare and fully make use of the characteristics of composite stimuli.

$$V_{am} = (A_s + a_c)\sin(2\pi f_c t) = (a_s\cos(2\pi f_s t) + a_c)\sin(2\pi f_c t) \tag{1}$$

$$V_{as} = A_s + A_c = a_s\sin(2\pi f_s t) + a_c\sin(2\pi f_c t) \tag{2}$$

where A_s, a_s are the first frequency (signal) waveform and amplitude, while A_c, a_c are those for the second (carrier) frequency.

Figure 4 shows the composed waveforms where the amplitude of 250 Hz (carrier) is varied at 50 Hz (signal). These waveforms were observed on the pin stimulator (Dual-Mode Lever System 300B, Aurora Scientific Inc.) that produced accurate waveforms. The stimulator pin is made of piano-wire 0.5 mm in diameter, the same size as in the TextureDisplay2R.

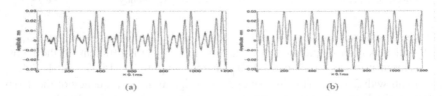

<table>
<tr><td>(a)</td><td>(b)</td></tr>
</table>

Fig. 4. (a) Waveform data generated by amplitude modulation, (b) waveform by additive synthesis (as=ac=15 μm, fs=50 Hz, fc=250 Hz)

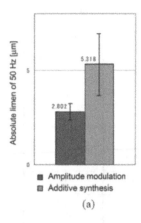
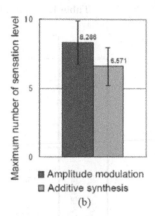

(a)   (b)

Fig. 5. (a) Absolute limen, and (b) sensation levels of 50 Hz stimulus under the constant 250 Hz component at 15 μm (Error bar indicates standard error

2.3 Sensation Scaling

The both waveforms were investigated in terms of sensation scaling to demonstrate difference between them. The procedure was the method of adjustment where the subjects were asked to find the jnd of the mixed stimulus. Here, the jnd for the amount of 50 Hz amplitude was the target value although there are many other values of interest in hybrid presentation. The base (carrier) frequency, 250 Hz, was constantly provided at 15 μm amplitude.

Figure 5(a) shows the absolute limen of 50 Hz component as a mean of seven subjects. The difference between the amplitude modulation and the additive synthesis was significant ($p=2.7 \times 10^{-6}$). The absolute threshold of the amplitude modulation was decreased in both waveforms from the data of single-frequency stimulation of about 7 μm as shown in Fig. 3. The reduction is remarkable in the case of the amplitude modulation. In addition, the standard error is smaller that means small individual difference leads to stable presentation.

Figure 5(b) shows the maximum number of sensation intensity. The amplitude modulation exhibited more number of levels within 15 μm amplitude. The difference was significant ($p=6.1 \times 10^{-10}$) that indicates the amplitude modulation is more usable in presenting multilevel textures.

2.4 Sensation Rating of Hardness

The two waveforms of the amplitude modulation and the additive synthesis differed in the quality of sensation. Many of the subjects of the measurement in the above experiment told that the additive synthesis was softer than the amplitude modulation. To show the fact quantitatively, we conducted subjective evaluation of hardness impression of composite stimulations by using a graph scale method that had seven indexes (very soft, moderately soft, slightly soft, standard stimulus, slightly hard, moderately hard, hard, very hard) with the standard stimulus of single-frequency

Table 1. Amplitude of two components

	Id	a_s, 50 Hz	a_c, 250 Hz
Amplitude modulation	A	3.75	15
	B	7.5	15
	C	11.25	15
	D	15.0	15
Additive synthesis	E	3.75	15
	F	7.5	15
	G	11.25	15
	H	15.0	15

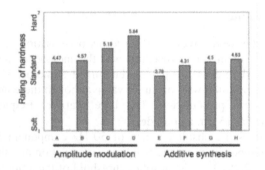

Fig. 6. Hardness ratings for mixed stimulus

stimulus of 15 μm at 250 Hz. The eight composite stimuli shown in Table 1 were compared with the standard stimulus in terms of hardness by the seven subjects.

Figure 6 shows the result. The amplitude modulation (left four bars) was harder in general than the additive synthesis (right four bars) as reported earlier by the subjects. The hardness increase along with the amount of 50 Hz component added was steeper in the amplitude modulation than in the additive synthesis. Only in the case of 'E' the tactile sensation was softer than the standard stimulus. In addition, some subjects commented that the additive synthesis imparted springy (elastic) impression.

3 A Tactile-Force Hybrid Realistic Haptic Display

Haptic exploration in the real space involves not only the tactile sensation but the proprioceptive (force) sensation. A hybrid haptic display was built for the two sensations [5]. The display provide both sensations in the real three dimensional space. Figure 7 shows the overview. The tactile sensation is evoked by a vibratory tactile stimulator that consists of ten pins driven independently at a 250 Hz. The contactor pins are arranged in a five-row two-column window with 3-mm spacing for the index fingerpad. The tactile display is mounted to the force display, the phantom 1.5, as shown in Fig. 8.

The 3D tactile presentation quality was evaluated by three-stage discrimination experiments in which the textures are presented on a 3D object. In the first and second stage one of the five surfaces was replaced only in the tactile texture data while the visual textures were not changed. In the third stage visual textures were masked and the standard texture was placed on the designated surface. The subject was asked to find the texture identical to the standard from the rest four surfaces.

Fig. 7. A 3D haptic display for both cutaneous and deep sensations. A stereoscopic view is provided on an 80-inch back-projection screen.

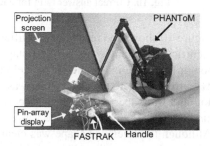

Fig. 8. Tactile stimulation display (pinarray) for 3D space presentation with force reflection. Pin array tactile display is mounted on the Phantom.

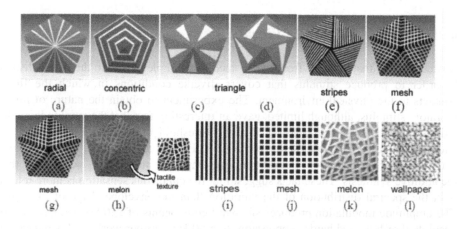

Fig. 9. Textures used in the evaluation experiment

Figure 9 shows the textures used for the evaluation of presentation accuracy. The textures were put on a surface of an icosahedron that has different surface normal vectors. The edge of the icosahedron was 5-cm long, and the width of lines in (a),(b) was 2 mm, and in (e),(f),(i),(j) 1 mm. The textures (k),(l) were presented in multilevel stimulus intensity (in fifteen intensity levels) whereas the other textures were presented in binary (zero or intensity-15) stimulation.

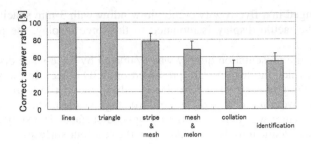

Fig. 10. Correct answer ratio for each condition. (Error bar shows SEM)

Figure 10 shows the results of identification of these textures. The lines (radial and concentric) and triangles as the first stage were perceived almost perfectly (100 %), although the stripe/mesh and stripe/melon as second stage were discriminated about 75 % correctly where the chance rate was 25 %. The test set involving the surface of a melon and wallpaper was difficult to perceive. The correct answer ratio decreased to around 50 % while the chance rate was 25 %.

Although the line/edge shape was clearly identified with visual-haptic comparison despite the large sampling interval, blind tactile identification was not easy for the subjects. One of the reasons of the degraded result in the second and the third stages seems to come from the density and layout of pin stimulators. The design improvement is needed under the requirements of a small size and weight to enable loading on a force display.

4   Discussion and Future Work

It is considered that multiple frequencies need to be implemented to the tactile display in order to produce stimulus that covers diverse conditions in which the finger contacts to the physical environment. The experiment to obtain the nature of mixed vibratory stimulus, although limited, gave an interesting fact that the amplitude modulation was perceived with a lower absolute threshold of 50 Hz vibration than the additive synthesis. The absolute threshold of 50 Hz was as small as a half of that in a single component condition. In addition, the amplitude modulation was harder than the additive synthesis. These facts suggest that the cutaneous sensation is more related with the spectral distribution of the vibration than the envelope shape of the wave. The amplitude modulation produces sideband components of 250 Hz that has smaller absolute threshold and harder impression than 50 Hz. Further work on this interpretation should be performed to clarify the characteristics of vibration perception.

The experiment of texture identification on the 3D surfaces suggested that the texture perception performance is subject to relative density of the display pins to the spatial density of the texture. The display density should be determined by the textures to be presented. A single edge can be presented with a very limited number of pins while the grayscale (multilevel) textures with a high spatial frequency requires high density of pins of less than 3-mm inter-pin distance. For the optimization of the vibratory pin layout that enables high perception, spatiotemporal characteristics of haptic perception need to be measured and modeled as a design base for the tactile/force displays.

Acknowledgments

The author would like to thank Hajime Kajitani and Kanako Nishimura for their considerable contribution to the data for the present paper.

References

1. Bliss, J.C., Katcher, M.H., Rogers, C.H., Shepard, R.P.: Optical-to-tactile image conversion for the blind. IEEE Transactions on Man-Machine Systems 11, 58–65 (1970)
2. Ikei, Y., Wakamatsu, K., Fukuda, S.: Vibratory tactile display of image-based textures. IEEE Computer Graphics and Applications 17(6), 53–61 (1997)
3. Summers, I.R., Chanter, C.M.: A broadband tactile array on the fingertip. J. Acoustical Soc. Am. 112(5), 2118–2126 (2002)
4. Ikei, Y., Yamada, M., Fukuda, S.: A new design of haptic texture display–texturedisplay2– and its preliminary evaluation. In: Proc. IEEE Virtual Reality 2001, pp. 21–28 (2001)
5. Ikei, Y., Shiratori, M.: TextureExplorer: A tactile and force display for virtual textures. In: Proc. 10th Sympo. Haptic Interfaces for Virtual Environment and Teleoperator Systems, pp. 327–334 (2002)

Analysis of Tactual Impression by Audio and Visual Stimulation for User Interface Design in Mixed Reality Environment

Mami Kagimoto[1], Asako Kimura[2], Fumihisa Shibata[1], and Hideyuki Tamura[1]

[1] Graduate School of Science and Engineering, Ritsumeikan University,
1-1-1 Noji-Higashi, Kusatsu, 525-8577, Shiga, Japan
[2] PRESTO, Japan Science and Technology Agency,
4-1-8 Honcho Kawaguchi, Saitama, Japan
kagimoto@rm.is.ritsumei.ac.jp

Abstract. In a mixed-reality (MR) environment, a touchable object can be made to change its appearance when a computer-generated image (MR visual stimulation) is superimposed onto it. In this research, we conduct experiments to study the effects of MR visual and audio stimuli on the tactual impression of the "roughness" of an object. We show that MR visual stimulation alters a subject's tactual impression of the roughness of an object and that the addition of MR audio stimulation intensifies that effect.

Keywords: Mixed Reality, Tactual Impression, Psychophysical Influence and Visual and Audio Stimulation.

1 Introduction

MR technology that merges real and virtual worlds has so far been investigated and implemented mainly in a visual sense [1][2]. MR is a powerful extension of conventional virtual reality (VR) technology, which deals with only a computer-generated electronic environment. The reason why MR is superior over VR is that everything in the experiencing environment need not be electronically modeled; that is, with MR, objects in the real world can be used without modification and only the necessary items are electronically modeled and merged to them.

There exist visual or auditory displays that are versatile and for general use. However, there are no displays in tactile or haptic functions, and only displays with the limited representative functions have been developed. In this regard, there is room for utilizing the MR technology. For example, a user would perceive the presence of a real object by grasping or pressing it, while electronic data is superimposed on it. The results of such studies could be highly useful for user-interface and other industrial design applications. For example, Ohshima et al. developed a system that enables automobile customers to test an automobile interior design in an MR environment (Fig. 1) [3]. Their system is capable of visual simulation of the interior design, where the customer touches real objects on which other images are superimposed in order to vary an object's color, shape, and material.

R. Shumaker (Ed.): Virtual and Mixed Reality, LNCS 5622, pp. 326–335, 2009.
© Springer-Verlag Berlin Heidelberg 2009

However, this study raises a question: how is a user's tactile perception of an object affected by the object's visual appearance? He/she might be discomforted when touching, but the tactile sense could be affected by visual sense. To address this question, we conducted experiments to analyze the influence of "MR visual stimulation" in which texture images were superimposed onto real objects, on the tactile sense (specifically "roughness perception") [4]. We obtained the following results:

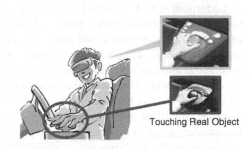

Fig. 1. Presentation of MR Visual Stimulation

- When objects of equal roughness appear to be of different roughness, people tend to perceive them to be tactually different.
- When objects of different roughness appear to be of equal roughness, people tend to perceive them to be tactually the same.
- In some cases, when a different material image is superimposed on a real object, people sometimes feel that they are touching an object of a different material.

Although these results did not occur in all cases, they did occur often enough to justify their use for industrial application, given the selection of suitable combinations of visual and tactual stimuli.

Moreover, these results suggest that one can intensify the limited "illusion of presenting materials" by changing the condition of presentation or adding other stimuli, which can be very useful for the simulation of user interface designs. For example, the sound generated when we touch an object (the "touch sound") also stimulates the audio sense. Thus, it is natural to suppose that the tactual impression (illusion) could be intensified by controlling the audio stimuli arbitrarily.

In this paper, expanding the systematic methodology of [4], we investigate how tactual impressions change with the addition of both visual and audio stimuli. Having found that the real touch sounds generated by touching experimental objects were insufficient for our experiment, we enhanced the touch sounds by mixing in friction and collision sounds. By making use of the sounds, we conducted the intended experiments and analyzed its results.

2 Related Work

Some studies exist on the influence of visual stimuli on the tactile sense. Lederman et al. [5] reported that when subjects looked at one sheet of sandpaper and touched another one of different roughness simultaneously, they perceived an intermediate roughness for both sandpapers. Biocca et al. [6] reported that subjects could feel physical resistance (e.g., gravity, inertia) while moving virtual objects with their first two fingers in a VR environment without any haptic devices. Based on these studies, Iesaki et al. [4] conducted experiments on the influence of MR visual stimuli. We also follow the same research approach.

Lederman et al. [7] studied the influence of audio stimuli on tactile sense. Subjects touched plastic plates with a patterned indented surface and evaluated the roughness of the plates under three conditions: only audio stimuli, only tactile stimuli, and both audio and tactile stimuli simultaneously. They reported that in the case presenting both audio and tactile stimuli, the subjects perceived the roughness to be intermediate between that with only audio and only tactile stimuli. Jousmäki et al. [8] reported that subjects felt their palmar skin to be drier when they heard the sound of hands rubbing together, amplified in the high-frequency range. Guest et al. [9] reported that subjects felt greater tactual roughness when they heard the sound of hands rubbing sandpaper, amplified in the high-frequency range. We focus on [8] and [9] using fabricated sounds different from the sound generated from the real object and adopt similar experimental methodologies.

3 Preparation and Evaluation of Audio Stimuli

3.1 Presentation Stimuli

Similar to the experiment in [4], we use tactual, visual, and audio stimuli, each with four levels of roughness (Fig. 2). We label the objects as follows: tactile stimuli Rough 1 to Rough 4, visual stimuli CGI 1 to CGI 4, and audio stimuli Sound 1 to Sound 4, in descending order of roughness. The real objects used in our experiments are rapid prototyping (RP) plates made from ABS plastic [11], whose roughnesses are fabricated to be discriminated tactually (Fig. 3). Similar to the experiment in [4], we use the pictured surface images of these plates as visual stimuli.

For audio stimuli, it is natural to use the touch sounds of the RP plates prepared for tactual stimulation without modification. However, as we recorded and compared the touch sounds of the four RP plates (Rough 1 to Rough 4), we found it difficult to discriminate among them.

Most people, when they touch an object without viewing it, cannot accurately guess the object's material or roughness from only the sound of touching the object. Conversely, when they view the object, they tend to presume what the touch sound will be produced. Our objective is to substantiate the existence of some type of "illusion", using touch sounds that emphasize their preconceptions. In other words, we create

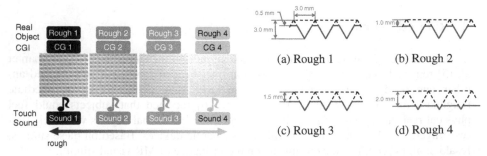

Fig. 2. Presentation Stimuli

Fig. 3. Artificial Rough Surface (solid lines are the surface line)

"touch sounds" and use them as audio stimuli in the experiments. These sounds should hear like touching the experimental objects and should make the roughnesses of different objects distinguishable. We defined these sound "emphasized touch sounds" meet the following requirements:

- The sounds are created by modifying the real touch sounds of the RP plates.
- Each object's roughness is distinguishable according to four emphasized touch sounds.
- The sounds are as natural as the touch sounds of the RP plates.

3.2 Preparation and Evaluation of Audio Stimuli

Analysis of real touch sounds. As shown in Fig. 3, the surface of each experimental RP plate consists of indentations and flat areas. As scraping these surfaces by a palm or fingernails, touch sounds are generated. We break up the sounds, and define them as following;

- Collision sound: sound generated by hitting at a dent edge (Fig. 4 (a))
- Friction sound: sound generated by friction at a flat area (Fig. 4 (b))

Because a rougher object has deeper and larger dents and smaller flat areas, it is likely that sounds caused by touch of these objects are the result of more collision sounds and fewer friction sounds. For a smoother object, the opposite would be the case. Based on this idea, we thought that we could create touch sounds that enhance differences in roughness by controlling the mixing rate of collision and friction sounds.

Meanwhile collision and friction sounds differ in energy according to the hardness or material of the touching medium. For example, when an object is stroked with a rigid and smooth touch medium such as fingernails, the collision sound can be heard clearly but the friction sound cannot. In contrast, when an object is stroked with a soft touch medium such as a finger cushion, only the friction sound can be heard; the collision sound is absorbed by the finger.

We recorded the real touch sounds that are generated by stroking the four RP plates with fingernailss and palm, and performed a frequency analysis of each. The stroking speed is one round trip (about 30 cm) per second and the sampling frequency of the recorded sounds is 48 kHz. Figs. 5 and 6 show the frequency analyses results of these touch sounds (half round trip). We found that the touch sounds of fingernailss have cyclical high-frequency energy parts (streaky part in Fig. 5)—the rougher the object surface, the higher the energy. On the other hand, the touch sounds of palms did not vary with roughness (Fig. 6).

Creation of Enhanced Touch Sounds. From the results described above, we decided to create enhanced touch sounds using the touch sounds of a fingernails (containing much collision sound) and of a palm (containing much friction sound) as follows:

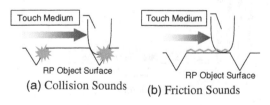

(a) Collision Sounds   (b) Friction Sounds

Fig. 4. Touch Sound Generated from RP Objects

(i) Normalize the fingernails and the palm touch sounds in all roughness to Rough 1. Each of the touch sounds of is clipped from the sounds recorded in 3.1. The length of each is one round trip (one second).

(ii) Attenuate fingernails touch sounds lower than 5 kHz by 20 dB. This is because the collision sounds of fingernails are too loud to mix without modification. At lower than 5 kHz, the energy of a fingernails touch sound is higher than that of a palm touch sound (Fig. 7), so the fingernails touch sounds are attenuated in this range to be natural after mixing.

(iii) Mix the fingernails and palm touch sounds at the rate shown in Table 1. In this step, the touch sounds of the RP plate corresponding to each roughness are mixed.

(iv) Normalize the mixed sound for all roughnesses to the sound of (i).

(v) Amplify the sound of (iv) at the rate shown in Table 1 to make the sound of rougher objects louder.

Evaluation Experiment. We conducted two preliminary experiments to determine whether subjects could distinguish the roughnesses of the four RP plate surfaces by hearing the four groups of audio stimuli (touch sounds of group A to D), and whether the sounds were as natural as the touch sounds of the RP plates shown in Fig. 2. We presented four round trips of the audio stimuli to 16 subjects with normal auditory sensation. The experimental description is as described below.

Preliminary Experiment 1

(1) The four audio stimuli of each group are presented one by one randomly. The interval time between each presentation is 1 second.

(2) After hearing all sounds, subjects report the order of roughness of the four audio stimuli.

(3) Step (1) and (2) are conducted in all groups (A to D) randomly.

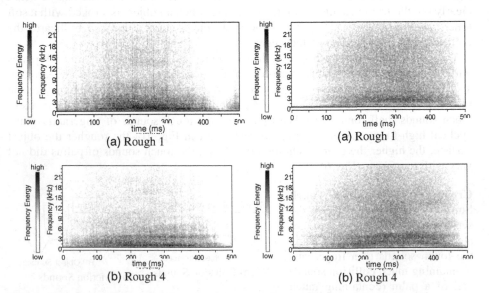

Fig. 5. Frequency Analysis Result of the Touch Sound (Fingernails)

Fig. 6. Frequency Analysis Result of the Touch Sound (Palm)

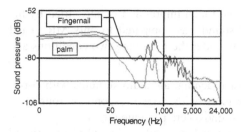

Fig. 7. Difference of Frequency Energy between Fingernails and Palm Touch Sound

Table 1. Fabricated Audio Stimulation

		Sound 1	Sound 2	Sound 3	Sound 4
The fingernail sound rate		1.0	1.0	1.0	1.0
Audio Stimuli A	The palm sound rate	0.9	1.0	1.1	1.2
	The amplification rate after the	1.1	1.0	0.9	0.8
Audio Stimuli B	The palm sound rate	0.9	1.0	1.1	1.2
	The amplification rate after the	1.2	1.0	0.8	0.6
Audio Stimuli C	The palm sound rate	0.8	1.0	1.2	1.4
	The amplification rate after the	1.1	1.0	0.9	0.8
Audio Stimuli D	The palm sound rate	0.8	1.0	1.2	1.4
	The amplification rate after the	1.2	1.0	0.8	0.6

Original sound volume: 1.0

Preliminary Experiment 2

(1) The four RP plates are placed in order of roughness in front of the subject, and the audio stimuli corresponding to each plate is presented in order. Only the groups of audio stimuli (group B and D) are used whose order was answered correctly in Preliminary Experiment 1. The presentation of audio stimuli is as for Preliminary Experiment 1.

(2) Subjects answer whether the four sounds are associated with each RP plate appearance.

(3) Step (1) and (2) are conducted in groups B and D randomly.

In Preliminary Experiment 1, the number of subjects who answered the order of roughness correctly are, in descending order, 13 in group D, 9 in group B, 7 in group C, and 6 in group A; all subjects answered correctly at least either group B or D. This result indicates that the difference of roughness in audio stimuli could be emphasized through the above procedure. In Preliminary Experiment 2, 13 out of 16 subjects answered that the audio stimuli of group B and/or D are associated with each RP plate appearance. Therefore, for this study, we adopted group B and D as the enhanced touch sounds that satisfied the three requirements in 3.1.

4   Experiment 1: Using Objects of Equal Surface Roughness

4.1   Purpose

Iesaki et al. [4] showed that the tactile sense was affected by MR visual stimuli under the following conditions:

- Two real RP plates of equal surface roughness are apposed.
- Two texture images of different surface roughness are superimposed onto each real object.
- The subjects answer which RP plate they tactually perceive to be rougher under the pair comparison method.

In this experiment, we investigate whether the touch impression is intensified by the addition of audio stimuli (enhanced touch sound), as compared to only MR visual stimuli. Specifically, we conduct experiments under the following two conditions and compare the results:

1a: Present combinations of a real object for touching, an audio stimulus with corresponding roughness, and a visual stimulus with noncorresponding roughness (similar to [4], except that natural touch sounds were presented in [4]).
1b: Present combinations of a real object for touching, and audio and visual stimuli with noncorresponding roughness.

4.2 Descriptions

Environment. Fig. 8 shows the experimental environment. The MR system configuration used in this study is similar to [4]. Subjects watch the MR space through a head-mounted display (HMD), and their head position and orientation is constantly tracked by a 3D laser tracker (Ascension laserBIRD). They hear the audio stimuli through inner-ear earphones (SANWA SUPPLY MM-HP106W) and wear earmuffs over them to insulate the real touch sounds generated when they actually stroke the objects.

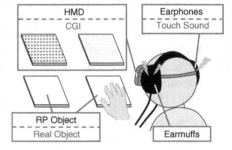

Fig. 8. Experimental Environment

Condition. Participants included 13 subjects who correctly associated enhanced touch sounds with object surface appearances in Preliminary Experiment 2. As the audio stimuli (enhanced touch sounds of group B or D) were presented, each subject answered associable with the roughness in Preliminary Experiment 2. The presentation time is six seconds, stroking one round trip per second. Preparation and procedure are as in Experiments 1a and b.

Preparation. (1) The subject practices stroking the RP plate, synchronizing hand motion with the touch sound. (2) He/she learns the roughness of touch sounds corresponding to the texture images. The four images of different surface roughness are placed in front of him/her wearing the HMD, and touch sounds corresponding to the roughness of the images are played.

Procedure. (3) Two RP plates of equal roughness, selected randomly, are placed in front of him/her. (4) Two texture images of different roughness are superimposed onto each object. (5) He/she strokes the RP plates one by one, just after each touch sound plays. Then he/she answers which plate is perceived to be tactually rougher (and is allowed the answer "indistinguishable"). (6) The RP plates are exchanged randomly, and steps (3) to (6) are repeated until all combinations of stimuli are presented.

4.3 Result and Discussion

Fig. 9 shows the result of Experiment 1. When only visual stimuli are changed (Experiment 1a), subjects tend to judge the visually rougher objects to be tactually rougher. In addition, they tend to judge the smoother objects to be indistinguishable (Rough 3 and Rough 4). In other words, the rougher surface object (Rough 1 and Rough 2) tends to be tactually perceived as being rougher by visual stimulation. These results are consistent with our previous study [4].

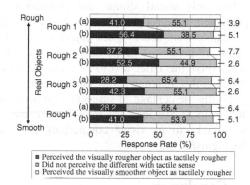

Fig. 9. Result of Experiment 1

When both visual and audio stimuli are changed (Experiment 1b), the percentage of subjects who felt the difference in roughness between two objects increases by 12–15% for all objects, as compared to Experiment 1a. Indeed, many subjects commented that when both visual and audio stimuli were changed, they perceived two identical objects to be tactually different. In addition, the tendency for rougher objects to be more affected by visual stimuli than smoother objects is as reported for Experiment 1a; however, in Experiment 1b, the number of subjects who felt the difference in roughness increases even for Rough 3 and Rough 4.

These results confirm that the influence of tactual impression (illusion) is intensified by adding both visual and audio fakes.

5 Experiment 2: Using Objects of Different Surface Roughness

5.1 Purpose

In Experiment 1, we confirm that the influence of tactual impression (illusion) is intensified by appending audio stimuli. In Experiment 2, we focus on the case of two real objects of different surface roughness. Specifically, we address two issues:

- Can a subject experience similar (Experiment 1) touch impressions when touching objects of different surface roughness?
- Can a subject perceive a rougher object (with appended visual and audio stimuli of smoothness) to be smoother than a smoother object (with appended stimuli of roughness)?

5.2 Descriptions

The experimental procedure (including environment, subjects, and stimuli) is as for Experiments 1a and b, except that objects are of different roughness. Objects are limited to only two RP plates (Rough 2 and Rough 3), so as to limit the trials to a number that avoids subject exhaustion and unwillingness or inability to continue.

5.3 Result and Discussion

When only visual stimuli are changed (Experiment 2a), the smoother object is perceived to be rougher than the rougher object 5.3% of the time and to be indistinguishable from the rougher object 10.1% of the time. When both visual and audio fakes are presented (Experiment 2b), these numbers change to 2.4% and 16.8%, respectively (the latter a 6.7% increase from the result of Experiment 2a) (Table 3). When both visual and audio stimuli of the same roughness are presented (Fig. 3 boxed cells), the percentage of subjects who perceive them to be indistinguishable grows to 46.2% (a 38.5% increase from Experiment 2a). These results show that by adding audio fake to its visual counterpart, differences in roughness become difficult to distinguish.

6 Conclusion

In this paper, we confirm that the tactual impression of the roughness of an object is intensified when audio stimuli are added to MR visual stimuli. As the real touch sounds generated by touching the experimental objects were not appropriate audio stimuli for the experiment, we created the audio stimuli (enhanced touch sounds), which were associated with the visual stimuli. Then we conducted the systematic and objective experiments.

We found that tactual impressions are intensified in the following cases:

- When subjects touch two objects of identical roughness, one of which is supplemented by visual and audio stimuli of different roughness from the object, they perceive the objects to be of different roughness.
- When subjects touch two objects of different roughness, one of which is supplemented by visual and audio stimuli of the same roughness as the other object, they find it difficult to perceive any difference in roughness.

As with the presentation of only MR visual stimuli, the results of these experiments are not applicable for every situation. However, they indicate that it is possible to intensify an intended illusion by selecting suitable stimuli. In other words, an impression can be changed (that is, one can be tricked more easily) by the addition of

Table 2. Result of Experiment 2b Number of Subjects Who Perceive Rough 3 as Rougher

	Real Object	Rough 3			
	CGI	CG 1	CG 2	CG 3	CG 4
Real Object / CGI	Touch Sound	Sound 1	Sound 2	Sound 3	Sound 4
Rough 2 / CG 1 / Sound 1		0 (+0)	0 (+0)	0 (+0)	0 (+0)
Rough 2 / CG 2 / Sound 2		3 (+3)	0 (+0)	0 (+0)	0 (+0)
Rough 2 / CG 3 / Sound 3		4 (+1)	1 (+0)	0 (+0)	0 (+0)
Rough 2 / CG 4 / Sound 4		4 (+1)	1 (-1)	3 (+1)	0 (+0)

unit: Number of People

※ the number in parenthesis shows increase-decrease values compared with the results of (a)
▇ : present same roughness CGI and touch sound
▨ : present smoother stimulation on rougher object and rougher stimulation on

Table 3. Result of Experiment 2b Number of Subjects Who Perceive the Objects to Be Indistinguishable

	Real Object	Rough 3			
	CGI	CG 1	CG 2	CG 3	CG 4
Real Object / CGI	Touch Sound	Sound 1	Sound 2	Sound 3	Sound 4
Rough 2 / CG 1 / Sound 1		8 (+7)	2 (-1)	0 (+0)	0 (-1)
Rough 2 / CG 2 / Sound 2		1 (-3)	6 (+4)	0 (-0)	0 (+0)
Rough 2 / CG 3 / Sound 3		0 (-1)	2 (+0)	3 (+2)	0 (+0)
Rough 2 / CG 4 / Sound 4		1 (+0)	2 (+1)	2 (+0)	7 (+7)

unit: Number of People

※ the number in parenthesis shows increase-decrease values compared with the results of (a)
▇ : present same roughness CGI and touch sound
▨ : present smoother stimulation on rougher object and rougher stimulation on

sounds. It is not easy to categorize and select suitable objects and stimuli; however, the existence of these objective facts is helpful for developing various MR application systems including product visualization for user interface design evaluation.

Acknowledgements. This research is supported by the Japan Society for the Promotion of Science through Grants-in-aid for Scientific Research (A), "A Mixed Reality system that merges real and virtual worlds with three senses."

References

1. Ohta, Y., Tamura, H. (eds.): Mixed Reality - Merging real and virtual worlds. Ohm-sha & Springer (1999)
2. MacIntyre, B., Livingston, M.A. (Special Session) Moving mixed reality into the real worlds. IEEE Computer Graphics and Applications 25(6), 22–56 (2005)
3. Ohshima, T., Kuroki, T., Yamamoto, H., Tamura, H.: A mixed reality system with visual and tangible interaction capability: Application to evaluating automobile interior design. In: Proc. 2nd IEEE and ACM Int. Symp. on Mixed and Augmented Reality (ISMAR 2003), pp. 284–285 (2003)
4. Iesaki, A., Somada, A., Kimura, A., Shibata, F., Tamura, H.: Psychophysical influence on tactual impression by mixed-reality visual stimulation. In: Proc. IEEE Virtual Reality 2008, pp. 265–267 (2008)
5. Lederman, S.J., Abott, S.G.: Texture perception: Studies on intersensory organization using a discrepancy paradigm and visual versus textual psychophysics. J. Experimental Psychology: Human Perception and Performance 7, 902–915 (1981)
6. Biocca, F., Kim, J., Choi, Y.: Visual touch in virtual environments: An exploratory study of presence, ultimodal interfaces, and cross-modal sensory illusions. Presence 10(3), 247–265 (2001)
7. Jousmäki, V., Hari, R.: Parchment-skin illusion: sound-biased touch. Current Biology 8, 190 (1998)
8. Guest, S., Catmur, C., Lloyd, D., Spence, C.: Audiotactile interactions in roughness perception. Experimental Brain Research 146, 161–171 (2002)
9. Constantinou, C.E., Omata, S., Murayama, Y.: Multisensory surgical support system incorporating, tactile, visual and auditory perception modalities. In: Proc. 4th Int. Conf. on Computer and Information Technology, pp. 870–874 (2004)
10. Xpress3D, http://www.xpress3d.com/Materials.aspx

Fundamental Research on Tactile Perception for Development of a Tactile Feel Display

Iyo Kunimoto[1], Naoki Saiwaki[1], Osamu Katayama[2], and Yasuji Inobe[2]

[1] Grad. School of Nara Women's Univ. Kitauoya Nishi-machi, Nara 630-8506, Japan
iyoyoyo4@yahoo.co.jp, saiwaki@cc.nara-wu.ac.jp
[2] Research Laboratories, DENSO CORPORATION 500-1 Minamiyama,
Komenoki-Cho, Nisshin-shi, Aichi 470-0111, Japan
okataya@rlab.denso.co.jp, YASUJI_INOBE@denso.co.jp

Abstract. In our daily life we use a large number of electronic devices incorporating a touch interface, e.g., mobile phones and the iPod Touch. This function is, however, in its infancy, permitting only input, with output being limited only to vibration to confirm input. Meanwhile, if we could create touch sensations with "qualitative information," such as the delicate sensation of materials or the feeling of touching an object, it would bring not only an improvement in the quality of touch sensations, but would also bring the possibility of developing new human interfaces such as more realistic VR systems and user-friendly universal communication tools for people with disability. Such human interfaces would be most effective if they did not require the development of special vibratory devices.On this basis, the authors have developed, based on knowledge gained from previous research, a prototype of a unique vibratory device employing a micro- motor, and employed it in evaluation experiment in which various differing tactile sensations are presented to study subjects.

1 Introduction

Conventional tactile feel displays such as Phantom are focused on presenting sensations of force such as shape and force feedback, and the texture was presented mainly through irregularities in the surface. As presented by the authors at HCI'05, an artificial tactile display is under development which will present the delicate sensations of non-rigid materials such as cloth [1]~[6]. This device is in the form of a small plate to which an ICPF (Ionic Conducting Polymer gel Film) has been applied, and produces minute vibrations when a voltage is applied to the film. By applying a signal incorporating a specific frequency component to multiple plates arrayed on a flat surface, a variety of tactile sensations can be created. On the other hand, manufacture of ICPF requires a considerable level of technology and generates large amounts of heat. The film has limited durability and is expensive, and its reliability leaves much to be desired. These defects have proved a hindrance to progress in research.This research has therefore employed cheap and readily available micro-motors, in the creation of a prototype system to present tactile sensations to the fingertips through mechanical vibration.[7]

R. Shumaker (Ed.): Virtual and Mixed Reality, LNCS 5622, pp. 336–345, 2009.
© Springer-Verlag Berlin Heidelberg 2009

Use of this system permits expression of tactile sensations with a number of variations, albeit in a comparatively simple manner. Evaluation of these sensations by users were investigated, and based on the results, conclusions were drawn for generation of more diverse tactile sensations.

2 Development of a Tactile Feel Display

Micro-motors are fitted with an eccentric counterweight on the shaft, resulting in vibration when the shaft rotates. The motors are approximately 1cm in diameter, and are therefore readily incorporated in miniaturized devices. They are activated by simple application of a voltage and consume very little power, and are therefore employed in such applications as mobile phones and game controllers.

The authors constructed a vibration device comprising 25 micro-motors arrayed on a flat square surface (see Figure 2). To provide a smooth vibrating surface and to ensure that vibrations are transmitted directly, a thin sheet of recycled paper was applied over the motors. As shown in Figure 3, the device is used by touching the forefinger, middle finger, third finger lightly on the surface of the device, and using the thumb and little finger to move the device in the same manner as a mouse. A film with low friction coefficient is applied to the bottom surface of the device, permitting a tactile vibration to be felt while sliding the device freely over the desk in a manner characteristic of natural touching.

The arrangement of the vibrators as shown in Figure 2 initially gave rise to fears that the vibration might be reduced or biased in some way due to interference between vibratory motors, and that localized heating might occur; however, a preparatory experiment showed that vibration at each fingertip on the touch surface was similar, and that almost no heating was apparent.

Fig. 1. Micro -motor

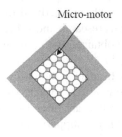

Fig. 2. Layout of micro-motors

Fig. 3. Tactile Feel Display

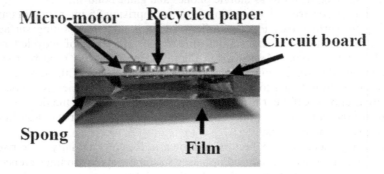

Fig. 4. Side View of Device

The voltage and frequency of the vibration applied to this tactile feel display is controlled with an oscillator able to generate any desired waveform. The signal from the oscillator is passed through an amplifier to the device to generate various vibrations, sensed by the fingertips as various sensations.

3   Method for Generating Tactile Sensations

This section describes the tactile sensation patterns created for evaluation experiments using the tactile feel display described in Section 2.

The authors varied the oscillator frequency, amplitude, offset and duty ratio to create six vibration patterns with distinctly different tactile sensations based on knowledge gained from previous research and subjective perceptions[1]~[6],[8],[9].

The vibration patterns were obtained with a programmable oscillator using the following parameters (see Figure 5).

Vibrations become finer as frequency increases from lower frequencies (e.g. 5Hz, 13Hz) to higher frequencies (e.g. 80Hz, 150Hz, 180Hz, 220Hz). The sensations associated with the changes in vibrations are often expressed subjectively with such terms as 'hard & lumpy', 'hard & grainy', 'slippery smooth' and 'dry smooth.'

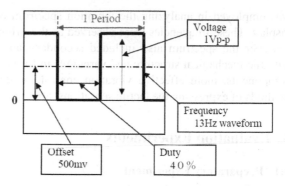

*Programmable parameters
Example
    Frequency : 13Hz
    Voltage   : 1Vp-p
    Offset   : 500mv
    Duty   : 40%

Fig. 5. Parameter Settings Example

On the other hand, offset, duty ratio and voltage were adjusted to improve the ability to sense these basic frequency characteristics at the fingertips. For instance, given the same voltage, vibrations are perceived to be transmitted to the fingertips less readily at higher frequencies than at lower frequencies. This is thought to be due to the fact that rotation characteristics of the micro-motor are such that when frequency increases, reverse rotation through a very small angle occurs repeatedly before sufficient torque develops, weakening the actual vibration produced.

In a preparatory experiment, it was found that doubling the voltage to 2_{Vp-p} at frequencies of 180Hz or more produced a strong perceived tactile sensation at the fingertips in a manner similar to that at frequencies below 180Hz. Following shows the tactile sensation patterns created for the evaluation experiments based on these observations.

Table 1. Six Tactile Sensation Patterns Employed in Evaluation Experiments

		Frequency (Hz)	Voltage (Vp-p)	Offset (mv)	Duty (%)
Fine-graininess	①	5	1	500	60
	②	13	1	500	40
Coarse	③	80	1	400	50
	④	150	1	400	50
	⑤	180	2	0	50
fain	⑥	220	2	100	50

1 Soft & airy 2 Soft & lumpy 3 Sharp 4 Hard & grainy 5 Slippery smooth 6 Silky smooth.

(From (1) to (6) are our subjective tactile sensations described using Japanese adjectives).

Note that frequency as used here is derived from the period of the alternating current signal presented to the tactile feel display, and is not the frequency component included in the vibration generated by the micro-motor. Laser distance measurement was employed in analyzing the vibration spectrum of the surface of the tactile feel display. These frequencies were observed as the primary component of the spectrum, however the spectrum also included secondary and tertiary frequencies associated with the mechanical structure and variations in torque. The effects of these subsidiary components, more effective vibration control incorporating these components, and methods of expressing the tactile sensations, are currently under consideration.

4 Evaluation Experiments

4.1 Preparatory Experiment

To investigate the relationship between the six basic tactile sensation patterns and the perceptions of these sensations by the subjects, an experiment was conducted in which patterns were applied randomly as stimuli. To isolate the subjects from information from other sensory organs, they were blindfolded and provided with earplugs. No limits were placed on the duration of exposure to the tactile sensations. Subjects were required to select from a list of 15 expressions describing the tactile sensations in a prepared questionnaire, or to enter responses in their own words.

The list of 15 expressions was as follows.

Slippery smooth	Slightly slippery-smooth	Silky smooth
Hard & grainy	Slightly hard & grainy	Sharp
Soft and airy	Slightly soft and airy	Pleasant
Dry smooth	Painful	Satiny
Soft	Normal	Don't know

The experiment showed that all subjects did not always employ the same expression each time to describe a given vibration pattern; however a definite tendency was apparent. For example, 'rocky ' appeared together with 'soft and airy', while not with 'fine-grained' or 'hard & grainy'. Furthermore, 'hard & grainy' and 'soft and airy' appearing frequently at low frequencies, and 'slippery smooth' and 'dry smooth' appearing frequently at high frequencies, were distinguishable in almost all cases. Overall, the experiment indicated that there are a number of categories expressing tactile sensations in an n-dimensional space. This is thought to show that the tactile feel display developed by the authors is able to present everyone with at least the number of categories of the differing tactile sensation stimuli, and that effective evaluation experiments are possible.

4.2 Evaluation Experiment

In this evaluation experiment the method of providing the tactile sensations, the questionnaire, the time for which the subjects were presented with the tactile sensations, the response time, and the method of operating the device were improved based on the results of the preparatory experiment. Practical details are as follows.

- Sequences of presenting tactile feel display patterns. Since changes were apparent in the evaluation criteria between the start and end of the experiment, tactile sensation patterns presented at the start were again presented at the end of the experiment to allow re-evaluation.
- Changes to questionnaire. The expressions 'pleasant' and 'soft', and 'hard & lumpy' and 'rocky', appearing frequently in entries in subjects' own words, were added to the questionnaire used in the preparatory experiment. In addition, fine-graininess and softness were evaluated on a five-point scale.
- Time for which subjects were presented with tactile sensations, and response time. Since considerable differences were apparent between subjects in the length of exposure to the tactile sensations, and in response time, exposure time and response time were both limited to a maximum of 30 seconds. Furthermore, since movement, and speed of movement, of the hand were thought to be important factors in analysis, the experiment was recorded on video.
- Touching the tactile feel display. A blindfold had been employed to eliminate the influence of vision when touching the tactile feel display. This methodology was recognized as insufficient, and made subjects feel uncomfortable. For the evaluation experiments, a screen was therefore constructed to ensure that subjects were unable to see hand movement.

Furthermore, application of the questionnaire to the screen was useful in that it presented subjects with the expressions simultaneously with exposure to the tactile sensations.

These improvements were implemented and six tactile sensation patterns presented to 12 female university students aged around 20, using three methods in which the sequence of presentation was changed between 'fine-graininess sequence', 'coarseness sequence' and 'random sequence'.

Three expressions were added to the 15 expressions employed in the preparatory experiment, so that a total of 18 expressions were provided in the questionnaire for subjects to describe the tactile stimuli. If a suitable expression was not available, subjects were able to describe sensations in their own words. Strength of expressions such as 'fine-grained' and 'soft' was evaluated subjectively on a five-point scale.

Examples of results obtained when presented in the random sequence are shown in Figure 6 and Figure 7. Using the tactile feel display, it was found that almost all subjects were able to perceive a hard, coarse vibration (hard & lumpy sensation) with a

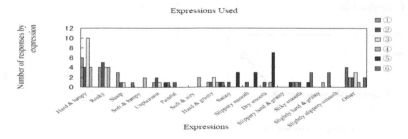

Fig. 6. Distribution of Expressions Used by Subjects to Describe Tactile Sensations for Presented Patterns

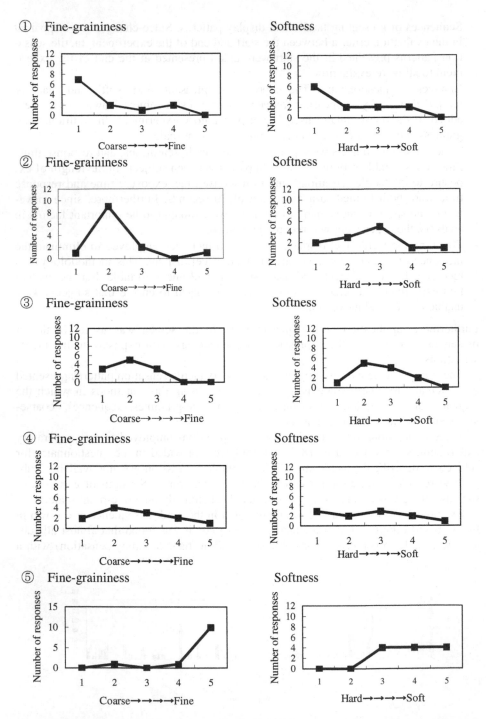

Fig. 7. Distribution of Evaluations of Fine-graininess and Softness for Tactile Sensation Patterns

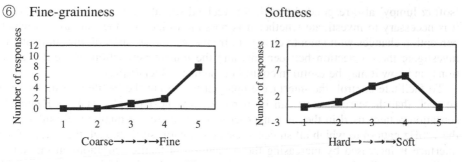

Fig. 7. (*continued*)

low frequency in the vicinity of 10Hz ((1) and (2)), and a fine soft vibration (slippery smooth sensation) with a high frequency in the vicinity of 200Hz. This corresponds accurately with a previously known model in which differing touch sensory nerves are stimulated by differing stimulating frequencies, resulting in differing sensations.

5 Observations and Topics for the Future

Results of evaluation of tactile sensation patterns in 4.2 may be summarized as follows.

1. Evaluation of the tactile sensation stimuli initially presented to the subjects contained considerable variation, and thus stimuli were presented again at the end of the experiment. Evaluation criteria were therefore not formulated the first time, and differences between individuals were considerable, however a variety of tactile sensations were experienced the second time, assisting in formulation of evaluation criteria. Responses of almost all subjects were then in agreement.
2. Results in Figure 7 show a mutual relationship between fine-graininess and softness. Subjects perceived fine-grained items as soft, and coarse items as hard, and indeed, textures such as fine-grained and hard rocks do exist in the real world. The ability to express and control these two qualities separately in the tactile feel display requires consideration.
3. In connection with the phenomena in (2) above, opinions as to whether the 150Hz tactile sensation patterns were soft or hard varied (see Figure 6 and Figure 7). This is thought to be due to variations between individuals; however, those considering the stimulus to be soft also selected 'soft & airy' and 'soft & lumpy', while those considering it to be hard tended to select 'hard & lumpy' and 'rocky'. The authors set the stimulus in reference to the intermediate 'hard & grainy.'

Consideration of the reason for the ambiguity surrounding the expression 'soft' leads to the conclusion that there exists a threshold around which the recognition result changes dynamically with minute changes in strength of vibrations with the frequency of the stimuli presented. Those replying with 'hard' and 'rocky' also responded that they perceived stimuli to be strong, while those replying with 'soft' and 'soft & lumpy' also responded that they perceived stimuli to be weak. For the future, it is necessary to investigate whether it is possible to identify the fine area in which perception changes with smooth change in frequency and strength of vibration, and to investigate the connection between this and the human perception of tactile sensations, and how it may be useful in control of the tactile feel display.

To facilitate control, the interface employed to present the tactile sensations must be such that these sensations can be perceived by most people. The 150Hz tactile sensation pattern used in the current experiments is therefore qualitatively inferior to the 180Hz pattern to which all subjects responded with 'soft', though the value of the interface is increased by increasing the perception of tactile sensations in this intermediate area. Furthermore, in order to investigate the flexibility inherent in the characteristics of human perception of tactile sensations, it was considered particularly effective to employ stimuli that can be perceived in different ways depending on the individual and on context in this manner. For example, it is possible that research may progress to a point at which differences in brain activity patterns between perception of, for instance, a presented 150Hz stimulus as hard or soft are analyzed using f-MRI. The authors have already commenced experiments in which f-MRI is employed to determine whether or not differences in perception of tactile sensations are able to be recognized.

4. When an 80Hz tactile stimulus was presented in the fine-graininess sequence, it was perceived as coarse and hard, though when presented in the coarseness sequence, it was perceived as slightly soft. This shows that the evaluation is affected by a comparison between the immediately previous and current stimuli.

The authors presented this stimulus as 'sharp', however only one subject responded with 'sharp', and most responded with 'hard & lumpy' or 'rocky'. The physical representations of the expressions 'sharp' and 'hard & lumpy' differ as 'sharp' and 'mild' vibrations respectively, with 'sharp' vibrations incorporating a greater high-frequency component. This may suggest that the authors, rather than the subjects, had become more sensitive to the high-frequency component during the progress of the experiments. Furthermore, passing signals with a considerable high-frequency component through a low pass filter (permitting user selection of cutoff frequency) before input to the tactile feel display may be able to create continuous changes in the tactile sensations.

5. The 13Hz tactile stimulus was intended to be perceived as 'soft & lumpy', however many subjects responded with 'hard & lumpy' or 'rocky'. One reason for this is the perception of the stimulus as 'hardness'. In contrast to the 80Hz tactile stimulus in (4) above, this shows the need to reduce the high-frequency component to present a 'rounder' sensation. As an aside, subjects responding to the effect that long-term application of this stimulus to the fingertips produced an unpleasant sensation noted that it occurred much more frequently than with any other tactile sensation pattern. This is thought to be due to a relationship with other bio-rhythms. While associated with LPF in (4) above, we intend to investigate the possibility of a tactile morphing providing a smooth transition from 'sharp' to 'soft & lumpy' sensations, and tactile equalizing in which a specific sensation is emphasized.

6. Based on the analysis by the authors of the factors in the evaluation of the tactile sensations of actual cloth, it is thought that if a distinct 'soft & airy' sensation can be presented, expression of tactile sensations to represent such aspects as 'fur liners' and 'piles' would be possible. However, in order to achieve this it is essential to control the sensation of an opposing force when pressed with the finger. A report has been received to the effect that a 'soft & airy' sensation is perceived when a low frequency is presented, however this is not a sponge-like sensation of an opposing force, and tends to be confused with softness.

Perception of tactile sensations suggest 'relativity', 'flexibility' and 'context dependency', and it is thought that consideration of these characteristics will permit highly realistic control of tactile sensations.

Keeping in mind the points noted in this paper, the authors wish to incorporate the tactile feel display in common devices used in daily life to create products useful in tactile communication.

References

1. Saiwaki, N., Taniguchi, M., Uchida, H., Kamitani, Y.: Basic Research on Brain Activity under Virtual Tactile Feeling Stimulus. The Japan Research Association for Textile End-Uses 47(12), 25–33 (2006)
2. Yoshida, A., Tadokoro, S., Saiwaki, N., Taniguchi, M.: Artificial Tactile Feel Display for Textile Fabrics. In: Human Computer Interaction (2005)
3. Taniguchi, M., Saiwaki, N., Yoshida, A., Tadokoro, S.: Basic Research on Brain Activity under Virtual Tactile Feeling Stimulus. Information Processing Society of Japan SIG Technical Reports, No.95 (HI-115), pp. 29–32 (2005)
4. Yoshida, A., Taniguchi, M., Saiwaki, N., Tadokoro, S.: Improvement of Tactile Feeling Display for reinforcement of a presented Sensation. In: Proceeding of FAN Symposium (2005)
5. Higashiwada, E., Saiwaki, N., Nagao, C., Taniguchi, M., Yoshida, A., Tadokoro, S.: Development of a Artificial Tactile Feel Display and Evaluation of User Interface. In: Proceeding of The Institute of Electrical Engineers of Japan (2006)
6. Saiwaki, N., Taniguchi, M., Uchida, H., Kamitani, Y., Konyo, M., Satoshi, T.: Fundamental Research on Presentation of Artificial Tactile stimuli and decoding method of f-MRI. In: Proceeding of Human Interface (2007)
7. Kunimoto, I., Saiwaki, N.: Fundamental Research on Tactile Perception for Development of a Tactile Feel Display. In: Proceeding of Japan Society of Home Economics Kansai Chapter (2008)
8. Higashiyama, A., Miyaoka, T., Taniguchi, T., Sato, A.: Tactile Sensation and Painful Sensation. Brain-shuppan, Japan (2000)
9. Iwamura, Y.: Touch. Igakuiin, Japan (2001)

Enhanced Industrial Maintenance Work Task Planning by Using Virtual Engineering Tools and Haptic User Interfaces

Simo-Pekka Leino[1], Salla Lind[1], Matthieu Poyade[2], Sauli Kiviranta[1],
Petteri Multanen[3], Arcadio Reyes-Lecuona[2], Ari Mäkiranta[3], and Ali Muhammad[3]

[1] VTT Technical Research Centre of Finland, Tekniikankatu 1, 33580, Finland
[2] Departamento de Tecnología Electrónica, ETSI de Telecomunicación,
Universidad de Málaga, Campus de Teatinos, s/n, 29071 Málaga, Spain
[3] Tampere University of Technology, IHA Department of Intelligent Hydraulics and
Automation, Finland
{simo-pekka.leino,salla.lind,sauli.kiviranta}@vtt.fi,
{matthieu.poyade,areyes}@uma.es,
{petteri.multanen,ari.makiranta,muhammad.ali}@tut.fi

Abstract. Good maintainability is an essential feature for machines and processes in industry. It promotes, among others, maintenance safety, post-maintenance reliability and cost-effective maintenance by ensuring quick and easy operation and short downtime. Virtual engineering tools provide an effective way for maintainability design already during the design phase. Machine designers may not consider maintenance tasks systematically, which can leave important task details open. The missing detail planning can contribute significantly to the probability of safety or reliability risks. So far, generic tools or facilities for planning demanding maintenance tasks in detail have not been available for companies' independent use. Another challenge is to develop and apply better user interfaces for design processes. Virtual engineering tools, such as virtual reality (VR) and haptics, provide a potential solution for improving maintenance planning and maintainability design. This paper introduces development and benefits of a new haptic interface for planning and training industrial maintenance tasks. The paper introduces a test with haptics tools in virtual maintenance case examples. As a conclusion we will sum up, whether the use of a haptic user interface would enhance task planning and maintainability design. In addition, we propose a set of recommendations regarding use of haptics in maintenance planning and maintainability design.

Keywords: Haptics, Virtual Environments, Maintenance.

1 Introduction

After-sales service is nowadays a focal part of business for machine manufacturers. For their customers, downtime of industrial plants is very expensive, which reflects as requirements for availability and effectiveness of maintenance services. Good maintainability is an essential feature for machines and processes in industry. It promotes, among others, maintenance safety, post-maintenance reliability and cost-effective

R. Shumaker (Ed.): Virtual and Mixed Reality, LNCS 5622, pp. 346–354, 2009.

maintenance by ensuring quick and easy operation and short downtime. Maintainability is also an inherent part of PLM, which emphasizes the users' viewpoint throughout the product lifecycle. [1]

Effectiveness of maintenance can be promoted with good maintenance task planning. However, generic tools or facilities for identifying and planning demanding maintenance tasks have not been available for companies' independent use. Another challenge is to develop and adopt better user interfaces for design processes. So far, design engineers have paid attention on higher level to maintenance tasks, leaving the task details open. The missing detail planning can contribute to the probability of safety or reliability risks [2]. As the current virtual engineering tools are lacking natural user interfaces, identification of the challenges of manual work tasks and circumstances is challenging using a CAD program in a desktop computer [3]. A potential solution for improving maintenance planning and maintainability design is using virtual engineering tools, such as virtual environments (VE) and haptics. However, the key challenge has been integrating such tools into the companies' production design processes.

In order to improve maintainability design and maintenance task planning, a research project called Virvo [2] was launched in 2006. In the research project we had two industrial case studies: maintenance of a heavy duty rock crusher and modernization of an elevator. The Virvo project has two main aims: 1) to develop a method for planning of critical maintenance work tasks in industry, and 2) to integrate the method to be a functional part of engineering processes.

This paper introduces development and implementation of a new haptic interface for maintenance task planning. The paper focuses on test of a haptic tool in virtual maintenance case examples. In these cases, a haptics tool was added to VE models with aim to find out if and how the use of haptics can produce information for maintainability design and maintenance task planning. As the maintenance test case had to be specific and independent from the confidential industrial case studies, we decided to make the test using a fictitious case on car maintenance. The relevant findings discussed with aim to consider their application in planning maintenance tasks in VE's. As a conclusion we will sum up, whether the use of a haptic user interface would enhance task planning and maintainability design. In addition, we propose a set of recommendations regarding use of haptics in maintenance planning and maintainability design.

2   Technical Background

2.1   Virtual Environments and Maintainability

Virtual Environment (VE) can be defined as a plausible artificial environment, which is created by technical means and allows interaction between the user and the environment [4]. Typically CAD-software enables one-way interaction, i.e. it reacts to commands given by the user, but does not provide real feedback to the user. Virtual environment system can consist of software, virtual models (CAD-models, digital humans, etc.), data communication, computers, display devices (monitors, immersive CAVEs), user interface devices, other devices and their drivers. The appropriate installation depends on the application.

The projection of a virtual model helps the users to understand the content of the design concept more reliably when compared to drawings and desktop display. Depending on the application the impressiveness of presentation can further emphasized by utilizing stereoscopic image, multiple projection or immersive virtual realities.

Currently only the most critical work tasks can be analyzed using VE tools, which can be costly or time-consuming to use. Thus, the tasks must be prioritized due to their criticality. Such tasks can be, for example, complex tasks or tasks involving high safety risks.

Maintainability can be defined quantitatively as the probability of performing a successful repair action within a given time [5]. Thus, maintainability can be defined quantitatively with equation (1), where μ is repair rate.

$$M(t) = 1 - e^{(\mu * t)} \ . \tag{1}$$

Following this definition, the qualitative maintainability features are those promoting ease and speed of maintenance task [5]. From the worker's viewpoint, system maintainability includes, among others, features affecting on ergonomics during the task execution. Certain maintainability indexes include in the concept of maintainability measurable variables, such as number of tasks to complete the operation, required time and number of tools. In addition, such indexes pay attention also to a system's qualitative features, such as accessibility and reachability. (see e.g. [6] [7]) The maintainability indexes aim to give maintainability a quantitative value based on qualitative and quantitative system and task features. The maintainability features can be assessed using virtual engineering tools. In addition, maintenance task details can be identified and analyzed in virtual environments already in the system design phase. The use of virtual technologies is of special interest in large-scale projects where the design and planning of maintenance devices and operations is heavily relied on virtual prototypes, due to the high costs, large size and complexity of physical prototypes. As an example, virtual models have been used extensively during the development of teleportation system for the maintenance of ITER divertor [8].

2.2 Haptics

The word 'haptics' refers to the sense of touch. This encompasses both tactile and kinesthetic sensory information [9], which suppose two different philosophies in touching and perceiving surrounded objects within an environment.

The use of haptic interfaces is becoming more typical. The haptic devices are small manipulators with several degrees of freedom with the capability of force reflection to the operator's hand (see e.g. [10]). The information about the operation is received from the virtual environment as sense of forces. Nowadays, several haptic devices are available in the market, providing a variety of workspaces and force feedback options. Irrespective their complexity, they all have force reflecting mechanisms. With controls and software tools, these devices can be applied in various ways to meet different user needs and requirements. The desired dynamics of the device can be modified in terms of mass, viscosity and stiffness to simulate the impedance matching with the maintenance task.

Applied to VEs, haptics results in the reciprocal communication between human and machine sensory motor channels [9], inducing force feedback enhancing strongly the tri-dimensional interaction in VEs [9] [11]. Furthermore, combined with VEs, haptic devices can provide new possibilities for the machine manufacturers. The manufacturers can interact with the product during the design phase and examine the associated maintenance procedures. This enables early improvement of maintainability through modification and possible redesign. For the customer, utilization of haptic devices and VEs helps planning, practicing and simulating maintenance task in the virtual environment before executing the task with the real product. In this way, a great number of errors and unpredictable situations can be identified and avoided before performing the actual maintenance task.

When implementing haptics in VEs, different software solutions are needed to integrate the required hardware. Usually, haptic interface manufacturers provide their own Application Programming Interface (API), which includes a set of functions in order to facilitate implementation onto VEs graphical engine. For example, Sensable Technologies provides the OpenHaptics® toolkit 2.0 [12], a free API oriented to OpenGL programming for Sensable Phantom® devices [13].

3 Methods

The paper bases on test of haptics tools in virtual maintenance case examples. Within these cases, a haptics interface, combined with VE models, was applied in maintenance planning process with aim to find out if and how the use of haptics can produce information for maintainability design and maintenance task planning. A driver was programmed in order to connect a haptic device with VE software. The test was carried out using a industrial rock crusher maintenance case and a fictitious car maintenance case.

First, we developed the necessary VE models. The development was carried out using Dassault/Virtools simulation software. We also described the data processing from CAD models to hapticalized virtual environment model. Second, we built a software interface (driver) between a commercial engineering tool (Dassault/Virtools) and a haptics device (SensAble Phantom®). Third, we created VE models for connecting VE with the haptic user interface for product development and maintenance planning processes. Fourth, we conducted a limited user test with 11 persons in order to explore usability and added value of haptic user interface in maintenance operations. The user tests consisted of three different test cases: 1) manipulation of 3D-parts in VE, 2) welding task of car maintenance, 3) re-assembly task of rock crusher maintenance. The most extensive tests were executed with the rock crusher. In that case, the actual test case is confidential, whereas the results regarding the use and feasibility of haptics are public.

3.1 Usability Test: Setting

In the welding task, test persons connected two parts of a rock crusher during reassembly task of crusher maintenance. The virtual model was built from CAD models, which were imported to Virtools simulation software. Haptic interface was built using the created haptics driver between Virtools and SensAble Phantom® device. The group of 11 test persons included: development engineer (3), project manager (2), machine engineer (2), mechanics engineer, mechanic, documentation engineer, design engineer. All of the test persons were employees of Metso Minerals company. During the test, they had the possibility to try a general haptics demo before the actual usability query. Each test person executed the welding task. After that, they filled a questionnaire form with ten statements. In addition to the statements, the questionnaire charted background information regarding persons' experience level (no experience, little experience, professional) with the different design tools and applications (3D models, CAD, VEs, simulation, haptics).

The questionnaire included the following ten statements: 1) haptic interface is easy to use, 2) user interface is natural, 3) haptics improves 6DOF navigation, 4) haptic device easier to use than 3D-mouse, 5) sense feedback helps me, 6) force feedback helps me, 7) haptics improves design work, 8) haptics improves training of work tasks, 9) I could adopt haptics as working tool, 10) overall attitude to haptics is positive. The statements had two answer options, i.e. yes and no. In addition, the test persons had also the possibility to give their free comments about haptics and ideas about haptics applications in industry.

3.2 Applied Software and Devices

The studies involved several tools and applications. Virtools™ is a comprehensive platform for creating highly interactive 3D applications. Programming is based on separation of objects, data and behaviors with intuitive user interface with real-time visualization window and graphical programming. With Virtools™ Scripting Language or the Virtools C++ SDK it is possible to implement customized functions and custom devices. (see: www.virtools.com)

Phantom Omni® and Desktop® interfaces are affordable electromechanical kinesthetic haptic desktop devices, manufactured by SensAble Technologies Inc®. The Phantom system provides a force reflecting interface between users and computers. It generates a pleasurable tri-dimensional haptic interaction with VEs due to the high degree of maneuverability. Depending on the configuration, the Phantom-based interaction can be realized through a stylus grip that users can comfortably handle as a pen, or a fingertip thimble [13].

The Phantom system tracks users' force and motion information to the 6 DOF of maneuverability. In turn, the Phantom system provides feedback to 3 DOF, high performance force effects [13], which maximum can reach 3.3 N for the Phantom Omni® and 7.9 N for the Phantom Desktop®.

Open-Haptics® toolkit 2.0 is a two layer haptic library. Higher level library, HLAPI, provides advanced support to haptic rendering, managed into a threading model. Haptic display, collision detection and Force Feedback are accomplished onto three separate threads that respectively update at 30, 100 and 1 KHz. OpenHaptics®

toolkit 2.0 provides a set of pre-written functions that allows setting up and combining various custom force effects, such as stiffness, damping, friction, dynamic friction and viscosity.

4 Results

The developed haptic interface enables the use of SensAble Phantom® haptic device with commercial Virtools VE development platform. The developed user interface for maintenance planning is integrated into a common product process of industrial companies (Fig. 1).

The product process includes following phases: concept design, detail design and engineering, prototyping and testing, production, operation and maintenance of products. Haptic interface is integrated into this process so, that 3D-models (CAD) generated in concept design and detail design (engineering) phases are exported into Virtual Environment. CAD-models are converted into proper file format of Virtools simulation software and simplified in order to reduce complexity of the model. Some additional models can be combined to VE, if needed.

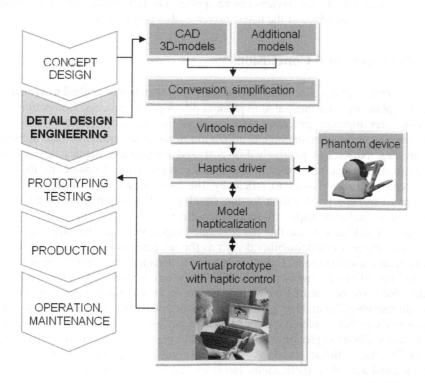

Fig. 1. Haptic user interface of maintenance planning integrated into a product process

Haptics driver connects SensAble Phantom® haptic device and Virtools. The haptic interface (driver) is introduced in more details in [14]. The driver also takes care of hapticalization of virtual models. The driver can be configured via graphical building block inside Virtools software. Engineers can plan and assess maintenance operations with haptics in Virtual Environment and give feedback into product process during prototyping phase.

The case studies explored the usability of the created methodology and haptic interface. Researchers and engineers of the partaking company assessed the related benefits. Haptic user interface was assessed to be easy to use and it has natural user interface. Following enhancements were reported during the user tests: Haptic interface improves 6 DOF navigation in a VE, haptic interface is easier to use than 3D-mouse, sense feedback of VE is moderate and force feedback is good. Half of the respondents considered haptics as a potential improvement in their design work, while all respondents found haptics as an improvement in industrial work task training. Half of the respondents considered it possible to adopt haptic interface as a work tool. Results from engineer user test are reported with more details in [14].

Haptic device has limitations on capability to process high accuracy models. However, while direct CAD models from industrial partners have been too heavy to process for the computers, there are now good possibilities to reduce model details in such a way that the haptic devices can be applies. Overall stability of the software has been very good. Interface of the haptic driver is also very easy to use.

5 Discussion and Conclusions

This paper introduces a new haptic user interface, which was applied to virtual maintenance planning, and integrated to product development process. Compatibility with product development processes and commercial engineering software tools can promote fluent implementation and utilization of the new haptic interface in industrial companies. Nowadays relatively low-cost and easy-to-use haptics devices enable cost-effective usage of haptics in maintenance engineering. Considering the relation between performance and cost efficiency, the introduced combination of device and software can be a good option for the development of inexpensive Virtual Reality applications including haptic tri-dimensional interaction.

The case studies indicate that the developed haptic interface enhances maintenance task planning and maintainability design as the interface is easy to use and it enables more natural user interface. Users can sense, for instance, the surfaces, mass and inertia feelings of the assembly parts in the maintenance work task. The interface provides also a six degree of freedom navigation in virtual environment and control of the disassembled/assembled parts. Furthermore, with haptics interface the design engineers can better identify difficulties and review the feasibility of maintenance work tasks. For example, force feedback could give a hint about mass of big machine parts. Training with haptics seems to be very promising application in industrial maintenance and assembly applications. However, adopting haptics as a design tool is up to the person.

During the studies, we identified some future improvements for the haptic interface. One technical drawback of the current driver was lack of capability to give feedback between manipulated object and environment. Furthermore, navigation inside VE may be challenging for the new users. Solutions for overcoming this problem include, for example, adding certain camera movement algorithms to improve sense of location. Best solution for this would be tracking for user's head motions, which would bring depth sensing to state of human's capability for sensing spatial locations in reality.

For maintenance planning and maintainability design, detailed planning using virtual engineering tools provide new possibilities to explore system features at an early stage. Such tools can help to assess, for example, reachability and accessibility to the maintenance area. They also help to estimate the complexity and feasibility of various maintenance tasks. In future applications, different kinds of haptics tools and VEs could also make it possible to identify and assess the task-related risks and complexity of the work phases during disassembly and reassembly. Moreover, haptics and VEs can have significant benefits in maintenance training and planning, as they provide a safe and realistic way to examine the tasks. However, some detailed studies are required to find the optimal solutions for generic industrial applications.

In future, the development should focus on collision feedback between manipulated object and the surrounding environment, which is essential in order to make assembly applications realistic. Building training simulators, requiring feedback only from the object surfaces, is probably more potential application than designing big machines in industry. With current virtual reality development tools, it is relatively easy to gather user performance data from such training simulators. Post processing this data for performance evaluation can be easily done in different software or can be shown in real time for the users. Sense and force feedback can be seen as good addition to VEs, but increased realism in haptics interfaces and enhanced exploitation of haptics in VEs still need development.

References

1. Lind, S., Leino, S.-P., Multanen, P., Mäkiranta, A., Heikkilä, J.: A virtual engineering based method for maintainability design. In: 4th International Conference on Maintenance and Facility Management, Rome, Italy, April 22-24 (2009)
2. Leino, S.-P., Helin, K., Lind, S., Viitaniemi, J., Multanen, P., Mäkiranta, A., Lahtinen, J., Nuutinen, P., Heikkilä, J., Martikainen, T.: Virtual engineering and remote operation in design, training and completion of demanding maintenance work tasks in challenging industrial plants (Virvo). In: MaSi Programme 2005-2009. Yearbook 2008. Tekes (2008)
3. Kimura, F., Yamane, N.: Haptic Environment for Designing Human Interface of Virtual Mechanical Products. The International Academy for Production Engineering, CIRP Annals - Manufacturing Technology 55, 127–130 (2006)
4. Reitmaa, I., Vanhala, J., Kauttu, A., Antila, M.: Virtuaaliympäristöt - kuvan sisälle vievät tekniikat. 2nd edn. TEKES, Helsinki (1996)
5. Sharma, R.K., Kumar, S.: Performance Modeling in Critical Systems Using RAM Analysis. Reliability Engineering and System Safety 93, 913–919 (2008)
6. SAE J817-2. Engineering Design Serviceability Guidelines – Construction and Industrial Machinery – Maintainability Index – Off-Road Work Machines. Surface Vehicle Information Report. Society of Automotive Engineers. Warrendale, PA (March 1991)

7. Wani, M.F., Gandhi, O.P.: Development of Maintainability Index for Mechanical Systems. Reliability Engineering and System Safety 65, 259–270 (1999)
8. Muhammad, A., Esque, S., Tolonen, M., Mattila, J., Nieminen, P., Linna, O., Vilenius, P.: Water hydraulic based teleoperation system for ITER. In: Tenth Scandinavian International Conference on Fluid Power, SICFP 2007, Tampere, Finland (2007)
9. Srinivasan, M.A., Basdogan, C.: Haptics in Virtual Environments: Taxonomy, Research Status and Challenges. Computer & Graphics 21, 393–404 (1997)
10. Sensable Technologies, http://www.sensable.com/haptic-phantom-omni.htm
11. MacLean, K.E., Hayward, V.: Do It yourself Haptics: Part II. IEEE Robotics & Automation Magazine, 104–119 (2008)
12. Itkowitz, B., Handley, J., Zhu, W.: The OpenHaptics™ Toolkit: A Library for Adding 3D Touch™ Navigation and Haptics to Graphics Applications. In: Proc. 1st Joint Eurohaptics Conf. and Symp. Haptic Interfaces for Virtual Environment and Teleoperator Systems, World Haptics, pp. 590–591. IEEE CS Press, Pisa (2005)
13. Potts, A.: Phantom-based haptic interaction. In: Proc. Comput. Sci. discipline semin. conf. CSCI 3901 (2000), http://mrs.umn.edu/~lopezdr/seminar/spring2000/potts.pdf
14. Poyade, M., Reyes Lecuona, A., Leino, S.-P., Kiviranta, S., Viciana Abad, R., Lind, S.: A High-Level Haptic Interface for Enhanced Interaction within Virtools™. In: 13th International Conference on Human-Computer Interaction, San Diego, USA, July 19-24 (2009)

Characterizing the Space by Thermal Feedback through a Wearable Device

Takuji Narumi[1,3], Akagawa Tomohiro[2], Young Ah Seong[1], and Michitaka Hirose[1]

[1] The University of Tokyo, 7-3-1 Hongo Bunkyo-ku, Tokyo Japan
{narumi,hirose}@cyber.t.u-tokyo.ac.jp,
yabird@hc.ic.i.u-tokyo.ac.jp
[2] Tokyo University of the Arts, 2-5-1 Shinko, Naka-ku, Yokohama, Japan
toakmoak@gsfnm.jp
[3] Japan Society for the Promotion of Science

Abstract. Thermal sensation is a kind of a haptic sensation and is very familiar feeling. However it is difficult to realize a thermal display which gives realistic thermal feedback because thermal characteristic has a larger ambiguity and is late-response. Alternatively, thermal feedback could be used as a new channel for the transmission of imaginary characteristics. We are aiming to add characteristics to the existing space by providing people with location-dependent thermal information. By manipulating thermal information presented to people, we can change implicit partitioning of the space without physically reconstructing it. "Thermotaxis" is a system that gives sensations of cool and warm to users by controlling thermoelectric devices wirelessly. In this system, the space is characterized as being cool or warm. Users experience the difference in temperatures while they walk in the space. Preliminary analysis shows that people stay close in the area of a comfortable temperature.

Keywords: Ambient Controlling, Characterizing the Space, Thermal Sensation, Thermal Feedback, Wearable Computing.

1 Introduction

Thermal sensation is a kind of a haptic sensation and is very familiar feeling. However, force and tactile feedback are the main sensory inputs presented to an operator using a haptic display and there is few example of the utility as a thermal interface or a thermal display. For example, there has been work on incorporating thermal feedback into haptic devices [1, 2]. Thermal feedback can be used to convey information about the thermal conductivity of objects encountered in an environment which can assist in object identification, or in the creation of a more realistic image of the object [1].

A thermal characteristic has a larger ambiguity than that of visual and audio information. And the response time is longer than visual and auditory sensation. These are the reasons why it is difficult to realize a thermal display which gives realistic thermal feedback. Alternatively, thermal feedback could be used as a new channel for the transmission of imaginary characteristics.

R. Shumaker (Ed.): Virtual and Mixed Reality, LNCS 5622, pp. 355–364, 2009.

In this paper we propose a method of characterizing the space by presenting thermal information. Although thermal sensing is slower in response time and lower in resolution than visual and audio sensing, it is suitable for informing users gradually, without giving a clear border.

Our research aims to make spatial design flexible. New characteristics are added to an existing space, so the relationship between the space and people within changes. In spatial information design, there are many studies on presenting information, including pervasive, ubiquitous and ambient computing [3]. Most of them focus on presenting additional information or information of distant place remotely [4, 5]. The kind of information we are interested in is not explanations about a location but part of a spatial structure that implicitly affects people's activity in the spaces. We call it ambient controlling of human behavior by presenting non-visual information.

In the rest of paper, we discuss an experiment of presenting thermal information to characterize the space. We also describe analysis of people's behavior in that space.

2   Characterizing the Space by Presenting Thermal Information

As discussed in the previous section, we introduce a thermal characteristic to a space. A thermal characteristic has a larger ambiguity than that of visual and audio information. And the response time is longer than visual and auditory sensation [6]. However, among all types of sensations, thermal sensing is effective in ambient controlling for presenting information non-intrusively. There are two advantages of using non-visual information presentation.

First, screens and displays force the eyes of users on them. For example, ambient display [4] was studied as a way of implicit information presentation. Without regular computer displays, users become free from the desktop to get information. There is still a drawback in this approach, however, that users are required to pay attention to where the information is presented, which constrains their activities.

Another example is the concept of ubiquitous computing and pervasive computing, which try to transform spaces that are filled with computers into intelligent spaces with communication capabilities [7-10]. Many of these studies, users have to walk around with mobile terminal or hand-held communication device to get annotated information. If users expect desired information, this can be available. But using devices with visual monitors are not applicable to implicit information presentation. It is because we want to encourage changing user's behavior regardless of whether the user expects it.

Second, information representation using auditory properties is susceptible to surrounding sound environment. Besides the sound can be intrusive noise for unconcerned people. One solution is providing a wearable headphone for each user.

The combinations of information technology and architecture have argued [11, 12]. The Austrian Architect, Hans Hollein has explored several possibilities of a new electronic media with architecture in 1960's [13]. In his claim, a space is as sculpture, or as a "determined activated region in indefinite three dimension".

Some applications have been developed that construct spatial structures using non-visual information presentation. "Monolith" is an LED sculpture by United Visual Artists [14]. This artwork is a symbolic responsive LED sculpture that makes a huge noise if the visitor comes close to it. By this behavior of the system, the visitor is forced to move toward moderately comfortable place. In this case, the sculpture creates a spatial structure by presenting audio information that affects users around it.

We have studied the recognition of a spatial structure without presenting visual information [15]. In this study, a spatial structure was not presented by blocking the visual information from the external world with the veil, and how the space was recognized by walking blind was investigated. This study indicated that people have more accuracy in recognizing topology than distance.

3 Thermotaxis

3.1 System Overview

In this section, we propose a system of controlling thermal characteristics and discuss how thermal information affects people's behavior.

Thermotaxis is a system that creates thermal sensory spots in an open space. It works as a spatial partitioning system without physical walls. Instead, it displays temperatures in several grades. In this system, we use earmuff like wearable devices that provide thermal sensation to ears depending on the location of people. We choose ears to present thermal information because cephalic part is the most sensitive to heat and cold stimuli [16]. By feeling the temperature, people distinguish different thermal areas, though there is no visual distinction between them.

Fig. 1. Thermotaxis

In Thermotaxis, space is divided into several thermal fields. The term "Thermotaxis" signifies a movement of a living organism in response to heat stimulation. Visitors are expected to walk around to find their comfortable position based on their thermal senses. Due to the variations of desired conditions and surrounding environment such as the air temperature, different positions are found to be comfortable by different visitors. For example, on a cold day in winter, a comfortable place would be warm unlike a summer day. People who have a similar preference would gather together. (Figure 1)

3.2 Hardware Configuration

The system is designed to be controlled by a computer as an operating unit via wireless communication, and all electronic modules that control temperature are installed in the earmuff.

This system consists of several earmuff-like wearable devices (Figure 2) and a control unit that controls the wearable devices and recognizes their locations. Figure 3 shows the configuration of devices.

Fig. 2. Earmuff device

An IEEE 1394 camera with an infrared filter for earmuff tracking is attached to the ceiling about 12 meters above the floor. Infrared LEDs are attached to the top of the earmuff device for camera tracking. Sensing with a camera is easy to install if the camera has a clear line of sight to all wearable devices. Figure 4 depicts the system layout. When the control unit requests locations of the wearable devices, the camera detects their positions by capturing blinking infrared LEDs mounted on their tops.

To build a wearable device that displays warm and cool temperatures, we use an Arduino Nano [17] as a microcontroller. It controls two Peltier devices in each side of the earmuff. It also controls infrared LEDs. There are five heating levels on the Peltier

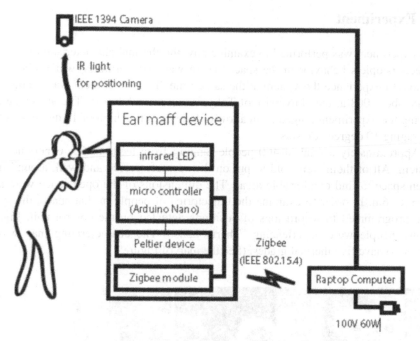

Fig. 3. Configuration of Earmuff Devices and Control Unit

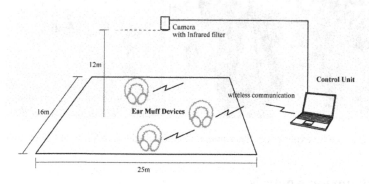

Fig. 4. System Layout

device control. Two of them are heating, two of them are cooling and one in the middle is without heating or cooling level. The difference in temperature created by these Peltier devices is about twenty degrees to forty degrees Celsius.

The control unit and the earmuff devices communicate via a Zigbee network. If the position is detected, the unit determines the heating level according to the thermal field and sends the temperature level to the earmuff device. Because the thermal fields are defined by software, we can change the map of fields dynamically.

4 Experiment

An experiment was performed to examine how the thermal characteristic of the space affects people's behavior in the space. There were six earmuffs, which allowed six people to experience the system at the same time. This experiment was conducted in December 2008 at the University of Tokyo as an art exhibition. The air temperature during the experiment ranged from a low of 8 degrees to a high of 12 degrees Celsius, averaging 10 degrees Celsius.

Approximately a total of 400 people ranging from teens to 60s experienced this system. All of them were told to put on the earmuff device and walk around in the open space to find comfortable areas. The dimensions of the open space were about 25m x 16m. In order to examine the trajectories of people in that space, the system was programmed to record logs of positions detected by the control unit. Figure 5 shows people were experiencing "Thermotaxis." The characterizing map was designed to have five thermal grades. (See the map of Figure 6).

Fig. 5. Visitors who experience "Thermotaxis" and a Bird's-Eye View of "Thermotaxis"

5 User Behavior Analysis

In this section, we present analysis of recorded data described earlier and discuss people's behavior in the space. This analysis consists of composed of following two points.

– The relation between area ratio and sojourn time in each area.
– The influence for other people on subject being in certain area.

The purpose of the first analysis is to determine which areas people prefer. The second analysis is to measure influences of one's location to other people.

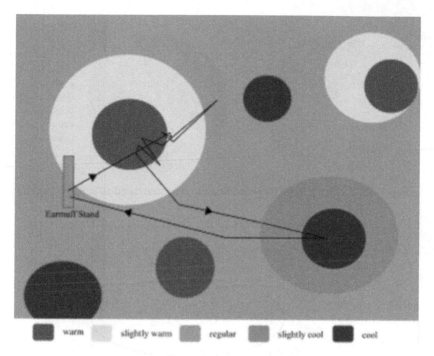

| warm | slightly warm | regular | slightly cool | cool |

Fig. 6. The Trajectories of People. In this map, red areas are warm, yellow areas are slightly warm and green areas are at a regular temperature area. All people standing in red area.

5.1 Thermal Area Ratio and Sojourn Time

Like open fires in winter and water places in summer, thermal locations have been work as attractive location since early times. A thermal spot has power to encourage people to gather together.

Figure 6 illustrates an example of user's trajectory. In this map, red areas are warm, yellow areas are slightly warm, cyan areas are slightly cool, blue areas are cool and green areas are at a regular temperature area. Left graph in Figure 7 compares areas of the thermal fields indicated in Figure 6. The regular area is largest, followed by the warm area. The cool, warm and slightly cool areas are approximately of the same size.

Right graph in Figure 7 shows the total sojourn time of all people. The total time spent in warm is the longest although the regular area is the largest. This result means that people preferred to stay longer in the warm area.

Figure 8 depicts a Venn diagram of arrival rate of each area. About 83 percent of people reached the warm area, while only 22 percent reached the cool area.

This result can be attributed to the topology of the map. As shown in Figure 6, the warm and slightly warm areas are closer to the earmuff stand which is the initial position of the trajectory. In other words, 80 percent of people searched near the starting point and about 60 percent were satisfied with the warm area. The air temperature may be a factor of this result. It is likely that people preferred to the warm area because of the low air temperature.

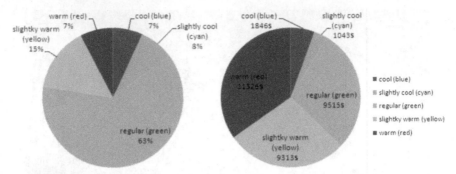

Fig. 7. Thermal Area Ratio (left) and Sojourn time summated all subjects (right)

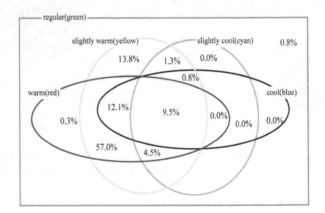

Fig. 8. Venn diagram of arrival factor

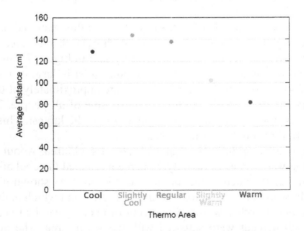

Fig. 9. Average Distance between People Sorted by Thermal Areas

5.2 Influences on Other Subjects

The visibility of other visitors also effects how visitors transition through the areas. In the open space, people can see each other. If one stays in a particular place, other people may be wonder why he or she is there. So, people influence each other by their positions.

Figure 9 shows average distance between people when one of them is in area. The average distances in the warm and slightly warm areas are small. There is little difference in the regular, slightly cool and cool area.

This result means that if there is at least one person in warm or slightly warm area, people tend to close each other. In other word, people stay close in the warm and slightly warm areas.

6 Conclusions

This paper discussed the idea of thermal feedback as a new channel for the transmission of imaginary characteristics. We proposed to characterize the space by presenting thermal information. Unlike physical walls or partitions, creating non-intrusive partition using information mapping onto an existing space enables us distinguish areas in space flexibly. In Thermotaxis, we characterize an open space with thermal information. Wearable thermal devices have been created to present an imaginary spatial structure.

We conclude that affecting people's behavior is possible by reconfiguring an open space with invisible spatial structure. In this paper, we have argued that the use of thermal information is useful for creating an implicit spatial structure. The result of our experiment shows that presenting thermal information affects people's behavior in making them get together in a warm area under certain conditions.

We need further investment about how people's behavior changes if the thermal map dynamically changes. We are also interested in using other media to perform ambient controlling. Although the use of visual or audio senses is reliable to deliver information accurately, there is an advantage of presenting information passively and unconsciously. We believe that it is worth investigating application of ambient controlling in new media.

Acknowledgements

We would like to thank Taro Suzuki, Tomohiro Tanikawa, Takashi Kiriyama, Takeshi Naemura and Hiroshi Harashima. This research is supported by JST(Japan Science and Technology Agency) CREST (Core Research for Evolutional Science and Technology) and by the Ministry of Education, Science, Sports and Culture, Grant-in-Aid for JSPS(Japan Society for the Promotion of Science) Fellows.

References

1. Ino, S., Shimizu, S., Odagawa, T., Sato, M., Takahashi, M., Izumi, T., Ifukube, T.: A tactile display for presenting quality of materials by changing the temperature of skin surface. In: Proc. 2nd IEEE Int. Workshop on Robot and Human Communication, pp. 220–224 (1993)
2. Yamamoto, A., Cros, B., Hashimoto, H., Higuchi, T.: Control of Thermal Tactile Display Based on Prediction of Contact Temperature. In: Proc. IEEE Int. Conf. on Robotics and Automation, pp. 1536–1541 (2004)
3. Weiser, M.: The computer for the 21st century. Scientific American (February 1991)
4. Wisneski, C., Ishii, H., Dahley, A., Gorbet, M., Brave, S., Ullmer, B., Yarin, P.: Ambient displays: Turning architectural space into an interface between people and digital information. LNCS, pp. 22–32. Springer, Heidelberg (1998)
5. Redström, J., Skog, T., Hallnäs, L.: Informative art: using amplified artworks as information displays. In: DARE 2000: Proceedings of DARE 2000 on Designing augmented reality environments, pp. 103–114. ACM Press, New York (2000)
6. Lederman, S.J., Klatzky, R.L.: Relative availability of surface and object properties during early haptic processing. Journal of Experimental Psychology: Human Perception and Performance 23, 1680–1707 (1997)
7. Shklovski, I., Chang, M.: Guest editors' introduction: Urban computing navigating space and context. Computer 39(9), 36–37 (2006)
8. Kindberg, T., Chalmers, M., Paulos, E.: Guest editors' introduction: Urban computing. Pervasive Computing 6(3), 18–20 (2007)
9. Wilson, J., Walker, B., Lindsay, J., Cambias, C., Dellaert, F.: Swan: System for wearable audio navigation. In: 11th IEEE International Symposium on Wearable Computers, October 2007, pp. 91–98 (2007)
10. Nishimura, T., Itoh, H., Nakamura, Y., Yamamoto, Y., Nakashima, H.: A Compact Battery-Less Information Terminal for Real World Interaction, pp. 124–139. Springer, Heidelberg (2004)
11. Maeda, E., Minami, Y.: Steps towards ambient intelligence. NTT Technical Review 4(1), 50–55 (2006)
12. Ujigawa, M., Hanazato, T.: A study on the influence of the information technologies to buildings. AIJ Journal of Technology and Design (22), 573–576 (2005)
13. Lefaivre, L.: Everything is architecture multiple hans hollein and the art of crossing over. Harvard Design Magazine (18) (Spring/Summer 2003)
14. Artists, U.V.: Monolith, http://www.uva.co.uk/archives/31
15. Narumi, T., Akagawa, T., Seong, Y.A., Hirose, M.: Absolute field: Proposal for a reconfigurable spatial structure. In: ACM International Conference on Advances in Computer Entertainment Technology (ACE 2008) (December 2008)
16. Nadel, E.R., Mitchell, J.W., Stolwijk, J.A.J.: Differential Thermal Sensitivity in the Human Skin. Pflugers Archiv European Journal of Physiology, Pflfigers Arch. 340, 71–76 (1973)
17. Arduino: Web page, http://www.arduino.cc/

A High-Level Haptic Interface for Enhanced Interaction within Virtools™

Matthieu Poyade[1], Arcadio Reyes-Lecuona[1], Simo-Pekka Leino[2], Sauli Kiviranta[2], Raquel Viciana-Abad[3], and Salla Lind[2]

[1] Departamento de Tecnología Electrónica, ETSI de Telecomunicación, Universidad de Málaga, Campus de Teatinos, s/n, 29071 Málaga, Spain
{matthieu.poyade,areyes}@uma.es
[2] Human-Machine Systems, VTT Technical Research Centre of Finland Tekniikankatu 1, FIN-33101, Tampere, Finland
{Simo-pekka.Leino,Sauli.Kiviranta,Salla.Lind}@vtt.fi
[3] Departamento de Ingeniería de Telecomunicación, Escuela Politécnica Superior de Linares, C/ Alfonso X El Sabio, 28, 23700 Linares, Spain
rviciana@ujaen.es

Abstract. Haptics is the outstanding technology to provide tri-dimensional interaction within Virtual Environments (VE). Nevertheless, many software solutions are not fully prepared to support Haptics. This paper presents a user-friendly implementation of Sensable Phantom haptic interfaces onto the interactive VE authoring platform, Virtools 4.0. Haptics implementation was realized using the Haptic Library (HLAPI) from OpenHaptics toolkit 2.0 which provides highly satisfactory custom forces effects. The integration of Phantom interaction at end-user development fulfils logical VE interactive authoring under Virtools. Haptics implementation was qualitatively assessed in a manual maintenance case, a welding task, as a part of the national Finnish project, VIRVO. Manipulation enhancements provided by the integration of Phantom interaction in Virtools suggest many further improvements for more complicated industrial pilot experiments as a part of the European Commission funded project ManuVAR.

Keywords: Virtual Reality, Haptics, OpenHaptics, Virtools™, Force Feedback.

1 Introduction

Haptic displays have been widely used for interaction technique to support manipulation tasks in Virtual Environments (VE) [1]. The haptic modality is included in a large number of commercial and non-commercial Virtual Reality (VR) applications, implicated in several industrial domains such as mechanical engineering. For instance, haptics was a significant issue in the national Finnish project VIRVO [2] [3], for the development of industrial virtual engineering tools and methods in order to improve maintainability design and maintenance task planning. Usability and benefits of virtual engineering tools were tested in two industrial case-studies related to mining and construction as well as elevator manufacturing and service business. In VIRVO project, haptics was also tested in several generic test cases. Furthermore, VR and

R. Shumaker (Ed.): Virtual and Mixed Reality, LNCS 5622, pp. 365–374, 2009.

haptics are strongly considered as a potential industrial solution in the European Commission funded project ManuVAR[1], to support manual work through Product Lifecycle Management (PLM).

The implementation of high performance Force Feedback (FF) haptic interfaces onto VE development platforms may strongly improve tri-dimensional interaction within VE. Nevertheless, most of haptic devices are not implemented onto VE development platforms graphical engines. This is the case of the Sensable Technologies OpenHaptics® toolkit onto the commercial VE development platform Virtools™ 4.0. So, it appears necessary to facilitate access to commercial VE development platform to inexpensive haptic interfaces users.

This paper presents a friendly end-user Sensable Technologies Phantom haptic interface implementation for Virtools™ 4.0 using Haptic Library (HLAPI) from OpenHaptics toolkit 2.0.

2   Technical Background

2.1   Virtual Environment Development Platform

The development of VEs requires powerful programming tools as software interfaces that ensure an optimum use of graphics hardware. The most commonly used is OpenGL [4] [5] which consists in a standard C++ based graphical platform API able to render two and three-dimensional objects geometric primitives through a series of processing stages known as OpenGL Rendering Pipeline. OpenGL programming is enhanced by additional libraries as the OpenGL Utility Library (GLU) and the OpenGL Utility Toolkit (GLUT). Recent developments concerning OpenGL have led to the rise of several toolkits as OpenSceneGraph [6], a high performance tri-dimensional graphics toolkit which uses a scene graph data structure to render objects geometric primitives.

VE development is strongly eased by visual programming software as Virtools™ [7], a development platform able to support key industry standard OpenGL, that allows intuitive authoring of tri-dimensional interactive graphic applications.

Virtools™ authoring development, also known as end-user development, is graphically-based on linking logical components, the Behavior Building Blocks (BBs), described into software libraries. High-end development consists in advanced programming using the Virtools™ development tools: Virtools™ Software Development Kit (SDK) and Virtools™ Script Language (VSL). Virtools™ SDK deals with standard C++ programming that provides access to rendering and behavioral engines allowing BBs programming in order to improve end-user development by implementing custom functions and VR device interfaces.

Virtools™ context is a real-time engine supported by a standalone threaded process loop, which includes behavioral and hierarchical graphical rendering sub-processes. So, primitive shapes are first vertex-based rendered and then hierarchically processed.

---

[1] ManuVAR is a European Union funded project, envisaged to start in spring 2009.

2.2 Haptics and Implementation on Virtual Environment Development Platforms

Haptics. Haptics refers to manual interaction with environments [1]. More specifically, it is associated to the ability of sensing and manipulating environment components through the sense of touch characterized by tactile and proprioceptive information [8].

Haptics in VEs is characterized by a multimodal real-time sensory-motor interaction between the human and the machine motor channels [1] [8], inducing reciprocal Force Feedback (FF). It is proved that haptic FF strongly improves task performance due to a higher maneuverability and enhances interaction making it more pleasurable [9] and environmentally more immersive [1].

Even though many works have successfully implemented the haptic modality in tri-dimensional interaction within VEs [9] [10] [11], managing with haptics interfaces keeps being a delicate labor that requires advanced programming knowledge.

Implementation of Haptics. The OpenHaptics® toolkit 2.0 [12] is an OpenGL-based haptic library for Phantom devices by SensAble Technologies Inc® providing a Phantom-based interaction [13].

OpenHaptics® toolkit has a two layered architecture: the Haptic Device API (HDAPI) and the Haptic Library API (HLAPI). HDAPI provides a low-level access to haptic device; it requires advanced programmer skills. HLAPI is a friendly high level rendering engine that uses a description of OpenGL's graphics stores graphic card buffers to display haptics. It offers several extension modules such as custom force effects (stiffness, damping, friction, dynamic friction, viscosity…) and threads management to support haptic rendering. The client thread (~30 Hz) supports graphical rendering. The collision thread (~100 Hz) supports collision detection. The servo thread (~1000 Hz) handles the position and orientation of the haptic device and updates forces.

Recent improvements in the brand new version OpenHaptics® toolkit 3.0 proposed an implementation of HLAPI pre-written functions and a top third layer API, Quick Haptics which shortens and simplifies OpenHaptics® programming in OpenGL.

There are plenty of other haptic APIs for non-commercial VR platforms. The most prominent are the SenseGraphics[2] H3DAPI and VHTK for OpenGL and osgHaptics for OpenSceneGraph.

The Haption Company [14] provides integration modules using haptic libraries corresponding to the Virtuose™ haptic devices onto various Dassault Systèmes industrial VR solutions like Virtools™ and Catia.

Concerning Phantom interaction onto Virtools™ platform, few works can be found. The Phantom interface was successfully implemented using the obsolete Sensable Technologies Ghost® SDK[3]. A much recent approach [15] used OpenHaptics® toolkit 2.0 HDAPI allowing a low level control of forces.

Our approach uses HLAPI which simplifies Virtools™ end-user authoring development and provides a wide set of customizable haptic force effects.

---

[2] SenseGraphics AB - Home, http://www.sensegraphics.com
[3] http://www.theswapmeet-forum.com/forum/download/file.php?id=1854

3 Description of the Developed Interface

3.1 Presentation of the Developed Interface

The proposed interface is a set of extension modules (BBs) for Virtools™ 4.0 platform that facilitate the integration of Sensable Technologies Phantom Omni and Desktop[4] haptic interfaces at end-user development stage. The integration of the extension modules at the end-user development stage can be easily realized regarding the Virtools™ logical components interlinking policy. Furthermore, the proposed extension allows adding and removing objects from the VE at end-user development stage.

3.2 Development of the Extension Modules

Basics of High-end Development. The Development of extension Modules for Virtools™ 4.0 platform results in a standard C++ programming using the Virtools™4.0 SDK pre-written functions. The whole project was compiled with Microsoft Visual Studio.NET 2003.

OpenHaptics programming using HLAPI requires setting up an alternative OpenGL context to store a copy of graphics vertices into specific buffers. This provides support to the average 1 KHz haptic rendering, which would be hardly achievable in a Virtools™ based context. The solution consists in supporting haptics within a hidden OpenGL context located on the top of the Virtools™ 3D Layout and then, proceeding with haptic coding using OpenHaptics® toolkit HLAPI programming.

Virtual objects geometries from Virtools™ are selectively processed in the alternative OpenGL context to render a vertex-based mapped haptic model which is a unique haptic shape that gathers all the Virtools™ objects to be hapticallized. The developed interface deals then with a real-time recognition of haptic geometries and their respective haptic characteristics while touching objects in the VE.

Basics of End-user Development. The interface extension results in a pair of BBs which facilitate end-user programming. These BBs were named "Phantom Sensable Waiter" and "Hapticallize Object", respectively shown in Fig 1.a and Fig 1.b.

"Phantom Sensable Waiter" BB launches the OpenGL context, initializes the Phantom haptic device, manages and outputs Phantom device 6 DOF sensing, handles object position and orientation, deals with collision detection and force feedback effects, scales manipulation area and sets up VE's viscosity. Fig 1.a details the input and output parameters of the "Phantom Sensable Waiter" BB that allow a natural integration into Virtools™ scenarios with interconnected BBs. The "Phantom Sensable Waiter" BB input parameters set up the haptic bounding box and its location into a VE in order to scale and position the manipulation area, to specify the group of touchable objects to which all hapticallized objects belong, and the viscosity parameter.

---

[4] The Phantom Omni and Desktop haptic interfaces are non-expensive 6 Degree-of-Freedom (DOF) position sensing electromechanical desktop devices with high fidelity Force Feedback output onto 3 DOF, with a maximum respectively set to 3.3N and 7.9N. Typical Phantom device configuration includes a stylus grip so that users can handle it as a pen.

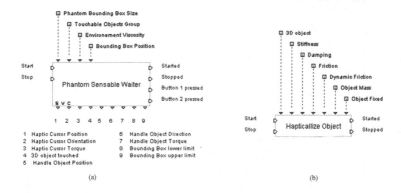

Fig. 1. (a) The Phantom Sensable Waiter BB and (b) the Hapticallize Object BB

"Hapticallize Object" BB supports as input parameters, the specification of the object to hapticallize, its mobility state and haptic characteristics as Stiffness, Damping, Friction, Dynamic Friction and Object Mass used to define object's weight and inertia. Haptic characteristics in the "Hapticallize Object" BB are quantified from 0 to 1, respectively representative of the null force level and the maximum force level applied by the Phantom haptic device[2]. Fig 1.b details the input parameters of the "Hapticallize Object" BB.

The implementation of the developed interface was tested in a simple Virtools™ generated VE consisting of basic geometric shapes as shown in Fig 2. This first trial allows examining the functionality of the implemented interface, so that objects contact and handling can be ensure as suitable.

The interconnectivity with other BBs is a key issue of the integration of the developed modules in Virtools™. "Phantom Sensable Waiter" and "Hapticallize Object" BBs must be connected into Virtools™ scenarios as shown in Fig 3.

"Hapticallize Object" BB specifies haptic characteristics of a unique object, so it is necessary to declare one BB per object.

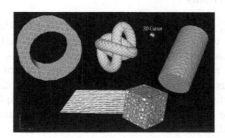

Fig. 2. The trial scene for rapid examination of the developed interface functionality

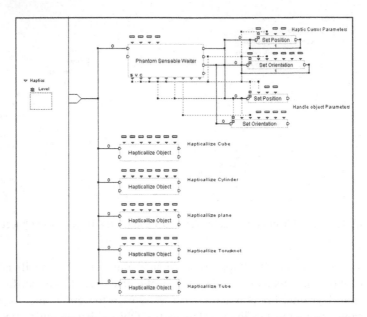

Fig. 3. An example Virtools™ scenario with interconnection on the developed interface

"Phantom Sensable Waiter" returns the haptic cursor and touched object position, direction and torque values. In order to see graphical shapes moving following haptics, it is necessary to assign position and orientation values to graphical shapes that represent the haptic cursor and the touched objects, by linking "Phantom Sensable Waiter" position and orientation output parameters to appropriate BBs input parameters. "Set Position" and "Set Orientation" BBs are required and connected to "Phantom Sensable Waiter" outputs to receive position and orientation data in order to graphically set up position and orientation of the haptic cursor and touched objects.

4   Assessment of the Developed Interface

4.1   Experimental Methods

In VIRVO project [3], a usability industrial test of new haptic user interface in VE was carried out. The test consisted in a virtual welding task using haptic device (SensAble Phantom) as a welding torch. In the welding task, testing subjects connected two parts of a rock crusher during reassembly task of crusher maintenance. The virtual model was built from CAD models imported into Virtools simulation software. Haptic interface was built using the developed haptics interface between Virtools and SensAble Phantom device. Fig. 4 shows a virtual welding task model dedicated to public audience.

There were 11 participants involved in usability test, three Development engineers, two project managers, two machine engineers, one mechanics engineer, one mechanic, one documentation engineer and one design engineer. All the testing subjects were employees of Metso Minerals Company.

Fig. 4. A virtual welding task for public audience

All participants had at least little experience of tri-dimensional models and CAD. Development engineers, mechanics engineer and design engineer got most experience. Most of the participants did not have experience of VR or simulation at all, while two development engineers and the mechanics engineer got little experience. Two development engineers got some experience of haptics, while the rest of tests persons had no experience at all.

Before the actual usability test, participants had possibility to practice onto a general assembly demo using haptics and leading with replacing a car pneumatic. Every test person did the welding task, and after the task, filled in a questionnaire form to qualitatively assess the haptic implementation. In the questionnaire, participants' experience level concerning tri-dimensional models, CAD, Virtual Environments, simulation, haptics was self-evaluated. Possible answers were no experience, little experience or professional.

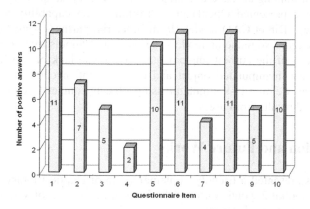

Fig. 5. Number of positive answers for each questionnaire item

The participants answered in questionnaire of 10 dichotomic items in which they have to report whether they agree or not to following statements: 1) Haptic interface is easy to use, 2) user interface is natural, 3) improved 6DOF navigation, 4) easier to use than tri-dimensional-mouse, 5) sense feedback improves interface, 6) force feedback improves interface, 7) haptics improves design work, 8) haptics improves training of work tasks, 9) I could adopt haptics as working tool and 10) positive attitude. The participants had also the possibility to give their free comments about haptics and ideas about haptics applications in industry.

4.2 Experimental Results

Users Experimentation Results. Fig. 5 summarizes all the experimental results. All participants assessed haptic user interface to be easy to use. Project managers and design engineers did not find haptics as natural user interface. Machine engineers and design engineers thought that haptic interface improves 6 DOF navigation in VE. Two development engineers found haptic interface easier to use than tri-dimensional mouse. All, but one project manager, assessed sense feedback of VE to be good and all participants appreciated force feedback. One development engineer, documentation engineer, design engineer and machine engineer assessed haptics to improve their design work. All persons thought that haptics improves work task training in industrial environments. Half of persons thought that they could adopt haptic interface into their work tools. Only one project manager did not have positive attitude against haptic interface.

The participants reported that haptic manipulation was surprisingly easy to learn but required more training in order to be considered its potential as design or training tool. As well, participants underlined that haptics is far away from realism but provide hints about mass of big machine parts, enhancing the objects manipulation and perception within VE.

End-User Development Comments. Performance of the haptics driver was well sufficient for end-user development of training applications. Performance of the driver was suitable for training task and overall stability was very satisfactory.

Haptic engine presented OpenHaptics limitations on capability to process high accuracy models. Direct CAD models from industrial partners were too complicated for the haptic engine, so reducing models' details was compulsory to use such device.

One drawback of the current implementation was the lack of capability to supply feedback between manipulated object and environment, needed in assembly tasks. On the contrary, welding task simulator using objects contact feedback received exceptionally good results from users.

5   Conclusion and Future Works

This paper has presented a friendly implementation of Haptic Library (HLAPI) from OpenHaptics® toolkit 2.0 onto Virtools™ 4.0, resulting in a set of Virtools BBs allowing an easy end-user development.

The developed interface was qualitatively assessed by VTT and industrial partners in a usability test case dealing with a virtual welding task onto a rock crusher during a reassembly task of crusher maintenance.

Experimental results showed usability of the developed haptic interface at user level. Those results supported haptics as a powerful interaction tool in virtual maintenance tasks even if participants felt that haptic force feedback was far away from realistic force models.

Comments by users and end-user developers from VTT suggested further improvements in order to improve end-user development and tri-dimensional haptic interaction in VEs generated with Virtools™ 4.0 and newer versions.

A firstly suggested improvement would consist in enhancing BBs with a scalable haptic bounding box so that haptic workspace would automatically fit to visual workspace. A secondly suggested improvement would provide haptic force feedback between manipulated objects and environment. This improvement would require solving the problem of complex collision detection at a high rate and the use of torque forces, but would result in strongly enhancing manipulation realism. A thirdly suggested improvement would remain in the implementation of a both hands interaction within VE through a set of two Phantom devices. Effectively, objects manipulation using both hands might appear more natural and immersive.

Furthermore end-user development would be strongly improved by implementing a database of most common haptic materials so that setting up materials of Virtools generated Objects would results as easy as selecting them from a collection of already defined OpenHaptics material.

Acknowledgements

This works was partially supported by the Spanish Ministry of Education and Sciences (Project TIN2006-15202-C03-02). Authors would like to thank Prof. Dr. Christian Geiger from the Düsseldorf University of Applied Sciences for sharing his knowledge about the integration of OpenHaptics on Virtools.

References

1. Srinivasan, M.A., Basdogan, C.: Haptics in Virtual Environements: Taxonomy, Research Status, and Challenges. Computers & Graphics 21(4), 393–404 (1997)
2. Leino, S.-P., Helin, K., Lind, S., Viitaniemi, J., Multanen, P., Mäkiranta, A., Lahtinen, J., Nuutinen, P., Heikkilä, J., Martikainen, T.: Virtual engineering and remote operation in design, training and completion of demanding maintenance work tasks in challenging industrial plants (VIRVO) - MASIT 15. In: MASI Programme 2005–2009, Yearbook 2008, Tekes, pp. 111–120 (2008)
3. Leino, S.-P., Lind, S., Poyade, M., Kiviranta, S., Multanen, P., Reyes-Lecuona, A., Mäkiranta, A., Muhammad, A.: Enhanced industrial maintenance work task planning by using virtual engineering and haptic user interfaces. In: HCI International 2009, 13th International Conference on Human-Computer Interaction, Springer, San Diego (2009)
4. Shreiner, D., Woo, M., Neider, J., Davis, T.: The OpenGL® Programming Guide: The Official Guide to Learning OpenGL®, Version 2, 5th edn. Addison-Wesley Professional, Reading (2005)
5. Shreiner, D.: OpenGL® Reference Manual: The Official Reference Document to OpenGL®, Version 1.4, 4th edn. Addison-Wesley Professional, Reading (2004)
6. Martz, P.: OpenSceneGraph Quick Start Guide: A Quick Introduction to the Cross-Platform Open Source Scene Graph API. Skew Matrix software LLC, Louisville (2007)

7. Agil, M., Balbed, M., Ibrahim, N., Yusof, A.M.: Implementation of Virtual Environment using VIRTOOLS. In: 5th Int. Conference on Computer Graphics, Imaging and Visualization, pp. 101–106. IEEE CS Press, Penang (2008)
8. MacLean, K.E., Hayward, V.: Do It yourself Haptics: Part II. IEEE Robotics & Automation Magazine, 104–119 (2008)
9. Dominjon, L., Lécuyer, A., Burkhardt, J.-M., Andrade-Barroso, G., Richir, S.: The Bubble technique: Interacting with Large Virtual Environment Using Haptic Devices with Limited Workspace. In: Proceedings of World Haptics Conference (joint Eurohaptics Conference and Haptics Symposium), pp. 639–640. IEEE CS Press, Pisa (2005)
10. Seth, A., Su, H.-J., Vance, J.M.: SHARP: A system for Haptic Assembly & Realistic Prototyping. In: Proceedings of the DETC 2006, ASME International Design Engineering Technical Conferences and Computers and Information in Engineering Conference, Philadelphia (2006)
11. Fischer, A., Vance, J.M.: Phantom Haptic Device Implemented in a Projection Screen Virtual Environment. In: Proceedings of Workshop on Virtual Environments 2003, ACM International Conferences Proceeding Series, Zurich, vol. 39, pp. 225–229 (2003)
12. Itkowitz, B., Handley, J., Zhu, W.: The OpenHaptics™ Toolkit: A Library for Adding 3D Touch™ Navigation and Haptics to Graphics Applications. In: Proceedings of World Haptics Conference (joint Eurohaptics Conference and Haptics Symposium), pp. 590–591. IEEE CS Press, Pisa (2005)
13. Potts, A.: Phantom-based haptic interaction. In: Proceedings of the Computer Sciences discipline Seminary Conference. CSCI 3901,
http://mrs.umn.edu/~lopezdr/seminar/spring2000/potts.pdf
14. Garrec, P., Friconneau, J.-P., Louvreau, F.: Virtuose 6D: A new Force-Control Master Arm Using Innovative Ball-Screw Actuators. In: 35th International Symposium of Robotics, Paris-Nord-Villepinte (2004)
15. Geiger, C., Klompmaker, F., Stoecklein, J., Fritze, R.: Development of an Augmented Reality Game by Extending a 3D Authoring System. In: Proceedings of the International Conference on Advances in Computer entertainment technology, ACM International Conference Proceeding Series, Salzburg, vol. 203, pp. 230–231 (2007)

A Study of the Attenuation in the Properties of Haptic Devices at the Limit of the Workspace

Jose San Martin

Universidad Rey Juan Carlos, 28933 Mostoles, Spain
jose.sanmartin@urjc.es

Abstract. In the context of the optimization in virtual reality systems involving a haptic device, this paper introduces a correction in the formula that defined the performance of the device near the boundary of its workspace. We introduce too corrections to an index based on the Manipulability which takes in account the frequency with which each zone of the application workspace is visited during the simulation process, in order to help the designer for obtaining the best positioning of the device respect to the virtual environment. We demonstrate the new formula studying three different tasks to be accomplished. Finally we look for this best positioning analyzing not only the displacement but the different orientations we can introduce in the virtual environment in order to take advantage of the best zones of the workspace in terms of Manipulability.

Keywords: Virtual reality, Haptic interface, Manipulability, Mechanical Performance, Optimal designing.

1 Introduction

The design of a virtual environment in occasions involves the integration of different mechanical devices. The system can include manipulators that, depending on the configuration can reach more or less easily the different points of the workspace. We defined Real Workspace (RW) as the volume corresponding to all points the end of a manipulator is capable of reaching (fig. 1). For each point there is calculated the value of the quality of the necessary configuration of the manipulator according to an index based on Manipulability criterion [1], [2]. This volume allows us to identify convenient zones to work [3], [4].

Studying this RW we have determined that as a representation of the performance of a mechanical device, near of the maximum range of the device, the algebraic values obtained in terms of Manipulability must be corrected. The paper presents an attenuation factor that solves this problem.

In previous works [5] we have studied the possibility of obtaining tools to help in the optimal designing of haptic devices. In order to accomplish this we studied the calculus of the best fitting of RW and the task to be realized, represented by a virtual environment.

A design criterion of a system that contains haptic devices is maximizing the efficiency of this relative positioning of the virtual environment inside of all the reachable space. Now we analyze for each relative positioning the possible orientation

R. Shumaker (Ed.): Virtual and Mixed Reality, LNCS 5622, pp. 375–384, 2009.

of the virtual environment (in fact it will involve the physical situation of the device in the Real World). So with this additional study we can improve the performance of the optimal solution.

2 Manipulability

Manipulability of a device is its ability to move freely in all directions into the workspace [6]. The first formulation that allowed a mathematical simple quantification was brought up by Yoshikawa [7]. We use the formulation of Manipulability proposed by Cavusoglu et al. [8]:

$$\mu = \sigma_{min}\,(J_u)/\sigma_{max}\,(J_u). \tag{1}$$

Where:

σ_{min} and σ_{max} are the minimum and maximum singular values of J_u, upper half of the manipulator Jacobian matrix.

In this terms the Manipulability index is a tool for evaluating the quality and the performance in the designing of a manipulator device [9], [10]. So the first step in the study of Manipulability is the analysis of the kinematics of a manipulator, in this case we have used the PHANToM OMNi of SensAble Technologies. From Jacobian we calculate using (1) the Manipulability measure for each point of the surrounding space the device can reach.

2.1 Manipulability Solid

We can extend the map 2D developed in figure 1 by analyzing the behavior of the device in its whole surrounding space. This RW defined in 3D is a volume of the space near of the OMNi that contains all points of the space that the End Effector can reach. If we assign to each of points the Manipulability measure calculated by (1), the resultant volume is the Manipulability Solid associated to the device.

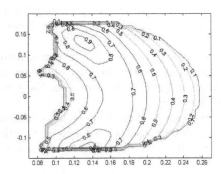

Fig. 1. OMNi device YZ Section from RW. Manipulability index values.

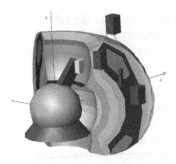

Fig. 2. 3D Map of Manipulability. Detail of the positioning of an AW inside the RW.

This map constitutes one important feature of the OMNi that we can consider to be physically joined the device. We can realize this map as a zone of influence of the device in its environment [5].

Figure 2 shows a representation of the OMNi device together with its 3D map of Manipulability. We use RW in the optimization of the design of Virtual Reality (VR) systems that integrate haptic devices. From whole the RW we select a portion, the virtual environment which we called Application Workspace (AW), in red in fig. 2. We place AW inside RW taking advantage of best zones according to Manipulability index. In the figure we appreciate different options of positioning an AW.

3 Attenuation at the Limit of RW

A problem exists near the limit of the RW (final range of the manipulator) and therefore near singular configurations. We need to characterize the attenuation of the properties in the limit zone of RW in terms of Manipulability, redefining RW. At the bottom of figure 1, at the frontier of RW, the value of Manipulability turns suddenly to zero. That it is not a real effect. To solve this problem, we first proposed an attenuation factor of Manipulability index to apply to the points to less distance than 10mm of the border. In the present paper a new factor is proposed in a more complex way, according to physical phenomenon beside introducing another idea: factor must not depend only on the distance to the border, but also on other points that surround it, being singular or not, definitively, with the shape of the surface at the border.

The value of the attenuation factor is depending, in each cell, of two circumstances: the first one is the distance to the boundary in each one of the three principal directions XYZ. A cell can be near of the boundary only across the X direction or in all directions (as a geographical cape). So we must penalize each one contribution to a very low value of Manipulability. In this case the attenuation is proportional to the distance.

Assuming a discretization in cells of the RW, the second factor that contributes to the attenuation is the feature of the surrounding cells, that is, depending of the geometry of the RW, a cell can have or not, bad neighbors in terms of Manipulability. This "bad neighbors" affects to the performance of the cell. So for each cell, we must study the surrounding cube of cells (26 cells) in terms of distance to the XYZ borders. After this we can recalculate the influence over the cell to study. Note that the new formulation will produce smoother surface of Manipulability than the algebraic one. Peaks are less high and valleys are less deep. We consider that these values are coherent with the conceptual definition of Manipulability.

4 Optimal Positioning

In addition we study the optimal positioning of a haptic device inside of a virtual environment. There are several scientific works aimed to develop methods of optimizing the use of manipulators [12]. Some of these works have used the measure of Manipulability as a criterion of optimization [13], [14], [15]. The design of a virtual reality system requires positioning the AW inside the solid of Manipulability. This intersection affect zones with different values of μ (different colored volumes v_i in fig. 2). In order to solve this problem, we have developed an automatic searching process based on Simulated Annealing [16], [17]. Every step of the algorithm, the system searches randomly a solution near the current one, according to a probability that depends on the current temperature (similar to the metallurgy concept of Annealing). The algorithm allows calculating an optimal positioning of AW that produces a maximum value of the cost function.

Generalizing optimal design we study not only the position but also the orientation of a generic haptic manipulator arm. First we discretize in cells the RW and obtain 3 principal axes of the solid AW. For each positioning of the AW inside the RW, we define a set of rotations (fig. 3) for AW around principal axes. The study is divided in two parts: first one a discretization of the space is defined with a low precision, so the possible positions (and the orientations in each case) to study are much more limited. Both cases we use Simulated Annealing for searching optimal positioning and orientation. The second study has a better precision, but studying only zones we have obtained optimal values of Manipulability index in the previous study.

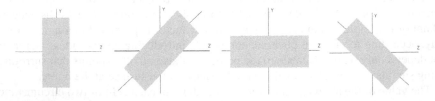

Fig. 3. Different orientations of the AW to study (0-45-90-135 grades) in each positioning

4.1 Frequency Map

Studying the problem of the optimal positioning we have seen that our application has zones of AW which are more used than others. These are, for instance in a simulation, the specific areas where the intervention is effectuated. It is desirable that the haptic device provides its best performance in the most visited zones.

So we propose, for the cases in which the use of the workspace is not homogeneous, to perform an additional analysis taking in account this heterogeneity. It involves the study of the End Effector movement across the AW during the simulation process. As a result of the trace of the navigation across the virtual environment, we can obtain data referred to the frequency each single cell of the AW is visited (f_{ijk}). With this value we can create a map of frequency for each task the device has to accomplish.

The optimal positioning is characterized by Useful Manipulability $\hat{\mu}_V$, considering a tri-dimensional grid of cells (i, j, k) of RW:

$$\hat{\mu}_v = \sum_{ijk} \mu_{vijk} \cdot f_{ijk} \tag{2}$$

Where:
  $\mu_{v\,ijk}$ volumetric average manipulability of a cell. We need to study the distribution of Manipulability inside of the cell and calculate an average value.
  f_{ijk} frequency of visits sampled during a task in each cell.

Note that if the size of cells (i,j,k) is small enough we can consider that Manipulability is constant and we can use the more simple formula:

$$\hat{\mu}_v = \sum_{ijk} \mu_{ijk} \cdot f_{ijk} \tag{3}$$

Where:
  μ_{ijk} is the Manipulability of a cell calculated by (1).
  With this criterion the best positioning of the OMNi in terms of frequency of use will produce maximum value of $\hat{\mu}_V$, which is the cost function in the Simulated Annealing process.

5 Results

The solution of the first proposed problem, the attenuation of the RW-Manipulability map near the frontier is formulated. Note that figure 4 represents only the part of the plane X=0 that corresponds with the real workspace. So we can see the attenuation factor at frontier zone (portion of the volume of thickness 10mm) in this figure. Contrasting fig. 4 and previous one without attenuation, figure 1, results that the Manipulability in the boundary limits falls smoothly and now the maximum, that it was at the border line, is clearly displaced inside the workspace.

5.1 Positioning and Orientation of the Virtual Environment

We use defined measures for Optimal designing to calculate the grade of suitability of a manipulator in a real application. As an example we use a previously developed simulation that consists of the positioning-orientation of an OMNi device used as a component of the mechanical platform of a Minimal Invasive Surgery Trainer [12]. The virtual environment is the internal cavity of a human shoulder (Figure 5).

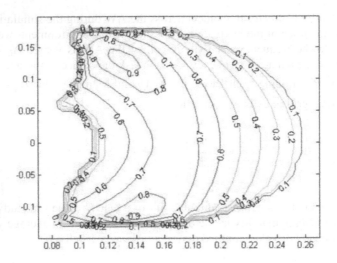

Fig. 4. OMNi device YZ Section from RW. Manipulability index including frontier-attenuation effect.

In order to introduce the study of the orientation of a generic haptic manipulator arm in a positioning, and taking in account the computational cost, the study is divided in two resolution parts. Both cases we use Simulated Annealing for searching optimal positioning and orientation.

In the first study we have used a resolution of 8mm of the cell side, with only 50000 cells to study. Using the above defined AW we calculate the best only-positioning of the AW inside the RW using (2). We obtain a value of cost function:

$$\hat{\mu}_V = 0.8521 \text{ as optimal solution.} \tag{4}$$

Now we remake the problem, with the same resolution, but including, for each possible positioning, 4 possible orientations, according to 0 grades (only positioning), 45, 90 and 135 grades of inclination (in fact other inclinations to consider are symmetrical to these). We study this cases for each axis XYZ. As a result we obtain:

$$\hat{\mu}_V = 0.8725 \text{ as optimal solution.} \tag{5}$$

So there is an option of the positioning-orientation (in the optimal orientation was 45 grades) that improves the only positioning study. The improvement is a very low percentage of 2.34%.

The second study has a better precision, cells of 2mm-side. In this case we must study near 2 million cells. The computational cost of this analysis is high so we

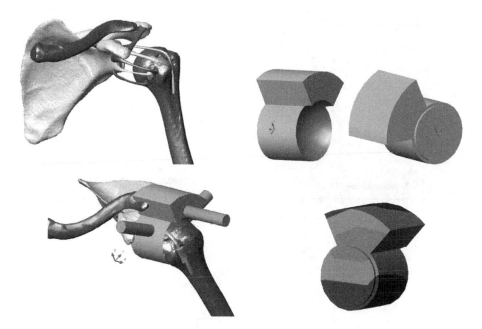

Fig. 5. Study of μv in a real implementation. 5-1 Anatomical model. 5-2 Two views of AW. 5-3 Shoulder view plus AW. Entry portals in green. 5-4 AW intersection with RW as the example indicated in figure 2.

decide to simplify the study: we consider only zones we have obtained good values of Manipulability index in the low resolution study. Again we introduce the three possible orientations in each XYZ axis. As a result of using (3) we obtain:

$$\hat{\mu}_V = 0.8838 \text{ as optimal solution.} \tag{6}$$

In this case the improvement is only of 1.28%.

5.2 Cases of Study: Frequency Map

In order to study the effect of realizing different tasks for the same haptic device in the same virtual environment, we select three tasks: task 1 is a simulation of a minimal invasive surgery, a shoulder arthroscopy (fig. 6-1) where most part of the work is most divided in two different zones (subacromial and glenohumeral). According to the trace of the movements of a surgeon in an intervention we have create the Frequency map of the figure. Note that in task 1 the navigation is located in two well-defined sectors.

The second task is a simulation of the movement of a probe-camera in the interior of a boiler in a operation searching for fissures. In this case most part of the navigation is in the frontier zone although all the movements pass through the center zone (fig. 6-2). The third task is a fictional task of the working of a machine tool. This task involves changing the tool, welding, coupling of parts, etc. Estimating the navigation across the virtual environment we can define its frequency map (fig. 6-3).

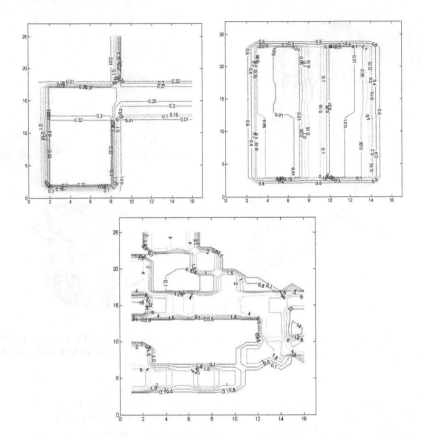

Fig. 6. Frequency map of tasks 1, 2 and 3 in the same Virtual Environment

So depending on the task, the optimal designing process defined previously concludes that haptic device must be placed in a different position of CG and orientation regard to principal axes in degrees:

Task 1. $\hat{\mu}_V$ =0.8042, AW at position XYZ (0.05, 0.13, 0.13).

Task 2. $\hat{\mu}_V$ =0.7911, AW at position XYZ (0.01, 0.13, 0.12).

Task 3. $\hat{\mu}_V$ =0.7717, AW at position XYZ (-0.02, 0.13, 0.115).

6 Conclusions

The definition of an attenuation factor solves the problem in the boundary of the current algebraic formulation and puts in hands of mechanical engineers a new tool to measure the performance of a manipulator taking in account the actual characteristics of the mechanical implementation.

In the generalization of the process of obtaining the optimal design the high resolution study indicate that the improvement of the global value of Manipulability index is small from preliminary study. We have defined an error value in percent when using the first test instead of the second. Our conclusion is that in most part of applications exists only a minimum error, and a search of optimal positioning with high resolution but without orientation study can be an acceptable search. We recommend the low resolution positioning-orientation option in cases where the RW is much bigger than virtual environment-AW.

Finally, we have demonstrated that the most important factor in order to select a haptic device to cope with a task is the kind of task to be done. It is obvious that the size of the AW defines a size of device in terms of a necessary RW, but through three examples we have seen that a same device in a same virtual environment has very different performance.

Acknowledgements

I would like to thank the anonymous reviewers for their helpful comments and to Gracian Trivino and the rest of the GMRV group at Universidad Rey Juan Carlos. This work was funded in part by the URJC - Comunidad de Madrid project CCG08-URJC/DPI-3647 and by the Spanish Ministry of Education and Science (grant TIN2007-67188).

References

1. Yoshikawa, T.: Foundations of Robotics: Analysis and Control. MIT Press, Cambridge (1990)
2. Yoshikawa, T.: Manipulability of Robotic Mechanisms. The International Journal of Robotics research (1985)
3. San Martin, J., Trivino, G.: Measurement of Suitability of a Haptic Device in a Virtual Reality System. In: Proc. 2nd International Conference on Virtual Reality HCII 2007 (July 2007)
4. Pham, H.H., Chen, I.-M.: Optimal Synthesis for Workspace and Manipulability of Parallel Flexure Mechanism. In: Proceeding of the 11th World Congress in Mechanism and Machine Science, Tianjin, China, August 18-21 (2003)
5. San Martin, J., Trivino, G.: Mechanical Design of a Minimal Invasive Surgery Trainer Using the Manipulability as Measure of Optimization. In: IEEE International Conference on Mechatronics ICM 2007, Kumamoto, Japan (May 2007)
6. Murray, R.M., Li, Z., Sastry, S.S.: A mathematical introduction to robotic manipulation. CRC Press, Inc., Boca Raton (1994)
7. Yoshikawa, T.: Manipulability and redundancy control of robotic mechanisms. In: Proceedings of IEEE International Conference on Robotics and Automation, March 1985, vol. 2, pp. 1004–1009 (1985)
8. Cavusoglu, M.C., Feygin, D., Tendick, F.: A Critical Study of the Mechanical and Electrical Properties of the PHANToM Haptic Interface and Improvements for High Performance Control. Teleoperators and Virtual Environments 11(6), 555–568 (2002)
9. Yamamoto, Y., Yun, X.: Unified analysis on mobility and manipulability of mobilemanipulators. In: Proceedings. 1999 IEEE International Conference on Robotics and Automation, Detroit, vol. 2, pp. 1200–1206 (1999)

10. Yokokohji, Y., Yoshikawa, T.: Guide of master arms considering operator dynamics. Journal of dynamic systems, measurement, and control 115(2A), 253–260 (1993)
11. Sobh, T.M., Toundykov, D.Y.: Optimizing the tasks at hand (robotic manipulators). Robotics & Automation Magazine 11(2), 78–85 (2004)
12. Alqasemi, R.M., McCaffrey, E.J., Edwards, K.D., Dubey, R.V.: Analysis, evaluation and development of wheelchair-mounted robotic arms. In: 9th International Conference on Rehabilitation Robotics, ICORR 2005, June 28-July 1, 2005, pp. 469–472 (2005)
13. Guilamo, L., Kuffner, J., Nishiwaki, K., Kagami, S.: Manipulability optimization for trajectory generation. In: Proceedings 2006 IEEE International Conference on Robotics and Automation, ICRA 2006, May 15-19, 2006, pp. 2017–2022 (2006)
14. Masuda, T., Fujiwara, M., Kato, N., Arai, T.: Mechanism Configuration Evaluation of a Linear-Actuated Parallel Mechanism Using Manipulability. In: Proceedings of the 2002 IEEE International Conference on Robotics 8 Automation, Washington, DC (May 2002)
15. Bayle, B., Fourquet, J.-Y., Renaud, M.: Manipulability of Wheeled Mobile Manipulators: Application to Motion Generation. The International Journal of Robotics Research 22(7-8), 565–581 (2003)
16. Kirkpatrick, S., Gelatt Jr., C.D., Vecchi, M.P.: Optimization by Simulated Annealing. Science (220), 671–680 (May 13, 1983)
17. Aragon, C.R., Johnson, D.S., McGeoch, L.A., Shevon, C.: Optimization by Simulated Annealing: An Experimental Evaluation; Part II, Graph Coloring and Number Partitioning. Operations Research 39(3), 378–406 (1991)

A Virtual Button with Tactile Feedback Using Ultrasonic Vibration

Kaoru Tashiro[1], Yuta Shiokawa[2], Tomotake Aono[3], and Takashi Maeno[2]

[1] Keio University, Graduate School of Integrated Design Engineering
Hiyoshi 3-14-1, Kohoku, Yokohama, Kanagawa, 223-8522, Japan
fr041303@a3.keio.jp
[2] Keio University, Graduate School of System Design and Management, Japan
[3] Kyocera Corporation, 1st Section 1st Department Yokohama R&D Center, Japan

Abstract. A virtual button with tactile feedback is realized by use of ultrasonic vibration with amplitude of a few micrometers. Button-like click feeling is displayed by recreating rapid change in reaction force arising from buckling of a mechanical push button utilizing squeeze film effect. First, click feeling display system was constructed based on the principle of perceiving click feeling when pushing a mechanical button. In the system, stimulation are applied to the operators at both buckling and restitution point. Then, by conducting several sensory evaluation experiments, the optimum parameters of the ultrasonic vibration was determined to display button-like click feeling. Finally, by conducting usability test, it was verified that the usability of the virtual button was equivalent to that of a mechanical button.

1 Introduction

With the diffusion of touchscreens, a number of attempts to display tactile information on touchscreens have been conducted. Establishment of the method to display click feeling to the touchscreen will lead to higher operation performance and decrease of unconscious incorrect input. As substitutes of tactile feedback, several methods are proposed, including displaying visual or auditory information such as screen effects and confirmation sound. However, it requires time and effort to recognize the visual information displayed on the screen. Even worse, operator's own finger disturbs seeing the screen. Moreover, as confirmation sounds are heard by people around, it is sometimes difficult to be used in public areas. Hence, displaying tactile information is necessary as an operating feedback for touchscreens. Past studies of tactile feedback for touchscreens include Touch Engine having function to vibrate the back side of the device [1] and Tactile Panel with function to display vibration on its touchscreen [2]. These touchscreens can generate various vibrations to operator's finger touching the touchscreen. The former utilizes piezoceramic bending motor and the latter utilizes conductivity type speaker as an actuator. Products having the same function as Touch Engine are recently being released. These products have minimum feedback performance. However, only simple monotonous vibration is used as feedback. Moreover, high voltage was necessary to recreate button stroke of approximately 100 μm using vibration. Meanwhile, tactile display using ultrasonic

R. Shumaker (Ed.): Virtual and Mixed Reality, LNCS 5622, pp. 385–393, 2009.

vibration has been attracting attention for creating large stimulation with low vibration amplitude because of squeeze film effect. We have confirmed that button-like click feeling can be displayed by applying ultrasonic vibration with appropriate amplitude and vibrating time in response to touch motion of an operator [5]. Hence, by creating tactile feedback to touchscreens using ultrasonic vibration, realistic click feeling can be displayed with amplitude of only a few micrometers.

In this study, we develop a virtual button with tactile feedback by utilizing ultrasonic vibration for displaying click feeling. In this study, click feeling is defined as the tactile sensation perceived when pushing a mechanical button such as PC mouse. By utilizing squeeze film effect due to ultrasonic vibration, we recreate buckling feeling that arises when mechanical buttons are being pushed at a certain suppress strength. Then, we verify the usability of the virtual button by conducting sensory evaluation experiments.

2 Principle of Displaying Click Feeling

In this chapter, we explain about the method for displaying click feeling using ultrasonic vibration. First, in 3.1, we explain about principle and characteristics of a mechanical push button. Then, in 3.2, we explain about the principle of perceiving click feeling when applying ultrasonic vibration to human finger pad in response to human touch motion.

2.1 Principle of Perceiving Click Feeling

Click feeling of a mechanical button is perceived when the dome structure of spring component buckles and restitutes as shown in Figure 1 [3]. Figure 2 (a) is a reaction force–stroke length (F-S) curve showing the relationship between reaction force and stroke length changes occurred in normal direction when a mechanical button is pushed or released vertically. In this study, F_b and F_r are defined as the force when buckling starts while pushing and the force when rapid restitution starts while releasing the button, respectively. As shown in Figure 2 (a), in the early stage of pushing phase, force and stroke are positively correlated. As the pushing force reach F_b, relationship between force and stroke turns to be negatively correlated.

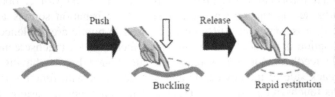

Fig. 1. Buckling and restitution of dome when pushing Button

Then, the relationship turns back to be positively correlated as the button is fully pushed because the whole button is deformed. In the releasing phase, the F-S curve follows the similar trajectory to that of pushing phase. When the pushing force comes

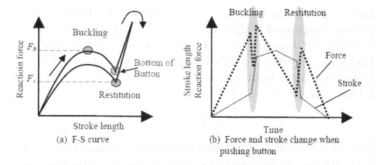

Fig. 2. Image of F-S curve and time scale change of F-S characteristic of push button

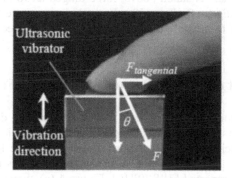

Fig. 3. Finger contact area of ultrasonic vibrator

down to F_r, the restitution force arises upward. Figure 2 (b) shows the rough image of time change in force and stroke of a general button pushing motion. As shown in Figure 2 (b), force and stroke change rapidly at buckling and restitution point. It is considered that click feeling is perceived due to the rapid change in force and stroke [5]. We have confirmed that the difference of buckling force was well distinguished whereas the difference in stroke length was difficult to be distinguished [4]. Hence, buckling force is an important factor for displaying click feeling whereas stroke length is not required to be recreated accurately.

2.2 Principle of Displaying Click Feeling Using Ultrasonic Vibration

In this study, click feeling is displayed by use of squeeze film effect. Squeeze film effect is phenomenon that occurs when two objects having sufficient area compared to the distance approach rapidly. When the fingertip is placed on a rapidly vibrating plate, the squeeze film is generated by the overpressure between the epidermal ridges [6]. It is known that coefficient of friction decreases due to squeeze film effect. In the case of this study, the displaying area of ultrasonic vibrator is touched as shown in Figure 3. In the proposed method, rapid change in force due to buckling of a mechanical button is recreated by temporary decreasing the coefficient of friction between operator's finger pad and displaying area of the ultrasonic vibrator.

Principle of perceiving click feeling is as follows: As shown in figure 3, it is assumed that the direction of pushing force F is θ in angle to normal direction when the operator pushes the displaying area. Therefore, normal and tangential forces applied by the operator to the vibrator are $F\cos\theta$ and $F\sin\theta$, respectively. Where coefficient of static friction between finger pad and the vibrator surface is μ, friction force is $\mu F\cos\theta$. Hence, finger slips when

$$\mu < |\tan\theta| \tag{1}$$

is satisfied $\tan\theta$ in pushing action was measured to be between -0.1 and 0.1. When finger slips, θ increases because of fingertip movement, resulting in increase of the right-hand value of (1). Therefore, resisting force tangential to human finger pad and normal force decrease. As stated above, force tangential to human finger pad can be decreased by changing coefficient of friction utilizing squeeze film effect. In this way, the rapid change in force and stroke due to buckling of mechanical buttons can be recreated.

3 Development of Virtual Button with Tactile Feedback

In this study, ultrasonic vibrator is used as the actuator for displaying click feeling. Ultrasonic vibrator is an actuator that consists of metal elastic body and piezoelectric device. It is characterized by high response, high generative force, minute amplitude control and quietness. Numbers of studies displaying various texture using ultrasonic vibration have been reported [7][8][9][10]. Figure 4 (a) shows the overall view of the push button display system. As an ultrasonic vibrator, the Langevin-type ultrasonic vibrator was used in the present study. Figure 4 (b) shows the detail of the vibrator. Driving frequency is close to 28.2 kHz, which is the natural frequency of primary longitudinal vibration mode. In this case, the vibrator vibrates in the direction as shown in Figure 4 (b) to create maximum amplitude of 20 μm. As shown in Figure 4 (a), upper side of the vibrator having flat metal surface is used as tactile displaying area.

(a) Overall view of push button display

(b) Ultrasonic vibrator

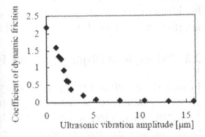

Fig. 4. Push button display

Fig. 5. Relationship between vibration amplitude and coefficient of dynamic friction

Therefore, the vibration is normal to human finger pad. In this case, squeeze film effect occurs between finger and displaying area. Figure 5 shows relationship between amplitude of ultrasonic vibration and coefficient of dynamic friction of the vibrator surface obtained by tracing tactile displaying area of the vibrator with finger pad. The coefficient of dynamic friction was calculated by measuring the tangential force when tracing on the excited vibrator with approximately 1 N of normal force. As shown in Figure 5, coefficient of dynamic friction of the vibrator surface is approximately 2.2 and it decreases to less than 0.5 when ultrasonic vibration with amplitude of 2.5 μm is excited. The displaying area measures 30 mm in width and 15 mm in depth. Operator pushes the displaying area like pushing a real button. By measuring strain of metal plates placed under the ultrasonic vibrator using strain gauge, normal force applied by operator to the vibrator can be measured, as shown in Figure 4 (a). In addition, as shown in Figure 4 (b), pick up sensor is placed in the vibrator. Voltage of sensor output is proportional to the vibration amplitude. Hence, monitoring and control of vibration amplitude is available by use of the sensor output. In this system, intended vibration amplitude can be obtained in spite of an operator's suppress strength by the control system built using FPGA (Field Programmable Gate Array) [11]. It is confirmed that vibration amplitude can be controlled with an uncertainty of 1 % using the system when load is under 10 N.

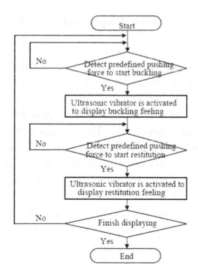

Fig. 6. Flow of the push button display system

One of the characteristics of our system is that operator's pushing force is used as the trigger for starting vibration. In most of the past studies of click feeling display [1][2], tactile feedbacks were displayed after configured time delay from touching the screen. The problem of this control method is that it has no robustness against various applications of buttons or characteristics of the operators because the same feedbacks are displayed in spite of various pushing motion. Moreover, it is difficult to display click feeling perceived when releasing a button using this control method because the stimulation was applied according to the configured time delay. In our system, we display more button-like click feeling compared to the past studies by displaying both pushing and releasing feeling of click utilizing the operator's pushing force information measured in real-time. Figure 6 shows the flow of the click feeling display system. In the system, ultrasonic vibration whose amplitude and vibrating time are configured in advance is excited when pushing force measured in real-time reaches the buckling load and restitution load, respectively. First, output obtained by strain gauge is converted to force in PC with control cycle of 1 KHz. When measured force reaches to predefined value, AC voltage with frequency of 28.2 kHz is applied to the vibrator via FPGA, oscillator and amplifier. Amplitude of ultrasonic vibration decayed by the operator's suppress strength measured by pick up sensor is fed back to FPGA and compensated to be intended amplitude. The response velocity of ultrasonic vibrator to excite intended vibration amplitude after activating signal is approximately 0.6 mm/s. Vibration amplitude, time and trigger force of both buckling and restitution can be set independently.

4 Verification

4.1 Survey of Parameter Value for Displaying Click Feeling

A simple sensory evaluation experiment was conducted to survey the appropriate value of vibration parameters for displaying click feeling. The task for examinees were to evaluate existence or non-existence of click feeling displayed using the constructed system on a 5-point scale, from 1 (do not perceive click feeling at all) to 5 (clearly perceive click feeling), when vibration amplitude, time and buckling load F_b of the system were changed, respectively. The averages of each evaluation value were calculated. Examinees were six males in their twenties. Sin curve with frequency of 28.2 kHz was utilized as the waveform of the vibration. Vibration amplitude and time of release click feeling were set to the same value as those of push click feeling. Restitution load F_r was set to 0.1 N less than buckling load F_b. Parameters not surveyed, for example vibration time and trigger force when surveying vibration amplitude, were set to intermediate value of surveying range of each parameter.

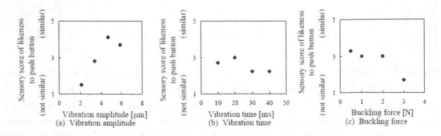

Fig. 7. Relationship of sensory evaluation score and changeable parameter

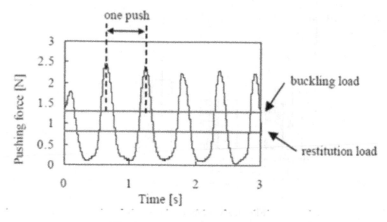

Fig. 8. Average of pushing force

Figure 7 (a), (b) and (c) show the results of the experiments to survey vibration amplitude, time and trigger force, respectively. As shown in Figure 7, click feeling was perceived when vibration amplitude was between 4 and 6 μm. Click feeling became more similar to real buttons when vibration time was between 50 and 100 ms and trigger force was between 0.5 and 2.0 N, respectively, compared to other values. Hence, click feeling more similar to real buttons can be displayed by combining the largest evaluated values of each parameter.

4.2 Usability Test

Experiment was conducted to verify the usability of the virtual button with tactile feedback. Examinees were asked to push two types of virtual button, with tactile feedback and without tactile feedback, 30 times, respectively. Each time examinees pushed the button normally, number shown in console increased so that examinees could count the number of pushes. Changes of pushing force of each examinee were measured throughout each test. The changes of values were compared to those measured when pushing a real mechanical button at the same experimental condition. Amplitude and vibrating time of ultrasonic vibration were set 4.7 μm and 20 ms, respectively, based on the result of previous section. Buckling and restitution load of the virtual button were set 1.3 N and 0.8 N, respectively, to coordinate with the mechanical button used for comparison. The task was conducted in two different conditions for each button. First, examinees were asked to push each button at a speed of two times per second, and second, four times per second. Examinees had at most 1 minute to practice pushing the button with correct rhythm before each task using metronome. Buttons were pushed with the most suitable way for each examinee. Examinees were ten males and females in their twenties, visual and auditory information masked. Considering difference between learning level, the tasks were conducted in different order among the examinees.

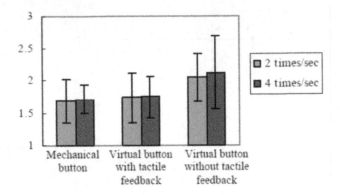

Fig. 9. Average of pushing force

Figure 9 shows an example of the change in pushing force of an examinee. One push was defined as the period between the point when pushing force exceeds the buckling load 1.3 N and fall below restitution load 0.8 N, as shown in Figure 9. Averages of twenty peak-to-peak values of the change in pushing force, from fifth to twenty-fifth push, were evaluated. Figure 10 shows the averages and standard deviations of the peak-to-peak values of the change in pushing force. From Figure 10, we can say that examinees applied larger force in virtual button without tactile feedback compared to other two buttons. By conducting one sided test, it was found that the difference of the averages between virtual button with tactile feedback and without tactile feedback was significant, whereas the difference of the averages between virtual button with tactile feedback and the real mechanical button was not significant, in 95% confidence interval. Moreover, by conducting interview, all examinees said that pushing the virtual button with tactile feedback was as easy as pushing the mechanical button. Hence, we can conclude that the virtual button with tactile feedback using ultrasonic vibration has similar usability as a real mechanical button.

5 Conclusion

We developed a virtual button with click feeling similar to real buttons by use of ultrasonic vibration with amplitude of a few micrometers. First, we constructed click feeling display system based on the principle of perceiving click feeling when pushing a mechanical button. The rapid change in force arising from buckling and restitution of mechanical buttons was recreated by utilizing decrease in friction due to squeeze film effect. In addition, by measuring operator's pushing force and utilizing it as the trigger for starting vibration, we enabled to display click feeling for both pushing and releasing. Then, simple sensory evaluation experiments were conducted to determine the appropriate value of vibration parameters for displaying click feeling. Finally, usability of the virtual button was verified. As a result, the usability of the virtual button was nearly equivalent to that of a real button. Precise examination for optimization of parameters and imitation of buttons is the challenge for the future.

References

1. Poupyrev, I., Maruyama, S., Rekimoto, J.: Ambient touch: designing tactile interfaces for handheld devices. In: Proceedings of the 15th annual ACM symposium on User interface software and technology, pp. 51–60 (2002)
2. Akabane, A., Murayama, J., Yamaguchi, T., Teranishi, N., Sato, M.: Examination on Signal Generating the Sensation of Depressing for a Touch Panel with a Tactile. Journal of Human Interface (in Japanese) 8(4), 591–598 (2006)
3. Ninomiya, K., Ymaji, T., Sakiyama, F., Kaizu, M., Yokoyama, T.: Metal Dome Sheet for Mobile Phones. Fujikura Technical Review (in Japanese) (99), 27–31 (2000)
4. Fujimoto, T.: Quantification and improvement of the touch in switch operation. Statistical Quality Control (in Japanese) 36, 1837–1843 (1985) (extra edn.)
5. Tashiro, K., Shiokawa, Y., Aono, T., Maeno, T.: Realization of Button Click Feeling by use of Ultrasonic Vibration and Force Feedback. In: World Haptics 2009 (in press)
6. Biet, M., Giraud, F., Lemaire-Semail, B.: Squeeze Film Effect for the Design of an Ultrasonic Tactile Plate. IEEE Transactions on Ultrasonics, Ferroelectrics, and Frequency Control 54(12), 2678–2688 (2007)
7. Watanabe, T., Fukui, S.: A Method for Controlling Tactile Sensation of Surface Roughness Using Ultrasonic Vibration. In: Proceedings of IEEE International Conference on Robotics and Automation, vol. 1, pp. 1134–1139 (1995)
8. Biet, M., Giraud, F., Lemaire-Semail, B.: New Tactile Devices using Piezoelectric Actuators. In: Proc. 10th International Conference on New Actuators, Germany, pp. 989–992 (2006)
9. Winfield, L., Glassmire, J., Edward Colgate, J., Peshkin, M.: T-PaD: Tactile Pattern Display through Variable Friction Reduction. In: World Haptics 2007, Japan, pp. 421–426 (2007)
10. Shiokawa, Y., Tazo, A., Konyo, M., Maeno, T.: Hybrid Display of Realistic Tactile Sense using Ultrasonic Vibrator and Force Display. In: IEEE/RSJ International Conference of Intelligent Robots and Systems, pp. 3008–3013 (2008)
11. Ogahara, Y., Maeno, T.: Torque Control of Traveling-Wave-Type Ultrasonic Motors using the Friction Contact Model. Transactions of the Japan Society of Mechanical Engineers, Series C 72(714), 441–448 (2006)

Enhancing Haptic Rendering through Predictive Collision Detection

Athanasios Vogiannou[1,2], Konstantinos Moustakas[2], Dimitrios Tzovaras[2], and Michael G. Strintzis[1,2]

[1] Electrical & Computer Engineering Department, Aristotle University of Thessaloniki, 54006 Thessaloniki, Greece
[2] Informatics and Telematics Institute, Centre for Research and Technology Hellas, P.O. Box 361, 57001, Thermi-Thessaloniki, Greece
{tvog,moustak,tzovaras,michael}@iti.gr

Abstract. This paper presents an efficient collision detection method for interactive haptic simulations of virtual environments that consist of both static and moving objects. The proposed method is based on a novel algorithm for predicting the time of proximity between a pair objects and the appropriate employment of the calculated prediction in a complex virtual scene with multiple objects. The user is able to interact with the virtual objects and receive real-time haptic feedback using the PHANToM Desktop haptic device, while the visual results are shown in the screen display. Experimental results demonstrate the efficiency and the reliability of the presented approach compared to state-of-the-art spatial subdivisions methods, especially for haptic rendering, where collision detection and response is a procedure of critical importance.

Keywords: collision detection and prediction, haptic interaction.

1 Introduction

The goal of Virtual Reality is the immersion of the user into a virtual environment by providing artificial input to its interaction sensors, for example the eyes, the ears and the hands. While the visual inputs are the most important factors in human-computer interaction, virtual reality applications will remain far from being realistic without providing to the user the sense of touch. The use of haptics augments the standard visual interface by offering to the user an alternative way of interaction with the components of the virtual environment. Haptic rendering provides a realistic human-computer interface for the manipulation of virtual objects, improving this way the level of immersion of the user into the virtual world. However, haptic interaction requires the integration of efficient modules for the dynamic generation of contact and friction information.

Collision detection is a major component of dynamic simulations responsible for enhancing interaction and realistic behavior between the virtual objects. Extended research has been performed in the area since the first applications of virtual reality emerged and excellent surveys of prior work can be found in [1], [2], [3] and [4].

The majority of the previous work in collision detection emphasizes on queries between a pair of objects. The dominant approach in this field is Bounding Volume

R. Shumaker (Ed.): Virtual and Mixed Reality, LNCS 5622, pp. 394–402, 2009.
© Springer-Verlag Berlin Heidelberg 2009

Hierarchies (BVH). The hierarchy consists of primitive objects like spheres [5], AABBs [6], OOBs [7] or discrete orientation polytopes [8]. The main characteristic of bounding volumes is the existence of efficient methods to test for intersection between them. If an intersection is detected in the root of the BVH tree, the algorithm proceeds by checking the volumes in the children of the root and so on, until the leaf nodes are reached and the accurate points of collision are found.

The previous methods are widely used for testing pairs of objects. However, as virtual environments become larger, and include more complex objects, problems arise by the high computational cost of testing each pair. In such scenes it is inefficient to employ the brute force approach of testing all possible pairs of objects because most of the time, the objects are far from each other. Many approaches have been introduced to overcome this difficulty by reducing the pairwise collision tests in large complicated 3D scenes. The most known are the Sweep and Prune technique [9, 10] and Space Partitioning methods [11, 12, 13, 14]. The Sweep and Prune technique can be used to maintain the objects of the scene in some sort of spatial ordering and therefore narrow down testing pairs to objects in adjacent positions of the sorted data structure. Space Partitioning methods divide space into regions and reduce testing in objects of the same region. The most notable of them is the Binary Space Partioning Hierarchy Tree [12], [13].

In this paper we present a new collision detection method for virtual environments containing a significant number of static and moving objects. The proposed method is based on a novel algorithm for predicting the time of proximity between a pair objects. Prediction is particularly useful in interactive haptic applications since with the appropriate object organization, the computational cost of collision detection can be dramatically reduced. In the rest of the text, the general aspects of the proposed framework are presented in section 2 while the implementation details of the approximate collision prediction algorithm are given in section 3. Further details about the interactive haptic rendering are presented in section 4 and the experimental results demonstrating the efficiency of the presented approach are given in section 5.

2   Collision Detection Framework

Broad/narrow phase methods have been widely used for collision detection between a large number of objects [16, 11]. In such systems, the broad phase is responsible for quickly eliminating tests between objects that are impossible to collide due to their distant positions [12, 13, 16], while the narrow phase performs collision tests in pairs of objects using accurate algorithms like in [6], [7] and [8]. From an abstract point of view, the two phases can be seen as ``black boxes". The objects of the scene are given as input to the broad phase. The produced output contains all the pairs of objects to be further checked for collision, i.e. the broad phase cannot decide that there is no collision for them. These pairs are the input of the narrow phase which returns the accurate collisions for every object in the scene.

In the broad phase of the proposed framework, collision prediction is employed in order to efficiently reduce the tested object pairs. The time value of possible collision for pairs of objects is estimated in continuous time, using a conservative prediction of the trajectories of the objects. The purpose of the prediction is to approximately determine the time when the two objects will be in close proximity. Further collision tests are not executed in every frame but only in the time intervals where the objects are close to each other. Proximity is explicitly defined using the bounding spheres of each object. When the spheres overlap, the objects are considered to be close to each other. Otherwise the objects are considered to be far enough to be excluded from the narrow phase tests.

The narrow phase follows tests each pair for collision using an external algorithm. By external we mean that it is not a structural part of the framework. If no collision is found for a testing pair, the objects of this pair remain in the narrow, until the respective bounding spheres stop overlapping. This feature differentiates the proposed broad/narrow phase approach from the usual one, as both phases function independently on the objects and not with the classical sequential method. Figure 1 displays the proposed approach for the broad/narrow phase.

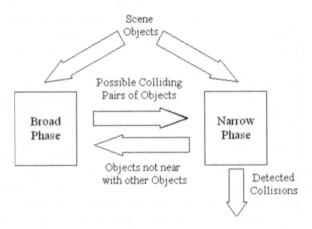

Fig. 1. The flow control diagram of the objects in the proposed framework

3   Approximate Collision Prediction

Prediction is performed utilizing the knowledge of the object's motion and a simple geometric representation of each object that consists of bounding spheres. Spheres are preferred to other bounding volumes, because a simple distance check is enough to determine if a point lies in the interior or the exterior of the sphere, while being also rotation invariant. Furthermore, the registration of the Phantom haptic device is quite straightforward using a sphere at the probe position.

In general, the objects are separated in Interactive Objects (IO) and Environment Objects (EO). IOs are considered to be controlled by the user while EOs are objects that "belong" entirely to the virtual environment. The substantial difference between them is that the motion of IOs cannot be defined accurately, while for the EOs it is well known. In common VR applications with haptic rendering there is only one IO in the scene, such as the Phantom probe. Both types of objects are considered to translate along a second degree curve for a specific time interval. Although this assumption may seem restrictive, the actual motion of the object is not restricted, since the prediction algorithm needs only a second degree estimation of the real path, even if it is not accurate. The Least Squares Curve Fitting method [15] can be used to calculate an approximation based on points from the real path.

We further extend this approach and instead of using just a specified path, a set of points around this path is considered to represent all the possible positions that the object could lie at a specified time. These points belong to the interior of an area defined by an absolute deviation from the predicted path. The deviation extends to all directions, so that the possible positions of the object form a spherical volume. The center of this sphere moves along the estimated curve while the radius depends on the deviation. A 2D projection of the resulting path is shown in Figure 2 where s(t) is the estimated path and R(t) the deviation.

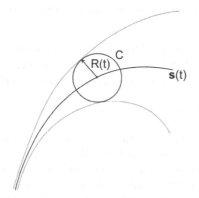

Fig. 2. Estimated path with deviation. The deviation R(t) extends the predicted path s(t) in all directions. All points inside C indicate a possible position of the object at time t.

R(t) is considered a simple second degree polynomial such as $R(t) = a + bt + ct^2$. Deviation is also considered positive and monotonically increasing because as time passes, is more probable that the object will diverge from the path. Hence, the deviation model should "tolerate" this change in order to have a valid estimated path for an acceptable time interval.

3.1 Estimation of Proximity

The bounding sphere of an object combined with the estimated path and the deviation, result in a moving bounding volume which increases with time, as shown in Figure 3, where S is the bounding sphere of the object and S´(t) is the extended moving bounding volume. The following analysis involves two objects with arbitrary deviation in their movement. It is then trivial to extend to the specific cases (EO-EO, IO-IO, EO-IO).

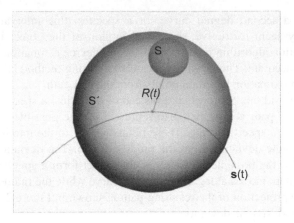

Fig. 3. Moving bounding volume. As the bounding sphere S of the object moves along the estimated path s(t), the deviation R(t) forms a new extended bounding volume S′(t).

Let $s_1(t)$ be the path, $R_1(t)$ the deviation and r_1 the radius of the bounding sphere of the first object and $s_2(t)$, $R_2(t)$ and r_2 for the second object respectively. The time of collision between the moving bounding spheres can be calculated by solving

$$|s_1(t) - s_2(t)| \le R_1(t) + R_2(t) + r .$$ (1)

for min(t > 0), where $r = r_1 + r_2$. Squaring the previous equation ends up to a fourth degree polynomial equation for t, as $R_1(t)$, $R_2(t)$, $|s_1(t)-s_2(t)|$ are second degree polynomials. The complexity of solving (1) is prohibitive for real-time applications. To reduce the computational cost, a linear approximation of each path is used. Let t_{init} and t_{final} be the minimum and maximum time values of the interval to check for collision. Let s(t) denote any of $s_1(t)$ or $s_2(t)$ and R(t) any of $R_1(t)$ or $R_2(t)$. Then s(t) can be approximated in $[t_{init}, t_{final}]$ from the line segment given by

$$s(m) = s(t_{init}) + mu .$$ (2)

for m in [0,1] and $u = s(t_{final}) - s(t_{init})$. The same approximation can be employed for the deviation R(t), where $R(m) = R(t_{init})+mDR$ and $DR = R(t_{final}) - R(t_{init})$. Figure 4-(a) shows the maximum error value caused by the approximation. To deal with this error, the bounding volume extends further in order to enclose the disregarded area (Figure 4-(b)).

Let t_{error} be the time of the maximum approximation error and $v_{error} = s(t_{error}) - s(t_{init})$ be the vector from the starting position of the estimation to the position of maximum error. It is trivial to prove that

$$t_{error} = t_{init} + (t_{final} - t_{init})/2 .$$ (3)

and the maximum error e_{max} equals to

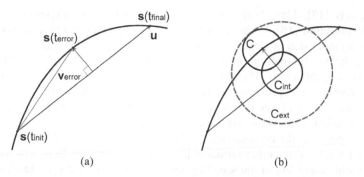

Fig. 4. Figure (a) displays the maximum absolute value of the approximation error which corresponds to the maximum distance between the linear approximation s(m) and the path s(t). The error is used to extend the bounding sphere C_{init}, moving along the linear interpolation, so that it includes the disregarded area of C, as displayed in (b).

$$e_{max} = \mid v_{error} \cdot \frac{u \times (v_{error} \times u)}{\mid u \times (v_{error} \times u) \mid} \mid . \tag{4}$$

The same error correction is not necessary for the approximation of R(t). As can be easily seen, R(t) is convex on the interval $[t_{init}; t_{final}]$. Consequently, the approximate deviation results to a larger moving bounding volume and no collision will be missed. Finally, equation (1) can be replaced by

$$\mid s_1(m) - s_2(m) \mid \leq R_1(m) + R_2(m) + r + e_1 + e_2 . \tag{5}$$

where e_1 and e_2 are the maximum approximation errors for the two objects. Let P(m) be the polynomial defined as

$$P(m) = \mid s_1(m) - s_2(m) \mid^2 - (R_1(m) + R_2(m) + r + e_1 + e_2)^2 . \tag{6}$$

Equation (5) holds when P(m) is negative or zero. Note that the valid approximation interval of m is [0,1] because outside this interval, m corresponds to time values outside $[t_{init}; t_{final}]$. That means that not every root of P(m) is a valid collision time. If m_s is a valid solution of P(m) according to the previous analysis, then the estimated time $t_{collision}$ of the next future collision can be approximated by

$$t_{collision} = t_{init} + m_s(t_{final} - t_{init}) . \tag{7}$$

If there is no possible collision, then we can be sure that there is no collision until t_{final}.

4 Interactive Haptic Rendering

Briefly, haptic rendering involves the process of detecting human-object collisions and generating the appropriate feedback depending on the texture and the "sense" of the virtual objects [17], [18], [19], [20]. While all modules are important in human-computer interaction [18], in this paper we focus only on collision detection. In particular we are interested in virtual environments with a significant number of objects.

For the haptic interaction in the experiments, we employed the PHANToM (http://www.sensable.com). The PHANToM is a general purpose haptic device from SensAble Technologies providing highend force feedback while being very simple to use. It has six degrees of freedom for reading the position of the probe and three or six degrees of freedom concerning the feedback, depending on the model.

In the proposed collision detection method, the probe acts as the single IO in the environment while all the other virtual objects are considered as EOs. The user is able to interact with every EO in the scene by setting it in motion, if it is static, or changing its direction, if it is already moving. The challenging part of this simulation is to handle collisions and contact in real-time.

For the rest of the haptic rendering update, force feedback is calculated using a standard spring force model. The force applied to the user is perpendicular to the object surface depending on the spring constant that which represents the physical properties of the simulated object and the penetration depth of the probe into the object.

5 Experimental Results

Experimental tests were conducted to evaluate the performance of the proposed framework. The results elaborate on the performance gain in a real-time application and the comparison with other state-of-the-art approaches for broad phase collision detection. The algorithms of the proposed framework were developed in C++. Other two software packages were used in the tests: SOLID 3.5 (http://www.dtecta.com/) and ODE 0.9 (http://www.ode.org/). SOLID is a collision detection software package containing both broad and narrow phase algorithms, described in detail in [21]. ODE is a general rigid body simulation library with a collision detection engine which employs a Multi-resolution Uniform Grid or a Quad Tree [11] in the broad phase. Tests were performed using a Core2 6600 2,4GHz CPU PC with 2GB of RAM and GeForce 7600 GS Graphics Card.

Table 1. Average performance gain of the proposed approach over state-of-the-art methods

Number of Objects	Brute Force	Sweep & Prune	Quad Tree	Uniform Grid
20	97.9%	83.3%	80.4%	82.1%
40	96.3%	51.8%	51.4%	49.9%
60	97.8%	60.7%	62.6%	64.6%
80	97.9%	46.1%	54.8%	59.7%
100	97.4%	32.7%	38.7%	39.9%

During the experimental tests, the user was free to "touch" a number of static or arbitrary moving virtual objects using the PHANToM probe. The comparative results concerning the performance are displayed in Table 1. The first thing to notice is that the brute force approach is an order of magnitude slower than the other methods, and the difference increases as more objects are added to the scene. This fact clearly suggests that the brute force approach is extremely aggregative for the application. Comparing the proposed method with the other methods, there is an almost constant improvement in the average performance. The update rate of the application varied from 80 Hz to 450 Hz. The improvement of the proposed method comprises a major advance in haptic interaction since it is very important to achieve very high update rates in order to produce realistic haptic feedback.

5.1 Performance Analysis

A concrete asymptotic analysis of the performance of the proposed method would conclude in a rather obscure result that could not give a clear picture of the algorithm. Therefore, it is preferred to describe the general characteristics of the proposed method. The overall performance highly depends on the frequency of collisions between the objects in the scene. Theoretically, the worst case is $O(n^2)$ and occurs when every object is near with all the other objects. However, the possibility of such a case is almost zero for large n in practical applications, as the usual case for the objects is to be near at discrete time intervals. The average performance can be roughly considered as $O(nc + k)$ where k is the number of pairs in the narrow phase and c is the number of objects that need estimation of future collision. The gain is higher for limited number of collisions in the scene, even for large number of objects, which can be relatively close to each other. It is also important to note that when no objects are near with each other, the performance is almost constant.

References

1. Jimenez, P., Thomas, F., Torras, C.: 3D Collision Detection: A Survey. Computer and Graphics 25, 269–285 (2001)
2. Lin, M.C., Gottschalk, S.: Collision Detection between Geometric Models: A Survey. In: IMA Conference on Mathematics of Surfaces (1998)
3. Hadap, S., Eberle, D., Volino, P., Lin, M.C., Redon, S., Ericson, C.: Collision Detection and Proximity Queries. In: ACM SIGGRAPH Course Notes (2004)
4. Teschner, M., Kimmerle, S., Zachmann, G., Heidelberger, B., Raghupathi, L., Fuhrmann, A., Cani, M.P., Faure, F., Magnetat-Thalmann, N., Strasser, W.: Collision Detection for Deformable Objects. In: Eurographics State-of-the-Art Report (EG-STAR), pp. 119–139 (2004)
5. Hubbard, P.: Approximating Polyhedra with Spheres for Time-Critical Collision Detection. ACM Transactions on Graphics 15, 179–210 (1996)
6. Bergen, G.v.d.: Efficient Collision Detection of Complex Deformable Models using AABB Trees. Journal of Graphics Tools 2, 1–14 (1997)
7. Gottschalk, S., Lin, M.C., Manocha, D.: OBBTree: A Hierarchical Structure for Rapid Interference Detection. Computer Graphics 30, 171–180 (1996)
8. Klosowski, J.T., Held, M., Mitchell, J.S.B., Sowizral, H., Zikan, K.: Efficient Collision Detection using Bounding Volume Hierarchies of k-DOPs. IEEE Transactions on Visualization and Computer Graphics 4, 21–36 (1998)

9. Cohen, J.D., Lin, M.C., Manocha, D., Ponagmi, M.: An Interactive and Exact Collision Detection System for Large-Scale Environments. In: Symposium on Interactive 3D Graphics, pp. 189–196 (1995)
10. Hudson, T., Lin, M.C., Cohen, J., Gottschalk, S., Manocha, D.: V-COLLIDE: Accelerated Collision Detection for VRML. In: VRML 1997: Second Symposium on the Virtual Reality Modeling Language (1997)
11. Ericson, C.: Real-time Collision Detection. Morgan Kaufmann, San Francisco (2005)
12. Luque, R., Comba, J., Freitas, C.: Broad-phase Collision Detection using Semi-Adjusting BSP-Trees. In: I3D 2005: Symposium on Interactive Graphics and Games, pp. 179–186 (2005)
13. Ar, S., Chazelle, B., Tal, A.: Self-customized BSP Trees for Collision Detection. Computational Geometry 15, 91–102 (2000)
14. Eitz, M., Lixu, G.: Hierarchical Spatial Hashing for Real-Time Collision Detection. In: IEEE International Conference on Shape Modeling and Applications, pp. 61–70 (2007)
15. Press, W., Teukolsky, S., Vetterling, T., Flannery, P.: Numerical Recipes in C: The Art of Scientific Computing. Cambridge University Press, Cambridge (1992)
16. Mirtich, B.: Efficient algorithms for two-phase collision detection. TR-97-23, Mitsubishi Electric Research Laboratory (1997)
17. Tzovaras, D., Nikolakis, G., Fergadis, G., Malasiotis, S., Stavrakis, M.: Design and implementation of haptic virtual environments for the training of visually impaired. IEEE Trans. Neural Syst. Rehabil. Eng., 266–278 (2004)
18. Otaduy, M.A., Lin, M.C.: Introduction to haptic rendering. In: ACM SIGGRAPH Courses (2005)
19. Basdogan, C., De, S., Kim, J., Muniyandi, M., Kim, H., Srinivasan, M.A.: Haptics in minimally invasive surgical simulation and training. IEEE Computer Graphics & Applications (2004)
20. Fritz, J.P.: Haptic rendering techniques for scientific visualization. Master thesis, University of Delaware, Newarty Delaware (1996)
21. Bergen, G.v.d.: Collision Detection in Interactive 3D Environments. Morgan Kaufmann, San Francisco (2003)

Part IV
Vision in Virtual and Mixed Reality

Shape Disparity Inspection of the Textured Object and Its Notification by Overlay Projection

Toshiyuki Amano and Hirokazu Kato

Graduate School of Information Science, Nara Institute of Science and Technology
Takayama 8916-5, Ikoma 630-0192, Japan
{amano,kato}@is.naist.jp

Abstract. In this paper we describe about use of the projector camera feedback system for shape disparity check of the textured object. Using the negative feedback in the proposed system, we realized real time shape disparity inspection and its visualization at the same time. In the experimental result, we confirmed the system has an ability to distinguish the 2 mm of shape disparity and its response time was 0.2 sec.

1 Introduction

With the factory automation growth, the visual inspection is the most widely used for many applications in the last few decades [1]. For example, the visual inspection is used for inspection of medicine tablet or capsule [2], engine valve [3], metallic industrial workpieces [4], aircraft surface [5], fabric texture [6] and other many applications and it includes apple quality evaluation [7]. In the visual inspection there are two strategies, those are full automatic inspection and semi-automatic inspection. If the inspection is able to implement by easy detection rule and it allows un-detection like a quality checking of the tablet, the automatic detection is suitable. Contrary, if it is complicated inspection and it never allows un-detection such as surface inspection of aircraft, semi-automatic detection that means assist of manual inspection for the operator is more suitable. Almost visual inspection system aims automatic and precise inspection, but the visualization was not considered well. In the semi-automatic process, the operator have to check corresponding defect in the inspected object to make sure its notification by the inspection result that was shown in the monitor display.

Recently, the research of projection based AR system is becoming active and it is useful for visualization of the visual inspection. Bimber et al. [8] proposed high dynamic range imaging technology that used optical projector with printed picture. The system enables boosting of the contrast of printed picture by the overwrap projection of the compensation light from the projector. This technique is proposed for new display technique. However, such like display technique that is projection-based AR technique is helpful not only for display technique but also as using as the inspection assist technique for the operator too. Amano et al. [9] proposed projector camera feedback system for the appearance enhancement of the less saturated picture in the realtime processing. This projector camera system realizes a realtime processing and its system achieved 15 fps processing for the appearance enhancement. Its real time

R. Shumaker (Ed.): Virtual and Mixed Reality, LNCS 5622, pp. 405–412, 2009.

processing enables assist of human visual perception in the manufacturing line. However, this system aims to enhance the object's appearance of color difference and brightness contrast caused by defects, so it cannot use for shape disparity inspection of free-form surface. However, its overlaying inspection result of shape disparity by using projection based AR technology is also useful for its visualization. Also, inspection of faint shape disparity is not easy for human perception.

From these reasons, we propose a visualization technique of the shape disparity inspection by the AR technology. Especially, we use a projector camera feedback due to realize realtime visualization that aims to human computer interaction.

2   Shape Disparity Inspection and Visualization

Typical flow of shape disparity inspection and visualization is illustrated in figure 1. In the shape disparity inspection process, we need a shape measurement. A rapid and cheapest shape measurement system is to employ space code projection such as gray code with commercial projector for the shape measurement. In this process, we have two problems. One is we need several times projection and it is processing time expensive for real time inspection. Other one is visually confusing. Because it is hard to distinguish projections for shape measurement and visual notification. Of course, we can use commercial range imaging system that used invisible light and has a capability of high speed measurement. However, it is expensive and whole inspection system is complicated because we need a projector for the visualization besides range imaging system. Therefore, we use a simple projector camera system, and we propose the method that makes whole shape measurement and visualization process more efficiently.

The core process of the shape measurement with the active stereo is calculating disparity between projector screen and camera image. This disparity is translated to 3-D shape by the camera and projector parameters. However, the calculation of calibrated

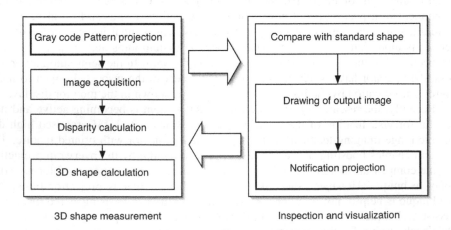

Fig. 1. Typical flow of the shape disparity inspection and visualization

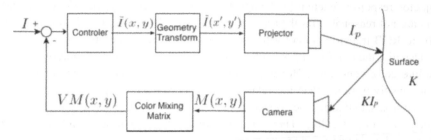

Fig. 2. A concept of projector camera negative feedback system

shape is unnecessary if we need only to check the match with a standard shape for inspecting dents. It is often required by quality check in the manufacturing line. The match of the disparity at a point of image plane is confirmed by checking of the space code, but its cost is equivalent with a conventional gray code projection. If we think about single point check, we can confirm its matching from whether a dot is projected on the corresponding point that is calculated by disparity of standard shape or not. However, in case of cell parallel processing, we have a problem of interference among neighbor projection points. Furthermore the system cannot realize continuous visualization because we need two projections of check and notification step. Therefore, we propose the single step projection method by the projector camera feedback that enables check and notification in the same time.

If we think about negative feedback system that is shown in figure 2, the projected light $\mathbf{I}_p \in \Re^3$ will converge along with to desired brightness $\mathbf{I} = \left[I_R, I_G, I_B\right]^T$. The negative feedback projector camera system was proposed by Nayar et al. [10][11], and that enables projection of images onto an arbitrary surface such that the effects of the surface imperfections are minimized.

In this paper, we regard the radiometric relation as rgb-color-channel model and we put compensation light power for time $t+1$ as:

$$\tilde{\mathbf{I}}(t+1) = \tilde{\mathbf{I}}(t) + G\left(\mathbf{I} - \mathbf{VM}(t)\right) \tag{1}$$

where $\tilde{\mathbf{I}} = \left[\tilde{I}_R, \tilde{I}_G, \tilde{I}_B\right]^T$ and $\tilde{\mathbf{I}}(0) = \mathbf{0}$. $\mathbf{G} \in \Re^{3\times3}$ is a diagonal matrix that gives feedback gain, $\mathbf{V} \in \Re^{3\times3}$ is color mixing matrix that compensate the difference of color space between projector and camera, $\mathbf{M} = \left[M_R, M_G, M_B\right]^T$ is acquired pixel value.

3 Color Calibration

The projector and camera have different color space since they have unique spectral sensitivity functions and non-linear illumination response curve functions. The general polynomial transformation for the camera sensitivity [12] and the calibration of projector response function [13] improve the color matching, but these calculation costs are not reasonable for the realtime processing. Therefore, we use a simple linear RGB to RGB transformation for the inter channel dispersion correction by the matrix $\mathbf{V}$. Usually, the color calibration chart is used for camera color calibration due to get absolute color sensitivity. However, our feedback system is not important absolute color sensitivity rather than the relation between camera and projector color spaces, because it is satisfied for the appearance enhancement if the system can project same color as the object color. Therefore, we compute its color space relation between camera and projector as below.

In the first step we project R, G, B plain color form the projector. At each projection, we get mean pixel value of each channel w_R, w_G and w_B at the whole projected area in the captured image. In the second step, we compute the mixing matrix as:

$$\mathbf{V} = \mathbf{W}^{-1} \det(\mathbf{W})$$ (2)

where

$$W = \begin{vmatrix} w_{R1} & w_{R2} & w_{R3} \\ w_{G1} & w_{G2} & w_{G3} \\ w_{B1} & w_{B2} & w_{B3} \end{vmatrix},$$

w_{*1}, w_{*2} and w_{*3} are meaning pixel values with R, G and B plain color projection respectively. We apply the mixing matrix after the image capture. Thus the color calibration is done by conversion of the camera color space to the projector color space.

4 Per-pixel Mapping Calculation

For the shape disparity inspection, we have to get the stereo disparity among projector and camera beforehand as a standard shape data. This stereo disparity is given by the part of conventional active stereo shape measurement process and is expressed by a per-pixel map between projection screen coordinate (x_p, y_p) and camera image plane coordinate (x_c, y_c). To compute lookup table for the per-pixel mapping, the gray code patterns projection by a complementary pattern projection that is the traditional method of the range image measurement is a robust way to get correspondence of coordinates (figure 3). Thus, we used vertical and horizontal gray code patterns for the calculation of lookup tables $x_p(x_c, y_c)$ and $y_p(x_c, y_c)$. In the actual implementation, we used inverse mapping $x_c(x_p, y_p)$ and $y_c(x_p, y_p)$ to reduce computational cost. These inverse mappings were generated by the voting with $x_p(x_c, y_c)$ and $y_p(x_c, y_c)$.

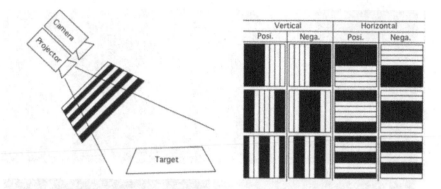

Fig. 3. Per-pixel mapping calculation by the complementary gray code pattern projection

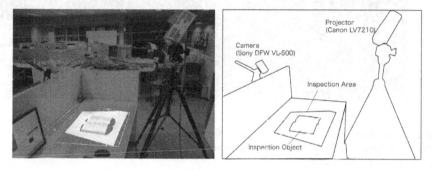

Fig. 4. The setup of the shape disparity inspection based on projector camera system

5 Experimental Result

Figure 4 shows the experimental setup. The camera (SONY DFW VL-500, RGB 8bit, 640 × 480 resolution) is put the front of the projector (CANON LV7210, RGB 8bit, 1024 × 768 resolution) and these were targeted on the same region of the worktable. For the system calibration, we calculate the color mixing matrix by (2) with RGB plain color projections. The feedback gain was set as $\mathbf{G} = diag(0.4, 0.4, 0.4)$ from our experience. The exact behavior of proposed negative feedback system was not considered by above theory. Therefore, in this research we tried to consider from its experimental results. To check its behavior, we used an opened book that is a smooth shape object shown in figure 5(a). The per-pixel map was calculated by gray code projection onto its opened book. With this per-pixel map, the appearance of the original shape is changed to figure 5(b) by the negative feedback and its texture is removed. This result is suitable for checking shape disparity, because often the texture confuses the projected notification. With the upper right 2 mm dent of inspection object the appearance was changed as shown in figure 5(c). The figure 5(d) shows a projected compensation pattern for figure 5(c).

Fig. 5. (a) Inspection object, (b) Negative feedback changes objects appearance and it removes texture. (c) With the 2mm displacement by the pushing, the stripe pattern (d) was projected at the dent area.

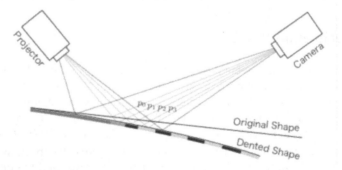

Fig. 6. The mechanism of stripe pattern generation

From this experimental result, we confirmed divergence of compensation light and it makes a striped pattern at the dented region. It is caused by in the figure 6 the projection light becomes over-power/under-power illumination at the point p1 since un-controllable because of a little disparity. For this over-power/under-power illumination neighbor point p2 becomes under-power/over-power illumination since it reference the point p1, and the stripe pattern is generated by its repeat. The width of stripe reflected a magnitude of dents depth geometrically, but it is not calibrated and also plus and minus is not measurable.

Our experiment was performed on a Core 2 Quad 2.66GHz PC with OpenMP library, and its processing frequency was reached 26 fps. We confirmed its striped pattern was stabled within around 5 frames by the step by step checking. Therefore the response time was about 0.2 sec.

6 Conclusion

This work shows the potential of the projector camera feedback system for the assistance system that aims the shape disparity inspection. In the conventional shape measurement method, we need several times of code pattern projection. Additionally, we need a projection of the inspection result for the AR based visualization. However our method integrated both projections by using of the projector camera feedback. In the experimental result, we confirmed the system has an ability to distinguish the 2 mm of shape disparity and its response time was 0.2 sec. In a future work, we need the theoretical analysis and development of inspection method of plus and minus of its dents.

Acknowledgement. A part of this work was supported by the Kayamori Foundation of Informational Science Advancement, Japan.

References

1. Li, Y., Gu, P.: Free-form surface inspection techniques state of the art review. In: Proc. of Computer-Aided Design, vol. 36, pp. 1395–1417 (2004)
2. Nakamura, K., Edamatsu, K., Sano, Y.: Auto-mated pattern inspection based on boundary length comparison method. In: Proc. International Joint Conference on Pattern Recognition, pp. 955–957 (1978)
3. Perkins, W.A.: Computer vision inspection of valve spring assemblies on engine heads. General Motors Research Laboratories, GMR-3369 (1980)
4. Bariani, M., Cucchiara, R., Mello, P., Piccardi, M.: Data mining for automated visual inspection. In: Proc. of PADD 1997, First Int. Conf. Practical Appl. Knowledge Discovery and Data Mining, London, UK, pp. 51–64 (1997); ISBN 0-9525554-7-6
5. Gunatilake, P., Siegel, M., Jordan, A., Podnar, G.: Image understanding algorithms for remote visual inspection of aircraft surfaces. In: Machine Vis. Appl. Indus Inspection V, vol. 3029, pp. 2–13 (1997)
6. Serdaroglu, A., Ertuzun, A., Ercil, A.: Defect Detection In Textile Fabric Images Using Wavelet Transforms And Independent Component Analysis. In: Proc. of PRIA 7, pp. 890–893 (2004)
7. Buisson, O., Bessere, B., Boukir, S., Helt, F.: Deterioration detection for digital film restoration. In: Proc. of Int. Conf. on CVPR, vol. 1, pp. 78–84 (1997)
8. Bimber, O., Iwai, D.: Superimposing dynamic range. In: Proc. of ACM SIGGRAPH 2008 new tech demos (2008)
9. Amano, T., Kato, H.: Real World Dynamic Appearance Enhancement with Procam Feedback. In: Proc. of Procams 2008 (2008)

10. Nayar, S.K., Peri, H., Grossberg, M.D., Belhumeur, P.N.: A projection system with radiometric compensation for screen imperfections. In: Proc. of ICCV Workshop on Projector-Camera Systems (2003)
11. Fujii, K., Grossberg, M.D., Nayar, S.K.: A Projector-Camera System with Real-Time Photometric Adaptation for Dynamic Environments. In: Proc. of CVPR 2005, pp. 814–821 (2005)
12. Ilie, A., Welch, G.: Ensuring color consistency across multiple cameras. In: ICCV 2005: Proceedings of the Tenth IEEE International Conference on Computer Vision, pp. 1268–1275. IEEE Computer Society, Washington (2005)
13. Ashdown, M., Okabe, T., Sato, I., Sato, Y.: Robust content-dependent photometric projector compensation. In: CVPRW 2006: Proceedings of the 2006 Conference on Computer Vision and Pattern Recognition Workshop, IEEE Computer Society, Washington (2006)

Complemental Use of Multiple Cameras for Stable Tracking of Multiple Markers

Yuki Arai and Hideo Saito

Department of Information and Computer Science,
Keio University, Yokohama, Japan
{araiguma,saito}@ozawa.ics.keio.ac.jp

Abstract. In many applications of Augmented Reality (AR), rectangular markers are tracked in real time by capturing with cameras. In this paper, we consider the AR application in which virtual objects are displayed onto markers while the markers and the cameras are freely moving. In this situation, the marker cannot be tracked when the marker is occluded by some objects. In this paper, we propose a method for tracking the projection matrix between the image and the marker even when the maker is occluded, by using cameras. In this method, we transfer the projection matrix for the marker that is detected by the cameras in order to estimate the relative projection matrix for the occluded marker. After computing the relative projection matrices using multiple cameras, we compute a more accurate projection matrix by using particle filter. As a result, we can continuously track the markers even when the marker is occluded.

Keywords: augmented reality, marker tracking, particle filter, multiple cameras.

1 Introduction

In recent years, Augmented Reality (AR) is well studied to present information for education or entertainment. AR is the combination of real-world and virtual reality, where computer generated virtual objects are overlaid onto video of the real world in real-time. "Magic Book" [1] is the example of AR. As marker is printed on the book, we can see virtual object on the book when we open the book. In order to achieve AR, we need to determine the camera pose accurately. Sensor based methods and vision based methods are well known for tracking the camera pose. Using sensors such as a magnetic sensor or a gyroscope are a robust way to rapid by track camera motion and change of lighting condition [2,3]. However sensor can not get enough information to calibrate accurate camera pose and has area that can be used. To compute camera pose, vision based method uses landmark in real space such as markers [4], interest points or edges [5,6], models that are pre-calibrated before using system [7]. Vision based methods do not need any particular device such as sensor, it is low cost and we can construct the system easily. In this paper, we propose marker based method since we can easily build the environment.

We use ARToolkit [8] to compute camera pose and position using rectangular markers. A unique pattern is drawn on each marker and the system can identify each

R. Shumaker (Ed.): Virtual and Mixed Reality, LNCS 5622, pp. 413–420, 2009.

marker using this pattern. Therefore the marker can easily be detected from input image so that we can achieve AR easily. However the marker can not be detected when the marker is occluded or illumination condition is not sufficient. There are many researches to solve such marker occlusion problem. Tateno et al. [9] have proposed nested marker to solve partial occlusion. The nested marker consists of several small markers. They employ small markers in the nested marker when the marker is occluded. They can display virtual object on the marker even when marker occlusion occurs. David et al. [10] have applied particle filter with tracking. They use markers to compute the projection matrix when the marker is not occluded. While marker occlusion occurs, they use marker corners as features for tracking using particle filter. David et al. use only one camera to solve partial occlusion of markers, while Pilet et al. [11] have used fixed multiple cameras to solve full occlusion of markers. As a pre-processing step, Pilet et al. calibrate all the cameras. Then they use another camera's information when the marker is occluded. This method can display a virtual object even if the camera can not see the marker perfectly. However this method requires to fix the cameras.

In this paper, we consider the AR application in which virtual objects are displayed onto markers while all the markers and the cameras are freely moving by users' interaction. In this situation, the marker cannot be tracked when the marker is occluded by some objects. For solving this problem, we propose a method for tracking the projection matrix between the image and the marker even when the maker is occluded, by complemental use of multiple cameras. In this method, all cameras share the projection matrices between the markers and the cameras for computing the relative projection matrix for occluded markers, so that virtual objects can be displayed onto the occluded markers.

2   System Description

In this paper, we consider the AR application in which virtual objects are displayed onto markers while all the markers and the cameras are freely moving by users' interaction. In the proposed method, we compute the projection matrix using ARToolkit when we can detect the marker from the image. While marker occlusion occurs, we compute projection matrix by sharing projection matrices between cameras. However the projection matrix computed from other cameras is not accurate, we optimize the projection matrix using particle filter.

2.1   Compute Projection Matrix Using Other Cameras

For computing a projection matrix between the camera and occluded marker, we compute extrinsic parameters between them using other cameras. Extrinsic parameters represent the rotation matrix and translation vector between two coordinates. For computing the extrinsic parameters between the camera and the occluded marker, we use common markers that are detected from more than two cameras. By multiplying extrinsic parameters computed for the common markers, we can compute extrinsic parameters between the camera and the occluded marker that are not computed directory using ARToolkit. After computing these parameters, we compute projection matrix using them and the intrinsic parameters of the camera that were previously estimated. Fig.1 shows the example for computing extrinsic parameters using other cameras. In Fig.1, straight arrows represent that the camera can detect the marker, so that the projection matrix between the camera and the marker can be computed using ARtoolkit. Then the extrinsic parameters between them can also be computed. We denote the extrinsic parameters between the camera c and the marker m by $\mathbf{M}[m{\leftarrow}c]$. The reverse extrinsic parameters are computed by inverting the matrix which we denote by $\mathbf{M}[c{\leftarrow}m]$. In Fig.1(a), occlusion occurs on the marker $m1$ from the camera $c3$, we can not compute $\mathbf{M}[m1{\leftarrow}c3]$. However we can compute $\mathbf{M}[m1{\leftarrow}c1]$, $\mathbf{M}[c1{\leftarrow}m2]$ and $\mathbf{M}[m2{\leftarrow}c3]$, then we can compute $\mathbf{M}[m1{\leftarrow}c3]$ from multiplying them.

In some case, there are many routes from the camera to the marker, so we have to select the best route. Fig.1 (b) shows the case using four cameras and three markers. In this case, camera $c4$ can not detect marker $m1$, so we can not compute $\mathbf{M}[m1{\leftarrow}c4]$ directory. However using common markers that can be detected from more than two cameras like marker $m2$, we can compute $\mathbf{M}[m1{\leftarrow}c4]$. Fig.1 (b) shows two routes to link camera $c4$ and marker $m1$. The $\mathbf{M}[m{\leftarrow}c]$ computed with a marker generally includes some errors, the errors are multiplied while passing other cameras. Therefore we have to select the route that is the most accurate. To select such route, we consider the least number of common markers for computing the objective extrinsic parameters. The reason to select the route that passes the least number of common markers is that the error can be increased by the number of common markers. We use the Dijkstra algorithm to select the shortest route. Dijkstra algorithm is famous to solve shortest path problem. When the number of common markers to pass is same, we select the path that includes more accurate extrinsic parameters. For evaluating the accuracy, we use the area of the common markers captured in the image.

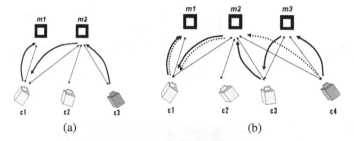

(a)   (b)

Fig. 1. Computing projection matrix from sharing projection matrices. Straight arrows represent the fact that the camera can detect the marker. (a) Computing extrinsic parameter using common marker $m2$. (b) There are some routes between camera $c4$ and marker $m1$. We have to select the shortest route.

2.2 Particle Filter Optimization

We denote the relative projection matrix using multiple cameras between the camera c and the marker m at time t by $\mathbf{P}_{tmp}(c,m,t)$, which was discussed in Section 2.1. The projection matrix computed with markers directly includes some error. The projection matrix $\mathbf{P}_{tmp}(c,m,t)$ still includes error as illustrated in Fig.2. For computing the correct projection matrix, we detect the occluded marker in the image using $\mathbf{P}_{\mathrm{tmp}}(c,m,t)$. The shape of the marker, projected by using $\mathbf{P}_{\mathrm{tmp}}(c,m,t)$, is almost correct even if the $\mathbf{P}_{\mathrm{tmp}}(c,m,t)$ includes error. So we can detect the occluded marker in the image to scale and translate the projected marker. In order to detect the occluded marker, we compute the matrix $\mathbf{H}_t$. $\mathbf{H}_t$ is affine transformation matrix at time t which transforms the marker projected by using $\mathbf{P}_{\mathrm{tmp}}(c,m,t)$ onto the occluded marker in the image. $\mathbf{H}_t$ is composed of parameters λ, u_x and u_y. λ indicates scale and u_x, u_y indicate the distance of translation. After detecting the marker in image using $\mathbf{P}_{\mathrm{tmp}}(c,m,t)$ and $\mathbf{H}_t$, we compute correct projection matrix using it.

$$\mathbf{H} = \begin{bmatrix} \lambda & 0 & u_x \\ 0 & \lambda & u_y \\ 0 & 0 & 1 \end{bmatrix} \tag{1}$$

In this section, we describe our method for estimating $\mathbf{H}_t$ by using a particle filter for each marker. We denote a particle by hypothesis $\mathbf{H}_t^i$ and weight w_t^i at time t. ($i=1...N$). N is the number of particles. The estimation of error from using a particle filter starts from the time that marker occlusion occurs ($t=t_0$). We assume that the marker in image is known at time t_0-1. We compute affine transformation matrix between the marker that is projected using $\mathbf{P}_{\mathrm{tmp}}(c,m,t_0)$ and the marker in image at time t_0-1. We set the initial parameter of $\mathbf{H}_t^i$ with the affine transformation matrix. When the route that is used to compute projection matrix from sharing projection matrices changes, we also initialize the particles.

After initialization, we estimate $\mathbf{H}_t^i$ from $\mathbf{H}_{t-1}^i$ sequentially. We have no prior knowledge of cause of error in each frame, we estimate $\mathbf{H}_t^i$ as:

$$\mathbf{H}_t^i = \mathbf{H}_{t-1}^i + \varepsilon = \begin{bmatrix} \lambda & 0 & u_x \\ 0 & \lambda & u_y \\ 0 & 0 & 1 \end{bmatrix} + \begin{bmatrix} \varepsilon_{scale} & 0 & \varepsilon_x \\ 0 & \varepsilon_{scale} & \varepsilon_y \\ 0 & 0 & 0 \end{bmatrix} \tag{2}$$

Fig. 2. Projecting marker using $\mathbf{P}_{\mathrm{tmp}}(c,m,t)$ computed by Section 2.1. $\mathbf{P}_{\mathrm{tmp}}(c,m,t)$ has error, projected marker does not match marker in image.

ε composed of ε_{scale}, ε_x and ε_y. Each parameter represents the random noise which has a normal distribution.

$$\varepsilon_{scale} = N(\,0\,,\sigma_{scale}{}^2)\tag{3}$$

$$\varepsilon_x,\varepsilon_y = N(\,0\,,\sigma_{trans}{}^2)\tag{4}$$

After estimating hypothesis at time t, we compute weight from input image for each particle. Since the weight indicates the confidence of the estimation, the particles that have a heavy weight indicate a correct hypothesis. We weight particles using the distance between the edge in input image and the projected marker that was computed with $\mathbf{H}_t^{\,i}$ and $\mathbf{P}_{tmp}(c,m,t)$. First we extract the edge from input image using a Canny edge detector, and then project the marker with $\mathbf{P}_{tmp}(c,m,t)$ and $\mathbf{H}_t^{\,i}$. Next we put sample points on the projected marker contour. Fig.3 shows the example of sample points ($K=20$). We scan the pixels along the marker contour normal from the sample points. We measure the distance d between the sample point and edge that is scanned. We compute distance d from each sample point and compute sum of distance. We represent the sum of distance as expectation c_t^i. After computing c_t^i for each particle, we weight the particles. We weight particle heavier when c_t^i is small by using a Gaussian function to weight the particles.

$$w_t^i \propto e^{-\frac{c_t^{i2}}{2\sigma^2}}\tag{5}$$

We normalize the weight so that:

$$\sum_{n=1}^{N} w_t^n = 1\tag{6}$$

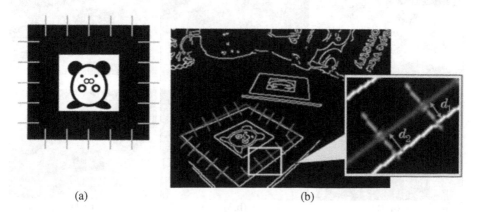

Fig. 3. (a) K sample points on the marker ($K = 20$). (b) Computing distance between projected marker using particle and edge in input image. We scan the pixels along the marker contour normal from all sample points.

After computing all weights for each particle, we evaluate the weights and select the particle that has the heaviest weight. We indicate the selected particle as the error at time t and compute projection matrix using the particle and $\mathbf{P}_{tmp}(c,m,t)$.

After computing the projection matrix, we remove particles that have small weight. After a few iterations, all but one particle will have negligible weight and reduce accuracy. To remove this particle, we eliminate particles which have small weight and concentrate on particles with large weights.

3 Experiments

In order to evaluate the performance of the method that we proposed, we track markers using multiple cameras. We move the markers on the desk and record the markers using three web cameras. The parameters that we use in the experiment are as follows: number of particle N=100, sample points on the marker K=20.

First, we changed the parameters σ_{scale} and σ_{trans}, and evaluated the accuracy of marker tracking. When σ_{scale} or σ_{trans} were too big, the marker position was not fixed.

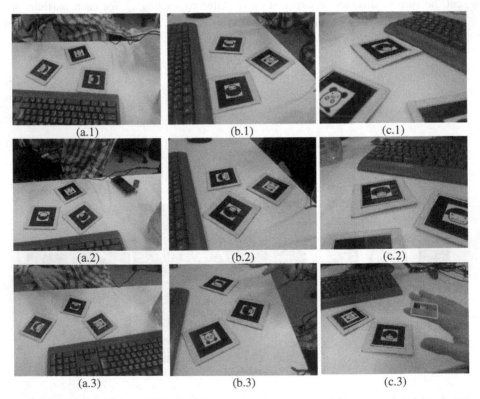

Fig. 4. The result of tracking markers. We track markers using the proposed method. (a)(b) Input image from cameras $c1$, $c2$. (c) Input image from camera $c3$ and projecting marker computed by proposed method on the image.

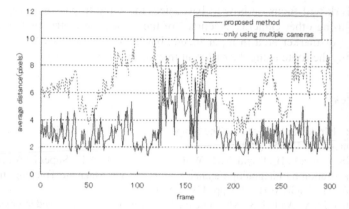

Fig. 5. A comparison of the accuracy of the proposed method and a method which does not use a particle filter

When σ_{scale} or σ_{trans} were too small, we could not adjust cause of error. After several tests, we have decided the parameter at σ_{scale}=0.05 and σ_{trans}=10.

After experimentally determining σ, we evaluated the accuracy of our method using a video sequence captured with three USB cameras. To evaluate the accuracy, we used the average distance between sample points on the marker that is projected using projection matrix and the edge in input image. The distance written in Section 2.2 is used for computing weight of each particle. In the video sequence, the cameras and markers move freely, and target marker is partially occluded. Target marker means the marker for which we estimate the projection matrix using our method. At least one marker can be seen from camera $c3$. The other cameras $c1$ and $c2$ see more than two markers in the sequence.

Fig.4 shows the input images from three cameras and marker tracking result when marker occlusion occurs or marker is partially out of the image. As we track markers using other cameras when marker occlusion occurs, we can track the marker which has full occlusion such as illustrated in Fig.4 (c.3). However, because we use the edge to optimize the marker position, we fail to track marker if the marker is completely occluded for a long time or the marker is near an edge that is parallel to the marker contour.

Fig.5 shows the average distance of the proposed method and the method which does not use a particle filter. Accuracy of the projection matrix computed by the proposed method is higher than the method which uses only multiple cameras.

4   Conclusion

In this paper, we presented a method that is robust enough to handle occlusion of markers by using multiple handheld cameras. When marker occlusion occurs, we share projection matrices between cameras and we can detect existence of marker even if marker is occluded.

Future work will focus on how to best select the route to pass to compute projection matrix using other cameras. Accuracy of the projection matrix depends not only on the result of marker area in input image, but also camera pose. We need to consider selecting the route using the different in camera poses as well.

References

1. Mark, B., Hirokazu, K., Ivan, P.: The Magic Book: a transitional AR interface. Computers & Graphics 25, 745–753 (2001)
2. Andrei, S., Gentaro, H., David, T.C., William, F.G., Mark, A.L.: Superior Augmented Reality Registration by Integrating Landmark Tracking and Magnetic Tracking. In: Proceedings of ACM SIGGRAPH 1996, pp. 429–438 (1996)
3. Livingston, M.A., Andrei, S.: Magnetic tracker calibration for improved augmented reality registration. Presence: Teleoperators and Virtual Environments 6(5), 532–546 (1997)
4. Xiang, Z., Stephan, F., Nassir, N.: Visual Marker Detection and Decoding in AR Systems: A Comparative Study. In: International Symposium on Mixed and Augmented Reality, p. 97 (2002)
5. Iryna, S., David, G.L.: Scene Modeling, Recognition and Tracking with Invariant Image Features. In: Proceedings of the Third IEEE and ACM International Symposium on Mixed and Augmented Reality, pp. 110–119 (2004)
6. Luca, V., Vincent, L., Pascal, F.: Combining edge and Texture Information for Real-Time accurate 3D Camera Tracking. In: Proceedings of the third IEEE and ACM International Symposium on mixed and Augmented Reality, pp. 18–56 (2004)
7. Harald, W., Florent, V., Didier, S.: Adaptive Line Tracking with Multiple Hypotheses for Augmented Reality. In: Fourth IEEE and ACM International Symposium on Mixed and Augmented Reality, pp. 62–69 (2005)
8. Kato, H., Billinghurst, M.: Marker Tracking and HMD Calibration for a video-based Augmented Reality Conferencing System. In: Proceedings of the 2nd International Workshop on Augmented Reality, San Francisco, USA (1999)
9. Tateno, K., Kitahara, I., Ohta, Y.: A Nested Marker for Augmented Reality. In: IEEE Virtual Reality Conference VR 2007, pp. 259–262 (2007)
10. David, M., Yannich, M., Yousri, A., Touradj, E.: Particle filter-based camera tracker fusing marker and feature point cues. In: Proc. of the IS and SPIE Conf. on Visual Communications and Image Processing (2007)
11. Julien, P., Andreas, G., Pascal, L., Vincent, L., Pascal, F.: An All-In-One Solution to Geometric and Photometric Calibration. In: Proceedings of the Third IEEE and ACM International Symposium on Mixed and Augmented Reality, pp. 69–78 (2006)

AR Display for Observing Sports Events Based on Camera Tracking Using Pattern of Ground

Akihito Enomoto and Hideo Saito

Department of Information and Computer Science, Keio University
3-14-1 Hiyoshi, Kohoku-ku, Yokohama , Yokohama 223-8522 Japan
{akihito,saito}@hvrl.ics.keio.ac.jp

Abstract. We present an AR display system for observing sports events on a desktop stadium based on fcamera tracking using pattern of the desktop ground by overlaying players in real sports events captured with multiple cameras. In this paper, we take soccer as the sports event. In the proposed system, the pose and the position of an observing camera are estimated in real-time by using a soccer field pattern on the desk top and an AR marker. The soccer field pattern in the desktop stadium on which the object soccer game is observed via AR display is previously registered with the real soccer stadium in which the real soccer game is captured with multiple cameras. In the previous procedure, we also estimate camera parameters (projection matrices) of the multiple cameras capturing the real soccer game using planar structures in the soccer field. Positions of soccer player and ball are also previously estimated based on the camera parameters. In the on-line procedure for AR display, the textures of the players captured in the multiple soccer video are simply overlaid onto AR camera videos with CG models which are generated for giving additional visual information.

Keywords: Augmented Reality, Free viewpoint videos, Multiple cameras.

1 Introduction

Computer vision and image processing technologies have extensively been applied to provide novel ways of viewing sports videos for various purposes in recent years. Such application can provide an immersive observation and additional information to viewers in broadcasting of sports games. We can see some examples, such as a virtual off-side line superimposing in soccer game broadcasting [1], world record line superimposing in swimming races, etc. Those additional effects definitely give exciting observing experiences that cannot be obtained by watching captured videos without any additional information. The information superimposing in input videos such as off-side line and world record line are considered as Augmented Reality (AR) video synthesis, in which the key technology is the way of estimating the position and pose of cameras capturing the sports events.

Besides, capturing using multiple cameras of object sports events also provides novel experiences of observation. Eye Vision [2] provides a sort of fly through viewing effect by switching cameras that capture the same sports event from multiple viewpoints.

R. Shumaker (Ed.): Virtual and Mixed Reality, LNCS 5622, pp. 421–430, 2009.

While Eye Vision is simply switching videos captured with multiple cameras, we can even synthesize a novel viewpoint video using videos captured with multiple cameras based on computer vision technology. Such method is called as free viewpoint synthesis, and has extensively been studied in recent 10 years [3,4,5,6]. Inamoto et al. [3] proposed a method for synthesizing intermediate viewpoint videos from videos captured with only weakly calibrated multiple cameras for real soccer match application. Jarusirisawad et al. [6] extended this method for applying to practical broadcasting of sports events.

Combining AR display and free viewpoint synthesis can also provide novel ways in order to provide immersive observation of such sports events. Uematsu et al. [7] has applied wide-area camera tracking method using multiple markers [8] to baseball observation onto a desktop baseball stadium model. Inamoto et al also proposed a system for AR observation of real soccer match onto a desktop soccer field model [9]. In this system, an user can observe objective soccer match on the soccer field model through HMD (Head Mounted Display) from arbitrary viewpoint. In this method, images of real players are registered with the field model image captured with the camera attached with HMD based on only projective geometry between the multiple viewpoint cameras capturing real soccer match for avoiding camera calibration procedure of the cameras. This implies that only image-based rendering can be augmented into the field model image, but virtual objects cannot be rendered in the AR display because of lack of 3D coordinate information. Such virtual object rendering is often useful for rendering objects that cannot be captured in input multiple viewpoint videos, as soccer goal, moving ball, etc.

In this paper, we propose a system for providing AR observation of soccer match onto a desktop field model using a video see through device, in which even CG rendering cab also be augmented into the field model image. In this system, we utilize the pattern on the field model for real-time estimation of camera parameters (projection matrix) of the observing camera with the help of an AR toolkit marker. The estimation of projection matrix of the observing camera enables to augment both rendered images by captured videos with real stadium cameras and CG images into the observing image. Additionally, CG generated players can also be rendered into the observing image, which is especially useful when the viewpoint of the observing camera is much different from the viewpoints of the real stadium cameras.

2 Proposed System

The data processing in the propose system can be divided into off-line phase and on-line phase. In the off-line phase, an objective soccer match is captured with multiple uncalibrated cameras from multiple view points in the stadium (we call those cameras as stadium cameras in this paper). Next, player region segmentation should be performed. The segmentation might be possible in automatic process by using state-of-art segmentation algorithms, but we performed with semi-automatic process with manual intervention. In addition to this segmentation, we also need to detect features in the videos for calibrating the capturing cameras such as lines of field pattern and the positions of the ball with manual operation. Such manual operation can be accepted because those procedures do not have to be performed in on-line phase.

Calibration

Selection of
Stadium Camera

AR Display

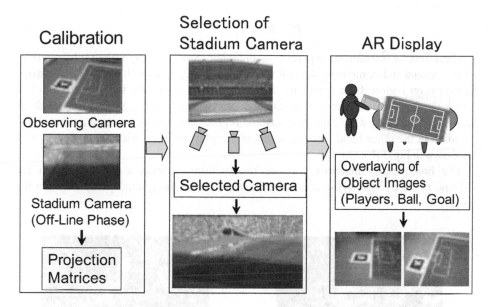

Fig. 1. Overview of the proposed method

In on-line phase, the segmented images of the players captured with the multiple cameras are overlaid onto the image of the filed model on the desktop captured with the observing camera. Fig.1 shows the overview of the on-line phase. First, four corner positions of the penalty area on the field pattern are detected in the image of the observing camera. Then using corresponding positions of the detected corners in the real stadium, the projection matrix of the observing camera onto the field of the real stadium is computed.

Next, according to the computed projection matrix of the observing camera, the stadium camera closest to the observing camera is selected. Then, the positions of players captured in the selected stadium camera are computed and transferred into the observing camera coordinates, so that the segmented player image of every player can be overlaid at the correct position into the observing camera.

2.1 Player Region Segmentation (Off-Line Phase)

The background subtraction is a generic way for player region segmentation, but it is not suitable especially when the shadow of the player exists. Recently, the graph-cut is often used for achieving robust segmentation [6], but it needs some manual intervention for each frame of input videos. For avoiding such problems, we employ a method for player region segmentation using plane constraint of the soccer field ground. We can assume all players do not lay down on the ground, but stand on the ground plane. This means that only the pixels of the ground can be transferred between different stadium cameras each other using homography matrix for the ground plane. Based on this assumption, we can assume that a pixel color P in a player region in a camera is not same as pixel colors P_i at transferred positions in the other cameras using homography matrices of the plane. This implies

$$P \neq P_1 \approx P_2 \tag{1}$$

Therefore, by transferring a pixel onto the other cameras using holography matrices of the ground and comparing the colors of them, we can decide that the pixel is inside in the player region if the colors are different. If we do not take this method, but just apply the background subtraction method, we will get the segmentation result as shown in Fig.2 (a), where the cast shadow regions are also segmented as the player region. On the other hand, we can segment the player region without shadow region as shown in Fig.2 (b).

The homography matrices between the stadium cameras are computed in the off-line phase by specifying correspondence points on the ground plane between the cameras.

 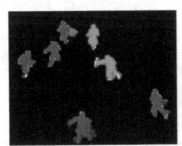

(a) Background Subtraction

(b) Segmentation using the ground plane constraint

Fig. 2. Comparison of segmented region

2.2 Detecting Penalty Area in Observing Camera (On-Line Phase)

In this system, we estimate the projection matrix P via the homograpy matrix H of the field plane. For estimating the homography matrix, the four corners of the penalty area of the field pattern are detected as the following procedure.

First, the positions of the corners are initially predicted by using AR marker that can easily be detected so that we can get the initial prediction of corner positions of the penalty area robustly in the on-line real-time processing. We employ ARTag [10] in this paper's experiment. According to the initial prediction, we detect accurate position of the corners using template matching.

In the template matching, we first set the searching area in the neighboring area of the initial predicted four points as shown in Fig.3 (a). We then transfer the captured image to the top-view image using the predicted four points. In the top view image, we take small window images at the initial predicted four points as template images, which are shown in Fig.3 (b). Then, each template image is searched within the searching area, so that we can get accurate corner positions of the penalty area as shown by the blue points in Fig.3 (c).

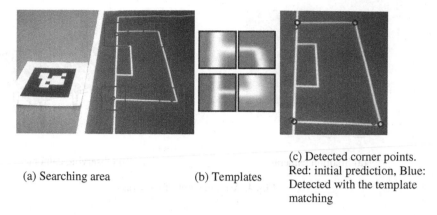

(a) Searching area   (b) Templates

(c) Detected corner points. Red: initial prediction, Blue: Detected with the template matching

Fig. 3. Detection of four corners of penalty area

If the initial predicted four points cannot be obtained because of miss-detection of AR marker, the detected four points in the previous frame are used as the predicted four points. This enables continuous estimation of the projection matrix of the observing camera even when the AR marker cannot be detected by the camera.

For estimating the projection matrix, we first compute homography H using the four corner points of the penalty area detected as described above. Then we do not use the positions of the corners of the penalty area in the stadium model, but in the real stadium, so that we can compute the projection matrix of the observing camera onto the real stadium position. This virtually connects the observing camera to the real stadium coordinate.

For upgrading homography to projection matrix, we employ the following equation [11][12].

$$
\begin{bmatrix} x \\ y \\ 1 \end{bmatrix} \sim H \begin{bmatrix} X \\ Y \\ 1 \end{bmatrix} \sim P \begin{bmatrix} X \\ Y \\ 0 \\ 1 \end{bmatrix}
\tag{2}
$$

As shown in Eq. (2), homography is equivalent with projection matrix when Z component is zero. This implies that we need to compute rotation vector for Z axis, which can be computed from rotation vectors for X and Y axis using the property of rotation matrix. Accordingly, we can get projection matrix of the observing cameras.

2.3 Selection of Stadium Camera for Overlay (On-Line Phase)

For each frame, we select the stadium camera closest to the observing camera using the estimated projection matrix as described above. In the experimental setting in this paper, we use the stadium cameras with the coordinate as shown in Fig. 4 (a), in which the goal area should be captured by all stadium cameras. In this case, the vertical axis on the field on the real stadium is set as Z axis, which implies that the most

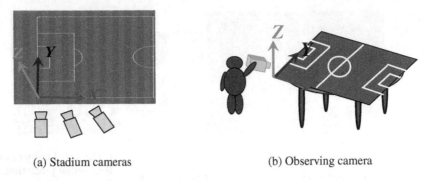

(a) Stadium cameras   (b) Observing camera

Fig. 4. Arrangement of cameras

significant direction of the stadium camera is the rotation around Z axis. Therefore, we evaluate only the direction around Z axis for finding the stadium camera closest to the observing camera. The direction can be computed from the projection matrix of every camera.

2.4 Computing Positions of Players and Ball (Off-Line Phase)

For overlaying the players and the ball onto the images captured with the observing camera, we need to compute the 3D positions of them in the coordinate of the field in the real stadium.

For the players' positions, we assume that the players are always standing on the ground by their foot, so that we can say that the position along Z axis for every player is always zero: $Z=0$. Then we can compute the positions on XY plane for every player from the foot position (x,y) of the player in the image captured in the stadium camera selected as described in the previous section by using the projection matrix of the stadium camera with the condition of $Z=0$.

For the ball position, we compute the 3D position from the ball positions detected in two images of arbitrarily selected two stadium cameras by using the projection matrices of both cameras. The 3D position can be computed according the following equation

$$\begin{pmatrix} p_{31}x - p_{11} & p_{32}x - p_{12} & p_{33}x - p_{13} \\ p_{31}y - p_{21} & p_{32}y - p_{22} & p_{33}y - p_{23} \\ p_{31}'x' - p_{11}' & p_{32}'x' - p_{12}' & p_{33}'x' - p_{13}' \\ p_{31}'y' - p_{21}' & p_{32}'y' - p_{22}' & p_{33}'y' - p_{23}' \end{pmatrix} \begin{pmatrix} X_B \\ Y_B \\ Z_B \end{pmatrix} = \begin{pmatrix} p_{14} - p_{34}x \\ p_{24} - p_{34}y \\ p_{14}' - p_{34}'x' \\ p_{24}' - p_{34}'y' \end{pmatrix} \tag{3}$$

where the projection matrices of the stadium cameras are represented as P and P', the ball positions in both cameras are indicated as (x,y), (x',y'), and the ball positions is (X_B, Y_B, Z_B).

2.5 AR Display (On-Line Phase)

For AR display onto the image captured with the observing camera, the players, the ball and the goal are overlaid at the projected positions from the computed 3D positions of them using the projection matrix of the observing camera. The position of the goal is previously computed by manual operation. For the images of the ball and the goal, we use simple CG models as shown in Fig.5 (c) and (d) because of CG image are more clear in visual appearance than segmented image from the input image captured with the stadium camera. For the player, we use the segmented image of each player shown in Fig.5 (a) or the CG model image as shown in Fig.5 (b). The CG model image is used particularly when the viewpoint of the observing camera is close to the top-down direction, because there is no image captured with the stadium cameras for such direction of observing camera.

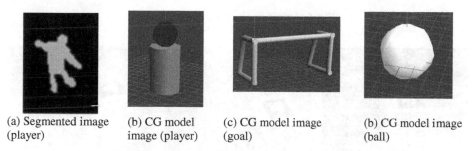

(a) Segmented image (player)   (b) CG model image (player)   (c) CG model image (goal)   (b) CG model image (ball)

Fig. 5. Images of various objects that are overlaid onto observing camera image

The size of the overlaid image is also very important for realistic AR display of those objects. The magnifying size is determined based on the position of the observing camera. The magnifying ratio s of the object images is decided based on the ratio of the norms of translational vectors T and T' of the selected stadium camera and the observing camera, respectively, by the following equation.

$$s = a \frac{|T|}{|T'|} \quad (a \text{ indicates a controlling coefficient}) \tag{4}$$

According to this equation, we can change the size of the object images by the distance between the stadium model and the observing camera.

3 Experiments

As the videos captured by the stadium cameras, we use the multiple viewpoint videos of the professional soccer match that are captured in Ajinomoto Stadium in Tokyo, Japan. We used three cameras that were located as shown in Fig. 6. The distance between camera 1 and camera 2 was 10m, and the distance between camera 2 and 3 was 20m. We also synchronized those cameras in frame.

As for the observing camera, we used WebCam Live!Pro of Creative. The size of captured images is 640 x 480pixels.

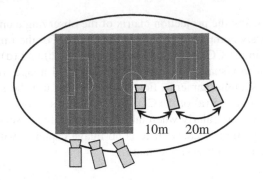

Fig. 6. Arrangement of stadium cameras

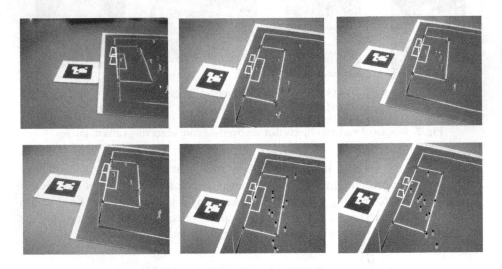

Fig. 7. The examples of AR display images

The examples of AR display images are shown in Fig.7. Please note that the player images in this example were intentionally painted by homogenous color by manually. This is because of the limitation of the video copyright of the professional soccer match. The example images demonstrate that we can correctly overlay the object onto the images captured with moving observing camera.

Fig. 8 demonstrates that the propose system can correctly track the observing camera even when the marker is occluded. Fig.8 (a) is the AR display on the observing camera without the template matching of the corners, in which the object images are overlaid at wrong positions in the observing images because of the occlusion of the maker. On the other hand, Fig. 8 (b) demonstrates that the projection matrix of the observing camera can be correctly estimated even when the marker is occluded, because the corners of the penalty area can correctly be detected.

Fig. 9 shows examples of the way to providing additional information of the soccer match, such as the off-side line and the trajectory of the ball.

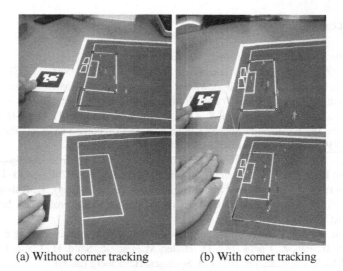

(a) Without corner tracking   (b) With corner tracking

Fig. 8. AR display in case of marker occlusion

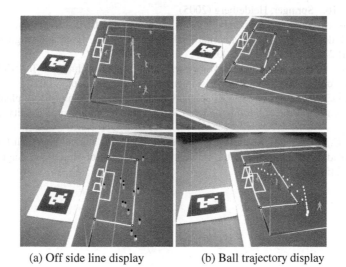

(a) Off side line display   (b) Ball trajectory display

Fig. 9. Adding information

4   Conclusion

In this paper, we present an AR display system for observing soccer match on a desktop stadium based on camera tracking using pattern of the desktop ground by overlaying players captured in real sports events with multiple stadium cameras. In the proposed system, the projection matrix of an observing camera is estimated in real-time by using a soccer field pattern on the desk top and an AR marker.

References

1. CyberPlay, `http://www.orad.co.il`
2. `http://www.ri.cmu.edu/events/sb35/tksuperbowls.html`
3. Inamoto, N., Saito, H.: Virtual viewpoint replay for a soccer match by view interpolation from multiple cameras. IEEE Trans. Multimedia 9(6), 1155–1166 (2007)
4. Kitahara, I., Saito, H., Akimichi, S., Ono, T., Ohta, Y., Kanade, T.: Large-scale virtualized reality. In: IEEE Computer Society Conference on Computer Vision and Pattern Recognition (CVPR2001), Technical Sketches (2001)
5. Yaguchi, S., Saito, H.: Arbitrary viewpoint video synthesis from multiple uncalibrated cameras. IEEE Trans. on Systems, Man and Cybernetics, Part B 34(1), 430–439 (2004)
6. Jarusirisawad, S., Hayashi, K., Saito, H., Inamoto, N., Kawamoto, T., Kubokawa, N., Fujiwara, T.: The intermediate view synthesis system for soccer broadcasts. In: Proceedings of ASIAGRAPH 2008, Shanghai (2008)
7. Uematsu, Y., Saito, H.: AR baseball presentation system with integrating multiple planar markers. In: Pan, Z., Cheok, D.A.D., Haller, M., Lau, R., Saito, H., Liang, R. (eds.) ICAT 2006. LNCS, vol. 4282, pp. 163–174. Springer, Heidelberg (2006)
8. Uematsu, Y., Saito, H.: Vision-based registration for augmented reality with integration of arbitrary multiple planes. In: Roli, F., Vitulano, S. (eds.) ICIAP 2005. LNCS, vol. 3617, pp. 151–162. Springer, Heidelberg (2005)
9. Inamoto, N., Saito, H.: Immersive Observation of Virtualized Soccer Match at Real Stadium Model. In: The Second International Symposium on Mixed and Augmented Reality (ISMAR 2003), pp. 188–197 (2003)
10. Fiala, M.: ARTag, a fiducial marker system using digital techniques. In: IEEE Computer Society Conference on Computer Vision and Pattern Recognition (2005)
11. Simon, G., Fitzgibbobo, A.W., Zisserman, A.: Markerles tracking using planar structures in the scene. In: Proc.of the International Symposium on Augmented Reality, pp. 120–128 (2000)
12. Simon, G., Berger, M.: Reconstructing while registering: a novel approach for markerless augmented reality. In: Proc.of the International Symposium Mixed and Augmented Reality, pp. 285–294 (2002)

Interactive Fluid Simulation Using Augmented Reality Interface

Makoto Fujisawa and Hirokazu Kato

Graduate School of Information Science, Nara Institute of Science and Technology,
8916-5 Takayama, Ikoma, Nara, Japan
{fujis,kato}@is.naist.jp

Abstract. This paper presents an interactive fluid simulation system using augmented reality interface. The presented system uses Smoothed Particle Hydrodynamics to simulate the behavior of liquid and adopts a particle-particle interaction approach to calculate the surface tension that becomes important in a small-scale liquid. Fluid-solid interaction can be calculated effectively by representing a solid as a distance function. Therefore, the shape of the solid can be represented precisely without increasing the number of the particles. Moreover, The system can directly operate the solid by augmented reality interface.

Keywords: real-time fluid simulation, surface tension, augmented reality interface.

1 Introduction

Fluid simulation has been mainly used in an industrial field to design products. In these fields, the accuracy is very important and then the computational time tends to be quite long. On the other hand, in computer graphics field, several methods for real-time fluid simulation had been developed in recent years. Especially, particle method, which is a technique of representing liquid by many particles, is used mainly for real-time application, game, and interactive system.

There are many researches to generate fluid animations such as ocean wave, explosion, and dam breaking. However, the many of fluid phenomena familiar to us are small-scale, for example, pouring water to the cup, flowing droplets. In such small-scale fluid phenomena, surface tension becomes a dominant factor. To realize the interaction with small-scale liquid such as water droplets, the fluid simulation must be stable and fast even though the surface tension is very large. We adopt Smoothed Particle Hydrodynamics (SPH) method with a particle-particle interaction approach for the surface tension calculation. In addition, to simulate high-viscosity fluid such as cream and incompressibility fluid, we use a double density relaxation method [3].

Interface is important part of the interactive fluid simulation system. Generally, movements of mouse in 2D are converted into limited movements in 3D space. However, this technique is not intuitive operation, and it is difficult to deal for inexperienced users. It is also possible to use 3D user interface such as PHANToM. But the cost is high. On the other hand, augmented reality (AR) interface is used as three dimensional interface that contains virtual and real objects simultaneously. AR

R. Shumaker (Ed.): Virtual and Mixed Reality, LNCS 5622, pp. 431–438, 2009.

interface only requires to a cheap camera and marker patterns which is printed on a paper, and provide more intuitive operations. The AR interface is used to operate a solid in our fluid simulator. The liquid represented by particles can control freely by using the solid. As a result, it is possible to use it as assistance for making CG animations.

The rest of the paper is organized as follows: Section 2 describes previous work and Section 3 details our fluid simulation techniques. Section 4 and 5 address our rendering method of liquid surface and AR interface used in the simulation. Section 6 shows the result of our method. Finally, we conclude the paper in section 7 with a discussion of future work.

2   Related Work

As a physical-based simulation, fluid dynamics have been used to animate complicated behaviors of water [4], gas [15], flames [14] etc. To capture a smooth interface of liquid, structured or unstructured grid has been used in computer graphics. The grid-based method, which known as a type of Eulerian approach, discretize the computational space by finite cells. Each cell contains a discriminant function (e.g. Level set function) to identify liquid region or not. This function represents the smooth surface of liquid. However, it is difficult to represent exact boundary of solid because of axis aligned grid. Losasso et al. [12] used an unstructured grid. The size of which is finer around free fluid and solid surfaces. However, a boundary region between the objects and fluid is represented by hexahedrons and good results are not always obtained. Klingner et al. [7] proposed a method in which tetrahedral grids are generated according to a boundary shape at each time step for interactions with moving solid objects. However, the generation of adaptive grids requires additional processing time.

The particle-based "Lagrangian" method abandons the grid completely. In this method, fluid is represented by a finite number of moving particles. Movement of the particle is equivalent to the movement of the fluid. The particle method can compute effectively as compared to the grid-based Eulerian approach that discretizes the whole space with the grids, because it only has to arrange the particles in the liquid domain where we want to calculate the movement. Therefore, the particle method frequently used for real-time applications. The most common of which include Moving Particle Semi-implicit(MPS) [8] and Smoothed Particle Hydrodynamics(SPH) [13]. MPS employed a semi-implicit algorithm to treat incompressible flows. The semi-implicit algorithm increases the computational cost. On the other hand, SPH that computes compressible flows, is often used in computer graphics because the computation cost of SPH is typically lower than that of MPS. Tartakovsky et al. [16] introduced a particle-particle interaction model in the calculation of SPH to represent the surface tension of liquid drop. The particle-particle interaction model was also applied to MPS by Liu et al. [10]. Harada et al. [5] proposed an improved calculation model of wall boundary computation. They used an implicit representation for solid surface. Clavet et al. [3] proposed a robust and stable method for viscoelastic fluid simulation. They adopted a prediction-relaxation scheme in SPH for numerical stability. The incompressibility was accomplished by a technique called "double density relaxation". For liquid simulation, we use the method of [3].

There are some researches which uses physic simulation in augmented reality environment. Allard and Raffin [1] developed a virtual reality system for augmenting real worlds with physical simulation and Chae and Ko [2] introduced rigid collisions by using Open Dynamics Engine. Kwatra et al. [9] used a fluid simulation and a complete 3D geometry reconstructed from binocular video sequences to enable one-way coupling from the video to the fluid. Imura et al. [6] integrated the particle-based fluid simulation method into augmented reality environment. We use SPH and the interaction between fluid and solids for operating the fluid as well as [6]. Our method also can treat highly viscous fluid and small-scale liquid phenomena such as water drops.

3 Fluid Simulation

3.1 Physical Quantity

In SPH, a physical property $\phi(\mathbf{x})$ is approximated by summing weighted properties of neighbor particles.

$$\phi(\mathbf{x}) = \sum_{j \in N} m_j \frac{\phi_j}{\rho_j} W(\mathbf{x}_j - \mathbf{x}, h) . \tag{1}$$

where N is the set of neighboring particles that are closer than the effective radius h. m_j and ρ_j are the mass and density of particle respectively. W is the kernel function.

The gradient of this property is approximated by using the derivative of the kernel function. The density ρ can be found from equation (1).

$$\rho(\mathbf{x}) = \sum_{j \in N} W(\mathbf{x}_j - \mathbf{x}, h) . \tag{2}$$

We assume all the particles have the unit mass (i.e. $m_j = 1$) for simplification. For density calculation, we employ $W = (1 - |\mathbf{x}_j - \mathbf{x}| / h)^2$ as a kernel function.

Given the density ρ, the pressure p is obtained from the equation of state.

$$p = k(\rho - \rho_0) . \tag{3}$$

where k is the stiffness parameter and ρ_0 is the rest density.

3.2 Incompressibility

SPH was developed for compressible flow in astrophysics, In order to simulate incompressibility and compute surface tension, we use a double density relaxation, and adopt a prediction relaxation approach for numerical stability [3].

The double density relaxation has two different particle densities: density and near-density. The near-density prevents particle clustering and provides surface tension effect without curvature evaluation.

A typical SPH computation updates the position and velocity of each particle by accumulating various forces. This explicit force integration tends to be unstable, particularly, when large time step is used and/or when large force is acted on particles (e.g. small water drop). The prediction relaxation avoids explicit force integration by using a technique more similar to an implicit scheme. At the start of the time step, predicted position of particle is computed from previous position and velocity. The predicted position is relaxed by relaxation displacements due to pressure, collision with solid, etc during the time step. The velocities are recomputed by subtracting previous positions from relaxed position at the end of the time step.

The density displacement between two particles is

$$D_{ij} = \Delta t^2 p_i \nabla W_p (\mathbf{x}_j - \mathbf{x}_i, h) .$$ (4)

where $W_p (\mathbf{x}_j - \mathbf{x}_i, h) = (1 - |\mathbf{x}_j - \mathbf{x}_i| / h)^2$ is the kernel function of the density relaxation. As described above, we use the near-density ρ^{near} in order to incompressibility and anti-clustering. The density displacement with the near-density is

$$D_{ij} = \Delta t^2 \left(p_i \nabla W_p (\mathbf{x}_j - \mathbf{x}_i, h) + p_i^{near} \nabla W_n (\mathbf{x}_j - \mathbf{x}_i, h) \right) .$$ (5)

where $W_n (\mathbf{x}_j - \mathbf{x}_i, h) = (1 - |\mathbf{x}_j - \mathbf{x}_i| / h)^3$ is the near-density kernel and the near-density is calculated by using this kernel as well as equation (2). $p^{near} = k^{near} \rho^{near}$ is the near-pressure. The near-density kernel acts as a repulsion force because its value becomes sharper near the center.

The surface tension force can be calculated by equation (5) as inter-particle force. There is another method for calculating surface tension that defines a color function to distinguish between liquid and non-liquid. The curvature of the liquid surface can be computed from the color function. Although the method using the color function works well with large-scale simulation, it is difficult to apply it to small-scale liquid phenomena such as small drop of water, because the method adds the force explicitly. Surface tension is physically caused by the forces acting on molecules at the surface. The forces can be modeled by the particle-particle interactions. We can include the surface tension in our simulation without using the color function which may cause numerical instability.

3.3 Interaction with Solid

Generally, a solid boundary in particle methods is represented as static particles. These particles are treated just like the fluid particles during the density and pressure calculations but the relative positions doesn't change. If we use this method, several layers of particles along the boundary is required. Furthermore, the particles can not accurately represent the boundary.

In order to improve these issues, Harada et al. [5] had introduced a precomputed wall weight function to compute the contribution of a boundary. The computation of fluid density with the wall weight function is

$$\rho(\mathbf{x}) = \sum_{j \in N_{fluid}} W(\mathbf{x}_j - \mathbf{x}, h) + \sum_{j \in N_{wall}} W_{wall}(\mathbf{x}_j - \mathbf{x}, h)$$

$$= \sum_{j \in N_{fluid}} W(\mathbf{x}_j - \mathbf{x}, h) + Z_{wall}(r_{iw}) \ . \tag{6}$$

where $Z_{wall}(r_{iw})$ is the wall weight function, r_{iw} is the distance between a particle i and wall. The wall weight function can be computed before the simulation step starts and simply referred in the step.

4 Rendering

The positions of particles have been computed, and then we have to visualize the free surface of liquid. One way to visualize the free surface of liquid is to render an iso surface of particles by using an additional field quantity called color field which is 1 at particle locations and 0 otherwise. The color field c_s can identify the free surface of liquid.

$$c_s(\mathbf{x}) = \sum_{j \in N} W_{cs}(\mathbf{x}_j - \mathbf{x}, h) \ . \tag{7}$$

We use Marching Cubes [11] to triangulate the iso-surface $c_s(\mathbf{x}) - T = 0$ where T is user defined threshold. We implemented Marching Cubes on GPU using CUDA to accomplish the real-time computation.

5 Augmented Reality Interface

AR interface is 3D input device that can be constructed at a low price, and we use this for the interaction with 3D flow simulation. The solid objects is moved by the AR interface, the user can operate the fluid through the solid. The solid objects can take any shape as described in section 0 because it is represented by a distance function.

6 Results

This section describes the results of our method. The results are performed on a PC with Core 2 Duo 3.16GHz CPU and 3.0GB RAM. The AR interface is implemented by AR Toolkit, and we make the two markers to indicate the environment and the user operation.

Fig. 1 shows the result of liquid in a tank and a solid ball augmented onto markers. The ball moves according to the movement of the marker and interacts with the liquid. The number of particles was about 800. Surface polygons were extracted from the particles using equation (7) and Marching Cubes and the process was accelerated

Fig. 1. Liquid in a tank interacting with a ball

by using GPU. The wall weight functions were used for the wall of the tank and the ball. Fig. 2 shows water drop simulation with a solid box rendered by wireframe. The shape of water drop is mainly governed by surface tension. Appropriate shape is reproduced by our stable surface tension calculation. The users can move the drop of water by using the solid. The drop of water spattered when the recognition of the marker becomes unstable depending on the environment and the marker moves too rapidly. It is necessary to improve it to become smooth movement by using Kalman filtering etc.

7 Conclusion and Future Work

We presented an interactive fluid simulation system using augmented reality interface. Our system adopted SPH to simulate the behavior of liquid and used the particle-particle interaction approach for the surface tension calculation. In addition, we used the double density relaxation method to simulate high-viscosity fluid and incompressibility fluid. In order to achieve intuitive operation, the augmented reality interface was used and fluid-solid interaction could be calculated effectively by representing the solid as a signed distance function.

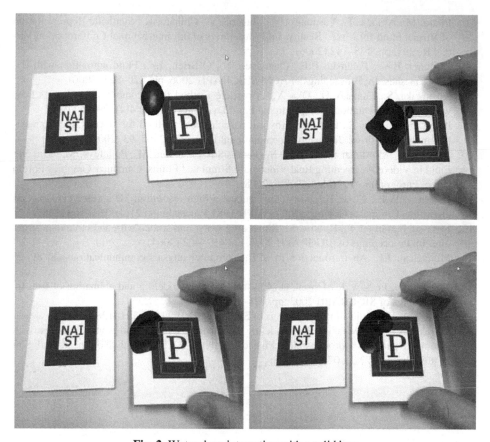

Fig. 2. Water drop interacting with a solid box

For future work, as mentioned in section 0, we may be able to estimate the solid motion using Kalman filtering. Other future research topics include a combination of another simulation and AR Interface, for example, elastic body deformation, air flow over the whole space etc.

References

1. Allard, J., Raffin, B.: Distributed Physical Based Simulations for Large VR Applications. In: VR 2006: Proceedings of the IEEE conference on Virtual Reality, pp. 89–96 (2006)
2. Chae, C., Ko, K.: Introduction of Physics Simulation in Augmented Reality. In: International Symposium on Ubiquitous Virtual Reality, pp. 37–40 (2008)
3. Clavet, S., Beaudoin, P., Poulin, P.: Particle-based Viscoelastic Fluid Simulation. In: ACM SIGGRAPH/Eurographics Symposium on Computer Animation, pp. 219–228 (2005)
4. Enright, D., Marschner, S., Fedkiw, R.: Animation and rendering of complex water surfaces. In: Proceedings of ACM SIGGRAPH 2002, pp. 736–744 (2002)
5. Harada, T., Koshizuka, S., Kawaguchi, Y.: Improvement of the Boundary Conditions in Smoothed Particle Hydrodynamics. Computer Graphics & Geometry 9(3), 2–15 (2007)

6. Imura, M., Amada, T., Yasumuro, Y., Manabe, Y., Chihara, K.: Synthetic Representation of Virtual Fluid for Mixed Reality. In: Proceedings of 8th International Conference on Virtual Reality, pp. 135–142 (2006)
7. Klingner, B.M., Feldman, B.E., Chentanez, N., O'Brien, J.F.: Fluid animation with dynamic meshes. In: Proceedings of ACM SIGGRAPH 2006, pp. 820–825 (2006)
8. Koshizuka, S., Tamako, H., Oka, Y.: A particle method for incompressible viscous flow with fluid fragmentation. Computational Fluid Dynamics Journal 4(4), 29–46 (1995)
9. Liu, J., Koshizuka, S., Oka, Y.: A hybrid particle-mesh method for viscous, incompressible, multiphase flows. Journal of Computational Physics 202, 65–93 (2005)
10. Kwatra, V., Mordohai, P., Narain, R., Penta, S.K., Carlson, M., Pollefeys, M., Lin, M.: Fluid in Video: Augmenting Real Video with Simulated Fluids. Computer Graphics Forum (Proc. Eurographics) 27(2), 487–496 (2008)
11. Lorensen, W.E., Cline, H.E.: Marching cubes: a high resolution 3D surface construction algorithm. Computer Graphics (SIGGRAPH 1987 Proceedings) 21(4), 163–169 (1987)
12. Losasso, F., Gibou, F., Fedkiw, R.: Simulating water and smoke with an octree data structure. In: Proceedings of SIGGRAPH 2004, pp. 457–462 (2004)
13. Monaghan, J.J.: An Introduction to SPH. Computer physics communications 48, 89–96 (1988)
14. Nguyen, D., Fedkiw, R., Jensen, H.: Physically based modeling and animation of fire. In: Proceedings of SIGGRAPH 2002, pp. 721–728 (2002)
15. Stam, J.: Stable fluids. In: Proceedings of SIGGRAPH 1999, pp. 121–128 (1999)
16. Tartakovsky, A., Meakin, P.: Modeling of surface tension and contact angles with smoothed particle hydrodynamics. Physical Review E (Statistical, Nonlinear, and Soft Matter Physics) 72(2), 026301 (2005)

Lens Accommodation to the Stereoscopic Vision on HMD

Satoshi Hasegawa[1], Masako Omori[2], Tomoyuki Watanabe[3],
Kazuhiro Fujikake[4], and Masaru Miyao[5]

[1] Department of Information Media, Nagoya Bunri University, Inazawa Aichi, Japan
shase@nagoya-u.jp
[2] Faculty of Home Economics, Kobe Women's University, Suma-ku Kobe, Japan
[3] Faculty of Psychological and Physical Science, Aichi Gakuin University, Aichi, Japan
[4] The Institute for Science of Labour , Kawasaki Kanagawa, Japan
[5] Graduate School of Information Science, Nagoya University, Chikusa-ku Nagoya, Japan

Abstract. The purpose of this study was to clarify the effect on visual function of gazing at stereoscopic images on a head mounted display (HMD). We measured visual accommodation during stereoscopic viewing while using a HMD by using our original instrument of measurement. The presented image was shown 3-dimensionally on an HMD set up at a visual distance of 3 cm. A spherical object moved back and forth toward and away from the observer in a 10 sec cycle. While the subjects were gazing at the 3D image with both eyes, the lens accommodation in the right eye was measured and recorded. Accommodation to the virtual objects was shown during the viewing of stereoscopic images of 3D computer graphics, but was not shown when the images were displayed without appropriate binocular parallax. It is suggested that stereoscopic moving images on HMD induced the visual accommodation by the expansion and contraction of the ciliary muscle, which is synchronizing with convergence.

Keywords: Binocular HMD, Stereoscopic image, 3-dimension, Visual function.

1 Introduction

Head mounted displays (HMDs) are now widely used in the world for viewing stereoscopic images. However, visual functions during stereoscopic vision on HMDs have been little studied. Lens accommodation with stereoscopic HMDs has not been measured, because the eyes are very close to the HMDs. To investigate the effects of stereoscopic images seen on HMDs on human vision, the authors measured lens accommodation in subjects as they watched stereoscopic images on an HMD.

Lens accommodation was measured for 40 sec as subjects gazed at 3D images on HMDs. Measurements were made when subjects gazed at 3D, Pseudo 3D, and 2D moving images with natural binocular vision.

We conducted the experiment using an HMD (Vuzix Corp; iWear AV920, 640 x 480 dot; Fig. 1) and Power 3D software (Olympus Visual Communications Corp).

Virtual images were created in the brain as shown in Fig. 2. The image was a sphere displayed stereoscopically on an HMD set at a visual distance of 3 cm.

To our knowledge there have been no reports on accommodation with stereoscopic HMDs. In this study we conducted an experiment on lens accommodation in response to 3D images on an HMD.

R. Shumaker (Ed.): Virtual and Mixed Reality, LNCS 5622, pp. 439–444, 2009.

Fig. 1. An HMD (iWear AV920, Vuzix Corporation; 640×480dot) used in the present experiment

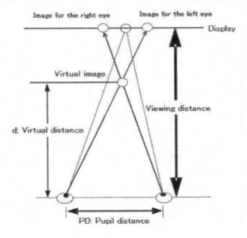

Fig. 2. Virtual image using convergence

2   Apparatus to Measure Lens Accommodation

A modified version of an original apparatus [1] to measure lens accommodation was used in the experiments. Accommodation was measured for 40 seconds under natural viewing conditions with binocular vision while a 3D image moved virtually toward and away from the subject on an HMD. For the accommodation measurements, the visual distance from the HMD to the subjects' eyes was 3 cm. The refractive index of the right lens was measured with an accommodo-refractometer (Nidek AR-1100) when the subjects gazed at the presented image via a small mirror with both eyes. The HMD was positioned so that it appeared in the upper portion of a dichroic mirror placed in front of the subject's eyes (Fig. 3). The 3D image was observed through the mirror. The stereoscopic image displayed in the HMD could be observed with natural binocular vision through reflection in the dichroic mirror, and refraction could be measured at the same time by transmitting infrared rays.

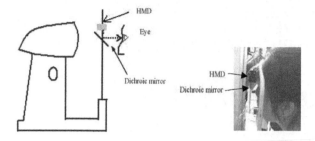

Fig. 3. Lens accommodation measured with a 3D content generation method on an HMD. An accommodo-refractometer (Nidek AR-1100) was used when the subjects gazed at the presented image via a small mirror with both eyes.

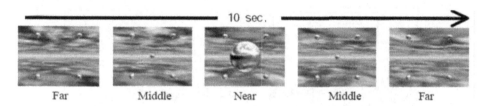

Fig. 4. Stereoscopic target movement

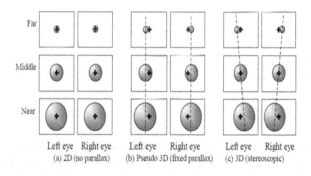

Fig. 5. Three parallax modes used in this experiment

The image was a sphere displayed stereoscopically on an HMD set at a visual distance of 3 cm. The sphere moved virtually in a reciprocating motion toward and away from the observer with the cycle of 10 seconds (Fig. 4).

The subjects were instructed to gaze at the center of the sphere, and the gaze time was set at 40 seconds. All subjects viewed tree types of images of 2D, pseudo 3D and 3D as shown in Fig.5. While both eyes were gazing at the stereoscopic image, the lens accommodation of the right eye was measured and recorded.

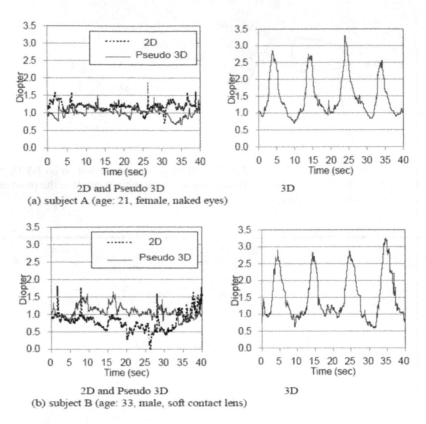

Fig. 6. Effect of different image content on lens accommodation. 2D, Pseudo 3D and 3D were shown in Fig. 5.

3   Results

The presented image was a 3-dimensionally displayed sphere that moved in a recipro-cating motion toward and away from the observer with the cycle of 10 sec. (Fig.4). The subjects gazed at the sphere for 40 seconds. The results for 2D, pseudo 3D and 3D (Fig. 5.) are shown in Fig. 6.

Fig.6 (a) is a result of subject A (age: 21, female, naked eyes), and (b) is of subject B (age: 33, male, soft contact lens).

The results showed that large amplitude of accommodation synchronizing with convergence are shown only in 3D mode.

Accommodation occurred together with the movement of the stereoscopic image in 3D mode on the HMD (Fig. 6), and the lens accommodated so that the near point focus corresponded to the time when the visual target reached the nearest point virtually. It was shown that the focus then moved to a distant point as the virtual movement of the visual target was away from the subject. The amplitude of accom-modation became smaller both in 2D and pseudo 3D.

Accommodation to the virtual objects was shown during the viewing of stereoscopic images of 3D computer graphics, but was not shown when the images were displayed without appropriate binocular parallax. It is suggested that stereoscopic moving images on HMD induced the visual accommodation by the expansion and contraction of the ciliary muscle, which is synchronizing with convergence.

4 Discussion

Lens accommodation was measured for 40 sec with subjects gazing at a 3D image under conditions of binocular vision using the HMD.

When the sphere moved closer, accommodation was made to approximately 3 Diopter in front of the eyes in the subject with the largest amplitude of accommodation. Immediately before the sphere reached the most distant point, the accommodation was about 1 Diopter. This demonstrates objectively that the ciliary muscle and ciliary zonule tense during near vision and relax during far vision, even when that vision is with virtual movement of a 3D image on an HMD.

Patterson and Martin [3] reviewed stereopsis and pointed out that perceived depth for crossed disparity follows predictions derived from constancy in most cases, whereas for uncrossed disparity perceived depth is frequently less than predicted. They reported that among several possible distance cues relating to the computation of perceived depth, one set of cues involves proprioceptive information from accommodation, convergence, or both.

To date there have been no reports on accommodation for stereoscopic HMDs. The present report showed the lens accommodation in response to 3D images on a HMD. There is empirical evidence that prolonged use of HMDs sometimes gives a feeling similar to motion sickness. The sensory conflict theory explains that motion sickness can occur when there are conflicting signals from the vestibular and visual systems [4]. In congruence with this theory, motion sickness can be induced without actual motion. Virtual reality systems are designed to be life-like [5], and the potential for visually induced motion sickness in virtual reality systems has been recognized [6]. Therefore, we are planning another experiment on the effects of stereoscopic views on HMDs on motion sickness, using stabilograms.

5 Conclusion

We investigated lens accommodation in stereoscopic vision on HMDs. Actual accommodation for stereoscopic views on HMDs was confirmed. Since HMDs are promising devices for ubiquitous virtual reality, further research, including that on 3D image sickness, is merited.

Acknowledgement

This study is supported by Olympus Visual Communications Corporation (OVC), Japan.

References

1. Miyao, M., Otake, Y., Ishihara, S.: A newly developed device to measure objective amplitude of accommodation and papillary response in both binocular and natural viewing conditions. Jpn. J. Ind. Health 34, 148–149 (1992)
2. Miyao, M., et al.: Visual accommodation and subject performance during a stereographic object task using liquid crystal shutters. Ergonomics 39(11), 1294–1309 (1996)
3. Patterson, R., Martin, W.L.: Human stereopsis. Human Factors 34, 669–692 (1992)
4. Reason, J.T.: Man in Motion. Wiedenfeld and Nicholson, London (1974)
5. Wells, M.J., Haas, M.: The human factors of helmet-mounted displays and sights. In: Karim, M. (ed.) Electro-optical Displays, Marcel Dekker, New York (1992)
6. Hettinger, L.J., Riccio, G.E.: Visually induced motion sickness in virtual reality system: implications for training and mission rehearsal. In: Interagency Conference on Visual Issues in Training and Simulation, Armstrong Laboratory, Aircrew Training Research Division, Williams Air Force Base, AZ (1991)

Acquiring a Physical World and Serving Its Mirror World Simultaneously

Seungpyo Hong[1,2], Jong-gil Ahn[1], Heedong Ko[1], and Jinwook Kim[1]

[1] Imaging Media Research Center, Korea Institute of Science and Technology
[2] Dept. of HCI and Robotics, University of Science and Technology, Korea
{junon,hide989,ko,jwkim}@imrc.kist.re.kr

Abstract. A mirror world, which is a virtual space modeling a physical space, attracts enormous interests from VR community recently. Various applications such as Second Life, Google Earth and Virtual Earth have proven their usefulness and potentialities. We introduce a novel method to build a mirror world by acquiring environment data represented as a point cloud. Since our system provides a streaming service of the mirror world while gathering the environment information simultaneously, users located in an immersive display system can navigate and interact in the mirror world reflecting the physical world of the present state. Mobile agent which is a mobile robot carrying two laser rangefinder is responsible for exploring the physical world and creating an environment model. Environment modeling involves position tracking method to merge scattered geometric data. Optimizing method is also need to reduce space complexity of environment model.

Keywords: Laser Rangefinder, Laser Scan, Environment Modeling, Mirror World.

1 Introduction

A mirror world is a kind of virtual world which is representing the real world. Mirror world gives a lot of opportunity which cannot be given in the real world. Mirror world applications such as Google Earth[16] and Virtual Earth[17] gives more realistic experience as if he or she had been there in addition to geographic information. Second Life[18] succeeded in making a virtual world to be a new life space. Many real companies and organization have their branch in the Second Life. As more mirror world services begin and mirror worlds become more complicated, it becomes harder to create and maintain the mirror world manually.

We introduce a novel type of mirror world which is constructed autonomously and shared in real-time. Our contribution is a novel tracking method which is essential for environment modeling and 3D reconstruction with restoring in between position sof mobile robot where each point of a scan was measured. Researches related with environment modeling are summarized in Section 2. After that, tracking, 3D reconstruction and optimizing issues are introduced in Section 3. Our mobile agent platform and example of environment model are also presented. At Section 4, sharing, rendering and navigating in the immersive VR environment are explained.

R. Shumaker (Ed.): Virtual and Mixed Reality, LNCS 5622, pp. 445–453, 2009.

2   Related Work

Autonomous 3D environment modeling has been intensively studied in many research fields such as robotics, virtual reality and computer vision. Related researches can be categorized by scale of modeling target and characteristic of sensory device which collect environment data. Targets of 3D environmental modeling are large-scale city, terrains, streets, buildings, corridors, rooms and so on. There is no solution that covers area from small scale objects to large scale city or terrain.

For the large scale city modeling, airplane with downside scanner is one of the best choices[7]. Using the GPS and navigation system, position of aircraft can be tracked during scanning process. 3D model data from laser scanning system and image data from satellite, airplane and ground are combined to create photorealistic virtual model. In this approach, main issues are detecting buildings and reconstructing them with plains to attach texture images.

3D environment modeling system which targets streets, building facades and small area terrain has many variations of sensory devices and vehicles. Truck[8], remotely controlled helicopter[9] and mobile robot[10][11][12] were used to carry sensory devices. 3D laser scanner which is 2D laser scanner with pan/tilt unit[10][11] or 2D laser scanner which scans vertically is used to collect geometric information. Inertia measurement unit and GPS are used to estimate accurate position[12]. Global road map from aerial map or digital surface model helps to correct the path of vehicle and close the loop when the vehicle moves along the roads[8].

Constructing the indoor map around the mobile robot has been a key issue in the area of robotics. Mapping and localization is chicken-egg problem which means that they cannot be solved independently. Researchers approach to the solution in terms of SLAM(Simultaneous Localization And Mapping)[13]. Recent researches tried to extend 2D mapping to 3D environment modeling. In a case of 3D indoor environment modeling, position of mobile robot is still in the two dimensional plane. The position of mobile is acquired from SLAM approach with 2D mapping, and 3D environment model can be acquired by combining and position from 2D map and environment data from another sensor which is 2D laser scan sensor, ultrasonic sensor or camera. Several researches are interested in how to simplify environment model with simple primitive geometries. Plane is one of the simplest primitives to model floors, walls and ceilings of building interior as well as artificial objects such as desks, bookshelves and doors. By approximating complicated mesh model to flat surfaces, complexity of environment model was reduced less than 10% of its original size[11]. Multi-planar environment model is acquired by expectation maximization algorithm which finds rectangular surface patches in real-time.

Image data make the environment model more realistic although the geometric model is not precise. In the Computer Vision field, there were many attempts to build environment map only with camera. In a case that the surrounding geometry is unknown, cube model with projected images looks realistic and quite useful for certain applications[14]. Only with 2D map from laser scan sensor and image from attached camera, several researches make nice results by extending 2D line to plane in 3D space and projecting the images as texture[22].

Fig. 1. Real world   **Fig. 2.** Mirror world

3 Environment Modeling

Environment modeling plays important role which is creating a mirrored world of the real world. Several sensors are available for acquiring environmental information. We used laser rangefinder which is one of the most widely used sensors. It measure the distance between sensor and obstacle directly, so it is not necessary to extract feature and guess how the world looks like. Our environment modeling system is based on mobile robot and two laser rangefinders. A mobile agent which is a mobile robot with two laser rangefinders freely wanders around the environment and scans the environment. One laser rangefinder which scans parallel to the ground is used to track the position of mobile agent, and another laser rangefinder which scans perpendicular to moving direction collects each slice of environment model.

3.1 Mobile Agent

Our mobile agent is a mobile robot which carries two laser rangefinders. Pioneer P3-AT[20] provides mobility and capability to carry sensors and laptop PC. Hokuyo URG-04LX and UTM-40LX are laser sensors which are suitable for mobile platform because of their low power consumption and light weight[16]. Laptop PC with Intel Core Duo 2.0Ghz CPU is responsible for connecting to laser rangefinders and robot, tracking the position of mobile agent, generating 3D point cloud from 2D scans and streaming the model data.

3.2 Tracking Strategy

Tracking the position of mobile is one of the most important parts of the suggested system. Our mobile agent freely wanders around the environment and collects the geometric information. It is hard to make a whole model only with slices of environmental data which is collected at different positions. A series of positions where each slice of environment model was captured is necessary to merge small slices into whole environment model.

Fig. 3. Mobile agent with two laser rangefinders

To know the mobile agent's position, a laser rangefinder that scans parallel to the ground is necessary. Scan matching method finds the relative position of mobile robot by comparing current scan and previous scan[1]. A number of methods have been suggested to estimate the displacement between two scans. Iterative Closest Point (ICP)[2] algorithm is a dominant algorithm to match scans. ICP algorithm finds the rigid transformation between two scans by iteratively finding the closest points. Our tracking algorithm applies ICP algorithm with distortion correction of scans

Scan matching method finds the relative position of current scan(X_k) comparing to previous scan(X_{k-1}) in terms of rotation R and translation p. R and p are solved by minimizing the objective function in equation (1) where x_i is i^{th} point in X_k and y_i is its corresponding point in X_{k-1}.

$$f(R, p) = \sum_{i=1}^{n} \|Rx_i + p - y_i\|^2 \tag{1}$$

The relative position is represented as described in equation (2) where T_k is a SE3 matrix[] which represents the position of mobile agent with respect to initial position.

$$T_{k-1}^{-1} T_k = \begin{bmatrix} R & p \\ 0 & 1 \end{bmatrix} \tag{2}$$

Relation between current scan and previous scan is

$$X_{k-1} \approx T_{k-1}^{-1} T_k X_k \tag{3}$$

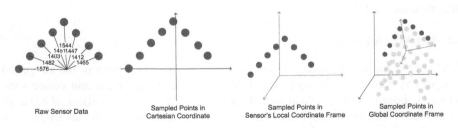

Fig. 4. Procedure of 3D Reconstruction

3.3 3D Reconstruction

A scan sensor which scans vertically collects the environmental data that consists of series of numbers representing distances which are measured during a rotation of motor, which means that the data is based on polar coordinate system originally. In order to convert raw point data to three dimensional points cloud, conversion process must include several computations as illustrated in Figure 3. First, raw scan is converted to points in two dimensional Cartesian coordinate system. Conversion is simply executed by sine and cosine arithmetic. Next, two dimensional points are transformed to three dimensional points based on laser rangefinder's local coordinate frame. Two laser rangefinder's motors have different rotation axis, because one scans horizontally and another scans vertically. And, they are assembled with offset due to physical limitation. From this physical configuration, transformation to sensor's local coordinate frame is constructed. Finally, rigid-transformation which is position of mobile agent is adopted to construct 3D model.

Each distance value in a same data set is scanned at different time, which means they are measured at different positions. However, tracking part of the mobile agent only reports the position at each time instances when horizontal laser rangefinder completes its one rotation of scan. By using the velocity of mobile agent, more accurate position where each distance is measured can be approximated. Current velocity, V_k is calculated by adopting matrix logarithm where n is total number of point in a scan and Δt is time interval between adjacent points.

$$V_k = \frac{1}{n\Delta t} \log T_{k-1}^{-1} T_k \tag{4}$$

Therefore, intermediate position when i^{th} point of kth scan was measured is

$$T_{k,i} = e^{i\Delta t V_k} T_k \tag{5}$$

3.4 Optimizing the Point Cloud

In order to reduce redundant points, a kind of spatial data structure is necessary. The distance between recently incoming point and its nearest point among previous points is compared with threshold which is the limit of resolution of modeled environment. If there exists previous point close enough to new point, new point will be rejected.

kd-tree[6] is one of the widely used spatial data structures and very efficient for searching the nearest neighbor node. If kd-tree guarantees that it is balanced, finding nearest neighbor requires time proportional to logarithm of total number of data which are already included in the tree structure. By using the kd-tree data structure, all the points are structured as a binary tree. Total number of points is determined by controlling threshold value. Fineness of model decreases while threshold of rejection increases as described in Table 1.

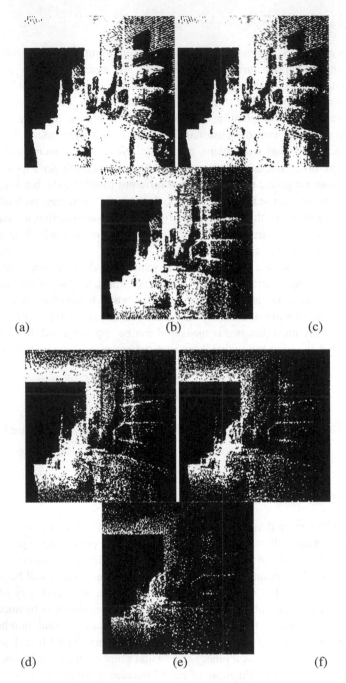

(a)   (b)   (c)

(d)   (e)   (f)

Fig. 5. Rendered image of mirror world with different level of detail

Table 1. Results of removing redundant points of mirror world

Level of Detail	Threshold	Number of Points	Survival Rate	Sample Image
0	0 cm(no rejection)	419362	100%	(a)
1	1 cm	197627	47.1%	(b)
2	2 cm	83370	19.9%	(c)
3	3 cm	43648	10.4%	(d)
4	4 cm	27258	6.5%	(e)
5	5 cm	18656	4.5%	(f)

4 Mirror World Application

Environment model consists of a large number of points which correspond to the points in real world. In order word, environment model represents real environment with its numerical data. Environment model can be shared through the network, rendered to remote displays and interacted with remote users.

4.1 Sharing the Environment Model

When the mobile agent construct and stream the environment model in real time, user in the remote side can share the space around the mobile agent at the same time. To make this possible, network based mirror world frame is necessary. NAVER[3] is one of the advanced network based VR framework, and VARU framework[4] successfully integrate VR, AR and real environment based on NAVER. In the core of the framework, object server is responsible for synchronizing all the states of objects in the virtual environment and real environment. The mobile agent that is responsible for constructing the environment model streams points cloud to object server, then object server updates the mirrored world. Concurrently, all of the NAVER client connecting to object server receive updated mirror world model and render the mirror world. Bottleneck of these processes is managing huge amount of point data in real time. Several methods such as reducing the points, compressing, culling and incremental updating are adapted to enhance the bottleneck.

4.2 Rendering and Navigation

Rendering is also based on NAVER framework which is optimized for multi-screen display. CAVE[] provides four screens on left, front, right side and bottom plane. User inside screen wall can experience being surrounded with points cloud and recognize the shape of surrounding geometry. Viewing direction and eye position is controlled by the user inside mirror world. Navigation manager transmits user's input to distributed NAVER clients to synchronize camera position and direction.

Fig. 6. Rendered image of mirror world in the immersive environment

5 Conclusion

In this paper, we suggested a novel approach to create, share, render and experience the mirror world. Our main contribution is autonomous environment modeling with mobile agent platform which employs two laser rangefinders. Exact position where each point was measured is restored by calculating the velocity and stamping the time instance. From the restored positions, all the points included in the environment model are refined to make more precise model. With our test bed environment, a real world where is explored by mobile agent is provided as a mirror world only a few second later. It means that a mirror world representing the real world also can be synchronized in terms of time. Each scan represents slice of environment data and has no idea to put them together. Along the tracked positions of mobile agent, sliced point data get accumulated to be a three dimensional environment model. Generated environment model is filtered and streamed via network so that remote user in an immersive VR environment can experience the mirror world.

References

1. Lu, F., Milios, E.: Robot Pose Estimation in Unknown Environments by Matching 2D Range Scans. Journal of Intelligent and Robotic Systems 18(3), 249–275 (1997)
2. Rusinkiewicz, S., Levoy, M.: Efficient variants of the icp algorithm. In: Proc. Intl. Conf. on 3D Digital Imaging and Modeling, pp. 145–152 (2001)
3. Park, C.H., Ko, H., Ahn, H., Kim, J.: NAVER: design and implementation of XML-based VR Framework on a PC cluster. In: The 8th International Conference on Virtual Systems and MultiMedia, Gyeongju, Korea, pp. 25–27 (2002)
4. Irawati, S., Ahn, S., Kim, J., Ko, H.: VARU Framework: Enabling Rapid Prototyping of VR, AR and Ubiquitous Applications. In: Virtual Reality Conference, VR 2008, pp. 201–208. IEEE, Los Alamitos (2008)

5. Hong, S., Ko, H., Kim, J.: Motion Tracking with Velocity Update and Distortion Correction from Planar Laser Scan Data. In: International Conference on Artificial Reality and Telexistence, pp. 315–318 (2008)
6. Bentley, J.L.: Multidimensional binary search trees used for associative searching. Commun. ACM 18(9), 509–517 (1975)
7. Hu, J., You, S., Neumann, U.: Approaches to large-scale urban modeling. Computer Graphics and Applications 23(6), 62–69 (2003)
8. Früh, C., Zakhor, A.: An Automated Method for Large-Scale, Ground-Based City Model Acquisition. Int. J. Comput. Vision 60(1), 5–24 (2004)
9. Thrun, S., Diel, M., Hahnel, D.: Scan alignment and 3d surface modeling with a helicopter platform. In: Proceedings of the International Conference on Field and Service Robotics, Lake Yamanaka, Japan (2003)
10. Pfaff, P., Triebel, R., Burgard, W.: An Efficient Extension to Elevation Maps for Outdoor Terrain Mapping and Loop Closing. The International Journal of Robotics Research 26, 217–230 (2007)
11. Hahnel, D., Burgard, W., Thrun, S.: Learning compact 3D models of indoor and outdoor environments with a mobile robot. Robotics and Autonomous Systems 44, 15–27 (2003)
12. Wolf, D., Howard, A., Sukhatme, G.S.: Towards geometric 3D mapping of outdoor environments using mobile robots. In: IEEE/RSJ International Conference on Intelligent Robots and Systems, pp. 1507–1512 (2005)
13. Leonard, J.J., Durrant-Whyte, H.F.: Simultaneous map building and localization for an autonomous mobile robot. In: IEEE/RSJ International Workshop on Intelligent Robots and Systems, Proceedings IROS 1991, vol. 3, pp. 1442–1447 (1991)
14. DiVerdi, S., Wither, J., Höllerer, T.: Envisor: Online Environment Map Construction for Mixed Reality. In: Virtual Reality Conference, VR 2008, pp. 19–26. IEEE, Los Alamitos (2008)
15. Ikeda, S., Miura, J.: 3D Indoor Environment Modeling by a Mobile Robot with Omnidirectional Stereo and Laser Range Finder. In: 2006 IEEE/RSJ International Conference on Intelligent Robots and Systems, pp. 3435–3440 (2006)
16. Kawata, H., Ohya, A., Yuta, S., Santosh, W., Mori, T.: Development of ultra-small lightweight optical range sensor system. In: IEEE/RSJ International Conference on Proc. Intelligent Robots and Systems, pp. 1078–1083 (2005)
17. Google Earth, http://earth.google.com/
18. Microsoft Virtual Earth,
    http://www.microsoft.com/virtualearth/
19. Second Life, http://secondlife.com/
20. Pioneer P3-AT,
    http://www.activrobots.com/ROBOTS/p2at.html

In-Situ 3D Indoor Modeler with a Camera and Self-contained Sensors

Tomoya Ishikawa[1], Kalaivani Thangamani[1,2],
Masakatsu Kourogi[1], Andrew P. Gee[3], Walterio Mayol-Cuevas[3],
Keechul Jung[4], and Takeshi Kurata[1]

[1] National Institute of Advanced Industrial Science and Technology, Japan
[2] University of Tsukuba, Japan
[3] University of Bristol, United Kingdom
[4] Soongsil University, Korea
tomoya-ishikawa@aist.go.jp

Abstract. We propose a 3D modeler for supporting in-situ indoor modeling effectively. The modeler allows a user easily to create models from a single photo by interaction techniques taking advantage of features in indoor space and visualization techniques. In order to integrate the models, the modeler provides automatic integration functions using Visual SLAM and pedestrian dead-reckoning (PDR), and interactive tools to modify the result. Moreover, for preventing shortage of texture images to be used for the models, our modeler automatically searches from 3D models created by the user for un-textured regions and intuitively visualizes shooting positions to take a photo for the regions. These functions make it possible that the user easily create photorealistic indoor 3D models that have enough textures on the fly.

Keywords: 3D indoor modeling, Mixed reality, Virtualized object, Visual SLAM, Pedestrian dead-reckoning, Self-contained sensor.

1 Introduction

Virtualized real objects made from photos enable virtual environments to enhance reality. This reduces the gap between the real and virtual world for a number of applications such as pre-visualization for online furniture-shopping, walk-through simulation, and so on. In particular, recently, establishing self-localisation methods [1] in indoor environment prompts some attempts in plants and offices for cut-down of unnecessary human movements and prediction of unsafe behaviors based on human traffic lines estimated by the methods. For analyzing these data by visualization, photorealistic indoor 3D models made from real environments are quite useful. In addition, 3D models have come into use for navigation systems [2] not only in outdoor but also indoor environments. In the system, 3D models similar to the real world are expected that they can help the users understand the position and direction intuitively. However, to create photorealistic indoor 3D models is still difficult task except for the professionals. In this research, we propose an interactive indoor 3D modeler which enables a user to create 3D models effectively and intuitively for augmenting the reality of the applications described above.

R. Shumaker (Ed.): Virtual and Mixed Reality, LNCS 5622, pp. 454–464, 2009.

In our proposed modeler, the user creates local models from input photos captured at different positions individually as a unit of modeling process. The local models are effectively integrated into a global model by using Visual SLAM [3] which can create "sparse" maps of landmarks from video sequences quickly, pedestrian dead-reckoning (PDR) [1] with self-contained sensors, and simple user interaction techniques. The 3D modeling based on a single photo allows the user to easily create photorealistic models which are texture-mapped with high-resolution and high-quality photos compared with video sequences which often contain motion blur and are generally lower-quality than photos. On the other hand, video sequences are suitable for capturing wide areas at a short time. Our modeler complementarily uses those properties for integrating local models.

In order to create indoor 3D models easily only from a single photo, our modeler utilizes interaction techniques taking advantages of features of indoor environments and geometric constraints from a photo, and also utilizes visualization techniques [4]. Hereby, it is possible to realize in-situ modeling. For stable and accurate integration of created local models, our modeler provides a two-stage registration function that consists of automatic functions and interaction techniques. Furthermore, the modeler helps the user creates more complete models by automatic un-textured-region detection and view recommendation to capture the regions.

This paper is organized as follows. Section 2 describes related works and Section 3, 4, and 5 present the overview of our proposed modeler, local modeling from a single photo, and global modeling for integrating local models respectively. Finally, in Section 6, conclusions and future prospects are summarized.

2 Related Work

3D modeling methods from photos can roughly be classified into two types. One is automatic modeling methods that can automatically reconstruct 3D models without interaction techniques. The other is manual / semi-automatic modeling methods with interaction techniques.

A state-of-the-art automatic modeling method has been proposed by Goesele et al. [5]. Their method reconstructs 3D models by using Structure-from-Motion (SfM) [6] which estimates camera parameters and 3D structural information of scenes by using stereo matching to obtain dense 3D shapes from photos. In stereo methods, the scene objects have to be captured at a number of different viewpoints observing overlapped regions for creating accurate 3D models. Therefore, it is time consuming to capture enough photos or video sequences of indoor environments which require inside-out video acquisition. In addition, the computational cost becomes higher when the video sequences are long, and the accuracy often does not meet the practical needs.

Manual / semi-automatic modeling methods can produce high-quality models by taking advantage of the users' knowledge. Google SketchUp [7] provides sketch interfaces on photos for creating 3D models, but the photos are used only for matching photos and 3D models. The system proposed by Oh et al. [8] utilizes geometric information from an input photo for constraining 3D models on LoS (Lines of Sight) while the user models and edits them. However, this system requires a large amount of time in order to divide the photo into regions.

All processes of modeling in automatic methods using SfM are broken down by failures of estimating correspondences among photos. To compensate for the weakness, Debevec et al. [9] have proposed the semi-automatic method that can carry out stable SfM and creation of models consisting of basic primitives by manually adding correspondences between edges on 3D primitives and of images. In this method, however, target objects have to be approximated by the pre-determined basic primitives.

Sinha et al. [10] and van den Hengel et al. [11] have proposed interactive 3D modelers using a sparse map and camera parameters estimated by SfM. These systems strongly utilize data from SfM for reducing manpower needed to modeling by assuming SfM must be able to estimate all parameters successfully. Accordingly, when SfM cannot work, all of the modeling processes are broken. Furthermore, in case that the created models have critical un-textured regions, the user has to re-visit the site for capturing texture images of the regions again.

A way for preventing such a shortage of texture images is to realize in-situ modeling. In terms of this strategy, Neubert et al. [12] and Bunnum and Mayol-Cuevas [13] have proposed 3D modelers, which can effectively and quickly creates 3D models nearby target objects. However, the created models are simple wireframe models for tracking the objects, so they are not suitable for our target applications.

3   Overview of 3D Indoor Modeler

Fig. 1 shows the flowchart of our proposed modeler. In the modeler, as the preprocessing, sparse maps in a global coordinate system are created by Visual SLAM and PDR for easily achieving integration process which describes below. Note that we assume intrinsic camera parameters are estimated by conventional camera calibration methods.

Then, the user takes a photo, creates a local model from the photo, and integrates it into the global coordinate system iteratively in order to create the global model as the whole indoor environment model. The local models are created in the local coordinate systems estimated from vanishing points on each input photo. In the local coordinate systems, the user can effectively create 3D models by interaction techniques utilizing features of indoor environments. Furthermore, during the local modeling, the user can easily comprehend the shapes of models being created by viewpoint change, real-time mixed mapping of projective texture mapping (PTM) and depth mapping, and smart secondary view, which is adaptively controlled. For integrating local models, our modeler estimates the transform parameters between the local and global coordinate systems by means of sparse maps of landmarks generated in pre-processing and the result of image feature matching, and also our modeler provides interactive tools for more stable parameter estimation. These functions enable the user to integrate models robustly without massive time consumption. After the integration, the modeler automatically detects un-textured regions in the global model and displays the regions, a recommended viewpoint for taking a texture image of the regions, and the position and direction of the user based on PDR for creating the more complete model. By above supportive functions, the user is able to create indoor 3D models effectively on the fly.

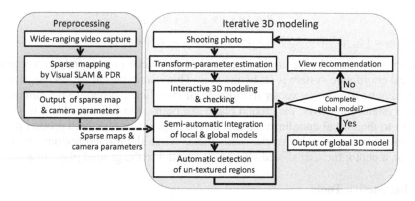

Fig. 1. Flowchart of our proposed modeler

4   Local Modeling from Single Photo

4.1   Transform-Parameter Estimation

In indoor spaces, floors, walls, and furniture are typically arranged in parallel or perpendicularly with respect to each others. Such features facilitate the modeling by applying an orthogonal coordinate system to floors and walls occupying large areas of a photo. Our proposed modeler utilizes these features and estimates transformation parameters between the local coordinate system and the camera coordinate system by CV-supported simple user interactions.

An local coordinate system can be constructed by selecting two pairs of lines that are parallel in the actual 3D room. The modeler first executes the Hough transform to detect lines on the photo, and then displays the lines to the user (Fig. 2-(a,b)). By clicking the displayed lines, the user can provide pairs of parallel lines to the modeler. The 2D intersection points of the selected lines are vanishing points for the photo. From the two vanishing points $\{e_1, e_2\}$ and the focal length f of the camera f, the rotation matrix between the local coordinate system and camera coordinate system $\mathbf{R}$ is given by the following equation.

Fig. 2. Transform-parameter estimation from single photo. (a): Input photo, (b): Detected lines by Hough transform, (c): Setting ground plane by user-interaction.

$$R = (\mathbf{v'}_1 \quad \mathbf{v'}_2 \quad \mathbf{v'}_1 \times \mathbf{v'}_2)$$

where $\mathbf{e}_i = (x_i, y_i)^T$ $(i = 1,2)$, $\mathbf{v}_i = (x_i, y_i, f)^T$, $\mathbf{v'}_i = \mathbf{v}_i / \|\mathbf{v}_i\|$.

After estimating R, the origin of ground plane which corresponds to x-y plane in the local coordinate system is set by the user. This manipulation allows the modeler to determine the translation vector from the local coordinate system to the camera coordinate system. Moreover, the ground plane can be used to place the local model from a photo to the global coordinate system on the assumption that both ground planes in each coordinate system lay on the same plane. When the ground regions are not captured on a photo, the user should set a plane parallel to the ground plane instead.

4.2   Interactive Tools

Assuming that each object in an indoor photo can be modeled with a set of quadrangular and freeform planes, our modeler provides two types of tools to create planes for the user.

- Quadrangular tool: creates a 3D quadrangular plane by giving the 3D coordinates of the opposing corners through mouse clicks. This tool is suitable for simple objects such as floors, walls, tables, and shelves.
- Freeform tool: creates a 3D freeform plane by giving a set of 3D points laying on the contour through repeated mouse clicks. This tool is used for more complex objects.

For both tools, the depth of the first established point can be given by calculating the intersection between the line of sight passing through the clicked point on the photo and the nearest plane to the optical center of the photo if there exists such an intersection. From the initial viewpoint corresponding to the optical center of the photo, the user can easily understand the correspondence between the photo and the model being created. In particular, in the case of the freeform tool, the interaction to set contour points in 3D planes is same as 2D interaction with the photos, thus the user can create models intuitively.

During these interactions, the normal of each plane can be toggled along several default directions such as the x-y, y-z, and z-x planes. The function is especially effective in artificial indoor environments. In addition, the user can create models by means of real-time mixed mapping of PTM and depth mapping as described below.

Fig. 3. Normal manipulation with geometric constraint (red-colored plane: plane being manipulated, green line: view-volume)

The created models can be translated, deformed, and deleted. In terms of translation and deformation, using the view-volume constraint, the user can control the depth and normal vector without changing 2D shapes projected onto the input photo (Fig. 3).

4.3 Visualization for Checking 3D Model

Texture-and-Depth Representation. The proposed modeler provides three types of texture-and-depth presentation modes to the user as follows (Fig. 4).

- Projective texture mapping (PTM): re-projects the texture in the photo onto 3D models and shows the correspondence between the shapes of the models and the textures.
- Depth mapping: displays the depth from the viewpoint to the models as a gray-scale view image and shows the shapes of the model clearly.
- Mixed mapping: displays the models by mixing PTM and depth mapping and shows a more shape-enhanced view image compared with PTM.

These modes of presentation can be rendered by a GPU in real-time not only while viewing the models but also while creating and editing the models. Therefore, it is effective for confirming the shape of models being created.

It is often difficult for the user to confirm shapes of models from the initial view-point using only PTM. In such cases, the depth mapping or mixed mapping provides good clues to confirm the shapes, to find lack of planes, and to adjust the depth.

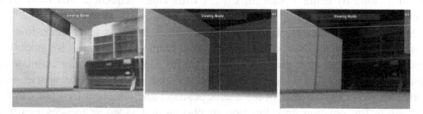

Fig. 4. Examples of PTM (left), depth mapping (center), and mixed mapping (right)

Smart Secondary View. In order to easily understand the shapes of models while they are being constructed, our modeler displays not only a primary view but also a secondary view (Fig. 5). This simultaneous representation helps the user intuitively carry out creation and confirmation of the models.

We define the criteria for determining the second view parameters as follows.

1. Update frequency: Viewing parameters should not be changed frequently.
2. Point visibility: The next point which will be created (corresponding to the mouse cursor) must not be occluded by the other planes.
3. Front-side visibility: The view must not show the backside of the target plane.
4. Parallelism: The view should be parallel to the target plane.
5. FoV difference: The view should have a wide field of view (FoV) when the primary view has narrow FoV, and vice versa.

Fig. 5. Close-up of secondary view (left) and primary view (right)

The modeler searches for the parameters of the second view based on the above criteria. For a real-time search of viewing parameters, the parameters are sampled coarsely.

5 Global Modeling from Local Models

5.1 Sparse Mapping Using Visual SLAM and Self-contained Sensors

Video sequences are suitable for capturing wide areas in a short time compared with photos. Our modeler generates sparse maps of indoor environments consisting of a set of point cloud by using Visual SLAM [3] with video sequences and PDR with self-contained sensors [1].

SfM generally requires high-computational cost and long calculation time to estimate accurate camera motion parameters and a map. Consequently, for smooth in-situ modeling operations, our modeler applies Visual SLAM, which can estimate camera motion parameters and a map simultaneously and quickly, to the sparse mapping. Furthermore, measurements of the user's position and direction by PDR can be used for setting the position and direction of photos and video sequences in the global coordinate system and the scale of the maps by simultaneously carrying out it PDR with Visual SLAM.

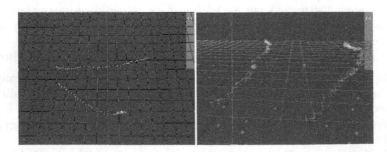

Fig. 6. Sparse maps by Visual SLAM and PDR in global coordinate system

When the modeler handles multiple maps, they are placed in a global coordinate system based on measurements from self-contained sensors. Additionally, the global coordinate system is configured as the Z axis and X-Y plane correspond to the upward vertical direction and the ground plane. Adjustments for rotation, translation, and scaling from initial parameters estimated by PDR can be done with interactive tools. Fig. 6 shows two maps placed in a global coordinate system and the camera paths. These sparse maps are used for semi-automatic functions of integrating local and global models.

5.2 Semi-automatic Integration of Local and Global Models

After creating a local model from a photo (Section 4), the local model is integrated into a global model. The integration process consists of automatic functions using Visual SLAM, PDR, and image-feature matching, and interactive tools with which the user gives information needed to integrate manually when the automatic functions fail to estimate transform parameters. This two-stage process enables the user to integrate local models into the global model effectively and reliably.

In the automatic functions, the modeler first carries out relocalisation toward the sparse maps using a photo used for local modeling by the relocalisation engine of Visual SLAM [3], and then the modeler takes camera motion parameters and its uncertainties for estimating transform parameters between the local and the global coordinate system. When the relocalisation succeeded for multiple maps, the modeler selects the most reliable camera motion parameters according to the uncertainties and the position and direction from PDR. In the case of failures of relocalisation, the modeler uses a position and direction only from PDR. However, the estimated camera motion parameters by Visual SLAM and PDR are not sufficiently accurate for registration of local models.

For more accurate registration, the modeler carries out image-feature matching between two photos; one is used for creating a local model, and the other is used for creating another local model nearest to the target local model. In recent years, robust feature detectors and descriptors such as SIFT [14] and SURF [15] have been proposed, and they are quite useful for such image-feature matching. The 2D point correspondences are converted into 3D point correspondences by using 3D local models created by the user. Then, the transform parameters between the local and global coordinate systems are estimated using RANSAC [16] robustly.

After automatic functions, the user confirms whether the local model is correctly integrated or not by viewing the displayed global model. Fig. 7 shows an example of automatic registration using functions described above. The integrated local model overlapping with a door of the global model is accurately registered in this figure. In the case that the accuracy of integration is not enough, the user can give 2D corresponding points manually or give the transform parameters (translation, rotation, and scaling) interactively.

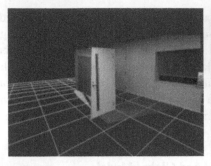

Fig. 7. Examples of automatic integration of local model. (left):global model before integration, (right): global model after integration.

5.3 Automatic Un-Textured-Region Detection and View Recommendation

For preventing shortages of texture images, our modeler automatically detects un-textured regions which correspond to occluded regions from all photos and presents a recommended shooting position to capture the region and the user's current position. This prompts the user to re-capture texture images intuitively.

Un-textured regions are detected from the integrated global model and intrinsic camera parameters and camera motion parameters of the photos in the global coordinate system. The automatic detector searches for planar regions occluded from all viewpoints of photos and finds a dominant region which has the highest density of the occluded regions by 3D window search. Then, the modeler searches for appropriate viewpoint to capture the region by estimating a cost function and recommends the viewpoint. The cost function is defined from the following criteria.

1. Observability: Viewpoint should capture a whole un-textured region.
2. Easiness: Viewpoint should be below the eye level of the users.
3. Parallelism: View-direction should be parallel to un-textured region.
4. Distance: Viewpoint should be close to un-textured region.

When the recommended viewpoint is placed in inapproachable positions, the user can interactively choose another viewpoint rated by the above cost function.

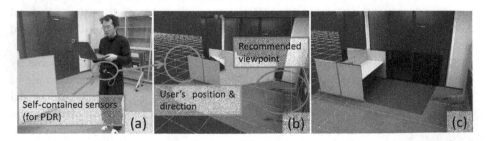

Fig. 8. (a) appearance of user confirming un-textured region, (b) detected un-textured region, recommended viewpoint, and the user's position, and (c) updated model

After estimating the recommended viewpoint, the user's position and direction are presented onto the monitor with the global model, un-textured region, and recommended viewpoint intuitively (Fig. 8).

6   Conclusions

We have proposed an in-situ 3D modeler that supports efficient modeling for indoor environments. The modeler provides the interaction techniques by taking advantage of the features that indoor environments inherently have and geometric constraints from a photo for easily creating 3D models, and provides intuitive visualization to confirm the shapes of created models. The created local models are integrated by semi-automatic functions robustly. Furthermore, presenting un-textured regions and recommended viewpoints to capture the regions make it possible that the user create more complete models on the fly.

Our near-term work is to evaluate the effectiveness of our proposed interaction techniques, visualization, and supportive functions by creating actual indoor environments. For more effective modeling, we plan to develop functions to optimize a global model overlapped with local models, to suggest initial 3D primitives by machine learning of features in indoor environments, and to inpaint small un-textured regions.

References

1. Kourogi, M., Sakata, N., Okuma, T., Kurata, T.: Indoor/Outdoor Pedestrian Navigation with an Embedded GPS/RFID/Self-contained Sensor System. In: Pan, Z., Cheok, D.A.D., Haller, M., Lau, R., Saito, H., Liang, R. (eds.) ICAT 2006. LNCS, vol. 4282, pp. 1310–1321. Springer, Heidelberg (2006)
2. Okuma, T., Kourogi, M., Sakata, N., Kurata, T.: A Pilot User Study on 3-D Museum Guide with Route Recommendation Using a Sustainable Positioning System. In: Proc. of Int. Conf. on Control, Automation and Systems (ICCAS 2007), pp. 749–753 (2007)
3. Gee, A.P., Chekhlov, D., Calway, A., Mayol-Cuevas, W.: Discovering Higher Level Structure in Visual SLAM. IEEE Trans. on Robotics 26(5), 980–990 (2008)
4. Ishikawa, T., Thangamani, K., Okuma, T., Jung, K., Kurata, T.: Interactive Indoor 3D Modeling from a Single Photo with CV Support. In: Electronic Proc. of IWUVR 2009 (2009)
5. Goesele, M., Snavely, N., Curless, B., Hoppe, H., Seitz, S.M.: Multi-View Stereo for Community Photo Collections. In: Proc. of Int. Conf. on Computer Vision (ICCV 2007), pp. 14–20 (2007)
6. Snavely, N., Seitz, S.M., Szeliski, R.: Modeling the World from Internet Photo Collections. Int. Journal of Computer Vision 80, 189–210 (2008)
7. Google SketchUp, http://sketchup.google.com/
8. Oh, B.M., Chen, M., Dorsey, J., Durand, F.: Image-Based Modeling and Photo Editing. In: Proc. of SIGGRAPH, pp. 433–442 (2001)
9. Debevec, P.E., Taylor, C.J., Malik, J.: Modeling and Rendering Architecture from Photographs: A Hybrid Geometry- and Image-Based Approach. In: Proc. of SIGGRAPH, pp. 11–20 (1996)

10. Sinha, S.N., Steedly, D., Szeliski, R., Agrawala, M., Pollefeys, M.: Interactive 3D Architectural Modeling from Unordered Photo Collections. ACM Trans. on Graphics 27(5), article 5 (2008)
11. van den Hengel, A., Dick, A., Thormahlen, T., Ward, B., Torr, P.H.S.: VideoTrace: Rapid Interactive Scene Modelling from Video. ACM Trans. on Graphics 26(3), article 86 (2007)
12. Neubert, J., Pretlove, J., Drummond, T.: Semi-Autonomous Generation of Appearance-based Edge Models from Image Sequences. In: Proc. of IEEE/ACM Int. Symp. on Mixed and Augmented Reality, pp. 79–89 (2007)
13. Bunnum, P., Mayol-Cuevas, W.: OutlinAR: An Assisted Interactive Model Building System with Reduced Computational Effort. In: Proc. of IEEE/ACM Int. Symp.on Mixed and Augmented Reality, pp. 61–64 (2008)
14. Lowe, D.G.: Distinctive image features from scale-invariant keypoints. Int. Journal of Computer Vision 60(2), 91–110 (2004)
15. Bay, H., Ess, A., Tuytelaars, T., Gool, L.V.: Speeded-Up Robust Features (SURF). Computer Vision and Image Understanding 110(3), 346–359 (2008)
16. Fischler, M.A., Bolles, R.C.: Random Sample Consensus: A Paradigm for model fitting with applications to image analysis and automated cartography. Communication of the ACM 24(6), 381–395 (1981)

Evaluation of Visually-Controlled Task Performance in Three Dimension Virtual Reality Environment

Chiuhsiang Joe Lin[1], Tien-Lung Sun[2], Hung-Jen Chen[1,*], and Ping-Yun Cheng[1]

[1] Department of Industrial and System Engineering, Chung-Yuan Christian University,
200, Chung Pei Rd., Chung-Li, Taiwan 32023, R.O.C.
[2] Department of Industrial Engineering and Management, Yuan-Ze University,
135, Yuan-Tung Rd., Chung-Li, Taiwan 32003, R.O.C.
[*]g9302405@cycu.edu.tw

Abstract. The present study aims to evaluate three commercial VR display devices on the market via a 3D Fitts' task. In addition, a Simulation Sickness Questionnaire (SSQ) was used to assess simulator sickness of participants. Ten participants performed repetitive pointing tasks over different conditions of varying display devices, movement directions and indices of difficulty. Based on the results, it seems that the 3D TV technology may not provide enough perceptual depth to enhance movement performance in a 3D VE. The projection display obtained the best performance and preference among the three display devices. The HMD gave the worst result in both the experimental task and the SSQ assessment due to the accompanied discomfort and fatigue.

Keywords: Fitts' law, virtual reality, projection display, HMD, 3D TV.

1 Introduction

Virtual Reality (VR) is a modern technology in the computer science field that offers huge potential impact at home, workplace and schools. Since inducted in 1960's, it has come up in a major way as architecture, interior design, medical, education, training and so forth. In the early period, more attention has been paid to development of the technology itself and potential application uses, but until recently little research and literature has been reported on usability and ergonomic issues associated with VR.

Virtual Environments (VE) can be described as computer-generated immersive surroundings where participants feel to be present and can interact intuitively with objects. The hardware of a typical immersive VR system will include: a computer, a display device and a hand-held input device. As the progress of computer technology, there are plenty of display devices on market could be adopted to present 3D virtual environments. However, the performance enhancement, comfort and fatigue of using these display devices to present a 3D VE are still indeterminate.

The 3D stereo television (3D TV) technology introduced by Philip [1] in 2006 is a breakthrough. This autostereoscopic 3D display provides stereo image that do not require users to wear special 3D glasses. However, in an interactive VE, the impact of the 3D TV on human motor performance is still unclear. For this reason, we apply Fitts' Law to this evaluation.

R. Shumaker (Ed.): Virtual and Mixed Reality, LNCS 5622, pp. 465–471, 2009.
© Springer-Verlag Berlin Heidelberg 2009

Fitts' Law [2] is well known to be an effective quantitative method for modeling user performance and evaluating manual input devices. Fitts' Law states that the time to move and point to a target of width W at a distance A is a logarithmic function of the spatial relative error (A/W), as shown in Equation (1).

$$MT = a + b \log_2(2A/W) .\tag{1}$$

where a and b are empirical constants determined through linear regression. The log term is called the index of difficulty (ID) and describes the difficulty of the motor task (bits).

Some variations of the law have been proposed, such as the Shannon formulation [3]. This equation (Equation (2)) differs only in the formulations for ID.

$$MT = a + b \log_2(A/W +1.0) .\tag{2}$$

The benefit of this equation is that it provides the best statistical fit, reflects the information theorem underlying Fitts' law, and always gives a positive ID. The throughput (TP) proposed by ISO [4] is the most familiar performance measurement of information capacity of human motor system. This approach combines the effects of the intercept and slope parameters of the regression model into one dependent measure that can easily be compared between studies [5]. As shown in Equation (3), MT was the mean movement time for all trials within the same condition, and ID = $\log_2(D/W+1)$.

$$Throughput = ID/MT .\tag{3}$$

Fitts' Law is an effective method in evaluating input devices. However, it has rarely been applied in comparing visual display devices. Fitts' pointing paradigm is a visually-controlled task, hence either input devices or display devices could influence performance of human motor system. In order to test whether Fitts' Law is applicable to compare display devices, Chun et al. [6] used Fitts' Law to evaluate four 3D stereo displays with same haptic input device. The results of this study demonstrated that Fitts' Law was applicable to the evaluation of visio-hoptic workstations.

Except performance measurement, subjective questionnaires were usually used to measure discomfort resulted from display devices in virtual reality environment. In 1997, Howarth and Costello [7] proposed a Simulation Sickness Questionnaire (SSQ) to compare head mounted display (HMD) and visual display unit (VDU). The results showed that HMD was rated with high scores than VDU in fatigue, headache, nausea and dizziness.

In summary, the present study attempts to evaluate the 3D TV and other two familiar display device, HMD and projection display, via Fitts' task and Simulator Sickness Questionnaire. From the results of this study, it will be shown that how is the influence of these three displays on human motor performance.

2 Methods

2.1 Subjects

Ten right-handed adult subjects participated in this experiment, aged 20-30 years old (six males and four females, mean age = 26.7 years, SD = 2.8 years), and were undergraduate Industrial and Systems Engineering students of Chung Yuan Christian University. All subjects had normal or corrected-to-normal vision with no other physical impairments.

2.2 Apparatus

Three display devices were used to present virtual reality interactive environment. The first display device adopted is the 3D stereo television (Philips 42" WOWvx). As illustrated in figure 1, the 3D TV is to get a distinct image into each eye of the viewer. From that point, the viewer's brain takes over, processing each image in the same, natural way in which it processes the images it receives from the three-dimensional world. The resolution of 3D TV is 1280×1024 pixels and refresh rate was 60 Hz. It is located in front of subjects in 1.5 meters and the field of view estimated is 32.8 degree.

Fig. 1. 3D stereo television Philips 42" WOWvx [1]

Fig. 2. Head mounted display i-glasses VIDEO 3D Pro [8]

The second display device head mounted display (i-glasses VIDEO 3D Pro) is shown on figure 2. It is worn like ordinary goggles. The resolution of HMD is 800×600 pixels, refresh rate is 60 Hz, and the field of view is 26 degree along the diagonal.

The third display device is Benq PB6100 projector (illustrated in figure 3) with a light output of 1500 ansilumens. At a three-meter distance, it projects a 1340 mm×1010 mm image with 1680 mm diagonal on a projective screen. The resolution is 800×600 pixels, refresh rate is 60 Hz, and the field of view is 25.2 degree.

Fig. 3. Projection display Benq PB6100 [9]

Fig. 4. Experiment environment

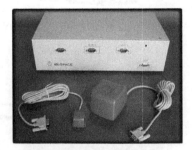

Fig. 5. Tracker VR SPACE Wintracker

Experiment environment created by EON professional 5.5 software is a 50cm × 50cm × 50cm cube. As shown in figure 4, the cube background is set to a white color, two dark gray tiles are drawn in the vertical plane at the right and left screen. The purpose of the cube is to enhance the perception of depth in our virtual reality environment. The cursor is shaped into a sphere and motivated by VR SPACE Wintracker (see figure 5) attached on subjects' base proximal phalange of medius. There were three red sphere targets located respectively in X, Y and Z directions.

2.3 Procedure

A 3×3×3 fully within subjects repeated measures design was used. The factors are three display devices (3D TV, HMD and projection display.), three movement directions(X, Y and Z direction) and three levels of ID (2, 3 and 4 bits). Movement directions Y was into the screen, X was horizontal across the screen and Z was vertical across the screen. IDs were produced by a constant target distance, 19 cm, and three target diameters. The C:D ratio was always 1:1. So, a hand movement in a particular distance resulted in an equal cursor movement.

At the start of each condition, subjects were allowed practice trials to familiarize tasks. Following this, subjects carried out all 27 experimental conditions in a random order to minimize the effect of learning and fatigue. Subjects were instructed to point as fast as possible while still maintaining high accuracy. Movement time started at the start point pressed and did not stop until correctly clicked inside the targets with a mouse grasped in hand. Each condition consisted of ten pointing trails, the average movement time and throughput of these ten pointing was recorded for ANOVA analysis.

After completion of each condition task, subjects were instructed to respond to an SSQ assessment questionnaire asking them to rate their experience of this condition. The questionnaire consisted of ten questions: discomfort, fatigue, boredom, headache, eyestrain, sweating, claustrophobia, disorientation, nausea and difficulty concentrating. Subjects were asked to respond to each question with a rating from low to high and these scores were collected and transferred to the Minitab software for the statistical analysis.

3 Results

3.1 Movement Time

Mean movement time for the three display devices: 3D TV, HMD and projection display respectively were 3689, 4324 and 3467 ms, there were significant differences between display devices in movement time ($F_{2, 234} = 34.31$, $p < 0.01$). The movement time for projection display was the fastest and HMD took the longest time. Further post-hoc Duncan test showed that the movement time of HMD was significantly longer than 3D TV and projection display. The main effect for movement directions ($F_{2, 234} = 35.04$, $p < 0.01$) and IDs ($F_{3, 234} = 190.82$, $p < 0.01$) were also significant in movement time. Movement time were 4323 ms for the highest Y direction, followed by Z direction (3709 ms) then the lowest X direction (3448 ms) and it increased with the level of indices of difficulty (2820 ms for 2 bits, 3075 ms for 3 bits and 4912 ms for 4 bits). Post-hoc Duncan showed that the movement time was different between the three movement directions and between the three levels of IDs statistically. There were significant IDs by display devices and IDs by movement directions interactions on movement time.

3.2 Throughput

Throughput computed for the projection display at 0.9144 bps was the highest. For 3D TV and HMD was 0.8610 and 0.7320 bps individually. The main effect for display devices was clearly significant ($F_{2, 234} = 35.01$, $p < 0.01$). Further Duncan test results showed that there was no significant difference between projection display and 3D TV, but both of them were obviously higher than HMD.

The ANOVA results also revealed significant differences between movement directions ($F_{2, 234} = 46.99$, $p < 0.01$) and IDs ($F_{2, 234} = 9.87$, $p < 0.01$). The post-hoc Duncan test showed that Y direction (0.7135 bps) was statistically lower than X (0.9210 bps) and Z (0.8729 bps) directions. Throughput for three levels of IDs was 0.7799, 0.8523 and 0.8752 bps in order and it increased with the level of ID. The post-hoc test showed that the throughput obtained at 2 bits was statistically lower then it obtained at 3 and 4 bits. There was a significant interaction between IDs and movement directions.

3.3 Simulation Sickness Questionnaire

The means and standard deviations of the responses on the six of ten questions of the SSQ are shown in Table 1. The remaining four questions, sweating, claustrophobia, disorientation, nausea, where participants didn't experience are excluded in this table. The results of the questionnaire analysis showed that all of these six responses are statistically significant between display devices. Subjects rated the discomfort, fatigue, boredom, headache and eyestrain higher scores while using HMD than using 3D TV and projection display obviously. These six questions mean were lowest for the projection display, it implies that subjects considered projection display was a more comfortable and did not induce fatigue, headache and eyestrain. Scores rated in discomfort, fatigue and eyestrain for 3D TV were near the midpoint, it did not induce headache as projection display.

It could be concluded from these questionnaire data that the SSQ assessment showed significant difference between the three display devices. Based on the results, subjects showed preference for projection display.

Table 1. Simulator Sickness Questionnaire rating of three display devices on 5-point scale

Variable	3D TV	HMD	Projection	P-value
Discomfort	2.90(1.02)[b]	4.60(0.54)[c]	1.00(0.00)[a]	0.000
Fatigue	2.89(0.77)[b]	4.44(0.50)[c]	1.08(0.27)[a]	0.000
Boredom	1.84(0.54)[b]	2.26(0.53)[c]	1.02(0.15)[a]	0.000
Headache	1.06(0.23)[a]	3.01(0.44)[b]	1.00(0.00)[a]	0.000
Eyestrain	2.68(0.90)[b]	4.47(1.03)[c]	1.09(0.39)[a]	0.000
Difficulty concentrating	1.99(0.57)[b]	2.79(1.27)[c]	1.09(0.32)[a]	0.000

1. Data are presented as mean (SD).
2. a, b, c groups from the post-hoc Duncan test.

4 Discussion and Conclusion

Based on the result of the study, it seems that the 3D stereo television technology introduced only recently may not provide enough perceptual depth to enhance movement performance of visually-controlled task in a 3D VE as one would have anticipated. The projection display obtained the best performance and preference among the three display devices. The HMD gave the worst result in both the experimental task and the SSQ assessment due to the accompanied discomfort and fatigue. Chun et al. [6] considered that it may be due to its limited configuration where the resolution is only 800×600 pixels with a small field of view. In all conditions, movement time increased linearly with levels of IDs. This is in line with previous studies that Fitts' Law was applicable to the performance evaluation of interaction with display devices. In addition, the predictive models developed by this study are reported as a reference for predicting interaction performance in the 3D virtual reality environment.

References

1. Philips, http://www.philips.com.tw/index.page
2. Fitts, P.: The information capacity of the human motor system in controlling the amplitude of movement. Journal of Experimental Psychology 47, 381–391 (1954)
3. MacKenzie, I.S.: A note on the information-theoretic basis for Fitts' law. Journal of Motor Behavior 21, 323–330 (1989)
4. ISO, ISO/DIS 9241-9 Ergonomic Requirements for Office Work with Visual Display Terminals, Non-keyboard Input Device Requirements, Draft International Standard, International Organization for Standardization (1998)
5. Soukoreff, R.W., MacKenzie, I.S.: Towards a standard for pointing device evaluation: Perspectives on 27 years of Fitts' law research in HCI. International Journal of Human-Computer Studies 61, 751–789 (2004)
6. Chun, K., Verplank, B., Barbagli, F., Salisbury, K.: Evaluating haptics and 3D stereo displays using Fitts' law. In: Proceeding of the 3rd IEEE Workshop on HAVE, pp. 53–58 (2004)
7. Howarth, P.A., Costello, P.J.: The occurrence of virtual simulation sickness symptoms when an HMD was used as a personal viewing system, Display 18, 107–116 (1997)
8. The i-glasses Video 3D Pro, http://www.i-glassesstore.com/ig-hrvpro.html
9. BENQ, http://www.benq.com.tw/benqstyle/model_index.cfm

Visual Data Mining in Immersive Virtual Environment Based on 4K Stereo Images

Tetsuro Ogi, Yoshisuke Tateyama, and So Sato

Graduate School of System Design and Management, Keio University
4-1-1 Hiyoshi, Kohoku-ku, Yokohama 233-8526, Japan
ogi@sdm.keio.ac.jp, tateyama@sdm.keio.ac.jp,
sosato@z8.keio.jp

Abstract. In this study, super high-definition immersive visual data mining environment using 4K stereo projector was developed. In this system, data can be represented with high accuracy in the three-dimensional space using the super high-definition stereo images, and the user can recognize the relation among several kinds of data by integrating them in the immersive environment using the plug-in function. This system was applied to the seismic data visualization and the effectiveness of this system was evaluated.

Keywords: Visual Data Mining, Immersive Virtual Environment, 4K Stereo Image, Seismic Data Analysis.

1 Introduction

In recent years, a large amount of data has been recorded in various fields according to the advance of database technologies. However, since the discovery of valuable information from the huge data is difficult, it is desired to establish a methodology to utilize these data effectively. Though data mining is one of the methods to solve such a problem, it was difficult for the user to understand the process of mining data and evaluate the result of it, because processing data is performed only in the computer in the usual data mining method [1]. Therefore, this study focuses on the visual data mining in which the user can analyze data interactively with the computer by visualizing the process and the result of the data mining.

In the visual data mining, it is expected that an new information can be discovered and analyzed by combining the ability of data processing and high-speed calculation of the computer with the human's ability such as intuition, common sense and creativity [2][3]. Particularly, this study aims at improving the effect of visual data mining by enhancing the ability of expressing data and interaction function by using the advanced display technologies. In this paper, system architecture and visualization ability of the super high-definition immersive visual data mining environment that was developed in this study are discussed and it was applied to the seismic data analysis.

2 Concept of Immersive Visual Data Mining

Visual data mining supports the user to analyze a large amount of data and to find new information by integrating the abilities of computer and human. The computer

R. Shumaker (Ed.): Virtual and Mixed Reality, LNCS 5622, pp. 472–481, 2009.

has large memory and high speed calculation capability. On the other hand, human is excellent in intuition, commonsense and creativity based on the visual information. By combining the information processes performed by computer and human, a large amount of data could be analyzed effectively to discover new information.

In this case, visualization technology is used to transmit the information from the computer to the human and interactive interface environment is used to support the collaboration between human and computer. If the expression abilities of information visualization and the interaction function between human and computer were increased, the performance of visual data mining would be improved based on the improvement of information processing of human and computer.

As for the increase of the expression ability in the information visualization, super high-definition image would enables the transmission of the detailed information from the computer to the human, and three-dimensional stereo image would be used effectively to represent the relationship among several kinds of data in the three-dimensional space. And as for the interaction between human and computer, immersive virtual environment could be used to enable the user to operate the visualized data directly and to explore data space as a first person experience [4][5][6]. Figure 1 shows the concept of super high-definition immersive visual data mining that is proposed in this study. In this figure, it is shown that the performance of visual data mining can greatly be improved by increasing the expression ability and the interaction function between computer and human.

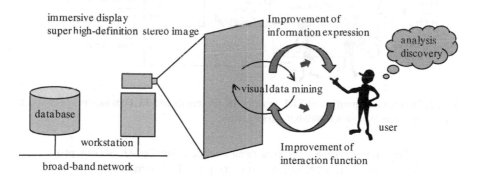

Fig. 1. Concept of super high-definition immersive visual data mining. Improvement of information expression and interaction function increase the performance of visual data mining.

3 Visual Data Mining Environment Using 4K Stereo Image

3.1 CDF System

In this study, CDF (Concurrent Design Facility) system that uses 4K stereo image was developed as a super high-definition immersive visual data mining environment. Figure 2 shows the appearance of the CDF system. CDF is designed for various purposes such as the collaborative design, presentation, and lecture in the university as well as for the visual data mining environment in which users can analyze data and find new knowledge while sharing the visualized data among users [7].

Fig. 2. CDF (Concurrent Design Facility) system. This system consists of 4K stereo projector and two LCD monitors.

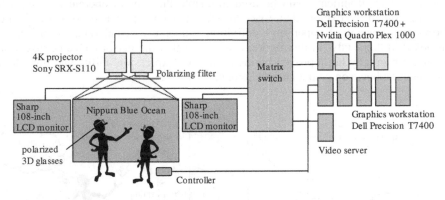

Fig. 3. System configuration of CDF system. 4K projectors and LCD monitors are connected to the graphics workstations through matrix switch.

The CDF consists of a 180-inch center screen for the 4K stereo projectors and two LCD 108-inch high-definition monitors placed at both sides. The center screen can be used not only to project 4K resolution stereo image but also to display four high-definition divided images as a multi screen monitor. Therefore, the whole of CDF system can display up to six high-definition images and it can be used as a data visualization and analysis environment in various application fields.

In order to generate images, eight graphics workstations (two workstations for 4K stereo image and six workstations for high-definition images) are used, and output image of the arbitrary graphics workstation can be sent to the arbitrary display area freely by switching the connections in the matrix switch. Figure 3 shows the system configuration of the CDF system.

3.2   4K Stereo Image

The main component of the CDF is 4K stereo projector system. 4K means super high resolution image of 4,096 x 2,160 pixels, and its image quality would be more than four times of the usual high-definition image [8]. This system uses stacked two 4K projectors (Sony, SRX-S110), and the images corresponding to the right eye and left eye positions of the user are projected. The image output from the projector is rear projected onto the screen through the polarizing filter, and the user can see the passive stereo image based on the binocular parallax by wearing the polarized 3D glasses.

The brightness of each 4K projector is 10,000 ANSI lumens, and an acrylic rear projection screen (Nippura, Blue Ocean Screen) is used to represent a high contrast image. As a result, the brightness of the images displayed on the center screen and the LCD monitors placed at both sides becomes almost same levels.

As for the computer to process data and generate 4K stereo image, two high-end workstations (Dell Precision T7400, 2xQuad Core Xeon 3.2GHz) with the graphics engine that has a genlock function (NVIDIA Quadro Plex 1000 Model IV) are used. In this system, interface devices such as an USB game controller and a wireless touch panel are used. The game controller is used to change the visualization method or move the view point, and the touch panel is used to switch the connections between the input images and the output devices. This system configuration of the CDF system realizes the super high-definition immersive visual data mining environment using the 4K resolution stereo image.

4 Data Representation Ability of CDF

In the data visualization using the 4K image, information can be represented with high accuracy based on the high resolution image compared with the visualization using the usual XGA or SXGA resolution image. Particularly, when the 4K stereo image is used, it is expected that the three-dimensional image with high spatial resolution can be displayed. In this study, the spatial resolution with which the visualized data can be represented in the three-dimensional space was experimentally measured.

In the experiment, the subjects sat at a position 3m away from the screen, and two parallel perpendicular lines with random intervals of 0.5mm, 1mm, 2.5mm, 5mm, or 10mm were displayed in the direction from the front to left. The subjects were asked to move the parallel lines in the depth direction using the controller, and to stop them at the limit position where they can recognize the displayed image as two lines and this position was recorded. Figure 4 shows the appearance of this experiment and Figure 5 shows the result of the experiment for five subjects with visual acuity of more than 1.0. In this graph, the contour lines are drawn by connecting the average values of the perceived depth positions for each interval of the parallel lines.

From this graph, we can understand that the data can be represented at the resolution of 10mm intervals at the distance of about 10m from the subjects, and it can be represented with high accuracy at the resolution of 0.5mm intervals at the distance of about 50cm. Though these values are a little bad compared with the theoretical values calculated from the interval of one pixel (0.97mm) on the screen, we can consider it is caused by the stereo vision image. In the inclined direction, the distance in which the subjects recognize the parallel lines becomes a little far, since the pixel interval on the screen looks narrow when it is seen from the slant direction. For example, the

Fig. 4. Appearance of the experiment on measuring the spatial resolution of data representation in CDF system

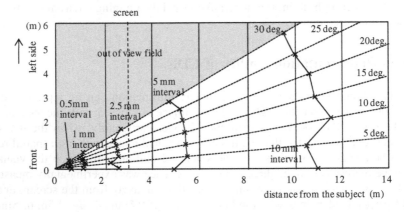

Fig. 5. Result of experiment on data representation ability of CDF system. Contour lines show the limit position where the subjects can recognize the parallel lines.

distance of the recognition of the parallel lines with 2.5mm interval in 30 degrees direction was about 1.2 times as long as the front direction. From the result, it is understood that the 4K stereo display can represent the detailed information with high accuracy, though the spatial resolution of the displayed image depends on the distance and direction from the user. Namely, this means that the visual data mining using the super high-definition stereo image has an ability to transmit a large amount of information from the computer to the user with high accuracy.

5   Application to Seismic Data Analysis

In this study, the super high-definition visual data mining environment was applied to the visualization and analysis of the earthquake data.

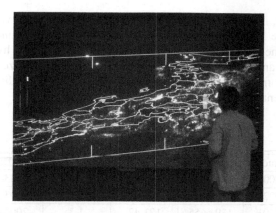

Fig. 6. Visualization of hypocenter data using 4K stereo projection system. User can recognize both each hypocenter data and distribution of whole data.

5.1 Distribution of Hypocenter Data

In Japan, since a lot of earthquakes occur every year, it is very important to analyze the feature of the hypocenter distribution for the earthquake prediction and the damage measure [9]. However, it was difficult to observe both the individual location and the overall distribution of the hypocenter data and to understand the feature of three-dimensional distribution of the earthquake by visualizing data using the conventional two-dimensional display. Therefore, the visualization system for the hypocenter data was constructed by using the super high-definition immersive visual data mining environment.

Figure 6 shows that the hypocenter data recorded in the past three years in Earthquake Research Institute of the University of Tokyo is visualized by using the 4K projection system. In the super high-definition display, the user can recognize the individual hypocenter while seeing the spatial distribution of the hypocenter in the whole of Japan, since the data can be represented with high resolution in the three-dimensional space with wide field of view. In this system, when the 1:10,000 scale map is displayed, the user can recognize the hypocenter positions located 5m away between each other at 50cm away in front of him. By using this system, the user could understand intuitively that the depths of hypocenters in west Japan is relatively shallow and hypocenters occurred in Tokai and Kanto area are distributed along a plate.

5.2 Relationship between Hypocenter and Other Data

Next, this system was applied to analyze the relationship between data by integrating different kinds of visualization data. In this application, map data, hypocenter data, terrain data, basement depth data and plate structure data were integrated in the immersive visualization environment. Though these data are stored in different database, they have location information. Therefore, they can be related with each other using the location information as a reference key. Table 1 to Table 4 show the database structure used in this system. Though the terrain data originally consist of altitude information corresponding to the latitude and longitude on the lattice, they are stored as data sets for the divided areas in the database.

In this system, the user can accesses these databases from the virtual environment and visualize the retrieved data by specifying the necessary condition. Thus, this system enables the user to understand the relationship among the hypocenter, terrain, basement depth, and plate structure data intuitively, and to analyze the feature of the earthquake phenomenon, by overlapping these data in the three-dimensional visualization environment.

Table 1. Database structure of hypocenter data

Latitude	Longitude	Depth	Magnitude	Date
36.3005	139.9837	40.68	0.8	2003-01-01
36.0927	138.7390	153.97	1.7	2003-01-01
36.2901	139.6655	121.42	1.3	2003-01-01
……	……	……	……	……

Table 2. Database structure of basement depth data

Latitude	Longitude	Depth
36. 505	138.510	3.057
36.505	138.515	2.801
36.505	138.520	2.661
……	……	……

Table 3. Database structure of plate structure data

Latitude	Longitude	Depth
36.510	138.460	151.827
36.510	138.465	151.103
36.510	138.470	151.371
……	……	……

Table 4. Database structure of terrain data

North edge in latitude	West edge in latitude	South edge in latitude	East edge in latitude	Filename
36.6051	139.8046	36.5895	139.8202	N36.6051_E139.8046.dat
36.6051	139.8202	36.5895	139.8358	N36.6051_E139.8202.dat
36.6051	139.8358	36.5895	139.8514	N36.6051_E139.8358.dat
……	……	……	……	……

As for the mechanism of integrating the visualized data in the virtual space, the plug-in function of the OpenCABIN library was used [10]. In this method, each data is visualized by different application programs and they are integrated in the three-dimensional space in the runtime. Figure 7 and Figure 8 show that several visualization data are integrated in the same space. In these examples, visualization programs for hypocenter data, terrain data, basement depth data and plate structure data are plugged-in to represent the relation among the data. The hypocenter data is visualized using the sphere, and the size of it indicates the magnitude of the earthquake. The terrain data is created by mapping the texture image captured from the satellite onto the shape model. And the basement depth and the plate structure data are represented using the colors that indicate the depth values.

Fig. 7. Integrating visualization data in CDF. The relation between terrain data and hypocenter data are shown.

Fig. 8. Integrating visualization data in CDF. User can understand the relation among hypocenter data, basement depth data and plate structure data.

When the several visualization programs are plugged-in, the toggle buttons that show the conditions of each data are displayed. The user can switch the visible condition of each data by using the toggle button in the virtual space. For example, the user can change the visualization data from the combination of hypocenter data and basement depth data to the combination of hypocenter data and plate structure data, while running the application programs in the virtual space. By using this method, the user can intuitively understand the feature of the distribution of hypocenter and the relation with other data. For example, user could see whether the attention data of the earthquake occurred on the plate or in the plate structure. Thus, this system could be effectively used to represent the relationship among several data in the three-dimensional space and to analyze the earthquake phenomenon.

6 Conclusions

In this study, the super high-definition immersive visual data mining environment that uses the 4K stereo projector was constructed. In this system, the effect of visual data mining based on the collaborative process between the user and the computer would be greatly improved, since the 4K stereo image increases the amount of information transmitted from the computer to the user and the interactive interface enables the user to explore the data space. The developed prototype system was applied to the seismic data analysis, and several kinds of visualization data such as map, hypo-center, terrain model, depth of basement and plate structure were integrated. Then, the effectiveness and possibility of the intuitive analysis in the immersive visual data mining environment were confirmed through the interactive operation to the visualized data. Future research will include developing more effective visual data mining method through the collaboration with the earthquake experts and applying this technology to other application fields.

Acknowledgements

This research was supported by G-COE (Center of Education and Research of Symbiotic, Safe and Secure System Design) program at Keio University. And we thank Dr. Takashi Furumura of the University of Tokyo, Dr. Shoji Itoh of Riken, and Satoshi Oonuki of University of Tsukuba for their support.

References

1. Kantardzic, M.: Data Mining: Concepts, Models, Methods, and Algorithms. Wiley-IEEE Press (2002)
2. Wong, P.C.: Visual Data Mining. Computer Graphics and Applications 19(5), 20–21 (1999)
3. Keim, D.A.: Information Visualization and Visual Data Mining. IEEE Transactions on Visualization and Computer Graphics 7(1), 100–107 (2002)
4. Ammoura, A., Zaïane, O.R., Ji, Y.: Immersed visual data mining: Walking the walk. In: Read, B. (ed.) BNCOD 2001. LNCS, vol. 2097, pp. 202–218. Springer, Heidelberg (2001)
5. Wegman, E.J., Symanzik, J.: Immersive Projection Technology for Visual Data Mining. Journal of Computational and Graphical Statistics 11, 163–188 (2002)
6. Ferey, N., Gros, P.E., Herisson, J., Gherbi, R.: Visual Data Mining of Genomic Databases by Immersive Graph-Based Exploration. In: Proc. of 3rd International Conference on Computer Graphics and Interactive Techniques in Australasia and South East Asia, pp. 143–146 (2005)
7. Ogi, T., Daigo, H., Sato, S., Tateyama, Y., Nishida, Y.: Super High Definition Stereo Image Using 4K Projection System. In: ICAT 2008, Proceedings of 18th International Conference on Artificial Reality and Telexistence, pp. 365–366 (2008)
8. Sony Press Release: Sony Unveils New "4K" Digital Cinema Projector (June 2004), http://news.sel.sony.com/pressrelease/4864

9. Furumura, T., Kennett, B.L.N.: Subduction Zone Guided Waves and the Heterogeneity Structure of the Subducted Plate: Intensity anomalies in northern Japan. Journal of Geophysical Research 110, B10302.1–B10302.27 (2005)
10. Tateyama, Y., Oonuki, S., Ogi, T.: K-Cave Demonstration: Seismic Information Visualization System Using the OpenCABIN Library. In: ICAT 2008, Proceedings of 18th International Conference on Artificial Reality and Telexistence, pp. 363–364 (2008)

MR-Mirror: A Complex of Real and Virtual Mirrors

Hideaki Sato, Itaru Kitahara, and Yuichi Ohta

Department of Intelligent Interaction Technologies,
Graduate School of Systems and Information Engineering, University of Tsukuba,
Tennodai 1-1-1, Tsukuba, Ibaraki, 305-8573, Japan
hsato@image.iit.tsukuba.ac.jp,
{kitahara,ohta}@iit.tsukuba.ac.jp

Abstract. MR-mirror is a novel Mixed-Reality (MR) display system created by using real and virtual mirrors. It merges real visual information reflected on a real mirror and a virtual one displayed on an electronic monitor. A user's body is presented by the reflection on the real mirror, and virtual objects are presented on a monitor that is visible through the real mirror. Users can observe an MR scene without wearing such devices as a head-mounted display and can interact with the virtual objects around them using their body motion in MR space. We implemented a prototype MR-mirror and a demonstration system.

Keywords: Mixed Reality, Virtual Mirror, Interaction.

1 Introduction

Mixed Reality (MR) is expected to develop novel user interfaces in such fields as medical welfare (rehabilitation), Computer Supported Cooperative Work (CSCW), education, and entertainment [1][2]. To realize such an advanced interface system, we have to consider immersive interaction in MR space that exploits user body motions. Body motion is important to express nonverbal information and to interact with real and virtual 3D objects in MR space.

Due to size and weight reductions, HMDs have become the most popular display system to observe all-around MR scenes [3]. However they need wired cables to supply electronic power and to transmit video signals. As a result, the user motions and the movable areas are limited by the length and weight of the cables. The user's field of view is determined by the HMD specifications, which however are generally not enough wide to cover the whole field-of-view of human eyes.

Projector-based MR systems display MR scenes using video projectors to cast the appearance of virtual objects onto the real world [4]. Since they make it possible to observe MR scenes without wearing any electronic devices, user motions are not restricted. However, displaying 3D virtual objects floating in midair is difficult.

This paper proposes our novel method, "MR-mirror," to realize immersive interaction in MR space. The overview of our MR-mirror is illustrated in figure 1. In the MR-mirror system, users observe the real world in a half mirror set in front of them. At the same time, they observe the virtual world in a monitor through a half mirror (virtual mirror technique [5]). By reproducing the optical characteristics of real mirrors on the virtual mirror, users can observe MR scenes. In the MR-mirror system,

R. Shumaker (Ed.): Virtual and Mixed Reality, LNCS 5622, pp. 482–491, 2009.

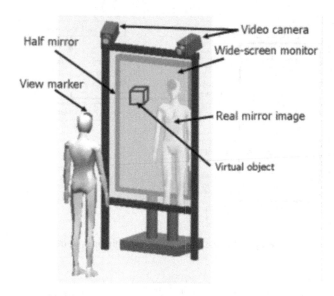

Fig. 1. Overview of MR-mirror system

users do not have to wear any electronic devices, and 3D virtual objects can be observed in the virtual mirror. Our system has another advantage: it can present the user's appearance without any calculation cost, since it is done by a natural phenomenon called specular reflection on the real mirror.

2 MR-Mirror System

As shown in figure 1, an MR-mirror system consists of a half mirror to reflect the real mirror image and a wide-screen monitor to show the virtual image. A view marker and two video cameras are used to calculate the user's viewing position necessary for generating the virtual mirror image. The two cameras, which are set at the top of the monitor, capture the user's body in front of the system.

Figure 2 shows the processing flow of the MR-mirror system. As a preparatory off-line process, we conducted camera calibration to estimate the intrinsic and extrinsic parameters of the stereo video cameras. Perspective projection matrixes of the two cameras are calculated with the parameters. The system extracts a view marker attached to the user's head in the captured stereo images and estimates the 3D position using the stereo-vision technique. By using the estimated 3D position of the view marker, the system calculates the virtual camera's position to generate mirror images of virtual objects. The virtual mirror images are displayed on the monitor. Finally, an "MR-mirror" is realized with which users can interact with virtual objects by watching their body motion in a real mirror.

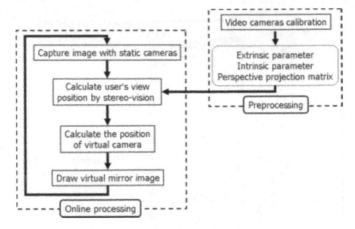

Fig. 2. Processing flow of MR-mirror system

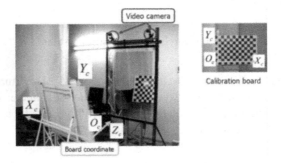

Fig. 3. Calibration of video cameras

3   Camera Calibration

Figure 3 shows an overview of the camera calibration procedure and the coordinate systems in the MR-mirror system. Using Zhang's camera calibration method [6], we calculated the intrinsic and extrinsic parameters of the video cameras based on board coordinate system *Wc*. The origin *Oc* of the coordinate system is at the bottom left corner of the calibration board. The *Xc*-axis is defined as the upward direction of the board's left side edge, and the *Yc*-axis is defined as the right direction of the bottom edge. The *Zc*-axis is defined by calculating the outer product of the *Xc* and *Yc* axes. As a result, the projective transformation is estimated, as shown in Eq. (1). Here, 3D point *(Xc,Yc,Zc)* in *Wc* is observed at *(u,v)* in a video camera image, and *Pc* is the projective matrix:

$$s(u,v,1)^T = P_c(X_c,Y_c,Z_c,1)^T . \tag{1}$$

4 3D Position Estimation of a Marker Using Stereo-Vision

The video cameras were calibrated as described above. The 3D position of a captured marker can be estimated with stereo-vision. The projective relationship between a 3D point $Mc(x_c, y_c, z_c)$ and observing point $m = [u, v]^T$ in an image is described in Eq. (2):

$$s\overline{m} = P_c \overline{M}_c. \tag{2}$$

As illustrated in Fig. 4. Stereo-vision

when 3D point Mc is observed at $m' = [u', v']^T$ in the other image, we have Eq. (3):

$$s'\overline{m}' = P'_c \overline{M}_c. \tag{3}$$

Here, $\overline{m}$, $\overline{m}'$, and $\overline{M}c$ are the homogeneous vectors of m, m', and Mc, respectively. s and s' are scalar with depth values and P and P' are the projection matrices of the video cameras .

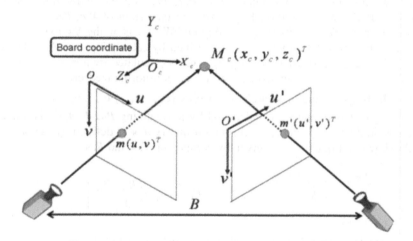

Fig. 4. Stereo-vision

Equation (4) is derived by merging Eqs. (2) and (3). p_{ij} and p'_{ij} are elements of projective matrices $P'c$ and Pc.

$$BM_c = b \tag{4}$$

$$B = \begin{bmatrix} up_{31} - p_{11} & up_{32} - p_{12} & up_{33} - p_{13} \\ up_{31} - p_{21} & up_{32} - p_{22} & up_{33} - p_{23} \\ up'_{31} - p'_{11} & up'_{31} - p'_{11} & up'_{31} - p'_{11} \\ up'_{31} - p'_{11} & up'_{31} - p'_{11} & up'_{31} - p'_{11} \end{bmatrix} \quad b = \begin{bmatrix} p_{14} - up_{34} \\ p_{24} - up_{34} \\ p'_{14} - up'_{34} \\ p'_{24} - up'_{34} \end{bmatrix}$$

When a pair of two corresponding points m and m' in the video camera images is known, we have four linear independent simultaneous equations. However, the number of unknown parameters is three (x_c, y_c, z_c). In such cases, the simultaneous equations can be solved with pseudo-inverse matrix $B+$, as described in Eq. (5):

$$M_c = B^+ b \quad B^+ = \left(B^T B\right)^{-1} B^T .$$

(5)

5   Integration of Coordinate Systems

Figure 5 illustrates the two coordinate systems used in the MR-mirror system. To integrate the captured real world and the 3D CG world, matrix Ccw, which transforms board coordinate system Wc to world coordinate system W, must be calculated. In the MR-mirror system, origin $Pw0$ of world coordinate system W is defined at the top left corner of the monitor. The Xw-axis is defined as the right direction of the monitor's upper edge, and the Yw-axis is defined as the upward direction of the left side edge. The Zw-axis is the outer product of the Xw and Yw axes and expresses the depth information of the user's view volume.

First, we measured six 3D points $\{Pc0, Pc1, Pc2\}$ on the calibration board and $\{Pw0, Pw1, Pw2\}$ on the monitor. Here, $Pc0$ is at the origin of Wc, $Pc1$ is on the Xc-axis, $Pc2$ is on the Yc-axis, $Pw0$ is at the origin of W, $Pw1$ is on the Xw-axis, and $Pw2$ is on the Yw-axis. Translation vector Tcw is defined by calculating $Pc0$- $Pw0$. The basis vectors of Wc are described as $\{e_{xc}, e_{yc}, e_{zc}\}$. e_{xc} is calculated by normalizing $Pc1$-$Pc0$, and e_{yc} is calculated by normalizing $Pc2$-$Pc0$. e_{zc} is a normalized cross product of e_{xc} and e_{yc}. The basis vectors of W are described as $\{e_{xw}, e_{yw}, e_{zw}\}$. e_{xw} is calculated by normalizing $Pw1$-$Pw0$, and e_{yw} is calculated by normalizing $Pw2$-$Pw0$. e_{zw} is a normalized cross product of e_{xw} and e_{yw}. 3D rotation matrix Rcw is defined by the basic vectors. As shown in Eq. (6), Ccw is given by composing Tcw and Rcw:

$$\begin{bmatrix} e_{xw} \\ e_{yw} \\ e_{zw} \end{bmatrix}^T = R_{cw} \begin{bmatrix} e_{xc} \\ e_{yc} \\ e_{zc} \end{bmatrix}^T \quad T_{cw} = P_{c0} - P_{w0} \quad C_{cw} = \begin{bmatrix} R_{cw} & T_{cw} \\ 0 & 1 \end{bmatrix}.$$

(6)

With calculated transformation matrix Ccw, the estimated 3D position of marker Mc is projected to M in the world coordinate system:

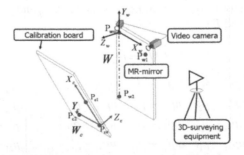

Fig. 5. Relation between two coordinate systems

6 Virtual Mirror Image Generation

6.1 Layout of a Virtual Camera and Virtual Objects

Figure 6 shows the geometrical relationship between the real and virtual worlds of the "MR-mirror". Although we only use the X_w-axis and the Z_w-axis to simply explain the geometry, the same relationship can be extended to the 3D world. When there is a real object at V_{obj}, and a user's viewpoint at V_v, objects are observed along with the solid line (line of sight) reflected on a mirror, as shown in **Fig. 6.** Geometric relation between real and virtual worlds in MR-mirror.

This optical phenomenon can be expressed without mirror reflection. In this case, the object is assumed to exist at V'_{obj}, where symmetry exists with the plane of the mirror, and the appearance is seen through the mirror along with the dotted line. The optical geometry is basically the same in both the real and virtual worlds. So generating a virtual mirror image is possible that displays a virtual object at V_{obj} by setting the virtual camera (V_{cam}) at V_v and the object at V'_{obj}. In an MR-mirror 3D coordinate system, the mirror plane coincides with the **Xw-Yw** plane. Thus, it is easy to generate virtual objects that have symmetry with the mirror to inverse the sign of the **Zw** (depth) value of the 3D data.

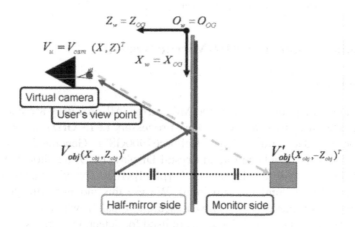

Fig. 6. Geometric relation between real and virtual worlds in MR-mirror

6.2 View Volume of a Virtual Camera

Since the observable region of the MR-mirror is limited by the monitor's area, rendering all virtual objects is not efficient, even out of the displaying area. Fig. 7. View volume of a virtual camera shows the change of the observable area (view volume) when a virtual camera moves from V_{cam} to V'_{cam}. To render only observable virtual objects, the MR-mirror system sets the view volume of a virtual camera depending on the monitor area and viewpoint V_{cam}. As illustrated in **Fig. 7.** View volume of a

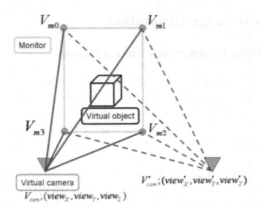

Fig. 7. View volume of a virtual camera

virtual camera, the 3D coordinates of the four vertices of the monitor are $Vm0$, $Vm1$, $Vm2$, and $Vm3$. Then the view volume is set as a square pyramid with a base comprised of $Vm0$, $Vm1$, $Vm2$, and $Vm3$ and a cone point set as V_{cam} . When the virtual camera moves, the square pyramid is deformed by moving the cone point. On the other hand, the base is fixed on the monitor.

7 Implementation of an MR-Mirror System

7.1 Specifications

Figure 8 shows the pilot system of the MR-mirror. All processes are executed by a single computer with two Intel Core2Duo processors (2.13 GHz), a 4-GB memory system, and a video card (nVidia "GeForce7900GS"). Generated virtual mirror images are displayed on a large Liquid Crystal Display (LCD) monitor (SHARP "PN-455R": 45 inches) that can display 1920 [pixel]×1080 [pixel] images and whose display size is 985.9 [mm] × 554.6 [mm]. We use this monitor with portrait style. IEEE1394b video cameras (Point Grey Research "Flea2"), which can capture 1024 [pixel]×768 [pixel] images with 30 [fps], are used for detecting markers.

7.2 Evaluation

We experimentally evaluated the feasibility of our proposed method. First, we confirmed whether the real and virtual objects are correctly overlapped on the MR-mirror. In the evaluation a real object, a gypsum cube, was set in front of the MR-mirror, as shown in Figure 8. A virtual object, a wire-frame cube with the same shape as the real object, was also set on the same position in 3D space. Instead of observation by a user, we put a digital camera to capture the sight. Figure 9 shows the images captured by the digital camera by moving it from right to left or up and down. We confirmed that the appearance of the virtual object is overlapped on the real object and that the geometry of the MR-mirror is adequately realized.

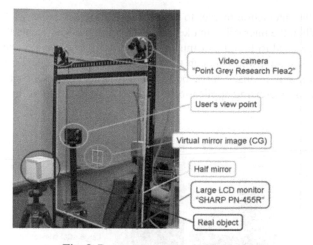

Fig. 8. Prototype system of MR-mirror

Fig. 9. Experimental results. Appearance of virtual object is overlapped on real object.

8   Game for MR-Mirror Demonstration

We developed a demonstration game system utilizing the effectiveness of the MR-mirror. Figure 10 shows the demonstration system. A player stands in front of the MR-mirror with two colored markers. The one on the player's head is a view marker to detect the viewpoint, and the other is an interaction marker to make contact with the virtual objects. In the MR scene (figure 10), some virtual objects (moving balls) are observed. The purpose of the game is to flick out the balls using body motion. The player moves the interaction marker to where a virtual object exists while observing the MR-mirror. When the interaction marker hits the ball in the MR scene, it is flicked out.

Since we are used to looking at mirrors in our daily life, we can easily understand the geometrical relationship between the real and virtual objects. To flick out all the balls, the player has to make large body motion. This suggests that the MR-mirror might be used for exercising applications, such as rehabilitation or the maintenance of good health.

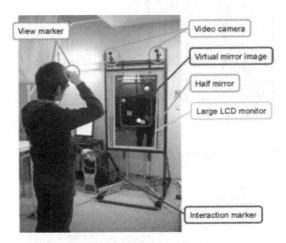

Fig. 10. Game for MR-mirror demonstration

9 Conclusion

This paper proposed an MR display method called "MR-mirror" that can display 3D virtual objects in midair without any wearable display devices. In the MR-mirror system, the appearance of real and virtual worlds is mixed using a half mirror. By integrating the 3D coordinate system between the real and virtual worlds and setting virtual objects to generate virtual mirror images, a user can observe an immersive MR scene without an HMD. We developed a prototype MR-mirror system to confirm its feasibility and effectiveness. Future works include the elimination of the half mirror's distortion or motion capture without colored markers. However, we confirmed the features of the MR-mirror with the developed system.

References

1. Minatani, S., Kitahara, I., Kameda, Y., Ohta, Y.: Face-to-Face Tabletop Remote Collaboration in Mixed Reality. In: ISMAR 2007, pp. 43–46 (2007)
2. Richard, E., Billaudeau, V., Richard, P.: Augmented reality for rehabilitation of disabled children: a preliminary study. In: Virtual Rehabilitation 2007, pp. 102–108 (2007)
3. Ohta, Y., Tamura, H.: Mixed Reality-Merging Real and Virtual Worlds. Ohmsha, Ltd. (1999)

4. Bimber, O., Raskar, R.: Spatial Augmented Reality Merging Real and Virtual Worlds. A.K. Peters, Ltd. (2005)
5. Ushida, K., Tanaka, Y., Naemura, T., Harashima, H.: i-mirror: An Interaction/ Information Environment Based on a Mirror Metaphor Aiming to Install into Our Life Space. In: Proceedings of the 12th International Conference on Artificial Reality and Telexistence (ICAT 2002) (December 2002)
6. Zhang, Z.: A Flexible new technique for camera calibration. IEEE Transaction on Pattern Analysis and Machine Intelligence (2000)
7. Jo, G., Tsuji, S.: Three dimensional vision (in Japanese), Kyoritsu Shuppan (1998); ISBN-13: 978-4320085220

A Novel Approach to On-Site Camera Calibration and Tracking for MR Pre-visualization Procedure

Wataru Toishita, Yutaka Momoda, Ryuhei Tenmoku, Fumihisa Shibata,
Hideyuki Tamura, Takafumi Taketomi, Tomokazu Sato, and Naokazu Yokoya

Ritsumeikan University, Nara Institute of Science and Technology, Japan
toishita@rm.is.ritsumei.ac.jp

Abstract. This paper presents camera calibration and tracking method for mixed reality based pre-visualization system for filmmaking. The proposed calibration method collects environmental information required for tracking efficiently since the rough camera path and target environment are known before actual shooting. Previous camera tracking methods using natural feature are suitable for outdoor environment. However, it takes large human cost to construct the database. Our proposed method reduces the cost of calibration process by using fiducial markers. Fiducial markers are used as reference points and feature landmark database is constructed automatically. In shooting phase, moreover, the speed and robustness of tracking are improved by using SIFT descriptor.

Keywords: Mixed Reality, Pre-visualization, Tracking, Natural Feature.

1 Introduction

Geometric registration is the most significant issue for mixed reality (MR) which can merge real and virtual worlds. This issue results in the real-time tracking problem of feature points in the real world. It's not an exaggeration to say that a large part of MR research focuses solving this problem. In early days, the most common approach is arranging fiducial markers in the real world in order to realize robust detection and tracking of feature points. On the other hands, a lot of markerless methods using natural feature points are popular in recent years [1]. In tracking techniques, some powerful methods are proposed recently [2,3]. However, there is no definitive method in the initial camera calibration, therefore, there is no all-round total geometric registration method.

We address MR-based pre-visualization in filmmaking (MR-PreViz, Fig.1) as an application of MR technology [4,5]. The purpose of MR-PreViz is pre-designing camerawork by superimposing the computer generated humans and creatures onto the real movie sets. To say in filmmaking terms, it corresponds to the real-time on-set 3D matchmove in the pre-production process of filmmaking. We develop software tools supporting this process. Here, the camera calibration and tracking play an important role.

We develop an on-site camera calibration and tracking method suitable for this purpose. Our proposed method cleverly innovates the initial camera calibration using fiducial markers and the markerless tracking technique. The basis of this method is

R. Shumaker (Ed.): Virtual and Mixed Reality, LNCS 5622, pp. 492–502, 2009.

Fig. 1. Conceptual image of MR-PreViz

the vision-based 6DOF tracking method using the landmark database constructed in advance by detecting natural feature points in the real scene [6]. We improved this method based on that MR-PreViz has the setup and the shooting phases. Our proposed method is a sustainable approach for the high-speed and complicated camera work of the actual shooting.

This paper is constructed as follows. Section 2 describes the outline of the proposed method. Sections 3 and 4 show the initial camera calibration and tracking techniques of the proposed method, respectively. Finally, Section 5 summarizes this paper.

2   New Tracking Method Suitable for MR-PreViz Shooting

2.1   Geometric Registration in MR-PreViz

Real-time estimation of camera position and pose is needed in MR-PreViz. Here, the following conditions are required.

- System performs in the outdoor and indoor environments.
- It doesn't take so much time and human costs to collect any environmental information.
- Tracking must be realized without any fiducial markers.

Considering these conditions, we decided to adopt Taketomi's method [6] to MR-PreViz. In the setup phase, we construct the landmark database of the MR-PreViz shooting site (e.g. the location sites, open sets, and indoor sets) before shooting MR-PreViz movies. In MR-PreViz shooting phase, the camera position and pose are estimated (calibrated and tracked) in real-time using the constructed landmark database. Taketomi's method [6] is the most appropriate method to fill the above conditions. This approach can estimate extrinsic camera parameters from the captured images using correspondences between landmarks of the database and natural feature points in the input image. The landmark database stores 3D positions of natural feature points and image templates around them.

However, there still remain the following improvements in simply adopting the previous method [6] to MR-PreViz procedures.

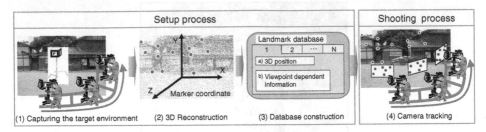

Fig. 2. Procedure of proposed method

- To reduce the human cost and computational time in constructing the landmark database
- To reduce the computational time of the initial camera calibration and tracking

In order to realize them, we propose the procedures that are described in the following section.

2.2 Procedures of Geometric Registration

The geometric registration procedures of the MR-PreViz system are shown in Fig.2. In the setup phase, as the first step, image sequences capturing the target environment in almost the same camera path as the MR-PreViz movie. In this step, the fiducial markers are arranged in the target environment to realize the robust and fast estimation of the camera path. Arranging fiducial markers makes it possible to reduce major part of the human cost. As the second step, 3D reconstruction of natural feature points except for the fiducial markers. As the third step, the system constructs the landmark database including 3D positions and viewpoint dependent information of the natural feature points. We aim that these procedures in the setup phase can be done within several tens of seconds ideally, within some minutes at most.

In the MR-PreViz shooting phase, MR-PreViz movie is shot in the condition of removing the fiducial markers from the target environment. The camera position and pose is estimated initially and tracked in real-time. Here, the target environment including the lighting condition doesn't change significantly even in the outdoor environment, since the landmark database can be constructed in a short time.

Fig. 3. Cubic marker

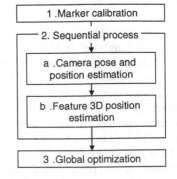

Fig. 4. Overview of 3D reconstruction

3 Construction of the Landmark Database

In MR PreViz, the landmark database should be constructed within minimal time and efforts, since the camera work and shooting sometimes changes at the location site. This section shows a rapid construction method of landmark database suitable for MR-PreViz.

3.1 3D Reconstruction

In order to estimate 3D position of feature points using structure-from-motion, the camera position and pose is required while capturing the feature points. The proposed method uses fiducial markers arranged in the real environment to estimate the camera position and pose. We adopted the cubic markers as shown in Fig.3 which are constructed by some ARToolKit markers [7], since such cubic markers make it possible to estimate camera position and pose more accurately than the planar markers. We assume multiple cubic markers are used to realize 3D reconstruction in wide area.

The flowchart of 3D reconstruction is shown in Fig.4. At first, relative positions of cubic markers have to be calculated (marker calibration). This process can be skipped if the target environment is covered by a single marker. Second, camera parameter and the 3D position of feature points are estimated for the captured image sequences. Image features are detected by FAST corner detector [12] which is known as one of the fastest detectors but has high repeatability. After detecting and identifying markers by an ARToolKit module, the camera parameters are estimated by solving PnP problems [11]. Finally, camera parameters in all frames and the 3D positions of natural feature points are refined by minimizing the formula (1).

$$E = \sum_{p} \sum_{f} \left| \mathbf{x}_{fp} - \hat{\mathbf{x}}_{fp} \right|^2 \tag{1}$$

Here, $\mathbf{x}_{fp}$ is the position of the detected image feature and $\hat{\mathbf{x}}_{fp}$ is the projected position of the feature point p in the frame f. This optimization is achieved by bundle adjustment using Levenberg-Marquardt method [8, 9].

3.2 Landmark Database

The each entry of the landmark database includes the following components:

(a) 3D position
(b) Viewpoint dependent information

- SIFT feature
- Scaling factor
- Position and pose of the camera

In order to realize rapid and robust tracking, we adopt SIFT feature for the matching. The scaling factor of every viewpoint is also required since the characteristic scale of SIFT is calculated by the distance between camera position and 3D position of landmarks in the proposed method. Details are described in section 4.1.

In addition to the landmark database, the key frame database is needed to estimate the initial camera parameter. The key frame database stores landmark data for each frame. Key frames are chosen automatically from captured image sequences at a regular interval. Each entry of the key frame database consists of 3D positions and SIFT features of visible landmarks.

3.3 Performance

We checked the performance of the proposed procedures of constructing the landmark database. In this experiment, we constructed the landmark database of Japanese traditional room from a 150 frames video sequence capturing a cubic marker. We used a PC (Xenon 3.4GHz, 2GB RAM) and a video camera (Sony, HDW-F900R, 720×364, 30fps) and the camera moved along the curved rail.

Fig.5 shows estimated 3D positions of tracked feature points and Fig.6 shows the estimated camera path from feature points and the cubic marker. Tab.1 shows the average processing time of every frame. Totally, it took about 27 seconds to estimate the 3D positions of all feature points.

Removing some feature points on the cubic marker from the 3D reconstruction result of the feature points, we constructed the landmark database including 288 feature points. Totally, it took about 40 seconds to construct the landmark database including the 3D reconstruction step. We can say that the proposed method for constructing the landmark database is enough fast and this method is suitable for MR-PreViz.

50th frame   100th frame   150th frame
(●detected landmarks, ×projected landmarks, ●tracked features)

Fig. 5. Estimation result of features

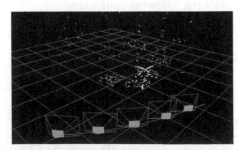

Fig. 6. Result of 3D reconstruction

Table 1. Processing time of 3D reconstruction (1 frame)

Process	Time (msec)
Camera parameter estimation	6.0
Feature 3D position estimation	45.5
Other processes	7.5
Total	59

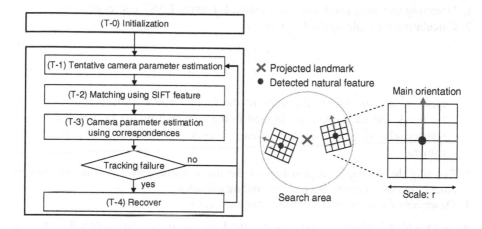

Fig. 7. Flow chart of tracking

Fig. 8. SIFT descriptor layout for 4×4 sub-regions

4 Camera Tracking

In the MR-PreViz shooting step, the camera position and pose is estimated in real-time using the landmark database (Fig.2.4). Fig.7 shows the flow chart of the camera tracking. At first, the initial camera parameter is estimated by using key frame database (T-0). Next, tentative camera parameter is estimated by matching landmarks between successive frames (T-1). Patches of a size of 10×10 pixels are extracted and the patch similarity is measured by a sum of absolute difference. To determine the correspondences between landmarks and feature points in an input image, SIFT features of landmarks are matched to input image (T-2). Finally, the camera parameter is estimated from the list of 2D and 3D correspondences (T-3). If tracking fails due to some problems, a recovering process resumes tracking (T-4).

4.1 Matching Using Modified SIFT

Previous method [6] needs a large computational cost because multi-scale image templates have to be constructed for matching landmarks to detected points. In order to reduce the computational cost, our approach uses a modified SIFT descriptor [10].

Generally, SIFT is not suitable for real time operations because it takes amount of time for calculation of the scale factor. Wagner [13] succeeds reducing computational cost by fixing the scale, but this method does not have the scale invariance. Therefore, when the distance between the camera and the feature point is changed, the feature quantity is also changed in Wagner's SIFT. Accordingly, our proposed method tries to reduce the computational cost and memory by calculating the scale from the distance D between the landmark and the camera. The layout of SIFT descriptor is shown Fig.8.

SIFT features used in our proposed method (modified SIFT) is obtained by the following steps.

1. Detecting matching candidates for landmark i using FAST corner detector
2. Calculating the scale by the formula (2)

$$r_i = \frac{r_i' \times d_i'}{d_i}.$$
(2)

Here, r' and d' means the scale of the feature and the distance between the landmark and the camera while used in the constructing the landmark database, respectively. d represents the distance between the tracked landmark and the camera.

3. Rotating the descriptor region toward the main orientation which is obtained by calculating the gradient orientations and magnitudes
4. Describing the normalized 128 dimensional vector

After matching landmarks to detected natural feature points, mismatched points are removed by PROSAC [14] and the final camera position and pose are estimated.

4.2 Recovering from Tracking Failure

Generally, camera tracking sometimes fails due to blurring or occlusions. Accordingly, the camera tracking method should be able to recover automatically form tracking failures. Our proposed method realizes automatic fast recovering from tracking failures on the assumption that the camera position and pose does not change significantly between before and after the tracking failure frame. Concretely, our proposed method solves the following problem.

The matching cost increases since all detected feature points from image have to be treated as matching candidates. All of them are matched to all landmarks. To solve this problem, our proposed method links feature points between before and after the tracking failure frame using the nearest neighbor search.

4.3 Initialization

In the first frame, the system has to estimate the camera position and pose without tracking techniques. The proposed method realizes the initialization on the assumption that the camera position is not so far from the camera path of the setup phase. This initialization is realized by using the key frame database.

The initialization consists of the following two steps.

1. Finding the nearest key frame
   As the first step, the system searches the nearest key frame by comparing the input image with key frame images of the key frame database. The similarity of images is given by the following formula

$$S_j = \sum_{i=1}^{L_j} \frac{1}{SSD(v_{ji}, v')},$$
(3)

where L_j is the number of landmarks registered in key frame j, and v_{ji} is the SIFT feature of landmark i in registered key frame j and v' represents the feature in current frame seemed to be the nearest neighbor of v_{ji}. This operation contributes to reduce the computational time and mismatching cases in the next step.

2. Matching using the nearest neighbor search

In the next step, the system matches landmarks of the nearest key frame to detected feature points from the input image using the nearest neighbor search.

4.4 Experiments

We had some experiments to show the effectiveness of the proposed tracking method, comparing with the previous method [6] in the computational time and robustness. In these experiments, a notebook PC (Core 2 Extreme 2.8GHz, 4GB RAM) and a video camera (Sony, DSR-PD170, 720×480, progressive scan, 15fps) are used. The landmark database were constructed by the captured image sequence consists of 400 frames. And 10 key frames were selected manually. The SIFT scale r' was 24.

First, we confirmed the proposed method can estimate the initial camera position and pose within 45 [ms] when the initial camera position is near the camera path during constructing the landmark database. The matching process in the initialization requires 1.41 [ms] averagely for every key frame. The camera positions which succeeded the initializing are shown in Fig.9.

Second, we compared the processing time of the proposed tracking method and [6]. Tab.2 shows the processing time of these methods. Tab.2 shows that the proposed method succeeds to reduce the processing time of whole processes, especially (T2) process, considerably.

Fig.10 shows the number of matched landmarks during the camera tracking using the proposed method. This chart shows the proposed method can recover the camera tracking after tracking failure frames.

Finally, Fig.11 shows example MR images based on the camera position and pose which were estimated by the proposed method. The arrows in the right figures represent the main orientation and the circle represents the described region.

Table 2. Processing time [ms]

Process	Previous method	Proposed method
Tentative camera parameter estimation (T1)	20.6	4.2
Matching using SIFT feature (T2)	35.1	3.6
Camera parameter estimation using correspondences (T3)	3.3	0.7
Total	59.0	8.5

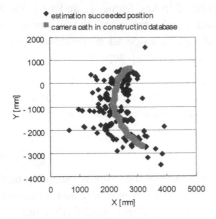

Fig. 9. Succeeded position to initialize

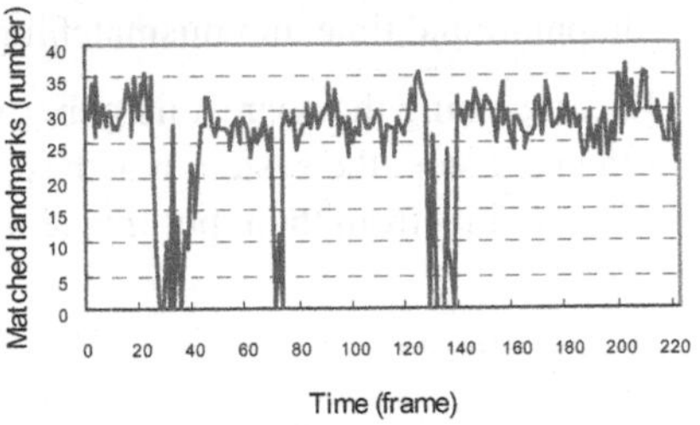

Fig. 10. The number of matched landmarks successfully

30th frame

60th frame

90th frame

Fig. 11. Left: MR images.right: Detected landmarks with SIFT

5   Conclusion

This paper describes a novel camera calibration and tracking method suitable for MR-PreViz. In the camera calibration, the proposed method tries to reduce the human and computational cost using fiducial markers. We also realized a fast and robust tracking by developing the traditional method [6] which uses the landmark database. Concretely speaking, modified SIFT and some devisal make it possible to reduce the computational costs so as to realize recovering from tracking failures.

In the future, we will shoot an MR-PreViz movie using the proposed method after polishing up the proposed method ongoingly.

Acknowledgements. This research is supported in part by Core Research for Evolutional Science and Technology (CREST) Program "Foundation of technology supporting the creation of digital media contents" of Japan Science and Technology Agency (JST).

References

1. Azuma, R., Baillot, Y., Behringer, R., Feiner, S., Julier, S., MacIntyre, B.: Recent advances in augmented reality. IEEE Computer Graphics and Applications 21(6), 34–47 (2001)
2. Klein, G., Murray, D.: Parallel tracking and mapping for small AR workspaces. In: Proc. 6th Int. Symp. on Mixed and Augmented Reality (ISMAR 2007), pp. 225–234 (2007)
3. Wagner, D., Reitmayr, G., Mulloni, A., Drummond, T., Schmalstieg, D.: Pose tracking from natural features on mobile phones. In: Proc. 7th Int. Symp. on Mixed and Augmented Reality (ISMAR 2008), pp. 125–134 (2008)
4. Tenmoku, R., Ichikari, R., Shibata, F., Kimura, A., Tamura, H.: Design and prototype implementation of MR pre-visualization workflow. In: DVD-ROM Proc. Int. Workshop on Mixed Reality Technology for Filmmaking, pp. 1–7 (2006)
5. Ichikari, R., Tenmoku, R., Shibata, F., Ohshima, T., Tamura, H.: Mixed reality pre-visualization for filmmaking: On-set camera-work authoring and action rehearsal. The International Journal of Virtual Reality 7(4), 25–32 (2008)
6. Taketomi, T., Sato, T., Yokoya, N.: Real-time camera position and posture estimation using a feature landmark database with priorities. In: CD-ROM Proc. 19th IAPR Int. Conf. on Pattern Recognition, ICPR 2008 (2008)
7. Kato, H., Billinghurst, M.: Marker tracking and HMD calibration for a video-based augmented reality conferencing system. In: Proc. 2nd Int. Workshop on Augmented Reality (IWAR 1999), pp. 85–94 (1999)
8. Triggs, B., McLauchlan, P., Hartley, R., Fitzgibbon, A.: Bundle adjustment – a modern synthesis. In: Proc. ICCV Workshop on Vision Algorithms, pp. 298–372 (1999)
9. Hartley, R., Zisserman, A.: Multiple View Geometry in Computer Vision, 2nd edn. Cambridge University Press, Cambridge (2004)
10. Lowe, D.: Distinctive image features from scale–invariant keypoints. Int J. Comput. Vision 60(2), 91–100 (2004)
11. Moreno-Noguer, F., Lepetit, V., Fua, P.: Accurate Non-Iterative O(n) Solution to the PnP Problem. In: Proc. 11th Int. Conf. on Computer Vision, pp. 1–8 (2007)

12. Rosten, E., Drummond, T.: Machine learning for high-speed corner detection. In: Leonardis, A., Bischof, H., Pinz, A. (eds.) ECCV 2006. LNCS, vol. 3951, pp. 430–443. Springer, Heidelberg (2006)
13. Wagner, D., Reitmayr, G., Mulloni, A., Drummond, T., Schmalstieg, D.: Pose tracking from natural features on mobile phones. In: Proc. 7th Int. Symp. on Mixed and Augmented Reality (ISMAR 2008), pp. 125–134 (2008)
14. Chum, O., Matas, J.: Matching with PROSAC – progressive sample consensus. In: Proc. IEEE Compt. Soc. Conf. on Computer Vision and Pattern Recognition (CVPR 2005), vol. 1, pp. 220–226 (2005)

Robust Hybrid Tracking with Life-Size Avatar in Mixed Reality Environment

Q.C.T. Tran, S.P. Lee, W.R. Pensyl, and D. Jernigan

Interaction & Entertainment Research Centre – IERC
Nanyang Technological University, Singapore
{qui_tran,splee,wrpensyl,DJernigan}@ntu.edu.sg

Abstract. We have developed a system which enables us to track participant-observers accurately in a large area for the purpose of immersing them in a mixed reality environment. This system is robust even under uncompromising lighting conditions. Accurate tracking of the observer's spatial and orientation point of view is achieved by using hybrid inertial sensors and computer vision techniques. We demonstrate our results by presenting life-size, animated human avatars sitting in real chairs, in a stable and low-jitter manner. The system installation allows the observers to freely walk around and navigate themselves in the environment even while still being able to see the avatars from various angles. The project installation provides and exciting way for cultural and historical narratives to be presented vividly in the real present world.

1 Objective and Significance

The objective of this project is to create a low-cost, easy-to-set-up, robust and reliable, interactive and immersive augmented and mixed reality system which presents life-size, animated human avatar in a cultural heritage environment.

The significance of this project is that it provides an environment where people can interact with historical human characters in a cultural setting. Other than for cultural and historical installation, this work has the potential of being further developed for the purpose of education, art, entertainment and tourism promotion.

2 Introduction

The motivation for developing this project is to allow people to experience pseudo-historical events impressed over present day real world environment (we have set our project at the famous Long Bar at the Raffles Hotel in Singapore). It is an augmented reality installation which involves re-enactment of the famous people who frequented the bar in the early 20th century. It uses augmented reality technology to develop both historical and legendary culturally significant events into interactive mixed reality experiences. Participants wearing head-mounted display systems witness virtual character versions of various notable figures, including Somerset Maugham, Joseph Conrad, and Jean Harlow, immersed within a real world environment modeled on the Raffles Hotel Long Bar they had frequented. Through the application of research in

R. Shumaker (Ed.): Virtual and Mixed Reality, LNCS 5622, pp. 503–510, 2009.

tracking, occlusion, and by embedding large mesh animated characters, this installation demonstrates the results of the technical research and the conceptual development and presentation in the installation. Moreover, requiring that our work eventually be located in the Long Bar provides us with the motivation to create a system that can accommodate compromising lighting conditions and large open spaces.

Tracking of human subjects in a large area indoor mixed reality application has always been a challenge. One of the most crucial parts of an appealing mixed reality presentation is the smooth, jitterless and accurate rendering of 3D virtual objects onto the physical real world. This involves primarily the tracking of user's point of view which in most cases are the spatial and orientation information of the viewing camera attached to user's head. Conventionally, fiducial markers are used in conjunction with ARToolkit [1] or MXRToolkit [2] in well-prepared, well-lit environment; however the use of markers poses several problems: they are not robust in a poor lighting environment; and placing and scattering markers in the environment makes the real world scene unaesthetic.

Previous work [3] tracked humans in an environment "whose only requirements are good, constant lighting and an unmoving background". In [4], capturing the human body requires a green recording room with consistent lighting. Our system, on the other hand, works in most unexpected, varying, artificial and/or ambient lighting condition.

The work in [5] provided excellent accounts and experimental results of hybrid inertial and vision tracking for augmented reality registration. The sensitivities of orientation tracking error were quantitatively analyzed, natural feature tracking and motion-based registration method that automatically computed the orientation transformation (among different coordinate systems) was presented. Our work is different in that the tracking cameras tracks only point light source, and they are statically mounted on the wall instead of attached to the observer/user's head.

3 Overview

This work was intended to be set up in the famous and historical Long Bar in Singapore. People wearing HMDs will be able to see virtual avatar of famous historical human character talking and interacting with them.

Our work uses a hybrid approach – tracking an active marker while at the same time tracking the movement of the observer's (camera's) frame with the use of inertial sensors. The active marker is made up of an infrared (IR) light-emitting diode (LED) mounted on the user's HMD. In our system, to detect IR LED, instead of using normal cameras, we use Nintendo Wii Remotes as vision tracking devices. This low-cost device can detect IR sources at up to 100 Hz, which is very suitable for real-time interaction systems. Furthermore, an inertial sensor consisting of 6DOF is attached to the HMD to detect the rotation and movement of user viewpoints.

There are two ways in which the user can interact with the virtual character. Upon request by the virtual character, the user could fill the physical glass with wine by first picking the glass up from the table. He will then "fill" the glass with "wine", and put the glass on anywhere on the table. The virtual character will then pick up the glass from that location. Another interaction is that when the virtual character asks the user

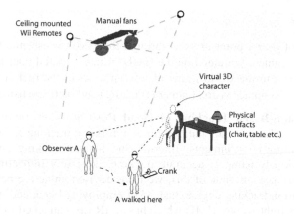

Fig. 1. Setup of the large area robust hybrid tracking system. The chair, table, lamp and glass are physical objects in the real world. The manual fan on the ceiling is virtual; it is controlled by a real physical crank. The "human" in dashed-line and sitting in the chair is a 3D avatar.

to crank up the virtual fans (which were installed on the ceiling) when it gets hot. The user then cranks up a physical device to control the speed of the fan. If the fans are too fast the virtual character will ask the user to slow down, and vice versa.

Figure 1 shows the system setup. The observer wears a HMD and can move freely around within the designated area. There is an empty chair, a table and other physical artifacts (glass, etc) in the demonstration area. As the observer looks at the chair, he sees a life size, 3D animated human character sitting in the chair.

4 System Details

4.1 System Block Diagram

Figure 2. shows the block diagrams of the system. The peripheral hardware are shaded in blue.

The details of each part will be described in the following subsections.

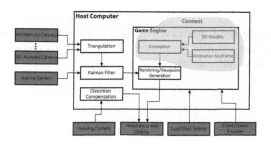

Fig. 2. Block diagram of the system

4.2 Tracking

The tracking of user's point of view through the HMD is essentially the continuous tracking of the camera (mounted on the HMD) frame's spatial coordinate and orientation, with respect to the world frame of reference set in the real environment. It is a combination of computer vision (camera tracking) and inertia sensing.

Low-cost Vision-Based Tracking of Head Position. Conventional ARToolkit or MXRToolkit markers are not suitable for vision-based tracking in large area, uncompromising lighting environments. Jittering and loss of tracking due to the lighting conditions seriously hampers accurate tracking, adversely impacting the audiences' aesthetic experience. In view of this, we have devised an active beacon by using IR LED as a position tracking device. Instead of employing black and white markers, the observer wears light-weight HMD which has an IR LED attached to it.

We use two Nintendo Wii Remotes as vision tracking devices. The Wii consists of a monochrome camera with resolution of 128x96 pixels, with an IR-pass filter in front of it. The Wii Remote cameras are installed in the ceiling to track the location of the observer. This tracking provides positional information only and does not provide the orientation information of the head.

The advantages of using Wii Remote cameras are manifold: low-cost, easy setup, high "frame rate" (in fact only processed images – the coordinates of the tracked points – are sent to the host) and wireless. The host computer is relieved from processing the raw image; and an optimal triangulation technique is all that is needed to obtain the depth information of the IR LED.

Inertial Sensor-based Tracking of Head Orientation. The inertial sensor is attached to the HMD, above the viewing camera. It provides drift-free 3D acceleration, 3D rate gyro and 3D earth-magnetic field data [6]. With sensor fusion algorithm, the 3D orientation (roll, pitch and yaw) data of the sensor's coordinate frame can be found.

As we are tracking different sources (IR LED for position and inertial sensor for rotation), the calibration process which is already important becomes even more critical. In the next part, we will describe the steps we have done in our calibration process.

4.3 Calibration

Intrinsic Calibration for Cameras. We used Camera Calibration Toolbox for Matlab [7] to calculate the intrinsic parameters of our viewing camera. The result we got from the Toolbox is an intrinsic matrix I:

$$I = \begin{bmatrix} f_x & S & O_x \\ 0 & f_y & O_y \\ 0 & 0 & 1 \end{bmatrix} \tag{1}$$

Where: f_x, f_y :   the focal length expressed in units of horizontal and vertical pixels.

O_x, O_y : the principal point coordinates.

S: the skew coefficient defining the angle between the x and y pixel axes.

From these parameters, the projection matrix that will be used in the game engine is calculated as follow: (in the same way as in ARToolkit [1])

$$P = \begin{bmatrix} \dfrac{2 \times f_x}{Width} & \dfrac{2 \times S}{Width} & \dfrac{2 \times O_x}{Width} - 1 & 0 \\[2ex] 0 & \dfrac{2 \times f_y}{Height} & \dfrac{2 \times O_y}{Height} - 1 & 0 \\[2ex] 0 & 0 & \dfrac{(gFar + gNear)}{(gFar - gNear)} & \dfrac{-2 \times gFar \times gNear}{(gFar - gNear)} \\[2ex] 0 & 0 & 1 & 0 \end{bmatrix} \qquad (2)$$

Where: *Width, Height*:   the resolution of the camera
         gFar, gNear: the far and near clipping planes

Similar to the viewing camera, the intrinsic parameters of the cameras inside wii-motes also need to be calculated. To do that, we use a small board with 4 IR LEDs. Wiimotes track these 4 IR sources simultaneously while the board is moved around. A few frames are captured and intrinsic parameters can be calculated.

Extrinsic Calibration. In this step, the transformation from the coordinate system of sensors to the coordinate system of the viewing camera needs to be calculated. To do that, we are using the method similar to the method described in [8].

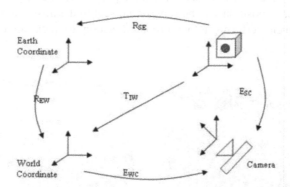

Fig. 3. The transformations between all the coordinate system

The relations between all the coordinate system are illustrated in Figure 3. In the figure, we use the following annotation: R for rotation, T for translation, E for trans-formation ($E = [R|T]$). R_{SE} is the rotation read from the inertial sensor, which is aligned to the Earth coordinate system. T_{IW} is the translation from the IR Led to the world coordinate system. T_{IW} is calculated by using the 2 wiimotes. E_{SC} and R_{EW} are the 2 unknown parameters that need to be calculated. As can be seen in Figure 3:

$$E_{SC} = E_{WC}\left[R_{Ew}R_{SE} \,{}^{|}T_{IW}\right]$$

$$\Rightarrow E_{SC} = [R_{WC}T_{WC}]\left[R_{Ew}R_{SE} \,{}^{|}T_{IW}\right] \tag{3}$$

$$\Rightarrow \begin{cases} R_{SC} = R_{WC}R_{Ew}R_{SE} \\ T_{SC} = R_{WC}T_{IW} + T_{WC} \end{cases}$$

During the calibration process, we put a chess board at the center of the world co-ordinate system to compute E_{WC}. At the same time, T_{IW} and R_{SE} are also captured. After capturing enough combinations (E_{wc}, T_{IW}, R_{SE}), R_{SC} and T_{SC} can be calculated in the form of solving the "AX=XB" equation system [8]. The same for R_{EW}.

4.4 Interaction

We provide two interesting scenarios in which user can interact with the 3D virtual human avatar. The first scenario is when the virtual human asks for his glass to be filled up with wine. The user himself, or another user (the bartender, as shown in Figure 4) will then pick up the physical glass from the table, fill it up, and put in on an arbitrary place on the table. The virtual human is supposed to pick up the glass from that location. A second scenario is that the user is supposed to respond to the avatar request of fanning the virtual ceiling fan. The details of the interaction and sensing techniques are described in the following sub-sections.

Arbitrary Placement of the Cup/Glass. Ferromagnetic metal detection sensors are installed at various spots under the table. A small, thin piece of iron is attached to the underneath of the glass. As user/bartender puts down the glass onto an arbitrary spot on the table, its position will be sensed and sent to the host computer. The virtual human avatar then performs a pre-animated action to pick up the virtual glass (Figure 4).

Fig. 4. First person view through the HMD. On the left figure, the virtual human pick up the "glass" (virtual) after the bartender put the glass (real) on the table. On the right, the virtual human puts the "glass" down and the bartender picks it up. Notice the virtual fans on the ceiling.

Cranking the Virtual Fan. A physical crank (Figure 5) is provided as a device to control the virtual ceiling fans. A rotary encoder is embedded inside the crank and it is used to measure the speed at which the user rotates the crank. Its rotational speed corresponds to that of the virtual ceiling fan. Notice in Figure 4 the virtual fans on the ceiling. The virtual human will react to the fan speed, such as complaining that the weather is hot and the fan is too slow.

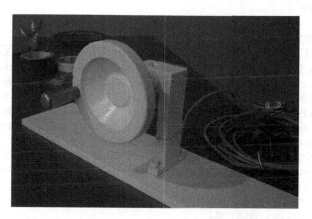

Fig. 5. The rotary crank used to control the virtual fan. It is connected to the host computer via a serial cable.

5 Conclusion and Future Work

This work provides users with enhanced experience in a large area immersive mixed reality world. The robust and stable rendering of the 3D avatars is made possible by accurate tracking which involves hybrid computer vision and inertial sensors. Users are able to interact with the avatars with the aids of various sensing techniques.

This work is originally intended for use in a cultural and heritage setting due to its large space and live-size avatars nature. However it can also be extended to applications such as online role-playing game, 3D social networking and military simulation.

One disadvantage of the hybrid tracking method is that inertial sensor and LEDs have to be mounted onto the HMD; this essentially makes it cumbersome and uncomfortable to wear. We propose to use, in next stage of development, natural feature tracking technique in place of the hybrid tracking. One such technique is parallel tracking and mapping (PTAM) [9].

Currently the position of the glass is discrete, since only a few ferromagnetic sensors are place underneath the table. Future version of this glass tracking technique would be a "continuous" and high resolution one; possible technologies which could be used are capacitive sensing and electric field sensing (similar to the tablet PC technology). Pre-animated pick-up-the-glass motion could not possibly be used because theoretically there are infinite picking up motions from infinite number of spots on the table. We propose that inverse kinematics be incorporated in the motion of the virtual human avatar when he picks up the glass from the table.

Physics would also be incorporated within the interaction scenarios to make it more realistic. For example, too strong the speed of the fan would blow the virtual human's hair and mess it up.

Haptics could also be used in this work. The user would be able to pat the virtual human's shoulder, or even shake hands with him.

References

1. ARToolkit, http://www.hitl.washington.edu/artoolkit
2. MXRToolkit, http://sourceforge.net/projects/mxrtoolkit
3. Sparacino, F., Wren, C., Davenport, G., Pentland, A.: Augmented Performance in Dance and Theatre. In: International Dance and Technology, ASU, Tempe, Arizona (1999)
4. Nguyen, T.H.D., Qui, T.C.T., Xu, K., Cheok, A.D., Teo, S.L., Zhou, Z.Y., Allawaarachchi, A., Lee, S.P., Liu, W., Teo, H.S., Thang, L.N., Li, Y., Kato, H.: Real Time 3D Human Capture System for Mixed-Reality Art and Entertainment. IEEE Transaction on Visualization and Computer Graphics (TVCG) 11(6), 706–721 (2005)
5. You, S., Neumann, U., Azuma, R.: Hybrid Inertial and Vision Tracking for Augmented Reality Registration. In: Proceedings of the IEEE Virtual Reality, Washington, DC (1999)
6. XSens: MTx 3DOF Orientation Tracker,
   http://www.xsens.com/Static/Documents/UserUpload/
   dl_42_leaflet_mtx.pdf
7. Camera Calibration Toolbox for Matlab,
   http://www.vision.caltech.edu/bouguetj/calib_doc/
8. Baillot, Y., Julier, S.J.: A Tracker Alignment Framework for Augmented Reality. In: Proceedings of 2nd IEEE and ACM International Symposium of Mixed and Augmented Reality (2003)
9. Klein, G., Murray, D.: Parallel Tracking and Mapping for Small AR Workspaces. In: Proceedings of 6th IEEE and ACM International Symposium on Mixed and Augmented Reality, ISMAR 2007 (2007)

Part V
VR Applications

Collaboration Design System Using Internet and Virtual Reality Technology

Hideki Aoyama[1] and Rie Iida[2]

[1] Keio University, Professor
3-14-1 Hiyoshi, Kohoku-ku, Yokohama 223-8522 Japan
haoyama@sd.keio.ac.jp
[2] Keio University, Master Course Student
3-14-1 Hiyoshi, Kohoku-ku, Yokohama 223-8522 Japan
rie-i@ina.sd.keio.ac.jp

Abstract. Globalization of manufacturing industry makes production bases covering two or more areas and countries. Moreover, in order to timely offer products which respond to consumer needs, it has been becoming important to shorten the lead time of product development. Opportunities to do collaboration work with designers/engineers existing different places are thus increasing. A support system for collaboration design work without physical moving of designers/engineers is strongly demanded to cut down time and cost. This research aims at proposing the intuitive 3-dimensional geometric model construction method and developing a system which supports collaboration design work for the discussion stage of ideas in the upstream of design processes. In this paper, a system which can intuitively build a 3D model and support collaboration design work for designers/engineers being different places by sharing mutually a design object through the Internet is described.

Keywords: Design Collaboration, Internet, Virtual Reality, 3D Modeling, Industry Product Design, Basic Design, CAD.

1 Introduction

Bases for design and development of industrial products are spreading to multiple areas and countries with globalization of manufacturing industry. Under such situation, opportunities to do collaboration work on design and development with remote places are increasing to create a new idea which cannot be hit by only one designer/engineer. This has been become one of the causes to increase time and cost in product development. On the other hand, in order to timely offer products which respond to consumer needs, it has been an important subject to shorten the lead time of product development and to decrease the cost for international competition. In order solve the problems, a technology to realize remote collaboration work on design and development of industrial products without physical moving of designers and engineers is demanded to create a new idea by stimulating each other and to decrease time and cost for the development.

As support systems for collaboration work on design and development of industrial products, systems [1], [2], [8] to collaboratively make and evaluate a product shape

R. Shumaker (Ed.): Virtual and Mixed Reality, LNCS 5622, pp. 513–521, 2009.

by communication between different places had been proposed. The target of these systems is for the downstream of design processes, in other word, for the detail design process. In these days, it is extremely hard to shorten the time from detail design to production because the streamline of the processes from detail design to production is becoming to the breaking point. Therefore, in order to decrease the lead time of product development, the upstream of design processes must be made higher efficiency [3]. For the upstream of design processes, the function to intuitively create and modify a shape is necessary [9], [10] than the function to strictly define a shape. Sometimes, the function to strictly define a shape disturbs creation of ideas due to its complicated operations required. A support system for the upstream of design processes requires the function to collaborate on discussion.

The objective of this research is to develop a system which enables designers and engineers to execute cooperative work between different places by applying virtual reality technology and communication technology with the Internet. The system supplies a virtual common space as an environment of discussion for designers and engineers being in different places. Since the system has a function to easily construct a three dimensional model by simple and intuitive operations, the intuitive modeling function and the discussion environment can support to create an idea in the upstream of design processes.

2 Outline of Proposed System

In order to realize a function to easily and intuitively construct a three dimensional model, a haptic device is utilized to develop the objective system. Fig. 1 shows the configuration of the proposed system. A haptic device: PHANToM Omni by Sensable Technologies inc., with a touching stylus is used as an operating equipment. It enables designers/engineers to intuitive operation for constructing a 3D model as if they are creating a model with touching. The device is a kind of force feedback display with 6-degree-of-freedom and has the range of 160*120*170 mm for detecting and has the

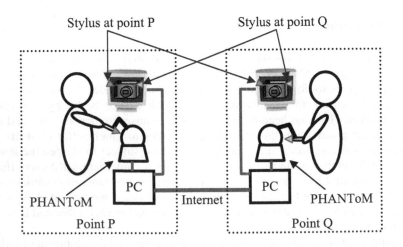

Fig. 1. Configuration of system

feedback force of 3.3 N in the maximum. Designers/engineers indicate the three dimensional position by the stylus of a haptic device, and the returned force from a three dimensional model is also given as touching feeling by the stylus [4]. A common space to discuss design is constructed and supplied for designers/engineers being in distributed places by such systems linked with the Internet.

A 3D model constructed at the point P by simple and intuitive operations using haptic devices is located in the common space and is simultaneously displayed on the both screens at the points P and Q. The 3D model constructed at the point P is also touched and remodeled at the point Q by using the devices. Therefore, a 3D model in the common space can be simultaneously operated by designers/engineers being in distributed points. The system then realizes cooperative and confrontational work by processes of constructing a 3D model and holding conversation each other from different places.

3   Method to Construct 3D Model

A currently used 3D CAD system constructs a model by set operations of fundamental forms so called primitives such as a cuboid, a cylinder, a sphere, etc. The primitives are defined by complex operations which are the indications of the type, the position, the direction and the form parameters. And the operations are executed on a display, in other words, a 2D space. The operations in a 2D space are not intuitive for 3D model construction. Such operations are convenient for detail design but they are not suitable for the early stage of design. For the problem, there have been research works to construct a 3D model by simple and intuitive operations. VLEGO [5] can intuitively build a 3D model by combining several primitives in a virtual space, but it is difficult to intuitively define each primitive. BlueGrotto [6] can input figure recognition by handwriting in a virtual space, and builds a 3D model more nearly intuitively. But, since BlueGrotto does not have feedback of the tactile sense in the construction process of a 3D model, it is difficult to intuitively specify the position and direction in the virtual space.

As mentioned above, the system proposed in this research enables designers/ engineers to construct a 3D model in a virtual space by simple and intuitive operations using a haptic device which can sensuously indicate the position and direction of primitives composing a 3D model in a 3D space. A basic system was developed to verify effectiveness of the proposed method. The system has the following functions;

- Construction of primitive shapes, that is, a cuboid and a cylinder,
- Construction of a 3D model by combining primitive shapes, and
- Shape modifications, that is, delete, enlargement/reduction, copy, movement, turn, and chamfering.

Fig. 2 shows a cuboid primitive and a cylinder primitive constructed by the developed system. A cuboid primitive is defined by the line AB which represents the diagonal line of a cuboid to be constructed and is given by a drag and drop operation of the stylus of a haptic device in a 3D space. A cylinder is also defined by same operation.

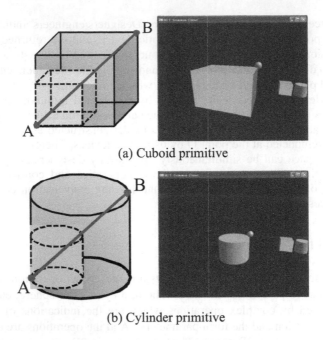

(a) Cuboid primitive

(b) Cylinder primitive

Fig. 2. Construction of primitives

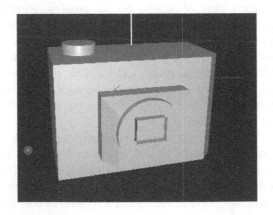

Fig. 3. An example: a constructed model

The position and direction for a primitive addition and a form modification are easily and intuitively specified according to the tactile sense given by the stylus of a haptic device.

Fig. 3 shows an example of 3D models constructed by the developed system. As shown in Fig. 3, a primitive has relationship with several primitives; in other words, a primitive is defined on another primitive. The relationship between primitives is defined as an object-oriented database by a hierarchical structure with a parent-child.

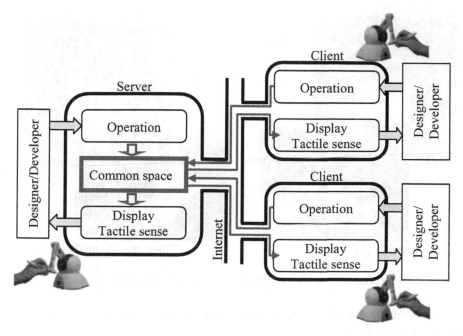

Fig. 4. Construction of common space

4 Construction Method of 3D Virtual Common Space

A 3D virtual common space is constructed by a Haptic Communication Toolkit [7] which is a kind of network library to communicate tactile sense information between haptic devices. In order to realize the frame rate of 1 kHz which is necessary for comfortable feeling in touching, the Haptic Communication Toolkit has restriction that transmitting and receiving data must be less than 256 bytes. As shown in Fig. 4, a 3D virtual common space is built in the server by making transmitting and receiving data limited in 256 bytes. The common space in which designers/engineers exist at the same time is realized by holding the information of the virtual space in common at the server and clients. The transmitting and receiving between the server and a client is executed in following processes.

As shown in Fig. 4, primitive information input by a designer/engineer on the site of a client is fed into the server and the unique ID is given to the primitive. The primitive with the unique ID is instantly constructed in the common space which is located in the server, and is identified and shared by the server and clients in real time. Primitive information input on the site of the server also constructs the primitive form in the common space by giving the unique ID, and the primitive is simultaneously identified by the server and clients. The model constructed in the common space by combining the primitives defined from the server site and client sites is shown on the displays of the server and clients and the tactile senses by haptic devices are returned to designers/engineers being in the sites of the server and clients, respectively.

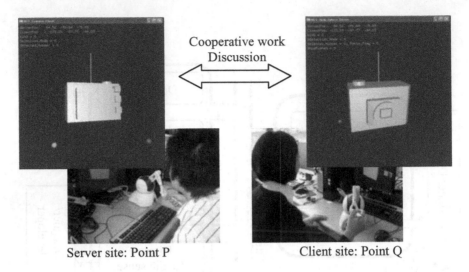

Server site: Point P   Client site: Point Q

Fig. 5. Cooperative design work between remote places

In the communication between the server and clients, 5 streams are prepared for the following data flow:

1. the coordinate values x, y, z of the stylus tip of a haptic device,
2. the direction vector of the stylus of a haptic device,
3. primitive information: the type, defining parameters, and parent-child relationship,
4. operation information: operation type and operating parameters, and
5. model information from the server to the clients.

As the results, designers/engineers can corporative design work with the 3D model constructed in the common space. The system can be applied for plural clients by constructing the server-clients structure. Fig. 5 shows the corporative work using the system. As shown in Fig. 5, designers/engineers are able to discuss design by constructing and modifying the design shape intuitively from different places as if they are staying in a same place.

5   Evaluation of Developed System

The aim of this research is to offer a system which enables designers/engineers existing different places to make cooperative work and discussion on product design by having a 3D virtual space in common. There have not been any ideas and methods to quantitatively evaluate the degree and depth of cooperative work and discussion. Therefore, in this research, the functionality for cooperative work and discussion is quantitatively judged by comparing the times to execute tasks by the developed system and a commercially available CAD system. A system having a shorter execution time of a task is evaluated as possessing high functionality for cooperative work and discussion than a system having a longer execution time of a task.

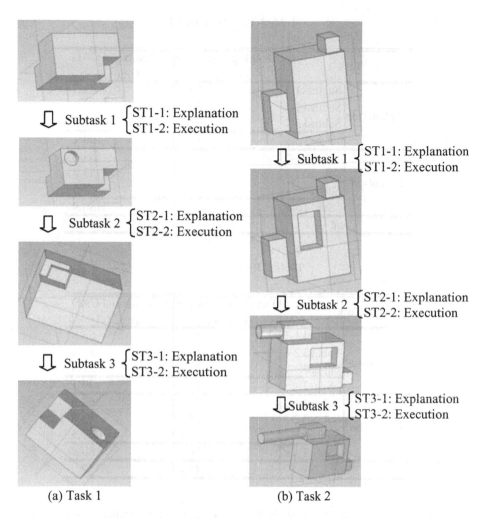

(a) Task 1   (b) Task 2

Fig. 6. Evaluation tests

The two tasks shown in Fig. 6: Task 1 and Task 2, were executed by 10 unaccustomed persons with from 22 to 24 years old. To execute the tasks, 5 persons of the 10 persons used the developed system and other 5 persons tried to use a commercially available CAD system: Solid Edge Ver19. As shown in Fig. 6, each task had three subtasks, and each subtask was executed in the two steps: the task explanation step and the task execution step. In the task explanation step, the specified person had the role to explain the subtask. The explanation for using the developed system was performed from the server site to a client site through the Internet. And the explanation for using the commercially available CAD system was carried out by only talking.

Table 1 and Table 2 show the results of the times to execute each subtask by the developed system and a commercial CAD system. As shown in Tables 1and 2, the times to understand the explanation of the subtasks by using the developed system

Table 1. Results of Task 1

Task 1		Developed system Time [s]	Commercial CAD Time [s]
Explanation	Subtask1-1	16.7	53.3
	Subtask2-1	26.8	88.3
	Subtask3-1	27.3	57.5
	Sub-Total	70.8	199.1
Execution	Subtask1-2	25.0	65.6
	Subtask2-2	18.0	57.8
	Subtask3-2	33.3	57.5
	Sub-Total	76.3	180.9
Total		147.1	380.0

Table 2. Results of Task 2

Task 1		Developed system Time [s]	Commercial CAD Time [s]
Explanation	Subtask1-1	16.7	53.3
	Subtask2-1	26.8	88.3
	Subtask3-1	27.3	57.5
	Sub-Total	70.8	199.1
Execution	Subtask1-2	25.0	65.6
	Subtask2-2	18.0	57.8
	Subtask3-2	33.3	57.5
	Sub-Total	76.3	180.9
Total		147.1	380.0

were from 30 to 40 % for the times in the case of using of a commercial CAD system. And the times to execute the subtasks by using the developed system were also from 30 to 40 % for the times in the case of using of the commercial CAD system. Therefore, it is understandable that the developed system has the effectiveness for understanding the will of a person existing in a remote place. It can be interpreted that the developed system is useful for cooperative work and discussion of designers/engineers being in different places. And the system is also useful for discussion to evaluate product design.

6 Conclusions

In this research, a method which enables designers and engineers existing in different places to execute cooperative work and discussion is proposed in order to hit new and unique idea. The method was realized by applying virtual reality technology and communication technology with the Internet. Virtual reality technology made simple operation to construct a 3D model and intuitive communication between designers and engineers being in different places. And the Internet constructed the virtual common space which realized a communication place without physical moving of designers and engineers. A basic system based on the proposed method was developed and the usefulness of the system was confirmed by simple experiment. According to the experiment results, understanding of will in the case of using of the developed system was improved from 30 to 40 % in comparison with non-using of it.

In this study, it was inspected by a basic system that a system to execute discussion using the Internet between designers/ engineers existing different places was useful for cooperative design work of products. The development of practical systems will support to cooperate on design work between remote places without physical movement and to create novel ideas from discussion.

References

1. Haoxue, M.A.: RISCH Tore: A database approach for information communication in a peer-to-peer collaborative CAD environment. Software Pract. Exp. 37(11), 1193–1213 (2007)
2. Masashi, O., Tomio, W., Satoshi, K.: Embodied Collaboration support system for 3D shape evaluation by using network virtual reality. In: Proceedings of the ASME 2007 International Design Engineering Technical Conferences & Computers and Information in Engineering Conference, pp. 1–8 (2007) (CD-ROM)
3. Tetsuya, T.: The 3-dimensional-CAD practice utilizing method (in Japanese). Japan Society for Design Engineering, p. 242 (2006)
4. Kim, L., Sukhatme, G.S., Desbrun, M.: A haptic-rendering technique based on hybrid surface representation. IEEE Computer Graphics and Applications 24(2), 66 (2004)
5. Kiyoshi, K., Haruo, T., Yoshiaki, K., Hidehiko, I., Naokazu, Y.: VLEGO: A Simple Two-Handed 3-D Modeler in a Virtual Environment. The transactions of the institute of electronics, information and communication engineers. A J80-A(9), 1517–1526 (1997)
6. Tomoharu, I., Naoki, N., Nobuaki, S., Naohumi, Y., Sato, S.: A 3-D Modeling Interface BlueGrotto on the Basis of Drawing Gesture Identification in Virtual Space. The transactions of the Institute of Electronics, Information and Communication Engineers. D-2 87-D-2(6), 1309–1318 (2004)
7. Goncharenko, S.M., Matsumoto, S., Masui, Y., Kanou, Y., Hosoe, S.: Cooperative Conrol with Haptic Visualization in Shared Virtual Environments. In: Proceedings of the 8th International conference on Information Visualization, pp. 533–538 (2004)
8. Okubo, M., Watanabe, T.: Embodied Collaboration Support System for 3D Shape Evaluation by Using Network Virtual Reality. In: Proceeding of the ASME 2007 International Design Engineering Technical Conference & Computer and Information in Engineering Conference, IDETC/CIE, pp. 1–8 (2007) (CD-ROM)
9. Zeleznik, R., Herndon, K., Hughes, J.: SKETCH: An Interface for Sketching 3D Scenes. In: SIGGRAPH Conference Proceedings, vol. 1996, pp. 163–170 (1996)
10. Igarashi, T., Matsuoka, S., Tanaka, H.: Teddy: A Sketching Interface for 3D Freeform Design. In: ACM SIGGRAPH 1999, pp. 409–416 (1999)

Evaluating the Potential of Cognitive Rehabilitation with Mixed Reality

Nicholas Beato, Daniel P. Mapes, Charles E. Hughes,
Cali Fidopiastis, and Eileen Smith

University of Central Florida
Orlando, FL 32816
nbeato@eecs.ucf.edu, dmapes@ist.ucf.edu,
ceh@eecs.ucf.edu, cfidopia@ist.ucf.edu, esmith@ist.ucf.edu

Abstract. We describe the development and use of a mixed reality (MR) test-bed to evaluate potential scenarios that may alleviate performance deficits in subjects who may be experiencing cognitive deficiencies, such as posttraumatic stress disorder (PTSD). The system blends real world sensory data with synthetic enhancements in the visual and aural domains. It captures user actions (movement, view direction, environment interaction, and task performance) and psychophysical states (engagement, workload, and skin conductivity) during an MR-enabled experience in order to determine task performance in the context of a variety of stimuli (visual and aural distracters in time-constrained activities). The goal is to discover triggers that affect stress levels and task performance in order to develop individualized plans for personal improvement.

Keywords: Mixed reality, post traumatic stress disorder, psychophysical sensing, medical rehabilitation, cognitive rehabilitation.

1 Introduction

In cognitive rehabilitation, it is vital that a patient's training generalizes and transfers to everyday situations. Environmental and economical factors have motivated medical researchers to explore alternatives including virtual environments in order to provide safe, reusable, and cost-effective recovery [4]. A drawback to virtual reality (VR) technology is that a patient only interacts with two senses, sight and sound, which the system overrides with artificial content. Seemingly normal expectations, such as manipulating physical objects with your hands, may prevent the patient from fully investing in the experience, compromising treatment. Mixed reality (MR) technology aims to seamlessly and believably combine virtual and real world content in a safe and controlled setting. To apply such technology to rehabilitation of cognitive disorders, it is necessary to evaluate treatment scenarios in a safe, cost-effective, and non-subjective manner. Our MR toolkit augments the visual and auditory senses while allowing the other senses to draw from the actual environment. With the addition of psychophysical sensors, we hypothesize that monitoring healthy participants may aid the efficacy of particular environments for the treatment of cognitive disorders [3], [4].

R. Shumaker (Ed.): Virtual and Mixed Reality, LNCS 5622, pp. 522–531, 2009.

2 Mixed Reality: What, Why, How?

2.1 What Is MR?

As defined by Milgram et al. [6], MR covers the spectrum of experiences ranging from almost purely virtual to almost purely physical. That is, an MR experience must involve some virtual and some real world aspects, with the amount of each highly dependent upon the application's requirements. Real experiences with added virtual overlays are categorized as augmented reality (AR). Synthetic experiences with added real world components are categorized as augmented virtuality (AV). In the case of AR, we generally overlay virtual objects on top of real ones, e.g., adding identifiers like textual or iconic information that make a visual landscape more understandable. In the case of AV, we typically place a small interactive set in a virtual surround, e.g., the user sits on a real chair at a real table interacting with other people within the context of a virtual restaurant.

The most interesting and challenging part of the MR spectrum lies in the middle, where virtual and real objects coexist. In order for these objects to coexist, they must interact with each other based on the user's viewpoint. Obviously, it's trivial for real objects to coexist with other real objects, and virtual objects to coexist with other virtual objects. The challenge lies in the interaction between the real and virtual.

2.2 Why MR versus VR?

VR can be viewed as the extreme limit of MR in which all assets are synthetic. A primary attribute of VR is that it dominates users' senses, separating them from the real world in order to provide a purely synthetic experience. While such isolation from reality is useful in some applications, it is very limiting in others, especially those in which people are performing tasks in a context that involves all their senses or relies on triggering memories in order to interact with objects and people [4]. In effect, VR takes its users away from the physical context, whereas MR enhances the physical context. This is a very important distinction for cognitive assessment and rehabilitation, where we often want to determine and address a subject's deficiencies at performing tasks in a specific, realistic context.

VR tends to be a visual and aural experience, with other senses only peripherally addressed. Because MR can take advantage of the real world, it usually involves all senses, with the visual and aural being a blend of real and synthetic, and the other senses generally being real. For instance, a rehabilitation experience could take place in a MR replica of a patient's kitchen [3], where the counters, the cabinets and their contents, a refrigerator, a toaster oven, a coffee maker and an accompanying therapist are real. These real assets are augmented by virtual textures on the counters and cabinets. The scene might also include a virtual wall with a virtual window and its accompanying virtual landscaping, a virtual eating area, and optional virtual aural cues to help the patient carry out tasks in the correct sequence. Passive and active haptics are provided by the environment's real objects, e.g., you can lean against the counters while opening the cabinets. The smell of food, e.g., a bagel toasting, and its taste are real. This combination of real and virtual content makes for a rich experience that may trigger old memories for patient assessment and build multiple pathways to new and existing ones for rehabilitation.

2.3 How Can We Achieve MR?

The most recognizable aspect of a functioning MR system is the ability to trick the brain into perceiving the presence of things that are not really there. Visually, we must enhance the appearance of the real world from the user's point-of-view. While other techniques exist, a see-through head-mounted display (ST-HMD) is a common way to accomplish this. We specifically use a video ST-HMD (VST-HMD), a device that allows us to capture the user's view, in stereo, from optically aligned mounted cameras, process the video on a computer system in real-time, and display the composited result, properly registered, via small LCDs in front of the user's eyes. Because the system acquires video and augments it before the user perceives the real content (as opposed to rendering on a transparent screen, as done on an optical ST-HMD in AR), we have much more control over the registration and synchronization of the real and virtual worlds. This control is a necessity, as the experiences we develop often require multiple, alternating layers of real and virtual content.

Although audio is often deferred to the end of production in the development of multimedia experiences, it is integral to a person's experiences and their recollection. Thus, for any MR experience intended for assessment or rehabilitation or for that matter nearly any interactive experience, the aural components are as important as the visual, and should be part of the entire design process, not a last-minute add-on. Just as the visual component, the aural part of MR involves many challenges. The challenges are understanding the sources of real audio, especially when there are multiple, concurrent origins; blending the real and virtual; and delivering this blend into a complex landscape [5].

To properly register the virtual content, whether visual or aural, in relation to the real, the underlying MR software needs to know the user's head position and orientation. Detecting an object's 3D position and orientation in physical space is commonly referred to as six degrees of freedom (6DOF) tracking. Until recently, accurate 6DOF tracking of people and objects in an MR setting was a costly proposition, involving expensive magnetic, acoustical, optical and/or inertial systems. In contrast, newer technology, such as infrared cameras, now provides the basis for very inexpensive yet accurate tracking. Advances that must still be made are in the vision algorithms for detecting and differentiating markers, and for recognizing gestures in order to provide semantic interpretation to people's non-verbal communication. Having an understanding of the meaning of movements allows one to use the human body as an interface device, to easily compress communications of actions for networked multi-player experiences and to drive a simulation based on a user's body language.

In order to capture a reasonably complete picture of an experience, MR systems must continuously record a user's movement, view direction, interaction with environment and task performance. This must all be correlated with the participant's psychophysical states, which can be monitored through unobtrusive, wireless biosensors (EEG, ECG and respiratory, temperature and electrodermal) [1]. EEG measures of engagement and workload can assist in determining the efficacy of a MR based rehabilitation environment within the feasibility stage [2]. These combined data recordings can be used to determine how well subjects perform tasks in the context of a variety of stimuli (visual and aural distracters, and time-constrained activities). Most importantly, the captured data can be visualized and then used by therapists to understand the patient's unique condition.

In order for commercialization to be an eventual outcome of a research project, one must address the important criteria of reliability, scalability and cost. Reliability is approached primarily through the use of commercial off-the-shelf hardware and strong software engineering practices. Scalability is insured by designing experiences that can be delivered in a tiered fashion, ranging from a VST-HMD to a full surround (circular or four-wall) stereo to a single wall stereo or mono version. Cost is addressed through the use of commodity hardware, free-license software, vision-based tracking, and the development of carefully crafted stories as a way to deliver contextually meaningful experiences with commodity hardware.

3 Software Infrastructure

3.1 DNA Engine

To facilitate agile development of low-cost, reliable and scalable scenarios ranging from VR to AR, the Media Convergence Lab (MCL) is iteratively developing a component-based engine, dubbed DNA, which loads and configures seemingly complex objects from reusable modules via XML. Modules may provide direct interfacing to available pre-existing libraries or may be user-friendly proxies to ongoing research code. The main development goal is to allow non-programmers to quickly assemble experiences using examples as templates. In other words, we note that project code is mostly "copy/paste" code that is thrown together, so we encourage this process by providing working examples for different aspects of the system and keeping this methodology in data files rather than source files when possible.

To allow rapid prototyping of new features, MCL has chosen to find suitable open-source or free-license libraries and progressively expose these libraries on an as-needed basis to the DNA loader as plug-ins. Such bindings can typically be done by directly mapping necessary library objects to XML elements, where public data members have XML attributes with identical naming conventions. This strategy allows us to point scenario developers to existing library documentation when such documentation is available.

For MR experiences, the DNA engine has several components that we repeatedly employ. On the display side of things, we expose Object-Oriented Graphics Rendering Engine (OGRE) for modern graphics presentation, which is capable of supporting VST-HMDs without any additional source code, and Cross-Platform Audio Creation Tool (XACT) for audio delivery, which enables custom source-to-speaker attenuation for non-conventional speaker configurations. In addition to synthetic contributions, we also have controls for digital multiplexing (DMX) to manipulate most powered real-world devices. On the input side of things, we have access to the basic keyboard and mouse though Object-Oriented Input System (OIS), but we also provide modules for a large number of devices including the WiiMote, 6DOF tracking, and bar code scanners. There are also a few hybrid libraries providing features such as multi-touch surface support.

A particularly useful feature of the DNA engine is that all data is exposed in the XML document. By cleverly nesting elements, we can quickly find pertinent information in another component, allowing specialized code to either subscribe as a data consumer or publish as a data provider. This dataflow approach decouples source from unnecessary dependencies and allows easy modification for both debugging and project changes. A particularly useful application of this feature arises during after-action review (AAR). For example, since we are interested in logging the position of a user for later playback, we can subscribe to the element that represents the user's position in the document and log changes observed in the element's attributes over time. Furthermore, the changes can occur from another, unknown element, such as a 6DOF tracker, network device, or keyboard that interprets values acquired from hardware. To construct an AAR tool for an experiment, we replace XML elements that interactively update the system state with proxies capable of loading recorded data files and mimicking the interactive modules. With other additions, such as the ability to manipulate system time and visual enhancements of important events, we can prototype project-specific AAR systems in a short amount of time and add metrics as researchers require them.

3.2 Blue-Screening

Chroma-keying, commonly referred to as blue-screening, is a viable method to inject virtual objects into the background of a video. Most chroma-keying tools target ideal cameras and lighting when applied in real-time, such as live news broadcasts. In MR, this problem is complicated by the sheer amount of processor time required by other aspects of the system and the relatively poor quality VST-HMD cameras. To alleviate these concerns and apply chroma-keying, we developed a GPU-based algorithm to detect and modify blue (or whatever color is used in the background) pixels.

The primary goal of our chroma-keying method is to provide a basic semi-automated interface for quick calibration in controlled environments that may be performed by non-experts. To realize this goal, we note that a camera digitizes the physical chroma-key material in such environments as a near solid color. The training step requires a user to view the surrounding material, allowing the system to statistically analyze the color and produce a parameterized, iterative fragment program capable of determining a good estimate of the opacity of each pixel in parallel on a GPU. This step may be done by a participant during the scenario, but is better suited for a setup procedure. There are two optional parameters exposed for tweaking that indicate confidence intervals, in standard deviations, of the training data. These parameters are necessary in ill-conditioned setups, such as situations in conference hall lighting and experiences with noisy VST-HMD cameras. Otherwise, the system can interactively determine the alpha matte from a video for virtual scene compositing with no user input aside from the initial training capture.

We note that under our camera restrictions and delivery method, dependent on noisy video input and real-time stereo rendering, we tend to aggressively key pixels and attempt error correction by adapting foreground extraction techniques. This methodology is not well-suited for off-line processing of high quality video, as it results in some misclassifications, especially in shadows and around objects, than what is commonly seen and accepted in the industry. Advances in VST-HMD, MR, and image matting technology will account for these downfalls in time. Our focus is to allow quick calibration in the field and deliver a believable experience to the user.

4 The MR Warehouse

For a first phase project, our goal is to develop a system capable of recording data that may eventually aid in the assessment and treatment of cognitive disorders, such as posttraumatic stress disorder (PTSD). As a feasibility test, we developed a MR scenario that puts a healthy participant into the role of a warehouse employee using a Canon COASTAR VST-HMD [7]. Our goal is to capture data to determine whether or not post-session analysis can evaluate the scenario's efficacy. For each test, the participant is responsible for several tasks, including buzzing in delivery trucks, fulfilling printed orders, and keeping track of inventory. Baseline tasks are performed in a quiet room to calibrate the sensors, and then they run through the full-fledged MR system. The system monitors both the user actions (gaze direction, movement, task performance, and environment interaction) and physiological state (EEG, ECG and respiratory, temperature, and electrodermal). This provides several metrics (such as engagement, workload, and skin conductivity) capable of correlating the physical state of a participant to task performance. In order for these metrics to have useful meaning, we must make the scenario interactive and realistic. This allows us to safely determine the difficulty of a set of tasks for an impaired subject by validating and inferring from test run on healthy people.

To provide tactical response to the virtual environment, we utilize chroma-key blue paint for the work surface and large cabinet. The virtual environment contributes to the appearance of these objects.

Fig. 1. In the physical environment, we have a combination of chroma-key blue material objects and visible objects. The chroma-key allows overriding the appearance of real objects, enabling the patient to believably touch virtual surfaces.

Fig. 2. The hazardous environment is purely virtual (including audio). This allows us to cheaply and safely introduce distracters into the rehabilitation scenario.

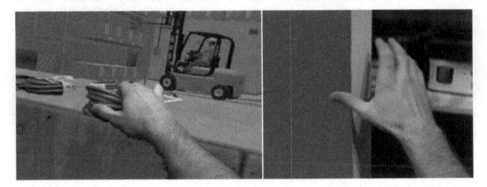

Fig. 3. The MR world allows the participant to see, hear, and feel a blending of the real and virtual worlds

We also use real objects as interactive props, such as the printer, buzzer, scanner, and inventory items, for order fulfillment and inventory stocking (Figure 1).

In the MR experience, the user can physically interact with these objects as one would in the real world, something that is infeasible in VR right now.

The real environment is then augmented with 3D graphics and spatial audio. These extensions safely immerse the subject in an otherwise hazardous environment, where moving forklifts, delivery trucks, and heavy boxes could cause complications or injury (Figure 2 and Figure 3). In addition, the physical setting, including both aural and visual, primarily occurs in the virtual world, allowing the scenario to restart (or run multiple times) with substantially less effort for a new participant, thus reducing the cost of subsequent evaluations. This also aids the portability of the experience.

Tracking user's interaction with the environment poses some difficult questions. To address these concerns, we use story as a seemingly natural interface to the simulation system. In particular, there are two types of tasks we must detect: item tracking and environmental awareness. Each time a participant focuses on a real item and moves it, the system should reliably react. To accomplish this, we require the participant to scan the item, taken from a known location, and to sort it by both picture and name in the destination storage cabinet. While this might seem unnecessarily complex, creative use of story and experiment design allows these steps to seem like a natural part of the task. Specifically, we instruct the user that filling an order, as a job requirement, includes the responsibility of tracking each item with a barcode scanner. Similarly, automated detection of the user's awareness of incoming delivery trucks (which is primarily heard in audio, but is also visible with the opening and closing of delivery bay doors) requires that the user presses a button to notify the manager. Through the use of story and context, this input seems natural, if not necessary, to the user. In reality, it gives us a means to track the user's situational awareness when trucks arrive in the scenario. In both situations, we motivate the user to provide us with systematic, reliable feedback by using story to reinforce that the performed action is both necessary and reasonable.

5 Experimental Findings

Since only five of twelve healthy individuals who participated in our study provided reliable data (others recorded too much noise during aspects of the scenario), we cannot draw any general conclusions. However, we can note common observations. Overall, participants showed a mix of both high and low engagement with frequent distractions. Distraction was mostly associated with the audio stimuli for the printer. Spikes ranging from 50 to 70% distraction were classified within 10 seconds of one or more printer audio cues. This quantifiably indicates that a particular scenario event had a negative effect on the participants without the use of post-test questionnaires, allowing us to make alterations to the environment.

When looking at workload through the scenario, the participants show phases of high and low levels. The changes in workload are not correlated with any particular aspect of the scenario. Further analysis of individual performance including task strategy may show distinct associations between tasks that demand more cognitive resources than others. We also observed that users only buzzed the manager when they visibly saw the first delivery truck. The average high workload prior to the arrival of all trucks is relatively high (near 60%), with the remainder dominated by moderate workload. For reference, this is enough to burn out a healthy employee within a week. From this, we can tell that participants were too focused on the current task, to the point that environmental awareness was compromised. This could explain why the sound of trucks was missed. However, we can also assume that the audio cues were not prevalent enough in the simulation and adjust settings accordingly. The important point is that we know that we overloaded healthy patients. So, we can detect this during the experiments provided we have a baseline to compare against.

Overall, the results show that the EEG measures of engagement and workload are good indicators of how the tasks affected the healthy participants. This data can be analyzed individually and in aggregate to obtain an understanding of cognitive aspects of the tasks that may pose challenges to head injured patients. For example, we can safely determine that a task is too hard for a healthy human, concluding that it would frustrate a rehabilitation patient with potential negative consequences. Furthermore, we can detect this during an experiment. This information is imperative to know for not only virtual rehabilitation therapy protocols, but also the field of rehabilitation in general.

6 Conclusions and Future Work

The primary goal of MR-enabled treatment is to alleviate a subject's deficits as regards task performance in real-world contexts. We have demonstrated that a combination of psychophysical and simulation-oriented data metrics promises to provide useful indicators of the effects of scenarios on participants. Specifically, we found that pre-experience calibrations and experience-time data capture allowed us to assess the stress level changes in healthy subjects in the context of task performance and simulation events. This provides encouraging indications that MR can be used in the assessment of affected populations and that the results of these MR-enabled patient assessments might be used to create therapeutic plan. Once such a plan is developed, traditional and/or MR-enabled therapy can be applied. In the case of MR-enabled therapies, we note that the system described here allows a therapist or technician to modify such a plan during run-time, potentially improving the course of treatment.

Based on our current findings, our next step is to apply these MR techniques to an affected population. If the outcomes are successful in isolating triggers that adversely affect performance of affected individuals, as they were with the unaffected population, then we will proceed to our primary goal, that of applying MR during the rehabilitation phase, using it to improve performance and, where appropriate, stimulate and enhance cognitive functions and induce positive neuroplastic changes.

Acknowledgments

The research presented here is partially supported by the National Science Foundation (IIP0750551 and DRL0638977) and the Air Force Office of Scientific Research.

References

1. Berka, C., Levendowski, D.J., Cvetinovic, M., Petrovic, M.M., Davis, G.F., Lumicao, M.N., Popovic, M.V., Zivkovic, V.T., Olmstead, R.E., Westbrook, P.: Real-time Analysis of EEG Indices of Alertness, Cognition and Memory Acquired with a Wireless EEG Headset. Special Issue of the International Journal of Human-Computer Interaction on Augmented Cognition 17(2), 151–170 (2004)
2. Fidopiastis, C.M., Hughes, C.E., Smith, E.M., Nicholson, D.M.: Assessing Virtual Rehabilitation Design with Biophysiological Metrics. In: Proceedings of Virtual Rehabilitation, p. 86. IEEE, Venice, Italy (2007)
3. Fidopiastis, C.M., Stapleton, C.B., Whiteside, J.D., Hughes, C.E., Fiore, S.M., Martin, G.A., Rolland, J.P., Smith, E.M.: Human Experience Modeler: Context Driven Cognitive Retraining to Facilitate Transfer of Training. CyberPsychology and Behavior 9(2), 183–187 (2006)

4. Fidopiastis, C.M., Weiderhold, M.: Mindscape Retuning and Brain Reorganization with Hybrid Universes: The Future of Virtual Rehabilitation. In: Schmorrow, D., Cohn, J., Nicholson, D. (eds.) The PSI Handbook of Virtual Environments for Training & Education: Developments for the Military and Beyond, vol. 3, pp. 427–434. Praeger Security International, Westport, CT (2008)
5. Hughes, D.E.: Defining an Audio Pipeline for Mixed Reality. In: Proceedings of Human Computer Interfaces International, Lawrence Erlbaum Assoc., Las Vegas (2005)
6. Milgram, P., Takemura, H., Utsumi, A., Kishino, F.: Augmented Reality: A Class of Displays on the Reality-Virtuality Continuum. In: Telemanipulator and Telepresence Technologies, vol. 2351, pp. 282–292 (1994)
7. Uchiyama, S., Takemoto, K., Satoh, K., Yamamoto, H., Tamura, H.: MR Platform: A Basic Body on Which Mixed Reality Applications Are Built. In: IEEE and ACM International Symposium on Mixed and Augmented Reality, pp. 246–256. IEEE Computer Society Press, Darmstadt, Germany (2002)

Augmented Reality Video See-through HMD Oriented to Product Design Assessment

Giandomenico Caruso and Umberto Cugini

Politecnico di Milano, Dipartimento di Meccanica, Via G. La Masa 1,
20156 Milano, Italy
{giandomenico.caruso,umberto.cugini}@polimi.it

Abstract. Current state of the art technology offers various solutions for developing virtual prototyping applications that also allow the interaction with the real environment. In particular, Augmented Reality (AR) technologies include tracking systems, stereoscopic visualization systems, photorealistic rendering tools, hi-resolution video overlay systems that allow us to create various types of applications where the virtual prototype is contextualized within the real world. One application domain is product design: AR technologies allow designers to perform some evaluation tests on the virtual prototype of industrial products without the necessity to produce a physical prototype. This paper describes the development of a new Video See-Through Head Mounted Display (VST-HMD) that is high-performing and based on stereoscopic visualization. The developed display system overcomes some issues concerning the correct visualization of virtual objects that are close to the user's point of view. The paper also presents the results of some tests about an AR application developed for product design assessment.

Keywords: Augmented Reality, Head Mounted Display, Video See-Through HMD, Design Assessment.

1 Introduction

Today, the aesthetic impact of products is an important aspect that may contribute in making the difference in respect to products that are technologically similar and with same functionalities. The product development process of products includes a phase dedicated to the design assessment, which is a crucial phase where various experts cooperate in selecting the optimal product shape. Although computer graphics allows us to create very realistic virtual representations of the products, it is not uncommon that designers decide to build physical mock-ups of their newly conceived products because they need to physically interact with the prototype and also to evaluate the product within a plurality of real contexts.

Current state of the art technology offers various solutions for developing virtual prototyping applications that also allow the interaction with the real environment. In particular, Augmented Reality (AR) technologies include tracking systems, stereoscopic visualization systems, photorealistic rendering tools, hi-resolution video overlay systems that allow us to create various types of applications where the virtual prototype is contextualized within the real world.

R. Shumaker (Ed.): Virtual and Mixed Reality, LNCS 5622, pp. 532–541, 2009.

In case of an AR application for supporting the assessment of designed products, it is very important that the designers are able to see the virtual object from different points of view, in a stereoscopic modality, and inserted within a real context. This can be achieved using a tracked Video See-Through Head Mounted Display (VST-HMD). This type of display system simulates the user's eyes viewing system. Although this solution allows a user to see the virtual objects in a stereoscopic modality, many problems arise when the user tries to see virtual objects that are near and far from the user's point of view. These problems are related to the cameras convergence angle. In most of the video see-through display systems the cameras position is fixed, while in order to solve convergence problems the angle between the two cameras should be accommodated according to the convergence value as our eyes do.

This paper describes a VST–HMD system that we have developed where cameras convergence issues have been addressed and solved. The VST–HMD system here presented is an initial prototype that has been developed in order to investigate issues regarding visual parameters and ergonomic aspects.

In addiction we have implemented an AR application for product design assessment where users can interact with various 3D models of a product through the use of an input remote control with the aim of assessing the designs.

The paper is organized as follows. Section 2 includes an overview of related works. Section 3 describes the design and development of the HMD. In Section 4 we present the AR application developed for product design assessment that has been used for validating the design and performances of the HMD.

2 Related Works

The selection of a specific visual display technology for an AR application depends on various factors [1] including: the type of objects to see, activities to be carried out, the environment where the application is performed (internal or external workspace), role of the user, etc.. With regard to our design assessment application the most appropriate visualization technological solution is a kind of VST-HMD system where the user is able to see a three-dimensional representation of a Virtual Prototype (VP) of a product from different points of view and in a natural way. Commercial VST-HMD are rare [2] and are mostly dedicated to a specific application purpose, and in addiction have several limitations. For this reason, many research groups have worked on the development of different types of VST-HMD oriented to their specific purposes.

One of the first examples of stereoscopic VST-HMD was developed by mounting small cameras onto a commercial Virtual Reality (VR) HMD [3]. This is a quick solution for the development of a VST-HMD and many research groups, including ours, are using this solution to create and evaluate AR applications with the aim of performing preliminary tests. Unfortunately, this solution does not guarantee high visual performances and the supported configuration involves several issues which must be addressed. The following reports some issues that may occur. The misalignment between the cameras and the user's eyes produces a parallax effect that leads to a spatial perception error [4] with the consequent feeling of incongruity especially at close distance [5]. The peripheral imagery does not match with the imagery inside the display: this may confuse the user who needs to see, at the same time, the display and the external surrounding environment [6]. Fixed cameras position does not allow users to reconstruct correctly objects that are near and far from the users' point of view. Fixed displays position does not allow users, with different interpupillar distance (IPD), to see properly the acquired scene. The initial experimental VST-HMD prototypes have proposed various solutions for solving these issues.

Fuchs et al. [7] describe a VST-HMD prototype implementation of a three-dimensional visualization system to assist laparoscopic surgical procedures. This device has two "eye-pods" consisting of a compact display and a lipstick camera. Takagi et al. [8] describe the studies and the experiments which led to the development of the Canon-MR HMD System [9]. The optical system of this VST-HMD is based on two prisms with a particular geometry that, by defining a specific optical path, allow the development of a compact and light optical system without parallax effect. Unfortunately this configuration does not allow users to see correctly the objects that are near from the users' point of view [2].

A solution for improving the visualization of close objects is to modify the convergence angle between the cameras accordingly to the user's point of view. A first attempt based on this approach has been implemented is a teleoperation system including two motion-controlled cameras, which dynamically converge onto the target object [10]. In this system the output stereoscopic imagery are displayed on a monitor and the user wears active polarized goggles. Actually, this is not a VST-HMD device but the results obtained using this particular acquisition system are indeed very interesting.

A different solution was described in [11] where, instead of rotating the cameras physically for changing the convergence angle, the authors have developed a software algorithm that allows them to simulate cameras rotation. They used a VST-HMD whose video cameras have a much larger field of view (fov) than the display unit. On the basis of this prototype they have developed another VST-HMD using commercial components and a mount manufactured through rapid prototyping methods [2].

3 VST-HMD Development

In current VST-HMD state of the art there are many examples of experimental devices created for specific purpose but a commercial product that solves all of the visual issues discussed in the previous session doesn't exist. Consequently we have developed a VST-HMD device which supports our application for product design assessment and which solves the issue related to the visualization of objects closely. The proposed solution for solving the visualization issue is to control the convergence angle of the cameras by using two micro servos. The main objective of our research was to demonstrate the feasibility of such visualization system; for this reason we have developed a prototype based on commercial component. The real scene is acquired by two Logitech QuickCam® Pro for Notebooks webcams that have these specifications: resolution of 640X480 @ 30fps. The display system is based on two Liteye monocular Full Color OLED display with a resolution of 800X600. The two cameras are handled by two Dong Yang analog servos that, although having small dimensions (19.8mm X 8.0mm X 22.5mm) and weight of 4.4 g, allow us to provide a torque of 0.8kg/cm and a speed of 0.12/60° values, which is more than enough for our purposes. All components were arranged on a light safety helmet by using a specific frame designed in order to provide all of degrees of freedom for a correct registration. Before physically making our device, we investigated some aspects in order to define the best layout of the components, and we performed a preliminary test in order to optimize the algorithm for the cameras control.

3.1 Cameras Control System

The geometrical studies discussed in [8] reveal that camera and display must be always aligned. However, like it has been demonstrated in [5], the human eye is able to adjust, in a short time, to small visual incongruities and consequently to reconstruct the three-dimensional image correctly. Starting from these assumptions we would like to demonstrate that the user can reconstruct a good three-dimensional image by using our system where the monocular displays are parallel while the cameras automatically converge toward the target object. This solution allows us to see far objects (parallel cameras and displays) and near objects (parallel displays and angled cameras) without the need of a manual registration.

The value of the convergence angle (β) of the cameras varies according to the following formula that was derived from a simple geometrical consideration.

$$\beta = arccos \frac{\sqrt{l^2 - \frac{d^2}{4}}}{l} \tag{1}$$

In this formula l is the distance between the object and the camera while d is the user's IPD. This function, however, doesn't consider the object dimension because the distance l is calculated from the centre of the virtual object thus, when the user tries to see a large model, the real distance l is lower. In order to solve this issue we have corrected the formula according to the size of the virtual object that was approximated whit a sphere (bounding sphere).

$$\beta = arccos \frac{\sqrt{l^2 - \frac{d^2}{4}} - r}{\sqrt{\left(l^2 - \frac{d^2}{4} - r\right)^2 + \frac{d^2}{4}}} \tag{2}$$

where r is the sphere radius.

3.2 Preliminary Test

In order to reduce the distortion due to the different convergent angle between cameras and displays we introduced in our cameras control software a constant value that was determined empirically through a preliminary test. During this test we also evaluated the differences perceive by the user when β is calculated using the formula (1) (normal method) or with the second one (2) (bounding sphere method). In order to perform this test we have developed a setup where the user can see through the fixed parallel display while the cameras are mounted on the servos and they are positioned on the desk (Fig.1).

Fig. 1. Setup of preliminary test

We performed the test with 10 users (7 male and 3 female) that have previous experience with stereoscopic viewing in order to set more significant conclusions. At the beginning of the test we measured the user's IPD and we set the distance between cameras and between displays to the same value of the user's IPD (this is the same registration that the user can set on our VST-HMD). The IPD value is also set on the cameras control software. During the test the user sees alternately three different virtual objects (elongated, squared and rounded) at different distances (2m, 80cm, 40cm, 15cm). For every object we proposed three different values of constant angle (0°, 3°, 6°) and the two different modalities to calculate the distance of the virtual object discussed in the previous section. The average duration of the test was 15-20 minutes.

The results of this preliminary test reveal that with the proposed configuration (parallel displays and converging cameras) there aren't problems when the user sees distant objects; while, when the objects are nearby, we observed that if the constant angle is between 0° and 3° the user improves the ability to reconstruct 3D images of near objects. The constant angle instead does not influence significantly the viewing of distant object. We also estimated that this value is proportional to the user's IPD that can be determined by this equation:

$$\beta' = \beta - IPD/35 \tag{3}$$

For what concerns the two different methods to calculate the distance of the objects, we observed that the normal method improves the viewing of the part of the object that is near to the marker while the bounding-sphere method improves the visualization of the part of the object that is near to the user's point of view. Obviously the use of the two methods does not influence the viewing of small objects but has a significant role for big ones. The effects of the bounding sphere method are also related to the geometry of the object. In fact the users have some viewing problems when they see the object where one or two dimensions are predominant respect to the other (elongated object).

3.3 Design of the VST-HMD

The layout of the components of the VST-HMD was designed in order to satisfy different morphological characteristics of the users. The optimization of the layout was

Fig. 2. Components layout configuration by using Tecnomatix Jack

Fig. 3. Digital and real models of the assembled VST-HMD

achieved by using the ergonomics and human factors software Tecnomatix Jack [12], which is generally used to improve the ergonomics of product designs and workplace tasks.

This software enables users to position biomechanically accurate digital humans of various sizes in virtual environments, assign them tasks and analyze their performance. Thanks to this software we implemented a simple routine that allowed to check the correct positions of the monocular displays for different virtual users with different IPD and head size (Fig. 2). The obtained results are used to defining the registration range of the three translational degrees of freedom (dof) of the monocular displays. These data were used to support the design of the frame where cameras, monocular displays and servos are mounted. The modeling and the virtual assembly into the digital model of the safety helmet of the frame were realized by using a CAD system.

After this developing phase of digital model of the frame, we made manually the frame with light material, like aluminium alloy and plexiglass; then we assembled the other components and we fix the frame onto the safety helmet. The weight of the device is about 850g. Fig. 3 shows the digital model and real model of the VST-HMD.

4 Application for Product Design Assessment

In order to evaluate the effectiveness of our VST-HMD we have developed an AR application by using the OSGART [13] library. The aim of this application is to perform some tests in order to collect, from a pool of testers, data and comments about usability and ergonomic aspects of the system. For what concerns the visualization, the AR application acquires the real scene from the cameras mounted on the VST-HMD and generates two images which are visualized on the VST-HMD displays by giving to the user the possibility to perceive the scene depth. In order to ensure a perfect overlapping of the right and left images, the convergence angle between the cameras is regulated according to the distance between the virtual object and the user's point of view as discussed in section 0. The AR application calculates this distance and sends the angle value to the servos that moves the cameras so that the user can see the virtual object properly both near and far. Correct position and orientation of the virtual object are guaranteed by a bi-dimensional marker: in addiction it is also possible to move, rotate and scale the virtual object by using a remote control system. In this case we have used the WiiMote [14] control system. The integration, between WiiMote and our AR application, was realized by using the Wiiyourself [15] library that allows us to acquire all information about the WiiMote integrated appliances. Furthermore, the AR application makes use of some combinations of pressed buttons and values coming from accelerometers that allow the user to interact with the virtual model.

4.1 Testing Scenario

The testing scenario, which we have developed for testing the use of our VST-HMD, concerns the validation of the re-design of the windscreen of an existing motorcycle. Initially we have digitalized the real motorcycle windscreen by using reverse engineering techniques; then a designer has made some aesthetic modifications on the digital model of the original windscreen and he created some new virtual prototypes of the new windscreen. In order to evaluate and appreciate the modified shapes of the windscreen, we proposed the use of our VST-HMD and our AR application that allows us to superimpose the virtual windscreen onto the existing motorcycle. In this AR environment the users could see and interact with the virtual prototypes in order to appreciate the differences among them.

The testing session preformed in our AR environment involved 5 users. The users included 4 engineers and 1 designer; all of them had previous experiences in using AR environments. The session was video recorded for subsequently analysis. When the users worn the VST-HMD, for the first time, they actually needed to accustom themselves to the stereoscopic visualization of the device but, after few seconds, they could see correctly. Before evaluating the mixed model the users tool in their hand the WiiMote control that was located on the table. In this first task the users hadn't great difficulty to localize and to reach the WiiMote.

The testers looked at the motorcycle and could see the mixed image: the real motorcycle and the virtual windscreen. In addition, by using the WiiMote control the testers were able to change the virtual model to display. When a tester went closer to the virtual windscreen, because he wanted to see better some details, the convergent

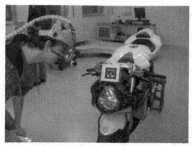

Fig. 4. User during the interaction and user's point of view

angle of the cameras changed according to the distance between the user's point of view and the virtual object. The testers were allowed to move, rotate and translate the virtual models by using the WiiMote.

After the testing session the users compiled a questionnaire about the efficiency of the system. They were asked to rate each answer from 1 (bad) to 6 (good). The questions and the average value of the answers are reported in the table below.

Table 1. Testing session questions and rates

Evaluation of the VST-HMD

A1. Video quality	4.8
A2. Is the representation of the windscreen realistic?	4.7
A3. Is the virtual windscreen integrated in the real scene?	4.4
A4. Do you perceive distortion or other visualization defect?	4.0
A5. Have you problems viewing or discomfort at the beginning of the test?	3.9
A6. Have you problems viewing or discomfort during the test?	2.7
A7. Do you perceive correctly the scene depth?	5.4
A8. Are you able to see the windscreen closely?	4.0
A9. Have you problems viewing or discomfort after the test?	2.0

Evaluation of the interactive AR design review

B1. Can you appreciate the difference among the models?	5.0
B2. Can you easily interact with the models?	4.7
B3. Do you consider that this methodology is effective ?	4.5

4.2 Evaluation Results

The testing sessions have allowed us to validate the use of VST-HMD visualization system and the interactive AR design review application. The first impression and comments on the visualization system from the testers was about the little field of view of the displays and about the little delay of the video streaming that, after all, is acceptable. All of the users saw the scene in the correct way by perceiving the depth sensation both of the real objects than the virtual ones.

The analysis of the answers to the questionnaire highlights that the VST-HMD gives the possibility to see the virtual and the real objects at the same time with good quality (question A1). The representation of the windscreen appears realistic enough and well integrated with the real motorcycle (questions A2, A3). Despite the fact that the users perceive correctly the scene depth (question A7) they found some defects and some distortions during the visualization. This phenomenon is most likely related to the quality of the commercial devices that we have used to assemble the VST-HMD and surely to the different fov between the cameras and the display. The control system, which controls the convergent angle of cameras, provides a correct regulation when the user tries to see the windscreen closely (question A8) and the speed of control seemed appropriate to the purpose. For what concerns issues about users' discomfort, the users did not report of any particular problem during and after the test (question A6, A9) while they felt some discomfort at the beginning of the test during a period of time required for eyes adaptation.

For what concerns the AR design review application, the users appreciate the possibility to switch among the different models in order to compare accurately the proposed solutions (question B1). The interaction, with the virtual model of the windscreen performed through the WiiMote control, is quite natural (question B2) and allows to extrapolate the virtual object from the real position in order to validate some aspects more easily. Globally the users consider the developed AR interactive environment very effective (question B3) and they supposed that the integration of the two proposed environments might reduce significantly the time for the industrial product development.

5 Conclusions

In this paper we have described the development of our VST-HMD prototype that allows us to solve the issues related to the viewing virtual objects closely. Our proposed solution is to control the cameras convergent angle by using two micro servos. This solution was validated by performing some preliminary tests. In addiction we also validate the use of the VST-HMD through a testing session performed with our AR application for design review. In this testing session the users could see and interact with the virtual prototypes in order to appreciate the differences among them. The results of this testing session reveal the effectiveness of the device and outlook the possibly use during the design review phase of the industrial product.

Acknowledgements

Special thanks go to Fabrizio Colombo and Guido Maria Re who have spent so much effort to help in implementing the control system of the cameras and to the physical realization of the VST-HMD.

References

1. Milgram, P., Kishino, F.: A Taxonomy of Mixed Reality Visual Displays. IEICE Transactions on Information Systems E77-D (1994)
2. State, A., Keller, K.P., Fuchs, H.: Simulation-based design and rapid prototyping of a parallax-free, orthoscopic video see-through head-mounted display. In: Proceedings. Fourth IEEE and ACM International Symposium on Mixed and Augmented Reality, pp. 28–31 (2005)

3. State, A., Livingston, M.A., Hirota, G., Garret, W.F., Whitton, M.C., Fuchs, H., Pisano, E.D.: Technologies for Augmented-Reality System: Realizing Ultrasound-Guided Needel Biopsies. In: Proceedings of SIGGRAPH 1996, New Orleans, LA, pp. 439–446 (1996)
4. Azuma, R.T.: A Survey of Augmented Reality. Presence 6, 355–385 (1997)
5. Rolland, J.P., Biocca, F.A., Barlow, T., Kancherla, A.: Quantification of adaptation to virtual-eye location in see-thru head-mounted displays. In: Proceedings of the Virtual Reality Annual International Symposium (VRAIS 1995), IEEE Computer Society, Los Alamitos (1995)
6. Drascic, D., Milgram, P.: Perceptual issues in augmented reality. In: Stereoscopic Displays and Virtual Reality Systems III, pp. 123–134. SPIE, San Jose (1996)
7. Fuchs, H., Livingston, M.A., Raskar, R., Keller, K., State, A., Crawford, J.R., Rademacher, P., Drake, S.H., Meyer, A.A.: Augmented reality visualization for laparoscopic surgery. In: Wells, W.M., Colchester, A.C.F., Delp, S.L. (eds.) MICCAI 1998. LNCS, vol. 1496, pp. 934–943. Springer, Heidelberg (1998)
8. Takagi, A., Yamazaki, S., Saito, Y., Taniguchi, N.: Development of a stereo video see-through HMD for AR systems. In: Proceedings. IEEE and ACM International Symposium on Augmented Reality (ISAR 2000), pp. 68–77 (2000)
9. Canon-MR HMD System,
http://www.canon.com/technology/canon_tech/explanation/mixed_reality.html
10. Matsunaga, K., Yamamoto, T., Shidoji, K., Matsuki, Y.: Effect of the ratio difference of overlapped areas of stereoscopic images on each eye in a teleoperation. In: Stereoscopic Displays and Virtual Reality Systems VII, pp. 236–243. SPIE, San Jose (2000)
11. State, A., Ackerman, J., Hirota, G., Lee, J., Fuchs, H.: Dynamic virtual convergence for video see-through head-mounted displays: maintaining maximum stereo overlap throughout a close-range work space. In: Proceedings. IEEE and ACM International Symposium on Augmented Reality, pp. 137–146 (2001)
12. Tecnomatix   Jack,   http://www.plm.automation.siemens.com/en_us/products/tecnomatix/assembly_planning/jack/index.shtml
13. OSGART, http://www.artoolworks.com/community/osgart/
14. WiiMote, http://www.wiili.org/Wiimote
15. WiiYourself, http://wiiyourself.gl.tter.org/

Mixed Reality Neurosurgical Microscope for Training and Intra-operative Purposes

Alessandro De Mauro[1], Joerg Raczkowsky[1], Marc Eric Halatsch[2], and Heinz Wörn[1]

[1] Institute for Process Control and Robotics, University of Karlsruhe (TH), Germany
[2] Department of Neurosurgery, University Hospital of Heidelberg, Germany
demauro@ira.uka.de

Abstract. In recent years, neurosurgery has been deeply influenced by new technologies. It requires fine techniques targeted to obtain treatments minimally invasive though often traumatic. The precision of the surgical gesture is related both to experience of the surgeon and accuracy of the available technological instruments. Computer Aided Surgery (CAS) can offer several benefits for the patient's safety. From a technological point of view we observe the use of the Virtual Reality (VR) for the surgeons training and Augmented Reality (AR) for the intra-operative aid for treatments. This paper presents a prototype for a mixed reality system for neurosurgical interventions embedded on a real surgical microscope for pre- and intra- operative purposes. Its main purposes are: the realistic simulation (visual and haptic) of the spatula palpation of low-grade glioma and also the stereoscopic visualization in AR of relevant 3D data for safe surgical movements in the image guided interventions.

Keywords: virtual and augmented reality, physical modeling, haptic feedback, training systems, neurosurgery.

1 Motivation and Medical Background

In recent years, neurosurgery has been deeply influenced by new technologies. It requires fine techniques targeted to obtain treatments minimally invasive and traumatic. Intra-operative false movements can be devastating, leaving patients paralyzed, comatose or dead. The precision of the surgical gesture is related both to experience of the surgeon and accuracy of the available technological instruments. Computer Aided Surgery (CAS) can offer several benefits for the patient safety. Traditional techniques for training in surgery include the use of animals, phantoms and cadavers. The main limitation of these approaches is that live tissue has different properties from dead tissue and also that animal anatomy is significantly different from the human. Nowadays, this classical training is improved by the use of well illustrated books and excellent training movies recorded directly in the Operating Room (OR) but the main training for surgeons is still performed on the real patient. It is shown [1] that virtual reality simulators can speed-up the learning process and improve the proficiency of surgeons prior to performing surgery on a real patient.

Low-grade gliomas are intrinsic brain tumors that typically occur in younger adults. The objective of related surgery is to remove as much of the tumor as possible while

R. Shumaker (Ed.): Virtual and Mixed Reality, LNCS 5622, pp. 542–549, 2009.

minimizing damage to the normal brain. One of the obstacles associated with the surgical resection of these tumors is that the pathological tissue may closely resemble normal brain parenchyma when looked at through the neurosurgical microscope.

As a result, efforts to remove all tumor cells inevitably remove some of the normal brain and can leave behind small sections of tumorous cells. The remaining glioma cells continue to grow, eventually causing additional damage to the remaining normal brain, and a recurrence of symptoms.

Neuro-navigation can help only partially because the brain shift phenomena effects the pre-operative patient data after craniotomy and tissue removal. The tactile appreciation of this difference, in consistency of the tumor compared to normal brain, requires considerable experience on the part of the neurosurgeon.

These previous considerations are the main reasons to develop a neurosurgical training system but this is only a preoperative task. As described later, microscope, surgical tools and patient data are commonly used in the OR during the image guided operation. The hardware (microscope, tracking system, tools) and the software (navigation system based on the patient dataset) are both involved in the training and intra-operative activities. These considerations justify the idea of a mixed reality system that uses similar environment and architecture setups for pre- and intra-operative use, in a natural continuum training system (based on VR) and in an intra-operative system (based on AR).

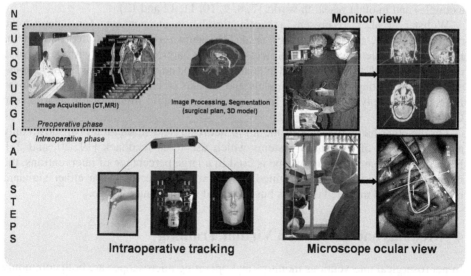

Fig. 1. Common steps in neurosurgery. Patient images are acquired and processed. 3D model of the region of interest are obtained. In the intra-operative phase this data are available on the screen and used for the navigation.

2 Neurosurgical Workflow

At this point, it is particularly important to give briefly an introduction about all the steps involved before and during the neurosurgical procedures. The geometric models of the organs or the region of interest (e.g. tumor) are reconstructed from data acquired by CT, MRI or other means by a radiologist. In the intra-operative phase a tracking system is used to track the relative positions of the patient, relevant tools, and microscope. All data are shown on the video using the normal three views (coronal, axial, sagittal). In the OR, a surgeon's eyes are typically on the microscope oculars but occasionally they need to see the screen in order to understand the correct position compared to the preoperative images (CT, MRI). The position and orientation of an active tool tracked by the infrared tracking system and it's relative position in the patient images are shown on the monitors. The two-dimensional contour of the region of interest is recognized as defined by the radiologist in the preoperative step. This two-dimensional shape is visible inside the commercial microscopes overlaid to the oculars views. The steps discussed here are shown in Fig.1. Nowadays, the three-dimensional environment reconstruction from two dimensions is another difficult and critical mental work for the surgeon.

3   State of the Art in Training Systems

The success of using haptic devices in medical training simulators has already been demonstrated by several commercial companies working in this field (Immersion Medical [3], Surgical Science [4], Mentice [5], and Reachin Technologies[6], for example) and in other research works [7, 8, 9, 10, 11, 12 and 13].

Webster et al. [14] present a haptic simulation environment for laparoscopic cholecystectomy, and Montgomery et al. [15] shows a simulation environment for laparoscopic hysteroscopy; both projects focus on haptic interaction with deformable tissue. Cotin et al. [16] present a haptic simulator for interventional cardiology procedures, incorporating blood flow models and models of cardiopulmonary physiology. De et al. [17] apply the method of finite spheres to a haptic simulator for laparoscopic GI surgery.

On the other hand, the state-of-the-art in neurosurgical simulation [18] shows only a few examples of VR based systems which use force feedback [19, 20, and 21]. Because a neurosurgical microscope is used in a large percentage of interventions, the realism of these simulators is limited by the architecture: they use either standard monitors or head mounted displays but not a real surgical microscope.

4   Methods and Tools for a Virtual Training

In neurosurgical interventions monitors and operating microscopes are both commonly employed. In order to understand the correct tumor position compared to the preoperative images (CT, MRI) a surgeon's eyes are normally on the microscope oculars and only occasionally glance at a larger screen. This second view is very important in image guided therapy to check the correct position of the surgical tools inside the patient brain. A complete simulation system for neurosurgical training requires:

- simulation of the virtual patient inside microscope oculars;
- force feedback rendering directly at the user's hand;
- navigation software actually used in OR (i.e. BrainLab or Stryker).

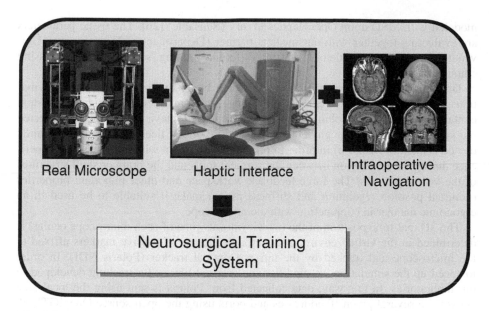

Fig. 2. Left: simulator concepts. Left: ocular views of the deformations of the 3D patient reconstructed from patient pre-operative images.

A virtual environment is geometrically built using real patients' data affected by a low grade glioma from the standard medical imaging devices. Human organs are accurately reconstructed from real patient images using the software package 3DSlicer [22]. A region growing algorithm has been used for segmentation, and next organ and region of interests (ROI) are classified. The 3D organ data obtained is imported directly into our application and the registration step between these two virtual environments is carried out. 3D models of the surgical tools are provided using a Laser ScanArm (FARO) [23].

The visual output is provided by the rendering software developed in C++ and built on the open source GPU licensed and cross-platform H3D [24] (version 2.0), a scene-graph API based on OpenGL is used for graphics rendering.

Collision detection modules based on the physical model for the simulation of tool interactions and brain deformations are developed on OpenGL to obtain high level performance and realism. Hierarchies of bounding volumes are used to perform fast collision detection between complex models, with the employed method based on model partition [25], the strategy of subdividing a set of objects into geometrically coherent subsets and computing a bounding volume for each subset of objects. The physical modeling method is based on mass-spring-damper (MSD) and consists of a mesh of point masses connected by elastic links and mapped onto the geometric representation of the virtual object. This method is employed in our prototype to describe the mechanical properties of the virtual bodies computing the force feedback to the haptics and the organ deformations to be visualised. It's a discrete method characterized by low computable load, simplicity, low accuracy and low risk of instability because it uses Newton dynamics to modify the point-masses positions and creates deformations with consideration to volume conservation. Brain tissue properties are modeled with MSD upon OpenHaptics library (Sensable) [26]. The tissue parameters are evaluating together with our medical partner (Department of Neurosurgery, University Hospital of Heidelberg) using different training sections and processing empiric data.

Different haptic renderings were tested for a better optimization of the deformations. In order to have a complete training platform a video navigation system containing different 3D volume views is required. To achieve this, we have connected our system with the image guided therapy module of 3DSlicer. We are using a haptic device (Phantom Desktop) in order to provide the surgeon with an immersive experience during the interaction between the surgical tools and the brain or skull structures of the virtual patients. The force feedback workspace and other important properties (nominal position resolution and stiffness range) make it suitable to be used in an ergonomic manner in conjunction with the microscope.

The 3D real-time position of the two viewpoints (one of each microscope ocular) is determined in the virtual environment through the use of passive markers affixed to the microscope and tracked by the infrared optical tracker (Polaris NDI). In order to speed up the simulation we modified the original library for tracking developed in our laboratories. In this way, data collected from Polaris is sent using the local area network to several given IP addresses and ports using the open-source OpenIGTLink of 3DSlicer modified for our needs. This allows a distributed architecture with the separation between rendering (graphical and haptic) and tracking PC with advantages in terms of computational load and realism (the average frame rate for graphical rendering is 31 fps and for the haptic 998 fps). The collisions between organs and surgical tools produce forces which have to be replicated by the haptic interface and organ deformations, which have to be graphically rendered.

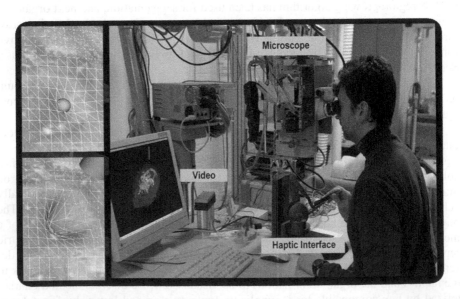

Fig. 3. Simulator. Left: brain tissue deformations. Right: complete prototype.

All the basic surgical operations on the brain are suitable to increase surgery skills in a fast and safe way using virtual reality. The main operating task simulated is the visual and tactile sensations of brain palpation (healthy or affected by low grade glioma) pushing aside the human tissue using a neurosurgical spatula.

The 3D environment description language used is X3D, which is the natural successor of the well known VRML. It means that the complete scene in the application can be rendered in a web browser for future extension as web- collaborative and distributed training.

5   Extension to Intra-operative Augmented Reality

The architecture described can be used for intra-operative purposes. In this instance, a surgeon needs to use the microscope, monitors and surgical tools. This is the basic setup for an image guided therapy interventions. The same virtual environment can be AR rendered in to the microscope optics with the difference that now the complete anatomy is considered rigid (deformations are not requested in this step).

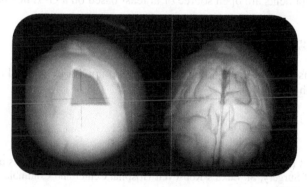

Fig. 4. Augmented reality microscope. Left: skull. Right: 3D model of the brain superimposed on the skull.

The haptic interface is no longer required and is replaced by new navigated infra-red active tools.

The prototype is capable of tracking, in real time, the microscope, the patient's head and one surgical tool (pointer with active markers).

Fig. 4 shows the augmented reality views inside the microscope oculars in which is possible identify 3D region of interest (in this example the brain surface is rendered). The microscope hardware related part was realized at our institute and described in a previous work [27]. Registration and camera calibration are required for a perfect alignment between real and virtual world. Both are off-line steps with similar approaches used in [27].

6 Conclusions

This paper presents the development of the first mixed reality system for training and intra-operative purposes in neurosurgery embedded on a real microscope. The main training task is the advanced simulation of brain tissue palpation enabling the surgeon to distinguish between normal brain tissue, and that tissue affected with a low grade glioma. Force feedback interaction with soft and hard tissues is provided to the surgeon's hands in order to provide a complete immersive experience.

The second feature allows the system to be employed as an augmented reality microscope inside the OR. In this case a complex 3D environment is rendered by a stereoscopic image injection directly inside the microscope oculars for a better real time brain navigation and space cognition. 3DSlicer is, in both previous functional modalities, directly connected to the NDI tracking system in order to provide the navigation inside the real patient's images on the screen. The previously described software architecture guarantees performances and portability.

The architecture and the main features were defined in tight collaboration with surgeon staff and we are evaluating other improvements in providing more specific simulation tasks extending this work.

All the components are open source or at least based on a GPL license.

Acknowledgments

This research is a part of the European project "CompuSurge" funded by EST "Marie Curie" research network.

References

1. Ro, C.Y., et al.: The LapSim. A learning environment for both experts and novices. Department of Surgery, St. Luke's-Roosevelt Hospital Center and Columbia University, New York, USA (2005)
2. Hill, D.L.G., Maurer Jr., C.R., Martin, A.J., Sabanathan, S., Hall, W.A., Hawkes, D.J., Rueckert, D., Truwit, C.L.: Assessment of intraoperative brain deformation using interventional MR imaging. In: Taylor, C., Colchester, A. (eds.) MICCAI 1999. LNCS, vol. 1679, pp. 910–919. Springer, Heidelberg (1999)
3. Immersion (status January 2008),
   http://www.immersion.com/
4. SurgicalScience (status January 2008), http://www.surgical-science.com/
5. Mentice (status January 2008), http://www.mentice.com/
6. Reachin (status January 2008), http://www.reachin.se/
7. Basdogan, C., Ho, C., Srinivasan, M.A.: Virtual Environments for Medical Training: Graphical and Haptic Simulation of Common Bile Duct Exploration. IEEE-ASME Trans. Mechatronics 6(3), 26–285 (2001)
8. Çakmak, H.K., Kühnapfel, U.: Animation and Simulation Techniques for VR-Training Systems in Endoscopic Surgery. In: Proc. Eurographics Workshop Animation and Simulation (EGCAS 2000), pp. 173–185 (2000)
9. Brown, J., et al.: Algorithmic Tools for Real-Time Microsurgery Simulation. Medical Image Analysis 6(3), 289–300 (2002)

10. Cotin, S., Delingette, H., Ayache, H.: Real-Time Elastic Deformations of Soft Tissues for Surgery Simulation. IEEE Trans. Visualization and Computer Graphics 5(1), 62–73 (1999)
11. Wu, X., et al.: Adaptive Nonlinear Finite Elements for Deformable Body Simulation Using Dynamic Progressive Meshes. In: Chalmers, A., Rhyne, T.-M. (eds.) Proc. Eurographics, Computer Graphics Forum, vol. 20(3), pp. 349–358 (2001)
12. Székely, G., Brechbühler, C., Hutter, R., Rhomberg, A., Schmid, P.: Modelling of Soft Tissue Deformation for Laparoscopic Surgery Simulation. In: Wells, W.M., Colchester, A.C.F., Delp, S.L. (eds.) MICCAI 1998. LNCS, vol. 1496, pp. 550–561. Springer, Heidelberg (1998)
13. O'Toole, R., et al.: Measuring and Developing Suturing Technique with a Virtual Reality Surgical Simulator. J. Am. College of Surgery 189, 114–128 (1999)
14. Webster, R., Haluck, R.S., Zoppeti, G., et al.: A haptic surgical simulator for laparoscopic cholecystectomy using real-time deformable organs. In: Proc. IASTED International Conference on Biomedical Engineering, Salzburg, Austria, June 25-27 (2003)
15. Montgomery, K., et al.: Surgical simulator for operative hysteroscopy. In: IEEE Visualization 2001, pp. 14–17 (2001)
16. Cotin, S., Dawson, S.L., Meglan, D., Shaffer, D.W., Farrell, M.A., Bardsley, R.S., Morgan, F.M., Nagano, T., Nikom, J., Sherman, P., Walterman, M.T., Wendlandt, J.: ICTS: An Interventional Cardiology Training System. In: Proceedings of Medicine Meets Virtual Reality, pp. 59–65 (2000)
17. De, S., Kim, J., Manivannan, M., Srinivasan, M.A., Rattner, D.: Multimodal Simulation of Laparoscopic Heller Myotomy Using a Meshless Technique. In: Proceedings of Medicine Meets Virtual Reality (MMVR), Newport Beach, pp. 127–132 (2002)
18. Goh, K.Y.C.: Virtual reality application in neurosurgery. In: Proceedings of the 2005 IEEE, Engineering in Medicine and Biology 27th Annual Conference, Shanghai (2005)
19. Luciano, C., Banerjee, P., Lemole, M.G., Charbel, F.: Second generation haptic ventriculostomy simulator using the immersivetouch™ system. In: Proceedings of Medicine Meets Virtual Reality 14, Long Beach, CA (2008)
20. Sato, D., Kobayashi, R., Kobayashi, A., Fujino, S., Uchiyama, M.: Soft tissue pushing operation using a haptic interface for simulation of brain tumor resection. Journal of robotics and mechatronics 18, 634–642 (2006)
21. Wiet, G., Bryan, J., Sessanna, D., Streadney, D., Schmalbrock, P., Welling, B.: Virtual temporal bone dissection simulation. In: Westwood, J.D. (ed.) Medicine Meets Virtual Reality 2000, Amsterdam, The Netherlands, pp. 378–384 (2000)
22. 3DSlicer (status January 2008), http://www.slicer.org/
23. Faro (status January 2008), http://www.faro.com
24. H3D (status January 2008), http://www.h3dapi.org/
25. Van den Bergen, C.: Collision detection in interactive 3D environment. Elsevier Morgan Kaufmann, S. Francisco, USA (2004)
26. OpenHaptics (status March 2009), http://www.sensable.com/products-openhaptics-toolkit.htm
27. Aschke, M., et al.: Augmented reality in operating microscopes for neurosurgical interventions. In: Wolf, Strock (eds.) Proceedings of 1st International IEEE EMBS Conference on Neural Engineering, pp. 652–655 (2003)

A Real-Virtual Mapping Method for Mechanical Product Assembly Process Planning in Virtual Assembly Environment

Xiumin Fan[1,2], Feng Gao[1], Hongmin Zhu[1], Dianliang Wu[1,2], and Qi Yin[1]

[1]CIM Institute of Shanghai Jiaotong University, Shanghai 200030, China
[2]Shanghai Key Laboratory of Advanced Manufacturing, Shanghai 200030, China
xmfan@sjtu.edu.cn

Abstract. In order to realize assembly process planning in virtual reality environment, an assembly process planning generation method based on real-virtual mapping of basic motion sequence is proposed. Based on the analysis of current assembly process content from enterprise, assembly process information is modeled; standard assembly operations and basic assembly motion are defined. The mapping matrix among standard assembly operations and basic assembly motions are set up. A method to get basic motion sequence in virtual environment during virtual assembling process by real user is put forward. A prototype system is developed based on these research results, and the system function is demonstrated through assembly process of automobile engine components. It shows that this assembly process generation method based on real-virtual mapping of motion sequence is feasible, and it also provides a new idea for the application of virtual assembly technique for product manufacturing process.

Keywords: Virtual reality; Virtual assembly; Assembly process planning; Standard assembly operation; Assembly basic motion; Real-virtual mapping.

1 Introduction

Mechanical product assembly belongs to the latter part of production work during the manufacturing process, it is a key link for product formation[1]. Mechanical assembly is a process to assemble components into subassembly, until the whole product. Mechanical assembly process plan is the reification of assembly process based on the product structure, manufacturing precision, and other factors. Assembly process planning includes information about assembly components and their assembly sequence, assembly tools and fixtures, assembly operation and assembly time and so on.

Assembly process plan is usually fulfilled by manufacturing engineer manually, and this procedure is depended on person's experience and knowledge to a large extent, and physical try out based on real prototype is necessary to check the process plan from time to time, it is inevitable low efficiency of this kind of assembly process planning. Therefore, computer aided assembly process planning can improve the efficiency of assembly planning, cut down the assembly cost and increase the degree of planning automation.

R. Shumaker (Ed.): Virtual and Mixed Reality, LNCS 5622, pp. 550–559, 2009.

In research area of computer aided assembly process planning, it focuses on two common problems: assembly path planning and assembly sequence planning. Literature [2] presented a model based on features for assembly sequence planning automatically. The basic assembly modeling strategy was based on the matching features of components, and a group of standards based on assembly feasibility, maneuverability, assembly direction, cost and stability were used to check whether the assembly sequence is good or not. Literature [3] built a model with three-layer assembly information, and presented assembly sequence reasoning method within layered structure model, which solving assembly sequence planning problem for complicated product, and the prototype system FVAPP was developed based on UG. There are shortcomings of the above methods, such as easy of leading combination explosion, assembly experience and knowledge of individual people in assembly process can not be considered fully.

In virtual assembly research area, VRCIM laboratory of Washington State University and American National Institute of Standards and Technology developed Virtual Assembly Design Environment (VADE) together, which integrated with commercial CAD system tightly, and fed virtual assembly results back to CAD system. Virtual Reality Applications Center (VRCA) of Iowa Sate University built an assembly planning and evaluation system IVY [5], where assembly planning and evaluation could be performed based on geometric models and assembly hierarchical structure data directly. CIM Research Institute from Shanghai Jiao Tong University developed a software system named Integrated Virtual Assembly Environment (IVAE) [6]. It is a general application system for virtual assembly of general mechanical products based on geometrical constraints and degree of freedom analysis, where users can assemble products through various interactive devices such as data glove, 3D mouse, voice command, virtual menu, etc.

Although computer aided assembly process planning has made great development, process plan generated by totally computer automatic reasoning is not so easy to put into real practical use. While research on virtual assembly at present is mainly focused on assembleability evaluation for product design. Virtual prototyping and virtual reality technology provide a new and effective approach for assembly process planning. With the characteristics of immersion, interaction and imagination from virtual reality, through the use of virtual reality peripherals, assembly planner can manipulate components and tools and fixtures more naturally, and do assembly process planning in a visualized, perceivable and traceable manner, so as to obtain process plan which is reasonable, practical, and meets ergonomic requirement.

For assembly process planning with virtual reality, as assembly planner conducts product assembly operation in virtual environment, a very important problem is how to capture all necessary information automatically by computer software system and map the information to assembly process plan.

2 General Idea for Virtual Assembly Process Planning

In order to solve the automatically mapping problem for mechanical product assembly process plan, a real-virtual operation mapping method based on Basic-motion-Sequence is proposed. The general idea includes following aspects, as shown in Fig.1.

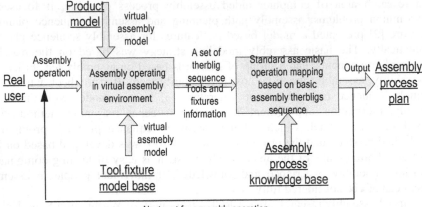

Fig. 1. General idea for assembly process planning based virtual assembly technology

A virtual assembly experimental environment is built where component assembly can be performed according to the mating constraint between each connected component. Assembly tools and fixtures database and Standard Assembly Process Knowledge base are built, and they act as support to do process planning. Product assembly tree model converted from CAD software system acts as input to the virtual assembly environment. With data glove and position tracking device, assembly planner can manipulate component with hand or with suitable assembly tool and fixture, and assemble components together to form the final product according to component's mating relation. During the assembly operation process for each component, software system can automatically record every set of complete virtual assembly operations in the form of basic-motion-sequence, together with information about operated component and assembly tool. Based on the mapping relation between basic-motion-sequence and Standard Assembly Operation, together with the type of component and type of assembly tool and so on, assembly process description information for each component and assembly time consumed for each assembly process can be generated automatically by searching in the standard assembly process knowledge base. After all the components have been assembled together, the software system will generate the final product assembly process plan. The key points of this basic idea are modeling of Standard Assembly Operation, modeling of Assembly Basic Motion, mapping between Standard Assembly Operation and Basic Motion Sequence, and acquisition of basic-motion-sequence during the virtual assembly operation. These key points are discussed in detail as follows.

3   Real-Virtual Mapping Method Based on Basic Motion Sequence

3.1   Modeling of Standard Assembly Operation

With the detail analysis of composition information about auto engine assembly process card from real industrial use, an assembly process information model is put forward which includes information about assembled component, assembly tool, assembly operation motion, assembly operation time, weight of assembled object and moving distance of assembly operation.

Among these information, assembled component, assembly tool and assembly operation motion are the most basic ones. Only when virtual assembly operations on components are described exactly and associated with real assembly operations that complete assembly process could be obtained, so as to generate assembly process plan. Therefore, the description of virtual assembly operation motion model is the base to build the description model of assembly process information.

With the analysis of assembly operation motion from real manufacturing process plan, assembly operation motions can be simplified and classified into 9 types, they are Prepare, Put-on, Insert, Screw, Fasten, Press, Knock-in, Load and Unload, which act as Standard Assembly Operation (SAO) in assembly process plan information model. These 9 types of Standard Assembly Operations cover most of the operation motion types in auto engine assembly work and with out any overlapping from the operation motion meaning point of view.

3.2 Modeling of Assembly Basic Motion

Taking the Method Time Measurement (MTM) [7] as reference, it shows that current feasible MTM therbligs includes 18 types, which can be classified into three categories as follows:

1. Effective therbligs, they are necessary motions during task operation, such as Reach, Grasp, Move, Position, Assemble, Disassemble, Use, Release, Inspect.
2. Assistant therbligs, they are necessary therbligs in order to complete task operation therbligs, and they will make task be delayed and consume much more time, and lead to low working efficiency, such as Search, Find, Select, Plan, Pre-position.
3. Ineffective therbligs, they are therbligs which have no any effect on task working operation, and should be managed to acquire in therblig analysis: Hold, Unavoidable Delay, Avoidable Delay, Rest.

In our research, Standard Assembly Operations and body motion can be described with the reference to MTM. But the description of MTM therbligs is too basic, how to make MTM therbligs aggregation to meet the requirement of practicability and applicability in virtual assembly should be well considered. Currently, subjective therbligs can not be defined easily in virtual reality environment, such as Search, Find, think, etc. And some therbligs are not necessary for virtual assembly, such as Hold, Unavoidable Delay, and Avoidable Delay. So, with reference to the uniform definition of basic therblig element from MTM standard criterion, 9 types of Assembly Basic Motion elements have been proposed for necessary used in virtual assembly environment, they are Reach, Grasp, Move, Turn, Apply Pressure, Disengage, Position, Position-Z, Release. The definition of Assembly Basic Motion element based on MTM is the foundation of aggregating Assembly Basic Motion to form Standard Assembly Operation.

The meaning of the above 9 Assembly Basic Motion Element which could be recorded in virtual assembly environment is described in detailed as follows:

1. **Reach**: Move empty hand to touch component object. Take the moment when the hand has the orientation of moving forward to destination object as the starting point of **Reach** motion, and the moment when the hand arrives at the destination object as the ending point of **Reach** motion.
2. **Grasp**: Use fingers or palm to fully control component object. Take the moment when fingers surround an object and try to control it as the starting point of **Grasp** motion, and the moment when the object has been fully controlled as the ending point of **Grasp** motion.
3. **Move**: Use hand or any other part of body moves an object from one place to another. Take the moment when hand with load has the orientation of moving forward to destination place as the starting point of **Move** motion, and the moment when hand with load arrives destination place as the ending point of **Move** motion.
4. **Turn**: Take forearm as rotation axis and rotate hand, wrist and forearm. This basic motion has two variation factors, the rotating angle and rotating weight or resistance force.
5. **Apply Pressure**: Append force to overcome resistance. Apply extra force when meeting larger resistance during assembly process.
6. **Disengage**: Make object disengage from other objects. Take the moment when object is under controlled (**Grasp**) and is ready to be disassembled as the starting point of **Disengage** motion, and the moment when the object has been disassembled completely as the ending point.
7. **Position**: Put object on a certain orientation. Take the moment when virtual hand with object in operation begins to sway, turn and slide to a certain orientation as the starting point of **Position** motion, and the moment when object has been put at a correct orientation as the ending point.
8. **Position-z**: Put an object on a given position. If the given orientation where the object is required to be positioned is an unambiguous point, the object should be allowed to be put anywhere within a certain range.
9. **Release**: Release grasped object. Take the moment when fingers begin to leave the grasped object as the starting point of **Release** motion, and the moment when fingers leave the object completely.

The definition of Assembly Basic Motion based on MTM method is the basis to aggregate Standard Assembly Operation from Assembly Basic Motion, and virtual assembly operation motion should be mapped according to these Assembly Basic Motion strictly.

3.3 Mapping between Standard Assembly Operation and Basic Motion Sequence

According to assembly operation motion in real assembly process, all operations can be classified into 9 basic ones without any overlapping in meaning, which are Prepare, Put-on, Insert, Screw, Fasten, Press, Knock-in, Load and Unload.

In virtual environment, Standard Assembly Operations could be aggregated according the combinations Assembly Basic Motion. In other words, a Standard Assembly Operation can be decomposed into Basic Motion sequence, and the Standard Assembly Operation and Assembly Basic Motion sequence has a unique mapping relationship with each other. During virtual assembly process, Basic Motion sequences in assembly

Table 1. Standard Assembly Operations and Basic Motion Mapping Matrix

Standard Assembly Operation \ Basic Motion	Reach	Grasp	Move	Turn	Apply Pressure	Disengage	Position	Position-z	Release	Mapping code
1. Prepare	X	X	X						X	111000001
2. Put-on	X	X	X					X	X	111000011
3. Insert	X	X	X				X		X	111000101
4. Screw	X	X	X	X			X		X	111100101
5. Fasten	X	X	X	X	X		X	X	X	111110111
6. Press	X	X	X		X		X	X	X	111010111
7. Knock-in	X	X	X		X		X		X	111010101
8. Load	X	X	X				X	X	X	111000111
9. Unload	X	X	X			X			X	111001001

operations are recorded according to virtual operation order, and then the Basic Motion sequences can be mapped to corresponding Standard Assembly Operation. The mapping matrix is shown in table 1, each row indicates a type of Standard Assembly Operation, and each column indicates a type of Basic Motion. Each Standard Assembly Operation is corresponding to a set of Basic Motions which forms a motion sequence; these corresponding Basic Motions are marked with letter 'X'. A 9 digital code is used to indicate the mapping relationship. For each row of Standard Assembly Operation, if the Basic Motion cell is marked with 'X', "1" is signed as the digital code number; if the Basic Motion cell is blank, "0" is signed as the digital code number. By this meaning, for each row, there is a 9 digital code, which is indicated at "Mapping code" column.

The Standard Assembly Operation and Basic Motion mapping matrix acts as the basis of Standard Assembly Operation's acquisition. During virtual assembly, when user manipulating some components, all Basic Motions are recorded. If a Basic Motion is applied during operating process, the digital code bit representing this Basic Motion will be signed as "1". After operations completed, Basic Motion sequences are generated from recorded Basic Motions, and mapped into unique Standard Assembly Operations separately.

3.4 Acquisition of Basic Motion Sequence during Virtual Assembly Operation

During virtual assembly, components are manipulated by virtual hand, Basic Motion sequence information for assembly operation is recorded, where basic motion **Reach** is set as the starting motion of basic motion sequence and **Release** as the end motion of basic motion sequence. As assembly operation in virtual assembly environment is quite different from that of real assembly operation, each Basic Motion digital code is set according to following rules:

Reach code: Reach acts as the beginning motion of each assembly operation during virtual assembly. When virtual hand touches component or tool, which can be determined with collision diction model, the operation motion is considered as Reach, and the **Reach** code is signed as '1'. As ineffective touch might occur between virtual hand and components from time to time during the virtual assembly procedure, only when Reach motion is combined with other basic motion (such as **Grasp** etc.), and only if the position of operated component has been changed, that the previous motion Reach is considered as effective motion.

Grasp code: If the virtual hand and component or tool is in the touch status, when operator sends a signal to grasp component or assembly tool, the **Grasp** motion code is set to '1'.

Release code: Release acts as the end motion of each assembly operation during virtual assembly, when operator sends a signal to release grasped object and the virtual hand leaves operated objects, the **Release** motion code is set to '1'. And all basic motions after **Reach** motion being recorded should be saved to get a mapping code, this mapping code is the basic information for motions-operation mapping.

Move code: when virtual hand is at state of grasping object, supposed that the object's position at beginning is $P1$, and the object's position at the end is $P2$, if $P1 \neq P2$, the **Move** motion code is set to '1'.

Turn code: when virtual hand is grasping objects, supposed that the object's orientation at beginning is $R1$, and the object's position at the end is $R2$, if $R1 \neq R2$, the **Turn** motion code is set to '1'.

Apply Pressure code: In virtual assembly, **Apply Pressure** can not be determined through signals sent by operator, but it can be determined by the final status of objects together with assembly process information. That is, check the object's ID to find out whether the object should be pressed during the assembly process, if yes, and then check whether the object is completely constrained, and if all the answers are yes, the **Apply Pressure** motion code is set to '1'.

Disengage code: By checking the status of operated component at the beginning and the end of operation separately, if the total number of parts of the assembled components is decreased, it means Disengage motion happens, the **Disengage** motion code is set to '1'.

Position code: When virtual hand is assembling a grasped object, if line-align-line constraint is confirmed, the **Position** motion code is set to '1'.

Position-z code: When virtual hand is assembling a grasped object, and if face-to-face constraint is confirmed, the **Position-z** motion code is set to '1'.

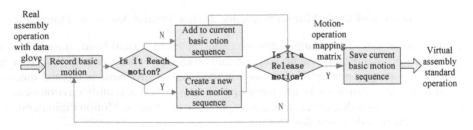

Fig. 2. Virtual assembly operation generating process

After virtual assembly operations, all basic motion sequences would be recorded as mapping codes, and Standard Assembly Operation could be acquired through mapping relationship shown in the motion-operation mapping matrix. The flow chat of real-virtual mapping process is shown in Fig.2. With these Standard Assembly Operations together with other assembly process information which are acquired at the same time during virtual assembly procedure, assembly process plan can be generated.

4 Example

The method mentioned above has been integrated into computer aided software named Virtual Assembly Process Planning Environment (VAPPE) which is developed by our research group. A type of auto engine has been selected as an example to verify the above method. Assembly tool and assembly fixture have been modeled and saved into database, standard assembly process knowledge for auto-engine assembly has also been modeled. After running the software system, VAPPE will read some initial files, such as product information and production environment information files, and set up virtual assembly environment, just as shown in Fig.3.

With data gloves, mouse or keyboard, operator can control virtual hand in the virtual environment to grasp and move components, and assemble components through constraint recognition and confirmation, so as to realize the assembly simulation function of virtual assembly system. Fig. 4 shows the assembling process of

Fig. 3. Auto engine virtual assembly operating simulation scene

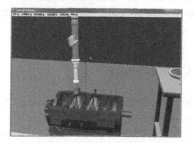

Fig. 4. Assembly process without tools   **Fig. 5.** Fasten bolts with semiautomatic tool

screwing 8 bolts into corresponding holes in bearing covers without tools. When the bolt is getting close enough to the mating hole, the system will highlight the potential constraints and prompt to operator with highlight line and/or face, and then operator can confirm these constraints in order to assemble components. After all the bolts are screwed to the right place, a semi-automatic tool is used to screw and fasten them, just as shown in Fig. 5.

During the virtual assembly operation, VAPPE system records all the basic motion sequences for every assembly operations and other assembly process information. After the virtual assembly operation completed, the software system runs the assembly process plan generation module. The module reads all virtual assembly basic motion sequence, and maps them into standard assembly operations according to motion-operation mapping matrix, as shown in table 2.

Table 2. Recorded assembly operation information

No.	Motion-operation mapping code	SAO	Component name	Tool name
1	111100101	screw	bolt CC4105Q-052004_2	No(hand)
9	111110111	Fasten	bolt CC4105Q-052004_2	Semi-automatic screwdriver

Table 3. Assembly process information corresponding to Table 2

No.	Content of process	time /s
1	Screw bolt CC4105Q-052004_2 with hand	2.2
9	Fasten bolt CC4105Q-052004_2 with semi-automatic screwdriver	2.7

Together with other assembly process information recorded during virtual assembly operation, VAPPE system will search corresponding standard assembly process in assembly process knowledge base to obtain standard assembly time, and shows the results in the interface. The processes corresponding to above standard assembly operations are shown in table 3. With this computer aided software, it is obvious that the assembly process plan efficiency can be increased. All the information about assembly process plan and workplaces can be saved into database and served for real assembly manufacturing process.

5   Conclusions

In order to realize assembly process planning in virtual reality environment, an assembly process planning generation method based on real-virtual mapping of basic motion sequence is proposed. In this paper, assembly process information is modeled; standard assembly operations and basic assembly motion are defined. The mapping matrix among standard assembly operations and basic assembly motions are set up. A method to get basic motion sequence in virtual environment during virtual assembling process by real user is put forward. A prototype system is developed based on these research results, and the system function is demonstrated through assembly process of automobile engine components. The application illustrates the feasibility of the proposed method; it also provides a new and effective approach for assembly process planning through operator's real experiencing in the virtual reality environment.

Acknowledgments

The work is supported by the National High-Tech Program of China (Grant No. 2006AA04Z141) and the Key Project from NSFC of China (Grant No. 90612017). The authors are also grateful to the editors and the anonymous reviewers for helpful comments.

References

1. Wang, X.K.: Mechanical assembly process, 3rd edn. Machinery Industry Press of China, Beijing (2008) (in Chinese)
2. Eng, T.H., Ling, Z.K., Olson, W.: Feature-based assembly modeling and sequence generation. Computers & Industrial Engineer 36, 17–33 (1999)
3. Pan, Y.Y.: Research on key technology of virtual assembly oriented process planning (in Chinese). Nanjing University of Technology and Engineering, master thesis (2003)
4. Jayaram, S.: VADE: a virtual assembly design environment. IEEE Computer Graphics and Application 19, 44–50 (1999)
5. Bob, K.A.: A Synthetic Environment for Assembly Planning and Evaluation (2005-10-9), http://www.cs.uiowa.edu/-cremer/.Sive-abstracts/kuehne.text
6. Yang, R.D., Fan, X.M., Wu, D.L., Yan, J.Q.: Virtual assembly technologies based on constraint and DOF analysis. Robotics and Computer-Integrated Manufacturing 23, 447–456 (2007)
7. Yang, R. D., Fan, X. M., Wu, D. L., Yan, J. Q.: A virtual reality-based experiment environment for engine assembly line workplace planning and ergonomics evaluation. In: Shumaker, R. (ed.) HCII 2007 and ICVR 2007. LNCS, vol. 4563, pp. 594–603. Springer, Heidelberg (2007)
8. Niebel, B.W., Freivalds, A.: Methods, standards, and work design. WCB/McGraw-Hill, Boston (1999c)

Rebalancing the Visual System of People with Amblyopia "Lazy Eye" by Using HMD and Image Enhancement

Sina Fateh[1] and Claude Speeg[2]

[1] Sina Fateh, Vision Performance Lab, Neuroptical Inc.
1931 Old Middlefield way, 94043 Mountain View, CA, USA
[2] Department of Ophthalmology, University of Strasbourg, France
SinaFateh,sfateh@neuroptical.com

Abstract. Amblyopia or "lazy eye" occurs when during early childhood visual information from one eye is absent or poorly transmitted to the brain. This visual deprivation causes poor vision and the eye gradually becomes weaker (amblyope) relative to the other eye which becomes stronger. The visual imbalance is caused by the brain's preference for the strong eye. To restore vision, conventional treatments use occlusion and vision penalization of the strong eye to force the brain to use the amblyope eye. Conventional treatments are regarded as effective in young children but impractical in older subjects and patient compliance remains the main cause of treatment failure. This presentation describes our preliminary efforts to develop a convenient and viable binocular head mounted display (HMD) interface. The goal is to rebalance the vision by using a simultaneous enhancing/attenuation image adjustment. The image presented to the normal eye will be attenuated while the image presented to the amblyope eye will be enhanced. During this operation the user will be engage in recreational activities such as watching movies, using internet or playing video games.

Keywords: Binocular HMD, amblyopia, vision restoration, enhancement/ attenuation, visual rebalance, compliance.

1 Introduction

Amblyopia or "lazy eye" is a visual imbalance that occurs in early childhood by either absence or poor image transmission from one eye to the brain and affects approximately 2% of the population (Figure 1). The treatment of amblyopia has two main objectives: 1) to restore and attain a normal level of vision in the amblyope eye, and 2) to maintain the visual gains and avoid regression.

The oldest treatment method for ambyopia is occlusion of the good eye. Occlusion was introduced in the 18th century [1] and is still the most common form of treatment today. Based on the subject's age and degree of amblyopia there are various forms and regimens tailored to fit the individual patient's needs.

Complete occlusion results in the most rapid visual improvement but has disadvantages such as poor compliance [2,3], risks of reversing the amblyopia, and disruption of an existing binocularity [4]. Partial occlusion, a modified form of treatment, promotes the use of the weak eye by using adhesive filters to attenuate the vision of

R. Shumaker (Ed.): Virtual and Mixed Reality, LNCS 5622, pp. 560–565, 2009.

Fig. 1. Simulation of an image seen by a normal eye (a) and image seen by an amblyopic eye (b)

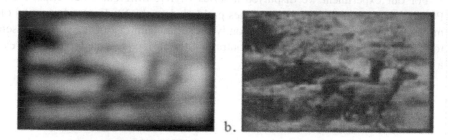

Fig. 2. Simulation of a penalization of the good eye (a) using pharmaceutically induced blur to force the brain to use the amblyope eye (b)

the good eye [5]. Another variation of the occlusion method is penalization, [6] where intentional visual blurring and distorting is used to reduce the vision of the good eye (Figure 2). The blurring is obtained optically using an over corrective lens or pharmaceutically by using atropine. Even after successful treatment visual regression is not uncommon. Approximately 25% of successfully treated cases lose some of their visual gain [8]. To prevent visual regression and preserve visual improvement eye care practitioners recommend continued part-time occlusion, optical overcorrection and pharmaceutical blur.

The conventional methods are regarded as effective in treating amblyopia before the age of 7, but their success is limited in older subjects. The high rate of failure in older subjects results from their lack of compliance and a reluctance to wear an eye patch due to cosmetic concerns. More importantly, it is inconvenient and onerous to rely solely on the amblyope eye for daily activities [9].

We propose to address the compliance issue and the risk of disrupting an existing binocular vision by using a combination of binocular head mounted display (HMD) and a monocular image alteration technique that could be used daily during recreational activities such as watching movies, using the internet, or playing video games.

2   Method and Implementation

The goal of our first phase is to develop a fully functional prototype which provides a flexible and convenient way to promote the vision of the amblyope eye without the unpleasant effect of impairing the good eye. The proposed system consists of a commercial binocular HMD, the Solo model from Myvu Corporation, a monocular image adjustment control and an Ipod video for providing the images. The HMD resolution of 320x240 was not ideal for our application; however, its modest weight of 90 grams and the possibility of adding optical correction by using a clip-on connector made it the best choice. Solo is compatible with the IPod video and DVD player and has two transmissive LCD micro displays. Having a separate image control for each eye is key to our application. We modified the commercial version by adding a separate image adjustment control to each LCD. The new configuration could host a second source of image for binocularity and anti suppression control.

For our experiment we displayed a series of five different video clips, a Power Point presentation, and two trivia games preloaded on the IPod video for a total of 25 minutes of viewing content. We randomly preset the contrast of the image presented to the left eye to a low level and the contrast of the image presented to the right eye to a high level (Figure 3).

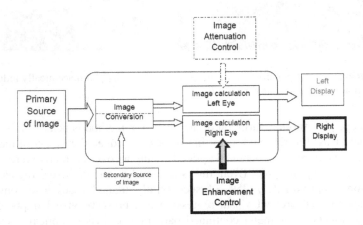

Fig. 3. The system configuration shows a separate image adjustment control for each LCD

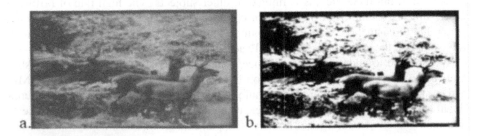

Fig. 4. Simulation of images perceived by each eye the low contrast image (a) and the high contrast image merged into one image

3 Results

Our subjective results show that the two images can reconcile into one perceived image. A similar device with a higher level of image enhancement/attenuation capability coffers a unique opportunity to treat moderate amblyopia by offering monocular image adjustment in a controlled binocular environment.

4 Discussion

Active stimulation techniques such as viewing high contrast targets as a supplement to conventional occlusion treatment have been proposed since late 1970s [10]. For example, the CAM vision simulator used rotating black and white strips to enhance the vision of the amblyope eye. While some studies reported some success [11], others found no significant difference compared to older forms of treatment [12].

However, recent studies on neuronal processes at the visual cortex [13,14] have enhanced our understanding of vision recovery and the maintenance mechanisms of some visual function.

Visual improvement demonstrated by perceptual learning in adults [15-18] confirms the possibility of restoring important visual function thought untreatable after age of 7. Extensive studies have shown the benefit of real time contrast enhancement [19,20] and its effect on improving vision [21,22].

Other studies have emphasized the role of the binocular interaction [23] in the vision recovery process [24].

Despite the encouraging results of these discoveries, the main obstacle to a successful vision recovery in amblyopia remains the compliance. Since compliance is a key issue, treatment methods that enable the subject to have enjoyment and recreation while simultaneously improving vision have the greatest chance for success. By combining the latest findings in neuroscience with technological advances in image processing, graphics technology, and the newest generation of HMD, we envision the development of a viable, convenient system that is effective for patients of any age.

The goal of our first phase was to evaluate the convenience of using a binocular HMD with enhanced/attenuated system to view video images. We are working on improved image adjustment control for our next phase.

5 Conclusion

We propose to use a binocular HMD with a monocular image enhancement/ attenuation control to rebalance the vision in mild amblyopia and recurring cases with binocularity.

In our anticipated second phase which includes a prospective clinical trial, we will use an improved HMD implementation with a higher resolution and higher level of image adjustment.

References

1. Buffon, G.L.: Sur la cause du strabisme ou des yeux louches, Memories de l'Academie des Sciences, Paris (1743)
2. Catford, G.V.: Amblyopic occlusion: The results of treatment. Transactions of the Ophthalmological Soc of UK (1987)
3. Oliver, M.: Compliance and results of treatment for amblyopia in children more than 8 years, old. Am. J. Ophthalmol. 102, 340–345 (1986)
4. Fawcett, S.L.: Disruption and reacquisition of binocular vision in childhood and in adulthood. Curr. Opin. Ophthalmol. 16(5), 298–302 (2005)
5. Charman, W.N.: Optical characteristics of Transpaseal as partial occluder. Am. J. Optom. Phys. Opt. 60, 846–850 (1983)
6. Von Norden, G.K., Milam, J.B.: Penalization in the treatment of amblyopia. Am. J. Ophthalmol. 88, 511–518 (1979)
7. Holmes, J.M., Beck, R.W., Kraker, R.T.: Risk of amblyopia recurrence after cessation of treatment. J. AAPOS 8, 420–428 (2004)
8. Flynn, J.T., Shiffman, J., Feyer, W., Corona: Trans. Am. Ophthalmol. Soc. 96, 431–450 (1998)
9. Fateh, S., Mawas, J.L.: Utilisation de telescope pour regarder la television afin d'ameliorer la vision de l'oeil amblyope. Con. An Orthop. Paris (1994)
10. Banks, R.V., Campell, F.W., Hess, R.A.: New treatment for amblyopia. Br. Orthot. J. 35, 1–12 (1978)
11. Watson, P.G., Banks, R.V.: Clinical assessment of a new treatment for amblyopia. Trans. Opthalmolo. Soc. UK 93, 201–208 (1978)
12. Lennerstrand, G., Samuelsson, B.: Amblyopia in 4 year-old children treated with grating stimulation and full time occlusion, A comparative study. Br. J. Ophtahlmol. 67, 181–190 (1983)
13. Hubel, D.H., Wiesel, T.N., Levay, S.: Plasticity of Ocular dominace clumuns in Monkey straite cortex. Phils. Trans. R Soc. Lon. Ser. B 278, 377–409 (1997)
14. Liao, D.S., Krahe, T., Prusky, G.T., Medina, A., Ramoa, A.S.: Recovery of cortical bicocularity and orientation selectivity after the critical period of ocular dominace plasticity. J. Neurophysiol 92, 2113–2121 (2004)
15. Levi, D.M., Polat, U., Hu, Y.S.: Improvement in vernier acuity in adults with amblyopia: practice makes better. Invest Ophthalmol. Vis. Sci. 38, 1493–1510 (1997)
16. Simmers, A.J., Gray, L.S.: Improvement of visual function in an adult amblyope. Optom. Vis. Sci. 76, 82–87 (1999)
17. Levi, D.M.: Perceptual Learning in Adults with Amblyopia: A Reevaluation of the Critical Periods in Human Vision. Dev. Psychobiol. 46, 222–232 (2005)
18. Polat, U., Ma-Naim, T., Belkin, M., Sagi, D.: Improving vision in adult amblyopia by perceptual learning. PNAS 101, 6692–6697 (2004)
19. Hier, R.G., Schmidt, G.W., Miller, R.S., Deforest, S.E.: Realtime locally adaptive Contrats enhancement a Practical Key to Overcoming Display and Human Visual System Limitations. In: SID Symposium Digest of technical Papers, pp. 491–494 (1993)
20. Fine, E., Peli, E., Brady, N.: Video enhancement improves performance of persons with moderate visual loss. In: Proceedings of the International Conference on Low Vision, Vision 1996, Madrid, Spain, pp. 85–92 (1997)

21. Peli, E., Goldstein, R.B., Young, G.M., Trempe, C.M., Buzney, S.M.: Image enhancement for the visually impaired: Simulations and experimental results. Invest. Ophthalmol. Vis. Sci. 32, 2337–2350 (1991)
22. Fullerton, M., Peli, E.: Post-transmission digital video enhancement for people with visual impairments. Journal of the Society for Information Display 14(1), 15–24 (2006)
23. Harrad, R.A., Hess, R.F.: Binocular Integration of Contrast Information in Amblyopia. Vision Res. 32(110), 21–35 (1992)
24. Baker, D.H., Meese, T.S., Mansouri, B., Hess, R.F.: Binocular Summation of Contrast remains intact in Strabismic Amblyopia. IOVS 48(11) (2007)

A Two-User Framework for Rapid Immersive Full Cycle Product Customization

Maxim Foursa, David d'Angelo, Gerold Wesche, and Manfred Bogen

Fraunhofer Institut für Intelligente Analyse- und Informationssyteme
Virtual Environments
53754 Sankt Augustin, Germany
{Maxim.Foursa,David.d-Angelo,
Gerold.Wesche,Manfred.Bogen}@iais.fraunhofer.de

Abstract. In this paper we present an approach for a full cycle product customization in Virtual Environments (VE). The main goal of our work is to develop an integrated immersive framework, which allows configuring products from a great number of parts. Our framework supports collaborative work of two users and operates both on desktop computers and in immersive environments. The framework is integrated into a manufacturing environment, thus making the immediate production of customized products possible. The integrated modules of the framework allow importing CAD files directly into VE, creation of new objects on the basis of constructive solid geometry principles, attaching virtual connectivity-describing attributes to parts, guided assembly of parts and comprehensive analysis of products. In order to identify the influence of immersion and collaboration on the performance in assembly and manipulation tasks in VE, we performed a quantitative assessment of user performance, which we also describe in the paper.

Keywords: Virtual Environment, Mass Customization, Product Development.

1 Introduction

The research on Virtual Reality (VR) technology and its applications in manufacturing industry has been actively performed during the last 15 years. Automotive companies, such as GM, Daimler-Chrysler and BMW [3], use VR applications in their production pipeline, but the technology as such is not yet fully integrated into the workflow and production process of most manufacturing enterprises. There are 3 main reasons for that. First of all, the hardware prices of VR installations have been quite high and became affordable only recently. Second, data formats used in VR applications were usually not compatible with common Computer-Aided Design (CAD) software and thereby prevented a seamless integration with traditional business processes. Third, the interfaces of VR applications have been quite complex, while their functional possibilities were limited and inflexible.

The European research project INT-MANUS [6] investigated between 2005 and 2008 the improvement potentials of flexibility and adaptability of manufacturing systems. The core technology of INT-MANUS is the Smart-Connected-Control platform (SCCP) [22], which integrates machines, robots and human personnel. The

R. Shumaker (Ed.): Virtual and Mixed Reality, LNCS 5622, pp. 566–575, 2009.

platform provides numerous services and provides specific interfaces for monitoring, controlling and configuring a production environment. Among other INT-MANUS achievements, we have developed a full cycle product customization framework for 3-D VR-based systems, which we present in this paper. The main purpose of this framework is to allow the configuration of products from a great number of parts, which can be modeled, attributed and assembled directly in the immersive environment and scheduled for immediate production. The framework is directly connected to the INT-MANUS SCCP platform, which allows automatic production rescheduling in response to configuration changes made in the framework.

Our framework combines two-dimensional menus with immersive three-dimensional widgets for a more effective interaction. It allows the team-work of two users not only by using special collaborative techniques, but also by providing correct 3-D perspective for each of the two co-workers. The framework can be used on desktop computers, although a two-user projection-based Virtual Environment allows a more effective benefit from the framework's potential. In the next sections we describe the related work and present the framework architecture and its modules.

2   Related Work

Virtual Prototyping is used to simulate assembly and to evaluate prototypes in different design stages [20]. It assists customized production development by virtual manufacturing simulation and visual evaluation on the basis of Virtual Reality technology, which generates 3-D immersive interactive worlds.

A part of manufacturing simulation is the assembly simulation, which involves packaging issues as well as determining required space regions by calculating assembly paths for parts. Several assembly simulation systems have been developed in the recent years [2, 9, 10, 11, 15, 21, 23, 27]. These simulation systems use physical-based [2, 9, 21, 27] or knowledge-based assembly constraints [10, 11, 15], as well as a combination of both [23]. Some systems have been developed for head-mounted displays [9, 15, 21, 27], while others used projection-based display systems [2, 10, 11, 23]. For example, Zachmann and Rettig [27] presented multimodal and spatial interaction for virtual assembly simulation and considered criteria like naturalness, robustness and precision for the development of grasping techniques and gestural input. Multimodal assembly and the extraction of connection properties from CAD files have been studied in [2]. The VADE system [9] is a fairly complex assembly simulation environment, which uses CAD models to represent the assembly area. Ma et al. [15] proposed a hierarchical-structured data model on the basis of positional relationships of feature elements.

A group of contributions focused on immersive modeling applications that support the assembly of complex models out of predefined parts. Jung [10] represents the connection sensitivity of part regions using so-called ports. From the rich connection semantics of those the constraints for part connections are derived. This includes analyzing the geometric relationships among the involved parts and allows finding a solution even for complex port configurations on multiple parts. The VLEGO modeler [11] allows assembling toys from blocks. Arising from the properties of those blocks and their studs, VLEGO restricts possible connections of blocks to discrete positions and orientations.

Collaborative object manipulation for two users wearing an HMD has been investigated by Pinho et al. [18]. They presented two kinds of collaborative manipulation tools; one is based on the separation of degrees of freedom for two users, whereas the other relies on the composition of user actions. They have observed increased performance and usability in difficult manipulation tasks. Another example of collaborative VE is the SeamlessDesign system of Kiyokawa et al. [12]. The system allows two users to model collaboratively, interactively combining geometric primitives with constraining primitives.

The integration between VR and CAD systems is an important issue [4, 7]. The aim of these researches is to allow modification of CAD-imported objects within Virtual Environments, in such a way that it becomes possible to reflect the modifications done in VR back to the CAD data. The coupling between VR and CAD functionality in both systems is done with OpenCascade technology[1], although the same approach can be also applied to more widely used CAD systems, such as CATIA [4].

The research on the benefits of VR technologies allows to understand better, in which tasks VR can be especially useful and how exactly it should be applied. For example, Zhang et al. [28] found out that the assembly task performance can be improved by visual and auditory feedback mechanisms. However, the hypothesis on the positive effects of immersion and natural 3D interaction for affective analysis of product design has been rejected [14]. Ye et al. [26] compared immersive VR, non-immersive desktop VR and traditional engineering environment in assembly planning tasks. He found out that performance time in the traditional environment was significantly longer than one in the desktop VR, and that the difference between the desktop VR and immersive VR was not significant.

Narayan et al. [16] investigated the effects of immersion on team performance in a collaborative environment for spatially separated users. He noticed that stereoscopic vision had a significant effect on team performance, unlike head tracking, which had no notable effect on the performance at all.

There are many user studies that compare the performance of different display systems for very simple object manipulation tasks. The results achieved so far are inconsistent and seem to depend on the kind of task to be performed [5, 24], although the effect of large displays is considered beneficial [17].

3   Framework Architecture and Its Use Cases

The pipeline of our product customization framework is presented in Fig.1. It consists of the following stages: import or immersive creation of product parts (1), visual attributing the parts with connection semantics (2) and interactive assembly of the virtual product from the part set (3).

---

[1] http://opencascade.org

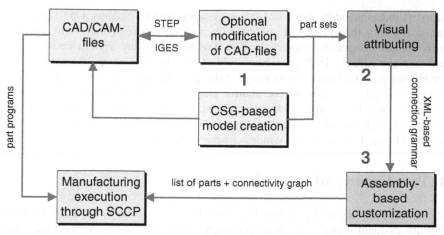

Fig. 1. The product customization pipeline

For a better understanding of the framework we want to consider an example – a company that produces complex products consisting of multiple parts in different variations. The company manufactures multiple product variants depending on the market situation or customer needs. The company may use our framework for the following purposes:

1. collaborative design evaluation in the immersive environment with possibilities to modify original CAD data and to create new 3-D objects from primitives on the basis of Boolean operations,
2. collaborative and interactive creation of connectivity semantics to simplify and guide assembly customization,
3. collaborative customization and evaluation of products by assembling them from great number of parts on the basis of the connectivity semantics,
4. supervised assembly training,
5. scheduling of production by sending the list of selected parts and their connectivity information to the manufacturing execution system through the SCCP platform.

Different collaboration modes are supported by the framework. For example, collaborative design evaluation would require a team-work of a designer and an engineer, while collaborative product assembly could be done with an engineer and a customer. Thus, the framework supports different roles, which define the functionalities available for a user.

The user interface of the framework is fully integrated into the immersive environment and uses context-based adapted two-dimensional menus as well as three-dimensional widgets for system control tasks. The widgets move functionality directly onto objects, allowing the exploitation of the full degrees of freedom of the three-dimensional workspace. The interface supports selection and manipulation of individual objects as well as groups of objects.

Our framework is based on the virtual reality framework Avango® [13], which supports different display systems from single-user desktop to multi-user projection-based virtual environments. We used the TwoView Virtual Environment [19], which supports independent head-tracked stereo viewing for two persons. Up to five persons can work with the systems simultaneously, but only two of them will see images with correct perspective projection. The TwoView display system consists of two active-stereo-capable DLP projectors behind a vertical 3 m x 2.4 m screen. Two simultaneously displayed stereo image pairs are separated by polarization filters in front of the projector lenses. The shutter glasses have corresponding filters, so that each user sees perceptively correct active stereo projection. The display system is integrated with an optical tracking system based on passive markers, which are attached to shutter-glasses and wireless interaction devices.

4   Part Import and Immersive Creation

Our framework allows importing part models from various standard CAD-formats that are frequently used in the industry, such as STEP or IGES. A new object can be directly created and modified in the immersive environment by applying constructive solid geometry (CSG) operations to geometrical primitives or imported models (see Fig. 2).

Fig. 2. Collaborative CSG-based creation of models in the TwoView Virtual Environment

The operations hierarchically combine objects on the basis of set operations like union, intersection and difference. Similar to [4, 7], our framework uses the Open-CASCADE geometric kernel to perform such operations. At the end of this activity, users can create sets of parts that may be connected together to form a product and save them in separate XML-based files. If geometry has been changed or created newly, the framework will send the new CAD file to the SCCP platform, which will create a request to produce respective part programs for manufacturing machines.

5 Visual Attributing with Connection Semantics

Our framework employs knowledge-based assembly constraints in the form of a grammar, which encodes the semantic connection information of all part models. The grammar is based on the concept of so-called *handles* [8]. These virtual objects can be directly attached to all parts in the immersive environment and configured to describe their connection semantics. Handles use geometric primitives, like points, vectors and coordinate systems. They have two main purposes: first, handles define the set of models constructible out of the set of given parts; second, handles support users by guiding them in the assembly process. Two parts can be connected at a common location if there is at least one pair of matching handles from each part.

Accurate positioning of handles in Virtual Environment is a challenging task, which requires visual guidance from the VE. We suggest the following assisting strategies, which should help a user of our framework to find optimal handle positions:

1. When requested, our system calculates a map of normals for all vertices of a 3-D model. The user can associate a handle with a normal, and move it along the surface (Fig. 3, left). In this case the accuracy of handle positioning is limited by the normal map sampling rate.
2. If the handle has to be positioned more accurately, the user can use assisting flat grids with variable size and sampling. This allows handle positioning with arbitrary accuracy in the coordinate system of the 3-D model (Fig. 3, right). This method is especially suited for flat surfaces.
3. Our system can also calculate assisting points of interests, such as the center of mass or the center of a flat geometrical primitive, which can help the user in estimating best positions for handles.
4. If two parts have to be marked as compatible and the positioning of handles is not important, the user simply moves the parts close together, and the framework calculates two normals with minimal distance for both adjacent surfaces and marks them as handles.

The strategies mentioned above rely on the polygonal mesh of a part, which actually is an approximation of the exact surface equation obtained by point sampling, i.e. by tessellation. In case the manufacturing process needs exact positioning of handles on the surface, we have to take the restrictions of existing strategies into account and apply additional ones, when necessary. If the vertices of a polygonal mesh coincide with the exact surface, handle placement only at these locations is exact. Arbitrary handle positioning on a curved or spherical surface can be achieved using the following additional strategies, which we are currently investigating:

1. In case of parametric surfaces, the parametric domain can be used as an assisting grid (see method 2 above) and mapped to the surface, so that the user can snap handles to exact surface positions.

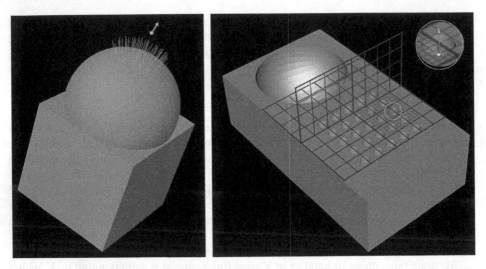

Fig. 3. Assisting strategies for handle positioning: map of normals in the vicinity of the handle (left) and assisting grids (right)

2. In case of implicit surfaces, the user can place handles exactly on the surface based on ray intersections.
3. For interactive searching for handle positions, the user can probe the surface and, based on the surface equation, can get information on the features of the surface, e.g. coordinate values, certain points like center points or mid-points, local extreme points, etc. Such positions are in many cases candidates for connecting other parts.

The output of this module is the XML-based file effectively describing possible set of part combinations, which may form the product. Additional information, such as time and costs needed for production of a part, can also be added to the grammar.

6 Assembly-Based Customization

The XML-based grammar produced in the previous steps to create part sets and constrain their connections is used as the basis for assembly-based product customization.

In addition to the selection and manipulation techniques mentioned above, this module of the framework supports the following tasks:

1. Add parts to the scene and remove them using drag-and-drop technique.
2. Assemble and disassemble compatible parts. As recommended in [28], the framework visually reacts on the actions of the user. When two parts with compatible handles are moved close enough to each other, the handles are highlighted. If the user continues bringing parts together, they will be automatically connected with the handles (snapped) and highlighted for a short time.
3. Visual inspection of parts, part groups and their connections. The user may alter material properties (textures), part transparencies and global illumination. In addition to that, the user sees the time and cost needed for production of a part group. However, the total production time is simply the sum of production times of all components, and the actual time may vary depending on parallelization.

4. Finally, assembled configurations may be saved and scheduled for production by sending the assembly graph containing the set of parts needed for production, their properties and connectivity information to the SCCP platform.

The details of this framework module may be found in [1].

7 Comparative Assessment of User Performance

In order to identify the influence of immersion and collaboration on the performance in assembly and manipulation tasks in a virtual environment, we performed a quantitative assessment of user performance in an assembly modeling application on the basis of our framework. We asked each of twenty participants to perform a specific task ten times in four modes: in single and collaborative two-user modes with stereoscopic and monoscopic vision for each mode. The participants had to assemble a table out of a table plate and four table legs and place it at a specific position on a floor plate. In each assembly task, the modeling parts were randomly positioned in space, while the sum of the inter-object distances was kept constant for all initial configurations. An automatic timer clock measured and logged the task completion times, starting with first and stopping with last assembly operations.

The results showed average speed-up factors of 1.6 and 1.4 for collaborative interaction and stereoscopic vision respectively. With both collaboration and stereo vision the performance of users could be increased by factor 2.2. Interestingly, early experiments on quantitative estimation of stereo vision benefits [25] showed that stereo allowed increasing the size of understandable abstract data in VE by factor 1.6, which is quite close to our results, despite the fact that the tasks are completely different. More details about our comparative assessment may be found in [1].

8 Conclusion and Future Work

We have shown that the immersive environment may be effectively used for a full cycle product customization: from creation of individual parts to scheduling of complete products. We described the coupling between VR environment and CAD functionality, the grammar-based assembly constraint and assembly-based product customization. The developed framework may be used in any production environment and can be easily adapted to different immersive display systems. The framework has also been used to evaluate the benefits of immersion and collaboration on task performance in assembly and manipulation operations. The results of the evaluation allowed measuring the benefits of stereoscopic vision and collaboration in Virtual Environments quantitatively. In our future work we are going to develop more sophisticated collaborative interaction techniques, integrate different interaction and haptic devices into the framework, and implement application-specific widgets to improve 3-D interaction.

Acknowledgments. The work is sponsored by the Commission of the European Union through the INT-MANUS project (NMP2-CT-2005-016550).

References

1. d'Angelo, D., Wesche, G., Foursa, M., Bogen, M.: The Benefits of Co-located Collaboration and Immersion on Assembly Modeling in Virtual Environments. In: Proceedings of the 4th International Symposium on Visual Computing, pp. 478–487 (2008)
2. Biermann, P., Jung, B., Latoschik, M., Wachsmuth, I.: Virtuelle werkstatt: A platform for Multimodal assembly in VR. In: Proc. of Virtual Reality International Conference 2002, pp. 53–62 (2002)
3. Bilalis, N., Petousis, M., Antoniadis, A.: Industrial Applications' Simulation Technologies in Virtual Environments - Part I: Virtual Prototyping. In: Proc. of New Horizons in Industry and Education conference, pp. 458-463 (2003)
4. Bourdot, P., Convard, T., Picon, F., Ammi, M., Touraine, D., Vezien, J.-M.: VR-CAD integration: Multimodal immersive interaction and advanced haptic paradigms for implicit edition of CAD models. Elsevier Computer-Aided Design journal (2008)
5. Figueroa, P., Bischof, W.F., Boulanger, P., Hoover, H.J.: Efficient comparison of platform alternatives in interactive virtual reality applications. Int. J. Hum.-Comput. Stud., 73–103 (January 2005)
6. Foursa, M., et al.: INT-MANUS: revolutionary controlling of production processes. In: ACM SIGGRAPH 2006, research poster and abstract, article No. 161. ACM, New York (2006)
7. Haselberger, F., Bues, M., Schuetz, T.: An immersive CAD testbed. In: Proceedings of the IPT-EGVE Symposium 2007, pp. 51–52 (2007)
8. Foursa, M., Wesche, G., D'Angelo, D., Bogen, M., Herpers, R.: A Two-User Virtual Environment for Rapid Assembly of Product Models within an Integrated Process Chain. In: Proceedings of the X Symposium on Virtual and Augmented Reality, pp. 143–150 (2008)
9. Jayaram, S., Jayaram, U., Wang, Y., Tirumali, H., Lyons, K., Hart, P.: Vade: A virtual assembly design environment. IEEE Comput. Graph. Appl. 19(6), 44–50 (1999)
10. Jung, B.: Task-Level Assembly Modeling in Virtual Environments, Computational Science and Its Applications. In: Kumar, V., Gavrilova, M.L., Tan, C.J.K., L'Ecuyer, P. (eds.) ICCSA 2003. LNCS, vol. 2669, pp. 721–730. Springer, Heidelberg (2003)
11. Kiyokawa, K., Takemura, H., Katayama, Y., Iwasa, H., Yokoya, N.: VLEGO: A Simple Two-handed Modeling Environment Based on Toy Blocks. In: Proc. ACM Virtual Reality Software and Technology, pp. 27–34 (1996)
12. Kiyokawa, K., Takemura, H., Yokoya, N.: SeamlessDesign: A Face-to-face Collaborative Virtual/Augmented Environment for Rapid Prototyping of Geometrically Constrained 3-D Objects. In: Proc. IEEE International Conference on Multimedia Computing and Systems, pp. 447–453 (1999)
13. Kuck, R., Wind, J., Riege, K., Bogen, M.: Improving the AVANGO VR/AR framework. In: Proc. of the 5th Workshop of GI-Fachgruppe VR/AR, pp. 209–220 (2008)
14. Lee, S., Chen, T., Kim, J., Kim, G.J., Han, S., Pan, Z.: Affective property evaluation of virtual product designs. In: Proc. of IEEE virtual reality conference, pp. 207–214 (2004)
15. Ma, W.Y., Zhong, Y.M., Tso, S.K., Zhou, T.X.: A Hierarchically Structured and Constraint-based Data Model for Intuitive and Precise Solid Modeling in a Virtual Reality Environment. Elsevier Computer-Aided Design Journal (2003)
16. Narayan, M., Waugh, L., Zhang, X., Bafna, P., Bowman, D.: Quantifying the benefits of immersion for collaboration in virtual environments. In: Proceedings of the ACM symposium on Virtual reality software and technology, pp. 78–81 (2005)
17. Ni, T., Bowman, D.A., Chen, J.: Increased display size and resolution improve task performance in Information-Rich Virtual Environments. In: Proceedings of Graphics Interface 2006, pp. 139–146 (2006)

18. Pinho, M., Bowman, D., Freitas, C.: Cooperative Object Manipulation in Immersive Virtual Environments: Framework and Techniques. In: Proc. ACM Virtual Reality Software and Technology, Hong Kong, pp. 171–178 (2002)
19. Riege, K., Holtkaemper, T., Wesche, G., Froehlich, B.: The bent pick ray: An extended pointing technique for multi-user interaction. In: 3DUI 2006: Proceedings of the 3D User Interfaces, pp. 62–65. IEEE Computer Society, Washington (2006)
20. Rix, J., Haas, S., Teixeira, J. (eds.): Virtual Prototyping: Virtual environments and the product design. Springer, Heidelberg (1995)
21. de Sa, A.G., Zachmann, G.: Virtual reality as a tool for verification of assembly and maintenance processes. Computers and Graphics 23(3), 389–403 (1999)
22. Schlegel, T., et al.: INT-MANUS: Interactive Production Control in a Distributed Environment. In: HCI applications and services, pp. 1150–1159. Springer, Berlin (2007)
23. Steffan, R., Kuhlen, T.: MAESTRO - a tool for Interactive assembly simulation in Virtual Environment. In: Fröhlich, B., Deisinger, J., Bullinger, H.-J. (eds.) Immersive Projection Technology and Virtual Environments, pp. 141–152. Springer, Wien, New York (2001)
24. Swan II, J.E., Gabbard, J.L., Hix, D., Schulman, R.S., Kim, K.P.: A Comparative Study of User Performance in a Map-Based Virtual Environment. In: Proceedings of the IEEE Virtual Reality, pp. 259–266 (2003)
25. Ware, C., Franck, G.: Evaluating stereo and motion cues for visualizing information nets in three dimensions. ACM Transactions on Graphics 15(2), 121–140 (1996)
26. Ye, N., Banerjee, P., Banerjee, A., Dech, F.: A Comparative Study of Assembly Planning in Traditional and Virtual Environments. IEEE Transactions on System, Man and Cybernetics 29(4), 546–555 (1999)
27. Zachmann, G., Rettig, A.: Natural and Robust Interaction in Virtual Assembly Simulation. In: Proc. Eighth ISPE International Conference on Concurrent Engineering: Research and Applications ISPE/CE 2001 (July 2001)
28. Zhang, Y., Sotudeh, R., Fernando, T.: The use of visual and auditory feedback for assembly task performance in a virtual environment. In: SCCG 2005: Proc. 21 spring conference on Computer graphics, pp. 59–66 (2005)

A Mixed Reality-Based Assembly Verification and Training Platform

Shiqi Li, Tao Peng, Chi Xu, Yan Fu, and Yang Liu

School of Mechanical Science & Engineering, Huazhong University of Science & Technology, Wuhan, Hubei Province, 430074, China
sqli@mail.hust.edu.cn, pntao@smail.hust.edu.cn,
tomxu2008@yahoo.com.cn, laura_fy@mail.hust.edu.cn,
liuyang-hust@tom.com

Abstract. Mixed reality (MR) based human-machine interaction provides a seamless interface between user and application environment, which synthesizes the advantages of the convenient interaction of virtual reality, and the strong realistic of augmented reality. In this paper, MR is applied in the context of industrial assembly process, and a MR based assembly verification and training platform is proposed. In the MR based assembly environment, virtual model, real images and augmented information are jointly displayed on the assembly scene, accessorizing multi-video display windows of different angles of view to browse the real assembly scene. Additionally, constraint proxies figuratively reconstruct part's constraint relationship in the MR environment, and avoid the complex calculation of constraint's match. By using a virtual hand with constraints guided to assemble, an effective and realistic assembly process experience is provided to the user.

Keywords: Mixed reality; Virtual assembly; Assembly verification; Assembly training.

1 Introduction

Modern design practice demands that the entire life cycle of a product be considered during the design stage. This requires that engineers be forward thinking and predict and design for the various stages of a product's life, from initial manufacturing a product to service, maintenance, and final disposal or recycling. In recent years, computers have provided engineers with increased computational capability and software tools that can assist in the design and testing of a product. Using the computer as a tool, researchers have developed virtual environments, which allow more realistic human-computer interactions and have become increasingly popular for engineering applications such as computer-aided design and process evaluation. Numerous virtual environments for assembly analysis exist or are under development, such as U.S. Washington State University's VADE system [1], Germany University of Bielefeld's CODY system [2], the U.S. University of Maryland's VTS system [3], China Zhejiang University's VDVAS system [4]. Milgram [5] firstly named the continuum of real-to-virtual environments as mixed reality (MR), referring to the merging of real and

R. Shumaker (Ed.): Virtual and Mixed Reality, LNCS 5622, pp. 576–585, 2009.

virtual worlds to produce new environments and visualizations, where physical and digital objects co-exist and interact in real time. With the help of MR technology, physical assembly space can be enhanced with various useful digital contents [6].

MR technology has offered a new low-cost and fast means for solving the problem of products assembly, and potential applications can be concluded into the following aspects: assembly feature design, assembly sequence evaluation, assembly training, assembly task guidance, and assembly inspection. In a MR system for assembly task application, MR displays can enhance the user's perception of the physical assembly working space and assembly constraint feature between virtual/physical parts, providing access to information the user can not directly perceive when unaided, while significantly shortening the time for skills training. We constructed a MR-based assembly verification and training platform, which provide the functions of automatic assembly demonstration, virtual hand operation, and augmented assembly guide. The platform has continued to use traditional mutual ways such as fictitious hands, the fictitious menu. Then the knowledge of assembling process in the virtual environment is presented to tip and guide users. At the same time with parts assembly constraints and matching rules to guide the assembly movement of virtual hand, it offers operator convenient assembly training experience.

2   Constraint Guided Assembly Verification

Geometric constraints are the necessary interactive ways to achieve precision operation directly in a virtual environment [7]. This paper created an assembly interactive method with virtual hand, under the guidance of assembly constrains. Using data glove and position tracker (Flock of Birds, FOB), relationship between real hand and virtual hand model in the assembly system can be established. Then the virtual hand comes to operate the virtual parts in accordance with the assembly demand, by the assist function of constraint capture and position.

2.1   Constraint Proxy and Assembly Positioning

In the CAD system, the assembly constraint information is included in the entity models, and the constraint relations between two geometric entities are identified by the fixed ID numbers. However, in a virtual assembly system, the geometric model based on surfaces does not contain any constraint information. In order to achieve the precise assembly in the virtual environment, we adopt a method on the basis of the proxy [8], which we named constraint proxy, and then solve the problem. Constraint proxies added on each part, contain the part's geometric constraint information, mainly expressed as plane and axis. It is stored as a serial of points, being extracted and simplified from the CAD system's constraint information. As shown in Fig. 1, it is the effect of constraint proxies added to the virtual parts.

During virtual assembly operating, the pose relations of virtual hands and operator's hands keep identical through the data glove that is worn. Firstly, the system calculates the global posture matrix of crawled part in the virtual environment, and then counts

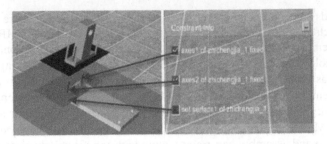

Fig. 1. Constraint proxies and corresponding information menu

the pose relations between the two parts real-time, according to the posture relationship between constraint proxies and virtual parts. Secondly, when the pose relations come to the margin of error advance sited to capture, angle or distance, then the system automatically capture the two constraints. Finally, according to the types of the geometric constant elements, recognition rules of constrain are divided into three kinds of situations:

    ① Plane—Plane: d_{P-P}, the distance from a point in the plane P_a to plane

        P_b; θ_{P-P}, Angle of the two planes;

    ② Plane—Line: d_{P-L}, the distance from a point in the line to the plane; θ_{P-L},

        Angle of the plane and line;

    ③ Line—Line: d_{L-L}, the distance from a point in one line to the other line; θ_{L-L},

        Angle of the two lines。

These angles and distances can be obtained from the known quantity above.

According to combinatorial analysis of axis and level constraint characteristic, we can draw the conclusion that three non-redundant constraints are enough for a full-targeted part [9]. In the assembly design, the Designers should choose no more than three axes or plane constraints, which mean that when the third constraint functions, the part can be totally restrained. This way of locating parts, need minimal maintenance in the process of assembly to realize positioning of the parts. So it is easy to realize the situation of multi-constraints acting on at the same.

2.2 Assembly Process Verification by Virtual Hand

In the process of assembly with virtual hand, the operator controls the movement of virtual hand in the virtual space, which is realized operated by transmitting the hand's operation information to the virtual hand model through the virtual peripheral hardware, to operate the virtual object in accordance with the task of assembly. When the collision happens between the virtual hand and parts, the virtual hand meets certain requirements of the gesture and the system achieves the crawl on parts. Then the component can be a free movement under the driven of virtual hand. When the operator's fingers are open, the assembly releasing operation is realized.

We should first initialize the entire virtual assembly scene, and then obtain the signal of data glove and FOB to drive virtual hand moving. Circular traversing the whole virtual assembly scenes and refreshing the motion state of virtual hand, testing the collision situation between the virtual hand and parts. When the collision occurs, the system judges the conditions of crawl, to solidify the coordinates of virtual part with the virtual hand. Driven with the FOB, virtual part translates and rotates with the virtual hand, thus the crawl operation completes. System traverses all the components that have already been assembled, and analyze the constraints information on these parts to identify the related constraints on the present operation, then it stores them in a constraint chain form which is waiting for capture [10]. System measures the pose relationship between the assembly part and goal part. When the two meet the error requirement scheduled, the constraints identified it and pose of the assembly part adjust. On the function of constraints, the movement of part is no longer driven solely by the virtual hand, but carried on the movement of navigating under constrains function. After constrains are confirmed sequentially, the system removes the consolidated relation between virtual hand and part which is assembled to the final position. Then destroy current operation related dynamic chain forms, virtual hand into the state of freedom of movement, and get ready for the assembly of the next part.

3 Information Augmentation for Assembly Training

During the virtual assembly-oriented training process information is indispensable and very important. In order to make it easier for operators to perceive the product assembly sequence and the effect, and complete the assembly process, it is necessary to display the assembly information in the virtual assembly environment, including step information, part information, path information and constraint information which can be acquired from CAD system and assembly planning system and organized according to the assembly information model.

3.1 Assembly Information Model

Information for virtual assembly environment is used mainly in assembling training and operating feedback, and provides user with a better understanding of the relationship between the parts in scene. These information are made up of four main aspects of components, assembly process information, part manage information, part geometric information and part topological information. We adopt the modeling method of the level [11] to built an assembly information model covered the information needed to strengthen in the virtual assembly scene, and described inter-relationship among the various information in the model. As shown in Fig. 2, we further refined the assembly process information and the part topological information, and assigned all the assembly information to three levels, assembles layer, parts layer and features layer. There are mapping relations among the three layers.

Every assembly steps in the assembly layer is corresponding to a definite part in the part layer, and each part includes a lot of definite characteristics in the feature layer. Starting from the assembly layer, we can get all the information needed by performing assembly step. This information is extracted sequentially according to the mapping relations among the layers, as the sequences of step ID information and

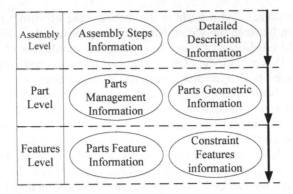

Fig. 2. Assembly information model

detail describe information of current assembly step, management information and geometric information of the part, assembly characteristic information and constraint information of the assembly part at present. We obtained all the assembly information needed by the model from CAD system and the assembly planning system.

3.2 Assembly Information Augmentation

In the virtual assembly scenes, all of the information in the assembly information level model can be summed up as two types, text information and features information. Text information is showed in the virtual scene mainly in three styles, being established as 2D or 3D text model, 3D information frame and text picture. Text model and 3D information frame can be imported directly from outside, and then established dynamically in the virtual scene. However, as the text picture style, the text exists in the form of picture, and it is comparatively difficult to establish it dynamically. So, we mainly adopt the preceding two styles to augment text information in the assembly scene.

Table 1. Parts assemble characteristic expressive methods

Characteristic type	Expressive methods
Axis	Axis, two extreme points P1, P2.
Level	Rectangle, four vertexes P1, P2, P3, P4.
Round cylinder	Two extreme points of centre line P1, P2; Radius r; Initial and stops angles of round cylinder α1, α2.
Sphere	The centre of Sphere O; Radius r.
Conical surface	Two extreme points of centre line P1, P2; Contained angle of axis and conical surface α; Initial and stops angles of conical surface α1, α2.
Regular curved surface	Triangular faces, vertexes meet the curved surface equation.

Augmentation of part assembly characteristic, includes axis, level, cylinder, sphere, etc., need to obtain the parameters of part characteristics, and then they are established dynamically in the virtual assembly scene. As shown in Table 1, it explains the methods to express assemble characteristic of various parts in the virtual assembly scene. Through the method of expressing assembly characteristic, as shown in Table 1, we can establish the augmented characteristic into virtual assemble scene. To display characteristics, axis and levels better, they are needed to expand them in the virtual scene.

4 MR-Based Assembly Operation

MR-based assembly combined the characteristics of immersion, interaction and imagination in virtual assembly environment, and the advantages of small scale modeling and high sense of reality in augmented reality technology, aiming at reducing costs and improving efficiency of production. In this paper, we analyzed the integration of virtual-physical scenes in augmented assembly system. The integration technology contains assembly model, augmented registration and video overlay.

4.1 MR-Based Assembly Modeling

MR-based assembly, a virtual assembly environment and human-computer interface using the virtual reality technology, superimposes virtual models, geometric features and information to the real assembly scene with augmented reality technology. With the real working scene window created in virtual assembly scene, it provided users with a virtual and real dual-channel visual experience and assembly navigation. MR models mainly include geometric model, the assembly constraint model and assembly level model.

From the solid model of CAD system, virtual assembly system extracts geometric information of parts, coordinates information, and assembles features information, then uses them assembly modeling. Parts geometric model have three main formats, that is, wire-frame model, the surface model and solid model. Assembly constraint model defined parts assembly features, constraints and pose matrix. In this paper, a chain structure [10] was used to organize and manage all constraint objects. Each constraint target has a unique number in the library, and is defined among the geometric elements of two parts. We use the tree-level assembly model describing the level of relations, mainly contains four kinds information of parts geometric model, spatial matrix, the assembly of characteristics and virtual or real signs of discrimination.

4.2 Integration of Virtual and Physical

To begin with, a virtual assembly scene as same as the real assembly scene is constructed. Then video signals captured from real scene cameras are processed with computer vision technique to process the image, extract element features, and calibrate the camera parameters as the translation and rotation of the camera with respect to the real scene. With the determined extrinsic camera parameters, it is able to register the virtual scene to the system and to determine the pose and gesture of virtual object. By real-time generating and rendering components in the virtual assembly

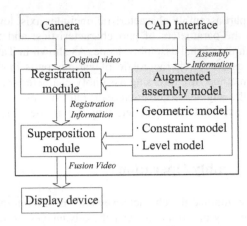

Fig. 3. Mixed reality assembly process

scenes, virtual scenes and real scenes merged together, then registration and superposition of virtual scene with real scene captured from video cameras realized. The process of MR-based assembly is shown in Fig.3.

For the contents of MR-based assembly scene superposed, the real part image is from the video of camera directly, and the virtual part images is produced and superposed from computer to the real scene. Superposing geometric model of virtual part, need to use part's registration information, projecting and transforming triangulated-surface model of part to the image plane of camera. Augmented text information, such as the name of product, ID number, assembling step information, position information, etc., was converted to digital maps in the process of superposing, and merge into MR scene piecemeal. Superpose to assemble characteristic information of vertex, surface and edge, adopt a firm way to unite information with part geometric model. The information changes with the part geometric models at the same time. An example for the mixed reality process is shown in Fig.4.

Fig. 4. An example for the mixed reality process

5   Prototype MR-Based Assembly Platform

We have developed a MR-based assembly verification and training system on the development platform of Microsoft Visual C++ 6.0. CAD model of the parts are established in Pro/Engineer Wildfire 2.0, and revealed in Open Inventor scene in the

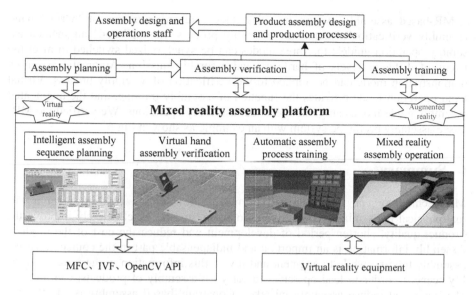

Fig. 5. Systematic structure of MR-based assembly platform

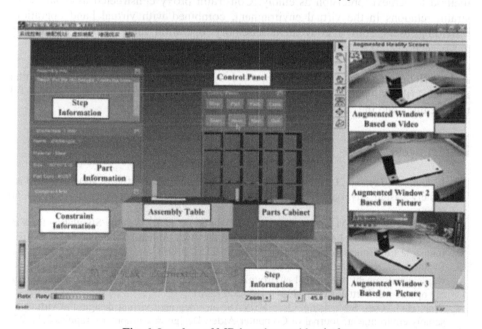

Fig. 6. Interface of MR-based assembly platform

form of IV file. Assembly feature rendering and depth image achievement by OpenGL; capturing video from camera by DirectShow; image processing and occlusion handling by open-source library OpenCV. Physical scene video is captured by camera, and virtual scene is generated by pc. The MR-based assembly platform structure is shown in Fig. 5.

MR-based assembly system provides three interactive modes of "virtual hand assembly verification", "automatic assembly process training" and "augmented assembly operation guide"; the three modes can be synchronized switched to meet the needs of different levels of hardware and assembly mission. Automatic assembly demonstration mode can be applied to the verification of assembly process. Virtual hand operation mode provides the function of assembly training, and the augmented assembly guide mode can guide the actual assembly operations. We verified the MR-based assembly prototype system with an example as show in Fig.6.

6 Summary

MR technology can be implicated in industrial assembly field to form a virtual/physical parts mixed assembly environment, and it can effectively improve the product quality, shorten period of development and reduce the cost of the product. Assembly information is an important and indispensable part in the course of virtual assembly training while to augment and reveal this information in the virtual assembly scene, in order to lead operators to carry on assembly of products, can improve efficiency and reduce assembly mistake. Constraint-based assembly is an effective method to achieve precision assembly. Constraint proxy constructed assembly constraint relations in the virtual environment, combined with virtual hand operation, providing users both a convenient assembly operation and realistic assembling experience.

Acknowledgments. The work is supported by the basic research project of China national 11th five-year plan (Grand No. B1420060173). The authors are also grateful to the editors and the anonymous reviewers for helpful comments.

References

1. Jayaram, S., Jayaram, U., Wang, Y., Tirumali, H., Lyons, K., Hart, P.: VADE: a virtual assembly design environment. IEEE Computer Graphics and Applications 19(6), 44–50 (1999)
2. Jung, B., Latoschik, M., Wachsmuth, I.: Knowledge -Based Assembly Simulation for Virtual Prototype Modeling. In: Proceedings of the 24th Annual Conference of the IEEE Industrial Electronics Society, vol. 4, pp. 2152–2157 (1998)
3. Brough, J.E., Schwartz, M., Gupta, S.K., Anand, D.K., Kavetsky, R., Pettersen, R.: Towards development of a virtual environment-based training system for mechanical assembly operations. Virtual Reality 11(4), 189–206 (2007)
4. Wan, H.G., Gao, S.M., Peng, Q.S.: VDVAS: an integrated virtual design and virtual assembly environment. Journal of Computer-Aided Design & Computer Graphics 7(1), 27–35 (2002)
5. Milgram, P., Kishino, F.: A taxonomy of mixed reality visual displays. IEICE Trans. on Information and Systems E77-D(12), 1321–1329 (1994)
6. Azuma, R.T.: A survey of augmented reality. J. Presence: Teleoperators and Virtual Environments 6(4), 355–385 (1997)
7. Wang, Y., Jayaram, U., Jayaram, S., Imtiyaz, S.: Methods and Algorithms for Constraint -based Virtual Assembly. Virtual Reality (6), 229–243 (2003)

8. Wang, Q.H., Li, J.R., Gong, H.Q.: A CAD-linked virtual assembly environment. Int. J. Prod. Res. 44(3), 467–486 (2006)
9. Wang, Y.: Physically Based Modeling in Virtual Assembly. Ph.D. dissertation, Washington State University (1998)
10. Xia, P.J., Yao, Y.X., Liu, J.S., Li, J.G.: Virtual Assembly Process Planning and Training System. Journal of Nanjing University of Science and Technology 29(5), 570–574 (2005)
11. Didier, S., Gudrun, K., Dirk, R.: A Fast and Robust Line-based Optical Tracker for Augmented Reality Application. In: Proceeding of the First International Workshop on Augmented Reality, pp. 129–145 (1998)

Trial of Formulating Affordance Features for Product Design

Tamotsu Murakami, Mariko Higuchi, and Hideyoshi Yanagisawa

The University of Tokyo, Department of Engineering Synthesis, 7-3-1 Hongo,
Bunkyo-ku, Tokyo 113-8656, Japan
murakami@mech.t.u-tokyo.ac.jp

Abstract. The aim of this research is to formulate relationships between the geometrical attributes of objects and affordance for operations as affordance features. If affordance features are well formulated, then they will allow designers to strengthen intended affordances for higher usability of products or to systematically examine and achieve product or interface shapes with both high usability and aestheticity or novelty. In this paper we show some affordance features and their relationships with quantitative conditions obtained from an analysis of user tests involving sample objects of various shapes.

Keywords: Affordance, feature, product design, usability, emotional design.

1 Introduction

The concept of "affordance" has been proposed and used in the fields of psychology and human interfaces. Affordance is defined as all possible actions latent in the environment that are objectively measurable and independent of the individual's ability to recognize them but are always in relation to the actor and therefore dependent on their capabilities [1], or those possible actions that are readily perceivable by an actor and are dependent not only on the physical capabilities of the actor, but also their goals, plans, values, beliefs and past experience [2][3]. If affordance is appropriately utilized in product design, people can intuitively understand the usage of the product and can easily use it, whereas inappropriate affordance may lead to incomprehensibility of the product and mistakes in its usage.

On the other hand, the concept of a "feature" has been proposed and used in the fields of machine design and CAD (computer-aided design). A feature is defined as a geometric form or entity that is meaningful to one or more design or manufacturing activities (i.e., function, manufacturability evaluation and serviceability) and is used to denote some aspect of a real-world entity of interest in a process [4]. A feature can be used as a type of heuristic method to formulate a relationship between object properties and human thought and activities.

The purpose of this study is to formulate the relationship between the geometrical attributes of an object and affordance regarding its operations, referred to as "affordance features". The formulation of affordance features may lead to the following merits in a product design process.

R. Shumaker (Ed.): Virtual and Mixed Reality, LNCS 5622, pp. 586–595, 2009.

– Designers can systematically verify the effect of affordance intentionally embodied for product usability [5] and detect unintentionally or accidentally existing wrong affordance that reduces product usability based on affordance features.
– Designers can obtain indications of how to reinforce their intended affordance or to weaken unintended or accidental wrong affordance to improve product usability by adding or removing the corresponding affordance features of the product.
– Designers can systematically examine and design a product in which high usability, aestheticity and novelty coexist.

2 Experiments and Shape Samples

2.1 Basic Approach of This Study

There is a related work exploring participant behavior arising from various characteristics (size, texture, color/pattern, weight, sound) of a shape (cube) [6]. In this study, we prepared parametric variations of samples of various shapes made of the same material (ABS plastic) (Fig. 1(a)(b)) by a rapid prototyping system (Stratasys FDM-8000). We showed the shapes oriented horizontally one by one (Fig. 1(c)) to examinees (masters course and undergraduate students in the mechanical engineering department) and asked the question: Suppose this object is an operator of some system. When you see this operator, which operation do you intuitively feel is possible? Choose up to two from the following: "push", "pull", "turn", "tilt", "slide", "other operation (please specify)", "none". Also, we asked the examinees to operate the object in the way they felt it should be operated, and we recorded the operation on a video for additional analyses afterwards. We gave a score of 2 points to their first choice from the above list and 1 point to their second choice, summed the scores for all operations for every sample shape and statistically analyzed the relationships between examinees' answers and the geometrical attributes of the samples used in the experiments [7].

2.2 Experiment 1 on Frustum-Shaped Samples

In this study, we made four types of samples based on different shapes for use in the experiments. The first three types were frustum-shaped samples. For each of the quadrilateral, isosceles triangular and elliptical frustums, we made 27 samples with 4 parameters, each taking 3 values (Table 1). We used the data for elliptical samples from our previous laboratory study [8]. The numbers of examinees were 12, 22 and 13 for experiments 1-Q (Jul. 2006), 1-T (Nov. 2006) and 1-E (Dec. 2005), respectively. For isosceles triangular samples, we considered the possibility that the affordance may depend on the orientation of the triangle, i.e., whether or not the triangle is inverted relative to the examinee. Therefore, we divided the 22 examinees into 2 groups and showed one group samples with the upright triangular orientation and one group samples with the inverted triangular orientation.

(a) Quadrilateral frustum samples.   (b) Triangular frustum samples.   (c) Experiment.

Fig. 1. Appearance of frustum-shaped samples

Table 1. Frustum-shaped samples (experiment 1)

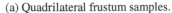

Experiment and sample shape	(1-Q) Quadrilateral	(1-T) Triangular	(1-E) Elliptical
Parameters	l_q = 10, 20, 40mm w_q = 10, 20, 40mm	l_t = 10, 20, 40mm θ = 30, 60, 120°	d_e = 10, 20, 40mm h_e = 5, 10, 30mm
	h_{qt} = 10, 25, 100mm, t_{qt} = 0.8, 1, 1.5		e = 0.3, 0.6, 1 t_e = 0, 1, 2
Square rate	min(l_q,w_q)/max(l_q, w_q)	min(l_n,w_t)/max(l_n,w_t)	e

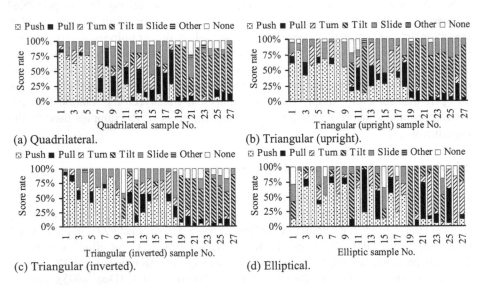

(a) Quadrilateral.

(b) Triangular (upright).

(c) Triangular (inverted).

(d) Elliptical.

Fig. 2. Aggregated answers for experiment 1 (experiments 1-Q, 1-T and 1-E)

The operation preferences of all examinees were aggregated by the scores obtained for each type of sample as shown in Fig. 2. For example, most examinees tended to push quadrilateral sample 1 whereas they tended to tilt sample 27, which indicates that the geometrical attributes have an effect on the answers.

2.3 Experiment 2 on Regular Polygonal and Circular Samples

The fourth type of samples were regular polygonal (triangular, square, pentagonal and hexagonal) and circular (Table 2, Fig. 3(a)). To give the impression of an equal horizontal cross-section area for each regular polygon and circle, we used the mean of the circumscribed and inscribed circle diameters of regular polygons (radius in the case of a circle) as the horizontal size factor. For regular polygonal samples, we considered the possibility that the affordance may depend on the orientation of the polygon, and we made two oppositely oriented samples for every polygon. By assigning one value to the height and three values to the mean diameter for every polygon and circle, we made 27 samples. The number of examinees was 11 for experiment 2 (Jan. 2007).

The answers obtained from all examinees were aggregated as shown in Fig. 3(b), which also indicates that the geometrical attributes have an effect on the answers.

Table 2. Regular polygonal and circular samples (experiment 2)

Horizontal section shape	Triangular	Square	Pentagonal	Hexagonal	Circular
Parameters	height h_r = 25mm, mean of circumscribed and inscribed circle diameters d_r = 24, 36, 48mm				

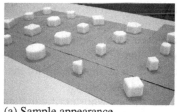

(a) Sample appearance.

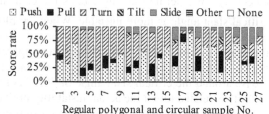

(b) Aggregated answers for experiment 2.

Fig. 3. Regular polygonal and circular samples

3 Affordance Feature of "Tilt"

3.1 Correlation between Affordance of "Tilt" and Instability of Shape

We analyzed the results in Fig. 2 and obtained the results shown in Fig. 4, indicating that samples of greater height obtained higher scores for "tilt". Furthermore, the recorded video indicates that examinees tended to tilt samples in the direction in which the shape was thin. These results indicate that being tall and thin, i.e., physically unstable (easily toppled), is relevant to the affordance of "tilt".

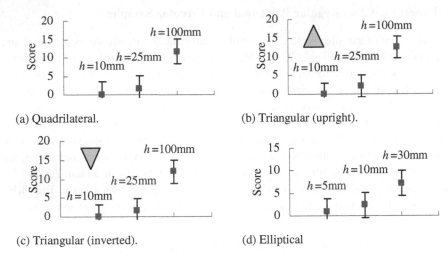

(a) Quadrilateral.   (b) Triangular (upright).

(c) Triangular (inverted).   (d) Elliptical

Fig. 4. Effect of sample height on "tilt" score

To confirm this quantitatively, we defined the critical slant angle of a shape (Fig. 5(a)). When we incline a 3D shape by angle ϕ_g so that the center of gravity is moved to a position above the boundary of the base (to be precise, its convex hull), the shape is in an unstable state (a critical state where the shape begins to topple spontaneously). We define this angle ϕ_g as the critical slant angle. A shape with a lower critical slant angle is more unstable. When we plot the relationship between the critical slant angle and the obtained score for "tilt" for the samples in Table 1, we obtain the graph shown in Fig. 5(b). There is an apparent negative correlation between the critical slant angle and the score for "tilt", and it appears that the score starts to increase around the critical slant angle of 30°. Therefore, we assume that the affordance of "tilt" is related to not the actual instability but the perceived instability.

To verify this assumption, we prepared figures of nine shapes whose critical slant angles were distributed almost uniformly from 15° to 60°. We showed the figures pairwise to examinees, based on a paired comparison method, and asked them to evaluate the relative stability of the two shapes on a five-point scale. By analyzing the result (Fig. 6), we found that the correlation coefficient between critical slant angle and perceived instability was $R = -0.93$ and that the border between perceived stability/instability was at about 30°, which supports our assumption.

Here is a summary of this section.

− The affordance feature of "tilt" is often attributed to shapes with a critical slant angle of less than about 30°.
− The reason for this is thought to be that a critical slant angle of about 30° may be the border at which a shape is perceived as stable or unstable. This result may be used for not only providing affordance but also in the perceptual and psychological design of shapes.

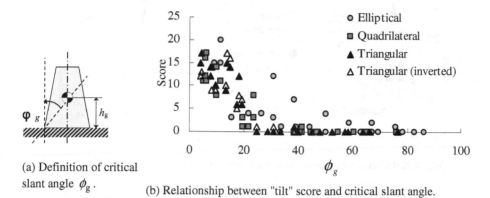

(a) Definition of critical slant angle ϕ_g.

(b) Relationship between "tilt" score and critical slant angle.

Fig. 5. Relationship between geometrical attribute and "tilt"

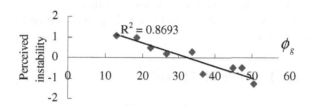

Fig. 6. Relationship between perceived instability and critical slant angle

3.2 Effect of Triangle Orientation

The recorded video of the experiment using triangular frustum samples indicates that the examinees tended to tilt the sample differently depending on the angle θ of the isosceles triangle (Table 1). Here we define the direction parallel to the shorter of l_n and w_t of the isosceles triangle in Table 1 as the "short direction" and the direction parallel to the longer of l_n and w_t as the "long direction". By classifying the scores based on the direction in which examinees tilted triangular frustum samples, we obtain Fig. 7. Here we observed the following tendency regardless of whether the shapes were presented to the examinees as an upright triangle or inverted triangle

- For samples of $\theta = 120°$ (obtuse triangle), most examinees tilted the samples in the short direction.
- For samples of $\theta = 30°$ (acute triangle), some examinees tilted the samples in the short direction and others tilted them in the long direction.

Triangular frustum samples are toppled more easily in the short direction than in the long direction. An isosceles triangle can also be represented by the direction from the center of its base to its vertex, identical to the direction indicated by a triangular arrow symbol. We define this direction as the "arrow direction" of the triangle. The above observations may be explained as follows.

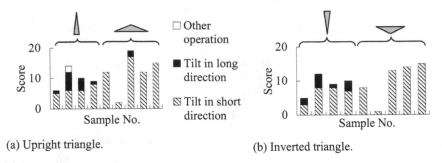

(a) Upright triangle.   (b) Inverted triangle.

Fig. 7. Relationship between geometrical attribute and "tilt" (triangular frustum)

– For samples of $\theta = 120°$, the toppling direction and the arrow direction defined above coincide.
– For samples of $\theta = 30°$, the toppling direction and the arrow direction are orthogonal; thus, there were two possible directions of tilting.

This observation suggests that both the toppling direction and the arrow direction may affect the affordance of tilt.

4   Affordance Feature of "Turn"

4.1   Quadrilateral and Elliptical Frustum Shapes

In Table 1 we define the square rate of the horizontal cross section of the samples. The square rate has a maximum value of 1 when the cross section is a square or circle, and takes a smaller value when the cross section is longer and narrower.

Here we define a space with length $\max(l_q, w_q)$ for the horizontal cross section of quadrilateral samples plotted on the x-axis and the square rate of the cross section plotted on the y-axis. When we represent the scores for "turn" for all quadrilateral samples by the area of a circle and plot them in the space, we obtain the result in Fig. 8(a). Similarly, we define a space where the x-axis is the major axis d_e of elliptical samples and the y-axis is the square rate. When we represent the scores for "turn" for all elliptical samples by the area of a circle and plot them in the space, we obtain the result in Fig. 8(b). These results indicate that the examinees tended to turn the quadrilateral samples when they were longer and narrower, whereas they tended to turn the elliptical samples when they were more circular. Although this result may be supported by the existence of dials in the shape of a quadrilateral frustum as shown in Fig. 8(c), it is possible that either such dials are designed on the basis of human behavior, exemplified by the answers of the examinees, or the examinees' answers are based on their knowledge and experience of such existing dials.

4.2   Triangular Frustum Shape

We analyzed the scores for "turn" obtained for the triangular samples. The result indicates that the orientation of the triangle affects the affordance of "turn" as follows.

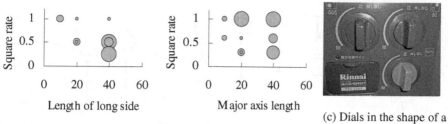

(a) Quadrilateral frustum. (b) Elliptical frustum. (c) Dials in the shape of a quadrilateral frustum.

Fig. 8. Relationship between geometrical attributes and "turn" (quadrilateral and elliptical frustum)

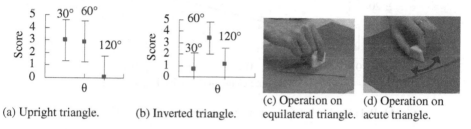

(a) Upright triangle. (b) Inverted triangle. (c) Operation on equilateral triangle. (d) Operation on acute triangle.

Fig. 9. Relationship between geometrical attribute and "turn" (isosceles triangular frustum)

- When upright triangular samples are presented, the examinees turned acute ($\theta = 30°$) and equilateral ($\theta = 60°$) samples but did not turn obtuse ($\theta = 120°$) samples (Fig. 9(a)).
- When inverted triangular samples are presented, the examinees turned equilateral ($\theta = 60°$) samples but did not turn acute ($\theta = 30°$) or obtuse ($\theta = 120°$) samples (Fig. 9(b)).

To find the reason for this difference, we observed the recorded video and noticed that many examinees held equilateral triangular samples in a "surrounding" manner as shown in Fig. 9(c), whereas they held acute triangular samples in a pinching manner as in Fig. 9(d). It appears that the orientation of the triangle does not have a significant difference when holding it in a surrounding manner. However, it is more natural to hold acute upright triangular samples in a pinching manner than inverted triangular samples because the former looks like the direction indicator of a rotating dial. Also, it may be easier to grip an upright triangle than an inverted triangle by pinching without slipping.

4.3 Regular Polygonal and Circular Shapes

By plotting the scores for "turn" for regular polygonal and circular samples in Table 2, we obtain Fig. 10. Basically, regular polygons with more edges obtain higher scores for "turn". This tendency is applicable to a square when it is oriented as a diamond (so that its one of its vertices is toward the examinees), but not applicable when

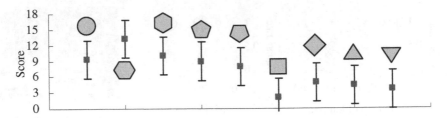

Fig. 10. Relationship between geometrical attribute and "turn" (regular polygonal and circular samples)

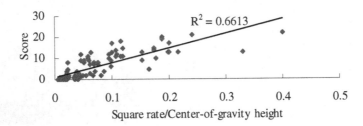

Fig. 11. Relationship between square rate/center-of-gravity height and "push"

it is placed as a square (oriented so that one of its edges is toward the examinees). A possible reason for this difference is that the horizontal and vertical edges of a square may give a stronger impression of stability than the slanted edges of a diamond. Similarly, the circle obtains rather small scores, in contrast to the overall tendency. A possible reason for this difference is that a circle has the affordance of not only "turn" but also other operations such as "push" (as explained later in Fig. 11), and thus the scores are divided between various affordances, reducing their values.

5   Affordance Feature of "Push"

By analyzing the scores for "push" for quadrilateral, triangular and elliptical samples, we obtained the result that the height and horizontal cross section shape affect the score for "push". Samples of lower height obtain higher scores for "push". Regarding the horizontal cross section shape, squares, regular triangles and circles, which have high square rates, obtain higher scores than other quadrilateral, triangular and elliptical shapes. Therefore, we plot the results for quadrilateral, triangular and elliptical samples on a plane where the x-axis is square rate / center-of-gravity height and the y-axis is the score for "push" (Fig. 11). The correlation coefficient between square rate / center-of-gravity height and the score for "push" was $R = 0.81$, indicating a reasonably strong positive correlation. Thus, shapes with a lower center of gravity and a horizontal cross section with a higher square rate may have the affordability of "push".

6 Conclusions

In this study, we proposed and investigated the concept of affordance features, which are the affordances for specific operations, on the basis of the geometrical attributes of objects.

Through experiments using quadrilateral, triangular and elliptical frustum-shaped samples and regular polygonal and circular samples and analyses based on the experimental results, we demonstrated the possibility of formulating the affordance features of "tilt", "turn" and "push" both qualitatively and quantitatively.

This paper is our first trial of formulating affordance features, and our future direction of research will include the following issues.

- Consideration of not only the geometrical attributes of shapes but also the context of operations (e.g., goals, plans and past experience).
- More systematic experiments and analyses with a larger number of examinees.
- Verification of our formulation by applying formulated affordance features to some design problems.

References

1. Gibson, J.J.: The Ecological Approach to Visual Perception. Houghton Mifflin, Boston (1979) (Japanese Translation)
2. Norman, D.A.: The Psychology of Everyday Things. Basic Books, New York (1988) (Japanese Translation)
3. Norman, D.A.: Affordances, Conventions, and Design. Interactions, pp. 38–42 (May/June 1999)
4. Dixon, J.R., Cunningham, J.J., Simmons, M.K.: Research in Designing with Features. In: Yoshikawa, H., Gossard, D. (eds.) Intelligent CAD, I, pp. 137–148. North-Holland, Amsterdam (1989)
5. ISO 9241-11: Ergonomic Requirements for Office Work with Visual Display Terminals (VDTs) - Guidance on Usability (1998)
6. Sheridan, J.G., Short, B.W., Van Laerhoven, K., Villar, N., Kortuem, G.: Exploring Cube Affordance: Towards a Classification of Non-verbal Dynamics of Physical Interfaces for Wearable Computing. In: IEE Eurowearable 2003, pp. 113–118 (2003)
7. Washio, Y.: Introduction to Design of Experiments. Japanese Standards Association, Tokyo (1997) (in Japanese)
8. Liu, M.C.: Research on Formulization of Affordance Features for Design. Graduation Thesis, Department of Engineering Synthesis, The University of Tokyo (2006)

An Empirical Study of Assembly Error Detection Using an Augmented Vision System

Barbara Odenthal, Marcel Ph. Mayer, Wolfgang Kabuß,
Bernhard Kausch, and Christopher M. Schlick

Institute of Industrial Engineering and Ergonomics at RWTH Aachen University,
Bergdriesch 27, 52062 Aachen, Germany
{b.odenthal,m.mayer,w.kabuss,b.kausch,
c.schlick}@iaw.rwth-aachen.de

Abstract. Within the Cluster of Excellence "Integrative Production Technology for High-Wage Countries" of RWTH Aachen University a numerical control unit and its ergonomic human-machine interface are developed for a robotized production unit. In order to cope with novel systems, the human operator will have to meet new challenges regarding the work requirements. Therefore, a first prototype of an augmented vision system to assist the human operator is developed dealing with the task of error detection and identification in an assembly object. Laboratory tests have been performed to find a preferable solution to display information.

Keywords: Augmented Reality, Assembly.

1 Introduction

Within the Cluster of Excellence "Integrative Production Technology for High-Wage Countries" of RWTH Aachen University a numerical control for a robotized production unit cell and an ergonomic human-machine interface are designed and developed.

Based on a representation of the target state (e.g. 3D-assembly object) the numerical control unit itself works out an assembly plan and performs according to it. During the execution, a critical error or mistake can occur that is only qualitatively able to be detected, meaning it is not possible to detect and identify the error. It is only possible to pass information to the skilled worker that an error has occurred. In that case (e.g. mistakes in the plan of the assembly process, mistakes in the implementation of the control programs of the elements of the production plant, unforeseen failure of a machine of the production plant), the error must be identified by the skilled worker in order to be able to correct it. A first prototype of an assistance system is developed dealing with the task of error detection in an assembly object (incorrect construction/composition of the assembly object). More precisely in this case, a prototype of an augmented vision system was developed and implemented with the focus on the presentation of the assembly information. The aim of using this system is to place the human operator in a position to detect the construction errors in a fast and adequate way. Due to this reason, laboratory tests are being performed to find a preferable

R. Shumaker (Ed.): Virtual and Mixed Reality, LNCS 5622, pp. 596–604, 2009.

ergonomic solution to display information. The augmented reality technology in the form of a head mounted display (HMD) has been used for the laboratory tests, so that additional synthetic assembly information or unit information can be displayed in the natural field of view of the human operator next to the real assembly object.

2 Method

Based on the common techniques for designing written assembly instructions from the domain of the technical writing [1], different modes of visual presentation were designed and developed. In general, assembly instructions are synthesized of different information objects: exploded views of parts to be assembled, textual or graphical step-by-step instructions of the assembly procedure, wiring diagrams, schematics, rules, shipment, assembly tools etc. [1], [4], [5]. Regarding the assistance system to detect assembly errors, the exploded views and graphical step-by-step instructions are considered [8]. The parts were modeled as 3D solids and were displayed in 3D stereo.

2.1 Experimental Design

The experimental design distinguishes three factors (each with two levels) representing different modes of presentation (and interaction) of synthetic assembly information, see Fig. 1: the so-called augmented vision mode (factor AVM), the a priori presentation of the goal state of the completely assembled LEGO model (factor APP), and the mode for interactively composing and decomposing the LEGO model during the error detection and identification process (factor DCM).

A full factorial design with repeated measures was used in the laboratory study and therefore eight experimental (2 x 2 x 2) conditions were distinguished.

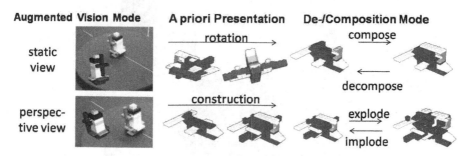

Fig. 1. Factors and factor levels in the laboratory study

Augmented Vision Mode (AVM):

1. Perspective View: The virtual LEGO model is aligned with the position and orientation of the real object in the field of view and is positioned to its left at a distance of 4 cm. A motion of the real model or a head movement leads to the redrawing of the virtual model, so that the perspectives accord.

2. Static View: In this case the virtual LEGO model is fixed to a position relative to the screen coordinates of the HMD. In the experiments the virtual object was displayed under an inclination angle of 20 degrees to its vertical axis in the third quadrant of the binocular screens.

A Priori Presentation (APP):

1. Rotation: the completely assembled virtual LEGO model rotates once on a predefined rotation axis with an inclination angle of 20 degrees and an angular velocity of 3.2 seconds for 360 degrees.
2. Construction: the virtual model is composed step-by-step by the single bricks with a cycle time of 1.2 seconds per element.

Decompostion/Composition Mode (DCM):

1. Step-by-step: the user can interactively decompose or compose the virtual LEGO model in relation to the goal state step-by-step and self-paced using two keys on a tablet.
2. Exploded view: the user is able to interactively either explode or implode the virtual model using a different key on a tablet.

2.2 Apparatus

The LEGO models with the assembly errors to be detected were placed on a small turntable (Fig. 2, left). The position and orientation of the HMD and the small turntable were tracked by the infrared real time tracking system smARTtrack of A.R.T. GmbH. A binocular optical see-through Head Mounted Display (nVisorST by NVIS Inc.) was used to display the synthetic assembly information.

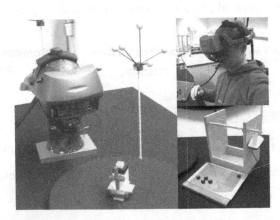

Fig. 2. Main components of the Augmented Vision System

A color marker pen was used by the subjects to mark the assembly error directly by hand on the corresponding LEGO brick. The pen was located behind a transparent lid (Fig. 2, top right). When grasping the pen behind the lid, a microswitch connected to the lid registered the point in time of error detection. The keys for manipulating the virtual LEGO models were mounted on a magnetic key tablet (Fig. 2, top right).

2.3 Procedure

The procedure was divided into two major phases:

1. **Pretests and training under experimental conditions:** First, the personal data were collected, e.g. age, profession, experiences with computers, experiences with virtual and augmented reality systems as well as assembly skills concerning LEGO models. Furthermore, a visual acuity test, a stereo vision test and a color test according to Ishiara are processed by means of a vision test device (Rodatest 302 by Vistec Vision Technologies). Third, the "dice test" of IST 2000-R (module: figural intelligence) [7] was carried out in order to quantify the imagination of spatial visualization. After completing the pretests, the subjects have some minutes to get familiar with the system.

2. **Data acquisition:** Each subject conducted eight trials. The procedure was as follows: Start of trial by the a priori presentation of the goal state of the LEGO model. The virtual assembly sequence was presented to the subjects without having the real object in their field of view. After the a priori presentation of the goal state, the real model with the assembly error was presented on the small turntable by the experimenter. It was possible to manipulate the corresponding virtual object with the keys on the tablet either by stepwise decomposing/composing it or by exploding/imploding it (factor DCM). The subjects could replay the a priori sequence at its full length in between without the possibility to abort the sequence or to further manipulate it. After the detection of the error, the erroneous brick had to be marked with the color marker pen and the difference had to be written down on an error identification sheet. It was possible that the subject could not find any difference between the real and the virtual LEGO model. In this case, it had to be indicated in the error identification sheet as well. Finally, in the post test the participant had to take the HMD off and had to fill in the cited questionnaire about visual fatigue. The total time-on-task was approximately two hours for each participant. The subjects were balanced in the experimental conditions.

2.4 Dependant Variables

The following four dependent variables were considered:

- Detection time: The detection time represents the time elapsed from the trial start until either an assembly error is detected and identified by the participant or the participant indicates the absence of an assembly error. The start and finish events were measured by the introduced apparatus. The detection time was limited to a maximum of 15 minutes.
- Quality of error detection in terms of frequency that the participant detected and identified the error correctly by marking the correct brick in the real model, frequency that the participant detected and identified the error incorrectly by marking an incorrect brick in the real model and frequency that the participant did not detect the error.

2.5 Subjects

A total of 24 subjects, 16 male and 8 female, participated in the laboratory study. All of them satisfied the requirements concerning stereo vision, color vision and em-metropia. Moreover, the imagination of spatial visualization was measured by the means of a "dice test" of IST 2000-R (module: figural intelligence) [7]. On average, the subjects allocated 13 of 20 dices correctly.

The age of the subjects was between 19 and 36 years (mean 26.8 years, SD 4.4). 37.5% of the subjects had prior experience with 3D computer games. The average weekly play time was approx. 4 hours. The average experience in assembling LEGO models was 3 (SD 1.4) on a scale ranging from 0 (low) to 5 (high). Eight persons stated problems in the past after working with electronic information displays.

2.6 Hypotheses

The following null hypotheses were formulated:

- Detection Time: The augmented vision mode (H_{01}), the a priori presentation of synthetic assembly information (H_{02}) and the decomposition/composition mode of the virtual model (H_{03}) do not significantly influence the detection time.
- Frequency of error detection: The augmented vision mode (H_{04}), the a priori presentation of synthetic assembly information (H_{05}) and the decomposition/composition mode of the virtual model (H_{06}) do not significantly influence the frequency of correctly detected and identified errors.

2.7 Correlation

The detection time is not correlated with the imagination of spatial visualization (H_{07}), and the LEGO-assembly experience (H_{08}).

The frequency of error detection is not correlated with the imagination of spatial visualization (H_{09}), and the LEGO-assembly experience (H_{10}).

A three-way analysis of variance (ANOVA) with repeated measures was calculated to test the hypotheses H_{01} - H_{03} (significance level $\alpha=0.05$). The means and the 95% confidence intervals of the detection times under the different experimental conditions are shown in Fig. 3.

In order to investigate the correlation, tests according to Pearson (H_{07}) and Spearman-Rho (H_{08} - H_{10}) were calculated to test the hypotheses (significance level $\alpha=0.05$).

3 Results

3.1 Detection Time

The augmented vision mode (AVM) significantly influenced the detection time ($F(1,22)=8.088$, $p=0.009$), so that null hypothesis H_{01} was rejected. On the other hand, neither the a priori presentation of synthetic assembly information (factor APP) nor

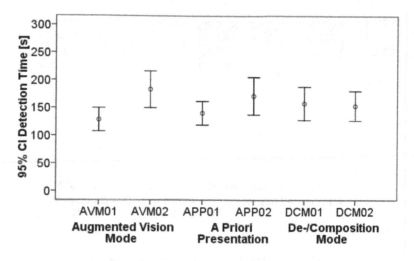

Fig. 3. Detection times [s] under the experimental conditions

the de-/composition mode (factor DCM) had significant effects on the detection time and the null hypotheses H_{02} and H_{03} were not rejected. According to Fig. 3 the average detection time under the static view condition of the augmented vision mode was on average 42.5% longer than under the perspective view condition.

Using the static view mode (instead of the perspective view mode), the users frequently had to process a mental rotation of the virtual LEGO model under consideration during the error search, which is a straining and time consuming operation. Since the classic works of SHEPARD & METZLER (1971) [10] it is known that the reaction time of a subject to decide if two items match or not is proportional to the rotation angle between them and our data confirms these findings. The reaction time also increased with the complexity level of the presented object [3]. The perspective view mode allowed a recognition-primed comparison between the goal and the given assembly state without the need to allocate significant cognitive resources for mental rotations or translations.

3.2 Frequency of Error Detection

According to Fig. 4, when comparing both augmented vision modes, the perspective view mode lead on average to a 19% higher frequency of correctly detected and identified errors than the static view mode. A rotating LEGO model for the a priori presentation of the product structure enabled the users to detect and identify 16% more errors correctly than under the alternative step-by-step construction. The frequency difference between step-by-step decomposition/composition and the exploded view was considerably smaller with 6% for correctly detected and identified errors. However, these frequency differences are not significant and therefore the null hypotheses H_{04}, H_{05} and H_{06} could not be rejected.

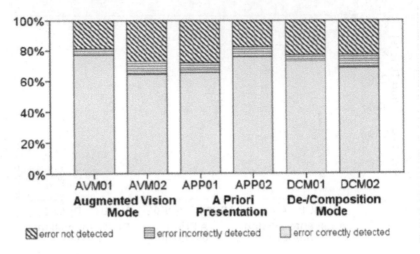

Fig. 4. Frequency of Error

3.3 Correlations

According to Fig. 5, on average, the subjects allocated 13 of 20 dices correctly (65%) regarding the imagination of spatial visualization. The average experience in assembling LEGO models was 3 (SD 1.4) on a scale ranging from 0 (low) to 5 (high).

The correlation between the experience in LEGO-assembly and error detection time (p=0.000) is significant. Hence, the null hypothesis H_{08} was rejected. The null hypotheses $H_{07,}$ H_{09} and H_{10} were not rejected.

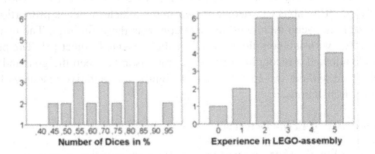

Fig. 5. Frequency of Number of Dices and Experience in LEGO-assembly

In Fig. 6 and Table 1, the weak negative correlation of the experience in LEGO-Assembly and error detection time (correlation coefficient = -0.261) is shown. The laboratory test confirms that a higher experience level leads to a lower detection time. Comparing the detection time of a subject with low experience and subjects with high experience, an average reduction of the detection time of 37.4% can be determined.

Table 1. Correlation Table

		Frequency of Error Detection	Error Detection Time
Experience in LEGO-Assembly	Correlation coefficient	0,014	-0,261*
	Significance level (2-sided)	0,851	0,000
Imagination of spatial visualization	Correlation coefficient	0.049	0.085
	Significance level (2-sided)	0.499	0.240

*) p<0.05 significant.

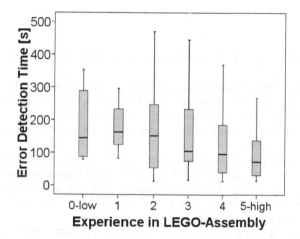

Fig. 6. Correlation between the error detection time and the experience in LEGO-assembly

Because of the fact, that the imagination of spatial visualization has no significant influence on the error detection and the error detection time, the assumption of a homogeny subject group can be confirmed. The differences in the detection time and in the frequency of error detection are due to the influence of the pre-knowledge of the subjects in the area of LEGO-assembly and to the influence of the investigated factors and factor levels (AVM, APP, DCM).

4 Future Work

Within this laboratory study of an augmented vision system, it was shown; that the influence of the augmented vision mode and the pre-knowledge in the area of the LEGO-assembly have significant influences on the error detection time.

Concerning future ergonomic studies of Augmented Vision Systems for self-optimizing assembly cells it is of special interest to analyze more complex work processes going beyond the admittedly simple assembly of LEGO bricks. Therefore, several products of medium complexity, e.g. a motorcycle carburetor, were already analyzed and it is planned to carry out similar laboratory study including also the robot motion. Due to the significant ageing of skilled operators in European manufacturing enterprises it is also of great interest to study age-related effects of visual perception and spatial visual memory when working with Augmented Vision Systems and to adapt the visualization and interaction modes to individual performance and workload.

Acknowledgement

The authors would like to thank the German Research Foundation DFG for the kind support within the Cluster of Excellence "Integrative Production Technology for High-Wage Countries".

References

1. Alred, G.J., Brusaw, C.T., Oliu, W.E.: Handbook of Technical Writing, Bedford/St. Martin's, Boston (2003)
2. Field, A.: Discovering Statistics Using SPSS. Sage Publications Ltd., London (2005)
3. Funke, J., Frensch, P.A.: Handbuch der Allgemeinen Psychologie – Kogition. Hogrefe Verlag GmbH & Co KG, Göttingen (2006) (in German)
4. Inaba, K., Parsons, S., Smillie, R.: Guidelines for Developing Instructions. CRC Press LLC, Boca Raton (2004)
5. Juhl, D.: Technische Dokumentation. Springer, Berlin (2005) (in German)
6. Kempf, T., Herfs, W., Brecher, C.: Cognitive Control Technology for a Self-Optimizing Robot Based Assembly Cell. In: Proceedings of the ASME 2008 International Design Engineering Technical Conferences & Computers and Information in Engineering Conference, American Society of Mechanical Engineers (2008)
7. Liepmann, D., Beauducel, A., Brocke, B., Amthauer, R.: IST 2000 R- Intelligenz Struktur Test 2000 R Manual (2007)
8. Odenthal, B., Mayer, M., Grandt, M., Schlick, C.: Examination of Visual Representation of Assembly Instructions for an Augmented Reality-based Support System of a Cognitive Production System. In: Proceedings of Applied Human Factors and Ergonomics 2nd International Conference, Las Vegas (2008)
9. Rasch, B., Friese, M., Hofmann, W., Naumann, E.: Quantitative Methoden, Band 1+2. Springer, Berlin (2004) (in German)
10. Shepard, R.N., Metzler, J.: Mental Rotation of Three-Dimensional Objects. Science 171(972), 701–703 (1971)
11. Wiedenmaier, S.: Unterstützung manueller Montage durch Augmented Reality-Technologien. Shaker, Aachen (2004) (in German)

Design and Implementation of Augmented Reality Environment for Complex Anatomy Training: Inguinal Canal Case Study

S. Sakellariou[1], B.M. Ward[2], Vassilis Charissis[3], D. Chanock[4], and P. Anderson[3]

[1] Aberdeen Royal Infirmary. Acute Medicine, Aberdeen, UK
s.sakellariou@nhs.net
[2] University of Edinburgh, UK
[3] University of Glasgow/ Glasgow School of Art, Digital Design Studio,
10 Dumbreck Road, G41 5BW, Glasgow, UK
v.charissis@ gsa.ac.uk
[4] Ayr Hospital Department of Radiology, Ayr, UK

Abstract. Adhering to contemporary requirements for reduction of cadaveric training of medical trainees we have developed a prototype augmented reality environment which investigates complex anatomical sections. A human 3D model has been implemented in order to facilitate educational tactics presented in a Virtual Reality (VR) environment. Opting for a sophisticated approach of interaction, the interface elements are based on simplified visual representation of real anatomical elements, and can be operated through haptic devices and surround auditory cues. This paper discusses the challenges involved in the development process of the augmented reality environment, and the HCI design, introduces the visual components of the interface and presents the outcome of a preliminary evaluation of the proposed VR training method on a group of twelve medical doctors. The paper concludes with a tentative plan of future work which aims to expand the context and interactivity of the system so as to enable the trainees to rehearse surgical methods in a simulated VR environment.

Keywords: Virtual Reality, Haptics, HCI, Inguinal Canal, Medical Training.

1 Introduction

The propagation of augmented reality representations and advanced human-computer interaction techniques presented momentous advances in the accretion of knowledge with regards to complex human-body regions [1, 2]. To this point it has to be noted that the knowledge acquisition and ultimately the understanding of such motley three-dimensional subjects typically entails a strong grasp of the 3D anatomy to which it relates [3, 4]. This is compounded when procedural techniques and specialist anatomy are effectively taught simultaneously. It has been shown however, that anatomy learning can be augmented by the use of high resolution 3D models and intuitive human-computer interaction [5, 6, 7, 8]. To this end, we have endeavoured in the investigation of various case studies which incorporate a high level of anatomical

R. Shumaker (Ed.): Virtual and Mixed Reality, LNCS 5622, pp. 605–614, 2009.

complexity which would demand for a highly versatile interface design. One such study, the inguinal canal region, was of particular interest, as the different abdominal layers forming the canal are exceptionally difficult to comprehend spatially.

Adhering to the aforementioned observations, a detailed 3D representation of the inguinal canal and the extended abdominal area was developed through the data acquisition by CT scans, laser scanning and MRI scans, under the consultation of the involved medical doctors. Utilising the departmental VR facilities we developed a custom user-interface which could facilitate a visual, haptic and auditory navigation throught the physical layers of the 3D model. The particular system entails real-time visualisation, gesture interaction with tactile feedback (CyberTouch™ sensored glove) and 3D sound developed around a Fakespace Immersive Workbench.

A comparative study between existing teaching material and the proposed VR training method was deemed necessary in order to identify the potential benefits, if any, of the proposed system.

Overall this study presents a concise but enlightening assessment on the involvement of a VR learning environment and advanced user-interfaces for medical training. The paper explores the empirical evidence regarding 3D visualisation and the enhancement of spatial learning and describes the integration of robust anatomical modeling techniques, intuitive human-computer interfaces (HCI) and current educational theory. The paper concludes with a succinct discussion of the deliverable feedback and suggestions from both trainee and consultant doctors and offers a provisional plan for further development.

2   Inguinal Canal Case Study

The inguinal canal region is broadly perceived in medical education as an explicitly arduous section of the human body; hence the medical doctors involved in this project suggested the particular section for further investigation through an augmented reality environment where physical constrains can be shifted.

The main difficulty towards the understanding of the special relation in –between the different elements occurs predominantly due to the complexity of the layered structure of muscles and fascias involved in the creation of the canal which forms the passage for the spermatic cord. Elaborating in the aforementioned observation it is evident that the male inguinal canal is the route by which the vas deferens and testicular neurovascular bundle passes through the musculature of the anterior abdominal wall. While the functionality of this system could be characterised as trivial in the female version, yet it poses a significant danger, as an area of potential flaws, in both sexes.

These flaws can be encountered typically in the form of three types of hernias which can appear at, or close to the inguinal region. Consequently these hernias can be named after their positioning attributes as direct or indirect inguinal and femoral hernias.

Contemporary educational methods for teaching complex anatomical regions are considered inadequate [1] as they typically lack the depiction of a 3D spatial issue in a three dimensional manner. As such the majority of explanatory illustrations are diagrammatic, 2D representations of pre-determined angles of depiction.

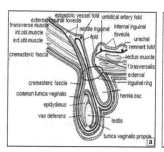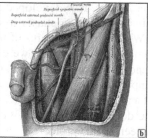

Fig. 1. Samples of teaching illustrations of the Inguinal Canal: (a) Simple 2D diagram, (b) More detailed 2D depiction, and (c) Screenshot from 3D model

Hence it is impossible for the trainee to investigate in depth the layered structures, their spatial relations and visit these complex structures from different angles which might enlighten their perception and understanding. Interestingly the explanatory text and the visual representations of the inguinal canal area appearing in a number of manuscripts are inadequate to convey the complexity and the volume of the information related to this region as presented in Figure 1. In contrary the text describes the position of each of the involved structures in explicit detail, convoluting even further the structural hierarchy of the region.

Notably the 2D representations were intended to be used as preparatory means of information to cadaveric dissections and demonstrations which can effectively present the three-dimensional relationships of the canal walls and openings.

However, the shortage of cadaveric material presented a significant issue in this training method which was inevitably reduced to the 2D representations as the main mean of teaching such regions. In the face of this major concern the only prominent method left to explore, was the digital reconstruction of the human body which offers a better real-life representation as well as a number of tools not applicable to a cadaver (i.e. infinite viewpoints, real-time highlights, colour coding etc.). Furthermore the indestructible ability of the digitised data offers infinite manipulation methods, minimum storage and maintenance requirements.

3   Development of 3D Dataset

Mindful of the aforementioned medical training issues, we opted initially for a realistic, yet stylised 3D representation of the human body, which would offer an uncluttered view (i.e. simplification of vein artery and nerves' routes) of the organs under investigation. The primary target of the evaluation was to highlight the spatial relation between different layers, organs and structures of the body. In order to achieve an adequate detail and precision to the final result we opted for a multidisciplinary group formed by specialists which included 3D visualisation experts, surgeons, anatomists, radiologists, medical educators, programmers, HCI scientists, and Human-Factor engineers. The derived high fidelity 3D representation of the inguinal canal was focused to compliment an existing activity based curriculum.

Adhering to the above objective we have developed a highly detailed 3D model of the inguinal canal region with particular emphasis in enhancing learning of human anatomy for trainee doctors. While the complexity of the human data was simplified we maintained a significant amount of details that were absolutely relevant to a surgical operation in that region and to the proper depiction of the different pathological cases. This exemplifies the importance of this collaborative methodology, and indeed the difference between taught and surgical operative anatomy.

Notably, each opening (the deep and superficial inguinal rings) was developed in order to be easily visible and seen to be "protected" by two of the muscle layers. The muscles and their aponeuroses were clearly defined and two of them (internal oblique and transversus abdominis) could be seen arching over the canal to form its roof and then its posterior wall (conjoint tendon) as depicted in Figure 2.

Particular emphasis was given to the detailed representation of relations between musculoskeletal parts and fascia layers. Furthermore, all the important surgical landmarks were visually clarified to the user. The final 3D model was in turn customised for stereoscopic viewing (Virtual reality representation) and haptic manipulation in an augmented reality facility.

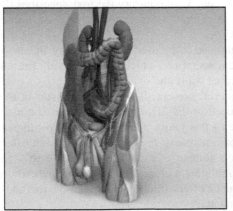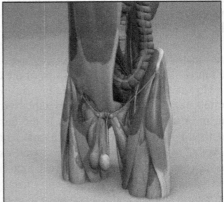

Fig. 2. (a) Real-time transparency change and layer appearance in the 3D Inguinal Canal, (b) Demonstration of different layers appearance and close-up investigation

4   Development of HCI for Medical Teaching

The purpose of developing such advanced VR system was not to exemplify any technological breakthroughs but to enhance the learning process in a very demanding profession. Hence our endeavour had as a main objective to assist this process by meaningful information provided in a simplistic manner. To this point we have to clarify that the proposed VR system did not aim to substitute the existing teaching methods; in contrary it was designed in conjunction to the existing curriculum so as to compliment the existing practices, yet to accelerate the learning progression and mentally imprint the crucial information.

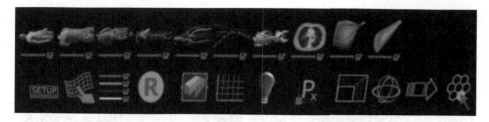

Fig. 3. Augmented Reality HCI: human layers (top), default actions (bottom)

To this end the interface development particularly aimed to depict meaningful information that could enhance the learning process of the trainee doctors in an augmented reality environment. Hence, our focusing point was the interface functionalities, which will enable the trainees to mentally perceive the three-dimensional structure of the human body and navigate through, discovering and understanding convoluted information with regard to complex anatomical regions, such as the inguinal canal.

These interface components present fresh opportunities for the portrayal of information using symbolic and alphanumeric representations and feature an infinite selection of viewing positions than was previously impossible in the cadaver. Our attempt to directly apply publicly accepted interface components to the medical training environment was a challenging process, as the icons had to be designed in accordance to the requirements of each section. To this end the icons were showing miniature representations of the layers as illustrated in the upper toolbar of Figure 3.

This was crucial in order to allow the doctors control of key muscular layers that obstruct ready access during hernia procedures thus allowing unparalleled investigative freedom.

Colour coding was also employed wherever required to aid the understanding of different tissues and functionalities. Notably the development of the 3D model, the VR environment and the proposed HCI aimed to lay the ground for primary laparoscopic surgical rehearsal.

5 Visualisation Requirements

The requirements for visualising and implementing the functionalities of the aforementioned interface were based on hardware equipment existing in the VR facility of Digital Design Studio. The system is designed based on a Fakespace Immersive Workbench and entails real-time visualisation, gesture interaction with tactile feedback (CyberTouch™ sensored glove) and 3D sound as depicted in figure 4 (a, b). Its semi-immersive design is particularly valuable in assisting with small group tutorial requirements.

The physical dimensions and shape of the table offered intriguingly similar position and dimensions to an operation table or an examination bed. For this reason the existing VR and haptic technology was repositioned in order to enhance this feeling, replicating as much as possible the position of a cadaveric examination as depicted in Figure 4.

Fig. 4. a) Haptic interface demonstration for the manipulation of the VR human section (b) The Fakespace Immersive Workbench with the CyberTouch™ sensored glove

The stereoscopic visualisation is provided by CrystalEyes shutter glasses, which could provide the trainee and the trainer to have an overall view of the table but also of the surrounding space and users around the table. However only one pair of glasses could be tracked by the table-sensors (typically the person using the haptic glove); therefore the rest of the viewers should be positioned as close as possible to that operating user in order to avoid visual distortion.

The "physical" interaction between user and the 3D model is achieved with the use of a tracked CyberTouch™ sensored glove with vibro-tactile stimulators on the fingers and palm. This glove can sense the bend and relative position of the fingers and thumb, allowing interaction via gesture; combined with tracking it can sense the hand's position in space, allowing the user to explore and manipulate the digital model directly in 3D space.

Finally 3D spatialised speakers provided the auditory cues. The speakers' network offered sound effects, which signalise a variety of different actions. The depth perception is extensively investigated with sound moves in space appropriate to the manipulation of the model.

6 Experiment Rationale

Subsequently a user-trial experiment was designed in an activity-based curriculum, in order to evaluate the responses of twelve medical trainees. These users were randomly selected to participate in this first phase of the experiment which involved manipulation of the 3D model and identification of each components starting from the pelvis and building up to the skin layer.

The evaluation aimed to contrast the potential benefits and pitfalls of a VR learning environment against the traditional anatomy teaching techniques. Feedback from laparoscopic surgeons was also derived in order to contrast it with the expectations and results of the trainees and their performance using the VR system. Notably the evaluation process involved trainee and fully trained doctors (consultant level) in order to cover both ends of the spectrum.

Their feedback and suggestions formed an initial appraisal of the benefits of the system but also highlighted its potential shortcomings. In general the system was praised for its efficiency in presenting complex 3D data in a comprehensive manner for the user, by circumventing the limitations of the traditional teaching tools. Finally the aforementioned feedback formed our tentative plan for future work which includes further development of the 3D model details and an extensive VR interface to include practical pre-operative surgical rehearsal for core surgical procedures.

The performance of the trainees was measured through a series of pre and post teaching tools as presented below. A usability questionnaire was employed to capture their thoughts and feedback with regards to these two diverse teaching techniques.

1. Pre assess Likert (demographics etc)
2. The pre-assessment quiz (10mins)
3. 5 minutes with the Inguinal Canal activator sheet
4. Intervention (15mins tutorial - focus on the structures on the CT)
5. Post assessment (Inguinal Canal spot test)
6. Usability questionnaire (no limit)

In this paper we are focusing our analysis on the pre and post-assessment results derived by Likert-scale questionnaires which can be indicative of the proposed systems positive aspects as well as the potential arising issues.

7 Results and Discussion

Analysis of the users' pre Likert questionnaires established that the two subgroups were comparable in respect to the following variables: stage of training (all being house officers), previous anatomy training (all being graduates of UK medical schools), exposure to pro-sections and dissections teaching methods (7-11 months), IT literacy, surgical hands-on experience (4-8 months) and focused anatomy training. None has had focused prior training on the inguinal canal region and none had yet attempted the surgical postgraduate exam.

The pre-assess Likert study also explored the users' views on current anatomy teaching and their learning behaviours on interpreting 3D data and complex regional anatomy for clinical use. Their responses were very similar, with no significant differences in p-values (t-Test: two sample assuming equal variance) in any of the attitude determining questions ($p>0.05$) between the subgroups. Notably, the trainees uniformly expressed the view that current anatomy teaching in undergraduate level and during clinical years is fragmented, limited and lacking in depth, whilst the teaching methods were described as time consuming and non-engaging.

The majority of users found it difficult to construct a mental 3D map of the human anatomy from studying 2D models and thus application of their anatomy knowledge in a clinical interpretation scenario was graded as inadequate for their clinical needs. 80% of users strongly agreed that further enhancement of their anatomy training will aid their clinical practice with the remaining agreeing with the aforementioned, but not as strongly. Access to 3D anatomical models for training needs was graded as limited and difficult by all users and they all agreed that anatomy is a hard subject to learn from books.

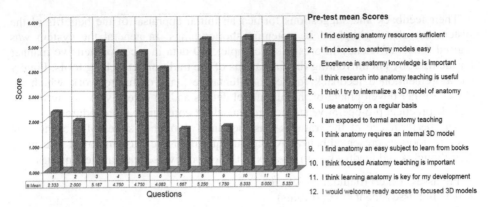

Pre-test mean Scores

1. I find existing anatomy resources sufficient
2. I find access to anatomy models easy
3. Excellence in anatomy knowledge is important
4. I think research into anatomy teaching is useful
5. I think I try to internalize a 3D model of anatomy
6. I use anatomy on a regular basis
7. I am exposed to formal anatomy teaching
8. I think anatomy requires an internal 3D model
9. I find anatomy an easy subject to learn from books
10. I think focused Anatomy teaching is important
11. I think learning anatomy is key for my development
12. I would welcome ready access to focused 3D models

Fig. 5. Pre-test mean scores in all 12 pre-assess Likert questions

The pre-assessment quiz consisted of open questions relating to the anatomy of the inguinal canal region. It aimed to establish the baseline knowledge of the users prior to any intervention and was compared with the post intervention assessment quiz. The aims of the exercise were two-fold: Identify the user's prior pure anatomy knowledge of the region and furthermore elucidate their ability to comprehend how anatomical structures relate to each other in a 3D environment. The latter was assessed by questions referring to space relations of the different structures in the 3D space.

It is of interest to note that overall the pre-intervention scores for both subgroups were disappointingly low, further enhancing the view that anatomy teaching in its current format lacks in its ability to provide in-depth understanding of complex anatomical relationships. Mean scores approached the 50% mark with no significant differences between subgroups (p=0.857) and almost negligible variance scores pre-intervention. Both groups improved on their scores after the teaching intervention, as expected, the traditional method group with a mean improvement in scores of 16%, whilst the VR method group with a mean percentage improvement of 25%. Scores were significantly different between the two groups post intervention (p=0.041) suggesting that users exposed to the VR method accumulated a better understanding of the spatial interrelationships of the structural elements of the canal compared to those taught in the traditional method. Furthermore, on further analysis of particular questions relating purely to the spatial relationship of structures, the VR group had an even higher advantage.

On concluding the experiment all users completed the usability questionnaire, where they were asked to grade their views about the educational approach. 25 statements were graded on a 6 point Likert scale (1 for strongly disagree to 6 for strongly agree). The views of the two groups were markedly different on almost all points with p values less than 0.001 on two sample t-testing. Positively phrased statements regarding the educational approach scored very highly in the VR group whilst scoring low in the traditional method group and vice versa for negatively phrased statements, as has been the case in every other case study we have investigated.

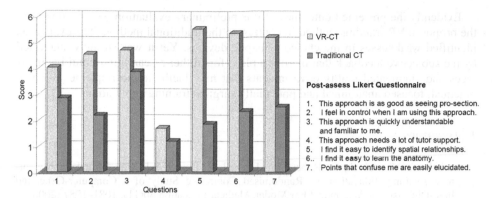

Fig. 6. Post-assess Likert scores in 7 selected questions relevant to the understanding of the 3D anatomical structures and the need of the tutor support

The only points that did not exhibit a significant difference related to the ease of use of the system and the familiarity with the interfaces. Remarkably even in these questions where one would have expected the responses to the VR approach to be more guarded, the responses were overall positive, with the majority of users finding the VR system more engaging, interesting and easy to use and more efficient in elucidating spatial inter-relationships of structures. Users preferred the VR system over traditional teaching methods and they were more inclined to recommend it to their peers (p<0.001 compared to the traditional method group responses) as Figure 5 illustrates.

8 Conclusions

Overall this paper presented the development process and the challenges that rose during the design and implementation of an augmented reality environment, and the HCI design. A succinct but informative introduction to the visual components of the interface offered a clear understanding of the aims of this work which focused primarily in the conveyance of meaningful information to the trainee in subjects that involve complex and convoluted anatomical structures. The suggested interface utilises simplicity to convey as seamlessly as possible the spatial information, facilitates interaction and limits extraneous and unnecessary data while achieving the required fidelity.

A presentation of the educational status quo in medicine offered the background and the reasoning for the development of an augmented reality inguinal canal. To this end it was evident that the present-day trainee remains reliant on inadequate cadaveric exposure, limited two-dimensional resources and inappropriate opportunistic learning through incisional 'windows' in the living patient. In this study we illuminated useful approaches to intuitive design aiming to allow trainees and trainers to maximise learning outcomes. In addition, through the development of appropriate, focused anatomical models we have explored important issues pertaining to the design of practical applications to augment anatomical training which could facilitate in the near future tools also applicable to surgical training in these complex regions.

Evidently the presented outcomes of this preliminary evaluation were in favour of the proposed VR training method in contrast to the traditional method. The evaluation identified weaknesses in the choice of haptic devices. Yet it was strongly suggested by the subjective feedback that there is a place for further research into intuitive interfaces and augmented reality environments that may facilitate the implementation of practical, focused anatomical and potentially surgical training applications.

References

1. Nicholson, D.T., Chalk, C., Robert, W., Funnell, J., Daniel, S.J.: Can Virtual Reality Improve Anatomy Education? A Randomised Controlled Study of a Computer-Generated Three-Dimensional Anatomical Ear Model. Medical Education 40(11), 1081–1087 (2006)
2. Lu, Q., Luo, S.: Primary Research of Digital Atlas of Human Anatomy on Virtual Reality. In: Proceedings of the 2nd International Conference on Bioinformatics and Biomedical Engineering (ICBBE 2008), Shanghai, China, pp. 2442–2445 (2008)
3. Turney, B.W.: Anatomy in a modern medical curriculum. Annals of the Royal College of Surgeons of England 89(2), 104–107 (2007)
4. Charissis, V., Ward, B.M., Naef, M., Rowley, D., Brady, L., Anderson, P.: An Enquiry into VR Interface Design for Medical Training: VR Augmented Anatomy Tutorials for Breast Cancer. In: Proceedings of the International Annual Symposium of SPIE, San Jose, California, USA, January 27-31 (2008)
5. Ornstein, M.H.: Virtual Reality and Laparoscopic Surgery. British Journal of Surgery 82(6), 854–855 (1995)
6. Sang-Hack, J., Bajcsy, R.: Learning Physical Activities in Immersive Virtual Environments. In: IEEE Proceedings of the International Conference on Computer Vision Systems, ICVS 2006, St. Johns University, Manhattan, New York City, USA (2006)
7. Ward, B.M., Charissis, V., Rowley, D., Anderson, P., Brady, L.: An Evaluation of Prototype VR Medical Training Environment: Applied Surgical Anatomy Training for Malignant Breast Disease. In: Proceedings of the 16th International Conference of Medicine Meets Virtual Reality, Long Beach, California, USA (2008)
8. Crossan, A., Brewster, S., Reid, S., Mellor, D.: Multi-Session VR Medical Training – The HOPS Simulator. In: The Proc. of British HCI Conference, London, UK, pp. 213–225. Springer, Heidelberg (2002)

The Use of Virtual Reality in the Treatment of Posttraumatic Stress Disorder (PTSD)

Deanne C. Simms, Susan O'Donnell, and Heather Molyneaux

National Research Council Canada Institute for Information Technology
46 Dineen Drive, Fredericton, New Brunswick, Canada, E3B 9W4
{Deanne.Simms,Susan.ODonnell,Heather.Molyneaux}@nrc-cnrc.gc.ca

Abstract. *Background.* Interest in the treatment of PTSD is increasing with concerns about the psychological effects of war on troops. *Objective.* We performed a comprehensive literature review on virtual reality (VR) for treating combat-related PTSD. *Methods.* Canada's primary institute for scientific and technical information (NRC-CISTI) performed the initial literature search in 2008. Of 296 items which met inclusion criteria, 20 pertained to VR in the treatment of mental health.. An additional 20 more recent items were added in 2009, making a total of 40 items reviewed. Of those, 6 empirical studies involved patients with PTSD [1, 2, 3, 4, 5, 6]. *Results.* VR exposure therapy (VRET) has been successfully used to treat anxiety and phobia disorders including PTSD [7, 8]. VRET may be particularly suitable for clients with combat-related PTSD as it aids in exposure treatments for these clients whom are often unable to engage in traditional therapy [9, 10]. Future research should include randomized, controlled studies employing large samples.

Keywords: Virtual reality, Posttraumatic stress disorder, treatment.

1 Introduction

Post traumatic stress disorder (PTSD) is an anxiety disorder characterized by feelings of intense horror, fear and helplessness as a result of exposure to a traumatic event when one experiences actual or threatened death or serious injury [11]. Individuals with PTSD persistently re-experience the trauma (e.g., nightmares, flashbacks), avoid stimuli that remind them of the trauma and often experience physiological hyper-arousal (e.g., sleep problems, irritability).

PTSD is a public health issue gaining prominence in Canada and many other countries. Since the start of the Canadian mission in Afghanistan, an increasing number of military personnel and veterans have been experiencing PTSD, and their families have been living with the associated stress and challenges. Assessing and treating PTSD is complex and costly. Veterans Affairs Canada – a federal government department – is mandated to provide health services to Canadian veterans. In 2002, Veterans Affairs Canada and the Department of National Defence (DND) launched a mental health initiative to support Canadian Forces members, veterans, and eligible RCMP officers who suffer from Operational Stress Injury (OSI) as a result of their

R. Shumaker (Ed.): Virtual and Mixed Reality, LNCS 5622, pp. 615–624, 2009.

service. The OSI initiative included opening and operating six OSI clinics across the country to provide specialized assessment and treatment services for a range of associated disorders, including PTSD.

In January 2008, an OSI clinic opened in Fredericton, New Brunswick to service all four Atlantic Provinces – a large geographical area. Fulfilling this mandate will require the best possible use of information and communication technologies (ICT). The National Research Council in Fredericton partnered with the Fredericton OSI Clinic in 2008 to conduct a comprehensive literature review on how ICT could be used effectively to assess and treat OSI and PTSD. The immediate goal of the review was to provide the Fredericton OSI clinic with information to support their decisions on the best ways to use ICT for OSI assessment and treatment for clients in Atlantic Canada [12]. Drawing on that larger study, the current paper discusses the literature related to VR and PTSD.

1.1 Rise of Combat-Related PTSD

The unique risks of trauma associated with working in a war environment (e.g., roadside bombs, seeing comrades killed etc.) places military soldiers at risk for developing mental health problems such as PTSD. Some authors suggest that the wars in Iraq and Afghanistan - which include novel battle situations such as terrorist tactics and pervasive battlefronts - have made currently-serving military service members (SM's) more at risk for PTSD than in the past [2]. Congruently, a recent review of the Canadian DND and Canadian Forces' action on OSI [13] suggests the level and intensity of combat operations in Afghanistan has increased significantly and that, as noted by the Canadian Surgeon General in 2008, a large number of soldiers are returning home from deployments with a range of mental health issues. The Ombudsman for National Defence and the Canadian forces concluded that PTSD was a very serious problem for hundreds - if not thousands - of Canadian Forces members but that the military's current approach to the treatment of mental health injuries was inadequate. Wood [14] and others warn that in order to decrease the future burden on the healthcare system early intervention is vital.

1.2 Traditional Approaches to PTSD Treatment

Traditional treatment interventions for PTSD include pharmacological treatments such as antidepressant and antipsychotic medication. However, some medications that attenuate anxiety (e.g., Alprazolam) may actually undermine therapy [15] and in many cases pharmacological treatments may only provide palliative solutions as opposed to the curative or prophylactic benefits some psychological interventions provide [16].

Efficacious treatments for PTSD include stress-inoculation training, cognitive reprocessing of the event and exposure techniques [16]. Among these and other techniques, Cognitive-Behavioral Therapy (CBT) has the best empirical evidence of its therapeutic efficacy [16, 17]. CBT interventions often include an element of exposure to anxiety provoking stimulus. For example, within the safety of the clinician's office, a person with a spider phobia may be exposed to a spider through its real (in-vivo exposure) or imagined presence (imaginal exposure). Originating from the

Emotion-Processing theory [18], exposure therapy serves to reduce anxiety by activating existing maladaptive fear structures (e.g., "Being near a spider will make me have a heart attack and die") and then incorporating information that is incompatible with the fear (e.g., "I am near the spider and I am not having a heart attack"). This allows the client to process their fearful emotions and relearn new, less anxious associations with the stimulus. In the case of PTSD the feared stimulus is traumatic memories which the patient is exposed to by imagining and narrating traumatic events from their past. Treatment guidelines for PTSD recommend CBT with exposure as the first-line therapy for PTSD [19].

1.3 VR in the Treatment of PTSD

Recently Virtual Reality (VR) has been introduced to exposure-based therapy of PTSD and is known as Virtual Reality Exposure Therapy or VRET [1, 4, 9]. VRET may benefit those with combat-related PTSD in its ability to present life-like scenarios via a medium which may be particularly suited to service members.

VR technology allows users to interact with a computer-simulated virtual environment (VE). In VR, input devices (e.g., head tracking devices) sense the user's motions and modify the synthetic environment accordingly, while output devices immerse the user in the VE by producing visual, auditory (through head-mounted devices with screens that project the sights and sounds of the VE), olfactory (by devices that emit scents) and haptic feed-back (e.g., vibration platforms located under the patient) sensations [9, 10, 20, 22, 23]. Currently, most VR systems include a clinical interface which displays the VE as seen by the patient [22, 23] and others also include non-invasive physiological measures both of which are displayed on a monitor allowing the clinician to observe the patient's experience and to adjust the intensity and duration of the exposure session accordingly [14].

Recent advances in VR technology have increased its therapeutic benefits. For example, Rizzo and colleagues [2, 22, 28] created a VR therapy application called *Virtual Iraq* made specifically for veterans of the Iraq war. This application features combat simulation scenarios based on the popular X-Box game *Full Spectrum Warrior,* as well as various auditory, visual and olfactory features specifically designed to replicate battle conditions in Iraq. In *Virtual Iraq*, users navigate through the VE using either a game pad controller or a replica M4 weapon with imbedded controls. The software features Middle Eastern themed city and desert road environments which include perspective shifts and realistic visual effects designed to resemble contexts that most SM's experience during deployment to Iraq. Preliminary data [2, 3] demonstrates that SM's who had recently returned from tour in Iraq found *Virtual Iraq* realistic and provided the 'feeling of being in Iraq'. This may be attributed to the iterative, user-centered design process wherein input from clinicians and SM's was continually solicited and utilized in modification of the software.

Due to its immersive nature (i.e., stimulus from the 'real world' is blocked out and only that from the VE is perceived), virtual reality exposure therapy (VRET) may potentially provide PTSD sufferers with more life-like simulations than traditional methods such as imaginal exposure. This 'presence' (i.e., the experience of an artificial stimulus as if it were real) which is an essential element of exposure therapy, contributes to the experience of anxiety and facilitates emotion processing [4, 10].

The use of VRET is relevant for clients with PTSD in particular because many are unwilling or unable to imagine or visualize traumatic events – in fact, avoidance of reminders of the trauma is a characteristic symptom of PTSD [10]. This is problematic as the inability to engage in treatment predicts worse outcomes [24]. Encouragingly, research suggests that VR may facilitate emotional engagement by augmenting patients' imaginative capacities while circumventing the natural avoidance tendency of patients with PTSD through delivering sensory cues without requiring the patient actively imagine their traumatic memories [3, 9]. This directive, multi-sensory experience helps recreate and reprocess traumatic memories and increases the engagement and efficacy of the therapeutic intervention [2, 9].

Active and veteran service members may be less likely to seek traditional talk therapies due to associated stigma [25]. In their survey, Hoge and colleagues [25] found that SM's who screened positive for a mental health disorder were two times as likely as others to report concern about stigma and barriers to mental health services. However, having previously used VR technologies in military training or recreation S.M.'s may find the virtual medium more appealing than other interventions [3]. In fact, Rizzo and colleagues [3] found that in their sample of SM's 71% were equally or more willing to use a form of technological treatment than traditional talk therapy alone. Despite its promise in the enhancement of exposure therapy, little research has been conducted assessing the efficacy of VRET specifically in the treatment of PTSD.

2 Method

The literature search was performed in 2008 by the National Research Council Canada Institute for Scientific and Technical Information (NRC-CISTI). The extensive search strategy was undertaken in five electronic databases (Inspec, El Compendex, Medline, CINAHL, and PsycInfo), using keywords including "Post Traumatic Stress Disorder" "Treat*", "Therapy", "e-therapy", "Computer Assisted Therapy", "Technolog*", "Virtual Reality" and "Software". A total of 570 potentially relevant papers were retrieved in the initial search. Among them, 296 items met inclusion criteria of being published between 2005 and present. Of those items, a final 20 articles were identified which pertained to VR in the treatment of mental health issues. In 2009, a further 20 articles were added to ensure the timeliness of this article for publication. Many of the retained articles were review articles (12) or technical papers (8). Of the empirical studies identified, 18 involved patients with specific phobias (9), social phobia (2) and PTSD (7).

3 Results

Our review of the selected articles revealed that in general, little research has been conducted involving randomized controlled trials of VRET. However, meta-anlalyses are a popular method of investigating the outcomes of VRET because they may be used to estimate effect sizes across studies while increasing statistical power. One of our main findings is that VRET has been successfully used since the mid 1990's to treat anxiety and phobia disorders and is acceptable to the majority of patients suffering from anxiety disorders [26]. Research suggests that participants with various anxiety disorders (e.g., social anxiety, specific phobias etc.) experience a reduction in anxiety symptoms after receiving VR based exposure therapy [27, 28, 29]. In fact, in a recent meta-analysis of 21 studies, [7] Parsons and Rizzo found that across anxiety disorders (i.e., social phobia, specific phobias, panic disorder with agoraphobia and PTSD) VRET resulted in clinically and statistically significant reductions in anxiety symptoms. However, the authors note that some of the studies included did not have control groups and others were not randomized, controlled trials which limits confidence in the findings. In their recent meta-analysis Powers and Emmelkamp [8] found that across 13 studies including individuals with specific phobia, social phobia, PTSD and panic disorder that VRET was significantly more effective at reducing anxiety in clients than both control and in vivo exposure conditions (although the effect size was small for the latter).

Our review also emphasized the mounting popularity of practitioners using VRET for PTSD specifically [1, 2, 29, 30, 31]. However, we were able to find few studies which examined the efficacy of VRET for PTSD specifically. Initial research conducted by Rothman and colleagues using a *Virtual Vietnam* scenario, including jungle and helicopter simulations, demonstrated the ability of VRET to reduce symptoms of PTSD in a Vietnam veteran [4]. Rothbaum's follow-up study [5] demonstrated significant reductions of PTSD in 10 Vietnam veterans although it did not utilize a control group. In their case study, Difede and Hoffman [1] found that their patient, who suffered PTSD as a result of the 9/11 attack on the World Trade Center, reported a 90% reduction rate of PTSD symptoms after completing VRET using a *Virtual World Trade Center* environment. In follow-up studies, Difede and colleagues [9, 30] also found that VRET was significantly more effective in PTSD symptom reduction than their waitlist control condition. In fact, in these methodologically rigorous studies, those in the treatment groups showed significant reductions in PTSD symptoms – seven of the ten participants no longer met criteria for PTSD following treatment [9]. Most recently, reports have shown positive preliminary support for *Virtual Iraq*. In their case study of a 29 year old SM, Gerardi and colleagues [31] documented a substantial reduction in the participant's PTSD symptoms after only a short treatment intervention (i.e., four sessions of VRET with *Virtual Iraq*) and, although the participant still met criteria for PTSD at posttreatment, he reported improved life functioning. Similarly, in their open clinical trial Rizzo and colleagues [3] used *Virtual Iraq* in their sample of 15 active duty SM's and found significant symptom reduction – twelve of the fifteen participants no longer met criteria for PTSD. Interestingly, two of the participants had mild to moderate traumatic brain injuries (TBI's) and were still able to receive treatment benefits suggesting that VRET may be suitable for those with cognitive limitations. Rizzo and colleagues [3] have also presented preliminary findings of a case study involving an SM with PTSD who received a lower frequency treatment schedule than usual (i.e., 11 sessions over seven months) using *Virtual Iraq*. At post-treatment, the SM no longer met criteria for PTSD which suggests that VRET may be effective enough to be implemented within a flexible time-frame.

3.1 Problems with the Use of VRET

The literature presents problems related to the use of VRET such as the patient's ability to use the tools and physical side effects. Gregg and Tarrier [29] suggest that the navigation of VR systems may prove problematic for clients with cognitive or motor difficulties and Rizzo [21] warns that the extra effort required to navigate the VR equipment may serve as a distraction and limit the treatment process. Also, cyber-sickness, a form of motion sickness, can result in a number of symptoms, including nausea and vomiting [21]. Other negative after-effects include motor disturbances, flashbacks, fatigue and drowsiness. However, some authors suggest repeated exposure could gradually reduce these side effects.

An important ethical consideration with the use of VRET is the clinician's competence with the technology. Clinicians should only employ treatments within their own area of expertise and Difede [9] suggests they should be trained in exposure therapy protocols before being trained in VRET. Further, as it is difficult to foresee how any client may respond to VRET and stress levels are difficult to predict, it is important that clinicians using this technology are well aware of potential side effects and reactions to the intervention and are prepared to respond appropriately if necessary.

3.2 Methodological Considerations

Although we found support for the use of VR within therapeutic interventions, many of the studies we reviewed contained methodological weaknesses. For example, many studies used a small number of participants. Gregg and Terrier [26] claim that in order to show a treatment effect studies must employ at least 27 participants; however, many of the studies reviewed had smaller sample sizes – particularly those related to PTSD (e.g., case studies; 18 participants). Further, some studies utilized unstandardized measures and others did not clearly describe their methodology (e.g., randomization process, treatment implementation). This is particularly problematic for meta-analyses for, although these studies may correct for small sample sizes, inaccuracies of methodologically flawed studies are exaggerated when amalgamated.

Although results from uncontrolled trials and case reports are encouraging, they cannot be generalized. Our findings further underscore the fact that more well-designed research is needed to verify the effectiveness of VRET over traditional therapeutic approaches. For example, many of the studies included in the review did not have control groups or used inactive treatments as comparison groups (e.g., wait-list). However, the inclusion of appropriate comparison groups such as traditional therapeutic approaches (e.g., CBT, stress-inoculation training, etc.) would help to more accurately estimate the effectiveness of VRET on the reduction of PTSD symptoms relative to other, established treatments.

Another methodological consideration is for greater attention to mediator and moderator effects. Analysis of the mechanisms through which treatments exert their effect (mediation) as well as the characteristics of the patient or population which make the treatment more or less successful (moderation) would serve to advance knowledge and improve patient care. For example, recent discoveries about neural mechanisms underlying exposure therapy have allowed researchers to augment traditional exposure therapy with use of pharmacological treatments to accelerate anxiety reduction [32]. It is also important to identify factors which may differentially impact treatment outcomes in order to better identify the most favorable treatment options for individual clients to optimize therapeutic change [8].

Overall, conducting controlled studies with randomized, between-groups design and utilizing large sample sizes with consideration of possible mediator and moderator variables would help to more confidently state the efficacy of VRET and enhance future treatment of PTSD.

4 Conclusion

VRET has many benefits including the ability to facilitate emotion processing by immersing clients within the virtual world – even for those who do not respond to traditional talk therapy. VR allows exposure to be repeated, gradual and prolonged (the three main tenants of exposure therapy) which facilitates maximally effective treatment. Further, VR allows exposure to stimuli which may otherwise be expensive, difficult to arrange or beyond the constraints of the real world – all within the clinician's control.

4.1 The Use of VRET in the Treatment of PTSD

VRET may be particularly suitable for military service members due to its format of delivery which may be similar to military training applications and, therefore, may be less stigmatized than traditional talk therapy. In their survey of service members, Rizzo and colleagues [3] found that 20% who stated they were not willing to seek traditional psychotherapy rated their willingness to use VR-based treatment as neutral to very willing.

4.2 Future Directions

In 2008, Canadian Ombudsman investigators found that the negative stigma associated with PTSD remains a real problem in military and civilian environments [13]. Mental health care providers from across Canada reported that stigma was one of the biggest challenges still facing the Canadian Forces [13]. Thus efforts need to be made not only in clearly identifying effective treatments for PTSD but also in initiatives to reduce stigma and barriers to treatment for SM's.

Traditionally, the health system has been a very conservative environment – particularly for new innovative technology. Within the system there exists great reluctance to invest in new methods of clinical care until conclusive demonstrations of efficacy and cost-effectiveness occur. In our work with Canadian OSI clinics there was notable interest amongst clinicians of the prospect of incorporating this treatment method into extant interventions for service members. However, currently there are no plans to employ VRET, in part due to cost concerns. VR units may be extremely costly - Gregg and Terrier [26] estimate the cost is from $2,000 to $5,000 for a Head Mounted Device, and up to $200,000 for a complete system. Although Parsons and Rizzo [7] claim the price of VR systems has decreased in the past 10 years (Rizzo [3] describes a base-level system for $1,500) they are still far too costly for many clinicians – particularly those in private practice – to afford them. Further, these lower-end systems may not feature the essential stimuli (e.g., olfactory, vibrotactile) which add to the immersive nature of VR and thus, may be less effective at creating an authentic, engaging experience for patients.

We hope that future research involving methodologically-sound study designs increases confidence in the technology and stimulates the creation of more cost-effective systems which may maximize access to clinicians. However, in the meantime, clinicians in traditional health care settings have turned to lower-cost alternatives. Following Rizzo and colleagues' claim that 'simple' video tools may also aid patients who are undergoing exposure therapy [33], practitioners in England have begun experimenting with Tetris video games and others in Newfoundland, Canada have begun using games for the Nintendo Wii gaming system (which include audio, visual and vibrotactile features) to treat PTSD and traumatic stress [35, 36]. Focusing on these low-cost alternatives may also stimulate interest among administrations and clinicians to conduct trials with different technologies in treating individuals with PTSD. We look forward to the findings of future research and the application of innovative technologies in the treatment of PTSD and hope for the invention of cost-effective treatment methods which increase accessibility to these worthwhile interventions.

Acknowledgements

The authors would like to thank their NRC colleagues and our research partners – the Fredericton OSI Clinic and River Valley Health in Fredericton, New Brunswick, Canada who provided helpful feedback. The authors gratefully acknowledge the helpful suggestions of anonymous peer-reviewers to an earlier version of this paper.

References

1. Difede, J., Hoffman, H.G.: Virtual Reality Exposure Therapy for World Trade Center Posttraumatic Stress Disorder: A Case Report. Cyber Psych. & Beh. 5, 529–535 (2002)
2. Rizzo, A.A., Rothbaum, B.O., Difede, J., Mclay, R.N., Johnston, S., Reger, et al.: Clinical Results from the Virtual Iraq Exposure Therapy Application for PTSD. In: The Proceedings of the 26th Annual Army Science Conference, Orlando, Fl (2008)
3. Rizzo, A.A., Reger, G., Gahm, G., Difede, J., Rothbaum, B.O.: Virtual Reality Exposure Therapy for Combat Related PTSD. In: Shiromani, P., Keane, T., LeDoux, J. (eds.) (in press)
4. Rothbaum, B.O., Hodges, L., Alarcon, R., Ready, D., Shahar, F., Graap, K., et al.: Virtual Reality Exposure Therapy for PTSD Vietnam Veterans: A Case Study. J. of Traum. Stress. 12, 263–271 (1999)
5. Rothbaum, B.O., Hodges, L., Ready, D., Graap, K., Alarcon, R.D.: Virtual Reality Exposure Therapy for Vietnam Veterans with Posttraumatic Stress Disorder. J. Clin. Psychiatry. 62, 617–622 (2001)
6. Rothbaum, B.O., Ruef, A.M., Litz, B.T., Han, H., Hodges, L.: Virtual Reality Exposure Therapy of Combat-Related PTSD: A Case Using Psychophysiological Indicators of Outcome. In: Taylor, S. (ed.) Advances in the Treatment of Posttraumatic Stress Disorder: Cognitive-Behavioral Perspectives. Springer, New York (2004)

7. Parsons, T.D., Rizzo, A.A.: Affective Outcomes of Virtual Reality Exposure Therapy for Anxiety and Specific Phobias: A Meta-analysis. J. Behav. Ther. Exp. Psychiatry. 39, 250–261 (2007)
8. Powers, M.B., Emmelkamp, P.M.G.: Virtual Reality Exposure Therapy for Anxiety Disorders: A Meta-analysis. J. Anx. Disord. 22, 561–569 (2007)
9. Difede, J., Cukor, J., Jayasinghe, N., Patt, I., Jedel, S., Spielman, L., et al.: Virtual Reality Exposure Therapy for the Treatment of Posttraumatic Stress Disorder Following September 11, 2001. J. Clin. Psychiatry 68, 1639–1647 (2007)
10. Pair, J., Allen, B., Dautricoutr, M., Treskunov, A., Liewer, M., Graap, K., et al.: A Virtual Reality Exposure Therapy Application for Iraq War Post Traumatic Stress Disorder. In: Proceedings of the IEEE conference on Virtual Reality, pp. 62–72. IEEE Press, New York (2006)
11. American Psychiatric Association: Diagnostic and Statistical Manual of Mental Disorders, 4th, Text Revision edn. American Psychiatric Association, Washington (2000)
12. Molyneaux, H., Gibson, K., Simms, D., O'Donnell, S., Oakley, P., Kondratova, I., et al.: Information and Communication Technologies for Assessing and Treating Operational Stress Injury (OSI). Fredericton: National Research Council. ERB-1159. NRC 50740 (2009)
13. McFadyen, M.: A Long Road to Recovery: Battling Operational Stress Injuries. Second Review of the Department of National Defence and Canadian Forces' Action on Operational Stress Injuries. Special Report, Ombudsman National Defence and Canadian Forces (2008)
14. Wood, D.P., Murphy, J., Center, K., McLay, R., Reeves, D., Pyne, J., et al.: Combat-Related Post-Traumatic Stress Disorder: A Case Report Using Virtual Reality Exposure Therapy with Physiological Monitoring. In: Westwood, J.D., et al. (eds.) Studies in Health Technology and Informatics, pp. 556–561. IOS Press, Amsterdam (2007)
15. Marks, I.M., Sweinson, R.P., Basoglu, M., Kuch, K., Noshivani, H., O'Sullivan, G., et al.: Alprazolam and Exposure Alone and Combined in Panic Disorder with Agoraphobia: A Controlled Study in London and Toronto. Br. J. of Psychiatry 162, 776–787 (1993)
16. Hollon, S.D., Stewart, M.O., Strunk, D.: Enduring Effects for Cognitive Behavior Therapy in the Treatment of Depression and Anxiety. Annu. Rev. Psycho. 57, 285–315 (2006)
17. Van Etten, M.L., Taylor, S.: Comparative Efficacy of Posttraumatic Stress Disorder: An Empirical Review. JAMA 268, 633–638 (1998)
18. Foa, E.B., Kozak, M.J.: Emotional Processing of Fear; Exposure to Corrective Information. Psych. Bull. 99, 20–35 (1986)
19. Foa, E.B., Davidosn, R.T., Frances, A.: Expert Consensus Guideline Series: Treatment of Posttraumatic Stress Disorder. Am. J. of Clin. Psychiatry. 60, 5–76 (1999)
20. Spira, J.L., Pyne, J.M.: Experiential Methods in the Treatment of Combat PTSD. Combat Stress Injury: Theory, research, and Management, pp. 205–218. Routledge, New York (2007)
21. Gorini, A., Riva, G.: Virtual Reality in Anxiety Disorders: The Past and the Future. Exp. Rev. Neurother. 8, 215–233 (2008)
22. Rizzo, A.A., Schultheis, M.T., Rothbaum, B.O.: Ethical Issues for the use of Virtual Reality in the Psychological Sciences. In: Bush, S.S., Drexler, M.L. (eds.) Ethical Issues in Clinical Neuropsychology, pp. 243–279 (2002)
23. Rizzo, A.A., Difede, J., Rothbaum, B.O., Johnston, S., Mclay, R.N., Reger, G., et al.: VR PTSD Exposure Therapy Results with Active Duty Iraq War Combatants. In: Westwood, J.D., et al. (eds.) Studies in Health Technology and Informatics. IOS Press, Amsterdam (January 2009) (in press)
24. Emmelkamp, P.M.G., Krijn, M., Hulsbosch, A.M., de Vries, S., Schueme, M.J., van der Mast, C.A.P.G.: Virtual Reality Treatment Versus Exposure In Vivo: A Comparative Evaluation in Acrophobia. Beh. Res. Ther. 40, 509–516 (2002)

25. Jaycox, L.H., Foa, E.B., Morral, A.R.: Influence of Emotional Engagement and Habituation on Exposure Therapy for PTSD. J. Consult. Clin. Psych. 66, 185–192 (1998)
26. Hoge, C.W., Castro, C.A., Messer, S.C., McGurk, D., Cotting, D.I., Koffman, R.L.: Combat Duty in Iraq and Afghanistan, Mental Health Problems, and Barriers to Care. N. Engl. J. Med. 351, 13–22 (2004)
27. Gregg, N., Tarrier, N.: Virtual Reality in Mental Health – A Review of the Literature. Soc. Psych. Psych. Epid. 42, 343–354 (2007)
28. Anderson, P., Rothbaum, B.O., Hodges, L.F.: Virtual Reality Exposure in the Treatment of Social Anxiety. Cognitive and Behavioral Practice 10, 240–247 (2003)
29. Garcia-Palacios, A., Botells, C., Hoffman, H., Fabregat, S.: Comparing Acceptance and Refusal Rates of Virtual Reality Exposure vs. In Vivo Exposure by Patients with Specific Phobias. Cyber Psych. & Beh. 10, 722–725 (2007)
30. Rothbaum, B.O., Schwartz, A.: Exposure Therapy for Posttraumatic Stress Disorder. Am. J. Psychother. 56, 59–75 (2002)
31. Difede, J., Cukor, J., Patt, I., Giosan, C., Hoffman, H.: The Application of Virtual Reality to the Treatment of PTSD Following the WTC Attack. Ann. NY Acad. Sci. 1071, 500–501 (2006)
32. Gerardi, M., Rothbaum, B.O., Ressler, K., Heekin, M., Rizzo, A.A.: Virtual Reality Exposure Therapy Using a Virtual Iraq: Case Report. J. Trauma. Stress. 21, 1–5 (2008)
33. Ressler, K.J., Rothbaum, B.O., Tannenbaum, L., Anderson, P., Zimand, E., Hodges, L., Davis, M.: Facilitation of Psychotherapy with D-Cyucloserine, a Putative Cognitive Enhancer. Arch. Gen. Psych. 61, 1136–1144 (2004)
34. Rizzo, A.A., Wiederhold, M., Buckwalter, J.G.: Basic Issues In the use of Virtual Environments for Mental Health Applications. In: Riva, G., Wiederhold, B.K., Molinari, E. (eds.) Virtual Environments in Clinical Psychology and Neuroscience, pp. 1–23. IOS Press, Amsterdam (1998)
35. BBC News, http://news.bbc.co.uk/2/hi/health/7813637.stm
36. The Whig Standard, http://thewhig.com/ArticleDisplay.aspx?e=1347494

Effect of an Eyesight Recovering Stereoscopic Movie System on Visual Acuity and Asthenopia

Akihiro Sugiura[1], Tetsuya Yamamoto[1], Hiroki Takada[1], and Masaru Miyao[2]

[1] Department of Radiology, Gifu University of Medical Science
795, 1, Ichihiraga Nagamine, Seki, Gifu, Japan
{asugiura,yamamoto,takada}@u-gifu-ms.ac.jp
[2] Central Information Center, Nagoya University
Huro-tyou, Chikusa-ku, Nagoya, Aichi, Japan
miyao@itc.nagoya-u.ac.jp

Abstract. Relaxing the contracted muscles involved in focus-adjustment around the eyeball, such as the ciliary body and extraocular muscles, is expected to improve pseudomyopia. This hypothesis has led to the development of Dr.REX— an apparatus for recovering eyesight by using a stereoscopic video. In this study, we verified the effects of this apparatus on visual acuity and asthenopia in the short and medium terms. Thirty-two myopic Japanese students participated in this study. We compared the severity of asthenopia in subjects who used Dr.REX and in those who performed close work on video display terminals (VDTs). We determined that the use of the apparatus improved visual acuity in both the short and medium terms. In addition, asthenopia seemed to be less severe in subjects who used Dr.Rex than in those who performed close work on VDTs.

Keywords: Pseudomyopia, visual acuity, asthenopia, stereoscopic video, visually induced motion sickness (VIMS).

1 Introduction

With the development of computers and the widespread use of the Internet, an increasing number of people need to perform close work (CW) such as operations on video display terminals (VDTs). Working under such conditions for many hours induces the contraction of the muscles involved in focus-adjustment around the eyeball, such as the ciliary body and extraocular muscles. Thus, it is possible that CW impairs focus adjustment—a symptom known as pseudomyopia [1]. In addition, CW has also been reported to induce cervicobrachial syndrome and psychoneurotic syndromes [2], [3].

Pseudomyopia is a symptom of refractive myopia. Relaxation of the contracted muscles involved in focus-adjustment is expected to alleviate pseudomyopia. An eyesight-recovering apparatus called MD-SS [4], developed by Kobayashi [5], is used to relax the contracted muscles. This apparatus works by using a Landolt ring drawn on a flat plate that moves back and forth over a distance of 2 m. Although the use of this apparatus is an effective way to improve eyesight, it is not an efficient solution because trainees are required to visit the clinic to use the apparatus, and hence, many

R. Shumaker (Ed.): Virtual and Mixed Reality, LNCS 5622, pp. 625–632, 2009.

trainees discontinue the training. The apparatus is also very expensive and large for trainees to buy privately. However, a new apparatus that delivers similar results was recently developed by Olympus Visual Communications [6]. This apparatus, called Dr.REX, uses stereoscopic video to overcome the problems associated with the old apparatus. In this paper, we verify the effect of this apparatus on visual acuity and asthenopia in the short and medium terms by conducting tests on myopic youths.

2   Materials and Methods

2.1   Outline of the Eyesight Recovering Stereoscopic Movie System

Dr.REX consists of a general-purpose personal computer, glasses with liquid crystal shutters, a liquid crystal display (LCD), a pair of speakers, and movie contents. We prepared images of a ball for the right and left eyes (Fig. 1). Each image was created using the POWER-3D method developed by Olympus Visual Communications. By simultaneously adjusting convergence, binocular parallax, and focus, the human eye can perceive images in three dimensions. A general stereoscopic image of an artificial object was constructed using fixed line of sight and without adjusting for convergence. Due to these measures, visually induced motion sickness (VIMS) occurred only infrequently [7]. However, images based on the POWER-3D method were constructed such that the contradiction between the experimental observations and actual conditions could be reconciled. Viewing the stereoscopic images effectively prevented VIMS in the observers. The right and left liquid crystal shutters in the glasses (Fig. 2) opened and shut in a synchronized fashion when the subjects viewed the images on the LCD. Furthermore, the right and left eyes alternately focused on each image. Hence, observers could perceive the images as a smooth stereoscopic movie at 60 Hz. The stereoscopic ball was first presented near the glasses and then moved far away from the glasses. As the movie was gradually moved closer or further away from the glasses, greater effort was required to adjust to the movie image on the LCD. Consequently, the muscles around the eyes were stimulated in such a way that observers could detect an improvement in their eyesight.

Apart from playing stereoscopic movies, Dr.REX also plays music, which had a relaxing effect on the observers. In this way, Dr.REX has not only a training effect on the observers but also a relaxing effect and thus attempts to improve eyesight using both physical and psychological methods.

2.2   Methods

A total of 32 myopic Japanese students (age, 20 ± 1 years; 16 men and 16 women) voluntarily participated in this study after signing informed consent forms.

The study participants were divided into 2 groups. Before the commencement of the study, we measured the far vision of the subjects by testing both eyes, right eye and left eye individually and simultaneously using the automatic optometer NV-300 (Nidek) (Pre). If the visual acuity, as measured by the automatic optometer, was <0.1, the visual acuity was measured using a Landolt chart posted on a wall. The protocol of this study is shown in Table 1. Under a controlled environment (mean illuminance: 240 lux, room temperature: 24 °C), the subjects in 1 group used the Dr.REX apparatus for 6 min; the subjects in the other group carried out CW on VDTs, which required them to maintain a steady gaze for the same amount of time. Each group carried out their assigned tasks every day for 11 days. Far-vision tests were carried out, and eye-strain was quantified using the visual analog scale (VAS[1]) immediately after loading. On days 5 and 11 (the final day), we made an addition to the far-vision tests before loading and filling out a simulator sickness questionnaire [8] (SSQ[2]) before and after loading. The degree of asthenopia calculated the SSQ was defined as SSQ-OD.

Fig. 1. An image produced using the POWER-3D method. The next image for the other eye is laterally shifted by a few centimeters due to the angle of convergence. An observer using glasses with liquid crystal shutters perceives the images in three dimensions.

Fig. 2. An observer uses the specially designed glasses. The right and left liquid crystal shutters in the glasses alternately open and shut at a frequency of 30 Hz. If the observer is myopic and cannot see the LCD without glasses, he/she wears both the glasses for myopia correction and the glasses with liquid crystal shutters.

---

[1] VAS, a visual assessment scale, is a 95-mm-long linear scale prepared such that moving the scale to the right increases the degree of asthenopia.

[2] Subscores were derived from the SSQ to measure the degree of VIMS. SSQ-OD was used to evaluate the degree of asthenopia.

Table 1. Study protocol. One group performed close work, and the other used the Dr.REX apparatus. The assignments were then switched between the groups, and the same protocol was followed. We intend to indicate results of an auto refractmeter in a next report.

Day	1-4	5	6-10	11
Protocol	Load 1[*] or Load 2[**] VAS[***] Far-vision[****]	SSQ[*****] Auto Refractometer Far-vision Load 1 or Load 2 SSQ VAS Auto Refractometer Far-vision	Load 1 or Load 2 VAS Far-vision	SSQ[****] Auto Refractometer Far-vision Load 1 or Load 2 SSQ VAS Auto Refractometer Far-vision

[*] Load1: Close work on video display terminals
[**] Load2: Using the Dr.REX   [****] Far-Vision was mesured without glasses.
[***] Visual Analog Scale   [*****] Simulator Sickness Questionnaire

Each group was required to take a 2-week break to expect the effects of loadings. The assignments were then switched, and the study was resumed with the same protocol. Thus, we obtained 32 datasets controlled the loading order.

3 Results

3.1 Visual Acuity

First, the geometrical mean of the visual acuity of the subjects before and after using Dr.REX on days 5 and 11 is shown in Table 2; these values were used to verify the short-term effects of the training. The visual acuity increased after using the apparatus on both days 5 and 11. Using the Wilcoxon matched-pairs signed-ranks test, a significant difference was found in the visual acuity of both eyes on day 11 and the left eye on days 5 and 11 ($P < 0.05$).

Next, in order to verify the effects in the medium term, the geometrical means of the visual acuity of the subjects after they had used the Dr.REX apparatus and performed CW are shown in Fig. 3-a and Fig. 3-b, respectively. The geometrical mean of the visual acuity was higher after using Dr.REX than it was before using this apparatus. The Friedman test revealed significant variations in the visual acuity in the all cases ($P < 0.01$) (Fig. 3-a). In addition, multiple comparisons showed significant differences in the pre- and post-test visual acuity of the right eye on days 8, 9, and 11 and of the left eye on days 8, 10, and 11 ($P < 0.05$). The Friedman test was also used to evaluate the differences in visual acuity after performing CW; no significant variations were found in the visual acuity.

3.2 Asthenopia

The degree of asthenopia was measured using the VAS. Significant variations in the VAS scores were not found in the short or medium term. In contrast, significant variations in the SSQ-OD scores were noted in the short term but not in the medium term. The mean SSQ-OD scores before and after using Dr.REX and performing CW on days 5 and 11 are shown in Table 3. The scores increased after each loading on both days. Using the paired t test, a significant difference was found only performing CW on day 5 ($P < 0.01$).

Table 2. Changes in the mean of visual acuity after using the Dr.REX apparatus on days 5 and 11. On both days, the visual acuity increased after the training.

Schedule (day)	5 (Before)	5 (After)	Increase	11 (Before)	11 (After)	Increase
Both eyes	0.145 ± 0.284	0.160 ± 0.282	0.015	0.138 ± 0.269	0.171 ± 0.267*	0.033
Right eye	0.114 ± 0.273	0.123 ± 0.272	0.009	0.126 ± 0.272	0.138 ± 0.246	0.012
Left eye	0.089 ± 0.440	0.106 ± 0.260*	0.017	0.101 ± 0.242	0.120 ± 0.240*	0.019

$*P < 0.05$

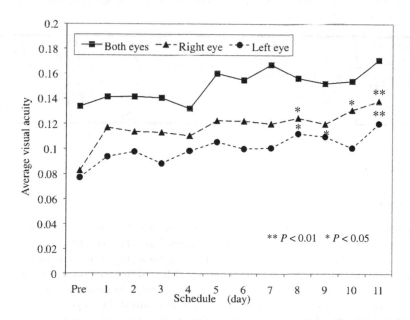

Fig. 3-a. Changes in the geometrical mean of visual acuity after using the Dr.REX apparatus

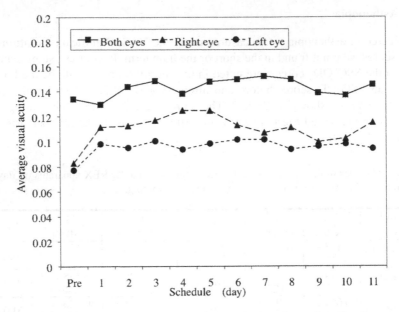

Fig. 3-b. Changes in the geometrical mean of visual acuity after performing close work

Table 3. Changes in the mean SSQ-OD scores before and after loadings on days 5 and 11. The scores increased after all loadings.

Schedule (day)	5 (Before)	5 (After)	Increase	11 (Before)	11 (After)	Increase
Dr.REX	4.26 ± 2.18	6.63 ± 2.25	2.37	5.92 ± 2.38	7.11 ± 2.28	1.18
CW	6.16 ± 2.08	9.71 ± 2.41**	3.55	5.92 ± 2.57	7.34 ± 2.68	1.42

$**P < 0.01$, CW: close work.

4 Discussion

4.1 Visual Acuity

First, the short-term effects of the apparatus on visual acuity were verified on the basis of the results of the far-vision tests on days 5 and 11. An improvement in visual acuity was noted so that the some mean of the visual acuity were increased. However, the increase in visual acuity was not significant for all the conditions shown in Table 2. The reason for the differences in the degree of improvement in visual acuity was the condition of the subjects' eyes. Subjects who strained their eyes before the measurements experienced the largest improvements since their muscles involved in focus-adjustment were strongly contracted. In contrast, subjects whose muscles were already relaxed experienced hardly any improvement.

Next, the effects of apparatus on visual acuity in the medium term were verified on the basis of the results of the far-vision tests performed over a period of 11 days. The increase in the visual acuity on the final day (day 11) considerably exceeded that in the pre-tests. Further, the difference in visual acuity was statistically significant. Thus, we concluded that an improvement in visual acuity was more effective in the medium term than in the short term so that the muscles involved in focus-adjustment, such as the ciliary body and extraocular muscles, are stimulated continuously. Moreover, we compared effects of the Dr.REX with the CW in Fig. 3. Visual acuity measured after loadings were a significantly difference on day 11 by using the Wilcoxon matched-pairs signed-ranks test ($P < 0.05$). This result suggests that the Dr.REX apparatus has a cumulative positive effect on eyesight and prevents the deterioration of visual acuity. After using this apparatus, some subjects experienced a large improvement in visual acuity, while others only experienced a slight improvement. We consider that the differences in the degree of improvement were attributable to differences among individuals.

4.2 Asthenopia

The differences in the degree of asthenopia after using Dr.REX and performing CW were verified on the basis of the asthenopic scores (VAS and SSQ-OD).

First, we evaluated the VAS scores after the subjects used Dr.REX and performed CW. The mean values for 11 days are shown in Fig. 4. The mean VAS scores after using Dr.REX were lower than the scores after performing CW. Further, a paired t test revealed that the difference in the scores was significant ($P < 0.01$).

With regard to the SSQ-OD scores, the mean score after performing CW was higher than that after using Dr.REX, but the difference was not significant. Since the assessment was subjective, we consider that these results depended on each subject's psychological condition or on the condition of the eyes.

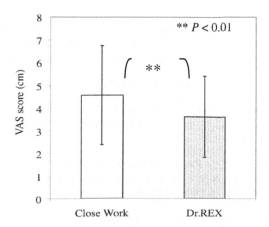

Fig. 4. Mean visual analog scale (VAS) scores after using the Dr.REX apparatus and after performing close work (CW). The mean VAS score after using the Dr.REX (0.948) is lower than that after performing CW.

The manufacturer of the Dr.REX apparatus recommends that the apparatus be used for 10 minutes at a time. Thus, in this study, we expected the degree of improvement in asthenopia to be low because the subjects were instructed to use the apparatus for only 6 min. Dr.REX had a relaxing effect on the subjects and a compulsory stretching effect on the muscles involved in focus-adjustment. We consider that these effects transiently induced asthenopia. On the other hand, the CW in this study was designed to induce asthenopia, and we consider that it did so in all the subjects. Thus, we estimated that asthenopia resulting from CW was more severe than that resulting from using Dr.REX. This conclusion, however, needs to be verified.

5 Conclusion

This study proves that pseudomyopia can be improved by relaxing the contracted muscles involved in focus-adjustment, such as the ciliary body and the extraocular muscles, by using a stereoscopic movie shown on an LCD. Furthermore, the apparatus used to present the movie, Dr.REX, is inexpensive and compact, as previously mentioned. With this apparatus, trainees are less likely to discontinue the training. Therefore, we conclude that the continual use of this apparatus improves visual acuity by relaxing contracted muscles involved in focus-adjustment.

Asthenopia induced by CW is more pronounced than that induced by the use of Dr.REX. However, no significant improvement of asthenopia was observed with the use of the Dr.REX apparatus. These results must be verified using other indexes of asthenopia.

In the future, we suggest that the apparatus be used for several months in order to verify its long-term effects on visual acuity and asthenopia. In addition, we intend to perform this study on older myopic people, and middle-aged and elderly presbyopic people.

References

1. Ohno, S., Kinoshita, S.: Standard ophthalmology. Igakusyoin, Tokyo (2007)
2. Nakazawa, T., Okubo, Y., Suwazono, Y., Kobayashi, E., Komine, S., Kato, N., Nogawa, K.: Association between duration of daily VDT use and subjective symptoms. Am. J. Ind. Med. 42, 421–426 (2002)
3. Gomzi, M.: Work environment and health in VDT use. An ergonomic approach. Arh. Hig. Rada. Toksikol. 45, 327–334 (1994)
4. Hiyoshi, I., Kodama, N., Wakui, A., Fukumoto, I.: A basic study of recovery pseudo-myopia using Purkinje-Sanson image measure method. IEICE technical report. ME and Bio-Cybernetics 100, 39–44 (2000)
5. Kobayashi, S.: Japan Patent 6-339501 (1994)
6. Nishihira, T., Tahara, H.: U.S. Patent US7404693B2 (2001)
7. Matsuda, T., Ohnaka, Y.: A note on the relation between trembling of pictorial image and visually included motion sickness. Ritsumeikan Journal of Human Sciences 9, 97–104 (2005)
8. Kennedy, R.S., Lane, N.E., Berbaum, K.S., Lilienthal, M.G.: A simulator sickness questionnaire (SSQ): An enhanced method for quantifying simulator sickness. Int. Aviat. Psychol. 3 (1993)

Augmented Reality System for Dental Implant Surgery

Satoshi Yamaguchi, Takafumi Ohtani, Hirofumi Yatani, and Taiji Sohmura

Department of Oromaxillofacial Regeneration,
Osaka University, 1-8 Yamadaoka, Suita, Osaka, Japan
{yamagu,takadent,yatani,sohmurat}@dent.osaka-u.ac.jp

Abstract. Recently, computer-assisted navigation systems have been developed to realize safe and precise surgery. In conventional systems, surgeons feel anxious intra-operatively because they have to watch a surgical monitor while operating instruments in the oral cavity. The objective of this study is to develop a novel dental implant navigation system by combining the retinal projection head mounted display (RPHMD) and the augmented reality techniques that can directly overlay pre-operative simulation images onto the real view of the surgeon. In this paper, we propose an image overlay procedure based on the RPHMD and verify its accuracy.

Keywords: Dental Implant Surgery, Augmented Reality, Surgical Navigation.

1 Introduction

As dental implants have been become an established dental treatment, the number of applications to difficult and aggressive cases with insufficient quantity and quality of bone has increased. To overcome these difficulties and realize safe and precise surgery, computer-assisted navigation systems have been developed [1]. In conventional systems, surgeons feel anxious intra-operatively because they have to operate instruments in the oral cavity while watching a surgical monitor. Thus, we develop a novel surgical navigation system by combining the retinal projection head mounted display (RPHMD) and the augmented reality (AR) techniques that can directly overlay pre-operative simulation images onto the real view of the surgeon. In this paper, we propose an image overlay procedure based on the RPHMD and verify its accuracy.

2 System Configuration

As shown in Fig. 1, our developed system consists of the RPHMD and Micron Tracker2 Sx60 (MT2) (Claron Technology Inc., USA). In our system, a simulation image of a dental implant placement position is directly overlaid onto surgeon's retina through the RPHMD. The surgeon can intuitively confirm the placement position and their view is not interrupted. To realize a registration of the simulation image and surgeon's view, we use a marker 1, a marker 2, and a marker 3 attached to a surgical stent, the RPHMD, and a implant drill respectively by the MT2 and calculate the

R. Shumaker (Ed.): Virtual and Mixed Reality, LNCS 5622, pp. 633–638, 2009.

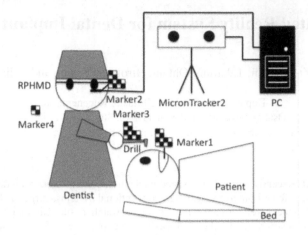

Fig. 1. System Configuration

translation matrixes. To calculate a projection matrix between surgeon's eye and the RPHMD, we also use a marker 4 to calibrate between the RPHMD coordinate and the surgeon's eye.

3   Methods

3.1   Pre-operative Procedures

1. To measure the position and posture of the marker 1, a surgical stent with marker1 attached thereto is placed inside oral cavity of the patient. CT scanning is performed and a 3-dimensional model from the CT images is reconstructed by using VGStudio Max 1.2 (Volume Graphics, GmbH, Germany).
2. A placement position of dental implants for the CT images is simulated by Free-FormModeling (SensAble Technologies, Inc., USA) and the 3-dimensional simulation image is generated. At this time, a translation matrix $_{maker1}^{implant}\mathbf{D}$ from a marker 1 to implants is recorded.
3. A translation matrix $_{maker2}^{eye}\mathbf{A}$ to surgeon's eye from the RPHMD with the marker 2 attached thereto is calculated. By using the marker 4 for calibration, the $_{maker2}^{eye}\mathbf{A}$ is calculated from 3-dimensional positions on the RPHMD coordinate system and its corresponding 2-dimensional positions on the surgeon's eye coordinate system [2].

3.2   Intra-operative Procedures

1. The marker 3 is also attached to the implant drill.
2. Translation matrixes $_{tracker}^{marker1}\mathbf{D}$, $_{tracker}^{marker2}\mathbf{D}$, and $_{tracker}^{marker3}\mathbf{D}$ are measured by the MT2 in real-time intra-operatively.

3. A translation matrix $^{eye}_{implant}\mathbf{P}$ is calculated from simulated dental implant CG image to the surgeon's eye as per the following equation (1). Finally, the CG image is projected onto the surgeon's view,

$$^{eye}_{implant}\mathbf{P} = {}^{marker1}_{implant}\mathbf{D}\ {}^{tracker}_{marker1}\mathbf{D}\ {}^{marker2}_{tracker}\mathbf{D}\ {}^{eye}_{maker2}\mathbf{A} \tag{1}$$

where, $^{marker1}_{implant}\mathbf{D} = {}^{implant}_{marker1}\mathbf{D}^{-1}$ and $^{tracker}_{marker1}\mathbf{D} = {}^{marker1}_{tracker}\mathbf{D}^{-1}$. And the translation matrix $^{eye}_{marker3}\mathbf{P}$ from the implant drill to the surgeon's view is calculated as per the following equation (2),

$$^{eye}_{marker3}\mathbf{P} = {}^{tracker}_{maker3}\mathbf{D}\ {}^{marker2}_{tracker}\mathbf{D}\ {}^{eye}_{marker2}\mathbf{A} \tag{2}$$

where, $^{tracker}_{marker3}\mathbf{D} = {}^{marker3}_{tracker}\mathbf{D}^{-1}$. Relationships between each coordinate system are shown in Fig. 2.

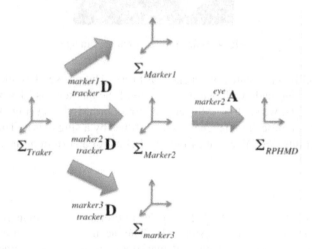

Fig. 2. Relationships of coordinate systems and translation matrixes

4 Experiment

To evaluate the proposed procedure, we performed an experiment using an optical see-through head mounted display (OSHMD) Data Glass 2 (SHIMAZU Inc., Japan) which replaced the RPHMD. The resolution of the OSHMD is 800 x 600 pixels. A USB camera was used in place of the user's eye. A ThinkPad X32 (IBM Inc., Japan) was used as a computer system to generate computer graphics (CG) as simulation

Fig. 3. Surgical stent with the marker 1

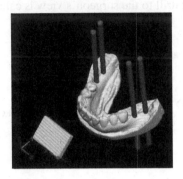

Fig. 4. 3-dimensional simulated image

image. The CG is represented by OpenGL Library. The marker 1 is attached to a tooh arrangement model made with plaster. The size of the marker 1 is 71 x 62 mm (Fig. 3). As dental implants, we set four cylinders into FreeFormModeling (Fig. 4).

The calibration procedure is repeated in 10 times by a single user. The user acquired 10 sampling points through a trial by mouse clicking of an origin of the marker 4.

5 Results

The dynamic RMS value of the MT2 was 70 micrometers less than 100 micrometers of accuracy in our previous system [3]. The accuracy of the translation matrix depends on the production accuracy of markers or acquisition accuracy of its corresponding point. Fig. 5 shows some examples of overlay images. Fig. 6 and Fig. 7 show reprojection errors on a x-axis and a y-axis respectively. As shown in Fig. 5, the virtual simulation image was overlaid onto the real surgical stent for any positions and postures through the OSHMD in real-time. As shown in Fig. 6 and Fig. 7, the maximum reprojection error in all trials was 26 pixels (3.25 %) for the x-axis and 17 pixels (2.83 %) for the y-axis. To reduce this error, we need to improve calibration procedure of the translation matrix $_{maker2}^{eye}\mathbf{A}$. One of the solutions is automatic sampling by using an image-processing technique [4].

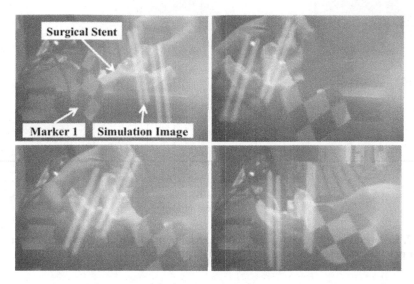

Fig. 5. Examples of overlay images: each image was taken from USB camera which was used in place of surgeon's eye through OSHMD. Four red cylinders are simulated images.

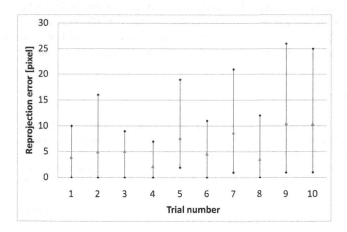

Fig. 6. Reprojection errors on an x-axis: the lower point of each trial shows minimum error, the upper point shows maximum error, and the middle point shows average error.

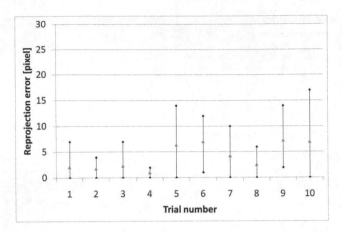

Fig. 7. Reprojection errors on a y-axis: the lower point of each trial shows minimum error, the upper point shows maximum error, and the middle point shows average error.

6 Conclusions

We proposed the dental implant surgical navigation system by using the RPHMD and its image overlay procedure. To verify its accuracy, we performed a basic experiment using OSHMD. As a result, our procedure could be performed as a real-time image overlay. With a view to the realization of the clinical applications, we will evaluate the size of markers, image overlay accuracy, measurable range, and light conditions.

References

1. Nardy, C., Alon, W., Nathan, P., Amir, S., Joshua, L.: Navigation Surgery for Dental Implants: Assessment of Accuracy of the Image Guided Implantology System. Journal of Oral Maxillofacial Surgery 62(suppl. 2), 116–119 (2004)
2. Hirokazu, K., Mark, B., Koichi, A., Keihachiro, T.: An Augmented Reality System and its Calibration based on Marker Tracking. Transaction on Virtual Reality Society of Japan 4(4), 607–616 (1999)
3. Takafumi, O., Naoki, K., Kazumichi, W., Shinichi, Y., Takashi, N., Youichi, K., Hirofumi, Y., Sohmura, T.: Application of Haptic Device to Implant Dentistry – Accuracy Verification of Drilling into a Pig Bone. Dental Material Journal 28(1), 75–81 (2009)
4. Satoshi, Y., Atsushi, N., Fumio, M., Junichi, S.: Robust Visual Tracking Method Based on the Optical Property of an Endoscopic Camera – Performance evaluation and application to direct calibration of endoscopic camera. Transactions of Japanese Society for Medical and Biological Engineering 45(1), 70–77 (2007)

A Feasible Tracking Method of Augmented Reality for Supporting Fieldwork of Nuclear Power Plant

Weida Yan[1], Hirotake Ishii[1], Hiroshi Shimoda[1], and Masanori Izumi[2]

[1] Graduate School of Energy Science, Kyoto University, 611-0011, Japan
yanweida@uji.energy.kyoto-u.ac.jp, hirotake@ieee.org,
shimoda@energy.kyoto-u.ac.jp
[2] FUGEN Decommissioning Engineering Center,
Japan Atomic Energy Agency, 914-8510, Japan
izumi.masanori@jaea.go.jp

Abstract. For the application of augmented reality in plant maintenance work, real-time tracking and technology with higher accuracy is necessary. This study focuses on the tracking method in vision based SLAM. In NPP, line features are abundant, and they are detected more easily and reliably than point features. Line features offer more information than points, but its tracking method is more complex. In this study, line features are used as landmark for tracking. The representation of the 3D line is relied on Plücker coordinates. A Gaussian sum approximates the feature initial state and is updated as new observations are gathered by the camera. Then extend Kalman filter is adopted for SLAM approach.

Keywords: Augmented Reality, Tracking, Line Feature, Plücker coordinates.

1 Introduction

The maintenance cost is the main cost during nuclear power generation. To improve the competition power of nuclear power, the cost needs to be reduced. It requires NPP field work to be more efficient to shorten the halting time for maintenance, be easier to reduce cost of training workers, and keep safety. Augmented Reality (AR) offers great possibilities to support NPP field work. It represents information more intuitively than with legacy interfaces such as paper-based instruction documents. It is expected that application of AR to support NPP maintenance can reduce human error and improve efficiency and security at the same time. In order to realize AR, a tracking system which can measure position of users in real time is necessary. Because the NPP environment is a very special environment which has lots of metal objects, only vision based sensor can be used. In this study, camera is the only sensor.

There are many methods on vision based SLAM (Simultaneous Localization and Mapping). *Michael Bosse* et,al[2] proposed a system for structure-from-motion using vanishing points and three-dimensional lines extracted from omni-directional video sequences. *Matthew N. Dailey* et,al[3] proposed the application of "FastSLAM" of estimating a map from observations of 3D line segments using a trinocular stereo

R. Shumaker (Ed.): Virtual and Mixed Reality, LNCS 5622, pp. 639–646, 2009.
© Springer-Verlag Berlin Heidelberg 2009

camera rig. *Paul Smith* et.al[4] proposed how straight lines can be added to a monocular EKF SLAM system in a manner that is both fast and which integrates easily with point features. *E. Rosten* et.al[5] addresses the problem of real-time 3D model based tracking by combining point-based and edge-based tracking systems.

Many methods are based on the point feature, because it is easy to detect the point in environment and establish the tracking model based on the point feature. This method, however, can not be applied in NPP, because of the complex environment in NPP, the point features detected by camera is not stable. There are many occlusions in environment, therefore many pseudo points are detected, and some real feature points are also not stable when the illumination or view angle changes. To avoid these disadvantages, line feature based model is chosen. In this model, the authors treat a line segments as an infinity line, so even if the segment extremities are not stable, the line is still detected easily.

In this paper, the authors employ the line feature represented by Plücker coordinates. The details of this model are described in Chapter 2. Chapter 3 describes the detail of the whole tracking flow. Chapter 4 then shows the tracking results of evaluation experiment.

2   3D Line Representation

Plücker coordinates are often used in the vision research field, because it is well adapted to the projection through a pinhole camera. As introduced in [1], the authors use the Euclidean Plücker coordinates, as the follow vector:

$$L_{(6\times 1)} = \left(\begin{matrix} n = h \bullet \bar{n} \\ \bar{u} \end{matrix} \right) \tag{1}$$

n is the normal to the plane containing the line and the origin O of the reference frame, h is the distance between O and the line and $\bar{u}$ is a unit vector which represents the direction of the line, as shown in Fig.1.

The projection of a 3D line L in an image is a 2D line l which is defined by the intersection of the image plane and the plane defined by n. The representation of l ($ax+by+c = 0$) in image coordinate is:

$$l = P_{l(3\times 3)} \left[l_{(3\times 3)} \ 0_{(3\times 3)} \right] L, l = (a, b, c)^t \tag{2}$$

P_l is the camera projection matrix for a Plücker line. It is defined based on the camera intrinsic calibration parameters. A common normalized parametrization for 2D lines is (ρ, θ). So l can be represented as: $l = (\cos\theta, \sin\theta, -\rho)$.

Given a reference frame transformation $(R, t)_{1-2}$, the Plücker coordinates of L in the two frames are related by:

$$L_2 = \begin{bmatrix} R & [t]_x R \\ 0_{(3\times 3)} & R \end{bmatrix} L_1 \tag{3}$$

Where $[t]_x$ denotes the matrix correspond to the cross product.

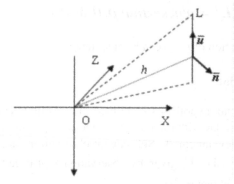

Fig. 1. The representation of a line L using Plücker coordinates

3   Line Based Tracking Algorithm

First of all, the image captured by camera was processed to detect the line feature. Histogram equalization method is applied for contrast enhancement of image to detect more features. Then the edge points are detected through Canny operator. Through IEPF (Iterative end point fit) method [6], the line features are identified from image. When a new line feature is observed, the representation of this feature is initialized with a sum of Gaussians [1]. Then, a process updates this initial state representation, until the feature can be declared as a landmark [7]. The new landmark is added in the state vector, which is managed by Extend Kalman Filter.

3.1   Initial State Approximation

First, the unit vector $\bar{n}$ is estimated and its PDF (Probability Density Function) is approximated by a single Gaussian. There are two quantities which prevent $p(L_c)$ from being a Gaussian: depth d and direction Φ of the line.

As presented in [1], In order to sample $p(L_c)$, a "generate" vector $\boldsymbol{g}$ is defined. The depth d of the line is defined along $\boldsymbol{g}$, and then $p(d)$ is sampled. $p(d)$ is a uniform distribution, its range is limited to $[d_{min}, d_{max}]$ by priori knowledge of the environment. As suggested in [7], [8], a Gaussian sum defined by a geometric series is a good approximation of $p(d)$. Similarly, the direction Φ of the line is defined with respect to $\boldsymbol{g}$, then $p(\Phi)$ is sampled. The plücker line can be represented as:

$$L_c^{i,j} = \begin{pmatrix} (d_i \sin\phi_j) \bullet \bar{n} \\ Rot(-\varphi_j \times \bar{n}) \bullet \bar{g} \end{pmatrix} \tag{4}$$

$Rot(x)$ is the (3×3) rotation matrix round the vector x. The original stochastic variables are the observation (ρ, θ), and the sampling variables over depth and direction. The following function can be formulated:

$$L_c^{i,j} = pluckerInit(\rho, \theta, d_i, \phi_j) \tag{5}$$

Then the approximation of $p(L_c)$ can be calculated through this formula.

3.2 Initial State Update

Once the set of Gaussian hypotheses is defined, the likelihoods computation and the selection process is similar with the one presented in [9]. The best hypothesis of line feature is added as a new landmark. Subsequent observations are used to compute the likelihood of each Gaussian Γ_i given by observation z_t at time t. The likelihood of a Gaussian of an observed feature is:

$$L_i^t = \frac{1}{\sqrt{2\pi|S_i|}} \exp\left(-\frac{1}{2}(z_t - \hat{z}_i)^T S_i^{-1}(z_t - \hat{z}_i)\right) \tag{6}$$

Where Si is the covariance of the innovation $z_t - \hat{z}_i$. $\hat{z}_i$ is the prediction of observation of feature. And the normalized likelihood for the hypothesis i is

$$\Lambda_i = \frac{\Pi_t L_i^t}{\Sigma_j \Pi_t L_j^t} \tag{7}$$

Then we can selete the bad hypotheses whose likelihood $\Lambda_{\psi}$is low and delete the associated Gaussian.

3.3 Structure of Kalman Filter

The state of the EKF is composed of the landmarks estimates, and current state of the camera. Although some past states of camere are still kept in the filter structure [9], here only the current state was save in filter for convenience. Namely some past states is stored in the structure of Landmark candidates. When a candidate was added as a new landmark, the past states were used to estimate the coordinates of landmark.The camera state is a 13 dimensions vector. (3D-position, 4D-quaternion, 3D-linear velocity, 3D- angular velocity).

When a feature is add as a new landmark, the state vector x and covariance matrix P is updated:

$$x^+ = \begin{pmatrix} x \\ x_f^j \end{pmatrix} \quad P^+ = \begin{pmatrix} P & P_{x,x_f^j} \\ P_{x_f^j,x} & P_{x_f^j} \end{pmatrix} \tag{8}$$

4 Evaluation Experiment

In order to evaluate the feasibility of this method, an evaluation experiment was conducted in Fugne NPP. The tracking result was compared with the true data measured by laser rangefinder.

4.1 Method

The experiment system includes a camera with 4mm focallength, and a computer connected to it. The program was developed from OPENCV in order to realize the proposed method mentioned in Chapter 3. The frame rate of the camera was set to 30fps. When tracking, camera can be moved arbitrarily in the environment. To compare the result with the real position, camera was fixed on a tripod, and a circular marker [10] was pasted on it for its position and orientation measurment. When moving the tripod, its position and orientation can be exactly measured by the laser rangefinder. 13 points were measured on the moving track of camera, and more than 4000 frames were captured. The total path length of the camera movement was approximately 10m.

In the experiment, a rectangle marker as shown in Fig.2 was pasted in the environment in advance. Its four edges were initial landmarks, and the position of the four corners of rectangle was measured by laser rangefinder beforehand.

4.2 Result and Discussion

Fig.3 shows the trajectory of the camera movement. Fig.4 shows the example image captured by the camera. There are lots of pipes in the image and they often cause occlusion problem if point feature method is applied. Fig.5 shows the position error of the camera tracked by the proposed method. As shown in Fig.5, the tracking error increases along with the camera moving. It is found that the error of y direction is much smaller than those of x, z direction. Because the y axis was defined vertical to the ground, and the position of y direction was changed a little, as shown in Fig.6 which indicates true position of the camera. In x and z direction, on the other hand, the error is larger. It is caused by the accumulation of error while camera moving, and the error of the position estimation of landmark.

In addition, the large error could appear when a shock on camera occurs. This is always observed when measuring the position of camera.

Fig. 2. Rectangle marker as initial landmark

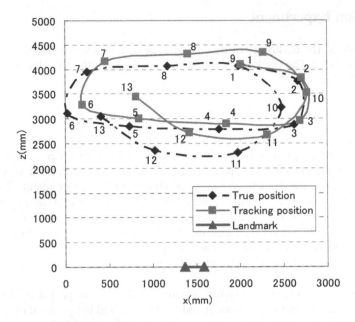

Fig. 3. The camera trajectory in top view of NPP field

Fig. 4. The image captured by camera (after contrast enhancement

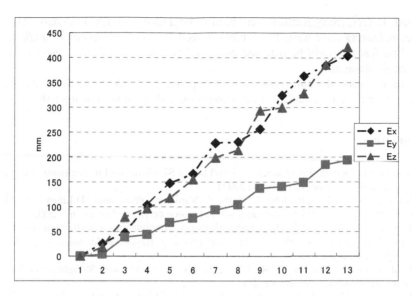

Fig. 5. Error on three directions (x, y, z) of camera. (Compare with the result measured by laser rangefinder)

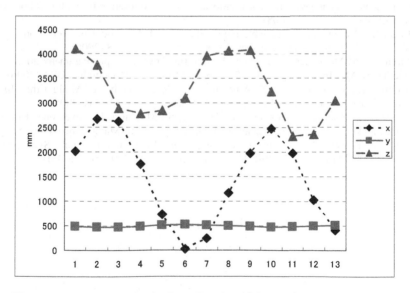

Fig. 6. True camera position in three directions (Measured by laser rangefinder)

5 Conclusion

In this paper, a feasible tracking method for NPP field has been proposed. Because of the special environment in NPP, the authors chose lines features as the landmark for tracking. The result of the evaluation experiment shows that the error can not be ignored. In fact, many features were hard to be added as a new landmark. This leads to the increasing error when the camera moved far from the rectangle marker. However, line feature could be detected more stably than point feature, especially when view angle changes.

In future work, the authors will try to improve the tracking model to be more robust, and improve the stability of line detection, and the matching algorithm.

References

1. Thomas, L., Simon, L.: Monocular-vision based SLAM using line segments. In: IEEE.Int. Conf. on Robotics & Automation (2007)
2. Michael, B., Richard, R., John, L., Seth, T.: Vanishing Points and 3D Lines From Omnidirectional Video. In: IEEE International Conference on Image Processing (2002)
3. Matthew, N.D., Manukid, P.: Landmark-based Simultaneous Localization and Mapping with Stereo Vision. In: Proc. Asian Conference on Industrial Automation and Robotics, Bangkok, Thailand (2005)
4. Paul, S., Ian, R., Andrew, D.: Real-Time Monocular SLAM with Straight Lines. In: British Machine Vision Conference (2006)
5. Edward, R., Tom, D.: Fusing Points and Lines for High Performance Tracking. In: Proc. IEEE International Conference on Computer Vision, Beijing, China, pp. 1508–1515 (2005)
6. Young-Ho, C., Tae-Kyeong, L., Se-Young, O.: A line feature based SLAM with low grade range sensors using geometric constraints and active exploration for mobile robot. Autonomous Robots 24, 13–18 (2008)
7. Eade, E., Drummond, T.: Scalable monocular SLAM. In: Proc. Conference on Computer Vision and Pattern Recognition, New York, USA, pp. 469–478 (2006)
8. Montiel, J.M.M., Javier, C., Andrew, D.: Unified Inverse Depth Parametrization for Monocular SLAM. In: Proc. Robotics: Science and Systems, Philadelphia, USA (2006)
9. Thomas, L., Simon, L., Joan, S.: A practical 3D Bearing-Only SLAM algorithm. In: IEEE International Conference on Intelligent Robots and Systems (August 2005)
10. Hirotake, I., Weida, Y., Shoufeng, Y., Hiroshi, S., Masanori, I.: Development of a Wide Area Tracking Method for Augmented Reality Applied to Maintenance Work Support in Nuclear Power Plants. In: Proceedings of Joint International Symposium of ISSNP2008/CSEPC2008/ISOFIC2008, vol. 1, pp. 22–28 (2008) (CD-ROM)

Author Index

Printed in the United States
By Bookmasters

Printed in the United States
By Bookmasters